The Complete Poetical Works of Oliver Wendell Holmes

Oliver Wendell Holmes

Copyright © BiblioLife, LLC

BiblioLife Reproduction Series: Our goal at BiblioLife is to help readers, educators and researchers by bringing back in print hard-to-find original publications at a reasonable price and, at the same time, preserve the legacy of literary history. The following book represents an authentic reproduction of the text as printed by the original publisher and may contain prior copyright references. While we have attempted to accurately maintain the integrity of the original work(s), from time to time there are problems with the original book scan that may result in minor errors in the reproduction, including imperfections such as missing and blurred pages, poor pictures, markings and other reproduction issues beyond our control. Because this work is culturally important, we have made it available as a part of our commitment to protecting, preserving and promoting the world's literature.

All of our books are in the "public domain" and some are derived from Open Source projects dedicated to digitizing historic literature. We believe that when we undertake the difficult task of re-creating them as attractive, readable and affordable books, we further the mutual goal of sharing these works with a larger audience. A portion of BiblioLife profits go back to Open Source projects in the form of a donation to the groups that do this important work around the world. If you would like to make a donation to these worthy Open Source projects, or would just like to get more information about these important initiatives, please visit www.bibliolife.com/opensource.

THE COMPLETE POETICAL WORKS OF OLIVER WENDELL HOLMES
Cambridge Edition

The Gambrel Roofed House, Cambridge

BOSTON AND NEW YORK
HOUGHTON, MIFFLIN AND COMPANY
The Riverside Press, Cambridge

PUBLISHERS' NOTE

THIS Cambridge Edition of *The Complete Poetic Works of Oliver Wendell Holmes* is the fourth in a series which includes the poems and dramas of Longfellow, Whittier, and Browning. It follows in its scheme the plan of the previous volumes. The editor was at some disadvantage in not being able to avail himself of the Life of Dr. Holmes which is now in preparation, but the frequent autobiographical passages in the writings of the author enabled him to illustrate a career devoid, even more than that of most poets, of adventure or dramatic incident. The head-notes, in like manner, could frequently be supplied from comment occurring in the author's prose writings and in prefaces to separate publications of poems, but very many of the poems are so self-explanatory that the reader requires no introduction.

The policy has been pursued, as in the former cases, of taking the latest collective edition issued in the poet's lifetime as the pattern to be followed both in text and in arrangement, but the opportunity has been used to include a few poems which were written after the latest edition appeared or had by some accident failed to receive the author's attention when he was making up his final collection; no attempt, however, has been made, in gathering the early poems, to go outside of the volumes in which they were originally included. It is assumed that Dr. Holmes when making up these volumes intentionally disregarded some of the poems scattered through periodicals. This is confirmed by the attitude which he took when his attention was called to the omission upon the occasion of the issue of the Riverside Edition. He refused to give them a refuge even in an appendix. The arrangement here is the same as in the Riverside Edition, with some slight modification, chiefly caused by the introduction of new material. In accordance with the plan of this series and with Dr. Holmes's original intention when the Riverside Edition was prepared, the *Juvenilia* are placed in an appendix in smaller type. Throughout the volume, whether in head-notes or in those placed in the appendix, the editor's work is distinguished by the use of brackets.

BOSTON, 4 PARK STREET, *October* 21, 1895.

TABLE OF CONTENTS

	PAGE
BIOGRAPHICAL SKETCH	xi
TO MY READERS	1
EARLIER POEMS (1830-1836).	
Old Ironsides	3
The Last Leaf	4
The Cambridge Churchyard	5
To an Insect	7
The Dilemma	7
My Aunt	8
Reflections of a Proud Pedestrian	8
Daily Trials, by a Sensitive Man	9
Evening, by a Tailor	9
The Dorchester Giant	10
To the Portrait of "A Lady"	11
The Comet	11
The Music-Grinders	12
The Treadmill Song	13
The September Gale	13
The Height of the Ridiculous	14
The Last Reader	14
Poetry: A Metrical Essay	15
POEMS PUBLISHED BETWEEN 1837 AND 1848.	
The Pilgrim's Vision	26
The Steamboat	28
Lexington	28
On Lending a Punch-Bowl	29
A Song for the Centennial Celebration of Harvard College, 1836	30
The Island Hunting-Song	31
Departed Days	32
The Only Daughter	32
Song written for the Dinner given to Charles Dickens, by the Young Men of Boston, February 1, 1842	33
Lines recited at the Berkshire Jubilee, Pittsfield, Mass., August 23, 1844	33
Nux Postcœnatica	35
Verses for After-Dinner	36

	PAGE
A Modest Request, complied with after the Dinner at President Everett's Inauguration	37
The Parting Word	40
A Song of Other Days	41
Song for a Temperance Dinner to which Ladies were invited (New York Mercantile Library Association, November, 1842)	42
A Sentiment	42
A Rhymed Lesson (Urania)	43
An After-Dinner Poem (Terpsichore)	54
MEDICAL POEMS.	
The Morning Visit	58
The Two Armies	59
The Stethoscope Song	60
Extracts from a Medical Poem	61
A Poem for the Meeting of the American Medical Association at New York, May 5, 1853	62
A Sentiment	63
Rip Van Winkle, M. D.	63
Poem read at the Dinner given to the Author by the Medical Profession of the City of New York, April 12, 1883	68
SONGS IN MANY KEYS (1849-1861).	
Prologue	72
Agnes	72
The Ploughman	79
Spring	80
The Study	82
The Bells	83
Non-Resistance	83
The Moral Bully	84
The Mind's Diet	85
Our Limitations	85
The Old Player	85
A Poem: Dedication of the Pittsfield Cemetery, September 9, 1850	87
To Governor Swain	89
To an English Friend	90

CONTENTS

After a Lecture on Wordsworth 90
After a Lecture on Moore . . 91
After a Lecture on Keats . 92
After a Lecture on Shelley . 92
At the Close of a Course of Lectures 93
The Hudson 94
The New Eden 94
Semi-centennial Celebration of the New England Society, New York, December 22, 1855 . . 96
Farewell to J. R. Lowell . . 97
For the Meeting of the Burns Club, 1856 97
Ode for Washington's Birthday 98
Birthday of Daniel Webster . 98
The Voiceless 99
The Two Streams 99
The Promise 100
Avis 100
The Living Temple 101
At a Birthday Festival: to J. R. Lowell 102
A Birthday Tribute to J. F. Clarke 102
The Gray Chief 102
The Last Look: W. W. Swain . 103
In Memory of Charles Wentworth Upham, Jr. . . . 103
Martha 104
Meeting of the Alumni of Harvard College, 1857 . . . 104
The Parting Song 106
For the Meeting of the National Sanitary Association, 1860 . 106
For the Burns Centennial Celebration, 1859 107
At a Meeting of Friends . . 108
Boston Common; Three Pictures 109
The Old Man of the Sea . . 109
International Ode 110
Vive la France 110
Brother Jonathan's Lament for Sister Caroline . . . 111

POEMS OF THE CLASS OF '29 (1851-1889).
Bill and Joe 113
A Song of "Twenty-Nine" . 114
Questions and Answers . . 115
An Impromptu 115
The Old Man dreams . . . 115
Remember — Forget . . . 116
Our Indian Summer . . . 117
Mare Rubrum 117
The Boys 118

Lines 119
A Voice of the Loyal North . 120
J. D. R. 120
Voyage of the Good Ship Union 120
"Choose you this day whom ye will serve" 121
F. W. C. 122
The Last Charge 123
Our Oldest Friend . . . 124
Sherman's in Savannah . . 124
My Annual 125
All Here 126
Once More 127
The Old Cruiser 128
Hymn for the Class-Meeting . 129
Even-Song 130
The Smiling Listener . . . 131
Our Sweet Singer: J. A. . . 133
H. C. M., H. S., J. K. W. . 133
What I have come for . . 134
Our Banker 135
For Class Meeting 136
"Ad Amicos" 137
How not to settle it . . . 138
The Last Survivor . . . 140
The Archbishop and Gil Blas . 141
The Shadows 142
Benjamin Peirce 143
In the Twilight 144
A Loving-Cup Song . . . 145
The Girdle of Friendship . . 145
The Lyre of Anacreon . . . 146
The Old Tune 146
The Broken Circle 147
The Angel-Thief 147
After the Curfew 148

POEMS FROM THE AUTOCRAT OF THE BREAKFAST-TABLE (1857-1858).
The Chambered Nautilus . . 149
Sun and Shadow 150
Musa 150
A Parting Health: to J. L. Motley 151
What We all think . . . 152
Spring has come 152
Prologue 153
Latter-Day Warnings . . . 154
Album Verses 155
A Good Time going! . . . 155
The Last Blossom 156
Contentment 157
Æstivation 158
The Deacon's Masterpiece; or, The Wonderful "One-Hoss Shay" 158
Prelude 160

Parson Turell's Legacy; or, The President's Old Arm-Chair	160
Ode for a Social Meeting, with Slight Alterations by a Teetotaler	162

POEMS FROM THE PROFESSOR AT THE BREAKFAST-TABLE (1858-1859).

Under the Violets	163
Hymn of Trust	163
A Sun-Day Hymn	163
The Crooked Footpath	164
Iris, Her Book	164
Robinson of Leyden	165
St. Anthony the Reformer	166
The Opening of the Piano	166
Midsummer	167
De Sauty	167

POEMS FROM THE POET AT THE BREAKFAST-TABLE (1871-1872).

Homesick in Heaven	169
Fantasia	170
Aunt Tabitha	171
Wind-Clouds and Star-Drifts	171
Epilogue to the Breakfast-Table Series	183

SONGS OF MANY SEASONS (1862-1874).

Opening the Window	185
Programme	185

In the Quiet Days.

An Old-Year Song	186
Dorothy Q.: A Family Portrait	186
The Organ-Blower	187
After the Fire	188
At the Pantomime	189
A Ballad of the Boston Tea-Party	190
Nearing the Snow-Line	191

In War Time.

To Canaan: A Puritan War-Song	191
"Thus saith the Lord, I offer Thee Three Things"	192
Never or Now	192
Hymn written for the Great Central Fair in Philadelphia, 1864	193
One Country	193
God Save the Flag!	194
Hymn after the Emancipation Proclamation	194
Hymn for the Fair at Chicago, 1865	194
Under the Washington Elm, Cambridge	195
Freedom, our Queen	195
Army Hymn	196
Parting Hymn	196
The Flower of Liberty	196
The Sweet Little Man	197
Union and Liberty	198

Songs of Welcome and Farewell.

America to Russia	198
Welcome to the Grand Duke Alexis	199
At the Banquet to the Grand Duke Alexis	199
At the Banquet to the Chinese Embassy	200
At the Banquet to the Japanese Embassy	201
Bryant's Seventieth Birthday	202
A Farewell to Agassiz	203
At a Dinner to Admiral Farragut	204
At a Dinner to General Grant	205
To H. W. Longfellow	206
To Christian Gottfried Ehrenberg	206
A Toast to Wilkie Collins	207

Memorial Verses.

For the Services in Memory of Abraham Lincoln, Boston, June 1, 1865	208
For the Commemoration Services, Cambridge, July 21, 1865	208
Edward Everett: January 30, 1865	210
Shakespeare Tercentennial Celebration, April 23, 1864	211
In Memory of John and Robert Ware, May 25, 1864	212
Humboldt's Birthday: Centennial Celebration, September 14, 1869	213
Poem at the Dedication of the Halleck Monument, July 8, 1869	214
Hymn for the Celebration at the Laying of the Corner-Stone of Harvard Memorial Hall, Cambridge, October 6, 1870	214
Hymn for the Dedication of Memorial Hall at Cambridge, June 23, 1874	215
Hymn at the Funeral Services of Charles Sumner, April 29, 1874	215

CONTENTS

RHYMES OF AN HOUR.
AN IMPROMPTU AT THE WALCKER DINNER UPON THE COMPLETION OF THE GREAT ORGAN FOR BOSTON MUSIC HALL IN 1863 . . . 215
ADDRESS FOR THE OPENING OF THE FIFTH AVENUE THEATRE, NEW YORK, DECEMBER 3, 1873 . . 216
A SEA DIALOGUE 218
CHANSON WITHOUT MUSIC . . 219
FOR THE CENTENNIAL DINNER OF THE PROPRIETORS OF BOSTON PIER, OR THE LONG WHARF, APRIL 16, 1873 220
A POEM SERVED TO ORDER . . 221
THE FOUNTAIN OF YOUTH . . . 222
NO TIME LIKE THE OLD TIME . 222
A HYMN OF PEACE, SUNG AT THE "JUBILEE," JUNE 15, 1869, TO THE MUSIC OF KELLER'S "AMERICAN HYMN" 223

BUNKER-HILL BATTLE AND OTHER POEMS (1874-1877).
GRANDMOTHER'S STORY OF BUNKER-HILL BATTLE 224
AT THE "ATLANTIC" DINNER, DECEMBER 15, 1874 227
"LUCY:" FOR HER GOLDEN WEDDING, OCTOBER 18, 1875 . . 228
HYMN FOR THE INAUGURATION OF THE STATUE OF GOVERNOR ANDREW, HINGHAM, OCTOBER 7, 1875 229
A MEMORIAL TRIBUTE TO DR. SAMUEL G. HOWE . . . , . 229
JOSEPH WARREN, M. D. . . . 230
OLD CAMBRIDGE, JULY 3, 1875 . 230
WELCOME TO THE NATIONS, PHILADELPHIA, JULY 4, 1876 . . . 232
A FAMILIAR LETTER . . . 232
UNSATISFIED 234
HOW THE OLD HORSE WON THE BET 234
AN APPEAL FOR "THE OLD SOUTH" 236
THE FIRST FAN 237
TO RUTHERFORD BIRCHARD HAYES 239
THE SHIP OF STATE . . . 239
A FAMILY RECORD 239

THE IRON GATE AND OTHER POEMS (1877-1881).
THE IRON GATE 243
VESTIGIA QUINQUE RETRORSUM . 244
MY AVIARY 247
ON THE THRESHOLD 249
TO GEORGE PEABODY . . . 249
AT THE PAPYRUS CLUB . . . 249

FOR WHITTIER'S SEVENTIETH BIRTHDAY 250
TWO SONNETS: HARVARD . . . 251
THE COMING ERA 251
IN RESPONSE 252
FOR THE MOORE CENTENNIAL CELEBRATION 253
TO JAMES FREEMAN CLARKE . . 255
WELCOME TO THE CHICAGO COMMERCIAL CLUB 255
AMERICAN ACADEMY CENTENNIAL CELEBRATION 256
THE SCHOOL-BOY 257
THE SILENT MELODY 263
OUR HOME — OUR COUNTRY . . 263
POEM AT THE CENTENNIAL ANNIVERSARY DINNER OF THE MASSACHUSETTS MEDICAL SOCIETY . 264
HARVARD 268
RHYMES OF A LIFE-TIME . . . 268

BEFORE THE CURFEW.
AT MY FIRESIDE 269
AT THE SATURDAY CLUB . . . 269
OUR DEAD SINGER. H. W. L. . 271
TWO POEMS TO HARRIET BEECHER STOWE ON HER SEVENTIETH BIRTHDAY.
  I. AT THE SUMMIT 272
  II. THE WORLD'S HOMAGE . 272
A WELCOME TO DR. BENJAMIN APTHORP GOULD 273
TO FREDERICK HENRY HEDGE ON HIS EIGHTIETH BIRTHDAY . . . 274
TO JAMES RUSSELL LOWELL . . 274
TO JOHN GREENLEAF WHITTIER ON HIS EIGHTIETH BIRTHDAY . 275
PRELUDE TO A VOLUME PRINTED IN RAISED LETTERS FOR THE BLIND 276
BOSTON TO FLORENCE . . . 276
AT THE UNITARIAN FESTIVAL, MARCH 8, 1882 277
POEM FOR THE TWO HUNDRED AND FIFTIETH ANNIVERSARY OF THE FOUNDING OF HARVARD COLLEGE 277
POST-PRANDIAL: PHI BETA KAPPA, 1881 284
THE FLÂNEUR: DURING THE TRANSIT OF VENUS, 1882 . . . 284
AVE 286
KING'S CHAPEL: READ AT THE TWO HUNDREDTH ANNIVERSARY . 286
HYMN FOR THE SAME OCCASION . 287
HYMN — THE WORD OF PROMISE . 288
HYMN READ AT THE DEDICATION OF THE OLIVER WENDELL HOLMES

CONTENTS

Hospital at Hudson, Wisconsin, June 7, 1887 288
On the Death of President Garfield 289
The Golden Flower . . . 290
Youth 290
Hail, Columbia! 290
Poem for the Dedication of the Fountain at Stratford-on-Avon, presented by George W. Childs, of Philadelphia . . . 291
To the Poets who only read and listen 292
For the Dedication of the New City Library, Boston . . 293
To James Russell Lowell, at the Dinner given in his honor at the Tavern Club, on his Seventieth Birthday, February 22, 1889 293
But One Talent 295
For the Window in St. Margaret's 296
James Russell Lowell: 1819-1891 . 296
In Memory of John Greenleaf Whittier: December 17, 1807 — September 7, 1892 . . 297
To the Teachers of America . 298
Hymn written for the Twenty-fifth Anniversary of the Reorganization of the Boston Young Men's Christian Union, May 31, 1893 298
Francis Parkman: September 16, 1823 — November 8, 1893 . 298

POEMS FROM OVER THE TEACUPS.

To the Eleven Ladies who presented me with a Silver Loving Cup 300
The Peau de Chagrin of State Street 300
Cacoethes Scribendi . . . 300
The Rose and the Fern . . 301
I Like you and I Love you . 301
La Maison d'Or (Bar Harbor) . 301
Too Young for Love . . . 301
The Broomstick Train; or, The Return of the Witches . . 301
Tartarus 304
At the Turn of the Road . 304
Invitâ Minervâ 305

READINGS OVER THE TEACUPS.

To my Old Readers . . . 306

The Banker's Secret . . . 307
The Exile's Secret 311
The Lover's Secret . . . 313
The Statesman's Secret . . 315
The Mother's Secret . . . 317
The Secret of the Stars . . 319

APPENDIX.

I. Verses from the Oldest Portfolio.
First Verses: Translation from the Æneid 321
The Meeting of the Dryads . 321
The Mysterious Visitor . . 322
The Toadstool 323
The Spectre Pig 323
To a Caged Lion 324
The Star and the Water-Lily . 325
Illustration of a Picture: "A Spanish Girl in Reverie" . 325
A Roman Aqueduct . . . 326
From a Bachelor's Private Journal 326
La Grisette 326
Our Yankee Girls 327
L'Inconnue 327
Stanzas 327
Lines by a Clerk 327
The Philosopher to his Love . 328
The Poet's Lot 328
To a Blank Sheet of Paper . 328
To the Portrait of "A Gentleman" in the Athenæum Gallery 329
The Ballad of the Oysterman . 329
A Noontide Lyric 330
The Hot Season 330
A Portrait 331
An Evening Thought, written at Sea 331
"The Wasp" and "The Hornet" 331
"Qui Vive?" 331
A Souvenir 332
The Dying Seneca . . . 332
The Last Prophecy of Cassandra 332
To my Companions . . . 333

II. Astræa: The Balance of Illusions 333

III. Notes and Addenda . . . 337

IV. A Chronological List of Dr. Holmes's Poems . . . 341

INDEX OF FIRST LINES . . . 345
INDEX OF TITLES 349

BIOGRAPHICAL SKETCH

DR. HOLMES had much to say in his writings of the problems of heredity, and was apparently as ready to recognize the caprices as the regular action of inherited tendencies. He may have speculated over his own descent when he wrote, in *The Poet at the Breakfast-Table*, "The various inherited instincts ripen in succession. You may be nine tenths paternal at one period of your life, and nine tenths maternal at another. All at once the traits of some immediate ancestor may come to maturity unexpectedly on one of the branches of your character, just as your features at different periods of your life betray different resemblances to your nearer or more remote relatives." One would fain believe that the thin poetic blood of his early ancestor Anne Bradstreet had been enriched by its secret passage through the veins of several generations before it issued in the warm pulsations of this poet of our day; but as for those generous, even passionate instincts of patriotism, and that strong impulse toward lawful freedom which characterized the wit and philosopher, one may readily take into account the whole strain of Dr. Holmes's ancestry on both sides.

With the exception of a Dutch strain a few generations before, these ancestors were of New England origin, going back to the early colonial days. John Holmes, of Puritan birth, settled in Woodstock, Connecticut, in 1686. His grandson, David Holmes, served as captain of British troops in the French and Indian war and later as a surgeon in the Revolutionary army. The son of this David was the Reverend Abiel Holmes, who was graduated at Yale College in 1782, and after a six years' pastorate in Georgia came to Cambridge, Massachusetts, where he was pastor over the first parish for forty years, and during his pastorate beside other writings and lectures compiled *The Annals of America*, a trustworthy and creditable historical survey. His second wife was a daughter of Oliver Wendell, and her ancestry besides its Dutch strain was connected with the Phillipses, Quincys, and other well-known New England families.

Oliver Wendell Holmes, the third child and eldest son of Abiel and Mary Wendell Holmes, was born at Cambridge, Massachusetts, August 29, 1809. "The year 1809," he says, in *Our Hundred Days in Europe*, "which introduced me to atmospheric existence, was the birth-year of Gladstone, Tennyson, Lord Houghton, and Darwin." But the circumstances of his birth were as distinct from those that attended the appearance of his illustrious contemporaries as New England was sharply discriminated from old England. The atmosphere, however, into which he was born, was a fresh, clear, and not unscholarly one. It was, moreover, charged with historical traditions. Cambridge was a village, but a village dominated by college life. The house in which the poet was born shared until a recent day the honors with the Craigie House, its neighbor. For in the early days of the Revolution, when studies at Harvard College were suspended, this old gambrel-roofed house had been the headquarters of General Artemas Ward and of the Committee of Safety. Upon the steps of the house stood President Langdon of Harvard College, so tradition says, and prayed for the men, who, halting there a few moments, marched forward under Colonel Prescott's lead to throw up entrenchments on Bunker Hill on the night of June 16, 1775; and in this house the boy's father, who had passed his own youth in the days of the Revolution, was collecting the memorabilia for his substantial contribution to American history. His mother, too, had her memory of a hurried exit from Boston during the siege, when she was six years old.

The appearance of the gambrel-roofed house has been preserved, fortunately, in various sketches and photographs; Dr. Holmes himself, who took a lively interest in the camera long before amateur photography was the fashion, made several copies of it from different points of view. But the most indelible picture of the house is in the affectionate portrait contained in Dr. Holmes's writings. It is a notable expression of the intense ardor with which he clung to places and scenes identified with his life and that of his forbears. By his literary workmanship he made the house, now vanished, a literary shrine. Not only in the detailed description contained in *The Poet at the Breakfast-Table*, but in random passages elsewhere, he delighted in recalling the dignified yet homely structure which was his first outward shell. "The slaughter of the Old Gambrel-roofed House," he says, "was a case of justifiable domicide," but he mourned over the necessity of its destruction. "Personally," he adds, "I have a right to mourn for it as a part of my life gone from me. . . . The house in which one drew his first breath and where he one day came into the consciousness that he was a personality, an *ego*, a little universe with a sky over him all his own, with a persistent identity, with the terrible responsibility of a separate, independent, inalienable existence, — that house does not ask for any historical associations to make it the centre of the earth for him."

In the Introduction to *A Mortal Antipathy*, Dr. Holmes has dwelt upon the conditions of his childish life, the rural simplicity of nature, the hills which were the playground of his imagination, the glimpses of sails in the distance, even though the water itself was invisible. "I am very thankful," he says, "that the first part of my life was not passed shut in between high walls and treading the unimpressible and unsympathetic pavement." The combination of almost rustic life with academic dignity and high breeding which he has witnessed to in autobiographic passages, which Lowell has described so felicitously in his *Cambridge Thirty Years Ago*, and which struck Clough so forcibly when he was a sojourner there a decade or two later, was a note of that culmination of New England provincialism so notably reflected in much of Holmes's writings. As we get farther away from the period roughly circumscribed between 1815 and 1850, we shall see more clearly that it was the flowering time of the plant whose seeds were sown in 1620–1640, and Holmes was instinctively its poet and historian, as he was in point of years the last of the remarkable group always to be associated with New England's intellectual aristocracy.

Holmes's early schooling after an initiation in a dame school, where a companion was the late Bishop Lee of Delaware, was under Master William Bigelow, and when ten years old he went to a school in Cambridgeport, where he had for schoolmates Margaret Fuller and Richard Henry Dana, whose famous kinsman, Washington Allston, glorified the rather unkempt Port with his studio. At fifteen he was sent for special preparation to Phillips Academy at Andover. His life there, and the companionship he enjoyed, he described in his pleasant paper *Cinders from the Ashes*, and touched with a kindly light in his reminiscent poem *The School-Boy*.

He spent a year at Andover and then entered Harvard College with the class which was to graduate in 1829. In those days the classes at college were smaller than now, and as they all joined in common studies, the members of a class came to know one another familiarly and to have such a sense of organic unity that long after college days, when the members were scattered and rarely came together, each still felt himself a member of his "class," as he might feel himself a citizen of some particular city. The complete roll of this class will be found in the appendix at the close of this volume, and though no titles or signs of honor are attached to the names, the reader will easily detect the presence of men who afterward came to great distinction, George Tyler Bigelow, for a while Chief Justice of the Supreme Court of Massachusetts; James Freeman Clarke, the humane, independent, and courageous preacher and public-spirited citizen; Benjamin Robbins Curtis, the eminent lawyer; Benjamin Peirce, the illustrious mathematician; Dr. S. F. Smith, who won national repute by writing four seven-line stanzas three years after leaving college; and others of less widespread fame, who yet were honored in their professions and offices. But the class enjoyed a distinction not granted to other classes, for though another college class, nine years later, had a great poet in James Russell Lowell, this alone had a poet who year after year at the class-meeting sang for them a song of memory and affection. It was the same song sung in many keys, and some of the music could not be shut up within narrow limits, but has found universal acceptance in such lines as *Bill and Joe*. The group of poems under the title *Poems of the Class of '29* extends from 1851 to 1889. On that sixtieth anniversary of their graduation, Holmes laid down his instrument with the tender lines *After the Curfew*. The class met once more at Parker's. Three only were present, Holmes, S. F. Smith, and Samuel May. Then came a meeting each of the few remaining years, at Dr. Holmes's house, quiet, social talks, with four at the most, five being the total number of the survivors; but no more poems.

The college, meanwhile, was so small a body, and was so representative of neighboring families, that Holmes naturally found comrades and intimate friends outside his own class. Charles Sumner was in the class below him, and two classes below were his own famous cousin, Wendell Phillips, and his life-long friend John Lothrop Motley. It became his privilege to write Motley's memoir, and the correspondence between the two, given in part in Curtis's *Letters of John Lothrop Motley*, intimates the closeness of their relation. As Holmes struck root deeply in the soil of his forefathers, so his nature went out in steadfast affection toward his fellows. His rosary of class poems shows this, and the many passages in which he recalls his early associates. When he had finished his memoir of Motley, he wrote in warm remembrance of his task : " Did not my own consciousness migrate, or seem, at least, to transfer itself into this brilliant life history, as I traced its glowing record ? I, too, seemed to feel the delight of carrying with me, as if they were my own, the charms of a presence which made its own welcome everywhere. I shared his heroic toils, I partook of his literary and social triumphs, I was honored by the marks of distinction which gathered about him, I was wronged by the indignity from which he suffered, mourned with him in his sorrow, and thus, after I had been living for months with his memory, I felt as if I should carry a part of his being with me so long as my self-consciousness might remain imprisoned in the ponderable elements."

The slight references which Dr. Holmes makes to his college life have to do with external things, trifling oddities which stick to the memory like burrs. The student life in its formal relation made but little impression on him apparently, and in later years he was more likely to take pride in the great advance made by the University than to dwell upon its worth in his own day. "During all my early years," he says, "our old Harvard Alma Mater sat still and lifeless as the colossi in the Egyptian desert. Then all at once, like the statue in Don Giovanni, she moved from her pedestal. The fall of that 'stony foot' has effected a miracle like the harp that Orpheus played, like the teeth that Cadmus sowed." But that was long after his own college days. His predilection for literature and his irrepressible humor were evident in the spontaneous, mirthful verses which came from him at this time, some before and some just after graduation. Many of them were printed in *The Collegian*, the college paper of the day, and in the collection of his poems they are divided between the group of *Earlier Poems* and the *Verses from the Oldest Portfolio*. The most active pen production was in the year after graduation, when he was studying law.

It was then that he wrote the poem *Old Ironsides*, in a burst of indignation as he has described in the note at the head of the poem. The verses are fresh evidence of that well of patriotism which lay near the surface of his nature, ever ready to spring forth into song or impassioned prose. It is notable that two young men of the same college class should so shortly after their graduation have produced two pieces of verse which are among the most famous of American patriotic poems, the one a fervent hymn, the other a trumpet call. The study of law was an experiment and apparently not carried on with very close or serious application. "For during that year," says Holmes, "I first tasted the intoxicating pleasure of authorship. A college periodical conducted by friends of mine, still undergraduates, tempted me into print, and there is no form of lead poisoning which more rapidly and thoroughly pervades the blood and bones and marrow than that which reaches the young author through mental contact with type-metal. . . . In that fatal year I had my first attack of author's lead-poisoning, and I have never quite got rid of it from that day to this."

Dr. Holmes, writing fifty years or more after first taking up the study of medicine, was unable to recall the precise reasoning which led him to make the change of intended profession. The aptitude which he disclosed for it is sufficient explanation now, and it is very possible that, though his tastes were strongly literary, he yielded to that conviction which so sane a man was sure to have, that it would be unwise to depend upon letters for his daily bread, and so chose a profession which appealed to the humane interest and the scientific temper which were scarcely less prominent in his make-up. He studied partly in a private medical school carried on then by physicians and surgeons in Boston in good practice, two of whom were also professors in the Harvard Medical School, and he attended lectures also in this school, a division probably not unlike that which still prevails more or less in the legal profession. In April, 1833, however, he went abroad to avail himself of the more considerable opportunities for study in Paris, and remained abroad until October, 1835.

Upon his return to America, Dr. Holmes began the practice of his profession in Boston, but a phrase or two in his reminiscences suggests one reason for the readiness with which he soon turned to academic work, and they substantiate the notion already formed of a very fundamental characteristic. In recalling his initiation into the study of medicine in Boston, he refers lightly to the first impressions produced upon him by the anatomical skeleton and the white faces of the patients in the hospital. "All this had to pass away in a little time," he adds. "I had chosen my profession, and must meet its painful and repulsive aspects until they lost their power over my sensibilities." A half-century after that first experience he could still write, upon the occasion of his second journey, after the long interval, to Paris, that he shrank from seeing La Pitié, the hospital where he worked in his student days. No one would know him there; they would scarcely remember anything of his old master, Louis, and besides, he goes on, "I have not been among hospital beds for many a year, and my sensibilities are almost as impressible as they were before daily habit had rendered them comparatively callous." Something, also, may have been due to the very close scientific methods with which he became enamored when studying in Paris, methods which constantly lend themselves to the service of the investigator, and tend to lead one to make his practice experimental rather than therapeutic. At any rate, he accepted the professorship of anatomy and physiology at Dartmouth College in 1839, though he remained in that position only a few months, not abandoning the practice of medicine in Boston ; he married Amelia Lee Jackson, daughter of Judge Charles Jackson of the Supreme Judicial Court of Massachusetts, and in 1847 was made Parkman Professor of Anatomy and Physiology in the Medical School of Harvard College, a position which he retained until the close of 1882.

In a biographical sketch designed to accompany a collection of Holmes's poems, it is not to be expected that much attention should be given to the scientific side of his activity, but it would be an unequal sketch which failed to take account of both sides of so animated a life, especially since they could not be, in the order of nature, absolutely dissociated. It is a coincidence worth noting that the year when Dr. Holmes took his degree as doctor of medicine, 1836, was the year also in which he published his first volume of verse. The Phi Beta Kappa society is a somewhat loose league of scholarship in American colleges, an order in which the merit system, as governed by the standard of collegiate rank, determines membership, though after admission to the league the members have nothing to do but to perpetuate it. At Harvard there has long been a double yearly function for the society, a dinner, at which wit is more abundant than wine, and a public meeting with an oration and poem. Oratory has flourished in this soil, and notable addresses have been made by Everett and Emerson in early days, by Adams and Fiske in later ones, and by many more who have chosen the occasion for saying what they have wished to say to an audience of their peers. But poetry, which shuns occasions, has only now and then jumped with the hour. Scarcely a poet of distinction, however, but has hoped he too might so force nature that poetry would somehow find wings for Phi Beta Kappa.

It is indicative of the reputation which Holmes had already formed that though he had been absent on his professional study for two or three years, he was called on, seven years after graduation, to deliver the poem at the commencement in 1836. With an instinct for what was appropriate on occasions which never failed him, he read the poem, *Poetry, a Metrical Essay,* which is included in the first division of his poetical writings. As the reader will see by the notes, the poem carried as interludes two lyrics already printed, *The Cambridge Churchyard* and *Old Ironsides.* The introduction of these verses was doubtless most effective in delivery, and served to interrupt the essay in an agreeable fashion, but both the body of the poem and the preface with which it was introduced, when shortly after it appeared with a collection of poems written in the interval since leaving college, as a single volume, indicate the seriousness with which the young poet regarded his vocation. Spontaneity was a birthright, but he did not therefore disregard or flout at traditional form and accepted standards. On the contrary, he showed unmistakably that he belonged to the order of poets, not to the disorder of the poetic mob, and thus the volume which heralded his accession to literature was a witness to the permanence of his foothold.

This volume *Poetry,* as we have said, was published in 1836, and the next year he published a medical treatise. Thus neck and neck at the start were the two horses he continued to ride for many years. He did not publish a volume of poetry again until 1847, the year in which he abandoned the practice of medicine, and then he gathered the fugitive poems which had been appearing in periodicals, or had been used on occasions since the publication of *Poetry*. It is interesting to note that among the occasional poems were some called out by his professional relations, as well as one or two, not occasional, which were inspired by his study and practice; so impossible was it for him to sever his life, as did Bryant, who seemed to keep journalism in one cell of his brain and poetry in another, each in solitary confinement and forbidden to hold intercourse with each other. The volume of 1847 contained also the contents of the volume of 1836, and the poetry in this consolidated volume was substantially that included in the first three divisions of the present collection and the group of poems which form the first section of the Appendix. The volume was reprinted in England, and for some time to come represented the claim which Holmes might make to a place among poets.

The decade which followed the publication of this volume was nevertheless a period both of ripening and of product. It was undoubtedly the time in which a large part of the work was done in the preparation of the long series of lectures which the Parkman professor delivered before his classes. The volume of *Medical Essays* in his collected works contain papers and discourses which belong to this decade and to the whole period of his professorship, but the printed matter bears a very small proportion to the whole volume of his professional writing and speaking. In his *Farewell Address* to the Medical School, delivered November 28, 1882, he says: "This is the thirty-sixth Course of Lectures in which I have taken my place and performed my duties as Professor of Anatomy. For more than half my term of office I gave instruction in Physiology, after the fashion of my predecessors and in the manner then generally prevalent in our schools, where the physiological laboratory was not a necessary part of the apparatus of instruction." President Eliot bore testimony to the fidelity with which he carried on his academic work: "He did a great deal to make the school what it has become. He lectured regularly five times a week throughout the school year, and never failed to be on hand. He was the most careful of men in preparation of his lectures, and very painstaking in his experiments. He was very exact in dissection. His prosectors, whose duty it was to prepare his dissections, were always kept on the *qui vive* and spurred to their very best effort." It should not be overlooked that one of his medical writings, *The Contagiousness of Puerperal Fever*, first published in 1843 and reissued in an enlarged form in 1855, was a distinct contribution to science and revolutionized the practice of physicians.

But the sessions of the medical school were not continuous through the year, and Dr. Holmes's intellectual activity, moreover, could not be confined within the limits of his professional duties. His scientific studies took him further afield, and his literary interests, with which we have mainly to do, had already been determined by his early taste and inclination. At the time of which we are writing, the lecture system was popular, and offered to men of letters a means of livelihood and a form of publication. As the lectures, however, were for the most part during the academic year, it was not expedient for Professor Holmes to stray very far from home; so, unlike Emerson, he was practically confined to a circle within a short radius of Boston. In the *Autocrat* he has given humorous reminiscences of some of his experience as a lecturer, and in a bit of scholastic fun has hinted at the very close connection between speaking and writing in the vocation of a man of letters. He made his own lectures also the occasion for postludes of song. This he did with special grace in a course before the Lowell Institute of Boston on *The English Poets of the Nineteenth Century*. The characterizations of Wordsworth, Moore, Keats, and Shelley were here produced. On special occasions, also, he was orator, though the more insistent demand was for his poetry.

Dr. Holmes is strongly identified with Cambridge and Boston by his residence in those two places; but, as some of his poems hint, he had another home at Pittsfield in the western part of the State, where he lived for seven summers. He was drawn to the locality by the association of Pittsfield with his great-grandfather, Colonel Jacob Wendell, who had a homestead there in the eighteenth century. In 1844 he was invited to attend the Berkshire Jubilee, where he read the lines beginning

"Come back to your mother, ye children, for shame."

He seems to have heeded his own invitation, for in the summer of 1848 he built a cottage on his inherited estate. Longfellow, who, through his wife's family, the Appletons, had also an interest in Pittsfield and spent many weeks there, wrote in his journal, under date of August 5, 1848 : " Drove over, in the afternoon, to Dr. Holmes's house on the old Wendell farm, — a snug little place, with views of the river and the mountains." And Dr. Holmes himself, writing in January, 1857, says, "Seven sweet summers, the happiest of my life. I would n't exchange the recollection of them for a suburban villa. One thing I shall always be glad of ; that I planted seven hundred trees for somebody to sit in the shade of." There is more than one reference in his writings to his country life there, and among his poems some which owed their origin to occasions in his neighborhood. Others there are which sang themselves out of the nature in which he lived. Indeed, as Mr. Smith points out in his interesting sketch,[1] the poems which were written in Berkshire were lacking in scientific reference and in fun ; " It is Nature herself that breathes through each and every line." Later in life he made a summer home for himself at Beverly Farms on the north shore of Massachusetts Bay.

With the close of this decade, 1847-1857, there came a new flowering forth of Holmes's genius, which took a form worth noting, since, being his own, it served most perfectly to embody his spiritual power. In the third of what is popularly known as The Breakfast-Table series, namely, *The Poet at the Breakfast-Table*, the author distinctly says, what the observant reader of the series will be pretty sure to discover for himself : —

"I have unburdened myself in this book, and in some other pages, of what I was born to say. Many things that I have said in my riper days have been aching in my soul since I was a mere child. I say aching, because they conflicted with many of my inherited beliefs, or rather traditions. I did not know then that two strains of blood were striving in me for the mastery, — two ! twenty, perhaps, — twenty thousand for aught I know, — but represented to me by two, — paternal and maternal. But I do know this : I have struck a good many chords, first and last, in the consciousness of other people. I confess to a tender feeling for my little brood of thoughts. When they have been welcomed and praised it has pleased me ; and if at any time they have been rudely handled and despitefully treated, it has cost me a little worry. I don't despise reputation, and I should like to be remembered as having said something worth lasting well enough to last."

This passage presents briefly three very noticeable characteristics of Dr. Holmes's prose as contained in the series of *Atlantic* papers and stories. They give the mature thought of the writer, held back through many years for want of an adequate occasion, and ripened in his mind during this enforced silence ; they illustrate the effect upon his thought of his professional studies, which predisposed him to treat of the natural history

[1] *The Poet Among the Hills.* Oliver Wendell Holmes, in Berkshire. By J. E. A. SMITH. Pittsfield, Massachusetts. George Blatchford, 1895.

of man, and to import into his analysis of the invisible organism of life the terms and methods employed in the science of the visible anatomy and physiology ; and finally they are warm with a sympathy for men and women, and singularly felicitous in their expression of many of the indistinct and half-understood experiences of life. Yet behind this threefold manifestation of individual genius one looks for the personality itself thus disclosed, and, guided by the clue offered in the biography of the author as already traced, sees the vivid nature, sensitive to impressions, yet stable through a substantial hold upon a highly developed community, the product of generations of specialized forces charged with electrical power and leaping into the light with gladness. We may please ourselves with the notion that the pent-up experience of New England found a vent in Dr. Holmes, but after all the nearest fact, behind which we need not go unless we choose, is that of a person speaking outright and not afraid of a large *I*. This note of egotism which was struck at once in the very title, so felicitous, of the first book, sounds throughout the series and gives it its undying charm ; for the man who does not shield himself behind the autobiographic form is rare, and the man who can dramatize other figures about a central one, and make that central one at once dramatic and dominant, is rarer still.

For the form of these writings, it may be said that the impression produced upon the reader of the *Autocrat* series, which was finally gathered into a volume, is of a growth rather than of a premeditated artistic completeness, and this makes more evident the mature character of the work and its closeness to the personality of the writer. The first suggestion, as Holmes points out in *The Autocrat's Autobiography*, is to be found in the two papers published, under the title of *The Autocrat of the Breakfast-Table*, in *The New England Magazine* for November, 1831, and January, 1832. These were written by Dr. Holmes shortly after his graduation from college, and before he entered on his medical studies. They consist of brief epigrammatic observations upon various topics, the desultory talk of a person engrossing conversation at a table. The form is monologue, with scarcely more than a hint at interruptions, and no attempt at characterizing the speaker or his listeners. Twenty-five years later, when *The Atlantic Monthly* was founded, the author remembering the fancy resumed it, and under the same title began a series of papers which at once had great favor and grew, possibly, beyond the writer's original intention. Twenty-five years had not dulled the wit and gayety of the exuberant young writer ; rather they had ripened the early fruit, and imparted a richness of flavor which greatly increased the value. The maturity was seen not only in the wider reach and deeper tone of the talk, but in the humanizing of the scheme. Out of the talk at the breakfast-table one began to distinguish characters and faces in the persons about the board, and before the *Autocrat* was completed there had appeared a series of portraits, vivid and full of interest.

Two characters meanwhile were hinted at by Dr. Holmes rather than described or very palpably introduced, — the Professor and the Poet. It is not difficult to see that these are thin disguises for the author himself, who, in the versatility of his nature, appeals to the reader now as a brilliant philosopher, now as a man of science, now as a seer and poet. *The Professor at the Breakfast-Table* followed, and there was a still stronger dramatic element ; some of the former characters remained, and others of even more positive individuality were added ; a romance was inwoven and something like a plot sketched, so that, while the talk still went on and eddied about graver subjects than before, the book which grew out of the papers had more distinctly the form of a series of sketches from life. It was followed by two novels, *Elsie Venner* and *The Guardian*

Angel. The talks at the breakfast-table had often gravitated toward the deep themes of destiny and human freedom ; the novels wrought the same subjects in the form of fiction, and action interpreted the thought, while still there flowed on the wonderful, apparently inexhaustible stream of wit, tenderness, passion, and human sympathy. Fourteen years after the appearance of the first of the series, came *The Poet at the Breakfast-Table.* A new group of characters, with slight reminders of former ones, occupied the pages ; again talk and romance blended ; and playfulness, satire, sentiment, wise reflection and sturdy indignation trooped across the pages.

The Breakfast-Table series forms a group independent of the intercalated novels, and with its frequent poems may be taken as an artistic whole. It is hardly too much to say, that it makes a new contribution to the forms of literary art. It was not altogether novel. Such a book as Southey's *The Doctor*, for example, might be cited as a progenitor. Still all that went before it were characterized more by negligence and an unordered freedom. The distinctive mark of the *Autocrat* and its fellows was, as we have hinted, the frank dominance of the author's personality. The elasticity of the scheme rendered possible a comprehensiveness of material ; the exuberance of the author's fancy and the fullness of his thought gave a richness to the fabric ; the poetic sense of fitness kept the whole within just bounds. It is illustrative of the native, personal character of this series, so stamped with his genius, that when in his old age Holmes felt a desire to write again, deliberately and at length, he returned to the same form, and in *Over the Teacups* essayed the old happy blending of prose and verse, the vivification of characters supposed to carry on discussion about a social board, when in reality one dominant voice, even if sometimes ventriloquial, is heard throughout, — that of the inventor of the characters. And it is interesting to observe how shadowy at the last these characters have become, so that they are scarcely more than numerical, and how instinctively the old man, musing over the board, has surrounded himself with the gracious presences of women.

The form of these books made poetical interludes easy and natural. Sometimes the verses introduced were not blossoms upon the wandering vine, but cut flowers fastened carelessly for the lightening of the effect ; for the most part, however, they seem to belong where we find them, and a survey of the groups as presented in this volume confirms this impression. When arranging his poems for a final collective edition, Dr. Holmes brought together in successive sections the poems from each of the Breakfast-Table series, but removed those poems which had been more arbitrarily placed first in these books, such as those more properly arranged under the heading *Poems of the Class of '29.* Thus the poems included in *The Professor* are quite distinctly the outgrowth of that strain of religious speculation which characterizes the work ; they are positive affirmations, as if the author found a relief in occasional clear poetic expression when engaged in the heat of theological discussion. The series *Wind-Clouds and Star-Drifts*, on the other hand, which constitutes the main poetic apparatus of *The Poet*, is more distinctly philosophical in its nature; but when one turns to the volume and notes the form of insertion, he is reminded that the whole book is soberer in tone and more taken up with the structural treatment of the mysteries of human life, whereas *The Professor* was quite as markedly critical and more than once destructive of notions and conventions. The poems in *The Autocrat* partake of the swift, varied play of that book, and those in *Over the Teacups* show the flaring up now and then of the old flame as the book itself is more or less of an effort.

For the purpose of treating this notable series as a whole, we have departed from a strictly chronological survey of Dr. Holmes's career. *The Autocrat* appeared in 1857-1858, *The Professor* in 1859. The gap of fourteen years which intervened between this book and *The Poet* is represented in the poetical writings by the collection under the title *Songs of Many Seasons*, and both the subdivisions of that section and the titles of many of the poems intimate how much the author's thoughts were upon the great affairs which stirred his own country, — the war, the restoration of peace, and the beginning of that second great ingathering of the nations which will render the period following the war a great period in American history. He has left his impressions both in prose and in verse. *The Atlantic Monthly* afforded a convenient vehicle, as did the several occasions now kept alive by his verses. One of his notable papers was that entitled *My Hunt after "the Captain,"* and details his experience when going to the seat of war in the fall of 1862 on the occasion of the wounding of a son, who bears his father's name and is now a justice on the bench of the Supreme Court of Massachusetts.

When John Lothrop Motley died, Dr. Holmes wrote a sketch of him for the Massachusetts Historical Society, which was afterward expanded and published as a volume. The book is more than a friendly testimony, it is an expression of patriotism. No one need be told who has read that, and the letters which he himself wrote to Motley, his *Bread and the Newspaper*, his oration on *The Inevitable Trial*, and the lyrics which are comprehended under the title *In War Time*, that the author of *Old Ironsides* had an ardent affection for the nation and a large-hearted belief in it. And yet great crises brought these expressions to pass; his familiar habit of mind was cordially local. His affection fastened upon his college, and in his college on his class; he had a worthy pride in the race from which he had sprung, and the noble clannishness which is one of the safeguards of social morality; he loved the city of his life, not with the merely curious regard of the antiquary, but with the passion of the man who can be at home only in one place; and he held to New England as to a substantial entity, not to a geographical section of some greater whole. He did not travel, because Boston and Berkshire contented him. His laboratory was at hand; human nature was under his observation from the vantage-ground of home. With the instinct of a man of science, he took for analysis that which was most familiar to him, assured that in the bit of the world where he was born, and out of which he had got his nourishment, he had all he needed for the exercise of his wit. There is no more pathetic yet kindly figure in our literature than Little Boston. With poetic instinct, Dr. Holmes made him deformed, but not ugly. He put into him a fiery soul of local patriotism, and transfigured him thus. Under the guise of a bit of nature's mockery he was enabled to give vent to a flood of feeling without arousing laughter or contempt. All Little Boston's vehemence of civic pride is a memorial inscription, and whatever may be the fortune of the city, however august may be its presence, there lies embedded in this figure of Little Boston a perpetual witness to an imperishable civic personality.

The poems which occupy the closing sections of this volume, *Bunker-Hill Battle and other Poems*, *The Iron Gate and other Poems*, and *Before the Curfew*, bear frequent witness to the strength of Dr. Holmes's fidelity to his people and his country. They hint also, as do his later writings, of that temper which was growing upon him, so beautifully reflected in his own verse : —

> "Youth longs and manhood strives, but age remembers,
> Sits by the raked-up ashes of the past,
> Spreads its thin hands above the whitening embers
> That warm its creeping life-blood till the last."

Thus he wrote for the breakfast given him by the publishers of *The Atlantic Monthly* at the close of 1879. Yet in 1886 he made with his daughter a journey to Europe. Most of the time was passed in England, where the journey was like a Royal Progress. "The travellers," says the London *Daily News*, "had barely arrived when invitations came pouring in upon them. They received their 'baptism of fire' in that long conflict which lasts through the London season, on the first evening of their arrival in town. It consisted of a dinner, where twenty guests, celebrities and agreeable persons, were assembled to meet them. The dinner was followed by a grand reception. Then began a perpetual round of social engagements. Breakfasts, luncheons, dinners, teas, receptions, two, three and four deep of the evening, was the order of the waking hours. Society was charmed with the genial philosopher and poet. His courteous manner, his ready wit, the fascinating nobility of his countenance, made up a charming personality. There was something magnetic in the glance of his blue-gray eye, in the hearty grasp of his hand. Dr. Holmes went to the Derby, impelled by the wish to live again the impressions of fifty years ago. But this time he went down in company with the Prince of Wales, and witnessed the race from the grand stand. The animation with which the old man describes Ormonde, the beautiful bay of the Duke of Westminster, flashing past ridden by Archer, belongs to spirits as buoyant as were those that stirred the blood of the youth half a century before." The record of the journey is preserved in *Our Hundred Days in Europe*.

He had a mellow evening of life. As one after another of his comrades left the world, he bade them good-by with a song. Thus in his old age he sang after Lowell and Whittier and Parkman; at last his own voice was silent, and there was no one left in his generation to sing his farewell, for he it was who brought up the rear of the procession of American writers of the great period, as one by one passed into the firmament of fame.

He died in his home in Boston suddenly, while talking with his son, at half-past one, Sunday afternoon, October 7, 1894, in the eighty-sixth year of his age.

H. E. S.

TO MY READERS

[Written to introduce the Blue and Gold edition of Holmes's Poe

Nay, blame me not; I might have spared
  Your patience many a trivial verse,
Yet these my earlier welcome shared,
  So, let the better shield the worse.

And some might say, "Those ruder songs
  Had freshness which the new have lost;
To spring the opening leaf belongs,
  The chestnut-burs await the frost."

When those I wrote, my locks were brown,
  When these I write — ah, well-a-day!
The autumn thistle's silvery down
  Is not the purple bloom of May!

Go, little book, whose pages hold
  Those garnered years in loving trust;
How long before your blue and gold
  Shall fade and whiten in the dust?

O sexton of the alcoved tomb,
  Where souls in leathern cerements lie,
Tell me each living poet's doom!
  How long before his book shall die?

It matters little, soon or late,
  A day, a month, a year, an age, —
I read oblivion in its date,
  And Finis on its title-page.

Before we sighed, our griefs were told;
  Before we smiled, our joys were sung;
And all our passions shaped of old
  In accents lost to mortal tongue.

In vain a fresher mould we seek, —
  Can all the varied phrases tell
That Babel's wandering children speak
  How thrushes sing or lilacs smell?

TO MY READERS

Caged in the poet's lonely heart,
  Love wastes unheard its tenderest tone;
The soul that sings must dwell apart,
  Its inward melodies unknown.

Deal gently with us, ye who read!
  Our largest hope is unfulfilled, —
The promise still outruns the deed, —
  The tower, but not the spire, we build.

Our whitest pearl we never find;
  Our ripest fruit we never reach;
The flowering moments of the mind
  Drop half their petals in our speech.

These are my blossoms; if they wear
  One streak of morn or evening's glow,
Accept them; but to me more fair
  The buds of song that never blow.
    April 8, 1862.

EARLIER POEMS

[THE printing of *Poetry: a Metrical Essay* was made the occasion by the author for publishing the first collection of his poems in 1836. This contained the group afterward designated *Earlier Poems*, as well as most of those now grouped at the end of this volume under the heading *Verses from the Oldest Portfolio;* for when the volume of his verse had become considerable, Dr. Holmes thought best to winnow his first gathering, and to retain under the title *Earlier Poems* those which he regarded as constituent parts of his poetical product. The following passages are from the *Preface*, dated Boston, 1 November, 1836, which introduced the volume.

"The shorter pieces are arranged mainly with reference to the dignity of their subjects. A few remarks with regard to a species of writing in which the author has occasionally indulged, are offered to the consideration of those who are disposed to criticise rigorously; without the intention, however, of justifying all or any attempts at comic poetry, if they are bad specimens of their kind.

"The *extravagant* is often condemned as unnatural; as if a tendency of the mind, shown in all ages and forms, had not its foundation in nature. A series of hyperbolical images is considered beneath criticism by the same judges who would write treatises upon the sculptured satyrs and painted arabesques of antiquity, which are only hyperbole in stone and colors. As material objects in different lights repeat themselves in shadows variously elongated, contracted, or exaggerated, so our solid and sober thoughts caricature themselves in fantastic shapes inseparable from their originals, and having a unity in their extravagance, which proves them to have retained their proportions in certain respects, however differing in outline from their prototypes. To illustrate this by an example. Our idea of a certain great nation, an idea founded in substantial notions of its geography, its statistics, its history, in one aspect of the mind stretches into the sublime in the image of *Britannia*, and in another dilates into the sub-ridiculous in the person of *John Bull*. Both these personifications partially represent their object; both are useful and philosophical. And I am not afraid to say to the declaimers upon dignity of composition, that a metrical arabesque of a storm or a summer, if its images, though hyperbolical, are conceivable, and consistent with each other, is a perfectly healthy and natural exercise of the imagination, and not, as some might think, a voluntary degradation of its office. I argue, as I said before, for a principle, and not for my own attempt at its illustration.

"I had the intention of pointing out some accidental plagiarisms, or coincidences as they might be more mildly called, discovered principally by myself after the composition of the passages where they occur; but as they are, so far as I know, both innocent and insignificant, and as I have sometimes had literary pickpockets at my own skirts, I will leave them, like the apples of Atalanta, as an encouragement to sagacious critics, should any such follow my footsteps.

"I have come before the public like an actor who returns to fold his robes and make his bow to the audience. Already engaged in other duties, it has been with some effort that I have found time to adjust my own mantle; and I now willingly retire to more quiet labors, which, if less exciting, are more certain to be acknowledged as useful and received with gratitude; thankful that, not having staked all my hopes upon a single throw, I can sleep quietly after closing the last leaf of my little volume."]

OLD IRONSIDES

This was the popular name by which the frigate Constitution was known. The poem was first printed in the *Boston Daily Advertiser*, at the time when it was proposed to break up the old ship as unfit for service. I subjoin the paragraph which led to the writing of the poem. It is from the *Advertiser* of Tuesday, September 14, 1830:—

"*Old Ironsides.* — It has been affirmed upon good authority that the Secretary of the Navy has recommended to the Board of Navy Commissioners to dispose of the frigate Constitution. Since it has been understood that such a step was in contemplation we have heard but one opinion expressed, and that in decided disapprobation of the measure. Such a national object of interest, so endeared to our national pride as Old Ironsides is, should never by any act of our government cease to belong to the Navy, so long as our country is to be found upon the map of nations. In England it was lately determined by the Admiralty to cut the Victory, a one-hundred gun ship (which it will be recollected bore the flag of Lord Nelson at the battle of Trafalgar), down to a seventy-four, but so loud were the lamentations of the people upon the proposed measure that the intention was abandoned. We confidently anticipate that the Secretary of the Navy will in like manner consult the general wish in regard to the Constitution, and either let her remain in ordinary or rebuild her whenever the public service may require." — *New York Journal of Commerce.*

The poem was an impromptu outburst of feeling and was published on the next day but one after reading the above paragraph. [When *Poetry: a Metrical Essay* was published this poem was introduced as an interlude at the close of the second section.]

AY, tear her tattered ensign down !
  Long has it waved on high,
And many an eye has danced to see
  That banner in the sky ;
Beneath it rung the battle shout,
  And burst the cannon's roar ; —
The meteor of the ocean air
  Shall sweep the clouds no more.

Her deck, once red with heroes' blood,
  Where knelt the vanquished foe,
When winds were hurrying o'er the flood,
  And waves were white below,
No more shall feel the victor's tread,
  Or know the conquered knee ; —
The harpies of the shore shall pluck
  The eagle of the sea !

Oh, better that her shattered hulk
  Should sink beneath the wave ;
Her thunders shook the mighty deep,
  And there should be her grave ;
Nail to the mast her holy flag,
  Set every threadbare sail,
And give her to the god of storms,
  The lightning and the gale !

THE LAST LEAF

The poem was suggested by the sight of a figure well known to Bostonians [in 1831 or 1832], that of Major Thomas Melville, "the last of the cocked hats," as he was sometimes called. The Major had been a personable young man, very evidently, and retained evidence of it in

"The monumental pomp of age," —

which had something imposing and something odd about it for youthful eyes like mine. He was often pointed at as one of the "Indians" of the famous "Boston Tea-Party" of 1774. His aspect among the crowds of a later generation reminded me of a withered leaf which has held to its stem through the storms of autumn and winter, and finds itself still clinging to its bough while the new growths of spring are bursting their buds and spreading their foliage all around it. I make this explanation for the benefit of those who have been puzzled by the lines,

"The last leaf upon the tree
  In the spring."

The way in which it came to be written in a somewhat singular measure was this. I had become a little known as a versifier, and I thought that one or two other young writers were following my efforts with imitations, not meant as parodies and hardly to be considered improvements on their models. I determined to write in a measure which would at once betray any copyist. So far as it was suggested by any previous poem, the echo must have come from Campbell's "Battle of the Baltic," with its short terminal lines, such as the last of these two,

"By thy wild and stormy steep,
  Elsinore."

But I do not remember any poem in the same measure, except such as have been written since its publication.

The poem as first written had one of those false rhymes which produce a shudder in all educated persons, even in the poems of Keats and others who ought to have known better than to admit them.

The guilty verse ran thus : —

"But now he walks the streets,
  And he looks at all he meets
    So forlorn,
  And he shakes his feeble head,
  That it seems as if he said,
    'They are gone' ! "

A little more experience, to say nothing of the sneer of an American critic in an English periodical, showed me that this would never do. Here was what is called a "cockney rhyme," — one in which the sound of the letter *r* is neglected — maltreated as the letter *h* is insulted by the average Briton by leaving it out everywhere except where it should be silent. Such an ill-mated pair as "forlorn" and "gone" could not possibly pass current in good rhyming society. But what to do about it was the question. I *must* keep

"They are gone!"

and I could not think of any rhyme which I could work in satisfactorily. In this perplexity my friend, Mrs. Folsom, wife of that excellent scholar, Mr. Charles Folsom, then and for a long time the unsparing and infallible corrector of the press at Cambridge, suggested the line,

"Sad and wan,"

which I thankfully adopted and have always retained.

Good Abraham Lincoln had a great liking for the poem, and repeated it from memory to Governor Andrew, as the Governor himself told me. I have a copy of it made by the hand of Edgar Allan Poe.

[When this poem was issued with an accompaniment of illustration and decoration in 1894, Dr. Holmes wrote to his publishers:—

"I have read the proof you sent me and find nothing in it which I feel called upon to alter or explain.

"I have lasted long enough to serve as an illustration of my own poem. I am one of the very last of the leaves which still cling to the bough of life that budded in the spring of the nineteenth century. The days of my years are threescore and twenty, and I am almost half way up the steep incline which leads me toward the base of the new century so near to which I have already climbed.

"I am pleased to find that this poem, carrying with it the marks of having been written in the jocund morning of life, is still read and cared for. It was with a smile on my lips that I wrote it; I cannot read it without a sigh of tender remembrance. I hope it will not sadden my older readers, while it may amuse some of the younger ones to whom its experiences are as yet only floating fancies."]

I SAW him once before,
As he passed by the door,
  And again
The pavement stones resound,
As he totters o'er the ground
  With his cane.

They say that in his prime,
Ere the pruning-knife of Time
  Cut him down,
Not a better man was found
By the Crier on his round
  Through the town.

But now he walks the streets,
And he looks at all he meets
  Sad and wan,
And he shakes his feeble head,
That it seems as if he said,
  "They are gone."

The mossy marbles rest
On the lips that he has prest
  In their bloom,
And the names he loved to hear
Have been carved for many a year
  On the tomb.

My grandmamma has said —
Poor old lady, she is dead
  Long ago —
That he had a Roman nose,
And his cheek was like a rose
  In the snow;

But now his nose is thin,
And it rests upon his chin
  Like a staff,
And a crook is in his back,
And a melancholy crack
  In his laugh.

I know it is a sin
For me to sit and grin
  At him here;
But the old three-cornered hat,
And the breeches, and all that,
  Are so queer!

And if I should live to be
The last leaf upon the tree
  In the spring,
Let them smile, as I do now,
At the old forsaken bough
  Where I cling.

THE CAMBRIDGE CHURCHYARD

[This poem was included as an interlude at the close of the first section in *Poetry: a Metrical Essay*, when that was published in book form.]

OUR ancient church! its lowly tower,
  Beneath the loftier spire,
Is shadowed when the sunset hour
  Clothes the tall shaft in fire;
It sinks beyond the distant eye

Long ere the glittering vane,
High wheeling in the western sky,
Has faded o'er the plain.

Like Sentinel and Nun, they keep
   Their vigil on the green;
One seems to guard, and one to weep,
   The dead that lie between;
And both roll out, so full and near,
   Their music's mingling waves,
They shake the grass, whose pennoned spear
   Leans on the narrow graves.

The stranger parts the flaunting weeds,
   Whose seeds the winds have strown
So thick, beneath the line he reads,
   They shade the sculptured stone;
The child unveils his clustered brow,
   And ponders for a while
The graven willow's pendent bough,
   Or rudest cherub's smile.

But what to them the dirge, the knell?
   These were the mourner's share, —
The sullen clang, whose heavy swell
   Throbbed through the beating air;
The rattling cord, the rolling stone,
   The shelving sand that slid,
And, far beneath, with hollow tone
   Rung on the coffin's lid.

The slumberer's mound grows fresh and green,
   Then slowly disappears;
The mosses creep, the gray stones lean,
   Earth hides his date and years;
But, long before the once-loved name
   Is sunk or worn away,
No lip the silent dust may claim,
   That pressed the breathing clay.

Go where the ancient pathway guides,
   See where our sires laid down
Their smiling babes, their cherished brides,
   The patriarchs of the town;
Hast thou a tear for buried love?
   A sigh for transient power?
All that a century left above,
   Go, read it in an hour!

The Indian's shaft, the Briton's ball,
   The sabre's thirsting edge,
The hot shell, shattering in its fall,
   The bayonet's rending wedge, —
Here scattered death; yet, seek the spot,
   No trace thine eye can see,
No altar, — and they need it not
   Who leave their children free!

Look where the turbid rain-drops stand
   In many a chiselled square;
The knightly crest, the shield, the brand
   Of honored names were there; —
Alas! for every tear is dried
   Those blazoned tablets knew,
Save when the icy marble's side
   Drips with the evening dew.

Or gaze upon yon pillared stone,
   The empty urn of pride;
There stand the Goblet and the Sun, —
   What need of more beside?
Where lives the memory of the dead,
   Who made their tomb a toy?
Whose ashes press that nameless bed?
   Go, ask the village boy!

Lean o'er the slender western wall,
   Ye ever-roaming girls;
The breath that bids the blossom fall
   May lift your floating curls,
To sweep the simple lines that tell
   An exile's date and doom;
And sigh, for where his daughters dwell,
   They wreathe the stranger's tomb.

And one amid these shades was born,
   Beneath this turf who lies,
Once beaming as the summer's morn,
   That closed her gentle eyes;
If sinless angels love as we,
   Who stood thy grave beside,
Three seraph welcomes waited thee,
   The daughter, sister, bride!

I wandered to thy buried mound
   When earth was hid below
The level of the glaring ground,
   Choked to its gates with snow,
And when with summer's flowery waves
   The lake of verdure rolled,
As if a Sultan's white-robed slaves
   Had scattered pearls and gold.

Nay, the soft pinions of the air,
   That lift this trembling tone,
Its breath of love may almost bear
   To kiss thy funeral stone;
And, now thy smiles have passed away,
   For all the joy they gave,

May sweetest dews and warmest ray
    Lie on thine early grave!

When damps beneath and storms above
    Have bowed these fragile towers,
Still o'er the graves yon locust grove
    Shall swing its Orient flowers;
And I would ask no mouldering bust,
    If e'er this humble line,
Which breathed a sigh o'er others' dust,
    Might call a tear on mine.

TO AN INSECT

The Katydid is "a species of grasshopper found in the United States, so called from the sound which it makes." WORCESTER.
I used to hear this insect in Providence, Rhode Island, but I do not remember hearing it in Cambridge, Massachusetts, where I passed my boyhood. It is well known in other towns in the neighborhood of Boston.

I LOVE to hear thine earnest voice,
    Wherever thou art hid,
Thou testy little dogmatist,
    Thou pretty Katydid!
Thou mindest me of gentlefolks, —
    Old gentlefolks are they, —
Thou say'st an undisputed thing
    In such a solemn way.

Thou art a female, Katydid!
    I know it by the trill
That quivers through thy piercing notes,
    So petulant and shrill;
I think there is a knot of you
    Beneath the hollow tree, —
A knot of spinster Katydids, —
    Do Katydids drink tea?

Oh, tell me where did Katy live,
    And what did Katy do?
And was she very fair and young,
    And yet so wicked, too?
Did Katy love a naughty man,
    Or kiss more cheeks than one?
I warrant Katy did no more
    Than many a Kate has done.

Dear me! I'll tell you all about
    My fuss with little Jane,
And Ann, with whom I used to walk
    So often down the lane,
And all that tore their locks of black,
Or wet their eyes of blue, —
Pray tell me, sweetest Katydid,
    What did poor Katy do?

Ah no! the living oak shall crash,
    That stood for ages still,
The rock shall rend its mossy base
    And thunder down the hill,
Before the little Katydid
    Shall add one word, to tell
The mystic story of the maid
    Whose name she knows so well.

Peace to the ever-murmuring race!
    And when the latest one
Shall fold in death her feeble wings
    Beneath the autumn sun,
Then shall she raise her fainting voice,
    And lift her drooping lid,
And then the child of future years
    Shall hear what Katy did.

THE DILEMMA

Now, by the blessed Paphian queen,
Who heaves the breast of sweet sixteen;
By every name I cut on bark
Before my morning star grew dark;
By Hymen's torch, by Cupid's dart,
By all that thrills the beating heart;
The bright black eye, the melting blue, —
I cannot choose between the two.

I had a vision in my dreams; —
I saw a row of twenty beams;
From every beam a rope was hung,
In every rope a lover swung;
I asked the hue of every eye
That bade each luckless lover die;
Ten shadowy lips said, heavenly blue,
And ten accused the darker hue.

I asked a matron which she deemed
With fairest light of beauty beamed;
She answered, some thought both were
    fair, —
Give her blue eyes and golden hair.
I might have liked her judgment well,
But, as she spoke, she rung the bell,
And all her girls, nor small nor few,
Came marching in, — their eyes were blue.

I asked a maiden; back she flung
The locks that round her forehead hung,

And turned her eye, a glorious one,
Bright as a diamond in the sun,
On me, until beneath its rays
I felt as if my hair would blaze ;
She liked all eyes but eyes of green ;
She looked at me ; what could she mean ?

Ah ! many lids Love lurks between,
Nor heeds the coloring of his screen ;
And when his random arrows fly,
The victim falls, but knows not why.
Gaze not upon his shield of jet,
The shaft upon the string is set ;
Look not beneath his azure veil,
Though every limb were cased in mail.

Well, both might make a martyr break
The chain that bound him to the stake ;
And both, with but a single ray,
Can melt our very hearts away ;
And both, when balanced, hardly seem
To stir the scales, or rock the beam ;
But that is dearest, all the while,
That wears for us the sweetest smile.

MY AUNT

My aunt ! my dear unmarried aunt !
　Long years have o'er her flown ;
Yet still she strains the aching clasp
　That binds her virgin zone ;
I know it hurts her, — though she looks
　As cheerful as she can ;
Her waist is ampler than her life,
　For life is but a span.

My aunt ! my poor deluded aunt !
　Her hair is almost gray ;
Why will she train that winter curl
　In such a spring-like way ?
How can she lay her glasses down,
　And say she reads as well,
When through a double convex lens
　She just makes out to spell ?

Her father — grandpapa ! forgive
　This erring lip its smiles —
Vowed she should make the finest girl
　Within a hundred miles ;
He sent her to a stylish school ;
　'T was in her thirteenth June ;
And with her, as the rules required,
　"Two towels and a spoon."

They braced my aunt against a board,
　To make her straight and tall ;
They laced her up, they starved her down,
　To make her light and small ;
They pinched her feet, they singed her hair,
　They screwed it up with pins ; —
Oh, never mortal suffered more
　In penance for her sins.

So, when my precious aunt was done,
　My grandsire brought her back ;
(By daylight, lest some rabid youth
　Might follow on the track ;)
" Ah ! " said my grandsire, as he shook
　Some powder in his pan,
" What could this lovely creature do
　Against a desperate man ! "

Alas ! nor chariot, nor barouche,
　Nor bandit cavalcade,
Tore from the trembling father's arms
　His all-accomplished maid.
For her how happy had it been !
　And Heaven had spared to me
To see one sad, ungathered rose
　On my ancestral tree.

REFLECTIONS OF A PROUD PEDESTRIAN

I saw the curl of his waving lash,
　And the glance of his knowing eye,
And I knew that he thought he was cutting a dash,
　As his steed went thundering by.

And he may ride in the rattling gig,
　Or flourish the Stanhope gay,
And dream that he looks exceeding big
　To the people that walk in the way ;

But he shall think, when the night is still,
　On the stable-boy's gathering numbers,
And the ghost of many a veteran bill
　Shall hover around his slumbers ;

The ghastly dun shall worry his sleep,
　And constables cluster around him,
And he shall creep from the wood-hole deep
　Where their spectre eyes have found him !

Ay! gather your reins, and crack your
    thong,
  And bid your steed go faster;
He does not know, as he scrambles along,
  That he has a fool for his master;

And hurry away on your lonely ride,
  Nor deign from the mire to save me;
I will paddle it stoutly at your side
  With the tandem that nature gave me!

DAILY TRIALS

BY A SENSITIVE MAN

    OH, there are times
When all this fret and tumult that we hear
Do seem more stale than to the sexton's
    ear
    His own dull chimes.

    Ding dong! ding dong!
The world is in a simmer like a sea
Over a pent volcano, — woe is me
    All the day long!

    From crib to shroud!
Nurse o'er our cradles screameth lullaby,
And friends in boots tramp round us as we
    die,
    Snuffling aloud.

    At morning's call
The small-voiced pug-dog welcomes in the
    sun,
And flea-bit mongrels, wakening one by
    one,
    Give answer all.

    When evening dim
Draws round us, then the lonely cater-
    waul,
Tart solo, sour duet, and general squall, —
    These are our hymn.

    Women, with tongues
Like polar needles, ever on the jar;
Men, plugless word-spouts, whose deep
    fountains are
    Within their lungs.

    Children, with drums
Strapped round them by the fond paternal
    ass;
Peripatetics with a blade of grass
    Between their thumbs.

    Vagrants, whose arts
Have caged some devil in their mad
    machine,
Which grinding, squeaks, with husky
    groans between,
    Come out by starts.

    Cockneys that kill
Thin horses of a Sunday, — men, with
    clams,
Hoarse as young bisons roaring for their
    dams
    From hill to hill.

    Soldiers, with guns,
Making a nuisance of the blessed air,
Child-crying bellman, children in despair,
    Screeching for buns.

    Storms, thunders, waves!
Howl, crash, and bellow till ye get your
    fill;
Ye sometimes rest; men never can be still
    But in their graves.

EVENING

BY A TAILOR

DAY hath put on his jacket, and around
His burning bosom buttoned it with stars.
Here will I lay me on the velvet grass,
That is like padding to earth's meagre ribs,
And hold communion with the things about
  me.
Ah me! how lovely is the golden braid
That binds the skirt of night's descending
  robe!
The thin leaves, quivering on their silken
  threads,
Do make a music like to rustling satin,
As the light breezes smooth their downy
  nap.

  Ha! what is this that rises to my touch,
So like a cushion? Can it be a cabbage?
It is, it is that deeply injured flower,
Which boys do flout us with; — but yet I
  love thee,
Thou giant rose, wrapped in a green sur-
  tout.

Doubtless in Eden thou didst blush as
    bright
As these, thy puny brethren; and thy
    breath
Sweetened the fragrance of her spicy air;
But now thou seemest like a bankrupt beau,
Stripped of his gaudy hues and essences,
And growing portly in his sober garments.

Is that a swan that rides upon the water?
Oh no, it is that other gentle bird,
Which is the patron of our noble calling.
I well remember, in my early years,
When these young hands first closed upon
    a goose;
I have a scar upon my thimble finger,
Which chronicles the hour of young ambition.
My father was a tailor, and his father,
And my sire's grandsire, all of them were
    tailors;
They had an ancient goose, — it was an
    heirloom
From some remoter tailor of our race.
It happened I did see it on a time
When none was near, and I did deal with it,
And it did burn me, — oh, most fearfully!

It is a joy to straighten out one's limbs,
And leap elastic from the level counter,
Leaving the petty grievances of earth,
The breaking thread, the din of clashing
    shears,
And all the needles that do wound the
    spirit,
For such a pensive hour of soothing silence.
Kind Nature, shuffling in her loose undress,
Lays bare her shady bosom; — I can feel
With all around me; — I can hail the
    flowers
That sprig earth's mantle, — and yon quiet
    bird,
That rides the stream, is to me as a brother.
The vulgar know not all the bidden pockets,
Where Nature stows away her loveliness.
But this unnatural posture of the legs
Cramps my extended calves, and I must go
Where I can coil them in their wonted fashion.

THE DORCHESTER GIANT

The "pudding-stone" is a remarkable conglomerate found very abundantly in the towns mentioned, all of which are in the neighborhood of Boston. We used in those primitive days to ask friends to *ride* with us when we meant to take them to *drive* with us. [It is interesting to see how the same subject presented itself to the poet in different moods. There is a passage in *The Professor at the Breakfast-Table* which begins, "I wonder whether the boys who live in Roxbury and Dorchester are ever moved to tears or filled with silent awe as they look upon the rocks and fragments of 'pudding-stone' abounding in those localities." Then follows a half page of eloquent speculation on the pudding-stone.]

THERE was a giant in time of old,
    A mighty one was he;
He had a wife, but she was a scold,
So he kept her shut in his mammoth fold;
    And he had children three.

It happened to be an election day,
    And the giants were choosing a king;
The people were not democrats then,
They did not talk of the rights of men,
    And all that sort of thing.

Then the giant took his children three,
    And fastened them in the pen;
The children roared; quoth the giant, "Be
    still!"
And Dorchester Heights and Milton Hill
    Rolled back the sound again.

Then he brought them a pudding stuffed
    with plums,
    As big as the State-House dome;
Quoth he, "There 's something for you to
    eat;
So stop your mouths with your 'lection
    treat,
    And wait till your dad comes home."

So the giant pulled him a chestnut stout,
    And whittled the boughs away;
The boys and their mother set up a shout,
Said he, "You 're in, and you can't get out,
    Bellow as loud as you may."

Off he went, and he growled a tune
    As he strode the fields along;
'T is said a buffalo fainted away,
And fell as cold as a lump of clay,
    When he heard the giant's song.

But whether the story's true or not,
    It is n't for me to show;

There 's many a thing that 's twice as queer
In somebody's lectures that we hear,
  And those are true, you know.

  . . . .

What are those lone ones doing now,
  The wife and the children sad?
Oh, they are in a terrible rout,
Screaming, and throwing their pudding about,
  Acting as they were mad.

They flung it over to Roxbury hills,
  They flung it over the plain,
And all over Milton and Dorchester too
Great lumps of pudding the giants threw;
  They tumbled as thick as rain.

  . . . .

Giant and mammoth have passed away,
  For ages have floated by;
The suet is hard as a marrow-bone,
And every plum is turned to a stone,
  But there the puddings lie.

And if, some pleasant afternoon,
  You 'll ask me out to ride,
The whole of the story I will tell,
And you shall see where the puddings fell,
  And pay for the punch beside.

TO THE PORTRAIT OF "A LADY"

IN THE ATHENÆUM GALLERY

[The companion piece, *To the Portrait of "A Gentleman" in the Athenæum Gallery*, was relegated by the author to *Verses from the Oldest Portfolio*, when he divided his first volume as stated in the introductory note.]

WELL, Miss, I wonder where you live,
  I wonder what 's your name,
I wonder how you came to be
  In such a stylish frame;
Perhaps you were a favorite child,
  Perhaps an only one;
Perhaps your friends were not aware
  You had your portrait done!

Yet you must be a harmless soul;
  I cannot think that Sin
Would care to throw his loaded dice,
  With such a stake to win;
I cannot think you would provoke
  The poet's wicked pen,
Or make young women bite their lips,
  Or ruin fine young men.

Pray, did you ever hear, my love,
  Of boys that go about,
Who, for a very trifling sum,
  Will snip one's picture out?
I 'm not averse to red and white,
  But all things have their place,
I think a profile cut in black
  Would suit your style of face!

I love sweet features; I will own
  That I should like myself
To see my portrait on a wall,
  Or bust upon a shelf;
But nature sometimes makes one up
  Of such sad odds and ends,
It really might be quite as well
  Hushed up among one's friends!

THE COMET

THE Comet! He is on his way,
  And singing as he flies;
The whizzing planets shrink before
  The spectre of the skies;
Ah! well may regal orbs burn blue,
  And satellites turn pale,
Ten million cubic miles of head,
  Ten billion leagues of tail!

On, on by whistling spheres of light
  He flashes and he flames;
He turns not to the left nor right,
  He asks them not their names;
One spurn from his demoniac heel, —
  Away, away they fly,
Where darkness might be bottled up
  And sold for "Tyrian dye."

And what would happen to the land,
  And how would look the sea,
If in the bearded devil's path
  Our earth should chance to be?
Full hot and high the sea would boil,
  Full red the forests gleam;
Methought I saw and heard it all
  In a dyspeptic dream!

I saw a tutor take his tube
    The Comet's course to spy;
I heard a scream, — the gathered rays
    Had stewed the tutor's eye;
I saw a fort, — the soldiers all
    Were armed with goggles green;
Pop cracked the guns! whiz flew the balls!
    Bang went the magazine!

I saw a poet dip a scroll
    Each moment in a tub,
I read upon the warping back,
    "The Dream of Beelzebub;"
He could not see his verses burn,
    Although his brain was fried,
And ever and anon he bent
    To wet them as they dried.

I saw the scalding pitch roll down
    The crackling, sweating pines,
And streams of smoke, like water-spouts,
    Burst through the rumbling mines;
I asked the firemen why they made
    Such noise about the town;
They answered not, — but all the while
    The brakes went up and down.

I saw a roasting pullet sit
    Upon a baking egg;
I saw a cripple scorch his hand
    Extinguishing his leg;
I saw nine geese upon the wing
    Towards the frozen pole,
And every mother's gosling fell
    Crisped to a crackling coal.

I saw the ox that browsed the grass
    Writhe in the blistering rays,
The herbage in his shrinking jaws
    Was all a fiery blaze;
I saw huge fishes, boiled to rags,
    Bob through the bubbling brine;
And thoughts of supper crossed my soul;
    I had been rash at mine.

Strange sights! strange sounds! O fearful dream!
    Its memory haunts me still,
The steaming sea, the crimson glare,
    That wreathed each wooded hill;
Stranger! if through thy reeling brain
    Such midnight visions sweep,
Spare, spare, oh, spare thine evening meal,
    And sweet shall be thy sleep!

THE MUSIC-GRINDERS

There are three ways in which men take
    One's money from his purse,
And very hard it is to tell
    Which of the three is worse;
But all of them are bad enough
    To make a body curse.

You're riding out some pleasant day,
    And counting up your gains;
A fellow jumps from out a bush,
    And takes your horse's reins,
Another hints some words about
    A bullet in your brains.

It's hard to meet such pressing friends
    In such a lonely spot;
It's very hard to lose your cash,
    But harder to be shot;
And so you take your wallet out,
    Though you would rather not.

Perhaps you're going out to dine, —
    Some odious creature begs;
You'll hear about the cannon-ball
    That carried off his pegs,
And says it is a dreadful thing
    For men to lose their legs.

He tells you of his starving wife,
    His children to be fed,
Poor little, lovely innocents,
    All clamorous for bread, —
And so you kindly help to put
    A bachelor to bed.

You're sitting on your window-seat,
    Beneath a cloudless moon;
You hear a sound, that seems to wear
    The semblance of a tune,
As if a broken fife should strive
    To drown a cracked bassoon.

And nearer, nearer still, the tide
    Of music seems to come,
There's something like a human voice,
    And something like a drum;
You sit in speechless agony,
    Until your ear is numb.

Poor "home, sweet home" should seem to be
    A very dismal place;

Your "auld acquaintance" all at once
  Is altered in the face;
Their discords sting through Burns and
    Moore,
  Like hedgehogs dressed in lace.

You think they are crusaders, sent
  From some infernal clime,
To pluck the eyes of Sentiment,
  And dock the tail of Rhyme,
To crack the voice of Melody,
  And break the legs of Time.

But hark! the air again is still,
  The music all is ground,
And silence, like a poultice, comes
  To heal the blows of sound;
It cannot be, — it is, — it is, —
  A hat is going round!

No! Pay the dentist when he leaves
  A fracture in your jaw;
And pay the owner of the bear
  That stunned you with his paw,
And buy the lobster that has had
  Your knuckles in his claw;

But if you are a portly man,
  Put on your fiercest frown,
And talk about a constable
  To turn them out of town;
Then close your sentence with an oath,
  And shut the window down!

And if you are a slender man,
  Not big enough for that,
Or, if you cannot make a speech,
  Because you are a flat,
Go very quietly and drop
  A button in the hat!

THE TREADMILL SONG

THE stars are rolling in the sky,
  The earth rolls on below,
And we can feel the rattling wheel
  Revolving as we go.
Then tread away, my gallant boys,
  And make the axle fly;
Why should not wheels go round about,
  Like planets in the sky?

Wake up, wake up, my duck-legged man,
  And stir your solid pegs!

Arouse, arouse, my gawky friend,
  And shake your spider legs;
What though you 're awkward at the
    trade,
  There's time enough to learn, —
So lean upon the rail, my lad,
  And take another turn.

They 've built us up a noble wall,
  To keep the vulgar out;
We 've nothing in the world to do
  But just to walk about;
So faster, now, you middle men,
  And try to beat the ends, —
It's pleasant work to ramble round
  Among one's honest friends.

Here, tread upon the long man's toes,
  He sha'n't be lazy here, —
And punch the little fellow's ribs,
  And tweak that lubber's ear, —
He's lost them both, — don't pull his
    hair,
  Because he wears a scratch,
But poke him in the further eye,
  That is n't in the patch.

Hark! fellows, there 's the supper-bell,
  And so our work is done;
It 's pretty sport, — suppose we take
  A round or two for fun!
If ever they should turn me out,
  When I have better grown,
Now hang me, but I mean to have
  A treadmill of my own!

THE SEPTEMBER GALE

This tremendous hurricane occurred on the 23d of September, 1815. I remember it well, being then seven years old. A full account of it was published, I think, in the records of the American Academy of Arts and Sciences. Some of my recollections are given in *The Seasons*, an article to be found in a book of mine entitled *Pages from an Old Volume of Life*.

I'M not a chicken; I have seen
  Full many a chill September,
And though I was a youngster then,
  That gale I well remember;
The day before, my kite-string snapped,
  And I, my kite pursuing,
The wind whisked off my palm-leaf hat;
  For me two storms were brewing!

It came as quarrels sometimes do,
  When married folks get clashing;
There was a heavy sigh or two,
  Before the fire was flashing, —
A little stir among the clouds,
  Before they rent asunder, —
A little rocking of the trees,
  And then came on the thunder.

Lord! how the ponds and rivers boiled!
  They seemed like bursting craters!
And oaks lay scattered on the ground
  As if they were p'taters;
And all above was in a howl,
  And all below a clatter, —
The earth was like a frying-pan,
  Or some such hissing matter.

It chanced to be our washing-day,
  And all our things were drying;
The storm came roaring through the lines,
  And set them all a flying;
I saw the shirts and petticoats
  Go riding off like witches;
I lost, ah! bitterly I wept, —
  I lost my Sunday breeches!

I saw them straddling through the air,
  Alas! too late to win them;
I saw them chase the clouds, as if
  The devil had been in them;
They were my darlings and my pride,
  My boyhood's only riches, —
"Farewell, farewell," I faintly cried, —
  "My breeches! O my breeches!"

That night I saw them in my dreams,
  How changed from what I knew them!
The dews had steeped their faded threads,
  The winds had whistled through them!
I saw the wide and ghastly rents
  Where demon claws had torn them;
A hole was in their amplest part,
  As if an imp had worn them.

I have had many happy years,
  And tailors kind and clever,
But those young pantaloons have gone
  Forever and forever!
And not till fate has cut the last
  Of all my earthly stitches,
This aching heart shall cease to mourn
  My loved, my long-lost breeches!

THE HEIGHT OF THE RIDICULOUS

I WROTE some lines once on a time
  In wondrous merry mood,
And thought, as usual, men would say
  They were exceeding good.

They were so queer, so very queer,
  I laughed as I would die;
Albeit, in the general way,
  A sober man am I.

I called my servant, and he came;
  How kind it was of him
To mind a slender man like me,
  He of the mighty limb.

"These to the printer," I exclaimed,
  And, in my humorous way,
I added, (as a trifling jest,)
  "There'll be the devil to pay."

He took the paper, and I watched,
  And saw him peep within;
At the first line he read, his face
  Was all upon the grin.

He read the next; the grin grew broad,
  And shot from ear to ear;
He read the third; a chuckling noise
  I now began to hear.

The fourth; he broke into a roar;
  The fifth; his waistband split;
The sixth; he burst five buttons off,
  And tumbled in a fit.

Ten days and nights, with sleepless eye,
  I watched that wretched man,
And since, I never dare to write
  As funny as I can.

THE LAST READER

I SOMETIMES sit beneath a tree
  And read my own sweet songs;
Though naught they may to others be,
  Each humble line prolongs
A tone that might have passed away,
But for that scarce remembered lay.

I keep them like a lock or leaf
  That some dear girl has given;
Frail record of an hour, as brief
  As sunset clouds in heaven,

But spreading purple twilight still
High over memory's shadowed hill.

They lie upon my pathway bleak,
    Those flowers that once ran wild,
As on a father's careworn cheek
    The ringlets of his child ;
The golden mingling with the gray,
And stealing half its snows away.

What care I though the dust is spread
    Around these yellow leaves,
Or o'er them his sarcastic thread
    Oblivion's insect weaves ?
Though weeds are tangled on the stream,
It still reflects my morning's beam.

And therefore love I such as smile
    On these neglected songs,
Nor deem that flattery's needless wile
    My opening bosom wrongs ;
For who would trample, at my side,
A few pale buds, my garden's pride ?

It may be that my scanty ore
    Long years have washed away,
And where were golden sands before
    Is naught but common clay ;
Still something sparkles in the sun
For memory to look back upon.

And when my name no more is heard,
    My lyre no more is known,
Still let me, like a winter's bird,
    In silence and alone,
Fold over them the weary wing
Once flashing through the dews of spring.

Yes, let my fancy fondly wrap
    My youth in its decline,
And riot in the rosy lap
    Of thoughts that once were mine,
And give the worm my little store
When the last reader reads no more !

POETRY

A METRICAL ESSAY, READ BEFORE THE PHI BETA KAPPA SOCIETY, HARVARD UNIVERSITY, AUGUST, 1836

TO CHARLES WENTWORTH UPHAM, THE FOLLOWING METRICAL ESSAY IS AFFECTIONATELY INSCRIBED.

This Academic Poem presents the simple and partial views of a young person trained after the schools of classical English verse as represented by Pope, Goldsmith, and Campbell, with whose lines his memory was early stocked. It will be observed that it deals chiefly with the constructive side of the poet's function. That which makes him a poet is not the power of writing melodious rhymes, it is not the possession of ordinary human sensibilities nor even of both these qualities in connection with each other. I should rather say, if I were now called upon to define it, it is the power of transfiguring the experiences and shows of life into an aspect which comes from his imagination and kindles that of others. Emotion is its stimulus and language furnishes its expression ; but these are not all, as some might infer was the doctrine of the poem before the reader.

A common mistake made by young persons who suppose themselves to have the poetical gift is that their own spiritual exaltation finds a true expression in the conventional phrases which are borrowed from the voices of the singers whose inspiration they think they share.

Looking at this poem as an expression of some aspects of the *ars poetica*, with some passages which I can read even at this mature period of life without blushing for them, it may stand as the most serious representation of my early efforts. Intended as it was for public delivery, many of its paragraphs may betray the fact by their somewhat rhetorical and sonorous character.

SCENES of my youth ! awake its slumber-
    ing fire !
Ye winds of Memory, sweep the silent lyre !
Ray of the past, if yet thou canst appear,
Break through the clouds of Fancy's wan-
    ing year ;
Chase from her breast the thin autumnal
    snow,
If leaf or blossom still is fresh below !

Long have I wandered ; the returning
    tide
Brought back an exile to his cradle's side ;
And as my bark her time-worn flag un-
    rolled,
To greet the land-breeze with its faded
    fold,
So, in remembrance of my boyhood's time,
I lift these ensigns of neglected rhyme ;
Oh, more than blest, that, all my wander-
    ings through,
My anchor falls where first my pennons
    flew !

The morning light, which rains its
    quivering beams
Wide o'er the plains, the summits, and the
    streams,
In one broad blaze expands its golden glow
On all that answers to its glance below ;
Yet, changed on earth, each far reflected
    ray
Braids with fresh hues the shining brow of
    day ;
Now, clothed in blushes by the painted
    flowers,
Tracks on their cheeks the rosy-fingered
    hours ;
Now, lost in shades, whose dark entangled
    leaves
Drip at the noontide from their pendent
    eaves,
Fades into gloom, or gleams in light again
From every dew-drop on the jewelled plain.

    We, like the leaf, the summit, or the
    wave,
Reflect the light our common nature gave,
But every sunbeam, falling from her throne,
Wears on our hearts some coloring of our
    own :
Chilled in the slave, and burning in the free,
Like the sealed cavern by the sparkling
    sea ;
Lost, like the lightning in the sullen clod,
Or shedding radiance, like the smiles of
    God ;
Pure, pale in Virtue, as the star above,
Or quivering roseate on the leaves of Love ;
Glaring like noontide, where it glows upon
Ambition's sands, — the desert in the
    sun, —
Or soft suffusing o'er the varied scene
Life's common coloring, — intellectual
    green.

    Thus Heaven, repeating its material
    plan,
Arched over all the rainbow mind of man ;
But he who, blind to universal laws,
Sees but effects, unconscious of their
    cause, —
Believes each image in itself is bright,
Not robed in drapery of reflected light, —
Is like the rustic who, amidst his toil,
Has found some crystal in his meagre soil,
And, lost in rapture, thinks for him alone
Earth worked her wonders on the spark-
    ling stone,

Nor dreams that Nature, with as nice a line,
Carved countless angles through the bound-
    less mine.

    Thus err the many, who, entranced to find
Unwonted lustre in some clearer mind,
Believe that Genius sets the laws at naught
Which chain the pinions of our wildest
    thought ;
Untaught to measure, with the eye of art,
The wandering fancy or the wayward heart ;
Who match the little only with the less,
And gaze in rapture at its slight excess,
Proud of a pebble, as the brightest gem
Whose light might crown an emperor's
    diadem.

    And, most of all, the pure ethereal fire
Which seems to radiate from the poet's lyre
Is to the world a mystery and a charm,
An Ægis wielded on a mortal's arm,
While Reason turns her dazzled eye away,
And bows her sceptre to her subject's sway ;
And thus the poet, clothed with godlike
    state,
Usurped his Maker's title — to create ;
He, whose thoughts differing not in shape,
    but dress,
What others feel more fitly can express,
Sits like the maniac on his fancied throne,
Peeps through the bars, and calls the world
    his own.

    There breathes no being but has some
    pretence
To that fine instinct called poetic sense :
The rudest savage, roaming through the
    wild ;
The simplest rustic, bending o'er his child ;
The infant, listening to the warbling bird ;
The mother, smiling at its half-formed
    word ;
The boy uncaged, who tracks the fields
    at large ;
The girl, turned matron to her babe-like
    charge ;
The freeman, casting with unpurchased
    hand
The vote that shakes the turret of the land ;
The slave, who, slumbering on his rusted
    chain,
Dreams of the palm-trees on his burning
    plain ;
The hot-cheeked reveller, tossing down the
    wine,

To join the chorus pealing "Auld lang
   syne;"
The gentle maid, whose azure eye grows
   dim,
While Heaven is listening to her evening
   hymn;
The jewelled beauty, when her steps draw
   near
The circling dance and dazzling chande-
   lier;
E'en trembling age, when Spring's renew-
   ing air
Waves the thin ringlets of his silvered
   hair; —
All, all are glowing with the inward flame,
Whose wider halo wreathes the poet's
   name,
While, unembalmed, the silent dreamer
   dies,
His memory passing with his smiles and
   sighs!

If glorious visions, born for all mankind,
The bright auroras of our twilight mind;
If fancies, varying as the shapes that lie
Stained on the windows of the sunset sky;
If hopes, that beckon with delusive gleams,
Till the eye dances in the void of dreams;
If passions, following with the winds that
   urge
Earth's wildest wanderer to her farthest
   verge; —
If these on all some transient hours bestow
Of rapture tingling with its hectic glow,
Then all are poets; and if earth had rolled
Her myriad centuries, and her doom were
   told,
Each moaning billow of her shoreless wave
Would wail its requiem o'er a poet's grave!

If to embody in a breathing word
Tones that the spirit trembled when it
   heard;
To fix the image all unveiled and warm,
And carve in language its ethereal form,
So pure, so perfect, that the lines express
No meagre shrinking, no unlaced excess;
To feel that art, in living truth, has taught
Ourselves, reflected in the sculptured
   thought; —
If this alone bestow the right to claim
The deathless garland and the sacred name,
Then none are poets save the saints on high,
Whose harps can murmur all that words
   deny!

But though to none is granted to reveal
In perfect semblance all that each may feel,
As withered flowers recall forgotten love,
So, warmed to life, our faded passions move
In every line, where kindling fancy throws
The gleam of pleasures or the shade of
   woes.

When, schooled by time, the stately queen
   of art
Had smoothed the pathways leading to the
   heart,
Assumed her measured tread, her solemn
   tone,
And round her courts the clouds of fable
   thrown,
The wreaths of heaven descended on her
   shrine,
And wondering earth proclaimed the Muse
   divine.
Yet if her votaries had but dared profane
The mystic symbols of her sacred reign,
How had they smiled beneath the veil to
   find
What slender threads can chain the mighty
   mind!

Poets, like painters, their machinery
   claim,
And verse bestows the varnish and the
   frame;
Our grating English, whose Teutonic jar
Shakes the racked axle of Art's rattling
   car,
Fits like mosaic in the lines that gird
Fast in its place each many-angled word;
From Saxon lips Anacreon's numbers
   glide,
As once they melted on the Teian tide,
And, fresh transfused, the Iliad thrills
   again
From Albion's cliffs as o'er Achaia's plain!
The proud heroic, with its pulse-like beat,
Rings like the cymbals clashing as they
   meet;
The sweet Spenserian, gathering as it
   flows,
Sweeps gently onward to its dying close,
Where waves on waves in long succession
   pour,
Till the ninth billow melts along the shore;
The lonely spirit of the mournful lay,
Which lives immortal as the verse of Gray,
In sable plumage slowly drifts along,
On eagle pinion, through the air of song;

The glittering lyric bounds elastic by,
With flashing ringlets and exulting eye,
While every image, in her airy whirl,
Gleams like a diamond on a dancing girl!

Born with mankind, with man's expanded range
And varying fates the poet's numbers change;
Thus in his history may we hope to find
Some clearer epochs of the poet's mind,
As from the cradle of its birth we trace,
Slow wandering forth, the patriarchal race.

I

When the green earth, beneath the zephyr's wing,
Wears on her breast the varnished buds of Spring;
When the loosed current, as its folds uncoil,
Slides in the channels of the mellowed soil;
When the young hyacinth returns to seek
The air and sunshine with her emerald beak;
When the light snowdrops, starting from their cells,
Hang each pagoda with its silver bells;
When the frail willow twines her trailing bow
With pallid leaves that sweep the soil below;
When the broad elm, sole empress of the plain,
Whose circling shadow speaks a century's reign,
Wreathes in the clouds her regal diadem, —
A forest waving on a single stem; —
Then mark the poet; though to him unknown
The quaint-mouthed titles, such as scholars own,
See how his eye in ecstasy pursues
The steps of Nature tracked in radiant hues;
Nay, in thyself, whate'er may be thy fate,
Pallid with toil or surfeited with state,
Mark how thy fancies, with the vernal rose,
Awake, all sweetness, from their long repose;
Then turn to ponder o'er the classic page,
Traced with the idyls of a greener age,
And learn the instinct which arose to warm
Art's earliest essay and her simplest form.

To themes like these her narrow path confined
The first-born impulse moving in the mind;
In vales unshaken by the trumpet's sound,
Where peaceful Labor tills his fertile ground,
The silent changes of the rolling years,
Marked on the soil or dialled on the spheres,
The crested forests and the colored flowers,
The dewy grottos and the blushing bowers, —
These, and their guardians, who, with liquid names,
Strephons and Chloes, melt in mutual flames,
Woo the young Muses from their mountain shade,
To make Arcadias in the lonely glade.

Nor think they visit only with their smiles
The fabled valleys and Elysian isles;
He who is wearied of his village plain
May roam the Edens of the world in vain.
'T is not the star-crowned cliff, the cataract's flow,
The softer foliage or the greener glow,
The lake of sapphire or the spar-hung cave,
The brighter sunset or the broader wave,
Can warm his heart whom every wind has blown
To every shore, forgetful of his own.

Home of our childhood! how affection clings
And hovers round thee with her seraph wings!
Dearer thy hills, though clad in autumn brown,
Than fairest summits which the cedars crown!
Sweeter the fragrance of thy summer breeze
Than all Arabia breathes along the seas!
The stranger's gale wafts home the exile's sigh,
For the heart's temple is its own blue sky!

Oh happiest they, whose early love unchanged,
Hopes undissolved, and friendship unestranged,
Tired of their wanderings, still can deign to see
Love, hopes, and friendship, centring all in thee!

And thou, my village! as again I tread
Amidst thy living and above thy dead;
Though some fair playmates guard with chaster fears
Their cheeks, grown holy with the lapse of years;
Though with the dust some reverend locks may blend,
Where life's last mile-stone marks the journey's end;
On every bud the changing year recalls,
The brightening glance of morning memory falls,
Still following onward as the months unclose
The balmy lilac or the bridal rose;
And still shall follow, till they sink once more
Beneath the snow-drifts of the frozen shore,
As when my bark, long tossing in the gale,
Furled in her port her tempest-rended sail!

What shall I give thee? Can a simple lay,
Flung on thy bosom like a girl's bouquet,
Do more than deck thee for an idle hour,
Then fall unheeded, fading like the flower?
Yet, when I trod, with footsteps wild and free,
The crackling leaves beneath yon linden-tree,
Panting from play or dripping from the stream,
How bright the visions of my boyish dream!
Or, modest Charles, along thy broken edge,
Black with soft ooze and fringed with arrowy sedge,
As once I wandered in the morning sun,
With reeking sandal and superfluous gun,
How oft, as Fancy whispered in the gale,
Thou wast the Avon of her flattering tale!
Ye hills, whose foliage, fretted on the skies,
Prints shadowy arches on their evening dyes,
How should my song with holiest charm invest
Each dark ravine and forest-lifting crest!
How clothe in beauty each familiar scene,
Till all was classic on my native green!

As the drained fountain, filled with autumn leaves,
The field swept naked of its garnered sheaves,
So wastes at noon the promise of our dawn,
The springs all choking, and the harvest gone.

Yet hear the lay of one whose natal star
Still seemed the brightest when it shone afar;
Whose cheek, grown pallid with ungracious toil,
Glows in the welcome of his parent soil;
And ask no garlands sought beyond the tide,
But take the leaflets gathered at your side.

II

But times were changed; the torch of terror came,
To light the summits with the beacon's flame;
The streams ran crimson, the tall mountain pines
Rose a new forest o'er embattled lines;
The bloodless sickle lent the warrior's steel,
The harvest bowed beneath his chariot wheel;
Where late the wood-dove sheltered her repose
The raven waited for the conflict's close;
The cuirassed sentry walked his sleepless round
Where Daphne smiled or Amaryllis frowned;
Where timid minstrels sung their blushing charms,
Some wild Tyrtæus called aloud, "To arms!"

When Glory wakes, when fiery spirits leap,
Roused by her accents from their tranquil sleep,
The ray that flashes from the soldier's crest
Lights, as it glances, in the poet's breast; —
Not in pale dreamers, whose fantastic lay

Toys with smooth trifles like a child at play,
But men, who act the passions they inspire,
Who wave the sabre as they sweep the lyre!

Ye mild enthusiasts, whose pacific frowns
Are lost like dew-drops caught in burning
  towns,
Pluck as ye will the radiant plumes of fame,
Break Cæsar's bust to make yourselves a
  name;
But if your country bares the avenger's
  blade
For wrongs unpunished or for debts unpaid,
When the roused nation bids her armies
  form,
And screams her eagle through the gather-
  ing storm,
When from your ports the bannered frigate
  rides,
Her black bows scowling to the crested tides,
Your hour has past; in vain your feeble
  cry
As the babe's wailing to the thundering sky!

Scourge of mankind! with all the dread
  array
That wraps in wrath thy desolating way,
As the wild tempest wakes the slumbering
  sea,
Thou only teachest all that man can be.
Alike thy tocsin has the power to charm
The toil-knit sinews of the rustic's arm,
Or swell the pulses in the poet's veins,
And bid the nations tremble at his strains.

The city slept beneath the moonbeam's
  glance,
Her white walls gleaming through the vines
  of France,
And all was hushed, save where the foot-
  steps fell,
On some high tower, of midnight sentinel.
But one still watched; no self-encircled
  woes
Chased from his lids the angel of repose;
He watched, he wept, for thoughts of bitter
  years
Bowed his dark lashes, wet with burning
  tears:
His country's sufferings and her children's
  shame
Streamed o'er his memory like a forest's
  flame;
Each treasured insult, each remembered
  wrong,
Rolled through his heart and kindled into
  song.
His taper faded; and the morning gales
Swept through the world the war-song of
  Marseilles!

Now, while around the smiles of Peace
  expand,
And Plenty's wreaths festoon the laughing
  land;
While France ships outward her reluctant
  ore,
And half our navy basks upon the shore;
From ruder themes our meek-eyed Muses
  turn
To crown with roses their enamelled urn.

If e'er again return those awful days
Whose clouds were crimsoned with the
  beacon's blaze,
Whose grass was trampled by the soldier's
  heel,
Whose tides were reddened round the rush-
  ing keel,
God grant some lyre may wake a nobler
  strain
To rend the silence of our tented plain!
When Gallia's flag its triple fold displays,
Her marshalled legions peal the Marseil-
  laises;
When round the German close the war-
  clouds dim,
Far through their shadows floats his battle-
  hymn;
When, crowned with joy, the camps of Eng-
  land ring,
A thousand voices shout, "God save the
  King!"
When victory follows with our eagle's
  glance,
Our nation's anthem pipes a country dance!

Some prouder Muse, when comes the
  hour a. last,
May shake our hillsides with her bugle-
  blast;
Not ours the task; but since the lyric dress
Relieves the statelier with its sprightliness,
Hear an old song, which some, perchance,
  have seen
In stale gazette or cobwebbed magazine.
There was an hour when patriots dared pro-
  fane
The mast that Britain strove to bow in vain;
And one, who listened to the tale of shame,

Whose heart still answered to that sacred name,
Whose eye still followed o'er his country's tides
Thy glorious flag, our brave Old Ironsides!
From yon lone attic, on a smiling morn,
Thus mocked the spoilers with his schoolboy scorn.

III

When florid Peace resumed her golden reign,
And arts revived, and valleys bloomed again,
While War still panted on his broken blade,
Once more the Muse her heavenly wing essayed.
Rude was the song: some ballad, stern and wild,
Lulled the light slumbers of the soldier's child;
Or young romancer, with his threatening glance
And fearful fables of his bloodless lance,
Scared the soft fancy of the clinging girls,
Whose snowy fingers smoothed his raven curls.
But when long years the stately form had bent,
And faithless Memory her illusions lent,
So vast the outlines of Tradition grew
That History wondered at the shapes she drew,
And veiled at length their too ambitious hues
Beneath the pinions of the Epic Muse.

Far swept her wing; for stormier days had brought
With darker passions deeper tides of thought.
The camp's harsh tumult and the conflict's glow,
The thrill of triumph and the gasp of woe,
The tender parting and the glad return,
The festal banquet and the funeral urn,
And all the drama which at once uprears
Its spectral shadows through the clash of spears,
From camp and field to echoing verse transferred,
Swelled the proud song that listening nations heard.

Why floats the amaranth in eternal bloom
O'er Ilium's turrets and Achilles' tomb?
Why lingers fancy where the sunbeams smile
On Circe's gardens and Calypso's isle?
Why follows memory to the gate of Troy
Her plumed defender and his trembling boy?
Lo! the blind dreamer, kneeling on the sand
To trace these records with his doubtful hand;
In fabled tones his own emotion flows,
And other lips repeat his silent woes;
In Hector's infant see the babes that shun
Those deathlike eyes, unconscious of the sun,
Or in his hero hear himself implore,
"Give me to see, and Ajax asks no more!"

Thus live undying through the lapse of time
The solemn legends of the warrior's clime;
Like Egypt's pyramid or Pæstum's fane,
They stand the heralds of the voiceless plain.
Yet not like them, for Time, by slow degrees,
Saps the gray stone and wears the embroidered frieze,
And Isis sleeps beneath her subject Nile,
And crumbled Neptune strews his Dorian pile;
But Art's fair fabric, strengthening as it rears
Its laurelled columns through the mist of years,
As the blue arches of the bending skies
Still gird the torrent, following as it flies,
Spreads, with the surges bearing on mankind,
Its starred pavilion o'er the tides of mind!

In vain the patriot asks some lofty lay
To dress in state our wars of yesterday.
The classic days, those mothers of romance,
That roused a nation for a woman's glance;
The age of mystery, with its hoarded power,
That girt the tyrant in his storied tower,
Have passed and faded like a dream of youth,
And riper eras ask for history's truth.

On other shores, above their mouldering towns,
In sullen pomp the tall cathedral frowns,
Pride in its aisles and paupers at the door,
Which feeds the beggars whom it fleeced of yore.
Simple and frail, our lowly temples throw
Their slender shadows on the paths below;
Scarce steal the winds, that sweep his woodland tracks,
The larch's perfume from the settler's axe,
Ere, like a vision of the morning air,
His slight-framed steeple marks the house of prayer;
Its planks all reeking and its paint undried,
Its rafters sprouting on the shady side,
It sheds the raindrops from its shingled eaves
Ere its green brothers once have changed their leaves.

Yet Faith's pure hymn, beneath its shelter rude,
Breathes out as sweetly to the tangled wood
As where the rays through pictured glories pour
On marble shaft and tessellated floor; —
Heaven asks no surplice round the heart that feels,
And all is holy where devotion kneels.

Thus on the soil the patriot's knee should bend
Which holds the dust once living to defend;
Where'er the hireling shrinks before the free,
Each pass becomes "a new Thermopylæ!"
Where'er the battles of the brave are won,
There every mountain "looks on Marathon!"

Our fathers live; they guard in glory still
The grass-grown bastions of the fortressed hill;
Still ring the echoes of the trampled gorge,
With *God and Freedom! England and Saint George!*
The royal cipher on the captured gun
Mocks the sharp night-dews and the blistering sun;
The red-cross banner shades its captor's bust,
Its folds still loaded with the conflict's dust;
The drum, suspended by its tattered marge,
Once rolled and rattled to the Hessian's charge;
The stars have floated from Britannia's mast,
The redcoat's trumpets blown the rebel's blast.

Point to the summits where the brave have bled,
Where every village claims its glorious dead;
Say, when their bosoms met the bayonet's shock,
Their only corselet was the rustic frock;
Say, when they mustered to the gathering horn,
The titled chieftain curled his lip in scorn,
Yet, when their leader bade his lines advance,
No musket wavered in the lion's glance;
Say, when they fainted in the forced retreat,
They tracked the snowdrifts with their bleeding feet,
Yet still their banners, tossing in the blast,
Bore *Ever Ready*, faithful to the last,
Through storm and battle, till they waved again
On Yorktown's hills and Saratoga's plain !

Then, if so fierce the insatiate patriot's flame,
Truth looks too pale and history seems too tame,
Bid him await some new Columbiad's page,
To gild the tablets of an iron age,
And save his tears, which yet may fall upon
Some fabled field, some fancied Washington!

IV

But once again, from their Æolian cave,
The winds of Genius wandered on the wave.
Tired of the scenes the timid pencil drew,
Sick of the notes the sounding clarion blew,
Sated with heroes who had worn so long
The shadowy plumage of historic song,
The new-born poet left the beaten course,
To track the passions to their living source.

Then rose the Drama; — and the world admired
Her varied page with deeper thought inspired:
Bound to no clime, for Passion's throb is one
In Greenland's twilight or in India's sun;
Born for no age, for all the thoughts that roll
In the dark vortex of the stormy soul,
Unchained in song, no freezing years can tame;
God gave them birth, and man is still the same.

So full on life her magic mirror shone,
Her sister Arts paid tribute to her throne;
One reared her temple, one her canvas warmed,
And Music thrilled, while Eloquence informed.
The weary rustic left his stinted task
For smiles and tears, the dagger and the mask;
The sage, turned scholar, half forgot his lore,
To be the woman he despised before.
O'er sense and thought she threw her golden chain,
And Time, the anarch, spares her deathless reign.

Thus lives Medea, in our tamer age,
As when her buskin pressed the Grecian stage;
Not in the cells where frigid learning delves
In Aldine folios mouldering on their shelves,
But breathing, burning in the glittering throng,
Whose thousand bravos roll untired along,
Circling and spreading through the gilded halls,
From London's galleries to San Carlo's walls!

Thus shall he live whose more than mortal name
Mocks with its ray the pallid torch of Fame;
So proudly lifted that it seems afar
No earthly Pharos, but a heavenly star,
Who, unconfined to Art's diurnal bound,
Girds her whole zodiac in his flaming round,
And leads the passions, like the orb that guides,
From pole to pole, the palpitating tides!

V

Though round the Muse the robe of song is thrown,
Think not the poet lives in verse alone.
Long ere the chisel of the sculptor taught
The lifeless stone to mock the living thought;
Long ere the painter bade the canvas glow
With every line the forms of beauty know;
Long ere the iris of the Muses threw
On every leaf its own celestial hue,
In fable's dress the breath of genius poured,
And warmed the shapes that later times adored.

Untaught by Science how to forge the keys
That loose the gates of Nature's mysteries;
Unschooled by Faith, who, with her angel tread,
Leads through the labyrinth with a single thread,
His fancy, hovering round her guarded tower,
Rained through its bars like Danae's golden shower.

He spoke; the sea-nymph answered from her cave;
He called; the naiad left her mountain wave:
He dreamed of beauty; lo, amidst his dream,
Narcissus, mirrored in the breathless stream,
And night's chaste empress, in her bridal play,
Laughed through the foliage where Endymion lay;
And ocean dimpled, as the languid swell
Kissed the red lip of Cytherea's shell:
Of power, — Bellona swept the crimson field,
And blue-eyed Pallas shook her Gorgon shield;
O'er the hushed waves their mightier monarch drove,
And Ida trembled to the tread of Jove!

So every grace that plastic language knows
To nameless poets its perfection owes.
The rough-hewn words to simplest thoughts confined
Were cut and polished in their nicer mind;
Caught on their edge, imagination's ray
Splits into rainbows, shooting far away; —

From sense to soul, from soul to sense, it flies,
And through all nature links analogies;
He who reads right will rarely look upon
A better poet than his lexicon!

There is a race which cold, ungenial skies
Breed from decay, as fungous growths arise;
Though dying fast, yet springing fast again,
Which still usurps an unsubstantial reign,
With frames too languid for the charms of sense,
And minds worn down with action too intense;
Tired of a world whose joys they never knew,
Themselves deceived, yet thinking all untrue;
Scarce men without, and less than girls within,
Sick of their life before its cares begin; —
The dull disease, which drains their feeble hearts,
To life's decay some hectic thrills imparts,
And lends a force which, like the maniac's power,
Pays with blank years the frenzy of an hour.

And this is Genius! Say, does Heaven degrade
The manly frame, for health, for action made?
Break down the sinews, rack the brow with pains,
Blanch the bright cheek and drain the purple veins,
To clothe the mind with more extended sway,
Thus faintly struggling in degenerate clay?

No! gentle maid, too ready to admire,
Though false its notes, the pale enthusiast's lyre;
If this be genius, though its bitter springs
Glowed like the morn beneath Aurora's wings,
Seek not the source whose sullen bosom feeds
But fruitless flowers and dark, envenomed weeds.

But, if so bright the dear illusion seems,
Thou wouldst be partner of thy poet's dreams,
And hang in rapture on his bloodless charms,
Or die, like Raphael, in his angel arms,
Go and enjoy thy blessed lot, — to share
In Cowper's gloom or Chatterton's despair!

Not such were they whom, wandering o'er the waves,
I looked to meet, but only found their graves;
If friendship's smile, the better part of fame,
Should lend my song the only wreath I claim,
Whose voice would greet me with a sweeter tone,
Whose living hand more kindly press my own,
Than theirs, — could Memory, as her silent tread
Prints the pale flowers that blossom o'er the dead,
Those breathless lips, now closed in peace, restore,
Or wake those pulses hushed to beat no more?

Thou calm, chaste scholar! I can see thee now,
The first young laurels on thy pallid brow,
O'er thy slight figure floating lightly down
In graceful folds the academic gown,
On thy curled lip the classic lines that taught
How nice the mind that sculptured them with thought,
And triumph glistening in the clear blue eye,
Too bright to live, — but oh, too fair to die!

And thou, dear friend, whom Science still deplores,
And Love still mourns, on ocean-severed shores,
Though the bleak forest twice has bowed with snow
Since thou wast laid its budding leaves below,
Thine image mingles with my closing strain,
As when we wandered by the turbid Seine,
Both blessed with hopes, which revelled, bright and free,
On all we longed or all we dreamed to be;

To thee the amaranth and the cypress fell, —
And I was spared to breathe this last farewell!

But lived there one in unremembered days,
Or lives there still, who spurns the poet's bays,
Whose fingers, dewy from Castalia's springs,
Rest on the lyre, yet scorn to touch the strings?
Who shakes the senate with the silver tone
The groves of Pindus might have sighed to own?
Have such e'er been? Remember Canning's name!
Do such still live? Let "Alaric's Dirge" proclaim!

Immortal Art! where'er the rounded sky
Bends o'er the cradle where thy children lie,
Their home is earth, their herald every tongue
Whose accents echo to the voice that sung.
One leap of Ocean scatters on the sand
The quarried bulwarks of the loosening land;
One thrill of earth dissolves a century's toil
Strewed like the leaves that vanish in the soil;
One hill o'erflows, and cities sink below,
Their marbles splintering in the lava's glow;
But one sweet tone, scarce whispered to the air,
From shore to shore the blasts of ages bear;
One humble name, which oft, perchance, has borne
The tyrant's mockery and the courtier's scorn,
Towers o'er the dust of earth's forgotten graves,
As once, emerging through the waste of waves,
The rocky Titan, round whose shattered spear
Coiled the last whirlpool of the drowning sphere!

POEMS PUBLISHED BETWEEN 1837 AND 1848

[An English and enlarged edition of Dr. Holmes's *Poems* followed the American edition of 1836, and was furnished with a biographical sketch of the poet, but the second American edition was copyrighted in 1848, and published nominally in 1849. It contained the poems already published and a further group, as here presented. The preface to the earlier volume was omitted, and the new edition was introduced by a note headed "From a letter of the Author to the Publishers," from which the following passages are taken.

"As these productions are to be given to the public again at your particular request, I must trust that you will make all proper explanations. I need hardly remind you that a part of them appeared in a volume published about a dozen years ago; that when this volume had been some time out of print, another edition was printed, at your suggestion, in London, but I suppose sold principally to this country; and that the present edition is published to please you rather than to gratify myself. You will, therefore, take the entire responsibility of the second and third appearances, except so far as my consent involved me in the transactions.

"Let me remark, also, that it was only to suit your wishes that several copies of verses, which sound very much like school exercises, were allowed to remain unexpunged. If anybody takes the trouble to attack them, you may say that they belong to the department of 'Early' or 'Juvenile' Poems, and should be so ticketed. But stand up for the new verses, especially those added in this edition. Say that those two names, 'Terpsichore' and 'Urania,' may perhaps sound a little fantastic, but were merely intended as suggestive titles, and fall back upon Herodotus. Say that many of the lesser poems were written for meetings more or less convivial, and must of course show something like the fire-work frames on the morning of July 5th. If any objection is made to that bacchanalian song, say that the author entirely recedes from several of the sentiments contained in it, especially that about strong drink being a natural want. But ask, if a few classical reminiscences at a banquet may not be quite as like to keep out something worse, as to stand in the way of something better.

"If anything pleasant should be said about 'the new edition,' you may snip it out of the paper and save it for me. If contrary opinions are expressed, be so good as *not* to mark with brackets, carefully envelop, and send to me, as is the custom with many friends."]

THE PILGRIM'S VISION

In the hour of twilight shadows
  The Pilgrim sire looked out;
He thought of the "bloody Salvages"
  That lurked all round about,
Of Wituwamet's pictured knife
  And Pecksuot's whooping shout;
For the baby's limbs were feeble,
  Though his father's arms were stout.

His home was a freezing cabin,
  Too bare for the hungry rat;
Its roof was thatched with ragged grass,
  And bald enough of that;
The hole that served for casement
  Was glazed with an ancient hat,
And the ice was gently thawing
  From the log whereon he sat.

Along the dreary landscape
  His eyes went to and fro,
The trees all clad in icicles,
  The streams that did not flow;
A sudden thought flashed o'er him, —
  A dream of long ago, —
He smote his leathern jerkin,
  And murmured, "Even so!"

"Come hither, God-be-Glorified,
  And sit upon my knee;
Behold the dream unfolding,
  Whereof I spake to thee
By the winter's hearth in Leyden
  And on the stormy sea.

THE PILGRIM'S VISION

True is the dream's beginning, —
  So may its ending be!

"I saw in the naked forest
  Our scattered remnant cast,
A screen of shivering branches
  Between them and the blast;
The snow was falling round them,
  The dying fell as fast;
I looked to see them perish,
  When lo, the vision passed.

"Again mine eyes were opened; —
  The feeble had waxed strong,
The babes had grown to sturdy men,
  The remnant was a throng;
By shadowed lake and winding stream,
  And all the shores along,
The howling demons quaked to hear
  The Christian's godly song.

"They slept, the village fathers,
  By river, lake, and shore
When far adown the steep of Time
  The vision rose once more:
I saw along the winter snow
  A spectral column pour,
And high above their broken ranks
  A tattered flag they bore.

"Their Leader rode before them,
  Of bearing calm and high,
The light of Heaven's own kindling
  Throned in his awful eye;
These were a Nation's champions
  Her dread appeal to try.
God for the right! I faltered,
  And lo, the train passed by.

"Once more; — the strife is ended,
  The solemn issue tried,
The Lord of Hosts, his mighty arm
  Has helped our Israel's side;
Gray stone and grassy hillock
  Tell where our martyrs died,
But peaceful smiles the harvest,
  And stainless flows the tide.

"A crash, as when some swollen cloud
  Cracks o'er the tangled trees!
With side to side, and spar to spar,
  Whose smoking decks are these?
I know Saint George's blood-red cross,
  Thou Mistress of the Seas,
But what is she whose streaming bars
  Roll out before the breeze?

"Ah, well her iron ribs are knit,
  Whose thunders strive to quell
The bellowing throats, the blazing lips,
  That pealed the Armada's knell!
The mist was cleared, — a wreath of stars
  Rose o'er the crimsoned swell,
And, wavering from its haughty peak,
  The cross of England fell!

"O trembling Faith! though dark the morn,
  A heavenly torch is thine;
While feebler races melt away,
  And paler orbs decline,
Still shall the fiery pillar's ray
  Along thy pathway shine,
To light the chosen tribe that sought
  This Western Palestine!

"I see the living tide roll on;
  It crowns with flaming towers
The icy capes of Labrador,
  The Spaniard's 'land of flowers'!
It streams beyond the splintered ridge
  That parts the northern showers;
From eastern rock to sunset wave
  The Continent is ours!"

He ceased, the grim old soldier-saint,
  Then softly bent to cheer
The Pilgrim-child, whose wasting face
  Was meekly turned to hear;
And drew his toil-worn sleeve across
  To brush the manly tear
From cheeks that never changed in woe,
  And never blanched in fear.

The weary Pilgrim slumbers,
  His resting-place unknown;
His hands were crossed, his lips were closed,
  The dust was o'er him strown;
The drifting soil, the mouldering leaf,
  Along the sod were blown;
His mound has melted into earth,
  His memory lives alone.

So let it live unfading,
  The memory of the dead,
Long as the pale anemone
  Springs where their tears were shed,

Or, raining in the summer's wind
  In flakes of burning red,
The wild rose sprinkles with its leaves
  The turf where once they bled!

Yea, when the frowning bulwarks
  That guard this holy strand
Have sunk beneath the trampling surge
  In beds of sparkling sand,
While in the waste of ocean
  One hoary rock shall stand,
Be this its latest legend,—
  HERE WAS THE PILGRIM'S LAND!

THE STEAMBOAT

SEE how yon flaming herald treads
  The ridged and rolling waves,
As, crashing o'er their crested heads,
  She bows her surly slaves!
With foam before and fire behind,
  She rends the clinging sea,
That flies before the roaring wind,
  Beneath her hissing lee.

The morning spray, like sea-born flowers,
  With heaped and glistening bells,
Falls round her fast, in ringing showers,
  With every wave that swells;
And, burning o'er the midnight deep,
  In lurid fringes thrown,
The living gems of ocean sweep
  Along her flashing zone.

With clashing wheel and lifting keel,
  And smoking torch on high,
When winds are loud and billows reel,
  She thunders foaming by;
When seas are silent and serene,
  With even beam she glides,
The sunshine glimmering through the green
  That skirts her gleaming sides.

Now, like a wild nymph, far apart
  She veils her shadowy form,
The beating of her restless heart
  Still sounding through the storm;
Now answers, like a courtly dame,
  The reddening surges o'er,
With flying scarf of spangled flame,
  The Pharos of the shore.

To-night yon pilot shall not sleep,
  Who trims his narrowed sail;
To-night yon frigate scarce shall keep
  Her broad breast to the gale;
And many a foresail, scooped and strained,
  Shall break from yard and stay,
Before this smoky wreath has stained
  The rising mist of day.

Hark! hark! I hear yon whistling shroud,
  I see yon quivering mast;
The black throat of the hunted cloud
  Is panting forth the blast!
An hour, and, whirled like winnowing chaff,
  The giant surge shall fling
His tresses o'er yon pennon staff,
  White as the sea-bird's wing!

Yet rest, ye wanderers of the deep;
  Nor wind nor wave shall tire
Those fleshless arms, whose pulses leap
  With floods of living fire;
Sleep on, and, when the morning light
  Streams o'er the shining bay,
Oh think of those for whom the night
  Shall never wake in day!

LEXINGTON

SLOWLY the mist o'er the meadow was
  creeping,
  Bright on the dewy buds glistened the
    sun,
When from his couch, while his children
    were sleeping,
  Rose the bold rebel and shouldered his
    gun.
    Waving her golden veil
    Over the silent dale,
Blithe looked the morning on cottage and
    spire;
    Hushed was his parting sigh,
    While from his noble eye
Flashed the last sparkle of liberty's fire.

On the smooth green where the fresh leaf
    is springing
  Calmly the first-born of glory have met;
Hark! the death-volley around them is
    ringing!
  Look! with their life-blood the young
    grass is wet!
    Faint is the feeble breath,
    Murmuring low in death,
"Tell to our sons how their fathers have
    died;"

Nerveless the iron hand,
Raised for its native land,
Lies by the weapon that gleams at its side.

Over the hillsides the wild knell is tolling,
From their far hamlets the yeomanry come;
As through the storm-clouds the thunder-burst rolling,
Circles the beat of the mustering drum.
Fast on the soldier's path
Darken the waves of wrath, —
Long have they gathered and loud shall they fall;
Red glares the musket's flash,
Sharp rings the rifle's crash,
Blazing and clanging from thicket and wall.

Gayly the plume of the horseman was dancing,
Never to shadow his cold brow again;
Proudly at morning the war-steed was prancing,
Reeking and panting he droops on the rein;
Pale is the lip of scorn,
Voiceless the trumpet horn,
Torn is the silken-fringed red cross on high;
Many a belted breast
Low on the turf shall rest
Ere the dark hunters the herd have passed by.

Snow-girdled crags where the hoarse wind is raving,
Rocks where the weary floods murmur and wail,
Wilds where the fern by the furrow is waving,
Reeled with the echoes that rode on the gale;
Far as the tempest thrills
Over the darkened hills,
Far as the sunshine streams over the plain,
Roused by the tyrant band,
Woke all the mighty land,
Girded for battle, from mountain to main.

Green be the graves where her martyrs are lying!
Shroudless and tombless they sank to their rest,
While o'er their ashes the starry fold flying
Wraps the proud eagle they roused from his nest.
Borne on her Northern pine,
Long o'er the foaming brine
Spread her broad banner to storm and to sun;
Heaven keep her ever free,
Wide as o'er land and sea
Floats the fair emblem her heroes have won!

ON LENDING A PUNCH-BOWL

This "punch-bowl" was, according to old family tradition, a *caudle-cup*. It is a massive piece of silver, its cherubs and other ornaments of coarse repoussé work, and has two handles like a loving-cup, by which it was held, or passed from guest to guest.

THIS ancient silver bowl of mine, it tells of good old times,
Of joyous days and jolly nights, and merry Christmas chimes;
They were a free and jovial race, but honest, brave, and true,
Who dipped their ladle in the punch when this old bowl was new.

A Spanish galleon brought the bar, — so runs the ancient tale;
'T was hammered by an Antwerp smith, whose arm was like a flail;
And now and then between the strokes, for fear his strength should fail,
He wiped his brow and quaffed a cup of good old Flemish ale.

'T was purchased by an English squire to please his loving dame,
Who saw the cherubs, and conceived a longing for the same;
And oft as on the ancient stock another twig was found,
'T was filled with caudle spiced and hot, and handed smoking round.

But, changing hands, it reached at length a Puritan divine,
Who used to follow Timothy, and take a little wine,
But hated punch and prelacy; and so it was, perhaps,
He went to Leyden, where he found conventicles and schnapps.

And then, of course, you know what's
   next: it left the Dutchman's shore
With those that in the Mayflower came, —
   a hundred souls and more, —
Along with all the furniture, to fill their
   new abodes, —
To judge by what is still on hand, at least
   a hundred loads.

'T was on a dreary winter's eve, the night
   was closing dim,
When brave Miles Standish took the bowl,
   and filled it to the brim;
The little Captain stood and stirred the
   posset with his sword,
And all his sturdy men-at-arms were
   ranged about the board.

He poured the fiery Hollands in, — the
   man that never feared, —
He took a long and solemn draught, and
   wiped his yellow beard;
And one by one the musketeers — the men
   that fought and prayed —
All drank as 't were their mother's milk,
   and not a man afraid.

That night, affrighted from his nest, the
   screaming eagle flew,
He heard the Pequot's ringing whoop, the
   soldier's wild halloo;
And there the sachem learned the rule he
   taught to kith and kin :
"Run from the white man when you find
   he smells of Hollands gin ! "

A hundred years, and fifty more, had
   spread their leaves and snows,
A thousand rubs had flattened down each
   little cherub's nose,
When once again the bowl was filled, but
   not in mirth or joy, —
'T was mingled by a mother's hand to
   cheer her parting boy.

Drink, John, she said, 't will do you good,
   — poor child, you 'll never bear
This working in the dismal trench, out in
   the midnight air;
And if — God bless me ! — you were hurt,
   't would keep away the chill.
So John *did* drink, — and well he wrought
   that night at Bunker's Hill !

I tell you, there was generous warmth in
   good old English cheer;
I tell you, 't was a pleasant thought to
   bring its symbol here.
'T is but the fool that loves excess; hast
   thou a drunken soul?
Thy bane is in thy shallow skull, not in my
   silver bowl !

I love the memory of the past, — its
   pressed yet fragrant flowers, —
The moss that clothes its broken walls, the
   ivy on its towers;
Nay, this poor bauble it bequeathed, — my
   eyes grow moist and dim,
To think of all the vanished joys that
   danced around its brim.

Then fill a fair and honest cup, and bear it
   straight to me;
The goblet hallows all it holds, whate'er
   the liquid be;
And may the cherubs on its face protect
   me from the sin
That dooms one to those dreadful words,
   — "My dear, where *have* you
   been ? "

A SONG

FOR THE CENTENNIAL CELEBRATION OF HARVARD COLLEGE, 1836

This song, which I had the temerity to sing myself (*felix audacia*, Mr. Franklin Dexter had the goodness to call it), was sent in a little too late to be printed with the official account of the celebration. It was written at the suggestion of Dr. Jacob Bigelow, who thought the popular tune "The Poacher's Song" would be a good model for a lively ballad or ditty. He himself wrote the admirable Latin song to be found in the record of the meeting.

WHEN the Puritans came over
   Our hills and swamps to clear,
The woods were full of catamounts,
   And Indians red as deer,
With tomahawks and scalping-knives,
   That make folks' heads look queer;
Oh the ship from England used to bring
   A hundred wigs a year !

The crows came cawing through the air
   To pluck the Pilgrims' corn,
The bears came snuffing round the door
   Whene'er a babe was born,
The rattlesnakes were bigger round
   Than the but of the old ram's horn
The deacon blew at meeting time
   On every "Sabbath" morn.

But soon they knocked the wigwams
   down,
And pine-tree trunk and limb
Began to sprout among the leaves
   In shape of steeples slim;
And out the little wharves were stretched
   Along the ocean's rim,
And up the little school-house shot
   To keep the boys in trim.

And when at length the College rose,
   The sachem cocked his eye
At every tutor's meagre ribs
   Whose coat-tails whistled by:
But when the Greek and Hebrew words
   Came tumbling from his jaws,
The copper-colored children all
   Ran screaming to the squaws.

And who was on the Catalogue
   When college was begun?
Two nephews of the President,
   And *the* Professor's son;
(They turned a little Indian by,
   As brown as any bun;)
Lord! how the seniors knocked about
   The freshman class of one!

They had not then the dainty things
   That commons now afford,
But succotash and hominy
   Were smoking on the board;
They did not rattle round in gigs,
   Or dash in long-tailed blues,
But always on Commencement days
   The tutors blacked their shoes.

God bless the ancient Puritans!
   Their lot was hard enough;
But honest hearts make iron arms,
   And tender maids are tough;
So love and faith have formed and fed
   Our true-born Yankee stuff,
And keep the kernel in the shell
   The British found so rough!

THE ISLAND HUNTING-SONG

The island referred to is a domain of princely proportions, which has long been the seat of a generous hospitality. Naushon is its old Indian name. William Swain, Esq., commonly known as "the Governor," was the proprietor of it at the time when this song was written. Mr. John M. Forbes is his worthy successor in territorial rights and as a hospitable entertainer. The *Island Book* has been the recipient of many poems from visitors and friends of the owners of the old mansion. [In *The Autocrat*, section ii., is an animated account of Naushon, followed by a poem, *Sun and Shadow*, written there.]

No more the summer floweret charms,
   The leaves will soon be sere,
And Autumn folds his jewelled arms
   Around the dying year;
So, ere the waning seasons claim
   Our leafless groves awhile,
With golden wine and glowing flame
   We'll crown our lonely isle.

Once more the merry voices sound
   Within the antlered hall,
And long and loud the baying hounds
   Return the hunter's call;
And through the woods, and o'er the hill,
   And far along the bay,
The driver's horn is sounding shrill, —
   Up, sportsmen, and away!

No bars of steel or walls of stone
   Our little empire bound,
But, circling with his azure zone,
   The sea runs foaming round;
The whitening wave, the purpled skies,
   The blue and lifted shore,
Braid with their dim and blending dyes
   Our wide horizon o'er.

And who will leave the grave debate
   That shakes the smoky town,
To rule amid our island-state,
   And wear our oak-leaf crown?
And who will be awhile content
   To hunt our woodland game,
And leave the vulgar pack that scent
   The reeking track of fame?

Ah, who that shares in toils like these
   Will sigh not to prolong

Our days beneath the broad-leaved trees,
  Our nights of mirth and song?
Then leave the dust of noisy streets,
  Ye outlaws of the wood,
And follow through his green retreats
  Your noble Robin Hood.

DEPARTED DAYS

Yes, dear departed, cherished days,
  Could Memory's hand restore
Your morning light, your evening rays,
  From Time's gray urn once more,
Then might this restless heart be still,
  This straining eye might close,
And Hope her fainting pinions fold,
  While the fair phantoms rose.

But, like a child in ocean's arms,
  We strive against the stream,
Each moment farther from the shore
  Where life's young fountains gleam;
Each moment fainter wave the fields,
  And wider rolls the sea;
The mist grows dark, — the sun goes down, —
  Day breaks, — and where are we?

THE ONLY DAUGHTER

ILLUSTRATION OF A PICTURE

They bid me strike the idle strings,
  As if my summer days
Had shaken sunbeams from their wings
  To warm my autumn lays;
They bring to me their painted urn,
  As if it were not time
To lift my gauntlet and to spurn
  The lists of boyish rhyme;
And were it not that I have still
  Some weakness in my heart
That clings around my stronger will
  And pleads for gentler art,
Perchance I had not turned away
  The thoughts grown tame with toil,
To cheat this lone and pallid ray,
  That wastes the midnight oil.

Alas! with every year I feel
  Some roses leave my brow;
Too young for wisdom's tardy seal,
  Too old for garlands now.

Yet, while the dewy breath of spring
  Steals o'er the tingling air,
And spreads and fans each emerald wing
  The forest soon shall wear,
How bright the opening year would seem,
  Had I one look like thine
To meet me when the morning beam
  Unseals these lids of mine!
Too long I bear this lonely lot,
  That bids my heart run wild
To press the lips that love me not,
  To clasp the stranger's child.

How oft beyond the dashing seas,
  Amidst those royal bowers,
Where danced the lilacs in the breeze,
  And swung the chestnut-flowers,
I wandered like a wearied slave
  Whose morning task is done,
To watch the little hands that gave
  Their whiteness to the sun;
To revel in the bright young eyes,
  Whose lustre sparkled through
The sable fringe of Southern skies
  Or gleamed in Saxon blue!
How oft I heard another's name
  Called in some truant's tone;
Sweet accents! which I longed to claim,
  To learn and lisp my own!

Too soon the gentle hands, that pressed
  The ringlets of the child,
Are folded on the faithful breast
  Where first he breathed and smiled;
Too oft the clinging arms untwine,
  The melting lips forget,
And darkness veils the bridal shrine
  Where wreaths and torches met;
If Heaven but leaves a single thread
  Of Hope's dissolving chain,
Even when her parting plumes are spread
  It bids them fold again;
The cradle rocks beside the tomb;
  The cheek now changed and chill
Smiles on us in the morning bloom
  Of one that loves us still.

Sweet image! I have done thee wrong
  To claim this destined lay;
The leaf that asked an idle song
  Must bear my tears away.
Yet in thy memory shouldst thou keep
  This else forgotten strain,
Till years have taught thine eyes to weep,
  And flattery's voice is vain;

Oh then, thou fledgling of the nest,
　Like the long-wandering dove,
Thy weary heart may faint for rest,
　As mine, on changeless love;
And while these sculptured lines retrace
　The hours now dancing by,
This vision of thy girlish grace
　May cost thee, too, a sigh.

SONG

WRITTEN FOR THE DINNER GIVEN TO CHARLES DICKENS BY THE YOUNG MEN OF BOSTON, FEBRUARY 1, 1842

The stars their early vigils keep,
　The silent hours are near,
When drooping eyes forget to weep, —
　Yet still we linger here ;
And what — the passing churl may ask —
　Can claim such wondrous power,
That Toil forgets his wonted task,
　And Love his promised hour ?

The Irish harp no longer thrills,
　Or breathes a fainter tone ;
The clarion blast from Scotland's hills,
　Alas ! no more is blown ;
And Passion's burning lip bewails
　Her Harold's wasted fire,
Still lingering o'er the dust that veils
　The Lord of England's lyre.

But grieve not o'er its broken strings,
　Nor think its soul hath died,
While yet the lark at heaven's gate sings,
　As once o'er Avon's side ;
While gentle summer sheds her bloom,
　And dewy blossoms wave,
Alike o'er Juliet's storied tomb
　And Nelly's nameless grave.

Thou glorious island of the sea !
　Though wide the wasting flood
That parts our distant land from thee,
　We claim thy generous blood;
Nor o'er thy far horizon springs
　One hallowed star of fame,
But kindles, like an angel's wings,
　Our western skies in flame !

LINES

RECITED AT THE BERKSHIRE JUBILEE, PITTSFIELD, MASS., AUGUST 23, 1844

[Before reading these *Lines*, the poet spoke as follows :
" One of my earliest recollections is of an annual pilgrimage made by my parents to the west. The young horse was brought up, fatted by a week's rest and high feeding, prancing and caracoling to the door. It came to the corner and was soon over the western hills. He was gone a fortnight ; and one afternoon — it always seems to me it was a sunny afternoon — we saw an equipage crawling from the west toward the old homestead ; the young horse, who set out fat and prancing, worn thin and reduced by a long journey — the chaise covered with dust, and all speaking of a terrible crusade, a formidable pilgrimage. Winter-evening stories told me where — to Berkshire, to the borders of New York, to the old domain, owned so long that there seemed a kind of hereditary love for it. Many years passed away, and I travelled down the beautiful Rhine. I wished to see the equally beautiful Hudson. I found myself at Albany ; a few hours' ride brought me to Pittsfield, and I went to the little spot, the scene of this pilgrimage — a mansion — and found it surrounded by a beautiful meadow, through which the winding river made its course in a thousand fantastic curves ; the mountains reared their heads around it, the blue air which makes our city-pale cheeks again to deepen with the hue of health, coursing about it pure and free. I recognized it as the scene of the annual pilgrimage. Since then I have made an annual visit to it.

"In 1735, Hon. Jacob Wendell, my grandfather in the maternal line, bought a township not then laid out — the township of Poontoosuck — and that little spot which we still hold is the relic of twenty-four thousand acres of baronial territory. When I say this, no feeling which can be the subject of ridicule animates my bosom. I know too well that the hills and rocks outlast our families. I know we fall upon the places we claim, as the leaves of the forest fall, and as passed the soil from the hands of the original occupants into the hands of my immediate ancestors, I know it must pass from me and mine ; and yet with pleasure and pride I feel I can take every inhabitant by the hand and say, If I am not a son or a grandson, or even a nephew of this fair county, I am at least allied to it by hereditary relation."]

COME back to your mother, ye children, for shame,
Who have wandered like truants for riches or fame !
With a smile on her face, and a sprig in her cap,
She calls you to feast from her bountiful lap.

Come out from your alleys, your courts, and your lanes,
And breathe, like young eagles, the air of our plains ;
Take a whiff from our fields, and your excellent wives
Will declare it 's all nonsense insuring your lives.

Come you of the law, who can talk, if you please,
Till the man in the moon will allow it 's a cheese,
And leave "the old lady, that never tells lies,"
To sleep with her handkerchief over her eyes.

Ye healers of men, for a moment decline
Your feats in the rhubarb and ipecac line;
While you shut up your turnpike, your neighbors can go
The old roundabout road to the regions below.

You clerk, on whose ears are a couple of pens,
And whose head is an ant-hill of units and tens,
Though Plato denies you, we welcome you still
As a featherless biped, in spite of your quill.

Poor drudge of the city ! how happy he feels,
With the burs on his legs and the grass at his heels !
No *dodger* behind, his bandannas to share,
No constable grumbling, " You must n't walk there ! "

In yonder green meadow, to memory dear,
He slaps a mosquito and brushes a tear;

The dew-drops hang round him on blossoms and shoots,
He breathes but one sigh for his youth and his boots.

There stands the old school-house, hard by the old church;
That tree at its side had the flavor of birch;
Oh, sweet were the days of his juvenile tricks,
Though the prairie of youth had so many "big licks."

By the side of yon river he weeps and he slumps,
The boots fill with water, as if they were pumps,
Till, sated with rapture, he steals to his bed,
With a glow in his heart and a cold in his head.

'T is past, — he is dreaming, — I see him again ;
The ledger returns as by legerdemain;
His neckcloth is damp with an easterly flaw,
And he holds in his fingers an omnibus straw.

He dreams the chill gust is a blossomy gale,
That the straw is a rose from his dear native vale ;
And murmurs, unconscious of space and of time,
"A 1. Extra super. Ah, is n't it PRIME ! "

Oh, what are the prizes we perish to win
To the first little "shiner" we caught with a pin !
No soil upon earth is so dear to our eyes
As the soil we first stirred in terrestrial pies !

Then come from all parties and parts to our feast ;
Though not at the " Astor," we 'll give you at least
A bite at an apple, a seat on the grass,
And the best of old — water — at nothing a glass.

NUX POSTCŒNATICA

I was sitting with my microscope, upon my parlor rug,
With a very heavy quarto and a very lively bug;
The true bug had been organized with only two antennæ,
But the humbug in the copperplate would have them twice as many.

And I thought, like Dr. Faustus, of the emptiness of art,
How we take a fragment for the whole, and call the whole a part,
When I heard a heavy footstep that was loud enough for two,
And a man of forty entered, exclaiming, "How d' ye do?"

He was not a ghost, my visitor, but solid flesh and bone;
He wore a Palo Alto hat, his weight was twenty stone;
(It 's odd how hats expand their brims as riper years invade,
As if when life had reached its noon it wanted them for shade!)

I lost my focus, — dropped my book, — the bug, who was a flea,
At once exploded, and commenced experiments on me.
They have a certain heartiness that frequently appalls, —
Those mediæval gentlemen in semilunar smalls!

"My boy," he said, (colloquial ways, — the vast, broad-hatted man,)
"Come dine with us on Thursday next, — you must, you know you can;
We 're going to have a roaring time, with lots of fun and noise,
Distinguished guests, et cetera, the JUDGE, and all the boys."

Not so, — I said, — my temporal bones are showing pretty clear.
It 's time to stop, — just look and see that hair above this ear;
My golden days are more than spent, — and, what is very strange,
If these are real silver hairs, I 'm getting lots of change.

Besides — my prospects — don't you know that people won't employ
A man that wrongs his manliness by laughing like a boy?
And suspect the azure blossom that unfolds upon a shoot,
As if wisdom's old potato could not flourish at its root?

It 's a very fine reflection, when you 're etching out a smile
On a copperplate of faces that would stretch at least a mile,
That, what with sneers from enemies and cheapening shrugs of friends,
It will cost you all the earnings that a month of labor lends!

It 's a vastly pleasing prospect, when you 're screwing out a laugh,
That your very next year's income is diminished by a half,
And a little boy trips barefoot that Pegasus may go,
And the baby's milk is watered that your Helicon may flow!

No; — the joke has been a good one, — but I 'm getting fond of quiet,
And I don't like deviations from my customary diet;
So I think I will not go with you to hear the toasts and speeches,
But stick to old Montgomery Place, and have some pig and peaches.

The fat man answered: Shut your mouth, and hear the genuine creed;
The true essentials of a feast are only fun and feed;
The force that wheels the planets round delights in spinning tops,
And that young earthquake t' other day was great at shaking props.

I tell you what, philosopher, if all the longest heads
That ever knocked their sinciputs in stretching on their beds
Were round one great mahogany, I 'd beat those fine old folks
With twenty dishes, twenty fools, and twenty clever jokes!

Why, if Columbus should be there, the company would beg
He 'd show that little trick of his of balancing the egg!
Milton to Stilton would give in, and Solomon to Salmon,
And Roger Bacon be a bore, and Francis Bacon gammon!

And as for all the "patronage" of all the clowns and boors
That squint their little narrow eyes at any freak of yours,
Do leave them to your prosier friends, — such fellows ought to die
When rhubarb is so very scarce and ipecac so high!

And so I come, — like Lochinvar, to tread a single measure, —
To purchase with a loaf of bread a sugar-plum of pleasure,
To enter for the cup of glass that 's run for after dinner,
Which yields a single sparkling draught, then breaks and cuts the winner.

Ah, that 's the way delusion comes, — a glass of old Madeira,
A pair of visual diaphragms revolved by Jane or Sarah,
And down go vows and promises without the slightest question
If eating words won't compromise the organs of digestion!

And yet, among my native shades, beside my nursing mother,
Where every stranger seems a friend, and every friend a brother,
I feel the old convivial glow (unaided) o'er me stealing, —
The warm, champagny, old-particular, brandy-punchy feeling.

We 're all alike; — Vesuvius flings the scoriæ from his fountain,
But down they come in volleying rain back to the burning mountain;
We leave, like those volcanic stones, our precious Alma Mater,
But will keep dropping in again to see the dear old crater.

VERSES FOR AFTER-DINNER

PHI BETA KAPPA SOCIETY, 1844

I WAS thinking last night, as I sat in the cars,
With the charmingest prospect of cinders and stars,
Next Thursday is — bless me! — how hard it will be,
If that cannibal president calls upon me!

There is nothing on earth that he will not devour,
From a tutor in seed to a freshman in flower;
No sage is too gray, and no youth is too green,
And you can't be too plump, though you 're never too lean.

While others enlarge on the boiled and the roast,
He serves a raw clergyman up with a toast,
Or catches some doctor, quite tender and young,
And basely insists on a bit of his tongue.

Poor victim, prepared for his classical spit,
With a stuffing of praise and a basting of wit,
You may twitch at your collar and wrinkle your brow,
But you 're up on your legs, and you 're in for it now.

Oh, think of your friends, — they are waiting to hear
These jokes that are thought so remarkably queer;
And all the Jack Horners of metrical buns
Are prying and fingering to pick out the puns.

Those thoughts which, like chickens, will always thrive best
When reared by the heat of the natural nest,
Will perish if hatched from their embryo dream
In the mist and the glow of convivial steam.

Oh pardon me, then, if I meekly retire,
With a very small flash of ethereal fire;
No rubbing will kindle your Lucifer match,
If the *fiz* does not follow the primitive scratch.

Dear friends, who are listening so sweetly the while,
With your lips double-reefed in a snug little smile,
I leave you two fables, both drawn from the deep, —
The shells you can drop, but the pearls you may keep.

. . . .

The fish called the FLOUNDER, perhaps you may know,
Has one side for use and another for show;
One side for the public, a delicate brown,
And one that is white, which he always keeps down.

A very young flounder, the flattest of flats,
(And they 're none of them thicker than opera hats,)
Was speaking more freely than charity taught
Of a friend and relation that just had been caught.

"My! what an exposure! just see what a sight!
I blush for my race, — he is showing his white!
Such spinning and wriggling, — why, what does he wish?
How painfully small to respectable fish!"

Then said an old SCULPIN, — "My freedom excuse,
You 're playing the cobbler with holes in your shoes;
Your brown side is up, — but just wait till you 're tried
And you 'll find that all flounders are white on one side."

. . . .

There 's a slice near the PICKEREL's pectoral fins,
Where the *thorax* leaves off and the *venter* begins,
Which his brother, survivor of fish-hooks and lines,
Though fond of his family, never declines.

He loves his relations; he feels they 'll be missed;
But that one little tidbit he cannot resist;
So your bait may be swallowed, no matter how fast,
For you catch your next fish with a piece of the last.

And thus, O survivor, whose merciless fate
Is to take the next hook with the president's bait,
You are lost while you snatch from the end of his line
The morsel he rent from this bosom of mine!

A MODEST REQUEST

COMPLIED WITH AFTER THE DINNER AT PRESIDENT EVERETT'S INAUGURATION

SCENE, — a back parlor in a certain square,
Or court, or lane, — in short, no matter where;
Time, — early morning, dear to simple souls
Who love its sunshine and its fresh-baked rolls;
Persons, — take pity on this telltale blush,
That, like the Æthiop, whispers, "Hush, oh hush!"

Delightful scene! where smiling comfort broods,
Nor business frets, nor anxious care intrudes;
O si sic omnia! were it ever so!
But what is stable in this world below?
Medio e fonte, — Virtue has her faults, —
The clearest fountains taste of Epsom salts;
We snatch the cup and lift to drain it dry, —
Its central dimple holds a drowning fly!
Strong is the pine by Maine's ambrosial streams,
But stronger augers pierce its thickest beams;

No iron gate, no spiked and panelled door,
Can keep out death, the postman, or the bore.
Oh for a world where peace and silence reign,
And blunted dulness terebrates in vain!
— The door-bell jingles, — enter Richard Fox,
And takes this letter from his leathern box.

"Dear Sir, —
In writing on a former day,
One little matter I forgot to say;
I now inform you in a single line,
On Thursday next our purpose is to *dine*.
The act of feeding, as you understand,
Is but a fraction of the work in hand;
Its nobler half is that ethereal meat
The papers call 'the intellectual treat;'
Songs, speeches, toasts, around the festive board
Drowned in the juice the College pumps afford;
For only water flanks our knives and forks,
So, sink or float, we swim without the corks.
Yours is the art, by native genius taught,
To clothe in eloquence the naked thought;
Yours is the skill its music to prolong
Through the sweet effluence of mellifluous song;
Yours the quaint trick to cram the pithy line
That cracks so crisply over bubbling wine;
And since success your various gifts attends,
We — that is, I and all your numerous friends —
Expect from you — your single self a host —
A speech, a song, excuse me, *and* a toast;
Nay, not to haggle on so small a claim,
A few of each, or several of the same.
(Signed),   Yours, *most truly*, —— "

No! my sight must fail, —
If that ain't Judas on the largest scale!
Well, this *is* modest; — nothing else than that?
My coat? my boots? my pantaloons? my hat?
My stick? my gloves? as well as all my wits,
Learning and linen, — everything that fits!

Jack, said my lady, is it grog you'll try,
Or punch, or toddy, if perhaps you're dry?
Ah, said the sailor, though I can't refuse,
You know, my lady, 't ain't for me to choose;
I'll take the grog to finish off my lunch,
And drink the toddy while you mix the punch.

THE SPEECH. (The speaker, rising to be seen,
Looks very red, because so very green.)
I rise — I rise — with unaffected fear,
(Louder! — speak louder! — who the deuce can hear?)
I rise — I said — with undisguised dismay —
— Such are my feelings as I rise, I say!
Quite unprepared to face this learned throng,
Already gorged with eloquence and song;
Around my view are ranged on either hand
The genius, wisdom, virtue of the land;
"Hands that the rod of empire might have swayed"
Close at my elbow stir their lemonade;
Would you like Homer learn to write and speak,
That bench is groaning with its weight of Greek;
Behold the naturalist who in his teens
Found six new species in a dish of greens;
And lo, the master in a statelier walk,
Whose annual ciphering takes a ton of chalk;
And there the linguist, who by common roots
Thro' all their nurseries tracks old Noah's shoots, —
How Shem's proud children reared the Assyrian piles,
While Ham's were scattered through the Sandwich Isles!
— Fired at the thought of all the present shows,
My kindling fancy down the future flows:
I see the glory of the coming days
O'er Time's horizon shoot its streaming rays;
Near and more near the radiant morning draws
In living lustre (rapturous applause);

From east to west the blazing heralds run,
Loosed from the chariot of the ascending
    sun,
Through the long vista of uncounted years
In cloudless splendor (three tremendous
    cheers).
My eye prophetic, as the depths unfold,
Sees a new advent of the age of gold;
While o'er the scene new generations press,
New heroes rise the coming time to bless, —
Not such as Homer's, who, we read in Pope,
Dined without forks and never heard of
    soap, —
Not such as May to Marlborough Chapel
    brings,
Lean, hungry, savage, anti-everythings,
Copies of Luther in the pasteboard style, —
But genuine articles, the true Carlyle;
While far on high the blazing orb shall
    shed
Its central light on Harvard's holy head,
And learning's ensigns ever float unfurled
Here in the focus of the new-born world!
The speaker stops, and, trampling down
    the pause,
Roars through the hall the thunder of ap-
    plause,
One stormy gust of long-suspended Ahs!
One whirlwind chaos of insane Hurrahs!

THE SONG. But this demands a briefer
    line, —
A shorter muse, and not the old long Nine;
Long metre answers for a common song,
Though common metre does not answer
    long.

She came beneath the forest dome
    To seek its peaceful shade,
An exile from her ancient home,
    A poor, forsaken maid;
No banner, flaunting high above,
    No blazoned cross, she bore;
One holy book of light and love
    Was all her worldly store.

The dark brown shadows passed away,
    And wider spread the green,
And where the savage used to stray
    The rising mart was seen;
So, when the laden winds had brought
    Their showers of golden rain,
Her lap some precious gleanings caught,
    Like Ruth's amid the grain.

But wrath soon gathered uncontrolled
    Among the baser churls,
To see her ankles red with gold,
    Her forehead white with pearls.
"Who gave to thee the glittering bands
    That lace thine azure veins?
Who bade thee lift those snow-white
    hands
    We bound in gilded chains?"

"These are the gems my children gave,"
    The stately dame replied;
"The wise, the gentle, and the brave,
    I nurtured at my side.
If envy still your bosom stings,
    Take back their rims of gold;
My sons will melt their wedding-rings,
    And give a hundred-fold!"

THE TOAST. Oh tell me, ye who thought-
    less ask
Exhausted nature for a threefold task,
In wit or pathos if one share remains,
A safe investment for an ounce of brains!
Hard is the job to launch the desperate
    pun,
A pun-job dangerous as the Indian one.
Turned by the current of some stronger
    wit
Back from the object that you mean to
    hit,
Like the strange missile which the Austra-
    lian throws,
Your verbal *boomerang* slaps you on the
    nose.
One vague inflection spoils the whole with
    doubt,
One trivial letter ruins all, left out;
A knot can choke a felon into clay,
A not will save him, spelt without the *k*;
The smallest word has some unguarded
    spot,
And danger lurks in *i* without a dot.

Thus great Achilles, who had shown his
    zeal
In healing wounds, died of a wounded heel;
Unhappy chief, who, when in childhood
    doused,
Had saved his bacon had his feet been
    soused!
Accursed heel that killed a hero stout!
Oh, had your mother known that you were
    out,

Death had not entered at the trifling part
That still defies the small chirurgeon's art
With corns and bunions, — not the glorious John,
Who wrote the book we all have pondered on,
But other bunions, bound in fleecy hose,
To "Pilgrim's Progress" unrelenting foes!

A HEALTH, unmingled with the reveller's wine,
To him whose title is indeed divine;
Truth's sleepless watchman on her midnight tower,
Whose lamp burns brightest when the tempests lower.
On, who can tell with what a leaden flight
Drag the long watches of his weary night,
While at his feet the hoarse and blinding gale
Strews the torn wreck and bursts the fragile sail,
When stars have faded, when the wave is dark,
When rocks and sands embrace the foundering bark!
But still he pleads with unavailing cry,
Behold the light, O wanderer, look or die!

A health, fair Themis! Would the enchanted vine
Wreathed its green tendrils round this cup of thine!
If Learning's radiance fill thy modern court,
Its glorious sunshine streams through Blackstone's port!
Lawyers are thirsty, and their clients too, —
Witness at least, if memory serve me true,
Those old tribunals, famed for dusty suits,
Where men sought justice ere they brushed their boots;
And what can match, to solve a learned doubt,
The warmth within that comes from "cold without"?

Health to the art whose glory is to give
The crowning boon that makes it life to live.
Ask not her home; — the rock where nature flings
Her arctic lichen, last of living things;
The gardens, fragrant with the orient's balm,
From the low jasmine to the star-like palm,
Hail her as mistress o'er the distant waves,
And yield their tribute to her wandering slaves.
Wherever, moistening the ungrateful soil,
The tear of suffering tracks the path of toil,
There, in the anguish of his fevered hours,
Her gracious finger points to healing flowers;
Where the lost felon steals away to die,
Her soft hand waves before his closing eye;
Where hunted misery finds his darkest lair,
The midnight taper shows her kneeling there!
VIRTUE, — the guide that men and nations own;
And LAW, — the bulwark that protects her throne;
And HEALTH, — to all its happiest charm that lends;
These and their servants, man's untiring friends:
Pour the bright lymph that Heaven itself lets fall,
In one fair bumper let us toast them all!

THE PARTING WORD

I MUST leave thee, lady sweet!
Months shall waste before we meet;
Winds are fair and sails are spread,
Anchors leave their ocean bed;
Ere this shining day grow dark,
Skies shall gird my shoreless bark.
Through thy tears, O lady mine,
Read thy lover's parting line.

When the first sad sun shall set,
Thou shalt tear thy locks of jet;
When the morning star shall rise,
Thou shalt wake with weeping eyes;
When the second sun goes down,
Thou more tranquil shalt be grown,
Taught too well that wild despair
Dims thine eyes and spoils thy hair.

All the first unquiet week
Thou shalt wear a smileless cheek;

In the first month's second half
Thou shalt once attempt to laugh;
Then in Pickwick thou shalt dip,
Slightly puckering round the lip,
Till at last, in sorrow's spite,
Samuel makes thee laugh outright.

While the first seven mornings last,
Round thy chamber bolted fast
Many a youth shall fume and pout,
"Hang the girl, she's always out!"
While the second week goes round,
Vainly shall they ring and pound;
When the third week shall begin,
"Martha, let the creature in."

Now once more the flattering throng
Round thee flock with smile and song,
But thy lips, unweaned as yet,
Lisp, "Oh, how can I forget!"
Men and devils both contrive
Traps for catching girls alive;
Eve was duped, and Helen kissed,—
How, oh how, can you resist?

First be careful of your fan,
Trust it not to youth or man;
Love has filled a pirate's sail
Often with its perfumed gale.
Mind your kerchief most of all,
Fingers touch when kerchiefs fall;
Shorter ell than mercers clip
Is the space from hand to lip.

Trust not such as talk in tropes,
Full of pistols, daggers, ropes;
All the hemp that Russia bears
Scarce would answer lovers' prayers;
Never thread was spun so fine,
Never spider stretched the line,
Would not hold the lovers true
That would really swing for you.

Fiercely some shall storm and swear,
Beating breasts in black despair;
Others murmur with a sigh,
You must melt, or they will die:
Painted words on empty lies,
Grubs with wings like butterflies;
Let them die, and welcome, too;
Pray what better could they do?

Fare thee well: if years efface
From thy heart love's burning trace,
Keep, oh keep that hallowed seat
From the tread of vulgar feet;
If the blue lips of the sea
Wait with icy kiss for me,
Let not thine forget the vow,
Sealed how often, Love, as now.

A SONG OF OTHER DAYS

As o'er the glacier's frozen sheet
  Breathes soft the Alpine rose,
So through life's desert springing sweet
  The flower of friendship grows;
And as where'er the roses grow
  Some rain or dew descends,
'T is nature's law that wine should flow
  To wet the lips of friends.
    Then once again, before we part,
      My empty glass shall ring;
    And he that has the warmest heart
      Shall loudest laugh and sing.

They say we were not born to eat;
  But gray-haired sages think
It means, Be moderate in your meat,
  And partly live to drink.
For baser tribes the rivers flow
  That know not wine or song;
Man wants but little drink below,
  But wants that little strong.
    Then once again, etc.

If one bright drop is like the gem
  That decks a monarch's crown,
One goblet holds a diadem
  Of rubies melted down!
A fig for Cæsar's blazing brow,
  But, like the Egyptian queen,
Bid each dissolving jewel glow
  My thirsty lips between.
    Then once again, etc.

The Grecian's mound, the Roman's urn,
  Are silent when we call,
Yet still the purple grapes return
  To cluster on the wall;
It was a bright Immortal's head
  They circled with the vine,
And o'er their best and bravest dead
  They poured the dark-red wine.
    Then once again, etc.

Methinks o'er every sparkling glass
  Young Eros waves his wings,

And echoes o'er its dimples pass
From dead Anacreon's strings;
And, tossing round its beaded brim
Their locks of floating gold,
With bacchant dance and choral hymn
Return the nymphs of old.
Then once again, etc.

A welcome then to joy and mirth,
From hearts as fresh as ours,
To scatter o'er the dust of earth
Their sweetly mingled flowers;
'T is Wisdom's self the cup that fills
In spite of Folly's frown,
And Nature, from her vine-clad hills,
That rains her life-blood down!
Then once again, before we part,
My empty glass shall ring;
And he that has the warmest heart
Shall loudest laugh and sing.

SONG

FOR A TEMPERANCE DINNER TO WHICH LADIES WERE INVITED (NEW YORK MERCANTILE LIBRARY ASSOCIATION, NOVEMBER, 1842)

[In the *Professor* Dr. Holmes makes the following reference to this song: —
"I once wrote a song about wine, in which I spoke so warmly of it, that I was afraid some would think it was written *inter pocula*; whereas it was composed in the bosom of my family, under the most tranquillizing domestic influences.
" — The divinity student turned towards me, looking mischievous. — Can you tell me, — he said, — who wrote a song for a temperance celebration once, of which the following is a verse? —

"Alas for the loved one, too gentle and fair
The joys of the banquet to chasten and share!
Her eye lost its light that his goblet might shine,
And the rose of her cheek was dissolved in his wine!

I did, — I answered. — What are you going to do about it? — I will tell you another line I wrote long ago: —

"Don't be 'consistent,' — but be simply *true*."]

A HEALTH to dear woman! She bids us untwine,
From the cup it encircles, the fast-clinging vine;
But her cheek in its crystal with pleasure will glow,
And mirror its bloom in the bright wave below.

A health to sweet woman! The days are no more
When she watched for her lord till the revel was o'er,
And smoothed the white pillow, and blushed when he came,
As she pressed her cold lips on his forehead of flame.

Alas for the loved one! too spotless and fair
The joys of his banquet to chasten and share;
Her eye lost its light that his goblet might shine,
And the rose of her cheek was dissolved in his wine.

Joy smiles in the fountain, health flows in the rills,
As their ribbons of silver unwind from the hills;
They breathe not the mist of the bacchanal's dream,
But the lilies of innocence float on their stream.

Then a health and a welcome to woman once more!
She brings us a passport that laughs at our door;
It is written on crimson, — its letters are pearls, —
It is countersigned *Nature*. — So, room for the Girls!

A SENTIMENT

THE pledge of Friendship! it is still divine,
Though watery floods have quenched its burning wine;
Whatever vase the sacred drops may hold,
The gourd, the shell, the cup of beaten gold,
Around its brim the hand of Nature throws
A garland sweeter than the banquet's rose.
Bright are the blushes of the vine-wreathed bowl.

Warm with the sunshine of Anacreon's soul,
But dearer memories gild the tasteless wave
That fainting Sidney perished as he gave.
'T is the heart's current lends the cup its glow,
Whate'er the fountain whence the draught may flow, —
The diamond dew-drops sparkling through the sand,
Scooped by the Arab in his sunburnt hand,
Or the dark streamlet oozing from the snow,
Where creep and crouch the shuddering Esquimaux;
Ay, in the stream that, ere again we meet,
Shall burst the pavement, glistening at our feet,
And, stealing silent from its leafy hills,
Thread all our alleys with its thousand rills, —
In each pale draught if generous feeling blend,
And o'er the goblet friend shall smile on friend,
Even cold Cochituate every heart shall warm,
And genial Nature still defy reform!

A RHYMED LESSON

(URANIA)

This poem was delivered before the Boston Mercantile Library Association, October 14, 1846.

Yes, dear Enchantress, — wandering far and long,
In realms unperfumed by the breath of song,
Where flowers ill-flavored shed their sweets around,
And bitterest roots invade the ungenial ground,
Whose gems are crystals from the Epsom mine,
Whose vineyards flow with antimonial wine,
Whose gates admit no mirthful feature in,
Save one gaunt mocker, the Sardonic grin,
Whose pangs are real, not the woes of rhyme
That blue-eyed misses warble out of time; —

Truant, not recreant to thy sacred claim,
Older by reckoning, but in heart the same,
Freed for a moment from the chains of toil,
I tread once more thy consecrated soil;
Here at thy feet my old allegiance own,
Thy subject still, and loyal to thy throne!

My dazzled glance explores the crowded hall;
Alas, how vain to hope the smiles of all!
I know my audience. All the gay and young
Love the light antics of a playful tongue;
And these, remembering some expansive line
My lips let loose among the nuts and wine,
Are all impatience till the opening pun
Proclaims the witty shamfight is begun.
Two fifths at least, if not the total half,
Have come infuriate for an earthquake laugh;
I know full well what alderman has tied
His red bandanna tight about his side;
I see the mother, who, aware that boys
Perform their laughter with superfluous noise,
Beside her kerchief brought an extra one
To stop the explosions of her bursting son;
I know a tailor, once a friend of mine,
Expects great doings in the button line, —
For mirth's concussions rip the outward case,
And plant the stitches in a tenderer place.
I know my audience, — these shall have their due;
A smile awaits them ere my song is through!

I know myself. Not servile for applause,
My Muse permits no deprecating clause;
Modest or vain, she will not be denied
One bold confession due to honest pride;
And well she knows the drooping veil of song
Shall save her boldness from the caviller's wrong.
Her sweeter voice the Heavenly Maid imparts
To tell the secrets of our aching hearts:
For this, a suppliant, captive, prostrate, bound,
She kneels imploring at the feet of sound;
For this, convulsed in thought's maternal pains,
She loads her arms with rhyme's resounding chains;

Faint though the music of her fetters be,
It lends one charm,— her lips are ever free!

Think not I come, in manhood's fiery noon,
To steal his laurels from the stage buffoon;
His sword of lath the harlequin may wield;
Behold the star upon my lifted shield!
Though the just critic pass my humble name,
And sweeter lips have drained the cup of fame,
While my gay stanza pleased the banquet's lords,
The soul within was tuned to deeper chords!
Say, shall my arms, in other conflicts taught
To swing aloft the ponderous mace of thought,
Lift, in obedience to a school-girl's law,
Mirth's tinsel wand or laughter's tickling straw?
Say, shall I wound with satire's rankling spear
The pure, warm hearts that bid me welcome here?
No! while I wander through the land of dreams,
To strive with great and play with trifling themes,
Let some kind meaning fill the varied line.
You have your judgment; will you trust to mine?

Between two breaths what crowded mysteries lie,—
The first short gasp, the last and long-drawn sigh!
Like phantoms painted on the magic slide,
Forth from the darkness of the past we glide,
As living shadows for a moment seen
In airy pageant on the eternal screen,
Traced by a ray from one unchanging flame,
Then seek the dust and stillness whence we came.

But whence and why, our trembling souls inquire,
Caught these dim visions their awakening fire?
Oh, who forgets when first the piercing thought
Through childhood's musings found its way unsought?
I AM;— I LIVE. The mystery and the fear
When the dread question, WHAT HAS BROUGHT ME HERE?
Burst through life's twilight, as before the sun
Roll the deep thunders of the morning gun!
Are angel faces, silent and serene,
Bent on the conflicts of this little scene,
Whose dream-like efforts, whose unreal strife,
Are but the preludes to a larger life?

Or does life's summer see the end of all,
These leaves of being mouldering as they fall,
As the old poet vaguely used to deem,
As WESLEY questioned in his youthful dream?
Oh, could such mockery reach our souls indeed,
Give back the Pharaohs' or the Athenian's creed;
Better than this a Heaven of man's device,—
The Indian's sports, the Moslem's paradise!

Or is our being's only end and aim
To add new glories to our Maker's name,
As the poor insect, shrivelling in the blaze,
Lends a faint sparkle to its streaming rays?
Does earth send upward to the Eternal's ear
The mingled discords of her jarring sphere
To swell his anthem, while creation rings
With notes of anguish from its shattered strings?
Is it for this the immortal Artist means
These conscious, throbbing, agonized machines?

Dark is the soul whose sullen creed can bind
In chains like these the all-embracing Mind;
No! two-faced bigot, thou dost ill reprove
The sensual, selfish, yet benignant Jove,
And praise a tyrant throned in lonely pride,
Who loves himself, and cares for naught beside;

A RHYMED LESSON

Who gave thee, summoned from primeval night,
A thousand laws, and not a single right, —
A heart to feel, and quivering nerves to thrill,
The sense of wrong, the death-defying will;
Who girt thy senses with this goodly frame,
Its earthly glories and its orbs of flame,
Not for thyself, unworthy of a thought,
Poor helpless victim of a life unsought,
But all for him, unchanging and supreme,
The heartless centre of thy frozen scheme!

Trust not the teacher with his lying scroll,
Who tears the charter of thy shuddering soul;
The God of love, who gave the breath that warms
All living dust in all its varied forms,
Asks not the tribute of a world like this
To fill the measure of his perfect bliss.
Though winged with life through all its radiant shores,
Creation flowed with unexhausted stores
Cherub and seraph had not yet enjoyed;
For this he called thee from the quickening void!
Nor this alone; a larger gift was thine,
A mightier purpose swelled his vast design:
Thought, — conscience, — will, — to make them all thine own,
He rent a pillar from the eternal throne!

Made in his image, thou must nobly dare
The thorny crown of sovereignty to share.
With eye uplifted, it is thine to view,
From thine own centre, Heaven's o'erarching blue;
So round thy heart a beaming circle lies
No fiend can blot, no hypocrite disguise;
From all its orbs one cheering voice is heard,
Full to thine ear it bears the Father's word,
Now, as in Eden where his first-born trod:
"Seek thine own welfare, true to man and God!"
Think not too meanly of thy low estate;
Thou hast a choice; to choose is to create!

Remember whose the sacred lips that tell,
Angels approve thee when thy choice is well;
Remember, One, a judge of righteous men,
Swore to spare Sodom if she held but ten!
Use well the freedom which thy Master gave,
(Think'st thou that Heaven can tolerate a slave?)
And He who made thee to be just and true
Will bless thee, love thee, — ay, respect thee too!

Nature has placed thee on a changeful tide,
To breast its waves, but not without a guide;
Yet, as the needle will forget its aim,
Jarred by the fury of the electric flame,
As the true current it will falsely feel,
Warped from its axis by a freight of steel;
So will thy CONSCIENCE lose its balanced truth
If passion's lightning fall upon thy youth,
So the pure effluence quit its sacred hold
Girt round too deeply with magnetic gold.
Go to yon tower, where busy science plies
Her vast antennæ, feeling through the skies:
That little vernier on whose slender lines
The midnight taper trembles as it shines,
A silent index, tracks the planets' march
In all their wanderings through the ethereal arch;
Tells through the mist where dazzled Mercury burns,
And marks the spot where Uranus returns.
So, till by wrong or negligence effaced,
The living index which thy Maker traced
Repeats the line each starry Virtue draws
Through the wide circuit of creation's laws;
Still tracks unchanged the everlasting ray
Where the dark shadows of temptation stray,
But, once defaced, forgets the orbs of light,
And leaves thee wandering o'er the expanse of night.

"What is thy creed?" a hundred lips inquire;
"Thou seekest God beneath what Christian spire?"

Nor ask they idly, for uncounted lies
Float upward on the smoke of sacrifice;
When man's first incense rose above the plain,
Of earth's two altars one was built by Cain!
  Uncursed by doubt, our earliest creed we take;
We love the precepts for the teacher's sake;
The simple lessons which the nursery taught
Fell soft and stainless on the buds of thought,
And the full blossom owes its fairest hue
To those sweet tear-drops of affection's dew.
  Too oft the light that led our earlier hours
Fades with the perfume of our cradle flowers;
The clear, cold question chills to frozen doubt;
Tired of beliefs, we dread to live without:
Oh then, if Reason waver at thy side,
Let humbler Memory be thy gentle guide;
Go to thy birthplace, and, if faith was there,
Repeat thy father's creed, thy mother's prayer!
  Faith loves to lean on Time's destroying arm,
And age, like distance, lends a double charm;
In dim cathedrals, dark with vaulted gloom,
What holy awe invests the saintly tomb!
There pride will bow, and anxious care expand,
And creeping avarice come with open hand;
The gay can weep, the impious can adore,
From morn's first glimmerings on the chancel floor
Till dying sunset sheds his crimson stains
Through the faint halos of the irised panes.
  Yet there are graves, whose rudely-shapen sod
Bears the fresh footprints where the sexton trod;
Graves where the verdure has not dared to shoot,
Where the chance wild-flower has not fixed its root,
Whose slumbering tenants, dead without a name,
The eternal record shall at length proclaim
Pure as the holiest in the long array
Of hooded, mitred, or tiaraed clay!

  Come, seek the air; some pictures we may gain
Whose passing shadows shall not be in vain;
Not from the scenes that crowd the stranger's soil,
Not from our own amidst the stir of toil,
But when the Sabbath brings its kind release,
And Care lies slumbering on the lap of Peace.

  The air is hushed, the street is holy ground;
Hark! The sweet bells renew their welcome sound:
As one by one awakes each silent tongue,
It tells the turret whence its voice is flung.

  The Chapel, last of sublunary things
That stirs our echoes with the name of Kings,
Whose bell, just glistening from the font and forge,
Rolled its proud requiem for the second George,
Solemn and swelling, as of old it rang,
Flings to the wind its deep, sonorous clang;
The simpler pile, that, mindful of the hour
When Howe's artillery shook its half-built tower,
Wears on its bosom, as a bride might do,
The iron breastpin which the "Rebels" threw,
Wakes the sharp echoes with the quivering thrill
Of keen vibrations, tremulous and shrill;
Aloft, suspended in the morning's fire,
Crash the vast cymbals from the Southern spire;
The Giant, standing by the elm-clad green,
His white lance lifted o'er the silent scene,
Whirling in air his brazen goblet round,
Swings from its brim the swollen floods of sound;
While, sad with memories of the olden time,
Throbs from his tower the Northern Minstrel's chime, —
Faint, single tones, that spell their ancient song,
But tears still follow as they breathe along.

Child of the soil, whom fortune sends to range
Where man and nature, faith and customs change,
Borne in thy memory, each familiar tone
Mourns on the winds that sigh in every zone.
When Ceylon sweeps thee with her perfumed breeze
Through the warm billows of the Indian seas;
When — ship and shadow blended both in one —
Flames o'er thy mast the equatorial sun,
From sparkling midnight to refulgent noon
Thy canvas swelling with the still monsoon;
When through thy shrouds the wild tornado sings,
And thy poor sea-bird folds her tattered wings, —
Oft will delusion o'er thy senses steal,
And airy echoes ring the Sabbath peal!
Then, dim with grateful tears, in long array
Rise the fair town, the island-studded bay,
Home, with its smiling board, its cheering fire,
The half-choked welcome of the expecting sire,
The mother's kiss, and, still if aught remain,
Our whispering hearts shall aid the silent strain.
Ah, let the dreamer o'er the taffrail lean
To muse unheeded, and to weep unseen;
Fear not the tropic's dews, the evening's chills,
His heart lies warm among his triple hills!

Turned from her path by this deceitful gleam,
My wayward fancy half forgets her theme.
See through the streets that slumbered in repose
The living current of devotion flows,
Its varied forms in one harmonious band:
Age leading childhood by its dimpled hand;
Want, in the robe whose faded edges fall
To tell of rags beneath the tartan shawl;
And wealth, in silks that, fluttering to appear,
Lift the deep borders of the proud cashmere.
See, but glance briefly, sorrow-worn and pale,
Those sunken cheeks beneath the widow's veil;
Alone she wanders where with *him* she trod,
No arm to stay her, but she leans on God.
While other doublets deviate here and there,
What secret handcuff binds that pretty pair?
Compactest couple! pressing side to side, —
Ah, the white bonnet that reveals the bride!
By the white neckcloth, with its straitened tie,
The sober hat, the Sabbath-speaking eye,
Severe and smileless, he that runs may read
The stern disciple of Geneva's creed:
Decent and slow, behold his solemn march;
Silent he enters through yon crowded arch.
A livelier bearing of the outward man,
The light-hued gloves, the undevout rattan,
Now smartly raised or half profanely twirled, —
A bright, fresh twinkle from the week-day world, —
Tell their plain story; yes, thine eyes behold
A cheerful Christian from the liberal fold.
Down the chill street that curves in gloomiest shade
What marks betray yon solitary maid?
The cheek's red rose that speaks of balmier air,
The Celtic hue that shades her braided hair,
The gilded missal in her kerchief tied, —
Poor Nora, exile from Killarney's side!
Sister in toil, though blanched by colder skies,
That left their azure in her downcast eyes,
See pallid Margaret, Labor's patient child,
Scarce weaned from home, the nursling of the wild,
Where white Katahdin o'er the horizon shines,
And broad Penobscot dashes through the pines.
Still, as she hastes, her careful fingers hold
The unfailing hymn-book in its cambric fold.
Six days at drudgery's heavy wheel she stands,
The seventh sweet morning folds her weary hands.
Yes, child of suffering, thou mayst well be sure
He who ordained the Sabbath loves the poor!

This weekly picture faithful Memory draws,
Nor claims the noisy tribute of applause;
Faint is the glow such barren hopes can lend,
And frail the line that asks no loftier end.
Trust me, kind listener, I will yet beguile
Thy saddened features of the promised smile.
This magic mantle thou must well divide,
It has its sable and its ermine side;
Yet, ere the lining of the robe appears,
Take thou in silence what I give in tears.

Dear listening soul, this transitory scene
Of murmuring stillness, busily serene, —
This solemn pause, the breathing-space of man,
The halt of toil's exhausted caravan, —
Comes sweet with music to thy wearied ear;
Rise with its anthems to a holier sphere!

Deal meekly, gently, with the hopes that guide
The lowliest brother straying from thy side:
If right, they bid thee tremble for thine own;
If wrong, the verdict is for God alone!

What though the champions of thy faith esteem
The sprinkled fountain or baptismal stream;
Shall jealous passions in unseemly strife
Cross their dark weapons o'er the waves of life?

Let my free soul, expanding as it can,
Leave to his scheme the thoughtful Puritan;
But Calvin's dogma shall my lips deride?
In that stern faith my angel Mary died;
Or ask if mercy's milder creed can save,
Sweet sister, risen from thy new-made grave?

True, the harsh founders of thy church reviled
That ancient faith, the trust of Erin's child;
Must thou be raking in the crumbled past
For racks and fagots in her teeth to cast?

See from the ashes of Helvetia's pile
The whitened skull of old Servetus smile!
Round her young heart thy "Romish Upas" threw
Its firm, deep fibres, strengthening as she grew;
Thy sneering voice may call them "Popish tricks,"
Her Latin prayers, her dangling crucifix,
But *De Profundis* blessed her father's grave,
That "idol" cross her dying mother gave!
What if some angel looks with equal eyes
On her and thee, the simple and the wise,
Writes each dark fault against thy brighter creed,
And drops a tear with every foolish bead!
Grieve, as thou must, o'er history's reeking page;
Blush for the wrongs that stain thy happier age;
Strive with the wanderer from the better path,
Bearing thy message meekly, not in wrath;
Weep for the frail that err, the weak that fall,
Have thine own faith, — but hope and pray for all!

Faith; Conscience; Love. A meaner task remains,
And humbler thoughts must creep in lowlier strains.
Shalt thou be honest? Ask the worldly schools,
And all will tell thee knaves are busier fools;
Prudent? Industrious? Let not modern pens
Instruct "Poor Richard's" fellow-citizens.

Be firm! One constant element in luck
Is genuine solid old Teutonic pluck.
See yon tall shaft; it felt the earthquake's thrill,
Clung to its base, and greets the sunrise still.

Stick to your aim: the mongrel's hold will slip,
But only crowbars loose the bulldog's grip;
Small as he looks, the jaw that never yields
Drags down the bellowing monarch of the fields!

A RHYMED LESSON

Yet in opinions look not always back, —
Your wake is nothing, mind the coming track;
Leave what you 've done for what you have to do;
Don't be "consistent," but be simply true.

Don't catch the fidgets; you have found your place
Just in the focus of a nervous race,
Fretful to change and rabid to discuss,
Full of excitements, always in a fuss.
Think of the patriarchs; then compare as men
These lean-cheeked maniacs of the tongue and pen!
Run, if you like, but try to keep your breath;
Work like a man, but don't be worked to death;
And with new notions, — let me change the rule, —
Don't strike the iron till it 's slightly cool.

Choose well your *set*; our feeble nature seeks
The aid of clubs, the countenance of cliques;
And with this object settle first of all
Your weight of metal and your size of ball.
Track not the steps of such as hold you cheap,
Too mean to prize, though good enough to keep;
The "real, genuine, no-mistake Tom Thumbs"
Are little people fed on great men's crumbs.
Yet keep no followers of that hateful brood
That basely mingles with its wholesome food
The tumid reptile, which, the poet said,
Doth wear a precious jewel in his head.

If the wild filly, "Progress," thou wouldst ride,
Have young companions ever at thy side;
But wouldst thou stride the stanch old mare, "Success,"
Go with thine elders, though they please thee less.
Shun such as lounge through afternoons and eves,

And on thy dial write, "Beware of thieves!"
Felon of minutes, never taught to feel
The worth of treasures which thy fingers steal,
Pick my left pocket of its silver dime,
But spare the right, — it holds my golden time!

Does praise delight thee? Choose some *ultra* side, —
A sure old recipe, and often tried;
Be its apostle, congressman, or bard,
Spokesman or jokesman, only drive it hard;
But know the forfeit which thy choice abides,
For on two wheels the poor reformer rides, —
One black with epithets the *anti* throws,
One white with flattery painted by the *pros*.

Though books on MANNERS are not out of print,
An honest tongue may drop a harmless hint.
Stop not, unthinking, every friend you meet,
To spin your wordy fabric in the street;
While you are emptying your colloquial pack,
The fiend *Lumbago* jumps upon his back.
Nor cloud his features with the unwelcome tale
Of how he looks, if haply thin and pale;
Health is a subject for his child, his wife,
And the rude office that insures his life.
Look in his face, to meet thy neighbor's soul,
Not on his garments, to detect a hole;
"How to observe" is what thy pages show,
Pride of thy sex, Miss Harriet Martineau!
Oh, what a precious book the one would be
That taught observers what they 're *not* to see!

I tell in verse — 't were better done in prose —
One curious trick that everybody knows;
Once form this habit, and it 's very strange
How long it sticks, how hard it is to change.
Two friendly people, both disposed to smile,
Who meet, like others, every little while,
Instead of passing with a pleasant bow,

And "How d' ye do?" or "How's your
  uncle now?"
Impelled by feelings in their nature kind,
But slightly weak and somewhat undefined,
Rush at each other, make a sudden stand,
Begin to talk, expatiate, and expand;
Each looks quite radiant, seems extremely
  struck,
Their meeting so was such a piece of luck;
Each thinks the other thinks he's greatly
  pleased
To screw the vice in which they both are
  squeezed;
So there they talk, in dust, or mud, or
  snow,
Both bored to death, and both afraid to
  go!
  Your hat once lifted, do not hang your
    fire,
Nor, like slow Ajax, fighting still, retire;
When your old castor on your crown you
  clap,
Go off; you've mounted your percussion
  cap.

  Some words on LANGUAGE may be well
    applied,
And take them kindly, though they touch
  your pride.
Words lead to things; a scale is more pre-
  cise, —
Coarse speech, bad grammar, swearing,
  drinking, vice.
Our cold Northeaster's icy fetter clips
The native freedom of the Saxon lips;
See the brown peasant of the plastic South,
How all his passions play about his mouth!
With us, the feature that transmits the
  soul,
A frozen, passive, palsied breathing-hole.
The crampy shackles of the ploughboy's
  walk
Tie the small muscles when he strives to
  talk;
Not all the pumice of the polished town
Can smooth this roughness of the barnyard
  down;
Rich, honored, titled, he betrays his race
By this one mark, — he's awkward in the
  face; —
Nature's rude impress, long before he
  knew
The sunny street that holds the sifted few.
  It can't be helped, though, if we're taken
    young,
We gain some freedom of the lips and
  tongue;
But school and college often try in vain
To break the padlock of our boyhood's
  chain:
One stubborn word will prove this axiom
  true, —
No quondam rustic can enunciate *view*.

  A few brief stanzas may be well em-
    ployed
To speak of errors we can all avoid.
  Learning condemns beyond the reach of
    hope
The careless lips that speak of sōap for
  sŏap;
Her edict exiles from her fair abode
The clownish voice that utters rōad for
  rŏad:
Less stern to him who calls his cōat a cŏat,
And steers his bōat, believing it a bŏat,
She pardoned one, our classic city's boast,
Who said at Cambridge mōst instead of
  mŏst,
But knit her brows and stamped her angry
  foot
To hear a Teacher call a rōot a rŏot.

  Once more: speak clearly, if you speak
    at all;
Carve every word before you let it fall;
Don't, like a lecturer or dramatic star,
Try over-hard to roll the British R;
Do put your accents in the proper spot;
Don't, — let me beg you, — don't say
  "How?" for "What?"
And when you stick on conversation's burs,
Don't strew your pathway with those
  dreadful *urs*.

  From little matters let us pass to less,
And lightly touch the mysteries of DRESS;
The outward forms the inner man reveal, —
We guess the pulp before we cut the peel.

  I leave the broadcloth, — coats and all
    the rest, —
The dangerous waistcoat, called by cock-
  neys "vest,"
The things named "pants" in certain
  documents,
A word not made for gentlemen, but
  "gents;"
One single precept might the whole con-
  dense:

Be sure your tailor is a man of sense;
But add a little care, a decent pride,
And always err upon the sober side.

Three pairs of boots one pair of feet demands,
If polished daily by the owner's hands;
If the dark menial's visit save from this,
Have twice the number, — for he 'll sometimes miss.
One pair for critics of the nicer sex,
Close in the instep's clinging circumflex,
Long, narrow, light; the Gallic boot of love,
A kind of cross between a boot and glove.
Compact, but easy, strong, substantial, square,
Let native art compile the medium pair.
The third remains, and let your tasteful skill
Here show some relics of affection still;
Let no stiff cowhide, reeking from the tan,
No rough caoutchouc, no deformed brogan,
Disgrace the tapering outline of your feet,
Though yellow torrents gurgle through the street.

Wear seemly gloves; not black, nor yet too light,
And least of all the pair that once was white;
Let the dead party where you told your loves
Bury in peace its dead bouquets and gloves;
Shave like the goat, if so your fancy bids,
But be a parent, — don't neglect your kids.

Have a good hat; the secret of your looks
Lives with the beaver in Canadian brooks;
Virtue may flourish in an old cravat,
But man and nature scorn the shocking hat.
Does beauty slight you from her gay abodes?
Like bright Apollo, you must take to *Rhoades*, —
Mount the new castor, — ice itself will melt!
Boots, gloves, may fail; the hat is always felt!

Be shy of breastpins; plain, well-ironed white,
With small pearl buttons, — two of them in sight, —
Is always genuine, while your gems may pass,
Though real diamonds, for ignoble glass.

But spurn those paltry Cisatlantic lies
That round his breast the shabby rustic ties;
Breathe not the name profaned to hallow things
The indignant laundress blushes when she brings!

Our freeborn race, averse to every check,
Has tossed the yoke of Europe from its neck;
From the green prairie to the sea-girt town,
The whole wide nation turns its collars down.
The stately neck is manhood's manliest part;
It takes the life-blood freshest from the heart.
With short, curled ringlets close around it spread,
How light and strong it lifts the Grecian head!
Thine, fair Erechtheus of Minerva's wall;
Or thine, young athlete of the Louvre's hall,
Smooth as the pillar flashing in the sun
That filled the arena where thy wreaths were won,
Firm as the band that clasps the antlered spoil
Strained in the winding anaconda's coil!
I spare the contrast; it were only kind
To be a little, nay, intensely blind.
Choose for yourself: I know it cuts your ear;
I know the points will sometimes interfere;
I know that often, like the filial John,
Whom sleep surprised with half his drapery on,
You show your features to the astonished town
With one side standing and the other down; —
But oh, my friend! my favorite fellow-man!
If Nature made you on her modern plan,
Sooner than wander with your windpipe bare, —
The fruit of Eden ripening in the air, —
With that lean head-stalk, that protruding chin,
Wear standing collars, were they made of tin!
And have a neckcloth — by the throat of Jove! —
Cut from the funnel of a rusty stove!

The long-drawn lesson narrows to its close,
Chill, slender, slow, the dwindled current flows;
Tired of the ripples on its feeble springs,
Once more the Muse unfolds her upward wings.

Land of my birth, with this unhallowed tongue,
Thy hopes, thy dangers, I perchance had sung;
But who shall sing, in brutal disregard
Of all the essentials of the "native bard"?
Lake, sea, shore, prairie, forest, mountain, fall,
His eye omnivorous must devour them all;
The tallest summits and the broadest tides
His foot must compass with its giant strides,
Where Ocean thunders, where Missouri rolls,
And tread at once the tropics and the poles;
His food all forms of earth, fire, water, air,
His home all space, his birthplace everywhere.

Some grave compatriot, having seen perhaps
The pictured page that goes in Worcester's Maps,
And read in earnest what was said in jest,
"Who drives fat oxen"—please to add the rest,—
Sprung the odd notion that the poet's dreams
Grow in the ratio of his hills and streams;
And hence insisted that the aforesaid "bard,"
Pink of the future, fancy's pattern-card,
The babe of nature in the "giant West,"
Must be of course her biggest and her best.

Oh! when at length the expected bard shall come,
Land of our pride, to strike thine echoes dumb,
(And many a voice exclaims in prose and rhyme,
It's getting late, and he's behind his time,)
When all thy mountains clap their hands in joy,
And all thy cataracts thunder, "That's the boy,"—

Say if with him the reign of song shall end,
And Heaven declare its final dividend!

Be calm, dear brother! whose impassioned strain
Comes from an alley watered by a drain;
The little Mincio, dribbling to the Po,
Beats all the epics of the Hoang Ho;
If loved in earnest by the tuneful maid,
Don't mind their nonsense,—never be afraid!

The nurse of poets feeds her wingèd brood
By common firesides, on familiar food;
In a low hamlet, by a narrow stream,
Where bovine rustics used to doze and dream,
She filled young William's fiery fancy full,
While old John Shakespeare talked of beeves and wool!

No Alpine needle, with its climbing spire,
Brings down for mortals the Promethean fire,
If careless nature have forgot to frame
An altar worthy of the sacred flame.
Unblest by any save the goatherd's lines,
Mont Blanc rose soaring through his "sea of pines;"
In vain the rivers from their ice-caves flash;
No hymn salutes them but the Ranz des Vaches,
Till lazy Coleridge, by the morning's light,
Gazed for a moment on the fields of white,
And lo! the glaciers found at length a tongue,
Mont Blanc was vocal, and Chamouni sung!

Children of wealth or want, to each is given
One spot of green, and all the blue of heaven!
Enough if these their outward shows impart;
The rest is thine,—the scenery of the heart.
If passion's hectic in thy stanzas glow,
Thy heart's best life-blood ebbing as they flow;
If with thy verse thy strength and bloom distil,
Drained by the pulses of the fevered thrill;
If sound's sweet effluence polarize thy brain,

And thoughts turn crystals in thy fluid strain, —
Nor rolling ocean, nor the prairie's bloom,
Nor streaming cliffs, nor rayless cavern's gloom,
Need'st thou, young poet, to inform thy line;
Thy own broad signet stamps thy song divine!
Let others gaze where silvery streams are rolled,
And chase the rainbow for its cup of gold;
To thee all landscapes wear a heavenly dye,
Changed in the glance of thy prismatic eye;
Nature evoked thee in sublimer throes,
For thee her inmost Arethusa flows, —
The mighty mother's living depths are stirred, —
Thou art the starred Osiris of the herd!

A few brief lines; they touch on solemn chords,
And hearts may leap to hear their honest words;
Yet, ere the jarring bugle-blast is blown,
The softer lyre shall breathe its soothing tone.

New England! proudly may thy children claim
Their honored birthright by its humblest name!
Cold are thy skies, but, ever fresh and clear,
No rank malaria stains thine atmosphere;
No fungous weeds invade thy scanty soil,
Scarred by the ploughshares of unslumbering toil.
Long may the doctrines by thy sages taught,
Raised from the quarries where their sires have wrought,
Be like the granite of thy rock-ribbed land, —
As slow to rear, as obdurate to stand;
And as the ice that leaves thy crystal mine
Chills the fierce alcohol in the Creole's wine,
So may the doctrines of thy sober school
Keep the hot theories of thy neighbors cool!

If ever, trampling on her ancient path,
Cankered by treachery or inflamed by wrath,
With smooth "Resolves" or with discordant cries,
The mad Briareus of disunion rise,
Chiefs of New England! by your sires' renown,
Dash the red torches of the rebel down!
Flood his black hearthstone till its flames expire,
Though your old Sachem fanned his council-fire!

But if at last, her fading cycle run,
The tongue must forfeit what the arm has won,
Then rise, wild Ocean! roll thy surging shock
Full on old Plymouth's desecrated rock!
Scale the proud shaft degenerate hands have hewn,
Where bleeding Valor stained the flowers of June!
Sweep in one tide her spires and turrets down,
And howl her dirge above Monadnock's crown!

List not the tale; the Pilgrim's hallowed shore,
Though strewn with weeds, is granite at the core;
Oh, rather trust that He who made her free
Will keep her true as long as faith shall be!
Farewell! yet lingering through the destined hour,
Leave, sweet Enchantress, one memorial flower!

An Angel, floating o'er the waste of snow
That clad our Western desert, long ago,
(The same fair spirit who, unseen by day,
Shone as a star along the Mayflower's way,) —
Sent, the first herald of the Heavenly plan,
To choose on earth a resting-place for man,
Tired with his flight along the unvaried field,
Turned to soar upwards, when his glance revealed
A calm, bright bay enclosed in rocky bounds,
And at its entrance stood three sister mounds.

The Angel spake: "This threefold hill shall be
The home of Arts, the nurse of Liberty!
One stately summit from its shaft shall pour
Its deep-red blaze along the darkened shore;
Emblem of thoughts that, kindling far and wide,
In danger's night shall be a nation's guide.
One swelling crest the citadel shall crown,
Its slanted bastions black with battle's frown,
And bid the sons that tread its scowling heights
Bare their strong arms for man and all his rights!
One silent steep along the northern wave
Shall hold the patriarch's and the hero's grave;
When fades the torch, when o'er the peaceful scene
The embattled fortress smiles in living green,
The cross of Faith, the anchor staff of Hope,
Shall stand eternal on its grassy slope;
There through all time shall faithful Memory tell,
'Here Virtue toiled, and Patriot Valor fell;
Thy free, proud fathers slumber at thy side;
Live as they lived, or perish as they died!'"

AN AFTER-DINNER POEM

(TERPSICHORE)

Read at the Annual Dinner of the Phi Beta Kappa Society, at Cambridge, August 24, 1843.

IN narrowest girdle, O reluctant Muse,
In closest frock and Cinderella shoes,
Bound to the foot-lights for thy brief display,
One zephyr step, and then dissolve away!

Short is the space that gods and men can spare
To Song's twin brother when she is not there.

Let others water every lusty line,
As Homer's heroes did their purple wine;
Pierian revellers! Know in strains like these
The native juice, the real honest squeeze, —
Strains that, diluted to the twentieth power,
In yon grave temple might have filled an hour.
Small room for Fancy's many-chorded lyre,
For Wit's bright rockets with their trains of fire,
For Pathos, struggling vainly to surprise
The iron tutor's tear-denying eyes,
For Mirth, whose finger with delusive wile
Turns the grim key of many a rusty smile,
For Satire, emptying his corrosive flood
On hissing Folly's gas-exhaling brood,
The pun, the fun, the moral, and the joke,
The hit, the thrust, the pugilistic poke, —
Small space for these, so pressed by niggard Time,
Like that false matron, known to nursery rhyme, —
Insidious Morey, — scarce her tale begun,
Ere listening infants weep the story done.

Oh, had we room to rip the mighty bags
That Time, the harlequin, has stuffed with rags!
Grant us one moment to unloose the strings,
While the old graybeard shuts his leather wings.
But what a heap of motley trash appears
Crammed in the bundles of successive years!
As the lost rustic on some festal day
Stares through the concourse in its vast array, —
Where in one cake a throng of faces runs,
All stuck together like a sheet of buns, —
And throws the bait of some unheeded name,
Or shoots a wink with most uncertain aim,
So roams my vision, wandering over all,
And strives to choose, but knows not where to fall.

Skins of flayed authors, husks of dead reviews,
The turn-coat's clothes, the office-seeker's shoes,

AN AFTER-DINNER POEM

Scraps from cold feasts, where conversation runs
Through mouldy toasts to oxidated puns,
And grating songs a listening crowd endures,
Rasped from the throats of bellowing amateurs;
Sermons, whose writers played such dangerous tricks
Their own heresiarchs called them heretics,
(Strange that one term such distant poles should link,
The Priestleyan's copper and the Puseyan's zinc);
Poems that shuffle with superfluous legs
A blindfold minuet over addled eggs,
Where all the syllables that end in èd,
Like old dragoons, have cuts across the head;
Essays so dark Champollion might despair
To guess what mummy of a thought was there,
Where our poor English, striped with foreign phrase,
Looks like a zebra in a parson's chaise;
Lectures that cut our dinners down to roots,
Or prove (by monkeys) men should stick to fruits, —
Delusive error, as at trifling charge
Professor Gripes will certify at large;
Mesmeric pamphlets, which to facts appeal,
Each facts as slippery as a fresh-caught eel;
And figured heads, whose hieroglyphs invite
To wandering knaves that discount fools at sight:
Such things as these, with heaps of unpaid bills,
And candy puffs and homœopathic pills,
And ancient bell-crowns with contracted rim,
And bonnets hideous with expanded brim,
And coats whose memory turns the sartor pale,
Their sequels tapering like a lizard's tail, —
How might we spread them to the smiling day,
And toss them, fluttering like the new-mown hay,
To laughter's light or sorrow's pitying shower,
Were these brief minutes lengthened to an hour.

The narrow moments fit like Sunday shoes, —
How vast the heap, how quickly must we choose!
A few small scraps from out his mountain mass
We snatch in haste, and let the vagrant pass.
This shrunken CRUST that Cerberus could not bite,
Stamped (in one corner) "Pickwick copyright,"
Kneaded by youngsters, raised by flattery's yeast,
Was once a loaf, and helped to make a feast.
He for whose sake the glittering show appears
Has sown the world with laughter and with tears,
And they whose welcome wets the bumper's brim
Have wit and wisdom, — for they all quote him.
So, many a tongue the evening hour prolongs
With spangled speeches, — let alone the songs;
Statesmen grow merry, lean attorneys laugh,
And weak teetotals warm to half and half,
And beardless Tullys, new to festive scenes,
Cut their first crop of youth's precocious greens,
And wits stand ready for impromptu claps,
With loaded barrels and percussion caps,
And Pathos, cantering through the minor keys,
Waves all her onions to the trembling breeze;
While the great Feasted views with silent glee
His scattered limbs in Yankee fricassee.

Sweet is the scene where genial friendship plays
The pleasing game of interchanging praise.
Self-love, grimalkin of the human heart,
Is ever pliant to the master's art;
Soothed with a word, she peacefully withdraws
And sheathes in velvet her obnoxious claws,
And thrills the hand that smooths her glossy fur
With the light tremor of her grateful purr.

But what sad music fills the quiet hall,
If on her back a feline rival fall!
And oh, what noises shake the tranquil house
If old Self-interest cheats her of a mouse!

Thou, O my country, hast thy foolish ways,
Too apt to purr at every stranger's praise;
But if the stranger touch thy modes or laws,
Off goes the velvet and out come the claws!
And thou, Illustrious! but too poorly paid
In toasts from Pickwick for thy great crusade,
Though, while the echoes labored with thy name,
The public trap denied thy little game,
Let other lips our jealous laws revile, —
The marble Talfourd or the rude Carlyle, —
But on thy lids, which Heaven forbids to close
Where'er the light of kindly nature glows,
Let not the dollars that a churl denies
Weigh like the shillings on a dead man's eyes!
Or, if thou wilt, be more discreetly blind,
Nor ask to see all wide extremes combined.
Not in our wastes the dainty blossoms smile
That crowd the gardens of thy scanty isle.
There white-cheeked Luxury weaves a thousand charms;
Here sun-browned Labor swings his naked arms.
Long are the furrows he must trace between
The ocean's azure and the prairie's green;
Full many a blank his destined realm displays,
Yet sees the promise of his riper days:
Far through yon depths the panting engine moves,
His chariots ringing in their steel-shod grooves;
And Erie's naiad flings her diamond wave
O'er the wild sea-nymph in her distant cave!
While tasks like these employ his anxious hours,
What if his cornfields are not edged with flowers?
Though bright as silver the meridian beams
Shine through the crystal of thine English streams,
Turbid and dark the mighty wave is whirled
That drains our Andes and divides a world!

But lo! a PARCHMENT! Surely it would seem
The sculptured impress speaks of power supreme;
Some grave design the solemn page must claim
That shows so broadly an emblazoned name.
A sovereign's promise! Look, the lines afford
All Honor gives when Caution asks his word:
There sacred Faith has laid her snow-white hands,
And awful Justice knit her iron bands;
Yet every leaf is stained with treachery's dye,
And every letter crusted with a lie.
Alas! no treason has degraded yet
The Arab's salt, the Indian's calumet;
A simple rite, that bears the wanderer's pledge,
Blunts the keen shaft and turns the dagger's edge;
While jockeying senates stop to sign and seal,
And freeborn statesmen legislate to steal.
Rise, Europe, tottering with thine Atlas load,
Turn thy proud eye to Freedom's blest abode,
And round her forehead, wreathed with heavenly flame,
Bind the dark garland of her daughter's shame!
Ye ocean clouds, that wrap the angry blast,
Coil her stained ensign round its haughty mast,
Or tear the fold that wears so foul a scar,
And drive a bolt through every blackened star!
Once more, — once only, — we must stop so soon:
What have we here? A GERMAN-SILVER SPOON;
A cheap utensil, which we often see
Used by the dabblers in æsthetic tea,
Of slender fabric, somewhat light and thin,
Made of mixed metal, chiefly lead and tin;
The bowl is shallow, and the handle small,
Marked in large letters with the name
JEAN PAUL.

Small as it is, its powers are passing strange,
For all who use it show a wondrous change;
And first, a fact to make the barbers stare,
It beats Macassar for the growth of hair.
See those small youngsters whose expansive ears
Maternal kindness grazed with frequent shears;
Each bristling crop a dangling mass becomes,
And all the spoonies turn to Absaloms!
Nor this alone its magic power displays,
It alters strangely all their works and ways;
With uncouth words they tire their tender lungs,
The same bald phrases on their hundred tongues:
"Ever" "The Ages" in their page appear,
"Alway" the bedlamite is called a "Seer;"
On every leaf the "earnest" sage may scan,
Portentous bore! their "many-sided" man, —
A weak eclectic, groping vague and dim,
Whose every angle is a half-starved whim,
Blind as a mole and curious as a lynx,
Who rides a beetle, which he calls a "Sphinx."
And oh, what questions asked in clubfoot rhyme
Of Earth the tongueless and the deaf-mute Time!
Here babbling "Insight" shouts in Nature's ears
His last conundrum on the orbs and spheres;
There Self-inspection sucks its little thumb,
With "Whence am I?" and "Wherefore did I come?"
Deluded infants! will they ever know
Some doubts must darken o'er the world below,
Though all the Platos of the nursery trail
Their "clouds of glory" at the go-cart's tail?
Oh might these couplets their attention claim
That gain their author the Philistine's name!
(A stubborn race, that, spurning foreign law,
Was much belabored with an ass's jaw.)

Melodious Laura! From the sad retreats
That hold thee, smothered with excess of sweets,
Shade of a shadow, spectre of a dream,
Glance thy wan eye across the Stygian stream!
The slipshod dreamer treads thy fragrant halls,
The sophist's cobwebs hang thy roseate walls,
And o'er the crotchets of thy jingling tunes
The bard of mystery scrawls his crooked "runes."
Yes, thou art gone, with all the tuneful hordes
That candied thoughts in amber-colored words,
And in the precincts of thy late abodes
The clattering verse-wright hammers Orphic odes.
Thou, soft as zephyr, wast content to fly
On the gilt pinions of a balmy sigh;
He, vast as Phœbus on his burning wheels,
Would stride through ether at Orion's heels.
Thy emblem, Laura, was a perfume-jar,
And thine, young Orpheus, is a pewter star.
The balance trembles, — be its verdict told
When the new jargon slumbers with the old!

Cease, playful goddess! From thine airy bound
Drop like a feather softly to the ground;
This light bolero grows a ticklish dance,
And there is mischief in thy kindling glance.
To-morrow bids thee, with rebuking frown,
Change thy gauze tunic for a home-made gown,
Too blest by fortune if the passing day
Adorn thy bosom with its frail bouquet,
But oh, still happier if the next forgets
Thy daring steps and dangerous pirouettes!

MEDICAL POEMS

[THIS division was made when the Riverside Edition was arranged, but by accident the last number in the division was at that time omitted.]

THE MORNING VISIT

A SICK man's chamber, though it often boast
The grateful presence of a literal toast,
Can hardly claim, amidst its various wealth,
The right unchallenged to propose a health;
Yet though its tenant is denied the feast,
Friendship must launch his sentiment at least,
As prisoned damsels, locked from lovers' lips,
Toss them a kiss from off their fingers' tips.

The morning visit, — not till sickness falls
In the charmed circles of your own safe walls;
Till fever's throb and pain's relentless rack
Stretch you all helpless on your aching back;
Not till you play the patient in your turn,
The morning visit's mystery shall you learn.

'T is a small matter in your neighbor's case,
To charge your fee for showing him your face;
You skip up-stairs, inquire, inspect, and touch,
Prescribe, take leave, and off to twenty such.

But when at length, by fate's transferred decree,
The visitor becomes the visitee,
Oh, then, indeed, it pulls another string;
Your ox is gored, and that's a different thing!

Your friend is sick: phlegmatic as a Turk,
You write your recipe and let it work;
Not yours to stand the shiver and the frown,
And sometimes worse, with which your draught goes down.
Calm as a clock your knowing hand directs,
Rhei, jalapæ ana grana sex,
Or traces on some tender missive's back,
Scrupulos duos pulveris ipecac;
And leaves your patient to his qualms and gripes,
Cool as a sportsman banging at his snipes.
But change the time, the person, and the place,
And be yourself "the interesting case,"
You'll gain some knowledge which it's well to learn;
In future practice it may serve your turn.
Leeches, for instance, — pleasing creatures quite;
Try them, — and bless you, — don't you find they bite?
You raise a blister for the smallest cause,
But be yourself the sitter whom it draws,
And trust my statement, you will not deny
The worst of draughtsmen is your Spanish fly!
It's mighty easy ordering when you please,
Infusi sennæ capiat uncias tres;
It's mighty different when you quackle down
Your own three ounces of the liquid brown.
Pilula, pulvis, — pleasant words enough,
When other throats receive the shocking stuff;
But oh, what flattery can disguise the groan
That meets the gulp which sends it through your own!

Be gentle, then, though Art's unsparing
    rules
Give you the handling of her sharpest
    tools;
Use them not rashly, — sickness is enough;
Be always "ready," but be never "rough."

Of all the ills that suffering man endures,
The largest fraction liberal Nature cures;
Of those remaining, 't is the smallest part
Yields to the efforts of judicious Art;
But simple *Kindness*, kneeling by the bed
To shift the pillow for the sick man's head,
Give the fresh draught to cool the lips that
    burn,
Fan the hot brow, the weary frame to
    turn, —
Kindness, untutored by our grave M. D.'s,
But Nature's graduate, when she schools to
    please,
Wins back more sufferers with her voice
    and smile
Than all the trumpery in the druggist's
    pile.

Once more, be *quiet :* coming up the stair,
Don't be a plantigrade, a human bear,
But, stealing softly on the silent toe,
Reach the sick chamber ere you 're heard
    below.
Whatever changes there may greet your
    eyes,
Let not your looks proclaim the least sur-
    prise;
It 's not your business by your face to show
All that your patient does not want to
    know;
Nay, use your optics with considerate care,
And don't abuse your privilege to stare.
But if your eyes may probe him overmuch,
Beware still further how you rudely touch;
Don't clutch his carpus in your icy fist,
But warm your fingers ere you take the
    wrist.
If the poor victim needs must be percussed,
Don't make an anvil of his aching bust;
(Doctors exist within a hundred miles
Who thump a thorax as they 'd hammer
    piles;)
If you must listen to his doubtful chest,
Catch the essentials, and ignore the rest.
Spare him; the sufferer wants of you and
    art
A track to steer by, not a finished chart.
So of your questions : don't in mercy try

To pump your patient absolutely dry ;
He 's not a mollusk squirming in a dish,
You 're not Agassiz, and he 's not a fish.

And last, not least, in each perplexing case,
Learn the sweet magic of a *cheerful face;*
Not always smiling, but at least serene,
When grief and anguish cloud the anxious
    scene.
Each look, each movement, every word and
    tone,
Should tell your patient you are all his
    own;
Not the mere artist, purchased to attend,
But the warm, ready, self-forgetting friend,
Whose genial visit in itself combines
The best of cordials, tonics, anodynes.

Such is the *visit* that from day to day
Sheds o'er my chamber its benignant ray.
I give his health, who never cared to claim
Her babbling homage from the tongue of
    Fame;
Unmoved by praise, he stands by all con
    fest,
The truest, noblest, wisest, kindest, best.

THE TWO ARMIES

[Written for and read at a meeting of the
Massachusetts Medical Society in 1858.
In printing these verses in the *Autocrat*,
where they are referred to the "Professor," the
poet says : "He introduced them with a few
remarks, he told me, of which the only one he
remembered was this : that he had rather
write a single line which one among them
should think worth remembering than set them
all laughing with a string of epigrams."]

As Life's unending column pours,
    Two marshalled hosts are seen, —
Two armies on the trampled shores
    That Death flows black between.

One marches to the drum-beat's roll,
    The wide-mouthed clarion's bray,
And bears upon a crimson scroll,
    "Our glory is to slay."

One moves in silence by the stream,
    With sad, yet watchful eyes.
Calm as the patient planet's gleam
    That walks the clouded skies.

Along its front no sabres shine,
　No blood-red pennons wave;
Its banner bears the single line,
　"Our duty is to save."

For those no death-bed's lingering shade;
　At Honor's trumpet-call,
With knitted brow and lifted blade
　In Glory's arms they fall.

For these no clashing falchions bright,
　No stirring battle-cry;
The bloodless stabber calls by night, —
　Each answers, "Here am I!"

For those the sculptor's laurelled bust,
　The builder's marble piles,
The anthems pealing o'er their dust
　Through long cathedral aisles.

For these the blossom-sprinkled turf
　That floods the lonely graves
When Spring rolls in her sea-green surf
　In flowery-foaming waves.

Two paths lead upward from below,
　And angels wait above,
Who count each burning life-drop's flow,
　Each falling tear of Love.

Though from the Hero's bleeding breast
　Her pulses Freedom drew,
Though the white lilies in her crest
　Sprang from that scarlet dew, —

While Valor's haughty champions wait
　Till all their scars are shown,
Love walks unchallenged through the gate,
　To sit beside the Throne!

THE STETHOSCOPE SONG

A PROFESSIONAL BALLAD

THERE was a young man in Boston town,
　He bought him a stethoscope nice and new,
All mounted and finished and polished down,
　With an ivory cap and a stopper too.

It happened a spider within did crawl,
　And spun him a web of ample size,
Wherein there chanced one day to fall
　A couple of very imprudent flies.

The first was a bottle-fly, big and blue,
　The second was smaller, and thin and long;
So there was a concert between the two,
　Like an octave flute and a tavern gong.

Now being from Paris but recently,
　This fine young man would show his skill;
And so they gave him, his hand to try,
　A hospital patient extremely ill.

Some said that his *liver* was short of *bile*,
　And some that his *heart* was over size,
While some kept arguing, all the while,
　He was crammed with *tubercles* up to his eyes.

This fine young man then up stepped he,
　And all the doctors made a pause;
Said he, The man must die, you see,
　By the fifty-seventh of Louis's laws.

But since the case is a desperate one,
　To explore his chest it may be well;
For if he should die and it were not done,
　You know the *autopsy* would not tell.

Then out his stethoscope he took,
　And on it placed his curious ear;
Mon Dieu! said he, with a knowing look,
　Why, here is a sound that's mighty queer!

The *bourdonnement* is very clear, —
　Amphoric buzzing, as I'm alive!
Five doctors took their turn to hear;
　Amphoric buzzing, said all the five.

There's *empyema* beyond a doubt;
　We'll plunge a *trocar* in his side.
The diagnosis was made out, —
　They tapped the patient; so he died.

Now such as hate new-fashioned toys
　Began to look extremely glum;
They said that *rattles* were made for boys,
　And vowed that his *buzzing* was all a hum.

There was an old lady had long been sick,
　And what was the matter none did know:
Her pulse was slow, though her tongue was quick;
　To her this knowing youth must go.

So there the nice old lady sat,
 With phials and boxes all in a row;
She asked the young doctor what he was at,
 To thump her and tumble her ruffles so.

Now, when the stethoscope came out,
 The flies began to buzz and whiz:
Oh, ho! the matter is clear, no doubt;
 An *aneurism* there plainly is.

The *bruit de râpe* and the *bruit de scie*
 And the *bruit de diable* are all combined;
How happy Bouillaud would be,
 If he a case like this could find!

Now, when the neighboring doctors found
 A case so rare had been descried,
They every day her ribs did pound
 In squads of twenty; so she died.

Then six young damsels, slight and frail,
 Received this kind young doctor's cares;
They all were getting slim and pale,
 And short of breath on mounting stairs.

They all made rhymes with "sighs" and "skies,"
 And loathed their puddings and buttered rolls,
And dieted, much to their friends' surprise,
 On pickles and pencils and chalk and coals.

So fast their little hearts did bound,
 The frightened insects buzzed the more;
So over all their chests he found
 The *râle sifflant* and the *râle sonore*.

He shook his head. There's grave disease, —
 I greatly fear you all must die;
A slight *post-mortem*, if you please,
 Surviving friends would gratify.

The six young damsels wept aloud,
 Which so prevailed on six young men
That each his honest love avowed,
 Whereat they all got well again.

This poor young man was all aghast;
 The price of stethoscopes came down;
And so he was reduced at last
 To practise in a country town.

The doctors being very sore,
 A stethoscope they did devise
That had a rammer to clear the bore,
 With a knob at the end to kill the flies.

Now use your ears, all you that can,
 But don't forget to mind your eyes,
Or you may be cheated, like this young man,
 By a couple of silly, abnormal flies.

EXTRACTS FROM A MEDICAL POEM

THE STABILITY OF SCIENCE

THE feeble sea-birds, blinded in the storms,
On some tall lighthouse dash their little forms,
And the rude granite scatters for their pains
Those small deposits that were meant for brains.
Yet the proud fabric in the morning's sun
Stands all unconscious of the mischief done;
Still the red beacon pours its evening rays
For the lost pilot with as full a blaze, —
Nay, shines, all radiance, o'er the scattered fleet
Of gulls and boobies brainless at its feet.
 I tell their fate, though courtesy disclaims
To call our kind by such ungentle names;
Yet, if your rashness bid you vainly dare,
Think of their doom, ye simple, and beware!
 See where aloft its hoary forehead rears
The towering pride of twice a thousand years!
Far, far below the vast incumbent pile
Sleeps the gray rock from art's Ægean isle;
Its massive courses, circling as they rise,
Swell from the waves to mingle with the skies;
There every quarry lends its marble spoil,
And clustering ages blend their common toil;
The Greek, the Roman, reared its ancient walls,
The silent Arab arched its mystic halls;
In that fair niche, by countless billows laved,
Trace the deep lines that Sydenham engraved;

On yon broad front that breasts the changing swell,
Mark where the ponderous sledge of Hunter fell;
By that square buttress look where Louis stands,
The stone yet warm from his uplifted hands;
And say, O Science, shall thy life-blood freeze,
When fluttering folly flaps on walls like these?

A PORTRAIT

Thoughtful in youth, but not austere in age;
Calm, but not cold, and cheerful though a sage;
Too true to flatter and too kind to sneer,
And only just when seemingly severe;
So gently blending courtesy and art
That wisdom's lips seemed borrowing friendship's heart.
Taught by the sorrows that his age had known
In others' trials to forget his own,
As hour by hour his lengthened day declined,
A sweeter radiance lingered o'er his mind.
Cold were the lips that spoke his early praise,
And hushed the voices of his morning days,
Yet the same accents dwelt on every tongue,
And love renewing kept him ever young.

A SENTIMENT

'Ο βίος βραχύς, — life is but a song;
Ἡ τέχνη μακρή, — art is wondrous long;
Yet to the wise her paths are ever fair,
And Patience smiles, though Genius may despair.
Give us but knowledge, though by slow degrees,
And blend our toil with moments bright as these;
Let Friendship's accents cheer our doubtful way,
And Love's pure planet lend its guiding ray, —
Our tardy Art shall wear an angel's wings,
And life shall lengthen with the joy it brings!

A POEM

FOR THE MEETING OF THE AMERICAN MEDICAL ASSOCIATION AT NEW YORK, MAY 5, 1853

I HOLD a letter in my hand, —
A flattering letter, more 's the pity, —
By some contriving junto planned,
And signed *per order of Committee.*
It touches every tenderest spot, —
My patriotic predilections,
My well-known — something — don't ask what, —
My poor old songs, my kind affections.

They make a feast on Thursday next,
And hope to make the feasters merry;
They own they're something more perplexed
For poets than for port and sherry.
They want the men of — (word torn out);
Our friends will come with anxious faces,
(To see our blankets off, no doubt,
And trot us out and show our paces.)

They hint that papers by the score
Are rather musty kind of rations, —
They don't exactly mean a bore,
But only trying to the patience;
That such as — you know who I mean —
Distinguished for their — what d' ye call 'em —
Should bring the dews of Hippocrene
To sprinkle on the faces solemn.

— The same old story: that 's the chaff
To catch the birds that sing the ditties;
Upon my soul, it makes me laugh
To read these letters from Committees!
They 're all *so* loving and *so* fair, —
All for *your* sake such kind compunction;
'T would save your carriage half its wear
To touch its wheels with such an unction!

Why, who am I, to lift me here
And beg such learned folk to listen,
To ask a smile, or coax a tear
Beneath these stoic lids to glisten?
As well might some arterial thread
Ask the whole frame to feel it gushing,
While throbbing fierce from heel to head
The vast aortic tide was rushing.

As well some hair-like nerve might strain
  To set its special streamlet going,
While through the myriad-channelled brain
  The burning flood of thought was flowing;
Or trembling fibre strive to keep
  The springing haunches gathered shorter,
While the scourged racer, leap on leap,
  Was stretching through the last hot quarter!

Ah me! you take the bud that came
  Self-sown in your poor garden's borders,
And hand it to the stately dame
  That florists breed for, all she orders.
She thanks you, — it was kindly meant —
  (A pale affair, not worth the keeping,) —
Good morning; and your bud is sent
  To join the tea-leaves used for sweeping.

Not always so, kind hearts and true, —
  For such I know are round me beating;
Is not the bud I offer you,
  Fresh gathered for the hour of meeting,
Pale though its outer leaves may be,
  Rose-red in all its inner petals ? —
Where the warm life we cannot see —
  The life of love that gave it — settles.

We meet from regions far away,
  Like rills from distant mountains streaming;
The sun is on Francisco's bay,
  O'er Chesapeake the lighthouse gleaming;
While summer girds the still bayou
  In chains of bloom, her bridal token,
Monadnock sees the sky grow blue,
  His crystal bracelet yet unbroken.

Yet Nature bears the selfsame heart
  Beneath her russet-mantled bosom
As where, with burning lips apart,
  She breathes and white magnolias blossom;
The selfsame founts her chalice fill
  With showery sunlight running over,
On fiery plain and frozen hill,
  On myrtle-beds and fields of clover.

I give you *Home!* its crossing lines
  United in one golden suture,
And showing every day that shines
  The present growing to the future, —
A flag that bears a hundred stars
  In one bright ring, with love for centre,
Fenced round with white and crimson bars
  No prowling treason dares to enter!

O brothers, home may be a word
  To make affection's living treasure,
The wave an angel might have stirred,
  A stagnant pool of selfish pleasure ;
HOME! It is where the day-star springs
  And where the evening sun reposes,
Where'er the eagle spreads his wings,
  From northern pines to southern roses!

A SENTIMENT

[Distributed among the members gathered at the meeting of the American Medical Association, in Philadelphia, May 1, 1855.]

A TRIPLE health to Friendship, Science, Art,
  From heads and hands that own a common heart !
Each in its turn the others' willing slave,
Each in its season strong to heal and save.

Friendship's blind service, in the hour of need,
Wipes the pale face, and lets the victim bleed.
Science must stop to reason and explain;
ART claps his finger on the streaming vein.

But Art's brief memory fails the hand at last ;
Then SCIENCE lifts the flambeau of the past.
When both their equal impotence deplore,
When Learning sighs, and Skill can do no more,
The tear of FRIENDSHIP pours its heavenly balm,
And soothes the pang no anodyne may calm !

RIP VAN WINKLE, M.D.

AN AFTER-DINNER PRESCRIPTION TAKEN BY THE MASSACHUSETTS MEDICAL SOCIETY, AT THEIR MEETING HELD MAY 25, 1870

CANTO FIRST

OLD Rip Van Winkle had a grandson Rip,
Of the paternal block a genuine chip, —

A lazy, sleepy, curious kind of chap;
He, like his grandsire, took a mighty nap,
Whereof the story I propose to tell
In two brief cantos, if you listen well.

The times were hard when Rip to manhood grew;
They always will be when there's work to do.
He tried at farming, — found it rather slow, —
And then at teaching — what he didn't know;
Then took to hanging round the tavern bars,
To frequent toddies and long-nine cigars,
Till Dame Van Winkle, out of patience, vexed
With preaching homilies, having for their text
A mop, a broomstick, aught that might avail
To point a moral or adorn a tale,
Exclaimed, "I have it! Now, then, Mr. V.!
He's good for *something*, — make him an M. D.!"

The die was cast; the youngster was content;
They packed his shirts and stockings, and he went.
How hard he studied it were vain to tell;
He drowsed through Wistar, nodded over Bell,
Slept sound with Cooper, snored aloud on Good;
Heard heaps of lectures, — doubtless understood, —
A constant listener, for he did not fail
To carve his name on every bench and rail.

Months grew to years; at last he counted three,
And Rip Van Winkle found himself M. D.
Illustrious title! in a gilded frame
He set the sheepskin with his Latin name,
RIPUM VAN WINKLUM, QUEM we — SCIMUS — know
IDONEUM ESSE — to do so and so.
He hired an office; soon its walls displayed
His new diploma and his stock in trade,
A mighty arsenal to subdue disease,
Of various names, whereof I mention these:
Lancets and bougies, great and little squirt,
Rhubarb and Senna, Snakeroot, Thoroughwort,
Ant. Tart., Vin. Colch., Pil. Cochiæ, and Black Drop,
Tinctures of Opium, Gentian, Henbane, Hop,
Pulv. Ipecacuanhæ, which for lack
Of breath to utter men call Ipecac,
Camphor and Kino, Turpentine, Tolu,
Cubebs, "Copeevy," Vitriol, — white and blue, —
Fennel and Flaxseed, Slippery Elm and Squill,
And roots of Sassafras, and "Sassaf'rill,"
Brandy, — for colics, — Pinkroot, death on worms, —
Valerian, calmer of hysteric squirms,
Musk, Assafœtida, the resinous gum
Named from its odor, — well, it does smell some, —
Jalap, that works not wisely, but too well,
Ten pounds of Bark and six of Calomel.

For outward griefs he had an ample store,
Some twenty jars and gallipots, or more:
Ceratum simplex — housewives oft compile
The same at home, and call it "wax and ile;"
Unguentum resinosum — change its name,
The "drawing salve" of many an ancient dame;
Argenti Nitras, also Spanish flies,
Whose virtue makes the water-bladders rise —
(Some say that spread upon a toper's skin
They draw no water, only rum or gin);
Leeches, sweet vermin! don't they charm the sick?
And Sticking-plaster — how it hates to stick!
Emplastrum Ferri — ditto *Picis*, Pitch;
Washes and Powders, Brimstone for the — which,
Scabies or *Psora*, is thy chosen name
Since Hahnemann's goose-quill scratched thee into fame,
Proved thee the source of every nameless ill,
Whose sole specific is a moonshine pill,
Till saucy Science, with a quiet grin,
Held up the Acarus, crawling on a pin?
— Mountains have labored and have brought forth mice:
The Dutchman's theory hatched a brood of — twice

I've wellnigh said them — words unfitting quite
For these fair precincts and for ears polite.

The surest foot may chance at last to slip,
And so at length it proved with Doctor Rip.
One full-sized bottle stood upon the shelf,
Which held the medicine that he took himself;
Whate'er the reason, it must be confessed
He filled that bottle oftener than the rest;
What drug it held I don't presume to know —
The gilded label said "Elixir Pro."

One day the Doctor found the bottle full,
And, being thirsty, took a vigorous pull,
Put back the "Elixir" where 't was always found,
And had old Dobbin saddled and brought round.
— You know those old-time rhubarb-colored nags
That carried Doctors and their saddle-bags;
Sagacious beasts! they stopped at every place
Where blinds were shut — knew every patient's case —
Looked up and thought — The baby's in a fit —
That won't last long — he'll soon be through with it;
But shook their heads before the knockered door
Where some old lady told the story o'er
Whose endless stream of tribulation flows
For gastric griefs and peristaltic woes.

What jack-o'-lantern led him from his way,
And where it led him, it were hard to say;
Enough that wandering many a weary mile
Through paths the mountain sheep trod single file,
O'ercome by feelings such as patients know
Who dose too freely with " Elixir Pro.,"
He tumbl — dismounted, slightly in a heap,
And lay, promiscuous, lapped in balmy sleep.

Night followed night, and day succeeded day,
But snoring still the slumbering Doctor lay.
Poor Dobbin, starving, thought upon his stall,
And straggled homeward, saddle-bags and all.
The village people hunted all around,
But Rip was missing, — never could be found.
"Drownded," they guessed; — for more than half a year
The pouts and eels *did* taste uncommon queer;
Some said of apple-brandy — other some
Found a strong flavor of New England rum.

Why can't a fellow hear the fine things said
About a fellow when a fellow's dead?
The best of doctors — so the press declared —
A public blessing while his life was spared,
True to his country, bounteous to the poor,
In all things temperate, sober, just, and pure;
The best of husbands! echoed Mrs. Van,
And set her cap to catch another man.

So ends this Canto — if it 's *quantum suff.*,
We 'll just stop here and say we 've had enough,
And leave poor Rip to sleep for thirty years;
I grind the organ — if you lend your ears
To hear my second Canto, after that
We 'll send around the monkey with the hat.

CANTO SECOND

So thirty years had passed — but not a word
In all that time of Rip was ever heard;
The world wagged on — it never does go back —
The widow Van was now the widow Mac —
France was an Empire — Andrew J. was dead,
And Abraham L. was reigning in his stead.
Four murderous years had passed in savage strife,
Yet still the rebel held his bloody knife.
— At last one morning — who forgets the day

When the black cloud of war dissolved
    away? —
The joyous tidings spread o'er land and
    sea,
Rebellion done for! Grant has captured
    Lee!
Up every flagstaff sprang the Stars and
    Stripes —
Out rushed the Extras wild with mammoth
    types —
Down went the laborer's hod, the school-
    boy's book —
"Hooraw!" he cried, "the rebel army's
    took!"
Ah! what a time! the folks all mad with
    joy;
Each fond, pale mother thinking of her
    boy;
Old gray-haired fathers meeting — "Have
    — you — heard?"
And then a choke — and not another word;
Sisters all smiling — maidens, not less dear,
In trembling poise between a smile and
    tear;
Poor Bridget thinking how she'll stuff the
    plums
In that big cake for Johnny when he comes;
Cripples afoot; rheumatics on the jump;
Old girls so loving they could hug the
    pump;
Guns going bang! from every fort and
    ship;
They banged so loud at last they wakened
    Rip.

I spare the picture, how a man appears
Who's been asleep a score or two of years;
You all have seen it to perfection done
By Joe Van Wink — I mean Rip Jefferson.
Well, so it was; old Rip at last came back,
Claimed his old wife — the present widow
    Mac —
Had his old sign regilded, and began
To practise physic on the same old plan.

Some weeks went by — it was not long
    to wait —
And "please to call" grew frequent on the
    slate.
He had, in fact, an ancient, mildewed air,
A long gray beard, a plenteous lack of
    hair, —
The musty look that always recommends
Your good old Doctor to his ailing friends.
— Talk of your science! after all is said

There's nothing like a bare and shiny head;
Age lends the graces that are sure to please;
Folks want their Doctors mouldy, like their
    cheese.

So Rip began to look at people's tongues
And thump their briskets (called it "sound
    their lungs"),
Brushed up his knowledge smartly as he
    could,
Read in old Cullen and in Doctor Good.
The town was healthy; for a month or two
He gave the sexton little work to do.

About the time when dog-day heats be-
    gin,
The summer's usual maladies set in;
With autumn evenings dysentery came,
And dusky typhoid lit his smouldering
    flame;
The blacksmith ailed, the carpenter was
    down,
And half the children sickened in the town.
The sexton's face grew shorter than be-
    fore —
The sexton's wife a brand-new bonnet
    wore —
Things looked quite serious — Death had
    got a grip
On old and young, in spite of Doctor Rip.

And now the Squire was taken with a
    chill —
Wife gave "hot-drops" — at night an In-
    dian pill;
Next morning, feverish — bedtime, getting
    worse —
Out of his head — began to rave and curse;
The Doctor sent for — double quick he
    came:
Ant. Tart. gran. duo, and repeat the same
If no et cetera. Third day — nothing new;
Percussed his thorax till 't was black and
    blue —
Lung-fever threatening — something of the
    sort —
Out with the lancet — let him bleed — a
    quart —
Ten leeches next — then blisters to his side;
Ten grains of calomel; just then he died.

The Deacon next required the Doctor's
    care —
Took cold by sitting in a draught of air —
Pains in the back, but what the matter is

Not quite so clear, — wife calls it "rheumatiz."
Rubs back with flannel — gives him something hot —
"Ah!" says the Deacon, "that goes *nigh* the spot."
Next day a *rigor* — "Run, my little man,
And say the Deacon sends for Doctor Van."
The Doctor came — percussion as before,
Thumping and banging till his ribs were sore —
"Right side the flattest" — then more vigorous raps —
"Fever — that's certain — pleurisy, perhaps.
A quart of blood will ease the pain, no doubt,
Ten leeches next will help to suck it out,
Then clap a blister on the painful part —
But first two grains of *Antimonium Tart.*
Last with a dose of cleansing calomel
Unload the portal system — (that sounds well!)"

But when the selfsame remedies were tried,
As all the village knew, the Squire had died;
The neighbors hinted: "This will never do;
He's killed the Squire — he'll kill the Deacon too."

Now when a doctor's patients are perplexed,
A *consultation* comes in order next —
You know what that is? In a certain place
Meet certain doctors to discuss a case
And other matters, such as weather, crops,
Potatoes, pumpkins, lager-beer, and hops.
For what's the use! — there's little to be said,
Nine times in ten your man's as good as dead;
At best a talk (the secret to disclose)
Where three men guess and *sometimes* one man knows.

The counsel summoned came without delay —
Young Doctor Green and shrewd old Doctor Gray —
They heard the story — "Bleed!" says Doctor Green,
"That's downright murder! cut his throat, you mean!

Leeches! the reptiles! Why, for pity's sake,
Not try an adder or a rattlesnake?
Blisters! Why bless you, they're against the law —
It's rank assault and battery if they draw!
Tartrate of Antimony! shade of Luke,
Stomachs turn pale at thought of such rebuke!
The portal system! What's the man about?
Unload your nonsense! Calomel's played out!
You've been asleep — you'd better sleep away
Till some one calls you."

"Stop!" says Doctor Gray —
"The story is you slept for thirty years;
With brother Green, I own that it appears
You must have slumbered most amazing sound;
But sleep once more till thirty years come round,
You'll find the lancet in its honored place,
Leeches and blisters rescued from disgrace,
Your drugs redeemed from fashion's passing scorn,
And counted safe to give to babes unborn."

Poor sleepy Rip, M. M. S. S., M. D.,
A puzzled, serious, saddened man was he;
Home from the Deacon's house he plodded slow
And filled one bumper of "Elixir Pro."
"Good-by," he faltered, "Mrs. Van, my dear!
I'm going to sleep, but wake me once a year;
I don't like bleaching in the frost and dew,
I'll take the barn, if all the same to you.
Just once a year — remember! no mistake!
Cry, 'Rip Van Winkle! time for you to wake!'
Watch for the week in May when laylocks blow,
For then the Doctors meet, and I must go."

Just once a year the Doctor's worthy dame
Goes to the barn and shouts her husband's name;
"Come, Rip Van Winkle!" (giving him a shake)

"Rip! Rip Van Winkle! time for you to wake!
Laylocks in blossom! 't is the month of May —
The Doctors' meeting is this blessed day,
And come what will, you know I heard you swear
You 'd never miss it, but be always there!"

And so it is, as every year comes round
Old Rip Van Winkle here is always found.
You 'll quickly know him by his mildewed air,
The hayseed sprinkled through his scanty hair,
The lichens growing on his rusty suit —
I 've seen a toadstool sprouting on his boot —
— Who says I lie? Does any man presume? —
Toadstool! No matter — call it a mushroom.
Where is his seat? He moves it every year;
But look, you 'll find him, — he is always here, —
Perhaps you 'll track him by a whiff you know —
A certain flavor of "Elixir Pro."

Now, then, I give you — as you seem to think
We can give toasts without a drop to drink —
Health to the mighty sleeper, — long live he!
Our brother Rip, M. M. S. S., M. D.!

POEM

READ AT THE DINNER GIVEN TO THE AUTHOR BY THE MEDICAL PROFESSION OF THE CITY OF NEW YORK, APRIL 12, 1883.

HAVE I deserved your kindness? Nay, my friends,
While the fair banquet its illusion lends
Let me believe it, though the blood may rush
And to my cheek recall the maiden blush
That o'er it flamed with momentary blaze
When first I heard the honeyed words of praise;
Let me believe it while the roses wear
Their bloom unwithering in the heated air;
Too soon, too soon, their glowing leaves must fall,
The laughing echoes leave the silent hall,
Joy drop his garland, turn his empty cup,
And weary Labor take his burden up, —
How weighs that burden they can tell alone
Whose dial marks no moment as their own.

Am I your creditor? Too well I know
How Friendship pays the debt it does not owe,
Shapes a poor semblance fondly to its mind,
Adds all the virtues that it fails to find,
Adorns with graces to its heart's content,
Borrows from love what nature never lent,
Till what with halo, jewels, gilding, paint,
The veriest sinner deems himself a saint.
Thus while you pay these honors as my due
I owe my value's larger part to you,
And in the tribute of the hour I see
Not what I am, but what I ought to be.

Friends of the Muse, to you of right belong
The first staid footsteps of my square-toed song;
Full well I know the strong heroic line
Has lost its fashion since I made it mine;
But there are tricks old singers will not learn,
And this grave measure still must serve my turn.
So the old bird resumes the selfsame note
His first young summer wakened in his throat;
The selfsame tune the old canary sings,
And all unchanged the bobolink's carol rings;
When the tired songsters of the day are still
The thrush repeats his long-remembered trill;
Age alters not the crow's persistent caw,
The Yankee's "Haow," the stammering Briton's "Haw;"
And so the hand that takes the lyre for you
Plays the old tune on strings that once were new.

Nor let the rhymester of the hour deride
The straight-backed measure with its stately stride;
It gave the mighty voice of Dryden scope;
It sheathed the steel-bright epigrams of Pope;
In Goldsmith's verse it learned a sweeter strain;
Byron and Campbell wore its clanking chain;
I smile to listen while the critic's scorn
Flouts the proud purple kings have nobly worn;
Bid each new rhymer try his dainty skill
And mould his frozen phrases as he will;
We thank the artist for his neat device;
The shape is pleasing, though the stuff is ice.

Fashions will change — the new costume allures,
Unfading still the better type endures;
While the slashed doublet of the cavalier
Gave the old knight the pomp of chanticleer,
Our last-hatched dandy with his glass and stick
Recalls the semblance of a new-born chick;
(To match the model he is aiming at
He ought to wear an eggshell for a hat;) —
Which of these objects would a painter choose,
And which Velasquez or Van Dyck refuse?

When your kind summons reached my calm retreat,
Who are the friends, I questioned, I shall meet?
Some in young manhood, shivering with desire
To feel the genial warmth of fortune's fire, —
Each with his bellows ready in his hand
To puff the flame just waiting to be fanned;
Some heads half-silvered, some with snow-white hair, —
A crown ungarnished glistening here and there,
The mimic moonlight gleaming on the scalps
As evening's empress lights the shining Alps;

But count the crowds that throng your festal scenes,
How few that knew the century in its teens!

Save for the lingering handful fate befriends,
Life's busy day the Sabbath decade ends;
When that is over, how with what remains
Of nature's outfit, muscle, nerve, and brains?
Were this a pulpit I should doubtless preach,
Were this a platform I should gravely teach,
But to no solemn duties I pretend
In my vocation at the table's end;
So as my answer let me tell instead
What Landlord Porter — rest his soul! — once said.

A feast it was that none might scorn to share;
Cambridge and Concord's demigods were there, —
"And who were they?" You know as well as I
The stars long glittering in our Eastern sky, —
The names that blazon our provincial scroll
Ring round the world with Britain's drumbeat roll!

Good was the dinner, better was the talk;
Some whispered, devious was the homeward walk;
The story came from some reporting spy, —
They lie, those fellows, — oh, how they *do* lie!
Not ours those foot-tracks in the new-fallen snow, —
Poets and sages never zigzagged so!

Now Landlord Porter, grave, concise, severe,
Master, nay, monarch in his proper sphere,
Though to belles-lettres he pretended not,
Lived close to Harvard, so knew what was what;
And having bards, philosophers, and such,
To eat his dinner, put the finest touch
His art could teach, those learned mouths to fill
With the best proofs of gustatory skill;

And finding wisdom plenty at his board,
Wit, science, learning, all his guests had stored,
By way of contrast, ventured to produce,
To please their palates, an inviting goose.
Better it were the company should starve
Than hands unskilled that goose attempt to carve;
None but the master-artist shall assail
The bird that turns the mightiest surgeon pale.

One voice arises from the banquet-hall.
The landlord answers to the pleading call;
Of stature tall, sublime of port he stands,
His blade and bident gleaming in his hands;
Beneath his glance the strong-knit joints relax
As the weak knees before the headsman's axe.

And Landlord Porter lifts his glittering knife
As some stout warrior armed for bloody strife;
All eyes are on him; some in whispers ask,
What man is he who dares this dangerous task?
When lo! the triumph of consummate art,
With scarce a touch the creature drops apart!
As when the baby in his nurse's lap
Spills on the carpet a dissected map.

Then the calm sage, the monarch of the lyre,
Critics and men of science all admire,
And one whose wisdom I will not impeach,
Lively, not churlish, somewhat free of speech,
Speaks thus: "Say, master, what of worth is left
In birds like this, of breast and legs bereft?"
And Landlord Porter, with uplifted eyes,
Smiles on the simple querist, and replies:
"When from a goose you've taken legs and breast,
Wipe lips, thank God, and leave the poor the rest!"

Kind friends, sweet friends, I hold it hardly fair
With that same bird your minstrel to compare,
Yet in a certain likeness we agree,
No wrong to him and no offence to me;
I take him for the moral he has lent,
My partner, — to a limited extent.

When the stern Landlord whom we all obey
Has carved from life its seventh great slice away,
Is the poor fragment left in blank collapse
A pauper remnant of unvalued scraps?

I care not much what Solomon has said,
Before his time to nobler pleasures dead;
Poor man! he needed half a hundred lives
With such a babbling wilderness of wives!
But is there nothing that may well employ
Life's winter months, — no sunny hour of joy?

While o'er the fields the howling tempests rage,
The prisoned linnet warbles in its cage;
When chill November through the forest blows,
The greenhouse shelters the untroubled rose;
Round the high trellis creeping tendrils twine,
And the ripe clusters fill with blameless wine;
We make the vine forget the winter's cold,
But how shall age forget its growing old?

Though doing right is better than deceit,
Time is a trickster it is fair to cheat;
The honest watches ticking in your fobs
Tell every minute how the rascal robs.
To clip his forelock and his scythe to hide,
To lay his hour-glass gently on its side,
To slip the cards he marked upon the shelf
And deal him others you have marked yourself,
If not a virtue cannot be a sin,
For the old rogue is sure at last to win.
What does he leave when life is well-nigh spent
To lap its evening in a calm content?
Art, letters, science, these at least befriend
Our day's brief remnant to its peaceful end, —
Peaceful for him who shows the setting sun
A record worthy of his Lord's Well done!

When he, the master whom I will not
   name,
Known to our calling, not unknown to
   fame,
At life's extremest verge, half conscious
   lay,
Helpless and sightless, dying day by day,
His brain, so long with varied wisdom
   fraught,
Filled with the broken enginery of thought,
A flitting vision often would illume
His darkened world, and cheer its deepen-
   ing gloom, —
A sunbeam struggling through the long
   eclipse, —
And smiles of pleasure play around his lips.
He loved the art that shapes the dome and
   spire;
The Roman's page, the ring of Byron's
   lyre,
And oft when fitful memory would return
To find some fragment in her broken urn,
Would wake to life some long-forgotten
   hour,
And lead his thought to Pisa's terraced
   tower,
Or trace in light before his rayless eye
The dome-crowned Pantheon printed on
   the sky;
Then while the view his ravished soul ab-
   sorbs
And lends a glitter to the sightless orbs,
The patient watcher feels the stillness
   stirred
By the faint murmur of some classic word,
Or the long roll of Harold's lofty rhyme,
"Simple, erect, severe, austere, sub-
   lime," —
Such were the dreams that soothed his
   couch of pain,
The sweet nepenthe of the worn-out brain.

Brothers in art, who live for others' needs
In duty's bondage, mercy's gracious deeds,
Of all who toil beneath the circling sun
Whose evening rest than yours more fairly
   won?
Though many a cloud your struggling
   morn obscures,
What sunset brings a brighter sky than
   yours?

I, who your labors for a while have shared,
New tasks have sought, with new com-
   panions fared,
For nature's servant far too often seen
A loiterer by the waves of Hippocrene;
Yet round the earlier friendship twines the
   new,
My footsteps wander, but my heart is
   true,
Nor e'er forgets the living or the dead
Who trod with me the paths where science
   led.

How can I tell you, O my loving friends!
What light, what warmth, your joyous
   welcome lends
To life's late hour? Alas! my song is
   sung,
Its fading accents falter on my tongue.
Sweet friends, if, shrinking in the banquet's
   blaze,
Your blushing guest must face the breath
   of praise,
Speak not too well of one who scarce will
   know
Himself transfigured in its roseate glow;
Say kindly of him what is, chiefly, true,
Remembering always he belongs to you;
Deal with him as a truant, if you will,
But claim him, keep him, call him brother
   still!

SONGS IN MANY KEYS

1849-1861

PROLOGUE

THE piping of our slender, peaceful reeds
Whispers uncared for while the trumpets bray;
Song is thin air; our hearts' exulting play
Beats time but to the tread of marching deeds,
Following the mighty van that Freedom leads,
Her glorious standard flaming to the day!
The crimsoned pavement where a hero bleeds
Breathes nobler lessons than the poet's lay.
Strong arms, broad breasts, brave hearts, are better worth
Than strains that sing the ravished echoes dumb.
Hark! 't is the loud reverberating drum
Rolls o'er the prairied West, the rockbound North:
The myriad-handed Future stretches forth
Its shadowy palms. Behold, we come, — we come!

Turn o'er these idle leaves. Such toys as these
Were not unsought for, as, in languid dreams,
We lay beside our lotus-feeding streams,
And nursed our fancies in forgetful ease.
It matters little if they pall or please,
Dropping untimely, while the sudden gleams
Glare from the mustering clouds whose blackness seems
Too swollen to hold its lightning from the trees.
Yet, in some lull of passion, when at last
These calm revolving moons that come and go —
Turning our months to years, they creep so slow —
Have brought us rest, the not unwelcome past
May flutter to thee through these leaflets, cast
On the wild winds that all around us blow.

May 1, 1861.

AGNES

The story of Sir Harry Frankland and Agnes Surriage is told in the ballad with a very strict adhesion to the facts. These were obtained from information afforded me by the Rev. Mr. Webster, of Hopkinton, in company with whom I visited the Frankland Mansion in that town, then standing; from a very interesting Memoir, by the Rev. Elias Nason, of Medford; and from the manuscript diary of Sir Harry, or more properly Sir Charles Henry Frankland, now in the library of the Massachusetts Historical Society.

At the time of the visit referred to, old Julia was living, and on our return we called at the house where she resided.[1] Her account is little more than paraphrased in the poem. If the incidents are treated with a certain liberality at the close of the fifth part, the essential fact that Agnes rescued Sir Harry from the ruins after the earthquake, and their subsequent marriage as related, may be accepted as literal truth. So with regard to most of the trifling details which are given; they are taken from the record.

It is greatly to be regretted that the Frankland Mansion no longer exists. It was accidentally burned on the 23d of January, 1858, a year or two after the first sketch of this ballad was written. A visit to it was like stepping out of the century into the years before the Revolution. A new house, similar in plan and arrangements to the old one, has been built upon its site, and the terraces, the clump of box, and the lilacs doubtless remain to bear witness to the truth of this story.

[1] She was living June 10, 1861, when this ballad was published.

The story, which I have told literally in rhyme, has been made the subject of a carefully studied and interesting romance by Mr. E. L. Bynner.

PART I. THE KNIGHT

The tale I tell is gospel true,
 As all the bookmen know,
And pilgrims who have strayed to view
 The wrecks still left to show.

The old, old story, — fair, and young,
 And fond, — and not too wise, —
That matrons tell, with sharpened tongue,
 To maids with downcast eyes.

Ah! maidens err and matrons warn
 Beneath the coldest sky;
Love lurks amid the tasselled corn
 As in the bearded rye!

But who would dream our sober sires
 Had learned the old world's ways,
And warmed their hearths with lawless fires
 In Shirley's homespun days?

'T is like some poet's pictured trance
 His idle rhymes recite, —
This old New England-born romance
 Of Agnes and the Knight;

Yet, known to all the country round,
 Their home is standing still,
Between Wachusett's lonely mound
 And Shawmut's threefold hill.

One hour we rumble on the rail,
 One half-hour guide the rein,
We reach at last, o'er hill and dale,
 The village on the plain.

With blackening wall and mossy roof,
 With stained and warping floor,
A stately mansion stands aloof
 And bars its haughty door.

This lowlier portal may be tried,
 That breaks the gable wall;
And lo! with arches opening wide,
 Sir Harry Frankland's hall!

'T was in the second George's day
 They sought the forest shade,
The knotted trunks they cleared away,
 The massive beams they laid,

They piled the rock-hewn chimney tall,
 They smoothed the terraced ground,
They reared the marble-pillared wall
 That fenced the mansion round.

Far stretched beyond the village bound
 The Master's broad domain;
With page and valet, horse and hound,
 He kept a goodly train.

And, all the midland county through,
 The ploughman stopped to gaze
Whene'er his chariot swept in view
 Behind the shining bays,

With mute obeisance, grave and slow,
 Repaid by nod polite, —
For such the way with high and low
 Till after Concord fight.

Nor less to courtly circles known
 That graced the three-hilled town
With far-off splendors of the Throne,
 And glimmerings from the Crown;

Wise Phipps, who held the seals of state
 For Shirley over sea;
Brave Knowles, whose press-gang moved of late
 The King Street mob's decree;

And judges grave, and colonels grand,
 Fair dames and stately men,
The mighty people of the land,
 The "World" of there and then.

'T was strange no Chloe's "beauteous Form,"
 And "Eyes' cœlestial Blew,"
This Strephon of the West could warm,
 No Nymph his Heart subdue!

Perchance he wooed as gallants use,
 Whom fleeting loves enchain,
But still unfettered, free to choose,
 Would brook no bridle-rein.

He saw the fairest of the fair,
 But smiled alike on all;
No band his roving foot might snare,
 No ring his hand enthrall.

PART II. THE MAIDEN

Why seeks the knight that rocky cape
  Beyond the Bay of Lynn?
What chance his wayward course may shape
  To reach its village inn?

No story tells; whate'er we guess,
  The past lies deaf and still,
But Fate, who rules to blight or bless,
  Can lead us where she will.

Make way! Sir Harry's coach and four,
  And liveried grooms that ride!
They cross the ferry, touch the shore
  On Winnisimmet's side.

They hear the wash on Chelsea Beach, —
  The level marsh they pass,
Where miles on miles the desert reach
  Is rough with bitter grass.

The shining horses foam and pant,
  And now the smells begin
Of fishy Swampscott, salt Nahant,
  And leather-scented Lynn.

Next, on their left, the slender spires
  And glittering vanes that crown
The home of Salem's frugal sires,
  The old, witch-haunted town.

So onward, o'er the rugged way
  That runs through rocks and sand,
Showered by the tempest-driven spray,
  From bays on either hand,

That shut between their outstretched arms
  The crews of Marblehead,
The lords of ocean's watery farms,
  Who plough the waves for bread.

At last the ancient inn appears,
  The spreading elm below,
Whose flapping sign these fifty years
  Has seesawed to and fro.

How fair the azure fields in sight
  Before the low-browed inn!
The tumbling billows fringe with light
  The crescent shore of Lynn;

Nahant thrusts outward through the waves
  Her arm of yellow sand,
And breaks the roaring surge that braves
  The gauntlet on her hand;

With eddying whirl the waters lock
  Yon treeless mound forlorn,
The sharp-winged sea-fowl's breeding-rock,
  That fronts the Spouting Horn;

Then free the white-sailed shallops glide,
  And wide the ocean smiles,
Till, shoreward bent, his streams divide
  The two bare Misery Isles.

The master's silent signal stays
  The wearied cavalcade;
The coachman reins his smoking bays
  Beneath the elm-tree's shade.

A gathering on the village green!
  The cocked-hats crowd to see,
On legs in ancient velveteen,
  With buckles at the knee.

A clustering round the tavern-door
  Of square-toed village boys,
Still wearing, as their grandsires wore,
  The old-world corduroys!

A scampering at the "Fountain" inn, —
  A rush of great and small,
With hurrying servants' mingled din
  And screaming matron's call!

Poor Agnes! with her work half done
  They caught her unaware;
As, humbly, like a praying nun,
  She knelt upon the stair;

Bent o'er the steps, with lowliest mien
  She knelt, but not to pray, —
Her little hands must keep them clean,
  And wash their stains away.

A foot, an ankle, bare and white,
  Her girlish shapes betrayed, —
"Ha! Nymphs and Graces!" spoke the Knight;
  "Look up, my beauteous Maid!"

She turned, — a reddening rose in bud,
  Its calyx half withdrawn, —
Her cheek on fire with damasked blood
  Of girlhood's glowing dawn!

He searched her features through and
    through,
  As royal lovers look
On lowly maidens, when they woo
  Without the ring and book.

"Come hither, Fair one! Here, my Sweet!
  Nay, prithee, look not down!
Take this to shoe those little feet,"—
  He tossed a silver crown.

A sudden paleness struck her brow,—
  A swifter blush succeeds;
It burns her cheek; it kindles now
  Beneath her golden beads.

She flitted, but the glittering eye
  Still sought the lovely face.
Who was she? What, and whence? and
    why
  Doomed to such menial place?

A skipper's daughter,—so they said,—
  Left orphan by the gale
That cost the fleet of Marblehead
  And Gloucester thirty sail.

Ah! many a lonely home is found
  Along the Essex shore,
That cheered its goodman outward bound,
  And sees his face no more!

"Not so," the matron whispered,—"sure
  No orphan girl is she,—
The Surriage folk are deadly poor
  Since Edward left the sea,

"And Mary, with her growing brood,
  Has work enough to do
To find the children clothes and food
  With Thomas, John, and Hugh.

"This girl of Mary's, growing tall,—
  (Just turned her sixteenth year,)—
To earn her bread and help them all,
  Would work as housemaid here."

So Agnes, with her golden beads,
  And naught beside as dower,
Grew at the wayside with the weeds,
  Herself a garden-flower.

'T was strange, 't was sad,—so fresh, so
    fair!
  Thus Pity's voice began.

Such grace! an angel's shape and air!
  The half-heard whisper ran.

For eyes could see in George's time,
  As now in later days,
And lips could shape, in prose and rhyme,
  The honeyed breath of praise.

No time to woo! The train must go
  Long ere the sun is down,
To reach, before the night-winds blow,
  The many-steepled town.

'T is midnight,—street and square are
    still;
Dark roll the whispering waves
That lap the piers beneath the hill
  Ridged thick with ancient graves.

Ah, gentle sleep! thy hand will smooth
  The weary couch of pain,
When all thy poppies fail to soothe
  The lover's throbbing brain!

'T is morn,—the orange-mantled sun
  Breaks through the fading gray,
And long and loud the Castle gun
  Peals o'er the glistening bay.

"Thank God 't is day!" With eager eye
  He hails the morning shine:—
"If art can win, or gold can buy,
  The maiden shall be mine!"

PART III. THE CONQUEST

"Who saw this hussy when she came?
  What is the wench, and who?"
They whisper. *Agnes*—is her name?
  Pray what has she to do?

The housemaids parley at the gate,
  The scullions on the stair,
And in the footmen's grave debate
  The butler deigns to share.

Black Dinah, stolen when a child,
  And sold on Boston pier,
Grown up in service, petted, spoiled,
  Speaks in the coachman's ear:

"What, all this household at his will?
  And all are yet too few?
More servants, and more servants still,—
  This pert young madam too!"

"*Servant!* fine servant!" laughed aloud
    The man of coach and steeds;
"She looks too fair, she steps too proud,
    This girl with golden beads!

"I tell you, you may fret and frown,
    And call her what you choose,
You'll find my Lady in her gown,
    Your Mistress in her shoes!"

Ah, gentle maidens, free from blame,
    God grant you never know
The little whisper, loud with shame,
    That makes the world your foe!

Why tell the lordly flatterer's art,
    That won the maiden's ear, —
The fluttering of the frightened heart,
    The blush, the smile, the tear?

Alas! it were the saddening tale
    That every language knows, —
The wooing wind, the yielding sail,
    The sunbeam and the rose.

And now the gown of sober stuff
    Has changed to fair brocade,
With broidered hem, and hanging cuff,
    And flower of silken braid;

And clasped around her blanching wrist
    A jewelled bracelet shines,
Her flowing tresses' massive twist
    A glittering net confines;

And mingling with their truant wave
    A fretted chain is hung;
But ah! the gift her mother gave, —
    Its beads are all unstrung!

Her place is at the master's board,
    Where none disputes her claim;
She walks beside the mansion's lord,
    His bride in all but name.

The busy tongues have ceased to talk,
    Or speak in softened tone,
So gracious in her daily walk
    The angel light has shown.

No want that kindness may relieve
    Assails her heart in vain,
The lifting of a ragged sleeve
    Will check her palfrey's rein.

A thoughtful calm, a quiet grace
    In every movement shown,
Reveal her moulded for the place
    She may not call her own.

And, save that on her youthful brow
    There broods a shadowy care,
No matron sealed with holy vow
    In all the land so fair!

PART IV. THE RESCUE

A ship comes foaming up the bay,
    Along the pier she glides;
Before her furrow melts away,
    A courier mounts and rides.

"Haste, Haste, post Haste!" the letters
    bear;
"Sir Harry Frankland, These."
Sad news to tell the loving pair!
    The knight must cross the seas.

"Alas! we part!" — the lips that spoke
    Lost all their rosy red,
As when a crystal cup is broke,
    And all its wine is shed.

"Nay, droop not thus, — where'er," he
    cried,
"I go by land or sea,
My love, my life, my joy, my pride,
    Thy place is still by me!"

Through town and city, far and wide,
    Their wandering feet have strayed,
From Alpine lake to ocean tide,
    And cold Sierra's shade.

At length they see the waters gleam
    Amid the fragrant bowers
Where Lisbon mirrors in the stream
    Her belt of ancient towers.

Red is the orange on its bough,
    To-morrow's sun shall fling
O'er Cintra's hazel-shaded brow
    The flush of April's wing.

The streets are loud with noisy mirth,
    They dance on every green;
The morning's dial marks the birth
    Of proud Braganza's queen.

At eve beneath their pictured dome
  The gilded courtiers throng;
The broad moidores have cheated Rome
  Of all her lords of song.

Ah! Lisbon dreams not of the day —
  Pleased with her painted scenes —
When all her towers shall slide away
  As now these canvas screens!

The spring has passed, the summer fled,
  And yet they linger still,
Though autumn's rustling leaves have spread
  The flank of Cintra's hill.

The town has learned their Saxon name,
  And touched their English gold,
Nor tale of doubt nor hint of blame
  From over sea is told.

Three hours the first November dawn
  Has climbed with feeble ray
Through mists like heavy curtains drawn
  Before the darkened day.

How still the muffled echoes sleep!
  Hark! hark! a hollow sound, —
A noise like chariots rumbling deep
  Beneath the solid ground.

The channel lifts, the water slides
  And bares its bar of sand,
Anon a mountain billow strides
  And crashes o'er the land.

The turrets lean, the steeples reel
  Like masts on ocean's swell,
And clash a long discordant peal,
  The death-doomed city's knell.

The pavement bursts, the earth upheaves
  Beneath the staggering town!
The turrets crack — the castle cleaves —
  The spires come rushing down.

Around, the lurid mountains glow
  With strange unearthly gleams;
While black abysses gape below,
  Then close in jagged seams.

The earth has folded like a wave,
  And thrice a thousand score,
Clasped, shroudless, in their closing grave,
  The sun shall see no more!

And all is over. Street and square
  In ruined heaps are piled;
Ah! where is she, so frail, so fair,
  Amid the tumult wild?

Unscathed, she treads the wreck-piled street,
  Whose narrow gaps afford
A pathway for her bleeding feet,
  To seek her absent lord.

A temple's broken walls arrest
  Her wild and wandering eyes;
Beneath its shattered portal pressed,
  Her lord unconscious lies.

The power that living hearts obey
  Shall lifeless blocks withstand?
Love led her footsteps where he lay, —
  Love nerves her woman's hand:

One cry, — the marble shaft she grasps, —
  Up heaves the ponderous stone: —
He breathes, — her fainting form he clasps, —
  Her life has bought his own!

PART V. THE REWARD

How like the starless night of death
  Our being's brief eclipse,
When faltering heart and failing breath
  Have bleached the fading lips!

She lives! What guerdon shall repay
  His debt of ransomed life?
One word can charm all wrongs away, —
  The sacred name of WIFE!

The love that won her girlish charms
  Must shield her matron fame,
And write beneath the Frankland arms
  The village beauty's name.

Go, call the priest! no vain delay
  Shall dim the sacred ring!
Who knows what change the passing day,
  The fleeting hour, may bring?

Before the holy altar bent,
  There kneels a goodly pair;
A stately man, of high descent,
  A woman, passing fair.

No jewels lend the blinding sheen
  That meaner beauty needs,
But on her bosom heaves unseen
  A string of golden beads.

The vow is spoke, — the prayer is said, —
  And with a gentle pride
The Lady Agnes lifts her head,
  Sir Harry Frankland's bride.

No more her faithful heart shall bear
  Those griefs so meekly borne, —
The passing sneer, the freezing stare,
  The icy look of scorn;

No more the blue-eyed English dames
  Their haughty lips shall curl,
Whene'er a hissing whisper names
  The poor New England girl.

But stay ! — his mother's haughty brow, —
  The pride of ancient race, —
Will plighted faith, and holy vow,
  Win back her fond embrace ?

Too well she knew the saddening tale
  Of love no vow had blest,
That turned his blushing honors pale
  And stained his knightly crest.

They seek his Northern home, — alas :
  He goes alone before; —
His own dear Agnes may not pass
  The proud, ancestral door.

He stood before the stately dame;
  He spoke; she calmly heard,
But not to pity, nor to blame;
  She breathed no single word.

He told his love, — her faith betrayed;
  She heard with tearless eyes;
Could she forgive the erring maid ?
  She stared in cold surprise.

How fond her heart, he told, — how true;
  The haughty eyelids fell; —
The kindly deeds she loved to do;
  She murmured, "It is well."

But when he told that fearful day,
  And how her feet were led
To where entombed in life he lay,
  The breathing with the dead,

And how she bruised her tender breasts
  Against the crushing stone,
That still the strong-armed clown protests
  No man can lift alone, —

Oh ! then the frozen spring was broke;
  By turns she wept and smiled; —
"Sweet Agnes !" so the mother spoke,
  "God bless my angel child !

"She saved thee from the jaws of death, —
  'T is thine to right her wrongs;
I tell thee, — I, who gave thee breath, —
  To her thy life belongs ! "

Thus Agnes won her noble name,
  Her lawless lover's hand;
The lowly maiden so became
  A lady in the land !

PART VI. CONCLUSION

The tale is done ; it little needs
  To track their after ways,
And string again the golden beads
  Of love's uncounted days.

They leave the fair ancestral isle
  For bleak New England's shore;
How gracious is the courtly smile
  Of all who frowned before !

Again through Lisbon's orange bowers
  They watch the river's gleam,
And shudder as her shadowy towers
  Shake in the trembling stream.

Fate parts at length the fondest pair;
  His cheek, alas ! grows pale;
The breast that trampling death could spare
  His noiseless shafts assail.

He longs to change the heaven of blue
  For England's clouded sky, —
To breathe the air his boyhood knew;
  He seeks them but to die.

Hard by the terraced hillside town,
  Where healing streamlets run,
Still sparkling with their old renown, —
  The " Waters of the Sun," —

The Lady Agnes raised the stone
  That marks his honored grave,

And there Sir Harry sleeps alone
  By Wiltshire Avon's wave.

The home of early love was dear;
  She sought its peaceful shade,
And kept her state for many a year,
  With none to make afraid.

At last the evil days were come
  That saw the red cross fall;
She hears the rebels' rattling drum, —
  Farewell to Frankland Hall!

I tell you, as my tale began,
  The hall is standing still;
And you, kind listener, maid or man,
  May see it if you will.

The box is glistening huge and green,
  Like trees the lilacs grow,
Three elms high-arching still are seen,
  And one lies stretched below.

The hangings, rough with velvet flowers,
  Flap on the latticed wall;
And o'er the mossy ridgepole towers
  The rock-hewn chimney tall.

The doors on mighty hinges clash
  With massive bolt and bar,
The heavy English-moulded sash
  Scarce can the night-winds jar.

Behold the chosen room he sought
  Alone, to fast and pray,
Each year, as chill November brought
  The dismal earthquake day.

There hung the rapier blade he wore,
  Bent in its flattened sheath;
The coat the shrieking woman tore
  Caught in her clenching teeth; —

The coat with tarnished silver lace
  She snapped at as she slid,
And down upon her death-white face
  Crashed the huge coffin's lid.

A graded terrace yet remains;
  If on its turf you stand
And look along the wooded plains
  That stretch on either hand,

The broken forest walls define
  A dim, receding view,
Where, on the far horizon's line,
  He cut his vista through.

If further story you shall crave,
  Or ask for living proof,
Go see old Julia, born a slave
  Beneath Sir Harry's roof.

She told me half that I have told,
  And she remembers well
The mansion as it looked of old
  Before its glories fell; —

The box, when round the terraced square
  Its glossy wall was drawn;
The climbing vines, the snow-balls fair,
  The roses on the lawn.

And Julia says, with truthful look
  Stamped on her wrinkled face,
That in her own black hands she took
  The coat with silver lace.

And you may hold the story light,
  Or, if you like, believe;
But there it was, the woman's bite, —
  A mouthful from the sleeve.

Now go your ways; — I need not tell
  The moral of my rhyme;
But, youths and maidens, ponder well
  This tale of olden time!

THE PLOUGHMAN

ANNIVERSARY OF THE BERKSHIRE AGRI-
CULTURAL SOCIETY, OCTOBER 4, 1849

[At this anniversary, Dr. Holmes not only read the following poem, but was chairman of the committee on the ploughing match, and read the report which will be found in the notes at the end of this volume.]

CLEAR the brown path, to meet his coulter's
    gleam!
Lo! on he comes, behind his smoking
    team,
With toil's bright dew-drops on his sun-
    burnt brow,
The lord of earth, the hero of the plough!

First in the field before the reddening
    sun,
Last in the shadows when the day is done,

Line after line, along the bursting sod,
Marks the broad acres where his feet have trod;
Still, where he treads, the stubborn clods divide,
The smooth, fresh furrow opens deep and wide;
Matted and dense the tangled turf upheaves,
Mellow and dark the ridgy cornfield cleaves;
Up the steep hillside, where the laboring train
Slants the long track that scores the level plain;
Through the moist valley, clogged with oozing clay,
The patient convoy breaks its destined way;
At every turn the loosening chains resound,
The swinging ploughshare circles glistening round,
Till the wide field one billowy waste appears,
And wearied hands unbind the panting steers.

These are the hands whose sturdy labor brings
The peasant's food, the golden pomp of kings;
This is the page, whose letters shall be seen
Changed by the sun to words of living green;
This is the scholar, whose immortal pen
Spells the first lesson hunger taught to men;
These are the lines which heaven-commanded Toil
Shows on his deed, — the charter of the soil!

O gracious Mother, whose benignant breast
Wakes us to life, and lulls us all to rest,
How thy sweet features, kind to every clime,
Mock with their smile the wrinkled front of time!
We stain thy flowers, — they blossom o'er the dead;
We rend thy bosom, and it gives us bread;
O'er the red field that trampling strife has torn,
Waves the green plumage of thy tasselled corn;
Our maddening conflicts scar thy fairest plain,
Still thy soft answer is the growing grain.
Yet, O our Mother, while uncounted charms
Steal round our hearts in thine embracing arms,
Let not our virtues in thy love decay,
And thy fond sweetness waste our strength away.

No! by these hills, whose banners now displayed
In blazing cohorts Autumn has arrayed;
By yon twin summits, on whose splintery crests
The tossing hemlocks hold the eagles' nests;
By these fair plains the mountain circle screens,
And feeds with streamlets from its dark ravines, —
True to their home, these faithful arms shall toil
To crown with peace their own untainted soil;
And, true to God, to freedom, to mankind,
If her chained baudogs Faction shall unbind,
These stately forms, that bending even now
Bowed their strong manhood to the humble plough,
Shall rise erect, the guardians of the land,
The same stern iron in the same right hand,
Till o'er their hills the shouts of triumph run,
The sword has rescued what the ploughshare won!

SPRING

WINTER is past; the heart of Nature warms
Beneath the wrecks of unresisted storms;
Doubtful at first, suspected more than seen,
The southern slopes are fringed with tender green;
On sheltered banks, beneath the dripping eaves,
Spring's earliest nurslings spread their glowing leaves,
Bright with the hues from wider pictures won,
White, azure, golden, — drift, or sky, or sun, —

SPRING

The snowdrop, bearing on her patient breast
The frozen trophy torn from Winter's crest;
The violet, gazing on the arch of blue
Till her own iris wears its deepened hue;
The spendthrift crocus, bursting through the mould
Naked and shivering with his cup of gold.
Swelled with new life, the darkening elm on high
Prints her thick buds against the spotted sky;
On all her boughs the stately chestnut cleaves
The gummy shroud that wraps her embryo leaves;
The house-fly, stealing from his narrow grave,
Drugged with the opiate that November gave,
Beats with faint wing against the sunny pane,
Or crawls, tenacious, o'er its lucid plain;
From shaded chinks of lichen-crusted walls,
In languid curves, the gliding serpent crawls;
The bog's green harper, thawing from his sleep,
Twangs a hoarse note and tries a shortened leap;
On floating rails that face the softening noons
The still shy turtles range their dark platoons,
Or, toiling aimless o'er the mellowing fields,
Trail through the grass their tessellated shields.

At last young April, ever frail and fair,
Wooed by her playmate with the golden hair,
Chased to the margin of receding floods
O'er the soft meadows starred with opening buds,
In tears and blushes sighs herself away,
And hides her cheek beneath the flowers of May.

Then the proud tulip lights her beacon blaze,
Her clustering curls the hyacinth displays;
O'er her tall blades the crested fleur-de-lis,
Like blue-eyed Pallas, towers erect and free;
With yellower flames the lengthened sunshine glows,
And love lays bare the passion-breathing rose;
Queen of the lake, along its reedy verge
The rival lily hastens to emerge,
Her snowy shoulders glistening as she strips,
Till morn is sultan of her parted lips.

Then bursts the song from every leafy glade,
The yielding season's bridal serenade;
Then flash the wings returning Summer calls
Through the deep arches of her forest halls, —
The bluebird, breathing from his azure plumes
The fragrance borrowed where the myrtle blooms;
The thrush, poor wanderer, dropping meekly down,
Clad in his remnant of autumnal brown;
The oriole, drifting like a flake of fire
Rent by a whirlwind from a blazing spire.
The robin, jerking his spasmodic throat,
Repeats, imperious, his *staccato* note;
The crack-brained bobolink courts his crazy mate,
Poised on a bulrush tipsy with his weight;
Nay, in his cage the lone canary sings,
Feels the soft air, and spreads his idle wings.

Why dream I here within these caging walls,
Deaf to her voice, while blooming Nature calls;
Peering and gazing with insatiate looks
Through blinding lenses, or in wearying books?
Off, gloomy spectres of the shrivelled past!
Fly with the leaves that fill the autumn blast!
Ye imps of Science, whose relentless chains
Lock the warm tides within these living veins,
Close your dim cavern, while its captive strays
Dazzled and giddy in the morning's blaze!

THE STUDY

Yet in the darksome crypt I left so late,
Whose only altar is its rusted grate, —
Sepulchral, rayless, joyless as it seems,
Shamed by the glare of May's refulgent
  beams, —
While the dim seasons dragged their
  shrouded train,
Its paler splendors were not quite in vain.
From these dull bars the cheerful firelight's
  glow
Streamed through the casement o'er the
  spectral snow;
Here, while the night-wind wreaked its
  frantic will
On the loose ocean and the rock-bound hill,
Rent the cracked topsail from its quiver-
  ing yard,
And rived the oak a thousand storms had
  scarred,
Fenced by these walls the peaceful taper
  shone,
Nor felt a breath to slant its trembling
  cone.

Not all unblest the mild interior scene
When the red curtain spread its falling
  screen;
O'er some light task the lonely hours were
  past,
And the long evening only flew too fast;
Or the wide chair its leathern arms would
  lend
In genial welcome to some easy friend,
Stretched on its bosom with relaxing nerves,
Slow moulding, plastic, to its hollow curves;
Perchance indulging, if of generous creed,
In brave Sir Walter's dream-compelling
  weed.
Or, happier still, the evening hour would
  bring
To the round table its expected ring,
And while the punch-bowl's sounding depths
  were stirred, —
Its silver cherubs smiling as they heard, —
Our hearts would open, as at evening's hour
The close-sealed primrose frees its hidden
  flower.

Such the warm life this dim retreat has
  known,
Not quite deserted when its guests were
  flown;

Nay, filled with friends, an unobtrusive set,
Guiltless of calls and cards and etiquette,
Ready to answer, never known to ask,
Claiming no service, prompt for every task.

On those dark shelves no housewife hand
  profanes,
O'er his mute files the monarch folio reigns;
A mingled race, the wreck of chance and
  time,
That talk all tongues and breathe of every
  clime,
Each knows his place, and each may claim
  his part
In some quaint corner of his master's
  heart.
This old Decretal, won from Kloss's hoards,
Thick-leaved, brass-cornered, ribbed with
  oaken boards,
Stands the gray patriarch of the graver
  rows,
Its fourth ripe century narrowing to its
  close;
Not daily conned, but glorious still to view,
With glistening letters wrought in red and
  blue.
There towers Stagira's all-embracing sage,
The Aldine anchor on his opening page;
There sleep the births of Plato's heavenly
  mind,
In yon dark tomb by jealous clasps con-
  fined,
"Olim e libris" (dare I call it mine?)
Of Yale's grave Head and Killingworth's
  divine!
In those square sheets the songs of Maro
  fill
The silvery types of smooth-leaved Basker-
  ville;
High over all, in close, compact array,
Their classic wealth the Elzevirs display.
In lower regions of the sacred space
Range the dense volumes of a humbler
  race;
There grim chirurgeons all their mysteries
  teach,
In spectral pictures, or in crabbed speech;
Harvey and Haller, fresh from Nature's
  page,
Shoulder the dreamers of an earlier age.
Lully and Geber, and the learned crew
That loved to talk of all they could not do.
Why count the rest, — those names of later
  days
That many love, and all agree to praise, —

Or point the titles, where a glance may read
The dangerous lines of party or of creed?
Too well, perchance, the chosen list would show
What few may care and none can claim to know.
Each has his features, whose exterior seal
A brush may copy, or a sunbeam steal;
Go to his study, — on the nearest shelf
Stands the mosaic portrait of himself.

What though for months the tranquil dust descends,
Whitening the heads of these mine ancient friends,
While the damp offspring of the modern press
Flaunts on my table with its pictured dress;
Not less I love each dull familiar face,
Nor less should miss it from the appointed place;
I snatch the book, along whose burning leaves
His scarlet web our wild romancer weaves,
Yet, while proud Hester's fiery pangs I share,
My old MAGNALIA must be standing *there!*

THE BELLS

WHEN o'er the street the morning peal is flung
From yon tall belfry with the brazen tongue,
Its wide vibrations, wafted by the gale,
To each far listener tell a different tale.
  The sexton, stooping to the quivering floor
Till the great caldron spills its brassy roar,
Whirls the hot axle, counting, one by one,
Each dull concussion, till his task is done.
  Toil's patient daughter, when the welcome note
Clangs through the silence from the steeple's throat,
Streams, a white unit, to the checkered street,
Demure, but guessing whom she soon shall meet;
The bell, responsive to her secret flame,
With every note repeats her lover's name.
  The lover, tenant of the neighboring lane,
Sighing, and fearing lest he sigh in vain,
Hears the stern accents, as they come and go,
Their only burden one despairing No!
  Ocean's rough child, whom many a shore has known
Ere homeward breezes swept him to his own,
Starts at the echo as it circles round,
A thousand memories kindling with the sound;
The early favorite's unforgotten charms,
Whose blue initials stain his tawny arms;
His first farewell, the flapping canvas spread,
The seaward streamers crackling overhead,
His kind, pale mother, not ashamed to weep
Her first-born's bridal with the haggard deep,
While the brave father stood with tearless eye,
Smiling and choking with his last good-by.

  'T is but a wave, whose spreading circle beats,
With the same impulse, every nerve it meets,
Yet who shall count the varied shapes that ride
On the round surge of that aerial tide!

  O child of earth! If floating sounds like these
Steal from thyself their power to wound or please,
If here or there thy changing will inclines,
As the bright zodiac shifts its rolling signs,
Look at thy heart, and when its depths are known,
Then try thy brother's, judging by thine own,
But keep thy wisdom to the narrower range,
While its own standards are the sport of change,
Nor count us rebels when we disobey
The passing breath that holds thy passion's sway.

NON-RESISTANCE

PERHAPS too far in these considerate days
Has patience carried her submissive ways;

Wisdom has taught us to be calm and
    meek,
To take one blow, and turn the other
    cheek;
It is not written what a man shall do
If the rude caitiff smite the other too!

   Land of our fathers, in thine hour of
    need
God help thee, guarded by the passive
    creed!
As the lone pilgrim trusts to beads and
    cowl,
When through the forest rings the gray
    wolf's howl;
As the deep galleon trusts her gilded
    prow
When the black corsair slants athwart her
    bow;
As the poor pheasant, with his peaceful
    mien,
Trusts to his feathers, shining golden-green,
When the dark plumage with the crimson
    beak
Has rustled shadowy from its splintered
    peak, —
So trust thy friends, whose babbling
    tongues would charm
The lifted sabre from thy foeman's arm,
Thy torches ready for the answering peal
From bellowing fort and thunder-freighted
    keel!

THE MORAL BULLY

You whey-faced brother, who delights to
    wear
A weedy flux of ill-conditioned hair,
Seems of the sort that in a crowded place
One elbows freely into smallest space;
A timid creature, lax of knee and hip,
Whom small disturbance whitens round
    the lip;
One of those harmless spectacled machines,
The Holy-Week of Protestants convenes;
Whom school-boys question if their walk
    transcends
The last advices of maternal friends;
Whom John, obedient to his master's sign,
Conducts, laborious, up to *ninety-nine*,
While Peter, glistening with luxurious
    scorn,
Husks his white ivories like an ear of
    corn;

Dark in the brow and bilious in the cheek,
Whose yellowish linen flowers but once a
    week,
Conspicuous, annual, in their threadbare
    suits,
And the laced high-lows which they call
    their boots,
Well mayst thou *shun* that dingy front
    severe,
But him, O stranger, him thou canst not
    fear!
   Be slow to judge, and slower to despise,
Man of broad shoulders and heroic size!
The tiger, writhing from the boa's rings,
Drops at the fountain where the cobra
    stings.
In that lean phantom, whose extended
    glove
Points to the text of universal love,
Behold the master that can tame thee
    down
To crouch, the vassal of his Sunday frown;
His velvet throat against thy corded wrist,
His loosened tongue against thy doubled
    fist!

   The MORAL BULLY, though he never
    swears,
Nor kicks intruders down his entry stairs,
Though meekness plants his backward-
    sloping hat,
And non-resistance ties his white cravat,
Though his black broadcloth glories to be
    seen
In the same plight with Shylock's gaber-
    dine,
Hugs the same passion to his narrow
    breast
That heaves the cuirass on the trooper's
    chest,
Hears the same hell-hounds yelling in his
    rear
That chase from port the maddened buc-
    caneer,
Feels the same comfort while his acrid
    words
Turn the sweet milk of kindness into
    curds,
Or with grim logic prove, beyond debate,
That all we love is worthiest of our hate,
As the scarred ruffian of the pirate's
    deck,
When his long swivel rakes the staggering
    wreck!

Heaven keep us all! Is every rascal clown
Whose arm is stronger free to knock us down?
Has every scarecrow, whose cachectic soul
Seems fresh from Bedlam, airing on parole,
Who, though he carries but a doubtful trace
Of angel visits on his hungry face,
From lack of marrow or the coins to pay,
Has dogged some vices in a shabby way,
The right to stick us with his cutthroat terms,
And bait his homilies with his brother worms?

THE MIND'S DIET

No life worth naming ever comes to good
If always nourished on the selfsame food;
The creeping mite may live so if he please,
And feed on Stilton till he turns to cheese,
But cool Magendie proves beyond a doubt,
If mammals try it, that their eyes drop out.

No reasoning natures find it safe to feed,
For their sole diet, on a single creed;
It spoils their eyeballs while it spares their tongues,
And starves the heart to feed the noisy lungs.

When the first larvæ on the elm are seen,
The crawling wretches, like its leaves, are green;
Ere chill October shakes the latest down,
They, like the foliage, change their tint to brown;
On the blue flower a bluer flower you spy,
You stretch to pluck it — 't is a butterfly;
The flattened tree-toads so resemble bark,
They 're hard to find as Ethiops in the dark;
The woodcock, stiffening to fictitious mud,
Cheats the young sportsman thirsting for his blood;
So by long living on a single lie,
Nay, on one truth, will creatures get its dye;

Red, yellow, green, they take their subject's hue, —
Except when squabbling turns them black and blue!

OUR LIMITATIONS

We trust and fear, we question and believe,
From life's dark threads a trembling faith to weave,
Frail as the web that misty night has spun,
Whose dew-gemmed awnings glitter in the sun.
While the calm centuries spell their lessons out,
Each truth we conquer spreads the realm of doubt;
When Sinai's summit was Jehovah's throne,
The chosen Prophet knew his voice alone;
When Pilate's hall that awful question heard,
The Heavenly Captive answered not a word.

Eternal Truth! beyond our hopes and fears
Sweep the vast orbits of thy myriad spheres!
From age to age, while History carves sublime
On her waste rock the flaming curves of time,
How the wild swayings of our planet show
That worlds unseen surround the world we know.

THE OLD PLAYER

The curtain rose; in thunders long and loud
The galleries rung; the veteran actor bowed.
In flaming line the telltales of the stage
Showed on his brow the autograph of age;
Pale, hueless waves amid his clustered hair,
And umbered shadows, prints of toil and care;
Round the wide circle glanced his vacant eye, —
He strove to speak, — his voice was but a sigh.

Year after year had seen its short-lived race
Flit past the scenes and others take their place;
Yet the old prompter watched his accents still,
His name still flaunted on the evening's bill.
Heroes, the monarchs of the scenic floor,
Had died in earnest and were heard no more;
Beauties, whose cheeks such roseate bloom o'erspread
They faced the footlights in unborrowed red,
Had faded slowly through successive shades
To gray duennas, foils of younger maids;
Sweet voices lost the melting tones that start
With Southern throbs the sturdy Saxon heart,
While fresh sopranos shook the painted sky
With their long, breathless, quivering locust-cry.
Yet there he stood, — the man of other days,
In the clear present's full, unsparing blaze,
As on the oak a faded leaf that clings
While a new April spreads its burnished wings.

How bright yon rows that soared in triple tier,
Their central sun the flashing chandelier!
How dim the eye that sought with doubtful aim
Some friendly smile it still might dare to claim!
How fresh these hearts! his own how worn and cold!
Such the sad thoughts that long-drawn sigh had told.
No word yet faltered on his trembling tongue;
Again, again, the crashing galleries rung.
As the old guardsman at the bugle's blast
Hears in its strain the echoes of the past,
So, as the plaudits rolled and thundered round,
A life of memories startled at the sound.
He lived again, — the page of earliest days, —
Days of small fee and parsimonious praise;

Then lithe young Romeo — hark that silvered tone,
From those smooth lips — alas! they were his own.
Then the bronzed Moor, with all his love and woe,
Told his strange tale of midnight melting snow;
And dark-plumed Hamlet, with his cloak and blade,
Looked on the royal ghost, himself a shade.
All in one flash, his youthful memories came,
Traced in bright hues of evanescent flame,
As the spent swimmer's in the lifelong dream,
While the last bubble rises through the stream.

Call him not old, whose visionary brain
Holds o'er the past its undivided reign.
For him in vain the envious seasons roll
Who bears eternal summer in his soul.
If yet the minstrel's song, the poet's lay,
Spring with her birds, or children at their play,
Or maiden's smile, or heavenly dream of art,
Stir the few life-drops creeping round his heart,
Turn to the record where his years are told, —
Count his gray hairs, — they cannot make him old!
What magic power has changed the faded mime?
One breath of memory on the dust of time.
As the last window in the buttressed wall
Of some gray minster tottering to its fall,
Though to the passing crowd its hues are spread,
A dull mosaic, yellow, green, and red,
Viewed from within, a radiant glory shows
When through its pictured screen the sunlight flows,
And kneeling pilgrims on its storied pane
See angels glow in every shapeless stain;
So streamed the vision through his sunken eye,
Clad in the splendors of his morning sky.
All the wild hopes his eager boyhood knew,
All the young fancies riper years proved true.

The sweet, low-whispered words, the winning glance
From queens of song, from Houris of the dance,
Wealth's lavish gift, and Flattery's soothing phrase,
And Beauty's silence when her blush was praise,
And melting Pride, her lashes wet with tears,
Triumphs and banquets, wreaths and crowns and cheers,
Pangs of wild joy that perish on the tongue,
And all that poets dream, but leave unsung!

In every heart some viewless founts are fed
From far-off hillsides where the dews were shed:
On the worn features of the weariest face
Some youthful memory leaves its hidden trace,
As in old gardens left by exiled kings
The marble basins tell of hidden springs,
But, gray with dust, and overgrown with weeds,
Their choking jets the passer little heeds,
Till time's revenges break their seals away,
And, clad in rainbow light, the waters play.

Good night, fond dreamer! let the curtain fall:
The world 's a stage, and we are players all.
A strange rehearsal! Kings without their crowns,
And threadbare lords, and jewel-wearing clowns,
Speak the vain words that mock their throbbing hearts,
As Want, stern prompter! spells them out their parts.
The tinselled hero whom we praise and pay
Is twice an actor in a twofold play.
We smile at children when a painted screen
Seems to their simple eyes a real scene;
Ask the poor hireling, who has left his throne
To seek the cheerless home he calls his own,
Which of his double lives most real seems,
The world of solid fact or scenic dreams?
Canvas, or clouds, — the footlights, or the spheres, —
The play of two short hours, or seventy years?
Dream on! Though Heaven may woo our open eyes,
Through their closed lids we look on fairer skies;
Truth is for other worlds, and hope for this;
The cheating future lends the present's bliss;
Life is a running shade, with fettered hands,
That chases phantoms over shifting sands,
Death a still spectre on a marble seat,
With ever clutching palms and shackled feet;
The airy shapes that mock life's slender chain,
The flying joys he strives to clasp in vain,
Death only grasps; to live is to pursue, —
Dream on! there's nothing but illusion true!

A POEM

DEDICATION OF THE PITTSFIELD CEMETERY, SEPTEMBER 9, 1850

Angel of Death! extend thy silent reign!
Stretch thy dark sceptre o'er this new domain!
No sable car along the winding road
Has borne to earth its unresisting load;
No sudden mound has risen yet to show
Where the pale slumberer folds his arms below;
No marble gleams to bid his memory live
In the brief lines that hurrying Time can give;
Yet, O Destroyer! from thy shrouded throne
Look on our gift; this realm is all thine own!

Fair is the scene; its sweetness oft beguiled
From their dim paths the children of the wild;
The dark-haired maiden loved its grassy dells,
The feathered warrior claimed its wooded swells,
Still on its slopes the ploughman's ridges show

The pointed flints that left his fatal bow,
Chipped with rough art and slow barbarian
    toil, —
Last of his wrecks that strews the alien
    soil!
    Here spread the fields that heaped their
        ripened store
Till the brown arms of Labor held no more;
The scythe's broad meadow with its dusky
    blush;
The sickle's harvest with its velvet flush;
The green-haired maize, her silken tresses
    laid,
In soft luxuriance, on her harsh brocade;
The gourd that swells beneath her tossing
    plume;
The coarser wheat that rolls in lakes of
    bloom, —
Its coral stems and milk-white flowers alive
With the wide murmurs of the scattered
    hive;
Here glowed the apple with the pencilled
    streak
Of morning painted on its southern cheek;
The pear's long necklace strung with golden
    drops,
Arched, like the banian, o'er its pillared
    props;
Here crept the growths that paid the la-
    borer's care
With the cheap luxuries wealth consents to
    spare;
Here sprang the healing herbs which could
    not save
The hand that reared them from the neigh-
    boring grave.

Yet all its varied charms, forever free
From task and tribute, Labor yields to thee:
No more, when April sheds her fitful rain,
The sower's hand shall cast its flying grain;
No more, when Autumn strews the flaming
    leaves,
The reaper's band shall gird its yellow
    sheaves;
For thee alike the circling seasons flow
Till the first blossoms heave the latest
    snow.
In the stiff clod below the whirling drifts,
In the loose soil the springing herbage lifts,
In the hot dust beneath the parching weeds,
Life's withering flower shall drop its
    shrivelled seeds;
Its germ entranced in thy unbreathing sleep
Till what thou sowest mightier angels reap!

Spirit of Beauty! let thy graces blend
With loveliest Nature all that Art can lend.
Come from the bowers where Summer's
    life-blood flows
Through the red lips of June's half-open
    rose,
Dressed in bright hues, the loving sun-
    shine's dower;
For tranquil Nature owns no mourning
    flower.
    Come from the forest where the beech's
        screen
Bars the fierce noonbeam with its flakes of
    green;
Stay the rude axe that bares the shadowy
    plains,
Stanch the deep wound that dries the
    maple's veins.
    Come with the stream whose silver-
        braided rills
Fling their unclasping bracelets from the
    hills,
Till in one gleam, beneath the forest's
    wings,
Melts the white glitter of a hundred
    springs.
    Come from the steeps where look majes-
        tic forth
From their twin thrones the Giants of the
    North
On the huge shapes, that, crouching at their
    knees,
Stretch their broad shoulders, rough with
    shaggy trees.
Through the wide waste of ether, not in
    vain,
Their softened gaze shall reach our distant
    plain;
There, while the mourner turns his aching
    eyes
On the blue mounds that print the bluer
    skies,
Nature shall whisper that the fading view
Of mightiest grief may wear a heavenly
    hue.
Cherub of Wisdom! let thy marble page
Leave its sad lesson, new to every age;
Teach us to live, not grudging every breath
To the chill winds that waft us on to death,
But ruling calmly every pulse it warms,
And tempering gently every word it forms.
Seraph of Love! in heaven's adoring zone,
Nearest of all around the central throne,
While with soft hands the pillowed turf we
    spread

That soon shall hold us in its dreamless bed,
With the low whisper, — Who shall first be
  laid
In the dark chamber's yet unbroken
  shade ? —
Let thy sweet radiance shine rekindled
  here,
And all we cherish grow more truly dear.
Here in the gates of Death's o'erhanging
  vault,
Oh, teach us kindness for our brother's
  fault:
Lay all our wrongs beneath this peaceful
  sod,
And lead our hearts to Mercy and its God.

FATHER of all ! in Death's relentless
  claim
We read thy mercy by its sterner name;
In the bright flower that decks the solemn
  bier,
We see thy glory in its narrowed sphere;
In the deep lessons that affliction draws,
We trace the curves of thy encircling laws;
In the long sigh that sets our spirits free,
We own the love that calls us back to
  Thee !

Through the hushed street, along the
  silent plain,
The spectral future leads its mourning train,
Dark with the shadows of uncounted bands,
Where man's white lips and woman's wring-
  ing hands
Track the still burden, rolling slow before,
That love and kindness can protect uo
  more;
The smiling babe that, called to mortal
  strife,
Shuts its meek eyes and drops its little
  life;
The drooping child who prays in vain to
  live,
And pleads for help its parent cannot give;
The pride of beauty stricken in its flower;
The strength of manhood broken in an
  hour;
Age in its weakness, bowed by toil and
  care,
Traced in sad lines beneath its silvered hair.

The sun shall set, and heaven's resplen-
  dent spheres
Gild the smooth turf unhallowed yet by
  tears,

But ah ! how soon the evening stars will
  shed
Their sleepless light around the slumbering
  dead !

Take them, O Father, in immortal trust !
Ashes to ashes, dust to kindred dust,
Till the last angel rolls the stone away,
And a new morning brings eternal day !

TO GOVERNOR SWAIN

[Mr. William W. Swain was a New Bedford merchant, who became the owner of the island of Naushon, where he exercised a generous hospitality, and was given the title of Governor in playful affection. He had a passionate love for every tree and stone on the island, and was buried in a beautiful open glade in the woods there. The island passed into the possession of Mr. John M. Forbes, who married Governor Swain's niece. Dr. Holmes speaks of his own entertainment at Naushon in the *Autocrat*, pp. 39–41. This poem was written at Pittsfield in 1851.]

DEAR GOVERNOR, if my skiff might brave
The winds that lift the ocean wave,
The mountain stream that loops and
  swerves
Through my broad meadow's channelled
  curves
Should waft me on from bound to bound
To where the River weds the Sound,
The Sound should give me to the Sea,
That to the Bay, the Bay to thee.

It may not be ; too long the track
To follow down or struggle back.
The sun has set on fair Naushon
Long ere my western blaze is gone ;
The ocean disk is rolling dark
In shadows round your swinging bark,
While yet the yellow sunset fills
The stream that scarfs my spruce-clad
  hills ;
The day-star wakes your island deer
Long ere my barnyard chanticleer;
Your mists are soaring in the blue
While mine are sparks of glittering dew.

It may not be; oh, would it might,
Could I live o'er that glowing night !
What golden hours would come to life,
What goodly feats of peaceful strife, —
Such jests, that, drained of every joke,

The very bank of language broke, —
Such deeds, that Laughter nearly died
With stitches in his belted side;
While Time, caught fast in pleasure's
    chain,
His double goblet snapped in twain,
And stood with half in either hand, —
Both brimming full, — but not of sand !

It may not be; I strive in vain
To break my slender household chain, —
Three pairs of little clasping hands,
One voice, that whispers, not commands.
Even while my spirit flies away,
My gentle jailers murmur nay;
All shapes of elemental wrath
They raise along my threatened path;
The storm grows black, the waters rise,
The mountains mingle with the skies,
The mad tornado scoops the ground,
The midnight robber prowls around, —
Thus, kissing every limb they tie,
They draw a knot and heave a sigh,
Till, fairly netted in the toil,
My feet are rooted to the soil.
Only the soaring wish is free ! —
And that, dear Governor, flies to thee !

TO AN ENGLISH FRIEND

THE seed that wasteful autumn cast
To waver on its stormy blast,
Long o'er the wintry desert tost,
Its living germ has never lost.
Dropped by the weary tempest's wing,
It feels the kindling ray of spring,
And, starting from its dream of death,
Pours on the air its perfumed breath.

So, parted by the rolling flood,
The love that springs from common blood
Needs but a single sunlit hour
Of mingling smiles to bud and flower;
Unharmed its slumbering life has flown,
From shore to shore, from zone to zone,
Where summer's falling roses stain
The tepid waves of Pontchartrain,
Or where the lichen creeps below
Katahdin's wreaths of whirling snow.

Though fiery sun and stiffening cold
May change the fair ancestral mould,
No winter chills, no summer drains
The life-blood drawn from English veins,
Still bearing whereso'er it flows
The love that with its fountain rose,
Unchanged by space, unwronged by time,
From age to age, from clime to clime !

AFTER A LECTURE ON WORDSWORTH

[In 1853 Dr. Holmes gave a course of lectures before the Lowell Institute in Boston on English Poetry of the Nineteenth Century, and this and the following five poems were postludes to the lectures.]

COME, spread your wings, as I spread mine,
    And leave the crowded hall
For where the eyes of twilight shine
    O'er evening's western wall.

These are the pleasant Berkshire hills,
    Each with its leafy crown;
Hark ! from their sides a thousand rills
    Come singing sweetly down.

A thousand rills; they leap and shine,
    Strained through the shadowy nooks,
Till, clasped in many a gathering twine,
    They swell a hundred brooks.

A hundred brooks, and still they run
    With ripple, shade, and gleam,
Till, clustering all their braids in one,
    They flow a single stream.

A bracelet spun from mountain mist,
    A silvery sash unwound,
With ox-bow curve and sinuous twist
    It writhes to reach the Sound.

This is my bark, — a pygmy's ship:
    Beneath a child it rolls;
Fear not, — one body makes it dip,
    But not a thousand souls.

Float we the grassy banks between;
    Without an oar we glide;
The meadows, drest in living green,
    Unroll on either side.

Come, take the book we love so well,
    And let us read and dream
We see whate'er its pages tell,
    And sail an English stream.

Up to the clouds the lark has sprung,
    Still trilling as he flies;

The linnet sings as there he sung;
  The unseen cuckoo cries,

And daisies strew the banks along,
  And yellow kingcups shine,
With cowslips, and a primrose throng,
  And humble celandine.

Ah foolish dream! when Nature nursed
  Her daughter in the West,
The fount was drained that opened first;
  She bared her other breast.

On the young planet's orient shore
  Her morning hand she tried;
Then turned the broad medallion o'er
  And stamped the sunset side.

Take what she gives, her pine's tall stem,
  Her elm with hanging spray;
She wears her mountain diadem
  Still in her own proud way.

Look on the forests' ancient kings,
  The hemlock's towering pride:
Yon trunk had thrice a hundred rings,
  And fell before it died.

Nor think that Nature saves her bloom
  And alights our grassy plain;
For us she wears her court costume, —
  Look on its broidered train;

The lily with the sprinkled dots,
  Brands of the noontide beam;
The cardinal, and the blood-red spots,
  Its double in the stream,

As if some wounded eagle's breast,
  Slow throbbing o'er the plain,
Had left its airy path impressed
  In drops of scarlet rain.

And hark! and hark! the woodland rings;
  There thrilled the thrush's soul;
And look! that flash of flamy wings, —
  The fire-plumed oriole!

Above, the hen-hawk swims and swoops,
  Flung from the bright, blue sky;
Below, the robin hops, and whoops
  His piercing Indian cry.

Beauty runs virgin in the woods
  Robed in her rustic green,

And oft a longing thought intrudes,
  As if we might have seen

Her every finger's every joint
  Ringed with some golden line,
Poet whom Nature did anoint!
  Had our wild home been thine.

Yet think not so; Old England's blood
  Runs warm in English veins;
But wafted o'er the icy flood
  Its better life remains:

Our children know each wildwood smell,
  The bayberry and the fern,
The man who does not know them well
  Is all too old to learn.

Be patient! On the breathing page
  Still pants our hurried past;
Pilgrim and soldier, saint and sage, —
  The poet comes the last!

Though still the lark-voiced matins ring
  The world has known so long;
The wood-thrush of the West shall sing
  Earth's last sweet even-song!

AFTER A LECTURE ON MOORE

SHINE soft, ye trembling tears of light
  That strew the mourning skies;
Hushed in the silent dews of night
  The harp of Erin lies.

What though her thousand years have past
  Of poets, saints, and kings, —
Her echoes only hear the last
  That swept those golden strings.

Fling o'er his mound, ye star-lit bowers,
  The balmiest wreaths ye wear,
Whose breath has lent your earth-born flowers
  Heaven's own ambrosial air.

Breathe, bird of night, thy softest tone,
  By shadowy grove and rill;
Thy song will soothe us while we own
  That his was sweeter still.

Stay, pitying Time, thy foot for him
  Who gave thee swifter wings,
Nor let thine envious shadow dim
  The light his glory flings.

If in his cheek unholy blood
 Burned for one youthful hour,
'T was but the flushing of the bud
 That blooms a milk-white flower.

Take him, kind mother, to thy breast,
 Who loved thy smiles so well,
And spread thy mantle o'er his rest
 Of rose and asphodel.

The bark has sailed the midnight sea,
 The sea without a shore,
That waved its parting sign to thee, —
 "A health to thee, Tom Moore!"

And thine long lingering on the strand,
 Its bright-hued streamers furled,
Was loosed by age, with trembling hand,
 To seek the silent world.

Not silent! no, the radiant stars
 Still singing as they shine,
Unheard through earth's imprisoning bars,
 Have voices sweet as thine.

Wake, then, in happier realms above,
 The songs of bygone years,
Till angels learn those airs of love
 That ravished mortal ears!

AFTER A LECTURE ON KEATS

"*Purpureos spargam flores.*"

THE wreath that star-crowned Shelley gave
Is lying on thy Roman grave,
Yet on its turf young April sets
Her store of slender violets;
Though all the Gods their garlands shower,
I too may bring one purple flower.
Alas! what blossom shall I bring,
That opens in my Northern spring?
The garden beds have all run wild,
So trim when I was yet a child;
Flat plantains and unseemly stalks
Have crept across the gravel walks;
The vines are dead, long, long ago,
The almond buds no longer blow.
No more upon its mound I see
The azure, plume-bound fleur-de-lis;
Where once the tulips used to show,
In straggling tufts the pansies grow;
The grass has quenched my white-rayed gem,
The flowering "Star of Bethlehem,"
Though its long blade of glossy green
And pallid stripe may still be seen.
Nature, who treads her nobles down,
And gives their birthright to the clown,
Has sown her base-born weedy things
Above the garden's queens and kings.
Yet one sweet flower of ancient race
Springs in the old familiar place.
When snows were melting down the vale,
And Earth unlaced her icy mail,
And March his stormy trumpet blew,
And tender green came peeping through,
I loved the earliest one to seek
That broke the soil with emerald beak,
And watch the trembling bells so blue
Spread on the column as it grew.
Meek child of earth! thou wilt not shame
The sweet, dead poet's holy name;
The God of music gave thee birth,
Called from the crimson-spotted earth,
Where, sobbing his young life away,
His own fair Hyacinthus lay.
The hyacinth my garden gave
Shall lie upon that Roman grave!

AFTER A LECTURE ON SHELLEY

ONE broad, white sail in Spezzia's treacherous bay;
 On comes the blast; too daring bark, beware!
The cloud has clasped her; lo! it melts away;
 The wide, waste waters, but no sail is there.

Morning: a woman looking on the sea;
 Midnight: with lamps the long veranda burns;
Come, wandering sail, they watch, they burn for thee!
 Suns come and go, alas! no bark returns.

And feet are thronging on the pebbly sands,
 And torches flaring in the weedy caves,
Where'er the waters lay with icy hands
 The shapes uplifted from their coral graves.

Vainly they seek; the idle quest is o'er;
 The coarse, dark women, with their hanging locks,

And lean, wild children gather from the shore
To the black hovels bedded in the rocks.

But Love still prayed, with agonizing wail,
"One, one last look, ye heaving waters, yield!"
Till Ocean, clashing in his jointed mail,
Raised the pale burden on his level shield.

Slow from the shore the sullen waves retire;
His form a nobler element shall claim;
Nature baptized him in ethereal fire,
And Death shall crown him with a wreath of flame.

Fade, mortal semblance, never to return;
Swift is the change within thy crimson shroud;
Seal the white ashes in the peaceful urn;
All else has risen in yon silvery cloud.

Sleep where thy gentle Adonais lies,
Whose open page lay on thy dying heart,
Both in the smile of those blue-vaulted skies,
Earth's fairest dome of all divinest art.

Breathe for his wandering soul one passing sigh,
O happier Christian, while thine eye grows dim, —
In all the mansions of the house on high,
Say not that Mercy has not one for him!

AT THE CLOSE OF A COURSE OF LECTURES

As the voice of the watch to the mariner's dream,
As the footstep of Spring on the ice-girdled stream,
There comes a soft footstep, a whisper, to me, —
The vision is over, — the rivulet free!

We have trod from the threshold of turbulent March,
Till the green scarf of April is hung on the larch,
And down the bright hillside that welcomes the day,
We hear the warm panting of beautiful May.

We will part before Summer has opened her wing,
And the bosom of June swells the bodice of Spring,
While the hope of the season lies fresh in the bud,
And the young life of Nature runs warm in our blood.

It is but a word, and the chain is unbound,
The bracelet of steel drops unclasped to the ground;
No hand shall replace it, — it rests where it fell, —
It is but one word that we all know too well.

Yet the hawk with the wildness untamed in his eye,
If you free him, stares round ere he springs to the sky;
The slave whom no longer his fetters restrain
Will turn for a moment and look at his chain.

Our parting is not as the friendship of years,
That chokes with the blessing it speaks through its tears;
We have walked in a garden, and, looking around,
Have plucked a few leaves from the myrtles we found.

But now at the gate of the garden we stand,
And the moment has come for unclasping the hand;
Will you drop it like lead, and in silence retreat
Like the twenty crushed forms from an omnibus seat?

Nay! hold it one moment, — the last we may share, —
I stretch it in kindness, and not for my fare;
You may pass through the doorway in rank or in file,
If your ticket from Nature is stamped with a smile.

For the sweetest of smiles is the smile as we part,
When the light round the lips is a ray from the heart;

And lest a stray tear from its fountain might swell,
We will seal the bright spring with a quiet farewell.

THE HUDSON

AFTER A LECTURE AT ALBANY

[Given in December, 1854.]

'TWAS a vision of childhood that came with its dawn,
Ere the curtain that covered life's day-star was drawn;
The nurse told the tale when the shadows grew long,
And the mother's soft lullaby breathed it in song.

"There flows a fair stream by the hills of the West," —
She sang to her boy as he lay on her breast;
"Along its smooth margin thy fathers have played;
Beside its deep waters their ashes are laid."

I wandered afar from the land of my birth,
I saw the old rivers, renowned upon earth,
But fancy still painted that wide-flowing stream
With the many-hued pencil of infancy's dream.

I saw the green banks of the castle-crowned Rhine,
Where the grapes drink the moonlight and change it to wine;
I stood by the Avon, whose waves as they glide
Still whisper his glory who sleeps at their side.

But my heart would still yearn for the sound of the waves
That sing as they flow by my forefathers' graves;
If manhood yet honors my cheek with a tear,
I care not who sees it, — nor blush for it here!

Farewell to the deep-bosomed stream of the West!
I fling this loose blossom to float on its breast;
Nor let the dear love of its children grow cold,
Till the channel is dry where its waters have rolled!

THE NEW EDEN

MEETING OF THE BERKSHIRE HORTICULTURAL SOCIETY, AT STOCKBRIDGE, SEPTEMBER 16, 1854

[Mr. J. E. A. Smith, in his *The Poet among the Hills*, says that the theme of this poem was suggested by the severe drought in Berkshire County in the summer of 1854, and that after delivering the poem Dr. Holmes acceded to the request of a local editor who wished to print it, on condition that he should have as many proofs and make as many alterations as he chose, and in the end a hundred copies of the poem printed by itself. He had sixteen proofs and doubled the length of the poem; besides giving it a more serious tone.]

SCARCE could the parting ocean close,
  Seamed by the Mayflower's cleaving bow,
When o'er the rugged desert rose
  The waves that tracked the Pilgrim's plough.

Then sprang from many a rock-strewn field
  The rippling grass, the nodding grain,
Such growths as English meadows yield
  To scanty sun and frequent rain.

But when the fiery days were done,
  And Autumn brought his purple haze,
Then, kindling in the slanted sun,
  The hillsides gleamed with golden maize.

The food was scant, the fruits were few:
  A red-streak glistening here and there;
Perchance in statelier precincts grew
  Some stern old Puritanic pear.

Austere in taste, and tough at core,
  Its unrelenting bulk was shed,
To ripen in the Pilgrim's store
  When all the summer sweets were fled.

Such was his lot, to front the storm
  With iron heart and marble brow,
Nor ripen till his earthly form
  Was cast from life's autumnal bough.

But ever on the bleakest rock
  We bid the brightest beacon glow,
And still upon the thorniest stock
  The sweetest roses love to blow.

So on our rude and wintry soil
  We feed the kindling flame of art,
And steal the tropic's blushing spoil
  To bloom on Nature's ice-clad heart.

See how the softening Mother's breast
  Warms to her children's patient wiles, —
Her lips by loving Labor pressed
  Break in a thousand dimpling smiles,

From when the flushing bud of June
  Dawns with its first auroral hue,
Till shines the rounded harvest-moon,
  And velvet dahlias drink the dew.

Nor these the only gifts she brings;
  Look where the laboring orchard groans,
And yields its beryl-threaded strings
  For chestnut burs and hemlock cones.

Dear though the shadowy maple be,
  And dearer still the whispering pine,
Dearest yon russet-laden tree
  Browned by the heavy rubbing kine!

There childhood flung its rustling stone,
  There venturous boyhood learned to climb, —
How well the early graft was known
  Whose fruit was ripe ere harvest-time!

Nor be the Fleming's pride forgot,
  With swinging drops and drooping bells,
Freckled and splashed with streak and spot,
  On the warm-breasted, sloping swells;

Nor Persia's painted garden-queen, —
  Frail Houri of the trellised wall, —
Her deep-cleft bosom scarfed with green, —
  Fairest to see, and first to fall.

When man provoked his mortal doom,
  And Eden trembled as he fell,
When blossoms sighed their last perfume,
  And branches waved their long farewell,

One sucker crept beneath the gate,
  One seed was wafted o'er the wall,
One bough sustained his trembling weight;
  These left the garden, — these were all.

And far o'er many a distant zone
  These wrecks of Eden still are flung:
The fruits that Paradise hath known
  Are still in earthly gardens hung.

Yes, by our own unstoried stream
  The pink-white apple-blossoms burst
That saw the young Euphrates gleam, —
  That Gihon's circling waters nursed.

For us the ambrosial pear displays
  The wealth its arching branches hold,
Bathed by a hundred summery days
  In floods of mingling fire and gold.

And here, where beauty's cheek of flame
  With morning's earliest beam is fed,
The sunset-painted peach may claim
  To rival its celestial red.

What though in some unmoistened vale
  The summer leaf grow brown and sere,
Say, shall our star of promise fail
  That circles half the rolling sphere,

From beaches salt with bitter spray,
  O'er prairies green with softest rain,
And ridges bright with evening's ray,
  To rocks that shade the stormless main?

If by our slender-threaded streams
  The blade and leaf and blossom die,
If, drained by noontide's parching beams,
  The milky veins of Nature dry,

See, with her swelling bosom bare,
  Yon wild-eyed Sister in the West, —
The ring of Empire round her hair,
  The Indian's wampum on her breast!

We saw the August sun descend,
  Day after day, with blood-red stain,
And the blue mountains dimly blend
  With smoke-wreaths from the burning plain;

Beneath the hot Sirocco's wings
  We sat and told the withering hours,
Till Heaven unsealed its hoarded springs,
  And bade them leap in flashing showers.

Yet in our Ishmael's thirst we knew
  The mercy of the Sovereign hand
Would pour the fountain's quickening dew
  To feed some harvest of the land.

No flaming swords of wrath surround
  Our second Garden of the Blest;
It spreads beyond its rocky bound,
  It climbs Nevada's glittering crest.

God keep the tempter from its gate!
  God shield the children, lest they fall
From their stern fathers' free estate, —
  Till Ocean is its only wall!

SEMI-CENTENNIAL CELEBRATION OF THE NEW ENGLAND SOCIETY

NEW YORK, DECEMBER 22, 1855

NEW ENGLAND, we love thee; no time can erase
From the hearts of thy children the smile on thy face.
'T is the mother's fond look of affection and pride,
As she gives her fair son to the arms of his bride.

His bride may be fresher in beauty's young flower;
She may blaze in the jewels she brings with her dower.
But passion must chill in Time's pitiless blast;
The one that first loved us will love to the last.

You have left the dear land of the lake and the hill,
But its winds and its waters will talk with you still.
"Forget not," they whisper, "your love is our debt,"
And echo breathes softly, "We never forget."

The banquet's gay splendors are gleaming around,
But your hearts have flown back o'er the waves of the Sound;
They have found the brown home where their pulses were born;
They are throbbing their way through the trees and the corn.

There are roofs you remember, — their glory is fled;
There are mounds in the churchyard, — one sigh for the dead.
There are wrecks, there are ruins, all scattered around;
But Earth has no spot like that corner of ground.

Come, let us be cheerful, — remember last night,
How they cheered us, and — never mind — meant it all right;
To-night, we harm nothing, — we love in the lump;
Here's a bumper to Maine, in the juice of the pump!

Here's to all the good people, wherever they be,
Who have grown in the shade of the liberty-tree;
We all love its leaves, and its blossoms and fruit,
But pray have a care of the fence round its root.

We should like to talk big; it 's a kind of a right,
When the tongue has got loose and the waistband grown tight;
But, as pretty Miss Prudence remarked to her beau,
On its own heap of compost no biddy should crow.

Enough! There are gentlemen waiting to talk,
Whose words are to mine as the flower to the stalk.
Stand by your old mother whatever befall;
God bless all her children! Good night to you all!

FAREWELL

TO J. R. LOWELL

[On the occasion of Lowell's going abroad in the spring of 1855.]

FAREWELL, for the bark has her breast to the tide,
And the rough arms of Ocean are stretched for his bride;
The winds from the mountain stream over the bay;
One clasp of the hand, then away and away!

I see the tall mast as it rocks by the shore;
The sun is declining, I see it once more;
To-day like the blade in a thick-waving field,
To-morrow the spike on a Highlander's shield.

Alone, while the cloud pours its treacherous breath,
With the blue lips all round her whose kisses are death;
Ah, think not the breeze that is urging her sail
Has left her unaided to strive with the gale.

There are hopes that play round her, like fires on the mast,
That will light the dark hour till its danger has past;
There are prayers that will plead with the storm when it raves,
And whisper "Be still!" to the turbulent waves.

Nay, think not that Friendship has called us in vain
To join the fair ring ere we break it again;
There is strength in its circle, — you lose the bright star,
But its sisters still chain it, though shining afar.

I give you one health in the juice of the vine,
The blood of the vineyard shall mingle with mine;
Thus, thus let us drain the last dew-drops of gold,
As we empty our hearts of the blessings they hold.

FOR THE MEETING OF THE BURNS CLUB

1856

THE mountains glitter in the snow
  A thousand leagues asunder;
Yet here, amid the banquet's glow,
  I hear their voice of thunder;
Each giant's ice-bound goblet clinks;
  A flowing stream is summoned;
Wachusett to Ben Nevis drinks;
  Monadnock to Ben Lomond!

Though years have clipped the eagle's plume
  That crowned the chieftain's bonnet,
The sun still sees the heather bloom,
  The silver mists lie on it;
With tartan kilt and philibeg,
  What stride was ever bolder
Than his who showed the naked leg
  Beneath the plaided shoulder?

The echoes sleep on Cheviot's hills,
  That heard the bugles blowing
When down their sides the crimson rills
  With mingled blood were flowing;
The hunts where gallant hearts were game,
  The slashing on the border,
The raid that swooped with sword and flame,
  Give place to "law and order."

Not while the rocking steeples reel
  With midnight tocsins ringing,
Not while the crashing war-notes peal,
  God sets his poets singing;
The bird is silent in the night,
  Or shrieks a cry of warning
While fluttering round the beacon-light, —
  But hear him greet the morning!

The lark of Scotia's morning sky!
  Whose voice may sing his praises?
With Heaven's own sunlight in his eye,
  He walked among the daisies,
Till through the cloud of fortune's wrong
  He soared to fields of glory;

But left his land her sweetest song
  And earth her saddest story.

'T is not the forts the builder piles
  That chain the earth together;
The wedded crowns, the sister isles,
  Would laugh at such a tether;
The kindling thought, the throbbing words,
  That set the pulses beating,
Are stronger than the myriad swords
  Of mighty armies meeting.

Thus while within the banquet glows,
  Without, the wild winds whistle,
We drink a triple health, — the Rose,
  The Shamrock, and the Thistle!
Their blended hues shall never fade
  Till War has hushed his cannon, —
Close-twined as ocean-currents braid
  The Thames, the Clyde, the Shannon!

ODE FOR WASHINGTON'S BIRTHDAY

CELEBRATION OF THE MERCANTILE LIBRARY ASSOCIATION, FEBRUARY 24, 1856

WELCOME to the day returning,
  Dearer still as ages flow,
While the torch of Faith is burning,
  Long as Freedom's altars glow!
See the hero whom it gave us
  Slumbering on a mother's breast;
For the arm he stretched to save us,
  Be its morn forever blest!

Hear the tale of youthful glory,
  While of Britain's rescued band
Friend and foe repeat the story,
  Spread his fame o'er sea and land,
Where the red cross, proudly streaming,
  Flaps above the frigate's deck,
Where the golden lilies, gleaming,
  Star the watch-towers of Quebec.

Look! The shadow on the dial
  Marks the hour of deadlier strife;
Days of terror, years of trial,
  Scourge a nation into life.
Lo, the youth, become her leader!
  All her baffled tyrants yield;
Through his arm the Lord hath freed her;
  Crown him on the tented field!

Vain is Empire's mad temptation!
  Not for him an earthly crown!
He whose sword hath freed a nation
  Strikes the offered sceptre down.
See the throneless Conqueror seated,
  Ruler by a people's choice;
See the Patriot's task completed;
  Hear the Father's dying voice!

"By the name that you inherit,
  By the sufferings you recall,
Cherish the fraternal spirit;
  Love your country first of all!
Listen not to idle questions
  If its bands may be untied;
Doubt the patriot whose suggestions
  Strive a nation to divide!"

Father! We, whose ears have tingled
  With the discord-notes of shame, —
We, whose sires their blood have mingled
  In the battle's thunder-flame, —
Gathering, while this holy morning
  Lights the land from sea to sea,
Hear thy counsel, heed thy warning;
  Trust us, while we honor thee!

BIRTHDAY OF DANIEL WEBSTER

JANUARY 18, 1856

WHEN life hath run its largest round
  Of toil and triumph, joy and woe,
How brief a storied page is found
  To compass all its outward show!

The world-tried sailor tires and droops;
  His flag is rent, his keel forgot;
His farthest voyages seem but loops
  That float from life's entangled knot.

But when within the narrow space
  Some larger soul hath lived and wrought,
Whose sight was open to embrace
  The boundless realms of deed and thought, —

When, stricken by the freezing blast,
  A nation's living pillars fall,
How rich the storied page, how vast,
  A word, a whisper, can recall!

No medal lifts its fretted face,
  Nor speaking marble cheats your eye,

Yet, while these pictured lines I trace,
A living image passes by:

A roof beneath the mountain pines;
The cloisters of a hill-girt plain;
The front of life's embattled lines;
A mound beside the heaving main.

These are the scenes: a boy appears;
Set life's round dial in the sun,
Count the swift arc of seventy years,
His frame is dust; his task is done.

Yet pause upon the noontide hour,
Ere the declining sun has laid
His bleaching rays on manhood's power,
And look upon the mighty shade.

No gloom that stately shape can hide,
No change uncrown its brow; behold!
Dark, calm, large-fronted, lightning-eyed,
Earth has no double from its mould!

Ere from the fields by valor won
The battle-smoke had rolled away,
And bared the blood-red setting sun,
His eyes were opened on the day.

His land was but a shelving strip
Black with the strife that made it free;
He lived to see its banners dip
Their fringes in the Western sea.

The boundless prairies learned his name,
His words the mountain echoes knew.
The Northern breezes swept his fame
From icy lake to warm bayou.

In toil he lived; in peace he died;
When life's full cycle was complete,
Put off his robes of power and pride,
And laid them at his Master's feet.

His rest is by the storm-swept waves
Whom life's wild tempests roughly tried,
Whose heart was like the streaming caves
Of ocean, throbbing at his side.

Death's cold white hand is like the snow
Laid softly on the furrowed hill,
It hides the broken seams below,
And leaves the summit brighter still.

In vain the envious tongue upbraids;
His name a nation's heart shall keep

Till morning's latest sunlight fades
On the blue tablet of the deep!

THE VOICELESS

["Read what the singing-women — one to ten thousand of the suffering women — tell us, and think of the griefs that die unspoken! Nature is in earnest when she makes a woman; and there are women enough lying in the next churchyard with very commonplace blue slate stones at their head and feet, for whom it was just as true that 'all sounds of life assumed one tone of love,' as for Letitia Landon, of whom Elizabeth Browning said it; but she could give words to her grief, and they could not. — Will you hear a few stanzas of mine?" *The Autocrat of the Breakfast Table*, p. 306.]

WE count the broken lyres that rest
    Where the sweet wailing singers slumber,
But o'er their silent sister's breast
    The wild-flowers who will stoop to number?
A few can touch the magic string,
    And noisy Fame is proud to win them: —
Alas for those that never sing,
    But die with all their music in them!

Nay, grieve not for the dead alone
    Whose song has told their hearts' sad story, —
Weep for the voiceless, who have known
    The cross without the crown of glory!
Not where Leucadian breezes sweep
    O'er Sappho's memory-haunted billow,
But where the glistening night-dews weep
    On nameless sorrow's churchyard pillow.

O hearts that break and give no sign
    Save whitening lip and fading tresses,
Till Death pours out his longed-for wine
    Slow-dropped from Misery's crushing presses, —
If singing breath or echoing chord
    To every hidden pang were given,
What endless melodies were poured,
    As sad as earth, as sweet as heaven!

THE TWO STREAMS

[In his paper, *My Hunt after the Captain*, Dr. Holmes has a paragraph upon an alleged plagiarism in this poem. It will be found in the Notes at the end of this volume.]

BEHOLD the rocky wall
  That down its sloping sides
Pours the swift rain-drops, blending, as they fall,
  In rushing river-tides!

Yon stream, whose sources run
  Turned by a pebble's edge,
Is Athabasca, rolling toward the sun
  Through the cleft mountain-ledge.

The slender rill had strayed,
  But for the slanting stone,
To evening's ocean, with the tangled braid
  Of foam-flecked Oregon.

So from the heights of Will
  Life's parting stream descends,
And, as a moment turns its slender rill,
  Each widening torrent bends, —

From the same cradle's side,
  From the same mother's knee, —
One to long darkness and the frozen tide,
  One to the Peaceful Sea!

THE PROMISE

NOT charity we ask,
  Nor yet thy gift refuse;
Please thy light fancy with the easy task
  Only to look and choose.

The little-heeded toy
  That wins thy treasured gold
May be the dearest memory, holiest joy,
  Of coming years untold.

Heaven rains on every heart,
  But there its showers divide,
The drops of mercy choosing, as they part,
  The dark or glowing side.

One kindly deed may turn
  The fountain of thy soul
To love's sweet day-star, that shall o'er thee burn
  Long as its currents roll!

The pleasures thou hast planned, —
  Where shall their memory be
When the white angel with the freezing hand
  Shall sit and watch by thee?

Living, thou dost not live,
  If mercy's spring run dry;
What Heaven has lent thee wilt thou freely give,
  Dying, thou shalt not die!

HE promised even so!
  To thee his lips repeat, —
Behold, the tears that soothed thy sister's woe
  Have washed thy Master's feet.

AVIS

This is a true story. Avis, Avise, or Avice (they pronounce it *Avvis*) is a real breathing person. Her home is not more than an hour and a half's space from the palaces of the great ladies who might like to look at her. They may see her and the little black girl she gave herself to, body and soul, when nobody else could bear the sight of her infirmity, — leaving home at noon, or even after breakfast, and coming back in season to undress for the evening's party.

I MAY not rightly call thy name, —
  Alas! thy forehead never knew
The kiss that happier children claim,
  Nor glistened with baptismal dew.

Daughter of want and wrong and woe,
  I saw thee with thy sister-band,
Snatched from the whirlpool's narrowing flow
  By Mercy's strong yet trembling hand.

"Avis!" — With Saxon eye and cheek,
  At once a woman and a child,
The saint uncrowned I came to seek
  Drew near to greet us, — spoke, and smiled.

God gave that sweet sad smile she wore
  All wrong to shame, all souls to win, —
A heavenly sunbeam sent before
  Her footsteps through a world of sin.

"And who is Avis?" — Hear the tale
  The calm-voiced matrons gravely tell, —
The story known through all the vale
  Where Avis and her sisters dwell.

With the lost children running wild,
　Strayed from the hand of human care,
They find one little refuse child
　Left helpless in its poisoned lair.

The primal mark is on her face, —
　The chattel-stamp, — the pariah-stain
That follows still her hunted race, —
　The curse without the crime of Cain.

How shall our smooth-turned phrase relate
　The little suffering outcast's ail?
Not Lazarus at the rich man's gate
　So turned the rose-wreathed revellers
　　pale.

Ah, veil the living death from sight
　That wounds our beauty-loving eye!
The children turn in selfish fright,
　The white-lipped nurses hurry by.

Take her, dread Angel! Break in love
　This bruisèd reed and make it thine! —
No voice descended from above,
　But Avis answered, "She is mine."

The task that dainty menials spurn
　The fair young girl has made her own;
Her heart shall teach, her hand shall learn
　The toils, the duties yet unknown.

So Love and Death in lingering strife
　Stand face to face from day to day,
Still battling for the spoil of Life
　While the slow seasons creep away.

Love conquers Death; the prize is won;
　See to her joyous bosom pressed
The dusky daughter of the sun, —
　The bronze against the marble breast!

Her task is done; no voice divine
　Has crowned her deeds with saintly fame.
No eye can see the aureole shine
　That rings her brow with heavenly flame.

Yet what has holy page more sweet,
　Or what had woman's love more fair,
When Mary clasped her Saviour's feet
　With flowing eyes and streaming hair?

Meek child of sorrow, walk unknown,
　The Angel of that earthly throng,
And let thine image live alone
　To hallow this unstudied song!

THE LIVING TEMPLE

[The Professor, who is credited with this verse, was supposed to call it *The Anatomist's Hymn.*]

NOT in the world of light alone,
Where God has built his blazing throne,
Nor yet alone in earth below,
With belted seas that come and go,
And endless isles of sunlit green,
Is all thy Maker's glory seen:
Look in upon thy wondrous frame, —
Eternal wisdom still the same!

The smooth, soft air with pulse-like waves
Flows murmuring through its hidden caves,
Whose streams of brightening purple rush,
Fired with a new and livelier blush,
While all their burden of decay
The ebbing current steals away,
And red with Nature's flame they start
From the warm fountains of the heart.

No rest that throbbing slave may ask,
Forever quivering o'er his task,
While far and wide a crimson jet
Leaps forth to fill the woven net
Which in unnumbered crossing tides
The flood of burning life divides,
Then, kindling each decaying part,
Creeps back to find the throbbing heart.

But warmed with that unchanging flame
Behold the outward moving frame,
Its living marbles jointed strong
With glistening band and silvery thong,
And linked to reason's guiding reins
By myriad rings in trembling chains,
Each graven with the threaded zone
Which claims it as the master's own.

See how yon beam of seeming white
Is braided out of seven-hued light,
Yet in those lucid globes no ray
By any chance shall break astray.
Hark how the rolling surge of sound,
Arches and spirals circling round,
Wakes the hushed spirit through thine ear
With music it is heaven to hear.

Then mark the cloven sphere that holds
All thought in its mysterious folds;
That feels sensation's faintest thrill,
And flashes forth the sovereign will;
Think on the stormy world that dwells

Locked in its dim and clustering cells !
The lightning gleams of power it sheds
Along its hollow glassy threads !

O Father ! grant thy love divine
To make these mystic temples thine !
When wasting age and wearying strife
Have sapped the leaning walls of life,
When darkness gathers over all,
And the last tottering pillars fall,
Take the poor dust thy mercy warms,
And mould it into heavenly forms !

AT A BIRTHDAY FESTIVAL

TO J. R. LOWELL

FEBRUARY 22, 1859

WE will not speak of years to-night, —
For what have years to bring
But larger floods of love and light,
And sweeter songs to sing ?

We will not drown in wordy praise
The kindly thoughts that rise;
If Friendship own one tender phrase,
He reads it in our eyes.

We need not waste our school-boy art
To gild this notch of Time; —
Forgive me if my wayward heart
Has throbbed in artless rhyme.

Enough for him the silent grasp
That knits us hand in hand,
And he the bracelet's radiant clasp
That locks our circling band.

Strength to his hours of manly toil !
Peace to his starlit dreams !
Who loves alike the furrowed soil,
The music-haunted streams !

Sweet smiles to keep forever bright
The sunshine on his lips,
And faith that sees the ring of light
Round nature's last eclipse !

A BIRTHDAY TRIBUTE

TO J. F. CLARKE. APRIL 4, 1860

WHO is the shepherd sent to lead,
Through pastures green, the Master's sheep ?
What guileless " Israelite indeed "
The folded flock may watch and keep ?

He who with manliest spirit joins
The heart of gentlest human mould,
With burning light and girded loins,
To guide the flock, or watch the fold;

True to all Truth the world denies,
Not tongue-tied for its gilded sin;
Not always right in all men's eyes,
But faithful to the light within;

Who asks no meed of earthly fame,
Who knows no earthly master's call,
Who hopes for man, through guilt and shame,
Still answering, " God is over all; "

Who makes another's grief his own,
Whose smile lends joy a double cheer;
Where lives the saint, if such be known ?—
Speak softly, — such an one is here !

O faithful shepherd ! thou hast borne
The heat and burden of the day;
Yet, o'er thee, bright with beams unshorn,
The sun still shows thine onward way.

To thee our fragrant love we bring,
In buds that April half displays,
Sweet first-born angels of the spring,
Caught in their opening hymn of praise.

What though our faltering accents fail,
Our captives know their message well,
Our words unbreathed their lips exhale,
And sigh more love than ours can tell.

THE GRAY CHIEF

FOR THE MEETING OF THE MASSACHUSETTS MEDICAL SOCIETY, 1859

[In honor of Dr. Jacob Bigelow.]

'T IS sweet to fight our battles o'er,
And crown with honest praise
The gray old chief, who strikes no more
The blow of better days.

Before the true and trusted sage
With willing hearts we bend,

When years have touched with hallowing age
Our Master, Guide, and Friend.

For all his manhood's labor past,
For love and faith long tried,
His age is honored to the last,
Though strength and will have died.

But when, untamed by toil and strife,
Full in our front he stands,
The torch of light, the shield of life,
Still lifted in his hands,

No temple, though its walls resound
With bursts of ringing cheers,
Can hold the honors that surround
His manhood's twice-told years!

THE LAST LOOK

W. W. SWAIN

[Written at Naushon, September 22, 1858. W. W. Swain was an only son of Governor Swain, mentioned before, p. 89, and lies by the side of his father and mother in the island grave.]

BEHOLD — not him we knew!
This was the prison which his soul looked through,
Tender, and brave, and true.

His voice no more is heard;
And his dead name — that dear familiar word —
Lies on our lips unstirred.

He spake with poet's tongue;
Living, for him the minstrel's lyre was strung:
He shall not die unsung!

Grief tried his love, and pain;
And the long bondage of his martyr-chain
Vexed his sweet soul, — in vain!

It felt life's surges break,
As, girt with stormy seas, his island lake,
Smiling while tempests wake.

How can we sorrow more?
Grieve not for him whose heart had gone before
To that untrodden shore!

Lo, through its leafy screen,
A gleam of sunlight on a ring of green,
Untrodden, half unseen!

Here let his body rest,
Where the calm shadows that his soul loved best
May slide above his breast.

Smooth his uncurtained bed;
And if some natural tears are softly shed,
It is not for the dead.

Fold the green turf aright
For the long hours before the morning's light,
And say the last Good Night!

And plant a clear white stone
Close by those mounds which hold his loved, his own, —
Lonely, but not alone.

Here let him sleeping lie,
Till Heaven's bright watchers slumber in the sky
And Death himself shall die!

IN MEMORY OF CHARLES WENTWORTH UPHAM, JR.

APRIL 15, 1860

HE was all sunshine; in his face
The very soul of sweetness shone;
Fairest and gentlest of his race;
None like him we can call our own.

Something there was of one that died
In her fresh spring-time long ago,
Our first dear Mary, angel-eyed,
Whose smile it was a bliss to know.

Something of her whose love imparts
Such radiance to her day's decline,
We feel its twilight in our hearts
Bright as the earliest morning-shine.

Yet richer strains our eye could trace
That made our plainer mould more fair,
That curved the lip with happier grace,
That waved the soft and silken hair.

Dust unto dust! the lips are still
  That only spoke to cheer and bless;
The folded hands lie white and chill
  Unclasped from sorrow's last caress.

Leave him in peace; he will not heed
  These idle tears we vainly pour,
Give back to earth the fading weed
  Of mortal shape his spirit wore.

"Shall I not weep my heartstrings torn,
  My flower of love that falls half blown,
My youth uncrowned, my life forlorn,
  A thorny path to walk alone?"

O Mary! one who bore thy name,
  Whose Friend and Master was divine,
Sat waiting silent till He came,
  Bowed down in speechless grief like thine.

"Where have ye laid him?" "Come," they say,
  Pointing to where the loved one slept;
Weeping, the sister led the way, —
  And, seeing Mary, "Jesus wept."

He weeps with thee, with all that mourn,
  And He shall wipe thy streaming eyes
Who knew all sorrows, woman-born, —
  Trust in his word; thy dead shall rise!

MARTHA

DIED JANUARY 7, 1861

[Written on the death of an old family servant.]

Sexton! Martha's dead and gone;
  Toll the bell! toll the bell!
Her weary hands their labor cease;
Good night, poor Martha, — sleep in peace!
  Toll the bell!

Sexton! Martha's dead and gone;
  Toll the bell! toll the bell!
For many a year has Martha said,
"I'm old and poor, — would I were dead!"
  Toll the bell!

Sexton! Martha's dead and gone;
  Toll the bell! toll the bell!
She'll bring no more, by day or night,
Her basket full of linen white.
  Toll the bell!

Sexton! Martha's dead and gone;
  Toll the bell! toll the bell!
'T is fitting she should lie below
A pure white sheet of drifted snow.
  Toll the bell!

Sexton! Martha's dead and gone;
  Toll the bell! toll the bell!
Sleep, Martha, sleep, to wake in light,
Where all the robes are stainless white.
  Toll the bell!

MEETING OF THE ALUMNI OF HARVARD COLLEGE

1857

I THANK you, MR. PRESIDENT, you're kindly broke the ice;
Virtue should always be the first, — I'm only SECOND VICE —
(A vice is something with a screw that's made to hold its jaw
Till some old file has played away upon an ancient saw).

Sweet brothers by the Mother's side, the babes of days gone by,
All nurslings of her Juno breasts whose milk is never dry,
We come again, like half-grown boys, and gather at her beck
About her knees, and on her lap, and clinging round her neck.

We find her at her stately door, and in her ancient chair,
Dressed in the robes of red and green she always loved to wear.
Her eye has all its radiant youth, her cheek its morning flame;
We drop our roses as we go, hers flourish still the same.

We have been playing many an hour, and far away we've strayed,
Some laughing in the cheerful sun, some lingering in the shade;

And some have tired, and laid them down
  where darker shadows fall, —
Dear as her loving voice may be, they cannot hear its call.

What miles we've travelled since we shook
  the dew-drops from our shoes
We gathered on this classic green, so famed
  for heavy dues!
How many boys have joined the game, how
  many slipped away,
Since we've been running up and down,
  and having out our play!

One boy at work with book and brief, and
  one with gown and band,
One sailing vessels on the pool, one digging
  in the sand,
One flying paper kites on change, one planting little pills, —
The seeds of certain annual flowers well
  known as little bills.

What maidens met us on our way, and
  clasped us hand in hand!
What cherubs, — not the legless kind, that
  fly, but never stand!
How many a youthful head we've seen put
  on its silver crown!
What sudden changes back again to youth's
  empurpled brown!

But fairer sights have met our eyes, and
  broader lights have shone,
Since others lit their midnight lamps where
  once we trimmed our own
A thousand trains that flap the sky with
  flags of rushing fire,
And, throbbing in the Thunderer's hand,
  Thought's million-chorded lyre.

We've seen the sparks of Empire fly beyond the mountain bars,
Till, glittering o'er the Western wave, they
  joined the setting stars;
And ocean trodden into paths that trampling giants ford,
To find the planet's vertebræ and sink its
  spinal cord.

We've tried reform, — and chloroform, —
  and both have turned our brain;
When France called up the photograph, we
  roused the foe to pain;
Just so those earlier sages shared the chaplet of renown, —
Hers sent a bladder to the clouds, ours
  brought their lightning down.

We've seen the little tricks of life, its varnish and veneer,
Its stucco-fronts of character flake off and
  disappear,
We've learned that oft the brownest hands
  will heap the biggest pile,
And met with many a "perfect brick" beneath a rimless "tile."

What dreams we've had of deathless name,
  as scholars, statesmen, bards,
While Fame, the lady with the trump, held
  up her picture cards!
Till, having nearly played our game, she
  gayly whispered, "Ah!
I said you should be something grand, —
  you'll soon be grandpapa."

Well, well, the old have had their day, the
  young must take their turn;
There's something always to forget, and
  something still to learn;
But how to tell what's old or young, the
  tap-root from the sprigs,
Since Florida revealed her fount to Ponce
  de Leon Twiggs?

The wisest was a Freshman once, just
  freed from bar and bolt,
As noisy as a kettle-drum, as leggy as a
  colt;
Don't be too savage with the boys, — the
  Primer does not say
The kitten ought to go to church because
  the cat doth prey.

The law of merit and of age is not the rule
  of three;
Non constat that A. M. must prove as busy
  as A. B.
When Wise the father tracked the son,
  ballooning through the skies,
He taught a lesson to the old, — go thou
  and do like Wise!

Now then, old boys, and reverend youth, of
  high or low degree,
Remember how we only get one annual out
  of three,

And such as dare to simmer down three dinners into one
Must cut their salads mighty short, and pepper well with fun.

I've passed my zenith long ago, it's time for me to set;
A dozen planets wait to shine, and I am lingering yet,
As sometimes in the blaze of day a milk-and-watery moon
Stains with its dim and fading ray the lustrous blue of noon.

Farewell! yet let one echo rise to shake our ancient hall;
God save the Queen, — whose throne is here, — the Mother of us all!
Till dawns the great commencement-day on every shore and sea,
And "Expectantur" all mankind, to take their last Degree!

THE PARTING SONG

FESTIVAL OF THE ALUMNI, 1857

THE noon of summer sheds its ray
  On Harvard's holy ground;
The Matron calls, the sons obey,
  And gather smiling round.

CHORUS

Then old and young together stand,
  The sunshine and the snow,
As heart to heart, and hand in hand,
  We sing before we go!

Her hundred opening doors have swung;
  Through every storied hall
The pealing echoes loud have rung,
  "Thrice welcome one and all!"
    Then old and young, etc.

We floated through her peaceful bay,
  To sail life's stormy seas;
But left our anchor where it lay
  Beneath her green old trees.
    Then old and young, etc.

As now we lift its lengthening chain,
  That held us fast of old,
The rusted rings grow bright again, —
  Their iron turns to gold.
    Then old and young, etc.

Though scattered ere the setting sun,
  As leaves when wild winds blow,
Our home is here, our hearts are one,
  Till Charles forgets to flow.
    Then old and young, etc.

FOR THE MEETING OF THE NATIONAL SANITARY ASSOCIATION

1860

WHAT makes the Healing Art divine?
  The bitter drug we buy and sell,
The brands that scorch, the blades that shine,
  The scars we leave, the "cures" we tell?

Are these thy glories, holiest Art, —
  The trophies that adorn thee best, —
Or but thy triumph's meanest part, —
  Where mortal weakness stands confessed?

We take the arms that Heaven supplies
  For Life's long battle with Disease,
Taught by our various need to prize
  Our frailest weapons, even these.

But ah! when Science drops her shield —
  Its peaceful shelter proved in vain —
And bares her snow-white arm to wield
  The sad, stern ministry of pain;

When shuddering o'er the fount of life,
  She folds her heaven-anointed wings,
To lift unmoved the glittering knife
  That searches all its crimson springs;

When, faithful to her ancient lore,
  She thrusts aside her fragrant balm
For blistering juice, or cankering ore,
  And tames them till they cure or calm;

When in her gracious hand are seen
  The dregs and scum of earth and seas,
Her kindness counting all things clean
  That lend the sighing sufferer ease;

Though on the field that Death has won,
  She save some stragglers in retreat;—
These single acts of mercy done
  Are but confessions of defeat.

What though our tempered poisons save
  Some wrecks of life from aches and ails;
Those grand specifics Nature gave
  Were never poised by weights or scales!

God lent his creatures light and air,
  And waters open to the skies;
Man locks him in a stifling lair,
  And wonders why his brother dies!

In vain our pitying tears are shed,
  In vain we rear the sheltering pile
Where Art weeds out from bed to bed
  The plagues we planted by the mile!

Be that the glory of the past;
  With these our sacred toils begin:
So flies in tatters from its mast
  The yellow flag of sloth and sin,

And lo! the starry folds reveal
  The blazoned truth we hold so dear:
To guard is better than to heal,—
  The shield is nobler than the spear!

FOR THE BURNS CENTENNIAL CELEBRATION

JANUARY 25, 1859

[In a passage at the close of *Mechanism in Thought and Morals*, Dr. Holmes applies the ninth, tenth and twelfth stanzas of this poem to Dickens.]

HIS birthday.— Nay, we need not speak
  The name each heart is beating,—
Each glistening eye and flushing cheek
  In light and flame repeating!

We come in one tumultuous tide,—
  One surge of wild emotion,—
As crowding through the Frith of Clyde
  Rolls in the Western Ocean;

As when yon cloudless, quartered moon
  Hangs o'er each storied river,
The swelling breasts of Ayr and Doon
  With sea-green wavelets quiver.

The century shrivels like a scroll,—
  The past becomes the present,—
And face to face, and soul to soul,
  We greet the monarch-peasant.

While Shenstone strained in feeble flights
  With Corydon and Phillis,—
While Wolfe was climbing Abraham's heights
  To snatch the Bourbon lilies,—

Who heard the wailing infant's cry,
  The babe beneath the sheeling,
Whose song to-night in every sky
  Will shake earth's starry ceiling,—

Whose passion-breathing voice ascends
  And floats like incense o'er us,
Whose ringing lay of friendship blends
  With labor's anvil chorus?

We love him, not for sweetest song,
  Though never tone so tender;
We love him, even in his wrong,—
  His wasteful self-surrender.

We praise him, not for gifts divine,—
  His Muse was born of woman,—
His manhood breathes in every line,—
  Was ever heart more human?

We love him, praise him, just for this:
  In every form and feature,
Through wealth and want, through woe and bliss,
  He saw his fellow-creature!

No soul could sink beneath his love,—
  Not even angel blasted;
No mortal power could soar above
  The pride that all outlasted!

Ay! Heaven had set one living man
  Beyond the pedant's tether,—
His virtues, frailties, HE may scan,
  Who weighs them all together!

I fling my pebble on the cairn
  Of him, though dead, undying;
Sweet Nature's nursling, bonniest bairn
  Beneath her daisies lying.

The waning suns, the wasting globe,
  Shall spare the minstrel's story,—
The centuries weave his purple robe,
  The mountain-mist of glory!

AT A MEETING OF FRIENDS

AUGUST 29, 1859

[The occasion was the fiftieth birthday of Dr. Holmes.]

I REMEMBER — why, yes! God bless me!
    and was it so long ago?
I fear I 'm growing forgetful, as old folks
    do, you know;
It must have been in 'forty — I would say
    'thirty-nine —
We talked this matter over, I and a friend
    of mine.

He said, "Well now, old fellow, I 'm
    thinking that you and I,
If we act like other people, shall be older
    by and by;
What though the bright blue ocean is
    smooth as a pond can be,
There is always a line of breakers to fringe
    the broadest sea.

"We 're taking it mighty easy, but that is
    nothing strange,
For up to the age of thirty we spend our
    years like change;
But creeping up towards the forties, as
    fast as the old years fill,
And Time steps in for payment, we seem
    to change a bill."

"I know it," I said, "old fellow; you
    speak the solemn truth;
A man can't live to a hundred and likewise
    keep his youth;
But what if the ten years coming shall
    silver-streak my hair,
You know I shall then be forty; of course
    I shall not care.

"At forty a man grows heavy and tired of
    fun and noise;
Leaves dress to the five-and-twenties and
    love to the silly boys;
No foppish tricks at forty, no pinching of
    waists and toes,
But high-low shoes and flannels and good
    thick worsted hose."

But one fine August morning I found my-
    self awake:
My birthday: — By Jove, I 'm forty! Yes,
    forty and no mistake!
Why, this is the very milestone, I think I
    used to hold,
That when a fellow had come to, a fellow
    would then be old!

But that is the young folks' nonsense;
    they 're full of their foolish stuff;
A man 's in his prime at forty, — I see *that*
    plain enough;
At *fifty* a man *is* wrinkled, and *may be* bald
    or gray;
I call men old at fifty, in spite of all they
    say.

At last comes another August with mist
    and rain and shine;
Its mornings are slowly counted and creep
    to twenty-nine,
And when on the western summits the fad-
    ing light appears,
It touches with rosy fingers the last of my
    fifty years.

There have been both men and women
    whose hearts were firm and bold,
But there never was one of fifty that loved
    to say "I 'm old;"
So any elderly person that strives to shirk
    his years,
Make him stand up at a table and try him
    by his peers.

Now here I stand at fifty, my jury gathered
    round;
Sprinkled with dust of silver, but not yet
    silver-crowned,
Ready to meet your verdict, waiting to
    hear it told;
Guilty of fifty summers; speak! Is the
    verdict *old?*

No! say that his hearing fails him; say
    that his sight grows dim;
Say that he 's getting wrinkled and weak in
    back and limb,
Losing his wits and temper, but pleading,
    to make amends,
The youth of his fifty summers he finds in
    his twenty friends.

BOSTON COMMON; THREE PICTURES

FOR THE FAIR IN AID OF THE FUND TO PROCURE BALL'S STATUE OF WASHINGTON

NOVEMBER 14, 1859

1630

ALL overgrown with bush and fern,
  And straggling clumps of tangled trees,
With trunks that lean and boughs that turn,
  Bent eastward by the mastering breeze, —
With spongy bogs that drip and fill
  A yellow pond with muddy rain,
Beneath the shaggy southern hill
  Lies wet and low the Shawmut plain.
And hark ! the trodden branches crack;
  A crow flaps off with startled scream;
A straying woodchuck canters back;
  A bittern rises from the stream;
Leaps from his lair a frightened deer;
  An otter plunges in the pool; —
Here comes old Shawmut's pioneer,
  The parson on his brindled bull !

1774

The streets are thronged with trampling feet,
  The northern hill is ridged with graves,
But night and morn the drum is beat
  To frighten down the " rebel knaves."
The stones of King Street still are red,
  And yet the bloody red-coats come:
I hear their pacing sentry's tread,
  The click of steel, the tap of drum,
And over all the open green,
  Where grazed of late the harmless kine,
The cannon's deepening ruts are seen,
  The war-horse stamps, the bayonets shine.
The clouds are dark with crimson rain
  Above the murderous hirelings' den,
And soon their whistling showers shall stain
  The pipe-clayed belts of Gage's men.

186–

Around the green, in morning light,
  The spired and palaced summits blaze,
And, sunlike, from her Beacon-height
  The dome-crowned city spreads her rays;
They span the waves, they belt the plains,
  They skirt the roads with bands of white,
Till with a flash of gilded panes
  Yon farthest hillside bounds the sight.
Peace, Freedom, Wealth ! no fairer view,
  Though with the wild-bird's restless wings
We sailed beneath the noontide's blue
  Or chased the moonlight's endless rings !
Here, fitly raised by grateful hands
  His holiest memory to recall,
The Hero's, Patriot's image stands;
  He led our sires who won them all !

THE OLD MAN OF THE SEA

A NIGHTMARE DREAM BY DAYLIGHT

Do you know the Old Man of the Sea, of the Sea ?
Have you met with that dreadful old man ?
If you have n't been caught, you will be, you will be;
For catch you he must and he can.

He does n't hold on by your throat, by your throat,
  As of old in the terrible tale;
But he grapples you tight by the coat, by the coat,
  Till its buttons and button-holes fail.

There 's the charm of a snake in his eye, in his eye,
  And a polypus-grip in his hands;
You cannot go back, nor get by, nor get by,
  If you look at the spot where he stands.

Oh, you 're grabbed ! See his claw on your sleeve, on your sleeve !
  It is Sindbad's Old Man of the Sea !
You 're a Christian, no doubt you believe, you believe :
  You 're a martyr, whatever you be !

Is the breakfast-hour past ? They must wait, they must wait,
  While the coffee boils sullenly down,
While the Johnny-cake burns on the grate, on the grate,
  And the toast is done frightfully brown

Yes, your dinner will keep; let it cool, let
    it cool,
And Madam may worry and fret,
And children half-starved go to school, go
    to school;
He can't think of sparing you yet.

Hark! the bell for the train! "Come
    along! Come along!
For there is n't a second to lose."
"ALL ABOARD!" (He holds on.) " Fsht!
    ding-dong! Fsht! ding-dong!" —
You can follow on foot, if you choose.

There 's a maid with a cheek like a peach,
    like a peach,
That is waiting for you in the church; —
But he clings to your side like a leech, like
    a leech,
And you leave your lost bride in the
    lurch.

There 's a babe in a fit, — hurry quick!
    hurry quick!
To the doctor's as fast as you can!
The baby is off, while you stick, while you
    stick,
In the grip of the dreadful Old Man!

I have looked on the face of the Bore, of
    the Bore;
The voice of the Simple I know;
I have welcomed the Flat at my door, at
    my door;
I have sat by the side of the Slow;

I have walked like a lamb by the friend, by
    the friend,
That stuck to my skirts like a bur;
I have borne the stale talk without end,
    without end,
Of the sitter whom nothing could stir:

But my hamstrings grow loose, and I shake,
    and I shake,
At the sight of the dreadful Old Man;
Yes, I quiver and quake, and I take, and I
    take,
To my legs with what vigor I can!

Oh the dreadful Old Man of the Sea, of the
    Sea!
He 's come back like the Wandering
    Jew!

He has had his cold claw upon me, upon
    me, —
And be sure that he 'll have it on you!

INTERNATIONAL ODE

OUR FATHERS' LAND

This ode was sung in unison by twelve hundred children of the public schools to the air of "God save the Queen" at the visit of the Prince of Wales to Boston, October 18, 1860.

GOD bless our Fathers' Land!
  Keep her in heart and hand
    One with our own!
From all her foes defend,
Be her brave People's Friend,
On all her realms descend,
    Protect her Throne!

Father, with loving care
Guard Thou her kingdom's Heir,
    Guide all his ways:
Thine arm his shelter be,
From him by land and sea
Bid storm and danger flee,
    Prolong his days!

Lord, let War's tempest cease,
Fold the whole Earth in peace
    Under thy wings!
Make all thy nations one,
All hearts beneath the sun,
Till Thou shalt reign alone,
    Great King of kings!

VIVE LA FRANCE

A SENTIMENT OFFERED AT THE DINNER TO H. I. H. THE PRINCE NAPOLEON, AT THE REVERE HOUSE, SEPTEMBER 25, 1861

THE land of sunshine and of song!
  Her name your hearts divine;
To her the banquet's vows belong
  Whose breasts have poured its wine;
Our trusty friend, our true ally
  Through varied change and chance:
So, fill your flashing goblets high, —
  I give you, VIVE LA FRANCE!

Above our hosts in triple folds
  The selfsame colors spread,
Where Valor's faithful arm upholds
  The blue, the white, the red;
Alike each nation's glittering crest
  Reflects the morning's glance, —
Twin eagles, soaring east and west:
  Once more, then, VIVE LA FRANCE!

Sister in trial! who shall count
  Thy generous friendship's claim,
Whose blood ran mingling in the fount
  That gave our land its name,
Till Yorktown saw in blended line
  Our conquering arms advance,
And victory's double garlands twine
  Our banners? VIVE LA FRANCE!

O land of heroes! in our need
  One gift from Heaven we crave
To stanch these wounds that vainly bleed, —
  The wise to lead the brave!
Call back one Captain of thy past
  From glory's marble trance,
Whose name shall be a bugle-blast
  To rouse us! VIVE LA FRANCE!

Pluck Condé's baton from the trench,
  Wake up stout Charles Martel,
Or find some woman's hand to clench
  The sword of La Pucelle!
Give us one hour of old Turenne, —
  One lift of Bayard's lance, —
Nay, call Marengo's Chief again
  To lead us! VIVE LA FRANCE!

Ah, hush! our welcome Guest shall hear
  But sounds of peace and joy;
No angry echo vex thine ear,
  Fair Daughter of Savoy!
Once more! the land of arms and arts,
  Of glory, grace, romance;
Her love lies warm in all our hearts:
  God bless her! VIVE LA FRANCE!

BROTHER JONATHAN'S LAMENT FOR SISTER CAROLINE

MARCH 25, 1861

SHE has gone, — she has left us in passion and pride, —
Our stormy-browed sister, so long at our side!
She has torn her own star from our firmament's glow,
And turned on her brother the face of a foe!

Oh, Caroline, Caroline, child of the sun,
We can never forget that our hearts have been one, —
Our foreheads both sprinkled in Liberty's name,
From the fountain of blood with the finger of flame!

You were always too ready to fire at a touch;
But we said, "She is hasty, — she does not mean much."
We have scowled, when you uttered some turbulent threat;
But Friendship still whispered, "Forgive and forget!"

Has our love all died out? Have its altars grown cold?
Has the curse come at last which the fathers foretold?
Then Nature must teach us the strength of the chain
That her petulant children would sever in vain.

They may fight till the buzzards are gorged with their spoil,
Till the harvest grows black as it rots in the soil,
Till the wolves and the catamounts troop from their caves,
And the shark tracks the pirate, the lord of the waves:

In vain is the strife! When its fury is past,
Their fortunes must flow in one channel at last,
As the torrents that rush from the mountains of snow
Roll mingled in peace through the valleys below.

Our Union is river, lake, ocean, and sky:
Man breaks not the medal, when God cuts the die!
Though darkened with sulphur, though cloven with steel,
The blue arch will brighten, the waters will heal!

Oh, Caroline, Caroline, child of the sun,
There are battles with Fate that can never be won !
The star-flowering banner must never be furled,
For its blossoms of light are the hope of the world !

Go, then, our rash sister ! afar and aloof,
Run wild in the sunshine away from our roof;
But when your heart aches and your feet have grown sore,
Remember the pathway that leads to our door !

POEMS OF THE CLASS OF '29

1851-1889

["THE class of 1829 at Harvard College, of which I am a member, graduated, according to the triennial, fifty-nine in number. It is sixty years, then, since that time; and as they were, on an average, about twenty years old, those who survive must have reached fourscore years. Of the fifty-nine graduates ten only are living, or were at the last accounts; one in six, very nearly. In the first ten years after graduation, our third decade, when we were between twenty and thirty years old, we lost three members,—about one in twenty; between the ages of thirty and forty, eight died,—one in seven of those the decade began with; from forty to fifty, only two,—or one in twenty-four; from fifty to sixty, eight,—or one in six; from sixty to seventy, fifteen,—or two out of every five; from seventy to eighty, twelve,—or one in two. The greatly increased mortality which began with our seventh decade went on steadily increasing. At sixty we come 'within range of the rifle-pits,' to borrow an expression from my friend Weir Mitchell." *Over The Teacups*, p. 28. A list of the members of the class is given in the Notes at the end of this volume, and will serve to identify the initials which stand at the head of one and another poem.]

BILL AND JOE

COME, dear old comrade, you and I
Will steal an hour from days gone by,
The shining days when life was new,
And all was bright with morning dew,
The lusty days of long ago,
When you were Bill and I was Joe.

Your name may flaunt a titled trail
Proud as a cockerel's rainbow tail,
And mine as brief appendix wear
As Tam O'Shanter's luckless mare;
To-day, old friend, remember still
That I am Joe and you are Bill.

You 've won the great world's envied prize,
And grand you look in people's eyes,
With H O N. and L L. D.
In big brave letters, fair to see,—
Your fist, old fellow! off they go!—
How are you, Bill? How are you, Joe?

You 've worn the judge's ermined robe;
You 've taught your name to half the globe;
You 've sung mankind a deathless strain;
You 've made the dead past live again:
The world may call you what it will,
But you and I are Joe and Bill.

The chaffing young folks stare and say
"See those old buffers, bent and gray,—
They talk like fellows in their teens!
Mad, poor old boys! That 's what it means,"—
And shake their heads; they little know
The throbbing hearts of Bill and Joe!—

How Bill forgets his hour of pride,
While Joe sits smiling at his side;
How Joe, in spite of time's disguise,
Finds the old schoolmate in his eyes,—
Those calm, stern eyes that melt and fill
As Joe looks fondly up at Bill.

Ah, pensive scholar, what is fame?
A fitful tongue of leaping flame;
A giddy whirlwind's fickle gust,
That lifts a pinch of mortal dust;
A few swift years, and who can show
Which dust was Bill and which was Joe?

The weary idol takes his stand,
Holds out his bruised and aching hand,
While gaping thousands come and go,—
How vain it seems, this empty show!
Till all at once his pulses thrill;—
'T is poor old Joe's "God bless you, Bill!"

And shall we breathe in happier spheres
The names that pleased our mortal ears;
In some sweet lull of harp and song
For earth-born spirits none too long,
Just whispering of the world below
Where this was Bill and that was Joe?

No matter; while our home is here
No sounding name is half so dear;
When fades at length our lingering day,
Who cares what pompous tombstones say?
Read on the hearts that love us still,
Hic jacet Joe.   *Hic jacet* Bill.

A SONG OF "TWENTY-NINE"
1851

THE summer dawn is breaking
  On Auburn's tangled bowers,
The golden light is waking
  On Harvard's ancient towers;
    The sun is in the sky
    That must see us do or die,
  Ere it shine on the line
    Of the CLASS OF '29.

At last the day is ended,
  The tutor screws no more,
By doubt and fear attended
  Each hovers round the door,
    Till the good old Præses cries,
    While the tears stand in his eyes,
  "You have passed, and are classed
    With the BOYS OF '29."

Not long are they in making
  The college halls their own,
Instead of standing shaking,
  Too bashful to be known;
    But they kick the Seniors' shins
    Ere the second week begins,
  When they stray in the way
    Of the BOYS OF '29.

If a jolly set is trolling
  The last *Der Freischutz* airs,
Or a "cannon bullet" rolling
  Comes bouncing down the stairs,
    The tutors, looking out,
    Sigh, "Alas! there is no doubt,

'T is the noise of the Boys
  Of the CLASS OF '29."

Four happy years together,
  By storm and sunshine tried,
In changing wind and weather,
  They rough it side by side,
    Till they hear their Mother cry,
    "You are fledged, and you must fly,"
  And the bell tolls the knell
    Of the days of '29.

Since then, in peace or trouble,
  Full many a year has rolled,
And life has counted double
  The days that then we told;
    Yet we 'll end as we 've begun,
    For though scattered, we are one,
  While each year sees us here,
    Round the board of '29.

Though fate may throw between us
  The mountains or the sea,
No time shall ever wean us,
  No distance set us free;
    But around the yearly board,
    When the flaming pledge is poured,
  It shall claim every name
    On the roll of '29.

To yonder peaceful ocean
  That glows with sunset fires,
Shall reach the warm emotion
  This welcome day inspires,
    Beyond the ridges cold
    Where a brother toils for gold,
  Till it shine through the mine
    Round the BOY OF '29.

If one whom fate has broken
  Shall lift a moistened eye,
We 'll say, before he 's spoken —
  "Old Classmate, don't you cry!
    Here, take the purse I hold,
    There 's a tear upon the gold —
  It was mine — it is thine —
    A'n't we BOYS OF '29?"

As nearer still and nearer
  The fatal stars appear,
The living shall be dearer
  With each encircling year,
    Till a few old men shall say,
    "We remember 't is the day —

Let it pass with a glass
 For the CLASS OF '29."

As one by one is falling
 Beneath the leaves or snows,
Each memory still recalling,
 The broken ring shall close,
Till the nightwinds softly pass
O'er the green and growing grass,
Where it waves on the graves
 Of the BOYS OF '29!

QUESTIONS AND ANSWERS

1852

WHERE, oh where are the visions of morning,
 Fresh as the dews of our prime?
Gone, like tenants that quit without warning,
 Down the back entry of time.

Where, oh where are life's lilies and roses,
 Nursed in the golden dawn's smile?
Dead as the bulrushes round little Moses,
 On the old banks of the Nile.

Where are the Marys, and Anns, and Elizas,
 Loving and lovely of yore?
Look in the columns of old Advertisers, —
 Married and dead by the score.

Where the gray colts and the ten-year-old fillies,
 Saturday's triumph and joy?
Gone, like our friend πόδας ὠκὺς Achilles,
 Homer's ferocious old boy.

Die-away dreams of ecstatic emotion,
 Hopes like young eagles at play,
Vows of unheard-of and endless devotion,
 How ye have faded away!

Yet, though the ebbing of Time's mighty river
 Leave our young blossoms to die,
Let him roll smooth in his current forever,
 Till the last pebble is dry.

AN IMPROMPTU

NOT PREMEDITATED

1853

THE clock has struck noon; ere it thrice tell the hours
We shall meet round the table that blushes with flowers,
And I shall blush deeper with shame-driven blood
That I came to the banquet and brought not a bud.

Who cares that his verse is a beggar in art
If you see through its rags the full throb of his heart?
Who asks if his comrade is battered and tanned
When he feels his warm soul in the clasp of his hand?

No! be it an epic, or be it a line,
The Boys will all love it because it is mine;
I sung their last song on the morn of the day
That tore from their lives the last blossom of May.

It is not the sunset that glows in the wine,
But the smile that beams over it, makes it divine;
I scatter these drops, and behold, as they fall,
The day-star of memory shines through them all!

And these are the last; they are drops that I stole
From a wine-press that crushes the life from the soul,
But they ran through my heart and they sprang to my brain
Till our twentieth sweet summer was smiling again!

THE OLD MAN DREAMS

1854

OH for one hour of youthful joy!
 Give back my twentieth spring!

I 'd rather laugh, a bright-haired boy,
  Than reign, a gray-beard king.

Off with the spoils of wrinkled age!
  Away with Learning's crown!
Tear out life's Wisdom-written page,
  And dash its trophies down!

One moment let my life-blood stream
  From boyhood's fount of flame!
Give me one giddy, reeling dream
  Of life all love and fame!

My listening angel heard the prayer,
  And, calmly smiling, said,
"If I but touch thy silvered hair
  Thy hasty wish hath sped.

"But is there nothing in thy track,
  To bid thee fondly stay,
While the swift seasons hurry back
  To find the wished-for day?"

"Ah, truest soul of womankind!
  Without thee what were life?
One bliss I cannot leave behind:
  I 'll take — my — precious — wife!"

The angel took a sapphire pen
  And wrote in rainbow dew,
The man would be a boy again,
  And be a husband too!

"And is there nothing yet unsaid,
  Before the change appears?
Remember, all their gifts have fled
  With those dissolving years."

"Why, yes;" for memory would recall
  My fond paternal joys;
"I could not bear to leave them all —
  I 'll take — my — girl — and — boys."

The smiling angel dropped his pen, —
  "Why, this will never do;
The man would be a boy again,
  And be a father too!"

And so I laughed, — my laughter woke
  The household with its noise, —
And wrote my dream, when morning broke,
  To please the gray-haired boys.

REMEMBER — FORGET

1855

And what shall be the song to-night,
  If song there needs must be?
If every year that brings us here
  Must steal an hour from me?
Say, shall it ring a merry peal,
  Or heave a mourning sigh
O'er shadows cast, by years long past,
  On moments flitting by?

Nay, take the first unbidden line
  The idle hour may send,
No studied grace can mend the face
  That smiles as friend on friend;
The balsam oozes from the pine,
  The sweetness from the rose,
And so, unsought, a kindly thought
  Finds language as it flows.

The years rush by in sounding flight,
  I hear their ceaseless wings;
Their songs I hear, some far, some near,
  And thus the burden rings:
"The morn has fled, the noon has past,
  The sun will soon be set,
The twilight fade to midnight shade;
  Remember — and Forget!"

Remember all that time has brought —
  The starry hope on high,
The strength attained, the courage gained,
  The love that cannot die.
Forget the bitter, brooding thought, —
  The word too harshly said,
The living blame love hates to name,
  The frailties of the dead!

We have been younger, so they say,
  But let the seasons roll,
He doth not lack an almanac
  Whose youth is in his soul.
The snows may clog life's iron track,
  But does the axle tire,
While bearing swift through bank and drift
  The engine's heart of fire?

I lift a goblet in my hand;
  If good old wine it hold,
An ancient skin to keep it in
  Is just the thing, we 're told.

We're grayer than the dusty flask, —
　We're older than our wine;
Our corks reveal the "white top" seal,
　The stamp of '29.

Ah, Boys! we clustered in the dawn,
　To sever in the dark;
A merry crew, with loud halloo,
　We climbed our painted bark;
We sailed her through the four years'
　cruise,
We'll sail her to the last,
Our dear old flag, though but a rag,
　Still flying on her mast.

So gliding on, each winter's gale
　Shall pipe us all on deck,
Till, faint and few, the gathering crew
　Creep o'er the parting wreck,
Her sails and streamers spread aloft
　To fortune's rain or shine,
Till storm or sun shall all be one,
　And down goes TWENTY-NINE!

OUR INDIAN SUMMER

1856

YOU'll believe me, dear boys, 't is a pleasure to rise,
With a welcome like this in your darling old eyes;
To meet the same smiles and to hear the same tone
Which have greeted me oft in the years that have flown.

Were I gray as the grayest old rat in the wall,
My locks would turn brown at the sight of you all;
If my heart were as dry as the shell on the sand,
It would fill like the goblet I hold in my hand.

There are noontides of autumn when summer returns,
Though the leaves are all garnered and sealed in their urns,
And the bird on his perch, that was silent so long,
Believes the sweet sunshine and breaks into song.

We have caged the young birds of our beautiful June;
Their plumes are still bright and their voices in tune;
One moment of sunshine from faces like these
And they sing as they sung in the green-growing trees.

The voices of morning! how sweet is their thrill
When the shadows have turned, and the evening grows still!
The text of our lives may get wiser with age,
But the print was so fair on its twentieth page!

Look off from your goblet and up from your plate,
Come, take the last journal, and glance at its date:
Then think what we fellows should say and should do,
If the 6 were a 9 and the 5 were a 2.

Ah, no! for the shapes that would meet with us here,
From the far land of shadows, are ever too dear!
Though youth flung around us its pride and its charms,
We should see but the comrades we clasped in our arms.

A health to our future — a sigh for our past,
We love, we remember, we hope to the last;
And for all the base lies that the almanacs hold,
While we've youth in our hearts we can never grow old!

MARE RUBRUM

1858

FLASH out a stream of blood-red wine,
　For I would drink to other days,
And brighter shall their memory shine,
　Seen flaming through its crimson blaze!
The roses die, the summers fade,
　But every ghost of boyhood's dream

By nature's magic power is laid
  To sleep beneath this blood-red stream!

It filled the purple grapes that lay,
  And drank the splendors of the sun,
Where the long summer's cloudless day
  Is mirrored in the broad Garonne;
It pictures still the bacchant shapes
  That saw their hoarded sunlight shed, —
The maidens dancing on the grapes, —
  Their milk-white ankles splashed with red.

Beneath these waves of crimson lie,
  In rosy fetters prisoned fast,
Those flitting shapes that never die, —
  The swift-winged visions of the past.
Kiss but the crystal's mystic rim,
  Each shadow rends its flowery chain,
Springs in a bubble from its brim,
  And walks the chambers of the brain.

Poor beauty! Time and fortune's wrong
  No shape nor feature may withstand;
Thy wrecks are scattered all along,
  Like emptied sea-shells on the sand;
Yet, sprinkled with this blushing rain,
  The dust restores each blooming girl,
As if the sea-shells moved again
  Their glistening lips of pink and pearl.

Here lies the home of school-boy life,
  With creaking stair and wind-swept hall,
And, scarred by many a truant knife,
  Our old initials on the wall;
Here rest, their keen vibrations mute,
  The shout of voices known so well,
The ringing laugh, the wailing flute,
  The chiding of the sharp-tongued bell.

Here, clad in burning robes, are laid
  Life's blossomed joys, untimely shed,
And here those cherished forms have strayed
  We miss awhile, and call them dead.
What wizard fills the wondrous glass?
  What soil the enchanted clusters grew?
That buried passions wake and pass
  In beaded drops of fiery dew?

Nay, take the cup of blood-red wine, —
  Our hearts can boast a warmer glow,
Filled from a vintage more divine,
  Calmed, but not chilled, by winter's snow!
To-night the palest wave we sip
  Rich as the priceless draught shall be
That wet the bride of Cana's lip, —
  The wedding wine of Galilee!

THE BOYS
1859

HAS there any old fellow got mixed with the boys?
If there has, take him out, without making a noise.
Hang the Almanac's cheat and the Catalogue's spite!
Old Time is a liar! We 're twenty to-night!

We 're twenty! We 're twenty! Who says we are more?
He 's tipsy, — young jackanapes! — show him the door!
"Gray temples at twenty?" — Yes! *white* if we please;
Where the snow-flakes fall thickest there 's nothing can freeze!

Was it snowing I spoke of? Excuse the mistake!
Look close, — you will see not a sign of a flake!
We want some new garlands for those we have shed, —
And these are white roses in place of the red.

We 've a trick, we young fellows, you may have been told,
Of talking (in public) as if we were old: —
That boy we call "Doctor," and this we call "Judge;"
It 's a neat little fiction, — of course it 's all fudge.

That fellow 's the "Speaker," — the one on the right;
"Mr. Mayor," my young one, how are you to-night?
That 's our "Member of Congress," we say when we chaff;
There 's the "Reverend" What 's his name? — don't make me laugh.

That boy with the grave mathematical look
Made believe he had written a wonderful book,
And the ROYAL SOCIETY thought it was true!
So they chose him right in; a good joke it was, too!

There's a boy, we pretend, with a three-decker brain,
That could harness a team with a logical chain;
When he spoke for our manhood in syllabled fire,
We called him "The Justice," but now he's "The Squire."

And there's a nice youngster of excellent pith, —
Fate tried to conceal him by naming him Smith;
But he shouted a song for the brave and the free, —
Just read on his medal, "My country," "of thee!"

You hear that boy laughing? — You think he's all fun;
But the angels laugh, too, at the good he has done;
The children laugh loud as they troop to his call,
And the poor man that knows him laughs loudest of all!

Yes, we're boys, — always playing with tongue or with pen, —
And I sometimes have asked, — Shall we ever be men?
Shall we always be youthful, and laughing, and gay,
Till the last dear companion drops smiling away?

Then here's to our boyhood, its gold and its gray!
The stars of its winter, the dews of its May!
And when we have done with our life-lasting toys,
Dear Father, take care of thy children, THE BOYS!

LINES
1860

I'M ashamed, — that's the fact, — it's a pitiful case, —
Won't any kind classmate get up in my place?
Just remember how often I've risen before, —
I blush as I straighten my legs on the floor!

There are stories, once pleasing, too many times told, —
There are beauties once charming, too fearfully old, —
There are voices we've heard till we know them so well,
Though they talked for an hour they'd have nothing to tell.

Yet, Classmates! Friends! Brothers! Dear blessed old boys!
Made one by a lifetime of sorrows and joys,
What lips have such sounds as the poorest of these,
Though honeyed, like Plato's, by musical bees?

What voice is so sweet and what greeting so dear
As the simple, warm welcome that waits for us here?
The love of our boyhood still breathes in its tone,
And our hearts throb the answer, "He's one of our own!"

Nay! count not our numbers; some sixty we know,
But these are above, and those under the snow;
And thoughts are still mingled wherever we meet
For those we remember with those that we greet.

We have rolled on life's journey, — how fast and how far!
One round of humanity's many-wheeled car,
But up-hill and down-hill, through rattle and rub,
Old, true Twenty-niners! we've stuck to our hub!

While a brain lives to think, or a bosom to
    feel,
We will cling to it still like the spokes of
    a wheel!
And age, as it chills us, shall fasten the
    tire
That youth fitted round in his circle of
    fire!

A VOICE OF THE LOYAL NORTH

1861

(JANUARY THIRD)

WE sing "Our Country's" song to-night
    With saddened voice and eye;
Her banner droops in clouded light
    Beneath the wintry sky.
We'll pledge her once in golden wine
    Before her stars have set:
Though dim one reddening orb may shine,
    We have a Country yet.

'T were vain to sigh o'er errors past,
    The fault of sires or sons;
Our soldier heard the threatening blast,
    And spiked his useless guns;
He saw the star-wreathed ensign fall,
    By mad invaders torn;
But saw it from the bastioned wall
    That laughed their rage to scorn!

What though their angry cry is flung
    Across the howling wave, —
They smite the air with idle tongue
    The gathering storm who brave;
Enough of speech! the trumpet rings;
    Be silent, patient, calm, —
God help them if the tempest swings
    The pine against the palm!

Our toilsome years have made us tame;
    Our strength has slept unfelt;
The furnace-fire is slow to flame
    That bids our ploughshares melt;
'T is hard to lose the bread they win
    In spite of Nature's frowns, —
To drop the iron threads we spin
    That weave our web of towns,

To see the rusting turbines stand
    Before the emptied flumes,
To fold the arms that flood the land
    With rivers from their looms, —

But harder still for those who learn
    The truth forgot so long;
When once their slumbering passions burn,
    The peaceful are the strong!

The Lord have mercy on the weak,
    And calm their frenzied ire,
And save our brothers ere they shriek,
    "We played with Northern fire!"
The eagle hold his mountain height, —
    The tiger pace his den!
Give all their country, each his right!
    God keep us all! Amen!

J. D. R.

1862

THE friends that are, and friends that
    were,
    What shallow waves divide!
I miss the form for many a year
    Still seated at my side.

I miss him, yet I feel him still
    Amidst our faithful band,
As if not death itself could chill
    The warmth of friendship's hand.

His story other lips may tell, —
    For me the veil is drawn;
I only knew he loved me well,
    He loved me — and is gone!

VOYAGE OF THE GOOD SHIP UNION

1862

'T is midnight: through my troubled
    dream
    Loud wails the tempest's cry;
Before the gale, with tattered sail,
    A ship goes plunging by.
What name? Where bound? — The
    rocks around
    Repeat the loud halloo.
— The good ship Union, Southward bound:
    God help her and her crew!

And is the old flag flying still
    That o'er your fathers flew,
With bands of white and rosy light,
    And field of starry blue?

"CHOOSE YOU THIS DAY WHOM YE WILL SERVE"

— Ay! look aloft! its folds full oft
  Have braved the roaring blast,
And still shall fly when from the sky
  This black typhoon has past!

Speak, pilot of the storm-tost bark!
  May I thy peril share?
— O landsman, there are fearful seas
  The brave alone may dare!
— Nay, ruler of the rebel deep,
  What matters wind or wave?
The rocks that wreck your reeling deck
  Will leave me naught to save!

O landsman, art thou false or true?
  What sign hast thou to show?
— The crimson stains from loyal veins
  That hold my heart-blood's flow!
— Enough! what more shall honor claim?
  I know the sacred sign;
Above thy head our flag shall spread,
  Our ocean path be thine!

The bark sails on; the Pilgrim's Cape
  Lies low along her lee,
Whose headland crooks its anchor-flukes
  To lock the shore and sea.
No treason here! it cost too dear
  To win this barren realm!
And true and free the hands must be
  That hold the whaler's helm!

Still on! Manhattan's narrowing bay
  No rebel cruiser scars;
Her waters feel no pirate's keel
  That flaunts the fallen stars!
— But watch the light on yonder height, —
  Ay, pilot, have a care!
Some lingering cloud in mist may shroud
  The capes of Delaware!

Say, pilot, what this fort may be,
  Whose sentinels look down
From moated walls that show the sea
  Their deep embrasures' frown?
The Rebel host claims all the coast,
  But these are friends, we know,
Whose footprints spoil the "sacred soil,"
  And this is? — Fort Monroe!

The breakers roar, — how bears the shore?
— The traitorous wreckers' hands
Have quenched the blaze that poured its rays
  Along the Hatteras sands.

— Ha! say not so! I see its glow!
  Again the shoals display
The beacon light that shines by night,
  The Union Stars by day!

The good ship flies to milder skies,
  The wave more gently flows,
The softening breeze wafts o'er the seas
  The breath of Beaufort's rose.
What fold is this the sweet winds kiss,
  Fair-striped and many-starred,
Whose shadow palls these orphaned walls,
  The twins of Beauregard?

What! heard you not Port Royal's doom?
  How the black war-ships came
And turned the Beaufort roses' bloom
  To redder wreaths of flame?
How from Rebellion's broken reed
  We saw his emblem fall,
As soon his cursèd poison-weed
  Shall drop from Sumter's wall?

On! on! Pulaski's iron hail
  Falls harmless on Tybee!
The good ship feels the freshening gales,
  She strikes the open sea;
She rounds the point, she threads the keys
  That guard the Land of Flowers,
And rides at last where firm and fast
  Her own Gibraltar towers!

The good ship Union's voyage is o'er,
  At anchor safe she swings,
And loud and clear with cheer on cheer
  Her joyous welcome rings:
Hurrah! Hurrah! it shakes the wave,
  It thunders on the shore, —
One flag, one land, one heart, one hand,
  One Nation, evermore!

"CHOOSE YOU THIS DAY WHOM YE WILL SERVE"

1863

Yes, tyrants, you hate us, and fear while you hate
The self-ruling, chain-breaking, throne-shaking State!
The night-birds dread morning, — your instinct is true, —
The day-star of Freedom brings midnight for you!

Why plead with the deaf for the cause of
    mankind?
The owl hoots at noon that the eagle is
    blind!
We ask not your reasons, — 't were wast-
    ing our time, —
Our life is a menace, our welfare a crime!

We have battles to fight, we have foes to
    subdue, —
Time waits not for us, and we wait not for
    you!
The mower mows on, though the adder
    may writhe
And the copper-head coil round the blade
    of his scythe!

"No sides in this quarrel," your statesmen
    may urge,
Of school-house and wages with slave-pen
    and scourge! —
No sides in the quarrel! proclaim it as
    well
To the angels that fight with the legions of
    hell!

They kneel in God's temple, the North and
    the South,
With blood on each weapon and prayers in
    each mouth.
Whose cry shall be answered? Ye Heav-
    ens, attend
The lords of the lash as their voices
    ascend!

"O Lord, we are shaped in the image of
    Thee, —
Smite down the base millions that claim to
    be free,
And lend thy strong arm to the soft-handed
    race
Who eat *not* their bread in the sweat of
    their face!"

So pleads the proud planter. What echoes
    are these?
The bay of his bloodhound is borne on the
    breeze,
And, lost in the shriek of his victim's
    despair,
His voice dies unheard. — Hear the Puri-
    tan's prayer!

"O Lord, that didst smother mankind in
    thy flood,

The sun is as sackcloth, the moon is as
    blood,
The stars fall to earth as untimely are
    cast
The figs from the fig-tree that shakes in
    the blast!

"All nations, all tribes in whose nostrils is
    breath
Stand gazing at Sin as she travails with
    Death!
Lord, strangle the monster that struggles
    to birth,
Or mock us no more with thy 'Kingdom
    on Earth'!

"If Ammon and Moab must reign in the
    land
Thou gavest thine Israel, fresh from thy
    hand,
Call Baal and Ashtaroth out of their graves
To be the new gods for the empire of
    slaves!"

Whose God will ye serve, O ye rulers of
    men?
Will ye build you new shrines in the slave-
    breeder's den?
Or bow with the children of light, as they
    call
On the Judge of the Earth and the Father
    of All?

Choose wisely, choose quickly, for time
    moves apace, —
Each day is an age in the life of our
    race!
Lord, lead them in love, ere they hasten in
    fear
From the fast-rising flood that shall girdle
    the sphere!

F. W. C.

1864

FAST as the rolling seasons bring
    The hour of fate to those we love,
Each pearl that leaves the broken string
    Is set in Friendship's crown above.
As narrower grows the earthly chain,
    The circle widens in the sky;
These are our treasures that remain,
    But those are stars that beam on high.

We miss — oh, how we miss! — *his* face, —
  With trembling accents speak his name.
Earth cannot fill his shadowed place
  From all her rolls of pride and fame.
Our song has lost the silvery thread
  That carolled through his jocund lips;
Our laugh is mute, our smile is fled,
  And all our sunshine in eclipse.

And what and whence the wondrous charm
  That kept his manhood boylike still, —
That life's hard censors could disarm
  And lead them captive at his will?
His heart was shaped of rosier clay, —
  His veins were filled with ruddier fire, —
Time could not chill him, fortune sway,
  Nor toil with all its burdens tire.

His speech burst throbbing from its fount
  And set our colder thoughts aglow,
As the hot leaping geysers mount
  And falling melt the Iceland snow.
Some word, perchance, we counted rash, —
  Some phrase our calmness might disclaim,
Yet 't was the sunset's lightning's flash,
  No angry bolt, but harmless flame.

Man judges all, God knoweth each;
  We read the rule, He sees the law;
How oft his laughing children teach
  The truths his prophets never saw!
O friend, whose wisdom flowered in mirth,
  Our hearts are sad, our eyes are dim;
He gave thy smiles to brighten earth, —
  We trust thy joyous soul to Him!

Alas! — our weakness Heaven forgive!
  We murmur, even while we trust,
"How long earth's breathing burdens live,
  Whose hearts, before they die, are dust!"
But thou! — through grief's untimely tears
  We ask with half-reproachful sigh —
"Couldst thou not watch a few brief years
  Till Friendship faltered, 'Thou mayst die'?"

Who loved our boyish years so well?
  Who knew so well their pleasant tales,
And all those livelier freaks could tell
  Whose oft-told story never fails?
In vain we turn our aching eyes, —
  In vain we stretch our eager hands, —
Cold in his wintry shroud he lies
  Beneath the dreary drifting sands!

Ah, speak not thus! *He* lies not there!
  We see him, hear him as of old!
He comes! He claims his wonted chair;
  His beaming face we still behold!
His voice rings clear in all our songs,
  And loud his mirthful accents rise;
To us our brother's life belongs, —
  Dear friends, a classmate never dies!

THE LAST CHARGE

1864

Now, men of the North! will you join in the strife
For country, for freedom, for honor, for life?
The giant grows blind in his fury and spite, —
One blow on his forehead will settle the fight!

Flash full in his eyes the blue lightning of steel,
And stun him with cannon-bolts, peal upon peal!
Mount, troopers, and follow your game to its lair,
As the hound tracks the wolf and the beagle the hare!

Blow, trumpets, your summons, till sluggards awake!
Beat, drums, till the roofs of the fainthearted shake!
Yet, yet, ere the signet is stamped on the scroll,
Their names may be traced on the blood-sprinkled roll!

Trust not the false herald that painted your shield:
True honor *to-day* must be sought on the field!
Her scutcheon shows white with a blazon of red, —
The life-drops of crimson for liberty shed!

The hour is at hand, and the moment draws nigh;
The dog-star of treason grows dim in the sky;

Shine forth from the battle-cloud, light of
   the morn,
Call back the bright hour when the Nation
   was born!

The rivers of peace through our valleys
   shall run,
As the glaciers of tyranny melt in the sun;
Smite, smite the proud parricide down
   from his throne, —
His sceptre once broken, the world is our
   own!

OUR OLDEST FRIEND

1865

I GIVE you the health of the oldest friend
That, short of eternity, earth can lend, —
A friend so faithful and tried and true
That nothing can wean him from me and
   you.

When first we screeched in the sudden
   blaze
Of the daylight's blinding and blasting rays,
And gulped at the gaseous, groggy air,
This old, old friend stood waiting there.

And when, with a kind of mortal strife,
We had gasped and choked into breathing
   life,
He watched by the cradle, day and night,
And held our hands till we stood upright.

From gristle and pulp our frames have
   grown
To stringy muscle and solid bone;
While we were changing, he altered not;
We might forget, but he never forgot.

He came with us to the college class, —
Little cared he for the steward's pass!
All the rest must pay their fee,
But the grim old dead-head entered free.

He stayed with us while we counted o'er
Four times each of the seasons four;
And with every season, from year to year,
The dear name Classmate he made more
   dear.

He never leaves us, — he never will,
Till our hands are cold and our hearts are
   still;

On birthdays, and Christmas, and New-
   Year's too,
He always remembers both me and you.

Every year this faithful friend
His little present is sure to send;
Every year, wheresoe'er we be,
He wants a keepsake from you and me.

How he loves us! he pats our heads,
And, lo! they are gleaming with silver
   threads;
And he's always begging one lock of hair,
Till our shining crowns have nothing to
   wear.

At length he will tell us, one by one,
"My child, your labor on earth is done;
And now you must journey afar to see
My elder brother, — Eternity!"

And so, when long, long years have passed,
Some dear old fellow will be the last, —
Never a boy alive but he
Of all our goodly company!

When he lies down, but not till then,
Our kind Class-Angel will drop the pen
That writes in the day-book kept above
Our lifelong record of faith and love.

So here's a health in homely rhyme
To our oldest classmate, Father Time!
May our last survivor live to be
As bald and as wise and as tough as he!

SHERMAN'S IN SAVANNAH

A HALF-RHYMED IMPROMPTU

1865

LIKE the tribes of Israel,
   Fed on quails and manna,
Sherman and his glorious band
Journeyed through the rebel land,
Fed from Heaven's all-bounteous hand,
   Marching on Savannah!

As the moving pillar shone,
   Streamed the starry banner
All day long in rosy light,
Flaming splendor all the night,
Till it swooped in eagle flight
   Down on doomed Savannah!

Glory be to God on high!
Shout the loud Hosanna!
Treason's wilderness is past,
Canaan's shore is won at last,
Peal a nation's trumpet-blast, —
Sherman's in Savannah!

Soon shall Richmond's tough old hide
Find a tough old tanner!
Soon from every rebel wall
Shall the rag of treason fall,
Till our banner flaps o'er all
As it crowns Savannah!

MY ANNUAL
1866

How long will this harp which you once
  loved to hear
Cheat your lips of a smile or your eyes of
  a tear?
How long stir the echoes it wakened of old,
While its strings were unbroken, untarnished its gold?

Dear friends of my boyhood, my words do
  you wrong;
The heart, the heart only, shall throb in
  my song;
It reads the kind answer that looks from
  your eyes, —
"We will bid our old harper play on till
  he dies."

Though Youth, the fair angel that looked
  o'er the strings,
Has lost the bright glory that gleamed on
  his wings,
Though the freshness of morning has
  passed from its tone,
It is still the old harp that was always
  your own.

I claim not its music, — each note it affords
I strike from your heart-strings, that lend
  me its chords;
I know you will listen and love to the last,
For it trembles and thrills with the voice
  of your past.

Ah, brothers! dear brothers! the harp
  that I hold
No craftsman could string and no artisan
  mould;
He shaped it, He strung it, who fashioned
  the lyres
That ring with the hymns of the seraphim
  choirs.

Not mine are the visions of beauty it brings,
Not mine the faint fragrance around it that
  clings;
Those shapes are the phantoms of years
  that are fled,
Those sweets breathe from roses your summers have shed.

Each hour of the past lends its tribute to
  this,
Till it blooms like a bower in the Garden
  of Bliss;
The thorn and the thistle may grow as
  they will,
Where Friendship unfolds there is Paradise
  still.

The bird wanders careless while summer
  is green,
The leaf-hidden cradle that rocked him
  unseen;
When Autumn's rude fingers the woods
  have undressed,
The boughs may look bare, but they show
  him his nest.

Too precious these moments! the lustre
  they fling
Is the light of our year, is the gem of its
  ring,
So brimming with sunshine, we almost forget
The rays it has lost, and its border of jet.

While round us the many-hued halo is shed,
How dear are the living, how near are the
  dead!
One circle, scarce broken, these waiting below,
Those walking the shores where the asphodels blow!

Not life shall enlarge it nor death shall
  divide, —
No brother new-born finds his place at my
  side;
No titles shall freeze us, no grandeurs infest,
His Honor, His Worship, are boys like the
  rest.

Some won the world's homage, their names
    we hold dear, —
But Friendship, not Fame, is the counter-
    sign here;
Make room by the conqueror crowned in
    the strife
For the comrade that limps from the battle
    of life!

What tongue talks of battle? Too long
    we have heard
In sorrow, in anguish, that terrible word;
It reddened the sunshine, it crimsoned the
    wave,
It sprinkled our doors with the blood of our
    brave.

Peace, Peace come at last, with her garland
    of white;
Peace broods in all hearts as we gather to-
    night;
The blazon of Union spreads full in the
    sun;
We echo its words, — We are one! We
    are one!

ALL HERE

1867

It is not what we say or sing,
    That keeps our charm so long unbroken,
Though every lightest leaf we bring
    May touch the heart as friendship's
    token;
Not what we sing or what we say
    Can make us dearer to each other;
We love the singer and his lay,
    But love as well the silent brother.

Yet bring whate'er your garden grows,
    Thrice welcome to our smiles and
    praises;
Thanks for the myrtle and the rose,
    Thanks for the marigolds and daisies;
One flower erelong we all shall claim,
    Alas! unloved of Amaryllis —
Nature's last blossom — need I name
    The wreath of threescore's silver lilies?

How many, brothers, meet to-night
    Around our boyhood's covered embers?
Go read the treasured names aright
    The old triennial list remembers;

Though twenty wear the starry sign
    That tells a life has broke its tether,
The fifty-eight of 'twenty-nine —
    God bless THE BOYS! — are all together!

These come with joyous look and word,
    With friendly grasp and cheerful greet-
    ing, —
Those smile unseen, and move unheard,
    The angel guests of every meeting;
They cast no shadow in the flame
    That flushes from the gilded lustre,
But count us — we are still the same;
    One earthly band, one heavenly cluster!

Love dies not when he bows his head
    To pass beyond the narrow portals, —
The light these glowing moments shed
    Wakes from their sleep our lost immor-
    tals;
They come as in their joyous prime,
    Before their morning days were num-
    bered, —
Death stays the envious hand of Time, —
    The eyes have not grown dim that slum-
    bered!

The paths that loving souls have trod
    Arch o'er the dust where worldlings
    grovel
High as the zenith o'er the sod, —
    The cross above the sexton's shovel!
We rise beyond the realms of day;
    They seem to stoop from spheres of glory
With us one happy hour to stray,
    While youth comes back in song and
    story.

Ah! ours is friendship true as steel
    That war has tried in edge and temper;
It writes upon its sacred seal
    The priest's *ubique — omnes — semper!*
It lends the sky a fairer sun
    That cheers our lives with rays as steady
As if our footsteps had begun
    To print the golden streets already!

The tangling years have clinched its knot
    Too fast for mortal strength to sunder;
The lightning bolts of noon are shot;
    No fear of evening's idle thunder!
Too late! too late! — no graceless hand
    Shall stretch its cords in vain endeavor
To rive the close encircling band
    That made and keeps us one forever!

So when upon the fated scroll
The falling stars have all descended,
And, blotted from the breathing roll,
Our little page of life is ended,
We ask but one memorial line
Traced on thy tablet, Gracious Mother:
"My children. Boys of '29.
In pace. How they loved each other!"

ONCE MORE

1868

Will I come? That *is* pleasant! I beg to inquire
If the gun that I carry has ever missed fire?
And which was the muster-roll — mention but one —
That missed your old comrade who carries the gun?

You see me as always, my hand on the lock,
The cap on the nipple, the hammer full cock;
It is rusty, some tell me; I heed not the scoff;
It is battered and bruised, but it always goes off!

"Is it loaded?" I 'll bet you! What does n't it hold?
Rammed full to the muzzle with memories untold;
Why, it scares me to fire, lest the pieces should fly
Like the cannons that burst on the Fourth of July!

One charge is a remnant of College-day dreams
(Its wadding is made of forensics and themes);
Ah, visions of fame! what a flash in the pan
As the trigger was pulled by each clever young man!

And love! Bless my stars, what a cartridge is there!
With a wadding of rose-leaves and ribbons and hair, —

All crammed in one verse to go off at a shot!
"Were there ever such sweethearts?" Of course there were not!

And next, — what a load! it will split the old gun, —
Three fingers, — four fingers, — five fingers of fun!
Come tell me, gray sages, for mischief and noise
Was there ever a lot like us fellows, "The Boys"?

Bump! bump! down the staircase the cannon-ball goes, —
Aha, old Professor! Look out for your toes!
Don't think, my poor Tutor, to *sleep* in your bed, —
Two "Boys"— 'twenty-niners — room over your head!

Remember the nights when the tar-barrel blazed!
From red "Massachusetts" the war-cry was raised;
And "Hollis" and "Stoughton" reëchoed the call;
Till P—— poked his head out of Holworthy Hall!

Old P——, as we called him, — at fifty or so, —
Not exactly a bud, but not quite in full blow;
In ripening manhood, suppose we should say,
Just nearing his prime, as we boys are to-day!

Oh say, can you look through the vista of age
To the time when old Morse drove the regular stage?
When Lyon told tales of the long-vanished years,
And Lenox crept round with the rings in his ears?

And dost thou, my brother, remember indeed
The days of our dealings with Willard and Read?

When "Dolly" was kicking and running away,
And punch came up smoking on Fillebrown's tray?

But where are the Tutors, my brother, oh tell! —
And where the Professors, remembered so well?
The sturdy old Grecians of Holworthy Hall,
And Latin, and Logic, and Hebrew, and all?

"They are dead, the old fellows" (we called them so then,
Though we since have found out they were lusty young men).
They are *dead*, do you tell me? — but how do you know?
You've filled once too often. I doubt if it's so.

I'm thinking. I'm thinking. Is this 'sixty-eight?
It's not quite so clear. It admits of debate.
I *may* have been dreaming. I rather incline
To think — yes, I'm certain — it is 'twenty-nine!

"By Zhorzhe!" — as friend Sales is accustomed to cry, —
You tell me they 're dead, but I know it's a lie!
Is Jackson not President? — What was 't you said?
It can't be; you're joking; what, — all of 'em dead?

Jim, — Harry, — Fred, — Isaac, — all gone from our side?
They could n't have left us, — no, not if they tried.
Look, — there's our old Præses, — he can't find his text;
See, — P—— rubs his leg, as he growls out "*The next!*"

I told you 't was nonsense. Joe, give us a song!
Go harness up "Dolly," and fetch her along! —

Dead! Dead! You false graybeard, I swear they are not!
Hurrah for Old Hickory! — Oh, I forgot!

Well, *one* we have with us (how could he contrive
To deal with us youngsters and still to survive?)
Who wore for our guidance authority's robe, —
No wonder he took to the study of Job!

And now, as my load was uncommonly large,
Let me taper it off with a classical charge;
When that has gone off, I shall drop my old gun —
And then stand at ease, for my service is done.

*Bibamus ad Classem vocatam " The Boys"
Et eorum Tutorem cui nomen est " Noyes;"
Et floreant, valeant, vigeant tam,
Non Peircius ipse enumeret quam!*

THE OLD CRUISER

1869

HERE's the old cruiser, 'Twenty-nine,
Forty times she's crossed the line;
Same old masts and sails and crew,
Tight and tough and as good as new.

Into the harbor she bravely steers
Just as she's done for these forty years, —
Over her anchor goes, splash and clang!
Down her sails drop, rattle and bang!

Comes a vessel out of the dock
Fresh and spry as a fighting-cock,
Feathered with sails and spurred with steam,
Heading out of the classic stream.

Crew of a hundred all aboard,
Every man as fine as a lord.
Gay they look and proud they feel,
Bowling along on even keel.

On they float with wind and tide, —
Gain at last the old ship's side;
Every man looks down in turn, —
Reads the name that's on her stern.

"Twenty-nine! — *Diable* you say!
That was in Skipper Kirkland's day!
What was the Flying Dutchman's name?
This old rover must be the same.

"Ho! you Boatswain that walks the deck,
How does it happen you 're not a wreck?
One and another have come to grief,
How have you dodged by rock and reef?"

Boatswain, lifting one knowing lid,
Hitches his breeches and shifts his quid:
"Hey? What is it? Who's come to grief?
Louder, young swab, I 'm a little deaf."

"I say, old fellow, what keeps your boat
With all you jolly old boys afloat,
When scores of vessels as good as she
Have swallowed the salt of the bitter sea?

"Many a crew from many a craft
Goes drifting by on a broken raft
Pieced from a vessel that clove the brine
Taller and prouder than 'Twenty-nine.

"Some capsized in an angry breeze,
Some were lost in the narrow seas,
Some on snags and some on sands
Struck and perished and lost their hands.

"Tell us young ones, you gray old man,
What is your secret, if you can.
We have a ship as good as you,
Show us how to keep our crew."

So in his ear the youngster cries;
Then the gray Boatswain straight replies: —
"All your crew be sure you know, —
Never let one of your shipmates go.

"If he leaves you, change your tack,
Follow him close and fetch him back;
When you 've hauled him in at last,
Grapple his flipper and hold him fast.

"If you 've wronged him, speak him fair,
Say you 're sorry and make it square;
If he 's wronged you, wink so tight
None of you see what 's plain in sight.

"When the world goes hard and wrong,
Lend a hand to help him along;

When his stockings have holes to darn,
Don't you grudge him your ball of yarn.

"Once in a twelvemonth, come what may,
Anchor your ship in a quiet bay,
Call all hands and read the log,
And give 'em a taste of grub and grog.

"Stick to each other through thick and thin;
All the closer as age leaks in;
Squalls will blow and clouds will frown,
But stay by your ship till you all go down!"

ADDED FOR THE ALUMNI MEETING,
JUNE 29, 1869.

So the gray Boatswain of 'Twenty-nine
Piped to "The Boys" as they crossed the line;
Round the cabin sat thirty guests,
Babes of the nurse with a thousand breasts.

There were the judges, grave and grand,
Flanked by the priests on either hand;
There was the lord of wealth untold,
And the dear good fellow in broadcloth old.

Thirty men, from twenty towns,
Sires and grandsires with silvered crowns, —
Thirty school-boys all in a row, —
Bens and Georges and Bill and Joe.

In thirty goblets the wine was poured,
But threescore gathered around the board, —
For lo! at the side of every chair
A shadow hovered — we all were there!

HYMN FOR THE CLASS-MEETING

1869

THOU Gracious Power, whose mercy lends
The light of home, the smile of friends,
Our gathered flock thine arms infold
As in the peaceful days of old.

Wilt thou not hear us while we raise,
In sweet accord of solemn praise,

The voices that have mingled long
 In joyous flow of mirth and song?

For all the blessings life has brought,
For all its sorrowing hours have taught,
For all we mourn, for all we keep,
The hands we clasp, the loved that sleep;

The noontide sunshine of the past,
These brief, bright moments fading fast,
The stars that gild our darkening years,
The twilight ray from holier spheres;

We thank thee, Father! let thy grace
Our narrowing circle still embrace,
Thy mercy shed its heavenly store,
Thy peace be with us evermore!

EVEN-SONG

1870

It may be, yes, it must be, Time that brings
 An end to mortal things,
That sends the beggar Winter in the train
 Of Autumn's burdened wain, —
Time, that is heir of all our earthly state,
 And knoweth well to wait
Till sea hath turned to shore and shore to sea,
 If so it need must be,
Ere he make good his claim and call his own
 Old empires overthrown, —
Time, who can find no heavenly orb too large
 To hold its fee in charge,
Nor any motes that fill its beam so small,
 But he shall care for all, —
It may be, must be, — yes, he soon shall tire
 This hand that holds the lyre.

Then ye who listened in that earlier day
 When to my careless lay
I matched its chords and stole their first-born thrill,
 With untaught rudest skill
Vexing a treble from the slender strings
 Thin as the locust sings
When the shrill-crying child of summer's heat
 Pipes from its leafy seat,
The dim pavilion of embowering green
 Beneath whose shadowy screen
The small sopranist tries his single note
 Against the song-bird's throat,
And all the echoes listen, but in vain;
 They hear no answering strain, —
Then ye who listened in that earlier day
 Shall sadly turn away,

Saying, "The fire burns low, the hearth is cold
 That warmed our blood of old;
Cover its embers and its half-burnt brands,
 And let us stretch our hands
Over a brighter and fresh-kindled flame;
 Lo, this is not the same,
The joyous singer of our morning time,
 Flushed high with lusty rhyme!
Speak kindly, for he bears a human heart,
 But whisper him apart, —
Tell him the woods their autumn robes have shed
 And all their birds have fled,
And shouting winds unbuild the naked nests
 They warmed with patient breasts;
Tell him the sky is dark, the summer o'er,
 And bid him sing no more!"

Ah, welladay! if words so cruel-kind
 A listening ear might find!
But who that hears the music in his soul
 Of rhythmic waves that roll
Crested with gleams of fire, and as they flow
 Stir all the deeps below
Till the great pearls no calm might ever reach
 Leap glistening on the beach, —
Who that has known the passion and the pain,
 The rush through heart and brain,
The joy so like a pang his hand is pressed
 Hard on his throbbing breast,
When thou, whose smile is life and bliss and fame
 Hast set his pulse aflame,
Muse of the lyre! can say farewell to thee?
 Alas! and must it be?

In many a clime, in many a stately tongue,
 The mighty bards have sung;
To these the immemorial thrones belong
 And purple robes of song;

Yet the slight minstrel loves the slender tone
His lips may call his own,
And finds the measure of the verse more sweet,
Timed by his pulse's beat,
Than all the hymnings of the laurelled throng.
Say not I do him wrong,
For Nature spoils her warblers, — them she feeds
In lotus-growing meads
And pours them subtle draughts from haunted streams
That fill their souls with dreams.

Full well I know the gracious mother's wiles
And dear delusive smiles!
No callow fledgling of her singing brood
But tastes that witching food,
And hearing overhead the eagle's wing,
And how the thrushes sing,
Vents his exiguous chirp, and from his nest
Flaps forth — we know the rest.
I own the weakness of the tuneful kind, —
Are not all harpers blind?
I sang too early, must I sing too late?
The lengthening shadows wait
The first pale stars of twilight, — yet how sweet
The flattering whisper's cheat, —
"Thou hast the fire no evening chill can tame,
Whose coals outlast its flame!"

Farewell, ye carols of the laughing morn,
Of earliest sunshine born!
The sower flings the seed and looks not back
Along his furrowed track;
The reaper leaves the stalks for other hands
To gird with circling bands;
The wind, earth's careless servant, truant-born,
Blows clean the beaten corn
And quits the thresher's floor, and goes his way
To sport with ocean's spray;
The headlong-stumbling rivulet scrambling down
To wash the sea-girt town,
Still babbling of the green and billowy waste
Whose salt he longs to taste,
Ere his warm wave its chilling clasp may feel
Has twirled the miller's wheel.

The song has done its task that makes us bold
With secrets else untold, —
And mine has run its errand; through the dews
I tracked the flying Muse;
The daughter of the morning touched my lips
With roseate finger-tips;
Whether I would or would not, I must sing
With the new choirs of spring;
Now, as I watch the fading autumn day
And trill my softened lay,
I think of all that listened, and of one
For whom a brighter sun
Dawned at high summer's noon. Ah, comrades dear,
Are not all gathered here?
Our hearts have answered. — Yes! they hear our call:
All gathered here! all! all!

THE SMILING LISTENER

1871

PRECISELY. I see it. You all want to say
That a tear is too sad and a laugh is too gay;
You could stand a faint smile, you could manage a sigh,
But you value your ribs, and you don't want to cry.

And why at our feast of the clasping of hands
Need we turn on the stream of our lachrymal glands?
Though we see the white breakers of age on our bow,
Let us take a good pull in the jolly-boat now!

It's hard if a fellow cannot feel content
When a banquet like this does n't cost him a cent,
When his goblet and plate he may empty at will,
And our kind Class Committee will settle the bill.

And here's your old friend, the identical bard
Who has rhymed and recited you verse by the yard
Since the days of the empire of Andrew the First
Till you're full to the brim and feel ready to burst.

It's awful to think of, — how year after year
With his piece in his pocket he waits for you here;
No matter who's missing, there always is one
To lug out his manuscript, sure as a gun.

"Why won't he stop writing?" Humanity cries:
The answer is briefly, "He can't if he tries;
He has played with his foolish old feather so long,
That the goose-quill in spite of him cackles in song."

You have watched him with patience from morning to dusk
Since the tassel was bright o'er the green of the husk,
And now — it's too bad — it's a pitiful job —
He has shelled the ripe ear till he's come to the cob.

I see one face beaming — it listens so well
There must be some music yet left in my shell —
The wine of my soul is not thick on the lees;
One string is unbroken, one friend I can please!

Dear comrade, the sunshine of seasons gone by
Looks out from your tender and tear-moistened eye,
A pharos of love on an ice-girdled coast, —
Kind soul! — Don't you hear me? — He's deaf as a post!

Can it be one of Nature's benevolent tricks
That you grow hard of hearing as I grow prolix?

And that look of delight which would angels beguile
Is the deaf man's prolonged unintelligent smile?

Ah! the ear may grow dull, and the eye may wax dim,
But they still know a classmate — they can't mistake him;
There is something to tell us, "That's one of our band,"
Though we groped in the dark for a touch of his hand.

Well, Time with his snuffers is prowling about
And his shaky old fingers will soon snuff us out;
There's a hint for us all in each pendulum tick,
For we're low in the tallow and long in the wick.

You remember Rossini — you've been at the play?
How his overture-endings keep crashing away
Till you think, "It's all over — it can't but stop now —
That's the screech and the bang of the final bow-wow."

And you find you're mistaken; there's lots more to come,
More banging, more screeching of fiddle and drum,
Till when the last ending is finished and done,
You feel like a horse when the winning-post's won.

So I, who have sung to you, merry, or sad,
Since the days when they called me a promising lad,
Though I've made you more rhymes than a tutor could scan,
Have a few more still left, like the razor-strop man.

Now pray don't be frightened — I'm ready to stop
My galloping anapests' clatter and pop —
In fact, if you say so, retire from to-day
To the garret I left, on a poet's half-pay.

And yet — I can't help it — perhaps — who
    can tell ?
You might miss the poor singer you treated
    so well,
And confess you could stand him five min-
    utes or so,
"It was so like old times we remember, you
    know."

'T is not that the music can signify much,
But then there are chords that awake with
    a touch, —
And our hearts can find echoes of sorrow
    and joy
To the winch of the minstrel who hails
    from Savoy.

So this hand-organ tune that I cheerfully
    grind
May bring the old places and faces to
    mind,
And seen in the light of the past we recall
The flowers that have faded bloom fairest
    of all !

OUR SWEET SINGER

J. A.

1872

One memory trembles on our lips;
    It throbs in every breast;
In tear-dimmed eyes, in mirth's eclipse,
    The shadow stands confessed.

O silent voice, that cheered so long
    Our manhood's marching day,
Without thy breath of heavenly song,
    How weary seems the way !

Vain every pictured phrase to tell
    Our sorrowing heart's desire, —
The shattered harp, the broken shell,
    The silent unstrung lyre;

For youth was round us while he sang;
    It glowed in every tone;
With bridal chimes the echoes rang,
    And made the past our own.

Oh blissful dream ! Our nursery joys
    We know must have an end,
But love and friendship's broken toys
    May God's good angels mend !

The cheering smile, the voice of mirth
    And laughter's gay surprise
That please the children born of earth,
    Why deem that Heaven denies ?

Methinks in that refulgent sphere
    That knows not sun or moon,
An earth-born saint might long to hear
    One verse of "Bonny Doon;"

Or walking through the streets of gold
    In heaven's unclouded light,
His lips recall the song of old
    And hum "The sky is bright."

And can we smile when thou art dead ?
    Ah, brothers, even so !
The rose of summer will be red,
    In spite of winter's snow.

Thou wouldst not leave us all in gloom
    Because thy song is still,
Nor blight the banquet-garland's bloom
    With grief's untimely chill.

The sighing wintry winds complain, —
    The singing bird has flown, —
Hark ! heard I not that ringing strain,
    That clear celestial tone ?

How poor these pallid phrases seem,
    How weak this tinkling line,
As warbles through my waking dream
    That angel voice of thine !

Thy requiem asks a sweeter lay;
    It falters on my tongue;
For all we vainly strive to say,
    Thou shouldst thyself have sung !

H. C. M. H. S. J. K. W.

1873

The dirge is played, the throbbing death-
    peal rung,
    The sad-voiced requiem sung;
On each white urn where memory dwells
The wreath of rustling immortelles
    Our loving hands have hung,
And balmiest leaves have strown and ten-
    derest blossoms flung.

The birds that filled the air with songs
    have flown,
    The wintry blasts have blown,
And these for whom the voice of spring
Bade the sweet choirs their carols sing
    Sleep in those chambers lone
Where snows untrodden lie, unheard the
    nightwinds moan.

We clasp them all in memory, as the vine
    Whose running stems untwine
The marble shaft, and steal around
The lowly stone, the nameless mound;
    With sorrowing hearts resign
Our brothers true and tried, and close our
    broken line.

How fast the lamps of life grow dim and die
    Beneath our sunset sky!
    Still fading, as along our track
    We cast our saddened glances back,
    And while we vainly sigh
The shadowy day recedes, the starry night
    draws nigh.

As when from pier to pier across the tide
    With even keel we glide,
The lights we left along the shore
Grow less and less, while more, yet more
    New vistas open wide
Of fair illumined streets and casements
    golden-eyed.

Each closing circle of our sunlit sphere
    Seems to bring heaven more near:
    Can we not dream that those we love
    Are listening in the world above
    And smiling as they hear
The voices known so well of friends that
    still are dear?

Does all that made us human fade away
    With this dissolving clay?
    Nay, rather deem the blessed isles
    Are bright and gay with joyous smiles,
    That angels have their play,
And saints that tire of song may claim
    their holiday.

All else of earth may perish; love alone
    Not heaven shall find outgrown!
    Are they not here, our spirit guests,
    With love still throbbing in their breasts?
    Once more let flowers be strown.
Welcome, ye shadowy forms, we count you
    still our own!

WHAT I HAVE COME FOR

1873

I HAVE come with my verses — I think I
    may claim
It is not the first time I have tried on the
    same.
They were puckered in rhyme, they were
    wrinkled in wit;
But your hearts were so large that they
    made them a fit.

I have come — not to tease you with more
    of my rhyme,
But to feel as I did in the blessed old time;
I want to hear him with the Brobdingnag
    laugh —
We count him at least as three men and a
    half.

I have come to meet judges so wise and so
    grand
That I shake in my shoes while they're
    shaking my hand;
And the prince among merchants who put
    back the crown
When they tried to enthrone him the King
    of the Town.

I have come to see George — Yes, I think
    there are four,
If they all were like these I could wish
    there were more.
I have come to see one whom we used to
    call "Jim,"
I want to see — oh, don't I want to see
    him?

I have come to grow young — on my word
    I declare
I have thought I detected a change in my
    hair!
One hour with "The Boys" will restore it
    to brown —
And a wrinkle or two I expect to rub down.

Yes, that's what I've come for, as all of
    us come;
When I meet the dear Boys I could wish I
    were dumb.
You asked me, you know, but it's spoiling
    the fun;
I have told what I came for; my ditty is
    done.

OUR BANKER

1874

OLD TIME, in whose bank we deposit our notes,
Is a miser who always wants guineas for groats;
He keeps all his customers still in arrears
By lending them minutes and charging them years.

The twelvemonth rolls round and we never forget
On the counter before us to pay him our debt.
We reckon the marks he has chalked on the door,
Pay up and shake hands and begin a new score.

How long he will lend us, how much we may owe,
No angel will tell us, no mortal may know.
At fivescore, at fourscore, at threescore and ten,
He may close the account with a stroke of his pen.

This only we know, — amid sorrows and joys
Old Time has been easy and kind with "The Boys."
Though he must have and will have and does have his pay,
We have found him good-natured enough in his way.

He never forgets us, as others will do, —
I am sure he knows me, and I think he knows you,
For I see on your foreheads a mark that he lends
As a sign he remembers to visit his friends.

In the shape of a classmate (a wig on his crown, —
His day-book and ledger laid carefully down)
He has welcomed us yearly, a glass in his hand,
And pledged the good health of our brotherly band.

He's a thief, we must own, but how many there be
That rob us less gently and fairly than he:
He has stripped the green leaves that were over us all,
But they let in the sunshine as fast as they fall.

Young beauties may ravish the world with a glance
As they languish in song, as they float in the dance, —
They are grandmothers now we remember as girls,
And the comely white cap takes the place of the curls.

But the sighing and moaning and groaning are o'er,
We are pining and moping and sleepless no more,
And the hearts that were thumping like ships on the rocks
Beat as quiet and steady as meeting-house clocks.

The trump of ambition, loud sounding and shrill,
May blow its long blast, but the echoes are still,
The spring-tides are past, but no billow may reach
The spoils they have landed far up on the beach.

We see that Time robs us, we know that he cheats,
But we still find a charm in his pleasant deceits,
While he leaves the remembrance of all that was best,
Love, friendship, and hope, and the promise of rest.

Sweet shadows of twilight! how calm their repose,
While the dewdrops fall soft in the breast of the rose!
How blest to the toiler his hour of release
When the vesper is heard with its whisper of peace!

Then here's to the wrinkled old miser, our friend;
May he send us his bills to the century's end,

And lend us the moments no sorrow alloys,
Till he squares his account with the last of
"The Boys."

FOR CLASS MEETING

1875

It is a pity and a shame — alas! alas! I
  know it is,
To tread the trodden grapes again, but so
  it has been, so it is;
The purple vintage long is past, with
  ripened clusters bursting so
They filled the wine-vats to the brim, —
  't is strange you will be thirsting so!

Too well our faithful memory tells what
  might be rhymed or sung about,
For all have sighed and some have wept
  since last year's snows were flung
  about;
The beacon flame that fired the sky, the
  modest ray that gladdened us,
A little breath has quenched their light, and
  deepening shades have saddened us.

No more our brother's life is ours for cheer-
  ing or for grieving us,
One only sadness they bequeathed, the sor-
  row of their leaving us;
Farewell! Farewell! — I turn the leaf I
  read my chiming measure in;
Who knows but something still is there a
  friend may find a pleasure in?

For who can tell by what he likes what other
  people's fancies are?
How all men think the best of wives their
  own particular Nancies are?
If what I sing you brings a smile, you will
  not stop to catechise,
Nor read Bœotia's lumbering line with
  nicely scanning Attic eyes.

Perhaps the alabaster box that Mary broke
  so lovingly,
While Judas looked so sternly on, the Mas-
  ter so approvingly,
Was not so fairly wrought as those that
  Pilate's wife and daughters had,
Or many a dame of Judah's line that drank
  of Jordan's waters had.

Perhaps the balm that cost so dear, as some
  remarked officiously,
The precious nard that filled the room with
  fragrance so deliciously,
So oft recalled in storied page and sung in
  verse melodious,
The dancing girl had thought too cheap, —
  that daughter of Herodias.

Where now are all the mighty deeds that
  Herod boasted loudest of?
Where now the flashing jewelry the te-
  trarch's wife was proudest of?
Yet still to hear how Mary loved, all tribes
  of men are listening,
And still the sinful woman's tears like stars
  in heaven are glistening.

'Tis not the gift our hands have brought,
  the love it is we bring with it, —
The minstrel's lips may shape the song, his
  heart in tune must sing with it;
And so we love the simple lays, and wish
  we might have more of them,
Our poet brothers sing for us, — there must
  be half a score of them.

It may be that of fame and name our voices
  once were emulous, —
With deeper thoughts, with tenderer throbs
  their softening tones are tremu-
  lous;
The dead seem listening as of old, ere
  friendship was bereft of them;
The living wear a kinder smile, the remnant
  that is left of them.

Though on the once unfurrowed brows the
  harrow-teeth of Time may show,
Though all the strain of crippling years the
  halting feet of rhyme may show,
We look and hear with melting hearts, for
  what we all remember is
The morn of Spring, nor heed how chill the
  sky of gray November is.

Thanks to the gracious powers above from
  all mankind that singled us,
And dropped the pearl of friendship in the
  cup they kindly mingled us,
And bound us in a wreath of flowers with
  hoops of steel knit under it; —
Nor time, nor space, nor chance, nor change,
  nor death himself shall sunder it!

"AD AMICOS"

1876

*" Dumque virent genua
Et decet, obducta solvatur fonte senectus."*

THE muse of boyhood's fervid hour
  Grows tame as skies get chill and hazy;
Where once she sought a passion-flower,
  She only hopes to find a daisy.
Well, who the changing world bewails?
  Who asks to have it stay unaltered?
Shall grown-up kittens chase their tails?
  Shall colts be never shod or haltered?

Are we "The Boys" that used to make
  The tables ring with noisy follies?
Whose deep-lunged laughter oft would shake
  The ceiling with its thunder-volleys?
Are we the youths with lips unshorn,
  At beauty's feet unwrinkled suitors,
Whose memories reach tradition's morn, —
  The days of prehistoric tutors?

"The Boys" we knew, — but who are these
  Whose heads might serve for Plutarch's sages,
Or Fox's martyrs, if you please,
  Or hermits of the dismal ages?
"The Boys" we knew — can these be those?
  Their cheeks with morning's blush were painted; —
Where are the Harrys, Jims, and Joes
  With whom we once were well acquainted?

If we are they, we're not the same;
  If they are we, why then they're masking;
Do tell us, neighbor What's-your-name,
  Who are you? — What's the use of asking?
You once were George, or Bill, or Ben;
  There's you, yourself — there's you, that other —
I know you now — I knew you then —
  You used to be your younger brother!

You both are all our own to-day, —
  But ah! I hear a warning whisper;
You roseate hour that flits away
  Repeats the Roman's sad *paulisper*.

Come back! come back! we've need of you
  To pay you for your word of warning;
We'll bathe your wings in brighter dew
  Than ever wet the lids of morning!

Behold this cup; its mystic wine
  No alien's lip has ever tasted;
The blood of friendship's clinging vine,
  Still flowing, flowing, yet unwasted:
Old Time forgot his running sand
  And laid his hour-glass down to fill it,
And Death himself with gentle hand
  Has touched the chalice, not to spill it.

Each bubble rounding at the brim
  Is rainbowed with its magic story;
The shining days with age grown dim
  Are dressed again in robes of glory;
In all its freshness spring returns
  With song of birds and blossoms tender;
Once more the torch of passion burns,
  And youth is here in all its splendor!

Hope swings her anchor like a toy,
  Love laughs and shows the silver arrow
We knew so well as man and boy, —
  The shaft that stings through bone and marrow;
Again our kindling pulses beat,
  With tangled curls our fingers dally,
And bygone beauties smile as sweet
  As fresh-blown lilies of the valley.

O blessed hour! we may forget
  Its wreaths, its rhymes, its songs, its laughter,
But not the loving eyes we met,
  Whose light shall gild the dim hereafter.
How every heart to each grows warm!
  Is one in sunshine's ray? We share it.
Is one in sorrow's blinding storm?
  A look, a word, shall help him bear it.

"The Boys" we were, "The Boys" we'll be
  As long as three, as two, are creeping;
Then here's to him — ah! which is he? —
  Who lives till all the rest are sleeping;
A life with tranquil comfort blest,
  The young man's health, the rich man's plenty,
All earth can give that earth has best,
  And heaven at fourscore years and twenty.

HOW NOT TO SETTLE IT
1877

I LIKE, at times, to hear the steeples'
chimes
With sober thoughts impressibly that
mingle;
But sometimes, too, I rather like — don't
you? —
To hear the music of the sleigh bells'
jingle.

I like full well the deep resounding swell
Of mighty symphonies with chords in-
woven;
But sometimes, too, a song of Burns —
don't you?
After a solemn storm-blast of Beetho-
ven.

Good to the heels the well-worn slipper
feels
When the tired player shuffles off the
buskin;
A page of Hood may do a fellow good
After a scolding from Carlyle or Ruskin.

Some works I find, — say Watts upon the
Mind, —
No matter though at first they seemed
amusing,
Not quite the same, but just a little tame
After some five or six times' reperusing.

So, too, at times when melancholy rhymes
Or solemn speeches sober down a dinner,
I 've seen it 's true, quite often, — have n't
you? —
The best-fed guests perceptibly grow
thinner.

Better some jest (in proper terms ex-
pressed)
Or story (strictly moral) even if musty,
Or song we sung when these old throats
were young, —
Something to keep our souls from get-
ting rusty.

The poorest scrap from memory's ragged
lap
Comes like an heirloom from a dear
dead mother —

Hush! there 's a tear that has no business
here,
A half-formed sigh that ere its birth we
smother.

We cry, we laugh; ah, life is half and half,
Now bright and joyous as a song of
Herrick's,
Then chill and bare as funeral-minded
Blair;
As fickle as a female in hysterics.

If I could make you cry I would n't try;
If you have hidden smiles I 'd like to
find them,
And that although, as well I ought to
know,
The lips of laughter have a skull behind
them.

Yet when I think we may be on the brink
Of having Freedom's banner to dispose
of,
All crimson-hued, because the Nation
would
Insist on cutting its own precious nose
off,

I feel indeed as if we rather need
A sermon such as preachers tie a text
on.
If Freedom dies because a ballot lies,
She earns her grave; 't is time to call the
sexton!

But if a fight can make the matter right,
Here are we, classmates, thirty men of
mettle;
We 're strong and tough, we 've lived nigh
long enough, —
What if the Nation gave it us to settle?

The tale would read like that illustrious
deed
When Curtius took the leap the gap
that filled in,
Thus: "Fivescore years, good friends, as
it appears,
At last this people split on Hayes and
Tilden.

"One half cried, 'See! the choice is S. J.
T.!'
And one half swore as stoutly it was t'
other;

Both drew the knife to save the Nation's life
By wholesale vivisection of each other.

"Then rose in mass that monumental Class, —
'Hold! hold!' they cried, 'give us, give us the daggers!'
'Content! content!' exclaimed with one consent
The gaunt ex-rebels and the carpet-baggers.

"Fifteen each side, the combatants divide,
So nicely balanced are their predilections;
And first of all a tear-drop each lets fall,
A tribute to their obsolete affections.

"Man facing man, the sanguine strife began,
Jack, Jim and Joe against Tom, Dick and Harry,
Each several pair its own account to square,
Till both were down or one stood solitary.

"And the great fight raged furious all the night
Till every integer was made a fraction;
Reader, wouldst know what history has to show
As net result of the above transaction?

"Whole coat-tails, four; stray fragments, several score;
A heap of spectacles; a deaf man's trumpet;
Six lawyers' briefs; seven pocket-handkerchiefs;
Twelve canes wherewith the owners used to stump it;

"Odd rubber-shoes; old gloves of different hues;
Tax-bills, — unpaid, — and several empty purses;
And, saved from harm by some protecting charm,
A printed page with Smith's immortal verses;

"Trifles that claim no very special name, —
Some useful, others chiefly ornamental;
Pins, buttons, rings, and other trivial things,
With various wrecks, capillary and dental.

"Also, one flag, — 't was nothing but a rag,
And what device it bore it little matters;
Red, white, and blue, but rent all through and through,
'Union forever' torn to shreds and tatters.

"They fought so well not one was left to tell
Which got the largest share of cuts and slashes;
When heroes meet, both sides are bound to beat;
They telescoped like cars in railroad smashes.

"So the great split that baffled human wit
And might have cost the lives of twenty millions,
As all may see that know the rule of three,
Was settled just as well by these civilians.

"As well. Just so. Not worse, not better. No,
Next morning found the Nation still divided;
Since all were slain, the inference is plain
They left the point they fought for undecided."

If not quite true, as I have told it you, —
This tale of mutual extermination,
To minds perplexed with threats of what comes next,
Perhaps may furnish food for contemplation.

To cut men's throats to help them count their votes
Is asinine — nay, worse — ascidian folly;
Blindness like that would scare the mole and bat,
And make the liveliest monkey melancholy.

I say once more, as I have said before,
If voting for our Tildens and our Hayeses
Means only fight, then, Liberty, good night!
Pack up your ballot-box and go to blazes!

Unfurl your blood-red flags, you murderous hags,
You *pétroleuses* of Paris, fierce and foamy;
We 'll sell our stock in Plymouth's blasted rock,
Pull up our stakes and migrate to Dahomey!

THE LAST SURVIVOR

1878

YES! the vacant chairs tell sadly we are going, going fast,
And the thought comes strangely o'er me, who will live to be the last?
When the twentieth century's sunbeams climb the far-off eastern hill,
With his ninety winters burdened, will he greet the morning still?

Will he stand with Harvard's nurslings when they hear their mother's call
And the old and young are gathered in the many alcoved hall?
Will he answer to the summons when they range themselves in line
And the young mustachioed marshal calls out "Class of '29"?

Methinks I see the column as its lengthened ranks appear
In the sunshine of the morrow of the nineteen hundredth year;
Through the yard 't is creeping, winding, by the walls of dusky red, —
What shape is that which totters at the long procession's head?

Who knows this ancient graduate of fourscore years and ten, —
What place he held, what name he bore among the sons of men?
So speeds the curious question; its answer travels slow;
"'T is the last of sixty classmates of seventy years ago."

His figure shows but dimly, his face I scarce can see, —
There's something that reminds me, — it looks like — is it he?

He? Who? No voice may whisper what wrinkled brow shall claim
The wreath of stars that circles our last survivor's name.

Will he be some veteran minstrel, left to pipe in feeble rhyme
All the stories and the glories of our gay and golden time?
Or some quiet, voiceless brother in whose lonely, loving breast
Fond memory broods in silence, like a dove upon her nest?

Will it be some old *Emeritus*, who taught so long ago
The boys that heard him lecture have heads as white as snow?
Or a pious, painful preacher, holding forth from year to year
Till his colleague got a colleague whom the young folks flocked to hear?

Will it be a rich old merchant in a square-tied white cravat,
Or selectman of a village in a pre-historic hat?
Will his dwelling be a mansion in a marble-fronted row,
Or a homestead by a hillside where the huckleberries grow?

I can see our one survivor, sitting lonely by himself, —
All his college text-books round him, ranged in order on their shelf;
There are classic "interliners" filled with learning's choicest pith,
Each *cum notis variorum, quas recensuit doctus* Smith;

Physics, metaphysics, logic, mathematics — all the lot
Every wisdom-crammed octavo he has mastered and forgot,
With the ghosts of dead professors standing guard beside them all;
And the room is full of shadows which their lettered backs recall.

How the past spreads out in vision with its far receding train,
Like a long embroidered arras in the chambers of the brain,

From opening manhood's morning when
    first we learned to grieve
To the fond regretful moments of our sor-
    row-saddened eve !

What early shadows darkened our idle
    summer's joy
When death snatched roughly from us that
    lovely bright-eyed boy !
The years move swiftly onwards ; the
    deadly shafts fall fast, —
Till all have dropped around him — lo,
    there he stands, — the last !

Their faces flit before him, some rosy-hued
    and fair,
Some strong in iron manhood, some worn
    with toil and care;
Their smiles no more shall greet him on
    cheeks with pleasure flushed !
The friendly hands are folded, the pleasant
    voices hushed !

. . . .

My picture sets me dreaming; alas ! and
    can it be
Those two familiar faces we never more
    may see ?
In every entering footfall I think them
    drawing near,
With every door that opens I say, "At
    last they 're here !"

The willow bends unbroken when angry
    tempests blow,
The stately oak is levelled and all its
    strength laid low ;
So fell that tower of manhood, undaunted,
    patient, strong,
White with the gathering snowflakes, who
    faced the storm so long.

And he, — what subtle phrases their vary-
    ing light must blend
To paint as each remembers our many-
    featured friend !
His wit a flash auroral that laughed in
    every look,
His talk a sunbeam broken on the ripples
    of a brook,

Or, fed from thousand sources, a fountain's
    glittering jet,
Or careless handfuls scattered of diamond
    sparks unset;

Ah, sketch him, paint him, mould him in
    every shape you will,
He was *himself* — the only — the one un-
    pictured still !

Farewell ! our skies are darkened and yet
    the stars will shine,
We 'll close our ranks together and still
    fall into line
Till one is left, one only, to mourn for all
    the rest;
And Heaven bequeath their memories to
    him who loves us best !

THE ARCHBISHOP AND GIL BLAS

A MODERNIZED VERSION

1879

I DON'T think I feel much older; I 'm
    aware I 'm rather gray,
But so are many young folks; I meet 'em
    every day.
I confess I 'm more particular in what I
    eat and drink,
But one's taste improves with culture;
    that is all it means, I think.

Can you read as once you used to ? Well,
    the printing is so bad,
No young folks' eyes can read it like the
    books that once we had.
Are you quite as quick of hearing ? Please
    to say that once again.
Don't I use plain words, your Reverence ?
    Yes, I often use a cane,
But it 's not because I need it, — no, I al-
    ways liked a stick;
And as one might lean upon it, 't is as well
    it should be thick.
Oh, I 'm smart, I 'm spry, I 'm lively, —
    I can walk, yes, that I can,
On the days I feel like walking, just as
    well as you, young man !

*Don't you get a little sleepy after dinner every
    day ?*
Well, I doze a little, sometimes, but that
    always was my way.

*Don't you cry a little easier than some twenty
  years ago?*
Well, my heart is very tender, but I think
  't was always so.

*Don't you find it sometimes happens that you
  can't recall a name?*
Yes, I know such lots of people, — but my
  memory's not to blame.
What! You think my memory's fail-
  ing! Why, it's just as bright and
  clear, —
I remember my great-grandma! She's
  been dead these sixty year!

Is your voice a little trembly? Well, it may
  be, now and then,
But I write as well as ever with a good old-
  fashioned pen;
It's the Gillotts make the trouble, — not
  at all my finger-ends, —
That is why my hand looks shaky when I
  sign for dividends.

Don't you stoop a little, walking? It's a
  way I've always had,
I have always been round-shouldered, ever
  since I was a lad.
Don't you hate to tie your shoe-strings? Yes,
  I own it — that is true.
Don't you tell old stories over? I am not
  aware I do.

*Don't you stay at home of evenings? Don't
  you love a cushioned seat
In a corner, by the fireside, with your slippers
  on your feet?
Don't you wear warm fleecy flannels? Don't
  you muffle up your throat?
Don't you like to have one help you when
  you're putting on your coat?*

*Don't you like old books you've dogs-eared,
  you can't remember when?
Don't you call it late at nine o'clock and go to
  bed at ten?
How many cronies can you count of all you
  used to know
Who called you by your Christian name some
  fifty years ago?*

*How look the prizes to you that used to fire
  your brain?
You've reared your mound — how high is it
  above the level plain?*

*You've drained the brimming golden cup that
  made your fancy reel,
You've slept the giddy potion off, — now tell
  us how you feel!*

*You've watched the harvest ripening till every
  stem was cropped,
You've seen the rose of beauty fade till every
  petal dropped,
You've told your thought, you've done your
  task, you've tracked your dial round,*
— I backing down! Thank Heaven, not
  yet! I'm hale and brisk and sound,

And good for many a tussle, as you shall
  live to see;
My shoes are not quite ready yet, — don't
  think you're rid of me!
Old Parr was in his lusty prime when he
  was older far,
And where will you be if I live to beat old
  Thomas Parr?

*Ah well, — I know, — at every age life has a
  certain charm, —
You're going? Come, permit me, please, I
  beg you'll take my arm.*
I take your arm! Why take your arm?
  I'd thank you to be told
I'm old enough to walk alone, but not so
  very old!

THE SHADOWS

1880

"How many have gone?" was the ques-
  tion of old
  Ere Time our bright ring of its jewels
  bereft;
Alas! for too often the death-bell has
  tolled,
  And the question we ask is, "How many
  are left?"

Bright sparkled the wine; there were *fifty*
  that quaffed;
  For a decade had slipped and had taken
  but three.
How they frolicked and sung, how they
  shouted and laughed,
  Like a school full of boys from their
  benches set free!

There were speeches and toasts, there were
    stories and rhymes,
The hall shook its sides with their mer-
    riment's noise;
As they talked and lived over the college-
    day times, —
No wonder they kept their old name of
    "The Boys"!

The seasons moved on in their rhythmical
    flow
With mornings like maidens that pouted
    or smiled,
With the bud and the leaf and the fruit
    and the snow,
And the year-books of Time in his al-
    coves were piled.

There were *forty* that gathered where fifty
    had met;
Some locks had got silvered, some lives
    had grown sere,
But the laugh of the laughers was lusty as
    yet,
And the song of the singers rose ringing
    and clear.

Still flitted the years; there were *thirty*
    that came;
"The Boys" they were still, and they
    answered their call;
There were foreheads of care, but the
    smiles were the same,
And the chorus rang loud through the
    garlanded hall.

The hour-hand moved on, and they
    gathered again;
There were *twenty* that joined in the
    hymn that was sung;
But ah! for our song-bird we listened in
    vain, —
The crystalline tones like a seraph's that
    rung!

How narrow the circle that holds us to-
    night!
How many the loved ones that greet us
    no more,
As we meet like the stragglers that come
    from the fight,
Like the mariners flung from a wreck on
    the shore!

We look through the twilight for those we
    have lost;
The stream rolls between us, and yet
    they seem near;
Already outnumbered by those who have
    crossed,
Our band is transplanted, its home is not
    here!

They smile on us still — is it only a
    dream? —
While fondly or proudly their names we
    recall;
They beckon — they come — they are
    crossing the stream —
Lo! the Shadows! the Shadows! room
    — room for them all!

BENJAMIN PEIRCE

ASTRONOMER, MATHEMATICIAN
1809–1880

1881

FOR him the Architect of all
Unroofed our planet's starlit hall;
Through voids unknown to worlds unseen
His clearer vision rose serene.

With us on earth he walked by day,
His midnight path how far away!
We knew him not so well who knew
The patient eyes his soul looked through;

For who his untrod realm could share
Of us that breathe this mortal air,
Or camp in that celestial tent
Whose fringes gild our firmament?

How vast the workroom where he brought
The viewless implements of thought!
The wit how subtle, how profound,
That Nature's tangled webs unwound;

That through the clouded matrix saw
The crystal planes of shaping law,
Through these the sovereign skill that
    planned, —
The Father's care, the Master's hand!

To him the wandering stars revealed
The secrets in their cradle sealed:

The far-off, frozen sphere that swings
Through ether, zoned with lucid rings;

The orb that rolls in dim eclipse
Wide wheeling round its long ellipse, —
His name Urania writes with these
And stamps it on her Pleiades.

We knew him not? Ah, well we knew
The manly soul, so brave, so true,
The cheerful heart that conquered age,
The childlike silver-bearded sage.

No more his tireless thought explores
The azure sea with golden shores;
Rest, wearied frame! the stars shall keep
A loving watch where thou shalt sleep.

Farewell! the spirit needs must rise,
So long a tenant of the skies, —
Rise to that home all worlds above
Whose sun is God, whose light is love.

IN THE TWILIGHT
1882

NOT bed-time yet! The night-winds blow,
The stars are out, — full well we know
  The nurse is on the stair,
With hand of ice and cheek of snow,
And frozen lips that whisper low,
"Come, children, it is time to go
  My peaceful couch to share."

No years a wakeful heart can tire;
Not bed-time yet! Come, stir the fire
  And warm your dear old hands;
Kind Mother Earth we love so well
Has pleasant stories yet to tell
Before we hear the curfew bell;
  Still glow the burning brands.

Not bed-time yet! We long to know
What wonders time has yet to show,
  What unborn years shall bring;
What ship the Arctic pole shall reach,
What lessons Science waits to teach,
What sermons there are left to preach,
  What poems yet to sing.

What next? we ask; and is it true
The sunshine falls on nothing new,
  As Israel's king declared?

Was ocean ploughed with harnessed fire?
Were nations coupled with a wire?
Did Tarshish telegraph to Tyre?
  How Hiram would have stared!

And what if Sheba's curious queen,
Who came to see, — and to be seen, —
  Or something new to seek,
And swooned, as ladies sometimes do,
At sights that thrilled her through and
      through,
Had heard, as she was "coming to,"
  A locomotive's shriek,

And seen a rushing railway train
As she looked out along the plain
  From David's lofty tower, —
A mile of smoke that blots the sky
And blinds the eagles as they fly
Behind the cars that thunder by
  A score of leagues an hour!

See to my *fiat lux* respond
This little slumbering fire-tipped wand, —
  One touch, — it bursts in flame!
Steal me a portrait from the sun, —
One look, — and lo! the picture done!
Are these old tricks, King Solomon,
  We lying moderns claim?

Could you have spectroscoped a star?
If both those mothers at your bar,
  The cruel and the mild,
The young and tender, old and tough,
Had said, "Divide, — you 're right, though
      rough," —
Did old Judea know enough
  To etherize the child?

These births of time our eyes have seen,
With but a few brief years between;
  What wonder if the text,
For other ages doubtless true,
For coming years will never do, —
Whereof we all should like a few,
  If but to see what next.

If such things have been, such may be;
Who would not like to live and see —
  If Heaven may so ordain —
What waifs undreamed of, yet in store,
The waves that roll forevermore
On life's long beach may cast ashore
  From out the mist-clad main?

Will Earth to pagan dreams return
To find from misery's painted urn
   That all save hope has flown, —
Of Book and Church and Priest bereft,
The Rock of Ages vainly cleft,
Life's compass gone, its anchor left,
   Left, — lost, — in depths unknown?

Shall Faith the trodden path pursue
The *crux ansata* wearers knew
   Who sleep with folded hands,
Where, like a naked, lidless eye,
The staring Nile rolls wandering by
Those mountain slopes that climb the sky
   Above the drifting sands?

Or shall a nobler Faith return,
Its fanes a purer gospel learn,
   With holier anthems ring,
And teach us that our transient creeds
Were but the perishable seeds
Of harvests sown for larger needs,
   That ripening years shall bring?

Well, let the present do its best,
We trust our Maker for the rest,
   As on our way we plod;
Our souls, full dressed in fleshly suits,
Love air and sunshine, flowers and fruits,
The daisies better than their roots
   Beneath the grassy sod.

Not bed-time yet! The full-blown flower
Of all the year — this evening hour —
   With friendship's flame is bright;
Life still is sweet, the heavens are fair,
Though fields are brown and woods are bare,
And many a joy is left to share
   Before we say Good-night!

And when, our cheerful evening past,
The nurse, long waiting, comes at last,
   Ere on her lap we lie
In wearied nature's sweet repose,
At peace with all her waking foes,
Our lips shall murmur, ere they close,
   Good-night! and not Good-by!

A LOVING-CUP SONG

1883

Come, heap the fagots! Ere we go
Again the cheerful hearth shall glow;
We'll have another blaze, my boys!
When clouds are black and snows are white,
Then Christmas logs lend ruddy light
   They stole from summer days, my boys,
      They stole from summer days.

And let the Loving-Cup go round,
The Cup with blessed memories crowned,
   That flows whene'er we meet, my boys;
No draught will hold a drop of sin
If love is only well stirred in
   To keep it sound and sweet, my boys,
      To keep it sound and sweet.

Give me, to pin upon my breast,
The blossoms twain I love the best,
   A rosebud and a pink, my boys;
Their leaves shall nestle next my heart,
Their perfumed breath shall own its part
   In every health we drink, my boys,
      In every health we drink.

The breathing blossoms stir my blood,
Methinks I see the lilacs bud
   And hear the bluebirds sing, my boys;
Why not? Yon lusty oak has seen
Full tenscore years, yet leaflets green
   Peep out with every spring, my boys,
      Peep out with every spring.

Old Time his rusty scythe may whet,
The unmowed grass is glowing yet
   Beneath the sheltering snow, my boys;
And if the crazy dotard ask,
Is love worn out? Is life a task?
   We'll bravely answer No! my boys,
      We'll bravely answer No!

For life's bright taper is the same
Love tipped of old with rosy flame
   That heaven's own altar lent, my boys,
To glow in every cup we fill
Till lips are mute and hearts are still,
   Till life and love are spent, my boys,
      Till life and love are spent.

THE GIRDLE OF FRIENDSHIP

1884

She gathered at her slender waist
   The beauteous robe she wore;
Its folds a golden belt embraced,
   One rose-hued gem it bore.

The girdle shrank; its lessening round
  Still kept the shining gem,
But now her flowing locks it bound,
  A lustrous diadem.

And narrower still the circlet grew;
  Behold! a glittering band,
Its roseate diamond set anew,
  Her neck's white column spanned.

Suns rise and set; the straining clasp
  The shortened links resist,
Yet flashes in a bracelet's grasp
  The diamond, on her wrist.

At length, the round of changes past
  The thieving years could bring,
The jewel, glittering to the last,
  Still sparkles in a ring.

So, link by link, our friendships part,
  So loosen, break, and fall,
A narrowing zone; the loving heart
  Lives changeless through them all.

THE LYRE OF ANACREON

1885

The minstrel of the classic lay
  Of love and wine who sings
Still found the fingers run astray
  That touched the rebel strings.

Of Cadmus he would fain have sung,
  Of Atreus and his line;
But all the jocund echoes rung
  With songs of love and wine.

Ah, brothers! I would fain have caught
  Some fresher fancy's gleam;
My truant accents find, unsought,
  The old familiar theme.

Love, Love! but not the sportive child
  With shaft and twanging bow,
Whose random arrows drove us wild
  Some threescore years ago;

Not Eros, with his joyous laugh,
  The urchin blind and bare,
But Love, with spectacles and staff,
  And scanty, silvered hair.

Our heads with frosted locks are white,
  Our roofs are thatched with snow,
But red, in chilling winter's spite,
  Our hearts and hearthstones glow.

Our old acquaintance, Time, drops in,
  And while the running sands
Their golden thread unheeded spin,
  He warms his frozen hands.

Stay, wingèd hours, too swift, too sweet,
  And waft this message o'er
To all we miss, from all we meet
  On life's fast-crumbling shore:

Say that, to old affection true,
  We hug the narrowing chain
That binds our hearts, — alas, how few
  The links that yet remain!

The fatal touch awaits them all
  That turns the rocks to dust;
From year to year they break and fall, —
  They break, but never rust.

Say if one note of happier strain
  This worn-out harp afford, —
One throb that trembles, not in vain, —
  Their memory lent its chord.

Say that when Fancy closed her wings
  And Passion quenched his fire,
Love, Love, still echoed from the strings
  As from Anacreon's lyre!

THE OLD TUNE

THIRTY-SIXTH VARIATION

1886

This shred of song you bid me bring
  Is snatched from fancy's embers;
Ah, when the lips forget to sing,
  The faithful heart remembers!

Too swift the wings of envious Time
  To wait for dallying phrases,
Or woven strands of labored rhyme
  To thread their cunning mazes.

A word, a sigh, and lo, how plain
  Its magic breath discloses
Our life's long vista through a lane
  Of threescore summers' roses!

One language years alone can teach:
  Its roots are young affections
That feel their way to simplest speech
  Through silent recollections.

That tongue is ours. How few the words
  We need to know a brother!
As simple are the notes of birds,
  Yet well they know each other.

This freezing month of ice and snow
  That brings our lives together
Lends to our year a living glow
  That warms its wintry weather.

So let us meet as eve draws nigh,
  And life matures and mellows,
Till Nature whispers with a sigh,
  "Good-night, my dear old fellows!"

THE BROKEN CIRCLE

1887

[What is half a century to a place like Stonehenge? Nothing dwarfs an individual life like one of these massive, almost unchanging monuments of an antiquity which refuses to be measured. . . . The broken circle of stones, some in their original position, some bending over like old men, some lying prostrate, suggested the thoughts which took form in the following verses. *Our Hundred Days in Europe*, pp. 110, 111.]

I stood on Sarum's treeless plain,
  The waste that careless Nature owns;
Lone tenants of her bleak domain,
  Loomed huge and gray the Druid stones.

Upheaved in many a billowy mound
  The sea-like, naked turf arose,
Where wandering flocks went nibbling round
  The mingled graves of friends and foes.

The Briton, Roman, Saxon, Dane,
  This windy desert roamed in turn;
Unmoved these mighty blocks remain
  Whose story none that lives may learn.

Erect, half buried, slant or prone,
  These awful listeners, blind and dumb,
Hear the strange tongues of tribes unknown,
  As wave on wave they go and come.

"Who are you, giants, whence and why?"
  I stand and ask in blank amaze;
My soul accepts their mute reply:
  "A mystery, as are you that gaze.

"A silent Orpheus wrought the charm
  From riven rocks their spoils to bring;
A nameless Titan lent his arm
  To range us in our magic ring.

"But Time with still and stealthy stride,
  That climbs and treads and levels all,
That bids the loosening keystone slide,
  And topples down the crumbling wall, —

"Time, that unbuilds the quarried past,
  Leans on these wrecks that press the sod;
They slant, they stoop, they fall at last,
  And strew the turf their priests have trod.

"No more our altar's wreath of smoke
  Floats up with morning's fragrant dew;
The fires are dead, the ring is broke,
  Where stood the many stand the few."

My thoughts had wandered far away,
  Borne off on Memory's outspread wing,
To where in deepening twilight lay
  The wrecks of friendship's broken ring.

Ah me! of all our goodly train
  How few will find our banquet hall!
Yet why with coward lips complain
  That this must lean, and that must fall?

Cold is the Druid's altar-stone,
  Its vanished flame no more returns;
But ours no chilling damp has known, —
  Unchanged, unchanging, still it burns.

So let our broken circle stand
  A wreck, a remnant, yet the same,
While one last, loving, faithful hand
  Still lives to feed its altar-flame!

THE ANGEL-THIEF

1888

Time is a thief who leaves his tools behind him;
  He comes by night, he vanishes at dawn;

We track his footsteps, but we never find
   him:
  Strong locks are broken, massive bolts
   are drawn,

And all around are left the bars and borers,
  The splitting wedges and the prying
   keys,
Such aids as serve the soft-shod vault-ex-
   plorers
  To crack, wrench open, rifle as they
   please.

Ah, these are tools which Heaven in mercy
   lends us!
  When gathering rust has clenched our
   shackles fast,
Time is the angel-thief that Nature sends us
  To break the cramping fetters of our
   past.

Mourn as we may for treasures he has
   taken,
  Poor as we feel of hoarded wealth bereft,
More precious are those implements for-
   saken,
  Found in the wreck his ruthless hands
   have left.

Some lever that a casket's hinge has
   broken
  Pries off a bolt, and lo! our souls are
   free;
Each year some Open Sesame is spoken,
  And every decade drops its master-key.

So as from year to year we count our treas-
   ure,
  Our loss seems less, and larger look our
   gains;
Time's wrongs repaid in more than even
   measure,—
  We lose our jewels, but we break our
   chains.

AFTER THE CURFEW

1889

[The only remaining meeting of the class at Parker's was in 1890, three present. There was no poem.]

The Play is over. While the light
  Yet lingers in the darkening hall,
I come to say a last Good-night
  Before the final *Exeunt all.*

We gathered once, a joyous throng:
  The jovial toasts went gayly round;
With jest, and laugh, and shout, and song,
  We made the floors and walls resound.

We come with feeble steps and slow,
  A little band of four or five,
Left from the wrecks of long ago,
  Still pleased to find ourselves alive.

Alive! How living, too, are they
  Whose memories it is ours to share!
Spread the long table's full array,—
  There sits a ghost in every chair!

One breathing form no more, alas!
  Amid our slender group we see;
With him we still remained "The Class,"—
  Without his presence what are we?

The hand we ever loved to clasp,—
  That tireless hand which knew no rest,—
Loosed from affection's clinging grasp,
  Lies nerveless on the peaceful breast.

The beaming eye, the cheering voice,
  That lent to life a generous glow,
Whose every meaning said "Rejoice,"
  We see, we hear, no more below.

The air seems darkened by his loss,
  Earth's shadowed features look less fair,
And heavier weighs the daily cross
  His willing shoulders helped us bear.

Why mourn that we, the favored few
  Whom grasping Time so long has spared
Life's sweet illusions to pursue,
  The common lot of age have shared?

In every pulse of Friendship's heart
  There breeds unfelt a throb of pain,—
One hour must rend its links apart,
  Though years on years have forged the
   chain.

So ends "The Boys,"— a lifelong play.
  We too must hear the Prompter's call
To fairer scenes and brighter day:
  Farewell! I let the curtain fall.

POEMS FROM THE AUTOCRAT OF THE BREAKFAST-TABLE

1857-1858

[THE collection under this heading is not complete, since a few of the poems had been placed by the author in other divisions. Inasmuch as the poems when first printed were in many cases introduced by a prose passage, these introductions are here reproduced, without the editorial brackets. The same method has been followed with the two succeeding groups.]

THE CHAMBERED NAUTILUS

We need not trouble ourselves about the distinction between this [the Pearly Nautilus] and the Paper Nautilus, the *Argonauta* of the ancients. The name applied to both shows that each has long been compared to a ship, as you may see more fully in *Webster's Dictionary* or the *Encyclopedia*, to which he refers. If you will look into Roget's *Bridgewater Treatise* you will find a figure of one of these shells and a section of it. The last will show you the series of enlarging compartments successively dwelt in by the animal that inhabits the shell, which is built in a widening spiral. [This poem seemed to share with Dorothy Q. Dr. Holmes's interest, if one may judge by the frequency with which he chose it for reading or for autograph albums. He says on receipt of an album from the Princess of Wales, "I copied into it the last verse of a poem of mine called *The Chambered Nautilus*, as I have often done for plain republican albums."]

THIS is the ship of pearl, which, poets feign,
    Sails the unshadowed main, —
    The venturous bark that flings
On the sweet summer wind its purpled wings
In gulfs enchanted, where the Siren sings,
    And coral reefs lie bare,
Where the cold sea-maids rise to sun their streaming hair.

Its webs of living gauze no more unfurl;
    Wrecked is the ship of pearl!
    And every chambered cell,
Where its dim dreaming life was wont to dwell,
As the frail tenant shaped his growing shell,
    Before thee lies revealed, —
Its irised ceiling rent, its sunless crypt unsealed!

Year after year beheld the silent toil
    That spread his lustrous coil;
    Still, as the spiral grew,
He left the past year's dwelling for the new,
Stole with soft step its shining archway through,
    Built up its idle door,
Stretched in his last-found home, and knew the old no more.

Thanks for the heavenly message brought by thee,
    Child of the wandering sea,
    Cast from her lap, forlorn!
From thy dead lips a clearer note is born
Than ever Triton blew from wreathèd horn!
    While on mine ear it rings,
Through the deep caves of thought I hear a voice that sings: —

Build thee more stately mansions, O my soul,
    As the swift seasons roll!
    Leave thy low-vaulted past!
Let each new temple, nobler than the last,
Shut thee from heaven with a dome more vast,

Till thou at length art free,
Leaving thine outgrown shell by life's unresting sea!

SUN AND SHADOW

[The isle where this poem was written was Naushon, already celebrated in the poems *To Governor Swain* and *The Island Hunting-Song.*] How can a man help writing poetry in such a place? When the sun is in the west, vessels sailing in an easterly direction look bright or dark to one who observes them from the north or south, according to the tack they are sailing upon. Watching them from one of the windows of the great mansion, I saw these perpetual changes, and moralized thus:—

As I look from the isle, o'er its billows of green,
To the billows of foam-crested blue,
Yon bark, that afar in the distance is seen,
Half dreaming, my eyes will pursue:
Now dark in the shadow, she scatters the spray
As the chaff in the stroke of the flail;
Now white as the sea-gull, she flies on her way,
The sun gleaming bright on her sail.

Yet her pilot is thinking of dangers to shun,—
Of breakers that whiten and roar;
How little he cares, if in shadow or sun
They see him who gaze from the shore!
He looks to the beacon that looms from the reef,
To the rock that is under his lee,
As he drifts on the blast, like a wind-wafted leaf,
O'er the gulfs of the desolate sea.

Thus drifting afar to the dim-vaulted caves
Where life and its ventures are laid,
The dreamers who gaze while we battle the waves
May see us in sunshine or shade;
Yet true to our course, though the shadows grow dark,
We'll trim our broad sail as before,
And stand by the rudder that governs the bark,
Nor ask how we look from the shore!

MUSA

The throbbing flushes of the poetical intermittent have been coming over me from time to time of late. Did you ever see that electrical experiment which consists in passing a flash through letters of goldleaf in a darkened room, whereupon some name or legend springs out of the darkness in characters of fire? There are songs all written out in my soul, which I could read, if the flash might pass through them,—but the fire must come down from heaven. Ah! but what if the stormy *nimbus* of youthful passion has blown by, and one asks for lightning from the ragged *cirrus* of dissolving aspirations, or the silvered cumulus of sluggish satiety? I will call on her whom the dead poets believed in, whom living ones no longer worship,—the immortal maid, who, name her what you will,—Goddess, Muse, Spirit of Beauty,—sits by the pillow of every youthful poet and bends over his pale forehead until her tresses lie upon his cheek and rain their gold into his dream.

O MY lost beauty!—hast thou folded quite
Thy wings of morning light
Beyond those iron gates
Where Life crowds hurrying to the haggard Fates,
And Age upon his mound of ashes waits
To chill our fiery dreams,
Hot from the heart of youth plunged in his icy streams?

Leave me not fading in these weeds of care,
Whose flowers are silvered hair!
Have I not loved thee long,
Though my young lips have often done thee wrong,
And vexed thy heaven-tuned ear with careless song?
Ah, wilt thou yet return,
Bearing thy rose-hued torch, and bid thine altar burn?

Come to me!—I will flood thy silent shrine
With my soul's sacred wine,
And heap thy marble floors
As the wild spice-trees waste their fragrant stores,
In leafy islands walled with madrepores

And lapped in Orient seas,
When all their feathery palms toss, plume-like, in the breeze.

Come to me! — thou shalt feed on honeyed words,
  Sweeter than song of birds; —
  No wailing bulbul's throat,
No melting dulcimer's melodious note
When o'er the midnight wave its murmurs float,
  Thy ravished sense might soothe
With flow so liquid-soft, with strain so velvet smooth.

Thou shalt be decked with jewels, like a queen,
  Sought in those bowers of green
  Where loop the clustered vines
And the close-clinging dulcamara twines, —
Pure pearls of Maydew where the moonlight shines,
  And Summer's fruited gems,
And coral pendants shorn from Autumn's berried stems.

Sit by me drifting on the sleepy waves, —
  Or stretched by grass-grown graves,
  Whose gray, high-shouldered stones,
Carved with old names Life's time-worn roll disowns,
Lean, lichen-spotted, o'er the crumbled bones
  Still slumbering where they lay
While the sad Pilgrim watched to scare the wolf away.

Spread o'er my couch thy visionary wing!
  Still let me dream and sing, —
  Dream of that winding shore
Where scarlet cardinals bloom — for me no more, —
The stream with heaven beneath its liquid floor,
  And clustering nenuphars
Sprinkling its mirrored blue like golden-chaliced stars!

Come while their balms the linden-blossoms shed! —
  Come while the rose is red, —
  While blue-eyed Summer smiles
On the green ripples round yon sunken piles

Washed by the moon-wave warm from Indian isles,
  And on the sultry air
The chestnuts spread their palms like holy men in prayer!

Oh for thy burning lips to fire my brain
  With thrills of wild, sweet pain! —
  On life's autumnal blast,
Like shrivelled leaves, youth's passion-flowers are cast, —
Once loving thee, we love thee to the last! —
  Behold thy new-decked shrine,
And hear once more the voice that breathed "Forever thine!"

A PARTING HEALTH

TO J. L. MOTLEY

[Upon his return to England after the publication of the *History of the Dutch Republic* in 1857.]

YES, we knew we must lose him, — though friendship may claim
To blend her green leaves with the laurels of fame;
Though fondly, at parting, we call him our own,
'T is the whisper of love when the bugle has blown.

As the rider that rests with the spur on his heel,
As the guardsman that sleeps in his corselet of steel,
As the archer that stands with his shaft on the string,
He stoops from his toil to the garland we bring.

What pictures yet slumber unborn in his loom,
Till their warriors shall breathe and their beauties shall bloom,
While the tapestry lengthens the life-glowing dyes
That caught from our sunsets the stain of their skies!

In the alcoves of death, in the charnels of time,

Where flit the gaunt spectres of passion and
    crime,
There are triumphs untold, there are mar-
    tyrs unsung,
There are heroes yet silent to speak with
    his tongue!

Let us hear the proud story which time has
    bequeathed
From lips that are warm with the freedom
    they breathed!
Let him summon its tyrants, and tell us
    their doom,
Though he sweep the black past like Van
    Tromp with his broom!

. . . .

The dream flashes by, for the west-winds
    awake
On pampas, on prairie, o'er mountain and
    lake,
To bathe the swift bark, like a sea-girdled
    shrine,
With incense they stole from the rose and
    the pine.

So fill a bright cup with the sunlight that
    gushed
When the dead summer's jewels were tram-
    pled and crushed:
The true Knight of Learning, — the
    world holds him dear, —
Love bless him, Joy crown him, God speed
    his career!

WHAT WE ALL THINK

I think few persons have a greater disgust for plagiarism than myself. If I had even suspected that the idea in question was borrowed, I should have disclaimed originality, or mentioned the coincidence, as I once did in a case where I had happened to hit on an idea of Swift's. — But what shall I do with these verses I was going to read you? I am afraid that half mankind would accuse me of stealing their thoughts, if I printed them. I am convinced that several of you, especially if you are getting a little on in life, will recognize some of these sentiments as having passed through your consciousness at some time. I can't help it, — it is too late now. The verses are written, and you must have them.

That age was older once than now,
    In spite of locks untimely shed,
Or silvered on the youthful brow;
    That babes make love and children wed

That sunshine had a heavenly glow,
    Which faded with those "good old days"
When winters came with deeper snow,
    And autumns with a softer haze.

That — mother, sister, wife, or child —
    The "best of women" each has known.
Were school-boys ever half so wild?
    How young the grandpapas have grown!

That *but for this* our souls were free,
    And *but for that* our lives were blest;
That in some season yet to be
    Our cares will leave us time to rest.

Whene'er we groan with ache or pain, —
    Some common ailment of the race, —
Though doctors think the matter plain, —
    That ours is "a peculiar case."

That when like babes with fingers burned
    We count one bitter maxim more,
Our lesson all the world has learned,
    And men are wiser than before.

That when we sob o'er fancied woes,
    The angels hovering overhead
Count every pitying drop that flows,
    And love us for the tears we shed.

That when we stand with tearless eye
    And turn the beggar from our door
They still approve us when we sigh,
    "Ah, had I but *one thousand more!*"

Though temples crowd the crumbled brink
    O'erhanging truth's eternal flow,
Their tablets bold with *what we think*,
    Their echoes dumb to *what we know;*

That one unquestioned text we read,
    All doubt beyond, all fear above,
Nor crackling pile nor cursing creed
    Can burn or blot it: God is Love!

SPRING HAS COME

INTRA MUROS

The sunbeams, lost for half a year,
    Slant through my pane their morning
        rays;

For dry northwesters cold and clear,
  The east blows in its thin blue haze.

And first the snowdrop's bells are seen,
  Then close against the sheltering wall
The tulip's horn of dusky green,
  The peony's dark unfolding ball.

The golden-chaliced crocus burns;
  The long narcissus-blades appear;
The cone-beaked hyacinth returns
  To light her blue-flamed chandelier.

The willow's whistling lashes, wrung
  By the wild winds of gusty March,
With sallow leaflets lightly strung,
  Are swaying by the tufted larch.

The elms have robed their slender spray
  With full-blown flower and embryo leaf;
Wide o'er the clasping arch of day
  Soars like a cloud their hoary chief.

See the proud tulip's flaunting cup,
  That flames in glory for an hour, —
Behold it withering, — then look up, —
  How meek the forest monarch's flower!

When wake the violets, Winter dies;
  When sprout the elm-buds, Spring is near;
When lilacs blossom, Summer cries,
  "Bud, little roses! Spring is here!"

The windows blush with fresh bouquets,
  Cut with their Maydew on the lips;
The radish all its bloom displays,
  Pink as Aurora's finger-tips.

Nor less the flood of light that showers
  On beauty's changed corolla-shades, —
The walks are gay as bridal bowers
  With rows of many-petalled maids.

The scarlet shell-fish click and clash
  In the blue barrow where they slide;
The horseman, proud of streak and splash,
  Creeps homeward from his morning ride.

Here comes the dealer's awkward string,
  With neck in rope and tail in knot, —
Rough colts, with careless country-swing,
  In lazy walk or slouching trot.

Wild filly from the mountain-side,
  Doomed to the close and chafing thills,
Lend me thy long, untiring stride
  To seek with thee thy western hills!

I hear the whispering voice of Spring,
  The thrush's trill, the robin's cry,
Like some poor bird with prisoned wing
  That sits and sings, but longs to fly.

Oh for one spot of living green, —
  One little spot where leaves can grow, —
To love unblamed, to walk unseen,
  To dream above, to sleep below!

PROLOGUE

Of course I wrote the prologue I was asked to write. I did not see the play, though. I knew there was a young lady in it, and that somebody was in love with her, and she was in love with him, and somebody (an old tutor, I believe) wanted to interfere, and, very naturally, the young lady was too sharp for him. The play of course ends charmingly; there is a general reconciliation, and all concerned form a line and take each other's hands, as people always do after they have made up their quarrels, — and then the curtain falls, — if it does not stick, as it commonly does at private theatrical exhibitions, in which case a boy is detailed to pull it down, which he does, blushing violently.

Now, then, for my prologue. I am not going to change my cæsuras and cadences for anybody; so if you do not like the heroic, or iambic trimeter brachycatalectic, you had better not wait to hear it.

A PROLOGUE? Well, of course the ladies know, —
I have my doubts. No matter, — here we go!
What is a Prologue? Let our Tutor teach:
Pro means beforehand; *logos* stands for speech.
'T is like the harper's prelude on the strings,
The prima donna's courtesy ere she sings;
Prologues in metre are to other *pros*
As worsted stockings are to engine-hose.
"The world's a stage," — as Shakespeare said, one day;
The stage a world — was what he meant to say.

The outside world 's a blunder, that is
    clear;
The real world that Nature meant is here.
Here every foundling finds its lost mamma;
Each rogue, repentant, melts his stern papa;
Misers relent, the spendthrift's debts are
    paid,
The cheats are taken in the traps they laid;
One after one the troubles all are past
Till the fifth act comes right side up at
    last,
When the young couple, old folks, rogues,
    and all,
Join hands, so happy at the curtain's fall.
Here suffering virtue ever finds relief,
And black-browed ruffians always come to
    grief.
When the lorn damsel, with a frantic
    screech,
And cheeks as hueless as a brandy-peach,
Cries, "Help, kyind Heaven!" and drops
    upon her knees
On the green — baize, — beneath the (can-
    vas) trees, —
See to her side avenging Valor fly: —
"Ha! Villain! Draw! Now, Terraitorr,
    yield or die!"
When the poor hero flounders in despair,
Some dear lost uncle turns up millionaire,
Clasps the young scapegrace with paternal
    joy,
Sobs on his neck, "*My boy!* My boy!!
    MY BOY!!!"

Ours, then, sweet friends, the real world
    to-night,
Of love that conquers in disaster's spite.
Ladies, attend! While woeful cares and
    doubt
Wrong the soft passion in the world with-
    out,
Though fortune scowl, though prudence
    interfere,
One thing is certain: Love will triumph
    here!
Lords of creation, whom your ladies rule, —
The world's great masters, when you 're
    out of school, —
Learn the brief moral of our evening's play:
Man has his will, — but woman has her
    way!
While man's dull spirit toils in smoke and
    fire,
Woman's swift instinct threads the electric
    wire, —

The magic bracelet stretched beneath the
    waves
Beats the black giant with his score of
    slaves.
All earthly powers confess your sovereign
    art
But that one rebel, — woman's wilful heart.
All foes you master, but a woman's wit
Lets daylight through you ere you know
    you 're hit.
So, just to picture what her art can do,
Hear an old story, made as good as new.

Rudolph, professor of the headsman's trade,
Alike was famous for his arm and blade.
One day a prisoner Justice had to kill
Knelt at the block to test the artist's skill.
Bare-armed, swart-visaged, gaunt, and
    shaggy-browed,
Rudolph the headsman rose above the
    crowd.
His falchion lighted with a sudden gleam,
As the pike's armor flashes in the stream.
He sheathed his blade; he turned as if to
    go;
The victim knelt, still waiting for the blow.
"Why strikest not? Perform thy mur-
    derous act,"
The prisoner said. (His voice was slightly
    cracked.)
"Friend, I *have* struck," the artist straight
    replied;
"Wait but one moment, and yourself de-
    cide."
He held his snuff-box, — "Now then, if
    you please!"
The prisoner sniffed, and, with a crashing
    sneeze,
Off his head tumbled, — bowled along the
    floor, —
Bounced down the steps; — the prisoner
    said no more!
Woman! thy falchion is a glittering eye;
If death lurk in it, oh how sweet to die!
Thou takest hearts as Rudolph took the
    head;
We die with love, and never dream we 're
    dead!

LATTER-DAY WARNINGS

I should have felt more nervous about the late comet, if I had thought the world was ripe. But it is very green yet, if I am not mistaken; and besides, there is a great deal

of coal to use up, which I cannot bring myself
to think was made for nothing. If certain
things, which seem to me essential to a millen-
nium, had come to pass, I should have been
frightened; but they have n't.

When legislators keep the law,
  When banks dispense with bolts and
    locks,
When berries — whortle, rasp, and straw —
  Grow bigger *downwards* through the
    box, —

When he that selleth house or land
  Shows leak in roof or flaw in right, —
When haberdashers choose the stand
  Whose window hath the broadest light, —

When preachers tell us all they think,
  And party leaders all they mean, —
When what we pay for, that we drink,
  From real grape and coffee-bean, —

When lawyers take what they would give,
  And doctors give what they would take, —
When city fathers eat to live,
  Save when they fast for conscience'
    sake, —

When one that hath a horse on sale
  Shall bring his merit to the proof,
Without a lie for every nail
  That holds the iron on the hoof, —

When in the usual place for rips
  Our gloves are stitched with special care,
And guarded well the whalebone tips
  Where first umbrellas need repair, —

When Cuba's weeds have quite forgot
  The power of suction to resist,
And claret-bottles harbor not
  Such dimples as would hold your fist, —

When publishers no longer steal,
  And pay for what they stole before, —
When the first locomotive's wheel
  Rolls through the Hoosac Tunnel's
    bore; —

Till then let Cumming blaze away,
  And Miller's saints blow up the globe;
But when you see that blessed day,
  Then order your ascension robe!

ALBUM VERSES

When Eve had led her lord away,
  And Cain had killed his brother,
The stars and flowers, the poets say,
  Agreed with one another

To cheat the cunning tempter's art,
  And teach the race its duty,
By keeping on its wicked heart
  Their eyes of light and beauty.

A million sleepless lids, they say,
  Will be at least a warning;
And so the flowers would watch by day,
  The stars from eve to morning.

On hill and prairie, field and lawn,
  Their dewy eyes upturning,
The flowers still watch from reddening
    dawn
  Till western skies are burning.

Alas! each hour of daylight tells
  A tale of shame so crushing,
That some turn white as sea-bleached
    shells,
  And some are always blushing.

But when the patient stars look down
  On all their light discovers,
The traitor's smile, the murderer's frown,
  The lips of lying lovers,

They try to shut their saddening eyes,
  And in the vain endeavor
We see them twinkling in the skies,
  And so they wink forever.

A GOOD TIME GOING!

[A farewell poem to Charles Mackay.]

Brave singer of the coming time,
  Sweet minstrel of the joyous present,
Crowned with the noblest wreath of rhyme,
  The holly-leaf of Ayrshire's peasant,
Good by! Good by! — Our hearts and
    hands,
Our lips in honest Saxon phrases,
Cry, God be with him, till he stands
  His feet among the English daisies!

'T is here we part; — for other eyes
  The busy deck, the fluttering streamer,
The dripping arms that plunge and rise,
  The waves in foam, the ship in tremor,
The kerchiefs waving from the pier,
  The cloudy pillar gliding o'er him,
The deep blue desert, lone and drear,
  With heaven above and home before him!

His home! — the Western giant smiles,
  And twirls the spotty globe to find it; —
This little speck the British Isles?
  'T is but a freckle, — never mind it!
He laughs, and all his prairies roll,
  Each gurgling cataract roars and chuckles,
And ridges stretched from pole to pole
  Heave till they crack their iron knuckles!

But Memory blushes at the sneer,
  And Honor turns with frown defiant,
And Freedom, leaning on her spear,
  Laughs louder than the laughing giant:
"An islet is a world," she said,
  "When glory with its dust has blended,
And Britain keeps her noble dead
  Till earth and seas and skies are rended!"

Beneath each swinging forest-bough
  Some arm as stout in death reposes, —
From wave-washed foot to heaven-kissed brow
  Her valor's life-blood runs in roses;
Nay, let our brothers of the West
  Write smiling in their florid pages,
One half her soil has walked the rest
  In poets, heroes, martyrs, sages!

Hugged in the clinging billow's clasp,
  From sea-weed fringe to mountain heather,
The British oak with rooted grasp
  Her slender handful holds together; —
With cliffs of white and bowers of green,
  And Ocean narrowing to caress her,
And hills and threaded streams between, —
  Our little mother isle, God bless her!

In earth's broad temple where we stand,
  Fanned by the eastern gales that brought us,
We hold the missal in our hand,
  Bright with the lines our Mother taught us.

Where'er its blazoned page betrays
  The glistening links of gilded fetters,
Behold, the half-turned leaf displays
  Her rubric stained in crimson letters!

Enough! To speed a parting friend
  'T is vain alike to speak and listen; —
Yet stay, — these feeble accents blend
  With rays of light from eyes that glisten.
Good by! once more, — and kindly tell
  In words of peace the young world's story, —
And say, besides, we love too well
  Our mothers' soil, our fathers' glory!

THE LAST BLOSSOM

Though young no more, we still would dream
  Of beauty's dear deluding wiles;
The leagues of life to graybeards seem
  Shorter than boyhood's lingering miles.

Who knows a woman's wild caprice?
  It played with Goethe's silvered hair,
And many a Holy Father's "niece"
  Has softly smoothed the papal chair.

When sixty bids us sigh in vain
  To melt the heart of sweet sixteen,
We think upon those ladies twain
  Who loved so well the tough old Dean.

We see the Patriarch's wintry face,
  The maid of Egypt's dusky glow,
And dream that Youth and Age embrace,
  As April violets fill with snow.

Tranced in her lord's Olympian smile
  His lotus-loving Memphian lies, —
The musky daughter of the Nile,
  With plaited hair and almond eyes.

Might we but share one wild caress
  Ere life's autumnal blossoms fall,
And Earth's brown, clinging lips impress
  The long cold kiss that waits us all!

My bosom heaves, remembering yet
  The morning of that blissful day,
When Rose, the flower of spring, I met,
  And gave my raptured soul away.

Flung from her eyes of purest blue,
  A lasso, with its leaping chain,
Light as a loop of larkspurs, flew
  O'er sense and spirit, heart and brain.

Thou com'st to cheer my waning age,
  Sweet vision, waited for so long!
Dove that would seek the poet's cage
  Lured by the magic breath of song!

She blushes! Ah, reluctant maid,
  Love's *drapeau rouge* the truth has told!
O'er girlhood's yielding barricade
  Floats the great Leveller's crimson fold!

Come to my arms! — love heeds not years;
  No frost the bud of passion knows.
Ha! what is this my frenzy hears?
  A voice behind me uttered, — Rose!

Sweet was her smile, — but not for me;
  Alas! when woman looks *too* kind,
Just turn your foolish head and see, —
  Some youth is walking close behind!

CONTENTMENT

"Man wants but little here below"

Should you like to hear what moderate wishes life brings one to at last? I used to be very ambitious, — wasteful, extravagant, and luxurious in all my fancies. Read too much in the *Arabian Nights*. Must have the lamp, — could n't do without the ring. Exercise every morning on the brazen horse. Plump down into castles as full of little milk-white princesses as a nest is of young sparrows. All love me dearly at once. — Charming idea of life, but too high-colored for the reality. I have outgrown all this; my tastes have become exceedingly primitive, — almost, perhaps, ascetic. We carry happiness into our condition, but must not hope to find it there. I think you will be willing to hear some lines which embody the subdued and limited desires of my maturity.

LITTLE I ask; my wants are few;
  I only wish a hut of stone,
(A *very plain* brown stone will do,)
  That I may call my own; —
And close at hand is such a one,
In yonder street that fronts the sun.

Plain food is quite enough for me;
  Three courses are as good as ten; —

If Nature can subsist on three,
  Thank Heaven for three. Amen!
I always thought cold victual nice; —
  My *choice* would be vanilla-ice.

I care not much for gold or land; —
  Give me a mortgage here and there, —
Some good bank-stock, some note of hand,
Or trifling railroad share, —
  I only ask that Fortune send
A *little* more than I shall spend.

Honors are silly toys, I know,
  And titles are but empty names;
I would, *perhaps*, be Plenipo, —
  But only near St. James;
I 'm very sure I should not care
To fill our Gubernator's chair.

Jewels are baubles; 't is a sin
  To care for such unfruitful things; —
One good-sized diamond in a pin, —
  Some, *not so large*, in rings, —
A ruby, and a pearl, or so,
Will do for me; — I laugh at show.

My dame should dress in cheap attire;
  (Good, heavy silks are never dear;) —
I own perhaps I *might* desire
  Some shawls of true Cashmere, —
Some marrowy crapes of China silk,
Like wrinkled skins on scalded milk.

I would not have the horse I drive
  So fast that folks must stop and stare;
An easy gait — two forty-five —
  Suits me; I do not care; —
Perhaps, for just a *single spurt*,
Some seconds less would do no hurt.

Of pictures, I should like to own
  Titians and Raphaels three or four, —
I love so much their style and tone,
  One Turner, and no more,
(A landscape, — foreground golden dirt, —
The sunshine painted with a squirt.)

Of books but few, — some fifty score
  For daily use, and bound for wear;
The rest upon an upper floor; —
  Some *little* luxury *there*
Of red morocco's gilded gleam
And vellum rich as country cream.

Busts, cameos, gems, — such things as these,
Which others often show for pride,
I value for their power to please,
And selfish churls deride; —
One Stradivarius, I confess,
Two Meerschaums, I would fain possess.

Wealth's wasteful tricks I will not learn,
Nor ape the glittering upstart fool; —
Shall not carved tables serve my turn,
But *all* must be of buhl?
Give grasping pomp its double share, —
I ask but *one* recumbent chair.

Thus humble let me live and die,
Nor long for Midas' golden touch;
If Heaven more generous gifts deny,
I shall not miss them *much*, —
Too grateful for the blessing lent
Of simple tastes and mind content!

ÆSTIVATION

AN UNPUBLISHED POEM, BY MY LATE LATIN TUTOR.

Your talking Latin — said I — reminds me of an odd trick of one of my old tutors. He read so much of that language, that his English half turned into it. He got caught in town, one hot summer, in pretty close quarters, and wrote, or began to write, a series of city pastorals. Eclogues he called them, and meant to have published them by subscription. I remember some of his verses, if you want to hear them. — You, Sir (addressing myself to the divinity-student), and all such as have been through college, or what is the same thing, received an honorary degree, will understand them without a dictionary. The old man had a great deal to say about "æstivation," as he called it, in opposition, as one might say, to *hibernation*. Intramural æstivation, or town-life in summer, he would say, is a peculiar form of suspended existence, or semi-asphyxia. One wakes up from it about the beginning of the last week in September. This is what I remember of his poem: —

IN candent ire the solar splendor flames;
The foles, languescent, pend from arid rames;
His humid front the cive, anheling, wipes,
And dreams of erring on ventiferous ripes.

How dulce to vive occult to mortal eyes,
Dorm on the herb with none to supervise,
Carp the suave berries from the crescent vine,
And bibe the flow from longicaudate kine!

To me, alas! no verdurous visions come,
Save yon exiguous pool's conferva-scum, —
No concave vast repeats the tender hue
That laves my milk-jug with celestial blue!

Me wretched! Let me curr to quercine shades!
Effund your albid hausts, lactiferous maids!
Oh, might I vole to some umbrageous clump, —
Depart, — be off, — excede, — evade, — erump!

THE DEACON'S MASTERPIECE

OR, THE WONDERFUL "ONE-HOSS SHAY"

A LOGICAL STORY

[The following note was prefaced to the poem when it appeared in an illustrated edition.]

"The Wonderful One-Hoss Shay" is a perfectly intelligible conception, whatever material difficulties it presents. It is conceivable that a being of an order superior to humanity should so understand the conditions of matter that he could construct a machine which should go to pieces, if not into its constituent atoms, at a given moment of the future. The mind may take a certain pleasure in this picture of the impossible. The event follows as a logical consequence of the presupposed condition of things.

There is a practical lesson to be got out of the story. Observation shows us in what point any particular mechanism is most likely to give way. In a wagon, for instance, the weak point is where the axle enters the hub or nave. When the wagon breaks down, three times out of four, I think, it is at this point that the accident occurs. The workman should see to it that this part should never give way; then find the next vulnerable place, and so on. until he arrives logically at the perfect result attained by the deacon.

HAVE you heard of the wonderful one-hoss shay,
That was built in such a logical way
It ran a hundred years to a day,

THE DEACON'S MASTERPIECE

And then, of a sudden, it — ah, but stay,
I 'll tell you what happened without delay,
Scaring the parson into fits,
Frightening people out of their wits, —
Have you ever heard of that, I say ?

Seventeen hundred and fifty-five.
Georgius Secundus was then alive, —
Snuffy old drone from the German hive.
That was the year when Lisbon-town
Saw the earth open and gulp her down,
And Braddock's army was done so brown,
Left without a scalp to its crown.
It was on the terrible Earthquake-day
That the Deacon finished the one-hoss shay.

Now in building of chaises, I tell you what,
There is always *somewhere* a weakest spot, —
In hub, tire, felloe, in spring or thill,
In panel, or crossbar, or floor, or sill,
In screw, bolt, thoroughbrace, — lurking still,
Find it somewhere you must and will, —
Above or below, or within or without, —
And that 's the reason, beyond a doubt,
That a chaise *breaks down,* but does n't *wear out.*

But the Deacon swore (as Deacons do,
With an " I dew vum," or an " I tell *yeou* ")
He would build one shay to beat the taown
'N' the keounty 'n' all the kentry raoun';
It should be so built that it *could n'* break daown:
"Fur," said the Deacon, " 't 's mighty plain
Thut the weakes' place mus' stan' the strain;
'N' the way t' fix it, uz I maintain,
Is only jest
T' make that place uz strong uz the rest."

So the Deacon inquired of the village folk
Where he could find the strongest oak,
That could n't be split nor bent nor broke, —
That was for spokes and floor and sills;
He sent for lancewood to make the thills;
The crossbars were ash, from the straightest trees,
The panels of white-wood, that cuts like cheese,
But lasts like iron for things like these;
The hubs of logs from the "Settler's ellum," —
Last of its timber, — they could n't sell 'em,
Never an axe had seen their chips,
And the wedges flew from between their lips,
Their blunt ends frizzled like celery-tips;
Step and prop-iron, bolt and screw,
Spring, tire, axle, and linchpin too,
Steel of the finest, bright and blue;
Thoroughbrace bison-skin, thick and wide;
Boot, top, dasher, from tough old hide
Found in the pit when the tanner died.
That was the way he "put her through."
" There ! " said the Deacon, "naow she 'll dew ! "

Do ! I tell you, I rather guess
She was a wonder, and nothing less !
Colts grew horses, beards turned gray,
Deacon and deaconess dropped away,
Children and grandchildren — where were they ?
But there stood the stout old one-hoss shay
As fresh as on Lisbon-earthquake-day !

EIGHTEEN HUNDRED; — it came and found
The Deacon's masterpiece strong and sound.
Eighteen hundred increased by ten; —
" Hahnsum kerridge " they called it then.
Eighteen hundred and twenty came; —
Running as usual; much the same.
Thirty and forty at last arrive,
And then come fifty, and FIFTY-FIVE.

Little of all we value here
Wakes on the morn of its hundredth year
Without both feeling and looking queer.
In fact, there 's nothing that keeps its youth,
So far as I know, but a tree and truth.
(This is a moral that runs at large;
Take it. — You 're welcome. — No extra charge.)

FIRST OF NOVEMBER, — the Earthquake-day, —
There are traces of age in the one-hoss shay,
A general flavor of mild decay,
But nothing local, as one may say.
There could n't be, — for the Deacon's art
Had made it so like in every part
That there was n't a chance for one to start.
For the wheels were just as strong as the thills,

And the floor was just as strong as the sills,
And the panels just as strong as the floor,
And the whipple-tree neither less nor more,
And the back crossbar as strong as the fore,
And spring and axle and hub *encore*.
And yet, *as a whole*, it is past a doubt
In another hour it will be *worn out!*

First of November, 'Fifty-five !
This morning the parson takes a drive.
Now, small boys, get out of the way !
Here comes the wonderful one-hoss shay,
Drawn by a rat-tailed, ewe-necked bay.
"Huddup!" said the parson. — Off went they.
The parson was working his Sunday's text, —
Had got to *fifthly*, and stopped perplexed
At what the — Moses — was coming next.
All at once the horse stood still,
Close by the meet'n'-house on the hill.
First a shiver, and then a thrill,
Then something decidedly like a spill, —
And the parson was sitting upon a rock,
At half past nine by the meet'n'-house clock, —
Just the hour of the Earthquake shock !
What do you think the parson found,
When he got up and stared around ?
The poor old chaise in a heap or mound,
As if it had been to the mill and ground !
You see, of course, if you 're not a dunce,
How it went to pieces all at once, —
All at once, and nothing first, —
Just as bubbles do when they burst.

End of the wonderful one-hoss shay.
Logic is logic. That 's all I say.

PRELUDE

[In introducing *Parson Turell's Legacy*, the Autocrat amused his readers with an account of his friend the Professor's experiments in chloroform. The Professor was about to read the poem, but upon delivering the *Prelude*, his MS. was taken from him by the Autocrat, who finished the reading.]

I 'M the fellah that tole one day
The tale of the won'erful one-hoss-shay.
Wan' to hear another ? Say.
— Funny, was n' it ? Made *me* laugh, —
I 'm too modest, I am, by half, —
Made me laugh '*s though I sh'd split*, —
Cahn' a fellah like fellah's own wit ?
— Fellahs keep sayin', — " Well, now that 's nice:
Did it once, but cahn' do it twice." —
Dŏn' you b'lieve the' 'z no more fat;
Lots in the kitch'n 'z good 'z that.
Fus'-rate throw, 'n' no mistake, —
Han' us the props for another shake; —
Know I 'll try, 'n' guess I 'll win;
Here sh' goes for hit 'm ag'in !

PARSON TURELL'S LEGACY
OR, THE PRESIDENT'S OLD ARM-CHAIR
A MATHEMATICAL STORY

FACTS respecting an old arm-chair.
At Cambridge. Is kept in the College there.
Seems but little the worse for wear.
That 's remarkable when I say
It was old in President Holyoke's day.
(One of his boys, perhaps you know,
Died, *at one hundred*, years ago.)
He took lodgings for rain or shine
Under green bed-clothes in '69.

Know old Cambridge ? Hope you do. —
Born there ? Don't say so ! I was, too.
(Born in a house with a gambrel-roof, —
Standing still, if you must have proof. —
" Gambrel ? — Gambrel ? " — Let me beg
You 'll look at a horse's hinder leg, —
First great angle above the hoof, —
That 's the gambrel; hence gambrel-roof.)
Nicest place that ever was seen, —
Colleges red and Common green,
Sidewalks brownish with trees between.
Sweetest spot beneath the skies
When the canker-worms don't rise, —
When the dust, that sometimes flies
Into your mouth and ears and eyes,
In a quiet slumber lies,
Not in the shape of unbaked pies
Such as barefoot children prize.

A kind of harbor it seems to be,
Facing the flow of a boundless sea.
Rows of gray old Tutors stand
Ranged like rocks above the sand;
Rolling beneath them, soft and green,
Breaks the tide of bright sixteen, —
One wave, two waves, three waves, four, —
Sliding up the sparkling floor:

PARSON TURELL'S LEGACY

Then it ebbs to flow no more,
Wandering off from shore to shore
With its freight of golden ore!
Pleasant place for boys to play; —
Better keep your girls away;
Hearts get rolled as pebbles do
Which countless fingering waves pursue,
And every classic beach is strown
With heart-shaped pebbles of blood-red stone.

But this is neither here nor there;
I'm talking about an old arm-chair.
You've heard, no doubt, of PARSON TU-RELL?
Over at Medford he used to dwell;
Married one of the Mathers' folk;
Got with his wife a chair of oak, —
Funny old chair with seat like wedge,
Sharp behind and broad front edge, —
One of the oddest of human things,
Turned all over with knobs and rings, —
But heavy, and wide, and deep, and grand, —
Fit for the worthies of the land, —
Chief Justice Sewall a cause to try in,
Or Cotton Mather to sit — and lie — in.
Parson Turell bequeathed the same
To a certain student, — SMITH by name;
These were the terms, as we are told:
"Saide Smith saide Chaire to have and holde;
When he doth graduate, then to passe
To y⁰ oldest Youth in y⁰ Senior Classe.
On payment of " — (naming a certain sum) —
" By him to whom y⁰ Chaire shall come;
He to y⁰ oldest Senior next,
And soe forever," — (thus runs the text,) —
" But one Crown lesse than he gave to claime,
That being his Debte for use of same."

Smith transferred it to one of the BROWNS,
And took his money, — five silver crowns.
Brown delivered it up to MOORE,
Who paid, it is plain, not five, but four.
Moore made over the chair to LEE,
Who gave him crowns of silver three.
Lee conveyed it unto DREW,
And now the payment, of course, was two.
Drew gave up the chair to DUNN, —
All he got, as you see, was one.
Dunn released the chair to HALL,
And got by the bargain no crown at all.

And now it passed to a second BROWN,
Who took it and likewise *claimed a crown*.
When *Brown* conveyed it unto WARE,
Having had one crown, to make it fair,
He paid him two crowns to take the chair;
And *Ware*, being honest, (as all Wares be,)
He paid one POTTER, who took it, three.
Four got ROBINSON; five got DIX;
JOHNSON *primus* demanded six;
And so the sum kept gathering still
Till after the battle of Bunker's Hill.

When paper money became so cheap,
Folks would n't count it, but said "a heap,"
A certain RICHARDS, — the books declare, —
(A. M. in '90? I 've looked with care
Through the Triennial, — *name not there,*) —
This person, Richards, was offered then
Eightscore pounds, but would have ten;
Nine, I think, was the sum he took, —
Not quite certain, — but see the book.
By and by the wars were still,
But nothing had altered the Parson's will.
The old arm-chair was solid yet,
But saddled with such a monstrous debt!
Things grew quite too bad to bear,
Paying such sums to get rid of the chair!
But dead men's fingers hold awful tight,
And there was the will in black and white,
Plain enough for a child to spell.
What should be done no man could tell,
For the chair was a kind of nightmare curse,
And every season but made it worse.

As a last resort, to clear the doubt,
They got old GOVERNOR HANCOCK out.
The Governor came with his Lighthorse Troop
And his mounted truckmen, all cock-a-hoop;
Halberds glittered and colors flew,
French horns whinnied and trumpets blew,
The yellow fifes whistled between their teeth,
And the bumble-bee bass-drums boomed beneath;
So he rode with all his band,
Till the President met him, cap in hand.
The Governor "hefted" the crowns, and said, —
" A will is a will, and the Parson's dead."
The Governor hefted the crowns. Said he, —

"There is your p'int. And here's my fee.
These are the terms you must fulfil, —
On such conditions I BREAK THE WILL!"
The Governor mentioned what these should be.
(Just wait a minute and then you'll see.)
The President prayed. Then all was still,
And the Governor rose and BROKE THE WILL!
"About those conditions?" Well, now you go
And do as I tell you, and then you'll know.
Once a year, on Commencement day,
If you'll only take the pains to stay,
You'll see the President in the CHAIR,
Likewise the Governor sitting there.
The President rises; both old and young
May hear his speech in a foreign tongue,
The meaning whereof, as lawyers swear,
Is this: Can I keep this old arm-chair?
And then his Excellency bows,
As much as to say that he allows.
The Vice-Gub. next is called by name;
He bows like t' other, which means the same.
And all the officers round 'em bow,
As much as to say that *they* allow.
And a lot of parchments about the chair
Are handed to witnesses then and there,
And then the lawyers hold it clear
That the chair is safe for another year.

God bless you, Gentlemen! Learn to give
Money to colleges while you live.
Don't be silly and think you'll try
To bother the colleges, when you die,
With codicil this, and codicil that,
That Knowledge may starve while Law grows fat;
For there never was pitcher that would n't spill,
And there's always a flaw in a donkey's will!

ODE FOR A SOCIAL MEETING

WITH SLIGHT ALTERATIONS BY A TEE-TOTALER

Here is a little poem I sent a short time since to a committee for a certain celebration. I understood that it was to be a festive and convivial occasion, and ordered myself accordingly. It seems the president of the day was what is called a "teetotaler." I received a note from him in the following words, containing the copy subjoined, with the emendations annexed to it.

"DEAR SIR, — Your poem gives good satisfaction to the committee. The sentiments expressed with reference to liquor are not, however, those generally entertained by this community. I have therefore consulted the clergyman of this place, who has made some slight changes, which he thinks will remove all objections, and keep the valuable portions of the poem. Please to inform me of your charge for said poem. Our means are limited, etc., etc., etc.

"Yours with respect."

Here it is with the slight alterations.

COME! fill a fresh bumper, for why should we go
While the ~~nectar~~ [logwood] still reddens our cups as they flow?
Pour out the ~~rich juices~~ [decoction] still bright with the sun,
Till o'er the brimmed crystal the ~~rubies~~ [dyestuff] shall run.

The ~~purple-globed clusters~~ [half-ripened apples] their life-dews have bled;
How sweet is the ~~breath~~ [taste] of the ~~fragrance they shed~~! [sugar of lead.]
For summer's ~~last roses~~ [rank poisons] lie hid in the ~~wines~~!!!
That were garnered by ~~maidens who laughed thro' the vines~~. [stable-boys smoking long-nines.]

Then a ~~smile~~ [scowl], and a ~~glass~~ [howl], and a ~~toast~~ [scoff], and a ~~cheer~~, [sneer,]
For all ~~the good wine, and we've some of it here~~! [strychnine and whiskey, and ratsbane and beer!]
In cellar, in pantry, in attic, in hall,
~~Long live the gay servant that laughs for us all~~! [Down, down with the tyrant that masters us all!]

POEMS FROM THE PROFESSOR AT THE BREAKFAST-TABLE

1858–1859

UNDER THE VIOLETS

HER hands are cold; her face is white;
  No more her pulses come and go;
Her eyes are shut to life and light; —
  Fold the white vesture, snow on snow,
  And lay her where the violets blow.

But not beneath a graven stone,
  To plead for tears with alien eyes;
A slender cross of wood alone
  Shall say, that here a maiden lies
  In peace beneath the peaceful skies.

And gray old trees of hugest limb
  Shall wheel their circling shadows round
To make the scorching sunlight dim
  That drinks the greenness from the ground,
  And drop their dead leaves on her mound.

When o'er their boughs the squirrels run,
  And through their leaves the robins call,
And, ripening in the autumn sun,
  The acorns and the chestnuts fall,
  Doubt not that she will heed them all.

For her the morning choir shall sing
  Its matins from the branches high,
And every minstrel-voice of Spring,
  That trills beneath the April sky,
  Shall greet her with its earliest cry.

When, turning round their dial-track,
  Eastward the lengthening shadows pass,
Her little mourners, clad in black,
  The crickets, sliding through the grass,
  Shall pipe for her an evening mass.

At last the rootlets of the trees
  Shall find the prison where she lies,
And bear the buried dust they seize
  In leaves and blossoms to the skies.
  So may the soul that warmed it rise!

If any, born of kindlier blood,
  Should ask, What maiden lies below?
Say only this: A tender bud,
  That tried to blossom in the snow,
  Lies withered where the violets blow.

HYMN OF TRUST

O LOVE Divine, that stooped to share
  Our sharpest pang, our bitterest tear,
On Thee we cast each earth-born care,
  We smile at pain while Thou art near!

Though long the weary way we tread,
  And sorrow crown each lingering year,
No path we shun, no darkness dread,
  Our hearts still whispering, Thou art near!

When drooping pleasure turns to grief,
  And trembling faith is changed to fear,
The murmuring wind, the quivering leaf,
  Shall softly tell us, Thou art near!

On Thee we fling our burdening woe,
  O Love Divine, forever dear,
Content to suffer while we know,
  Living and dying, Thou art near!

A SUN-DAY HYMN

LORD of all being! throned afar,
Thy glory flames from sun and star;
Centre and soul of every sphere,
Yet to each loving heart how near!

Sun of our life, thy quickening ray
Sheds on our path the glow of day;
Star of our hope, thy softened light
Cheers the long watches of the night.

Our midnight is thy smile withdrawn;
Our noontide is thy gracious dawn;
Our rainbow arch thy mercy's sign;
All, save the clouds of sin, are thine!

Lord of all life, below, above,
Whose light is truth, whose warmth is love,
Before thy ever-blazing throne
We ask no lustre of our own.

Grant us thy truth to make us free,
And kindling hearts that burn for thee,
Till all thy living altars claim
One holy light, one heavenly flame!

THE CROOKED FOOTPATH

Ah, here it is! the sliding rail
   That marks the old remembered spot,—
The gap that struck our school-boy trail,—
   The crooked path across the lot.

It left the road by school and church,
   A pencilled shadow, nothing more,
That parted from the silver-birch
   And ended at the farm-house door.

No line or compass traced its plan;
   With frequent bends to left or right,
In aimless, wayward curves it ran,
   But always kept the door in sight.

The gabled porch, with woodbine green,—
   The broken millstone at the sill,—
Though many a rood might stretch between,
   The truant child could see them still.

No rocks across the pathway lie,—
   No fallen trunk is o'er it thrown,—
And yet it winds, we know not why,
   And turns as if for tree or stone.

Perhaps some lover trod the way
   With shaking knees and leaping heart,—
And so it often runs astray
   With sinuous sweep or sudden start.

Or one, perchance, with clouded brain
   From some unholy banquet reeled,—
And since, our devious steps maintain
   His track across the trodden field.

Nay, deem not thus,— no earthborn will
   Could ever trace a faultless line;
Our truest steps are human still,—
   To walk unswerving were divine!

Truants from love, we dream of wrath;—
   Oh, rather let us trust the more!
Through all the wanderings of the path
   We still can see our Father's door!

IRIS, HER BOOK

I PRAY thee by the soul of her that bore
      thee,
By thine own sister's spirit I implore
      thee,
Deal gently with the leaves that lie before
      thee!

For Iris had no mother to infold her,
Nor ever leaned upon a sister's shoulder,
Telling the twilight thoughts that Nature
      told her.

She had not learned the mystery of awak-
      ing
Those chorded keys that soothe a sorrow's
      aching,
Giving the dumb heart voice, that else
      were breaking.

Yet lived, wrought, suffered. Lo, the pic-
      tured token!
Why should her fleeting day-dreams fade
      unspoken,
Like daffodils that die with sheaths un-
      broken?

She knew not love, yet lived in maiden
      fancies,—
Walked simply clad, a queen of high ro-
      mances,
And talked strange tongues with angels in
      her trances.

Twin-souled she seemed, a twofold nature
      wearing:
Sometimes a flashing falcon in her dar-
      ing,
Then a poor mateless dove that droops de-
      spairing.

Questioning all things: Why her Lord had
   sent her?
What were these torturing gifts, and where-
   fore lent her?
Scornful as spirit fallen, its own tormentor.

And then all tears and anguish: Queen of
   Heaven,
Sweet Saints, and Thou by mortal sorrows
   riven,
Save me! Oh, save me! Shall I die for-
   given?

And then — Ah, God! But nay, it little
   matters:
Look at the wasted seeds that autumn
   scatters,
The myriad germs that Nature shapes and
   shatters!

If she had — Well! She longed, and knew
   not wherefore.
Had the world nothing she might live to
   care for?
No second self to say her evening prayer
   for?

She knew the marble shapes that set men
   dreaming,
Yet with her shoulders bare and tresses
   streaming
Showed not unlovely to her simple seem-
   ing.

Vain? Let it be so! Nature was her
   teacher.
What if a lonely and unsistered creature
Loved her own harmless gift of pleasing
   feature,

Saying, unsaddened, — This shall soon be
   faded,
And double-hued the shining tresses
   braided,
And all the sunlight of the morning shaded?

This her poor book is full of saddest fol-
   lies,
Of tearful smiles and laughing melancholies,
With summer roses twined and wintry
   hollies.

In the strange crossing of uncertain chances,
Somewhere, beneath some maiden's tear-
   dimmed glances

May fall her little book of dreams and
   fancies.

Sweet sister! Iris, who shall never name
   thee,
Trembling for fear her open heart may
   shame thee,
Speaks from this vision-haunted page to
   claim thee.

Spare her, I pray thee! If the maid is
   sleeping,
Peace with her! she has had her hour of
   weeping.
No more! She leaves her memory in thy
   keeping.

ROBINSON OF LEYDEN

He sleeps not here; in hope and prayer
   His wandering flock had gone before,
But he, the shepherd, might not share
   Their sorrows on the wintry shore.

Before the Speedwell's anchor swung,
   Ere yet the Mayflower's sail was spread,
While round his feet the Pilgrims clung,
   The pastor spake, and thus he said: —

"Men, brethren, sisters, children dear!
   God calls you hence from over sea;
Ye may not build by Haerlem Meer,
   Nor yet along the Zuyder-Zee.

"Ye go to bear the saving word
   To tribes unnamed and shores untrod;
Heed well the lessons ye have heard
   From those old teachers taught of God.

"Yet think not unto them was lent
   All light for all the coming days,
And Heaven's eternal wisdom spent
   In making straight the ancient ways;

"The living fountain overflows
   For every flock, for every lamb,
Nor heeds, though angry creeds oppose
   With Luther's dike or Calvin's dam."

He spake; with lingering, long embrace,
   With tears of love and partings fond,
They floated down the creeping Maas,
   Along the isle of Ysselmond.

They passed the frowning towers of Briel,
  The "Hook of Holland's" shelf of sand,
And grated soon with lifting keel
  The sullen shores of Fatherland.

No home for these! — too well they knew
  The mitred king behind the throne; —
The sails were set, the pennons flew,
  And westward ho! for worlds unknown.

And these were they who gave us birth,
  The Pilgrims of the sunset wave,
Who won for us this virgin earth,
  And freedom with the soil they gave.

The pastor slumbers by the Rhine, —
  In alien earth the exiles lie, —
Their nameless graves our holiest shrine,
  His words our noblest battle-cry!

Still cry them, and the world shall hear,
  Ye dwellers by the storm-swept sea!
Ye *have* not built by Haerlem Meer,
  Nor on the land-locked Zuyder-Zee!

ST. ANTHONY THE REFORMER

HIS TEMPTATION

The Reformers have good heads, generally. Their faces are commonly serene enough, and they are lambs in private intercourse, even though their voices may be like

"The wolf's long howl from Oonalaska's shore,"

when heard from the platform. Their greatest spiritual danger is from the perpetual *flattery of abuse* to which they are exposed. These lines are meant to caution them.

No fear lest praise should make us proud!
  We know how cheaply that is won;
The idle homage of the crowd
  Is proof of tasks as idly done.

A surface-smile may pay the toil
  That follows still the conquering Right,
With soft, white hands to dress the spoil
  That sun-browned valor clutched in fight.

Sing the sweet song of other days,
  Serenely placid, safely true,
And o'er the present's parching ways
  The verse distils like evening dew.

But speak in words of living power, —
  They fall like drops of scalding rain
That plashed before the burning shower
  Swept o'er the cities of the plain!

Then scowling Hate turns deadly pale, —
  Then Passion's half-coiled adders spring,
And, smitten through their leprous mail,
  Strike right and left in hope to sting.

If thou, unmoved by poisoning wrath,
  Thy feet on earth, thy heart above,
Canst walk in peace thy kingly path,
  Unchanged in trust, unchilled in love, —

Too kind for bitter words to grieve,
  Too firm for clamor to dismay,
When Faith forbids thee to believe,
  And Meekness calls to disobey, —

Ah, then beware of mortal pride!
  The smiling pride that calmly scorns
Those foolish fingers, crimson dyed
  In laboring on thy crown of thorns!

THE OPENING OF THE PIANO

In the little southern parlor of the house
    you may have seen
With the gambrel-roof, and the gable look-
    ing westward to the green,
At the side toward the sunset, with the
    window on its right,
Stood the London-made piano I am dream-
    ing of to-night!

Ah me! how I remember the evening when
    it came!
What a cry of eager voices, what a group
    of cheeks in flame,
When the wondrous box was opened that
    had come from over seas,
With its smell of mastic-varnish and its
    flash of ivory keys!

Then the children all grew fretful in the
    restlessness of joy,
For the boy would push his sister, and the
    sister crowd the boy,
Till the father asked for quiet in his grave
    paternal way,
But the mother hushed the tumult with
    the words, "Now, Mary, play."

For the dear soul knew that music was a
　　very sovereign balm;
She had sprinkled it over Sorrow and seen
　　its brow grow calm,
In the days of slender harpsichords with
　　tapping tinkling quills,
Or carolling to her spinet with its thin metallic thrills.

So Mary, the household minstrel, who
　　always loved to please,
Sat down to the new "Clementi," and
　　struck the glittering keys.
Hushed were the children's voices, and
　　every eye grew dim,
As, floating from lip and finger, arose the
　　"Vesper Hymn."

Catharine, child of a neighbor, curly and
　　rosy-red,
(Wedded since, and a widow, — something
　　like ten years dead,)
Hearing a gush of music such as none before,
Steals from her mother's chamber and
　　peeps at the open door.

Just as the "Jubilate" in threaded whisper dies,
"Open it! open it, lady!" the little
　　maiden cries,
(For she thought 't was a singing creature
　　caged in a box she heard,)
"Open it! open it, lady! and let me see
　　the *bird!*"

MIDSUMMER

HERE! sweep these foolish leaves away,
I will not crush my brains to-day!
Look! are the southern curtains drawn?
Fetch me a fan, and so begone!

Not that, — the palm-tree's rustling leaf
Brought from a parching coral-reef!
Its breath is heated; — I would swing
The broad gray plumes, — the eagle's
　　wing.

I hate these roses' feverish blood! —
Pluck me a half-blown lily-bud,
A long-stemmed lily from the lake,
Cold as a coiling water-snake.

Rain me sweet odors on the air,
And wheel me up my Indian chair,
And spread some book not overwise
Flat out before my sleepy eyes.

Who knows it not — this dead recoil
Of weary fibres stretched with toil, —
The pulse that flutters faint and low
When Summer's seething breezes blow!

O Nature! bare thy loving breast,
And give thy child one hour of rest, —
One little hour to lie unseen
Beneath thy scarf of leafy green!

So, curtained by a singing pine,
Its murmuring voice shall blend with mine,
Till, lost in dreams, my faltering lay
In sweeter music dies away.

DE SAUTY

AN ELECTRO-CHEMICAL ECLOGUE

The first messages received through the submarine cable were sent by an electrical expert, a mysterious personage who signed himself De Sauty.

Professor　　　　　*Blue-Nose*

PROFESSOR

TELL me, O Provincial! speak, Ceruleo-Nasal!
Lives there one De Sauty extant now
　　among you,
Whispering Boanerges, son of silent thunder,
　　Holding talk with nations?

Is there a De Sauty ambulant on Tellus,
Bifid-cleft like mortals, dormient in nightcap,
Having sight, smell, hearing, food-receiving feature
　　Three times daily patent?

Breathes there such a being, O Ceruleo-Nasal?
Or is he a *mythus*, — ancient word for
　　"humbug," —
Such as Livy told about the wolf that wet-nursed
　　Romulus and Remus?

Was he born of woman, this alleged De Sauty?
Or a living product of galvanic action,
Like the *acarus* bred in Crosse's flint-solution?
Speak, thou Cyano-Rhinal!

BLUE-NOSE

Many things thou askest, jackknife-bearing stranger,
Much-conjecturing mortal, pork-and-treacle-waster!
Pretermit thy whittling, wheel thine ear-flap toward me,
Thou shalt hear them answered.

When the charge galvanic tingled through the cable,
At the polar focus of the wire electric
Suddenly appeared a white-faced man among us:
Called himself "DE SAUTY."

As the small opossum held in pouch maternal
Grasps the nutrient organ whence the term *mammalia*,
So the unknown stranger held the wire electric,
Sucking in the current.

When the current strengthened, bloomed the pale-faced stranger, —
Took no drink nor victual, yet grew fat and rosy, —
And from time to time, in sharp articulation,
Said, "*All right!* DE SAUTY."

From the lonely station passed the utterance, spreading
Through the pines and hemlocks to the groves of steeples,
Till the land was filled with loud reverberations
Of "*All right!* DE SAUTY."

When the current slackened, drooped the mystic stranger, —
Faded, faded, faded, as the stream grew weaker, —
Wasted to a shadow, with a hartshorn odor
Of disintegration.

Drops of deliquescence glistened on his forehead,
Whitened round his feet the dust of efflorescence,
Till one Monday morning, when the flow suspended,
There was no De Sauty.

Nothing but a cloud of elements organic,
C. O. H. N. Ferrum, Chlor. Flu. Sil. Potassa,
Calc. Sod. Phosph. Mag. Sulphur, Maug. (?) Alumin. (?) Cuprum, (?)
Such as man is made of.

Born of stream galvanic, with it he had perished!
There is no DE SAUTY now there is no current!
Give us a new cable, then again we'll hear him
Cry, "*All right!* DE SAUTY."

POEMS FROM THE POET AT THE BREAKFAST-TABLE

1871-1872

HOMESICK IN HEAVEN

Most people love this world more than they are willing to confess, and it is hard to conceive ourselves weaned from it so as to feel no emotion at the thought of its most sacred recollections, — even after a sojourn of years, as we should count the lapse of earthly time, — in the realm where, sooner or later, all tears shall be wiped away. I hope, therefore, the title of my lines will not frighten those who are little accustomed to think of men and women as beings in any state but the present.

THE DIVINE VOICE

Go seek thine earth-born sisters, — thus
    the Voice
  That all obey, — the sad and silent
    three;
These only, while the hosts of Heaven rejoice,
  Smile never; ask them what their sorrows be;

And when the secret of their griefs they
    tell,
  Look on them with thy mild, half-human
    eyes;
Say what thou wast on earth; thou
    knowest well;
  So shall they cease from unavailing
    sighs.

THE ANGEL

Why thus, apart, — the swift-winged
    herald spake, —
  Sit ye with silent lips and unstrung lyres
While the trisagion's blending chords
    awake
  In shouts of joy from all the heavenly
    choirs?

THE FIRST SPIRIT

Chide not thy sisters, — thus the answer
    came; —
  Children of earth, our half - weaned
    nature clings
To earth's fond memories, and her
    whispered name
  Untunes our quivering lips, our saddened
    strings;

For there we loved, and where we love is
    home,
  Home that our feet may leave, but not
    our hearts,
Though o'er us shine the jasper-lighted
    dome: —
  The chain may lengthen, but it never
    parts!

Sometimes a sunlit sphere comes rolling
    by,
  And then we softly whisper, — *can it be?*
And leaning toward the silvery orb, we try
  To hear the music of its murmuring sea;

To catch, perchance, some flashing glimpse
    of green,
  Or breathe some wild-wood fragrance,
    wafted through
The opening gates of pearl, that fold between
  The blinding splendors and the changeless blue.

THE ANGEL

Nay, sister, nay! a single healing leaf
  Plucked from the bough of yon twelve-
    fruited tree
Would soothe such anguish, — deeper
    stabbing grief
  Has pierced thy throbbing heart —

THE FIRST SPIRIT

     Ah, woe is me !
I from my clinging babe was rudely torn;
 His tender lips a loveless bosom pressed;
 Can I forget him in my life new born ?
Oh that my darling lay upon my breast !

THE ANGEL

And thou ? —

THE SECOND SPIRIT

   I was a fair and youthful bride,
The kiss of love still burns upon my cheek,
He whom I worshipped, ever at my side, —
 Him through the spirit realm in vain I seek.

Sweet faces turn their beaming eyes on mine;
 Ah ! not in these the wished-for look I read;
Still for that one dear human smile I pine;
 Thou and none other ! — is the lover's creed.

THE ANGEL

And whence *thy* sadness in a world of bliss
 Where never parting comes, nor mourner's tear ?
Art thou, too, dreaming of a mortal's kiss
 Amid the seraphs of the heavenly sphere ?

THE THIRD SPIRIT

Nay, tax not me with passion's wasting fire;
 When the swift message set my spirit free,
Blind, helpless, lone, I left my gray-haired sire;
 My friends were many, he had none save me.

I left him, orphaned, in the starless night;
 Alas, for him no cheerful morning's dawn !
I wear the ransomed spirit's robe of white,
 Yet still I hear him moaning, *She is gone !*

THE ANGEL

Ye know me not, sweet sisters ? — All in vain
Ye seek your lost ones in the shapes they wore;
The flower once opened may not bud again,
 The fruit once fallen finds the stem no more.

Child, lover, sire, — yea, all things loved below, —
 Fair pictures damasked on a vapor's fold, —
Fade like the roseate flush, the golden glow,
 When the bright curtain of the day is rolled.

I was the babe that slumbered on *thy* breast,
 And, sister, mine the lips that called *thee* bride.
Mine were the silvered locks *thy* hand caressed,
 That faithful hand, my faltering footstep's guide !

Each changing form, frail vesture of decay,
 The soul unclad forgets it once hath worn,
Stained with the travel of the weary day,
 And shamed with rents from every wayside thorn.

To lie, an infant, in *thy* fond embrace, —
 To come with love's warm kisses back to thee, —
To show *thine* eyes thy gray-haired father's face,
 Not Heaven itself could grant; this may not be !

Then spread your folded wings, and leave to earth
 The dust once breathing ye have mourned so long,
Till Love, new risen, owns his heavenly birth,
 And sorrow's discords sweeten into song !

FANTASIA

THE YOUNG GIRL'S POEM

Kiss mine eyelids, beauteous Morn,
Blushing into life new-born !
Lend me violets for my hair,
And thy russet robe to wear,

And thy ring of rosiest hue
Set in drops of diamond dew!

Kiss my cheek, thou noontide ray,
From my Love so far away!
Let thy splendor streaming down
Turn its pallid lilies brown,
Till its darkening shades reveal
Where his passion pressed its seal!

Kiss my lips, thou Lord of light,
Kiss my lips a soft good-night!
Westward sinks thy golden car;
Leave me but the evening star,
And my solace that shall be,
Borrowing all its light from thee!

AUNT TABITHA

THE YOUNG GIRL'S POEM

WHATEVER I do, and whatever I say,
Aunt Tabitha tells me that is n't the way;
When *she* was a girl (forty summers ago)
Aunt Tabitha tells me they never did so.

Dear aunt! If I only would take her advice!
But I like my own way, and I find it *so* nice!
And besides, I forget half the things I am told;
But they all will come back to me — when I am old.

If a youth passes by, it may happen, no doubt,
He may chance to look in as I chance to look out;
She would never endure an impertinent stare, —
It is *horrid*, she says, and I must n't sit there.

A walk in the moonlight has pleasures, I own,
But it is n't quite safe to be walking alone;
So I take a lad's arm, — just for safety, you know, —
But Aunt Tabitha tells me *they* did n't do so.

How wicked we are, and how good they were then!
They kept at arm's length those detestable men;
What an era of virtue she lived in! — But stay —
Were the *men* all such rogues in Aunt Tabitha's day?

If the men *were* so wicked, I 'll ask my papa
How he dared to propose to my darling mamma;
Was he like the rest of them? Goodness! Who knows?
And what shall *I* say, if a wretch should propose?

I am thinking if Aunt knew so little of sin,
What a wonder Aunt Tabitha's aunt must have been!
And her grand-aunt — it scares me — how shockingly sad
That we girls of to-day are so frightfully bad!

A martyr will save us, and nothing else can;
Let *me* perish — to rescue some wretched young man!
Though when to the altar a victim I go,
Aunt Tabitha 'll tell me *she* never did so!

WIND-CLOUDS AND STAR-DRIFTS

FROM THE YOUNG ASTRONOMER'S POEM

I

AMBITION

ANOTHER clouded night; the stars are hid,
The orb that waits my search is hid with them.
Patience! Why grudge an hour, a month, a year,
To plant my ladder and to gain the round
That leads my footsteps to the heaven of fame,
Where waits the wreath my sleepless midnights won?
Not the stained laurel such as heroes wear
That withers when some stronger conqueror's heel
Treads down their shrivelling trophies in the dust;
But the fair garland whose undying green
Not time can change, nor wrath of gods or men!

With quickened heart-beats I shall hear the tongues
That speak my praise; but better far the sense
That in the unshaped ages, buried deep
In the dark mines of unaccomplished time
Yet to be stamped with morning's royal die
And coined in golden days, — in those dim years
I shall be reckoned with the undying dead,
My name emblazoned on the fiery arch,
Unfading till the stars themselves shall fade.
Then, as they call the roll of shining worlds,
Sages of race unborn in accents new
Shall count me with the Olympian ones of old,
Whose glories kindle through the midnight sky:
Here glows the God of Battles; this recalls
The Lord of Ocean, and yon far-off sphere
The Sire of Him who gave his ancient name
To the dim planet with the wondrous rings;
Here flames the Queen of Beauty's silver lamp,
And there the moon-girt orb of mighty Jove;
But *this*, unseen through all earth's æons past,
A youth who watched beneath the western star
Sought in the darkness, found, and shewed to men;
Linked with his name thenceforth and evermore !
So shall that name be syllabled anew
In all the tongues of all the tribes of men:
I that have been through immemorial years
Dust in the dust of my forgotten time
Shall live in accents shaped of blood-warm breath,
Yea, rise in mortal semblance, newly born
In shining stone, in undecaying bronze,
And stand on high, and look serenely down
On the new race that calls the earth its own.

Is this a cloud, that, blown athwart my soul,
Wears a false seeming of the pearly stain
Where worlds beyond the world their mingling rays
Blend in soft white, — a cloud that, born of earth,
Would cheat the soul that looks for light from heaven ?
Must every coral-insect leave his sign
On each poor grain he lent to build the reef,
As Babel's builders stamped their sunburnt clay,
Or deem his patient service all in vain ?
What if another sit beneath the shade
Of the broad elm I planted by the way, —
What if another heed the beacon light
I set upon the rock that wrecked my keel, —
Have I not done my task and served my kind ?
Nay, rather act thy part, unnamed, unknown,
And let Fame blow her trumpet through the world
With noisy wind to swell a fool's renown,
Joined with some truth he stumbled blindly o'er,
Or coupled with some single shining deed
That in the great account of all his days
Will stand alone upon the bankrupt sheet
His pitying angel shows the clerk of Heaven.
The noblest service comes from nameless hands,
And the best servant does his work unseen.
Who found the seeds of fire and made them shoot,
Fed by his breath, in buds and flowers of flame ?
Who forged in roaring flames the ponderous stone,
And shaped the moulded metal to his need ?
Who gave the dragging car its rolling wheel,
And tamed the steed that whirls its circling round ?
All these have left their work and not their names, —
Why should I murmur at a fate like theirs ?
This is the heavenly light; the pearly stain
Was but a wind-cloud drifting o'er the stars !

II

REGRETS

Brief glimpses of the bright celestial spheres,
False lights, false shadows, vague, uncertain gleams,

Pale vaporous mists, wan streaks of lurid flame,
The climbing of the upward-sailing cloud,
The sinking of the downward-falling star, —
All these are pictures of the changing moods
Borne through the midnight stillness of my soul.

Here am I, bound upon this pillared rock,
Prey to the vulture of a vast desire
That feeds upon my life. — I burst my bands
And steal a moment's freedom from the beak,
The clinging talons and the shadowing plumes;
Then comes the false enchantress, with her song;
"Thou wouldst not lay thy forehead in the dust
Like the base herd that feeds and breeds and dies!
Lo, the fair garlands that I weave for thee,
Unchanging as the belt Orion wears,
Bright as the jewels of the seven-starred Crown,
The spangled stream of Berenice's hair!"
And so she twines the fetters with the flowers
Around my yielding limbs, and the fierce bird
Stoops to his quarry, — then to feed his rage
Of ravening hunger I must drain my blood
And let the dew-drenched, poison-breeding night
Steal all the freshness from my fading cheek,
And leave its shadows round my caverned eyes.
All for a line in some unheeded scroll;
All for a stone that tells to gaping clowns,
"Here lies a restless wretch beneath a clod
Where squats the jealous nightmare men call Fame!"

I marvel not at him who scorns his kind
And thinks not sadly of the time foretold
When the old hulk we tread shall be a wreck,
A slag, a cinder drifting through the sky
Without its crew of fools! We live too long,
And even so are not content to die,
But load the mould that covers up our bones
With stones that stand like beggars by the road
And show death's grievous wound and ask for tears;
Write our great books to teach men who we are,
Sing our fine songs that tell in artful phrase
The secrets of our lives, and plead and pray
For alms of memory with the after time,
Those few swift seasons while the earth shall wear
Its leafy summers, ere its core grows cold
And the moist life of all that breathes shall die;
Or as the new-born seer, perchance more wise,
Would have us deem, before its growing mass,
Pelted with star-dust, stoned with meteor-balls,
Heats like a hammered anvil, till at last
Man and his works and all that stirred itself
Of its own motion, in the fiery glow
Turns to a flaming vapor, and our orb
Shines a new sun for earths that shall be born.

I am as old as Egypt to myself,
Brother to them that squared the pyramids
By the same stars I watch. I read the page
Where every letter is a glittering world,
With them who looked from Shinar's clay-built towers,
Ere yet the wanderer of the Midland sea
Had missed the fallen sister of the seven.
I dwell in spaces vague, remote, unknown,
Save to the silent few, who, leaving earth,
Quit all communion with their living time.
I lose myself in that ethereal void,
Till I have tired my wings and long to fill
My breast with denser air, to stand, to walk
With eyes not raised above my fellow-men.
Sick of my unwalled, solitary realm,
I ask to change the myriad lifeless worlds
I visit as mine own for one poor patch
Of this dull spheroid and a little breath
To shape in word or deed to serve my kind.

Was ever giant's dungeon dug so deep,
Was ever tyrant's fetter forged so strong,
Was e'er such deadly poison in the draught
The false wife mingles for the trusting fool,
As he whose willing victim is himself
Digs, forges, mingles, for his captive soul?

III

SYMPATHIES

The snows that glittered on the disk of Mars
Have melted, and the planet's fiery orb
Rolls in the crimson summer of its year;
But what to me the summer or the snow
Of worlds that throb with life in forms unknown,
If life indeed be theirs; I heed not these.
My heart is simply human; all my care
For them whose dust is fashioned like mine own;
These ache with cold and hunger, live in pain,
And shake with fear of worlds more full of woe;
There may be others worthier of my love,
But such I know not save through these I know.

There are two veils of language, hid beneath
Whose sheltering folds, we dare to be ourselves;
And not that other self which nods and smiles
And babbles in our name; the one is Prayer,
Lending its licensed freedom to the tongue
That tells our sorrows and our sins to Heaven;
The other, Verse, that throws its spangled web
Around our naked speech and makes it bold.
I, whose best prayer is silence; sitting dumb
In the great temple where I nightly serve
Him who is throned in light, have dared to claim
The poet's franchise, though I may not hope
To wear his garland; hear me while I tell
My story in such form as poets use,
But breathed in fitful whispers, as the wind
Sighs and then slumbers, wakes and sighs again.

Thou Vision, floating in the breathless air
Between me and the fairest of the stars,
I tell my lonely thoughts as unto thee.
Look not for marvels of the scholar's pen
In my rude measure; I can only show
A slender-margined, unillumined page,
And trust its meaning to the flattering eye
That reads it in the gracious light of love.
Ah, would thou clothe thyself in breathing shape
And nestle at my side, my voice should lend
Whate'er my verse may lack of tender rhythm
To make thee listen.
                    I have stood entranced
When, with her fingers wandering o'er the keys,
The white enchantress with the golden hair
Breathed all her soul through some unvalued rhyme;
Some flower of song that long had lost its bloom;
Lo! its dead summer kindled as she sang!
The sweet contralto, like the ringdove's coo,
Thrilled it with brooding, fond, caressing tones,
And the pale minstrel's passion lived again,
Tearful and trembling as a dewy rose
The wind has shaken till it fills the air
With light and fragrance. Such the wondrous charm
A song can borrow when the bosom throbs
That lends it breath.
                    So from the poet's lips
His verse sounds doubly sweet, for none like him
Feels every cadence of its wave-like flow;
He lives the passion over, while he reads,
That shook him as he sang his lofty strain,
And pours his life through each resounding line,
As ocean, when the stormy winds are hushed,
Still rolls and thunders through his billowy caves.

IV

MASTER AND SCHOLAR

Let me retrace the record of the years
That made me what I am. A man most wise,
But overworn with toil and bent with age,

Sought me to be his scholar, — me, run
    wild
From books and teachers, — kindled in my
    soul
The love of knowledge; led me to his tower,
Showed me the wonders of the midnight
    realm
His hollow sceptre ruled, or seemed to rule,
Taught me the mighty secrets of the
    spheres,
Trained me to find the glimmering specks
    of light
Beyond the unaided sense, and on my chart
To string them one by one, in order due,
As on a rosary a saint his beads.
I was his only scholar; I became
The echo to his thought; whate'er he knew
Was mine for asking; so from year to year
We wrought together, till there came a time
When I, the learner, was the master half
Of the twinned being in the dome-crowned
    tower.

Minds roll in paths like planets; they re-
    volve,
This in a larger, that a narrower ring,
But round they come at last to that same
    phase,
That selfsame light and shade they showed
    before.
I learned his annual and his monthly tale,
His weekly axiom and his daily phrase,
I felt them coming in the laden air,
And watched them laboring up to vocal
    breath,
Even as the first-born at his father's board
Knows ere he speaks the too familiar jest
Is on its way, by some mysterious sign
Forewarned, the click before the striking
    bell.

He shrivelled as I spread my growing
    leaves,
Till trust and reverence changed to pitying
    care;
He lived for me in what he once had been,
But I for him, a shadow, a defence,
The guardian of his fame, his guide, his
    staff,
Leaned on so long he fell if left alone.
I was his eye, his ear, his cunning hand,
Love was my spur and longing after fame,
But his the goading thorn of sleepless age
That sees its shortening span, its lengthen-
    ing shades,
That clutches what it may with eager grasp,
And drops at last with empty, outstretched
    hands.
All this he dreamed not. He would sit
    him down
Thinking to work his problems as of old,
And find the star he thought so plain a
    blur,
The columned figures labyrinthine wilds
Without my comment, blind and senseless
    scrawls
That vexed him with their riddles; he
    would strive
And struggle for a while, and then his eye
Would lose its light, and over all his mind
The cold gray mist would settle; and ere-
    long
The darkness fell, and I was left alone.

V

ALONE

Alone! no climber of an Alpine cliff,
No Arctic venturer on the waveless sea,
Feels the dread stillness round him as it
    chills
The heart of him who leaves the slumber-
    ing earth
To watch the silent worlds that crowd the
    sky.

Alone! And as the shepherd leaves his
    flock
To feed upon the hillside, he meanwhile
Finds converse in the warblings of the
    pipe
Himself has fashioned for his vacant hour,
So have I grown companion to myself,
And to the wandering spirits of the air
That smile and whisper round us in our
    dreams.
Thus have I learned to search if I may
    know
The whence and why of all beneath the
    stars
And all beyond them, and to weigh my life
As in a balance, — poising good and ill
Against each other, — asking of the Power
That flung me forth among the whirling
    worlds,
If I am heir to any inborn right,
Or only as an atom of the dust
That every wind may blow where'er it will.

VI

QUESTIONING

I am not humble; I was shown my place,
Clad in such robes as Nature had at hand;
Took what she gave, not chose; I know no shame,
No fear for being simply what I am.
I am not proud, I hold my every breath
At Nature's mercy. I am as a babe
Borne in a giant's arms, he knows not where;
Each several heart-beat, counted like the coin
A miser reckons, is a special gift
As from an unseen hand; if that withhold
Its bounty for a moment, I am left
A clod upon the earth to which I fall.

Something I find in me that well might claim
The love of beings in a sphere above
This doubtful twilight world of right and wrong;
Something that shows me of the selfsame clay
That creeps or swims or flies in humblest form.
Had I been asked, before I left my bed
Of shapeless dust, what clothing I would wear,
I would have said, More angel and less worm;
But for their sake who are even such as I,
Of the same mingled blood, I would not choose
To hate that meaner portion of myself
Which makes me brother to the least of men.

I dare not be a coward with my lips
Who dare to question all things in my soul;
Some men may find their wisdom on their knees,
Some prone and grovelling in the dust like slaves;
Let the meek glowworm glisten in the dew;
I ask to lift my taper to the sky
As they who hold their lamps above their heads,
Trusting the larger currents up aloft,
Rather than crossing eddies round their breast,
Threatening with every puff the flickering blaze.

My life shall be a challenge, not a truce!
This is my homage to the mightier powers,
To ask my boldest question, undismayed
By muttered threats that some hysteric sense
Of wrong or insult will convulse the throne
Where wisdom reigns supreme; and if I err,
They all must err who have to feel their way
As bats that fly at noon; for what are we
But creatures of the night, dragged forth by day,
Who needs must stumble, and with stammering steps
Spell out their paths in syllables of pain?

Thou wilt not hold in scorn the child who dares
Look up to Thee, the Father, — dares to ask
More than thy wisdom answers. From thy hand
The worlds were cast; yet every leaflet claims
From that same hand its little shining sphere
Of star-lit dew; thine image, the great sun
Girt with his mantle of tempestuous flame,
Glares in mid-heaven; but to his noontide blaze
The slender violet lifts its lidless eye,
And from his splendor steals its fairest hue,
Its sweetest perfume from his scorching fire.

VII

WORSHIP

From my lone turret as I look around
O'er the green meadows to the ring of blue,
From slope, from summit, and from half-hid vale
The sky is stabbed with dagger-pointed spires,
Their gilded symbols whirling in the wind,
Their brazen tongues proclaiming to the world,
"Here truth is sold, the only genuine ware;
See that it has our trade-mark! You will buy
Poison instead of food across the way,
The lies of ——" this or that, each several name

The standard's blazon and the battle-cry
Of some true-gospel faction, and again
The token of the Beast to all beside.
And grouped round each I see a huddling crowd
Alike in all things save the words they use;
In love, in longing, hate and fear the same.

Whom do we trust and serve? We speak of one
And bow to many; Athens still would find
The shrines of all she worshipped safe within
Our tall barbarian temples, and the thrones
That crowned Olympus mighty as of old.
The god of music rules the Sabbath choir;
The lyric muse must leave the sacred nine
To help us please the dilettante's ear;
Plutus limps homeward with us, as we leave
The portals of the temple where we knelt
And listened while the god of eloquence
(Hermes of ancient days, but now disguised
In sable vestments) with that other god
Somnus, the son of Erebus and Nox,
Fights in unequal contest for our souls;
The dreadful sovereign of the under-world
Still shakes his sceptre at us, and we hear
The baying of the triple-throated hound;
Eros is young as ever, and as fair
The lovely Goddess born of ocean's foam.

These be thy gods, O Israel! Who is he,
The one ye name and tell us that ye serve,
Whom ye would call me from my lonely tower
To worship with the many-headed throng?
Is it the God that walked in Eden's grove
In the cool hour to seek our guilty sire?
The God who dealt with Abraham as the sons
Of that old patriarch deal with other men?
The jealous God of Moses, one who feels
An image as an insult, and is wroth
With him who made it and his child unborn?
The God who plagued his people for the sin
Of their adulterous king, beloved of him, —
The same who offers to a chosen few
The right to praise him in eternal song
While a vast shrieking world of endless woe
Blends its dread chorus with their rapturous hymn?
Is this the God ye mean, or is it he
Who heeds the sparrow's fall, whose loving heart
Is as the pitying father's to his child,
Whose lesson to his children is "Forgive,"
Whose plea for all, "They know not what they do"?

VIII

MANHOOD

I claim the right of knowing whom I serve,
Else is my service idle; He that asks
My homage asks it from a reasoning soul.
To crawl is not to worship; we have learned
A drill of eyelids, bended neck and knee,
Hanging our prayers on hinges, till we ape
The flexures of the many-jointed worm.
Asia has taught her Allahs and salaams
To the world's children, — we have grown to men!
We who have rolled the sphere beneath our feet
To find a virgin forest, as we lay
The beams of our rude temple, first of all
Must frame its doorway high enough for man
To pass unstooping; knowing as we do
That He who shaped us last of living forms
Has long enough been served by creeping things,
Reptiles that left their footprints in the sand
Of old sea-margins that have turned to stone,
And men who learned their ritual; we demand
To know Him first, then trust Him and then love
When we have found Him worthy of our love,
Tried by our own poor hearts and not before;
He must be truer than the truest friend,
He must be tenderer than a woman's love,
A father better than the best of sires;
Kinder than she who bore us, though we sin
Oftener than did the brother we are told
We — poor ill-tempered mortals — must forgive,
Though seven times sinning threescore times and ten.

This is the new world's gospel: Be ye men !
Try well the legends of the children's time;
Ye are the chosen people, God has led
Your steps across the desert of the deep
As now across the desert of the shore;
Mountains are cleft before you as the sea
Before the wandering tribe of Israel's sons;
Still onward rolls the thunderous caravan,
Its coming printed on the western sky,
A cloud by day, by night a pillared flame;
Your prophets are a hundred unto one
Of them of old who cried, "Thus saith the Lord;"
They told of cities that should fall in heaps,
But yours of mightier cities that shall rise
Where yet the lonely fishers spread their nets,
Where hides the fox and hoots the midnight owl;
The tree of knowledge in your garden grows
Not single, but at every humble door;
Its branches lend you their immortal food,
That fills you with the sense of what ye are,
No servants of an altar hewed and carved
From senseless stone by craft of human hands,
Rabbi, or dervish, brahmin, bishop, bonze,
But masters of the charm with which they work
To keep your hands from that forbidden tree !

Ye that have tasted that divinest fruit,
Look on this world of yours with opened eyes !
Ye are as gods ! Nay, makers of your gods, —
Each day ye break an image in your shrine
And plant a fairer image where it stood:
Where is the Moloch of your fathers' creed,
Whose fires of torment burned for span-long babes ?
Fit object for a tender mother's love !
Why not ? It was a bargain duly made
For these same infants through the surety's act
Intrusted with their all for earth and heaven,
By Him who chose their guardian, knowing well
His fitness for the task, — this, even this,
Was the true doctrine only yesterday
As thoughts are reckoned, — and to-day you hear
In words that sound as if from human tongues
Those monstrous, uncouth horrors of the past
That blot the blue of heaven and shame the earth
As would the saurians of the age of slime,
Awaking from their stony sepulchres
And wallowing hateful in the eye of day !

IX

RIGHTS

What am I but the creature Thou hast made ?
What have I save the blessings Thou hast lent ?
What hope I but thy mercy and thy love ?
Who but myself shall cloud my soul with fear ?
Whose hand protect me from myself but thine ?
 I claim the rights of weakness, I, the babe,
Call on my sire to shield me from the ills
That still beset my path, not trying me
With snares beyond my wisdom or my strength,
He knowing I shall use them to my harm,
And find a tenfold misery in the sense
That in my childlike folly I have sprung
The trap upon myself as vermin use,
Drawn by the cunning bait to certain doom.
Who wrought the wondrous charm that leads us on
To sweet perdition, but the selfsame power
That set the fearful engine to destroy
His wretched offspring (as the Rabbis tell),
And hid its yawning jaws and treacherous springs
In such a show of innocent sweet flowers
It lured the sinless angels and they fell ?
Ah ! He who prayed the prayer of all mankind
Summed in those few brief words the mightiest plea
For erring souls before the courts of heaven, —
Save us from being tempted, — lest we fall !

If we are only as the potter's clay
Made to be fashioned as the artist wills,
And broken into shards if we offend

The eye of Him who made us, it is well;
Such love as the insensate lump of clay
That spins upon the swift-revolving wheel
Bears to the hand that shapes its growing
　　form, —
Such love, no more, will be our hearts' re-
　　turn
To the great Master-workman for his
　　care, —
Or would be, save that this, our breathing
　　clay,
Is intertwined with fine innumerous threads
That make it conscious in its framer's
　　hand;
And this He must remember who has filled
These vessels with the deadly draught of
　　life, —
Life, that means death to all it claims.
　　Our love
Must kindle in the ray that streams from
　　heaven,
A faint reflection of the light divine;
The sun must warm the earth before the
　　rose
Can show her inmost heart-leaves to the
　　sun.

He yields some fraction of the Maker's right
Who gives the quivering nerve its sense of
　　pain;
Is there not something in the pleading eye
Of the poor brute that suffers, which ar-
　　raigns
The law that bids it suffer? Has it not
A claim for some remembrance in the book
That fills its pages with the idle words
Spoken of men? Or is it only clay,
Bleeding and aching in the potter's hand,
Yet all his own to treat it as He will
And when He will to cast it at his feet,
Shattered, dishonored, lost forevermore?
My dog loves me, but could he look beyond
His earthly master, would his love extend
To Him who — Hush! I will not doubt
　　that He
Is better than our fears, and will not wrong
The least, the meanest of created things!

He would not trust me with the smallest
　　orb
That circles through the sky; He would
　　not give
A meteor to my guidance; would not leave
The coloring of a cloudlet to my hand;
He locks my beating heart beneath its bars
And keeps the key himself; He measures
　　out
The draughts of vital breath that warm
　　my blood,
Winds up the springs of instinct which un-
　　coil,
Each in its season; ties me to my home,
My race, my time, my nation, and my
　　creed
So closely that if I but slip my wrist
Out of the band that cuts it to the bone,
Men say, "He hath a devil;" He has lent
All that I hold in trust, as unto one
By reason of his weakness and his years
Not fit to hold the smallest shred in fee
Of those most common things he calls his
　　own, —
And yet — my Rabbi tells me — He has
　　left
The care of that to which a million worlds
Filled with unconscious life were less than
　　naught,
Has left that mighty universe, the Soul
To the weak guidance of our baby hands,
Let the foul fiends have access at their will,
Taking the shape of angels, to our hearts, —
Our hearts already poisoned through and
　　through
With the fierce virus of ancestral sin;
Turned us adrift with our immortal charge,
To wreck ourselves in gulfs of endless woe.
If what my Rabbi tells me is the truth
Why did the choir of angels sing for joy?
Heaven must be compassed in a narrow
　　space,
And offer more than room enough for all
That pass its portals; but the under-world,
The godless realm, the place where demons
　　forge
Their fiery darts and adamantine chains,
Must swarm with ghosts that for a little
　　while
Had worn the garb of flesh, and being heirs
Of all the dulness of their stolid sires,
And all the erring instincts of their tribe,
Nature's own teaching, rudiments of "sin,"
Fell headlong in the snare that could not
　　fail
To trap the wretched creatures shaped of
　　clay
And cursed with sense enough to lose their
　　souls!
　　Brother, thy heart is troubled at my
　　word;
Sister, I see the cloud is on thy brow.

He will not blame me, He who sends not
  peace,
But sends a sword, and bids us strike amain
At Error's gilded crest, where in the van
Of earth's great army, mingling with the
  best
And bravest of its leaders, shouting loud
The battle-cries that yesterday have led
The host of Truth to victory, but to-day
Are watchwords of the laggard and the
  slave,
He leads his dazzled cohorts. God has
  made
This world a strife of atoms and of spheres;
With every breath I sigh myself away
And take my tribute from the wandering
  wind
To fan the flame of life's consuming fire;
So, while my thought has life, it needs
  must burn,
And, burning, set the stubble-fields ablaze,
Where all the harvest long ago was reaped
And safely garnered in the ancient barns.
But still the gleaners, groping for their
  food,
Go blindly feeling through the close-shorn
  straw,
While the young reapers flash their glittering steel
Where later suns have ripened nobler
  grain !

X

TRUTHS

The time is racked with birth-pangs; every
  hour
Brings forth some gasping truth, and truth
  newborn
Looks a misshapen and untimely growth,
The terror of the household and its shame,
A monster coiling in its nurse's lap
That some would strangle, some would only
  starve;
But still it breathes, and passed from hand
  to hand,
And suckled at a hundred half-clad breasts,
Comes slowly to its stature and its form,
Calms the rough ridges of its dragon-
  scales,
Changes to shining locks its snaky hair,
And moves transfigured into angel guise,
Welcomed by all that cursed its hour of
  birth,
And folded in the same encircling arms
That cast it like a serpent from their hold !

If thou wouldst live in honor, die in peace,
Have the fine words the marble-workers
  learn
To carve so well, upon thy funeral-stone,
And earn a fair obituary, dressed
In all the many-colored robes of praise,
Be deafer than the adder to the cry
Of that same foundling truth, until it
  grows
To seemly favor, and at length has won
The smiles of hard-mouthed men and
  light-lipped dames;
Then snatch it from its meagre nurse's
  breast,
Fold it in silk and give it food from gold;
So shalt thou share its glory when at last
It drops its mortal vesture, and, revealed
In all the splendor of its heavenly form,
Spreads on the startled air its mighty
  wings !

Alas ! how much that seemed immortal
  truth
That heroes fought for, martyrs died to
  save,
Reveals its earth-born lineage, growing old
And limping in its march, its wings un-
  plumed,
Its heavenly semblance faded like a dream !
  Here in this painted casket, just un-
  sealed,
Lies what was once a breathing shape like
  thine,
Once loved as thou art loved; there beamed
  the eyes
That looked on Memphis in its hour of
  pride,
That saw the walls of hundred-gated
  Thebes,
And all the mirrored glories of the Nile.
See how they toiled that all-consuming time
Might leave the frame immortal in its
  tomb;
Filled it with fragrant balms and odorous
  gums
That still diffuse their sweetness through
  the air,
And wound and wound with patient fold
  on fold
The flaxen bands thy hand has rudely torn !
Perchance thou yet canst see the faded stain
Of the sad mourner's tear.

XI
IDOLS

But what is this?
The sacred beetle, bound upon the breast
Of the blind heathen! Snatch the curious prize,
Give it a place among thy treasured spoils,
Fossil and relic, — corals, encrinites,
The fly in amber and the fish in stone,
The twisted circlet of Etruscan gold,
Medal, intaglio, poniard, poison-ring, —
Place for the Memphian beetle with thine hoard!

Ah! longer than thy creed has blest the world
This toy, thus ravished from thy brother's breast,
Was to the heart of Mizraim as divine,
As holy, as the symbol that we lay
On the still bosom of our white-robed dead,
And raise above their dust that all may know
Here sleeps an heir of glory. Loving friends,
With tears of trembling faith and choking sobs,
And prayers to those who judge of mortal deeds,
Wrapped this poor image in the cerement's fold
That Isis and Osiris, friends of man,
Might know their own and claim the ransomed soul.

An idol? Man was born to worship such!
An idol is an image of his thought;
Sometimes he carves it out of gleaming stone,
And sometimes moulds it out of glittering gold,
Or rounds it in a mighty frescoed dome,
Or lifts it heavenward in a lofty spire,
Or shapes it in a cunning frame of words,
Or pays his priest to make it day by day;
For sense must have its god as well as soul;
A new-born Dian calls for silver shrines,
And Egypt's holiest symbol is our own,
The sign we worship as did they of old
When Isis and Osiris ruled the world.

Let us be true to our most subtle selves,
We long to have our idols like the rest.

Think! when the men of Israel had their God
Encamped among them, talking with their chief,
Leading them in the pillar of the cloud
And watching o'er them in the shaft of fire,
They still must have an image; still they longed
For somewhat of substantial, solid form
Whereon to hang their garlands, and to fix
Their wandering thoughts and gain a stronger hold
For their uncertain faith, not yet assured
If those same meteors of the day and night
Were not mere exhalations of the soil.
Are we less earthly than the chosen race?
Are we more neighbors of the living God
Than they who gathered manna every morn,
Reaping where none had sown, and heard the voice
Of him who met the Highest in the mount,
And brought them tables, graven with His hand?
Yet these must have their idol, brought their gold,
That star-browed Apis might be god again;
Yea, from their ears the women brake the rings
That lent such splendors to the gypsy brown
Of sunburnt cheeks, — what more could woman do
To show her pious zeal? They went astray,
But nature led them as it leads us all.
We too, who mock at Israel's golden calf
And scoff at Egypt's sacred scarabee,
Would have our amulets to clasp and kiss,
And flood with rapturous tears, and bear with us
To be our dear companions in the dust;
Such magic works an image in our souls!

Man is an embryo; see at twenty years
His bones, the columns that uphold his frame
Not yet cemented, shaft and capital,
Mere fragments of the temple incomplete.
At twoscore, threescore, is he then full grown?
Nay, still a child, and as the little maids
Dress and undress their puppets, so he tries
To dress a lifeless creed, as if it lived,
And change its raiment when the world cries shame!
We smile to see our little ones at play
So grave, so thoughtful, with maternal care

Nursing the wisps of rags they call their babes; —
Does He not smile who sees us with the toys
We call by sacred names, and idly feign
To be what we have called them? He is still
The Father of this helpless nursery-brood,
Whose second childhood joins so close its first,
That in the crowding, hurrying years between
We scarce have trained our senses to their task
Before the gathering mist has dimmed our eyes,
And with our hollowed palm we help our ear,
And trace with trembling hand our wrinkled names,
And then begin to tell our stories o'er,
And see — not hear — the whispering lips that say,
"You know ——? Your father knew him. — This is he,
Tottering and leaning on the hireling's arm," —
And so, at length, disrobed of all that clad
The simple life we share with weed and worm,
Go to our cradles, naked as we came.

XII

LOVE

What if a soul redeemed, a spirit that loved
While yet on earth and was beloved in turn,
And still remembered every look and tone
Of that dear earthly sister who was left
Among the unwise virgins at the gate, —
Itself admitted with the bridegroom's train, —
What if this spirit redeemed, amid the host
Of chanting angels, in some transient lull
Of the eternal anthem, heard the cry
Of its lost darling, whom in evil hour
Some wilder pulse of nature led astray
And left an outcast in a world of fire, —
Condemned to be the sport of cruel fiends,
Sleepless, unpitying, masters of the skill
To wring the maddest ecstasies of pain
From worn-out souls that only ask to die, —
Would it not long to leave the bliss of heaven, —
Bearing a little water in its hand
To moisten those poor lips that plead in vain
With Him we call our Father? Or is all
So changed in such as taste celestial joy
They hear unmoved the endless wail of woe;
The daughter in the same dear tones that hushed
Her cradle slumbers; she who once had held
A babe upon her bosom from its voice
Hoarse with its cry of anguish, yet the same?

No! not in ages when the Dreadful Bird
Stamped his huge footprints, and the Fearful Beast
Strode with the flesh about those fossil bones
We build to mimic life with pygmy hands, —
Not in those earliest days when men ran wild
And gashed each other with their knives of stone,
When their low foreheads bulged in ridgy brows
And their flat hands were callous in the palm
With walking in the fashion of their sires,
Grope as they might to find a cruel god
To work their will on such as human wrath
Had wrought its worst to torture, and had left
With rage unsated, white and stark and cold,
Could hate have shaped a demon more malign
Than him the dead men mummied in their creed
And taught their trembling children to adore!
Made in *his* image! Sweet and gracious souls
Dear to my heart by nature's fondest names,
Is not your memory still the precious mould
That lends its form to Him who hears my prayer?
Thus only I behold Him, like to them,

Long-suffering, gentle, ever slow to wrath,
If wrath it be that only wounds to heal,
Ready to meet the wanderer ere he reach
The door he seeks, forgetful of his sin,
Longing to clasp him in a father's arms,
And seal his pardon with a pitying tear!

Four gospels tell their story to mankind,
And none so full of soft, caressing words
That bring the Maid of Bethlehem and her Babe
Before our tear-dimmed eyes, as his who learned
In the meek service of his gracious art
The tones which, like the medicinal balms
That calm the sufferer's anguish, soothe our souls.

Oh that the loving woman, she who sat
So long a listener at her Master's feet,
Had left us Mary's Gospel, — all she heard
Too sweet, too subtle for the ear of man!
Mark how the tender-hearted mothers read
The messages of love between the lines
Of the same page that loads the bitter tongue
Of him who deals in terror as his trade
With threatening words of wrath that scorch like flame!
They tell of angels whispering round the bed
Of the sweet infant smiling in its dream,
Of lambs enfolded in the Shepherd's arms,
Of Him who blessed the children; of the land
Where crystal rivers feed unfading flowers,
Of cities golden-paved with streets of pearl,
Of the white robes the winged creatures wear,
The crowns and harps from whose melodious strings
One long, sweet anthem flows forevermore!

We too had human mothers, even as Thou,
Whom we have learned to worship as remote
From mortal kindred, wast a cradled babe.
The milk of woman filled our branching veins,
She lulled us with her tender nursery-song,
And folded round us her untiring arms,
While the first unremembered twilight year
Shaped us to conscious being; still we feel
Her pulses in our own, — too faintly feel;
Would that the heart of woman warmed our creeds!

Not from the sad-eyed hermit's lonely cell,
Not from the conclave where the holy men
Glare on each other, as with angry eyes
They battle for God's glory and their own,
Till, sick of wordy strife, a show of hands
Fixes the faith of ages yet unborn, —
Ah, not from these the listening soul can hear
The Father's voice that speaks itself divine!
Love must be still our Master; till we learn
What he can teach us of a woman's heart,
We know not His whose love embraces all.

EPILOGUE TO THE BREAK-
FAST-TABLE SERIES

AUTOCRAT — PROFESSOR — POET

AT A BOOKSTORE

Anno Domini 1972

A CRAZY bookcase, placed before
A low-price dealer's open door;
Therein arrayed in broken rows
A ragged crew of rhyme and prose,
The homeless vagrants, waifs, and strays
Whose low estate this line betrays
(Set forth the lesser birds to lime)
YOUR CHOICE AMONG THESE BOOKS 1 DIME!

Ho! dealer; for its motto's sake
This scarecrow from the shelf I take;
Three starveling volumes bound in one,
Its covers warping in the sun.
Methinks it hath a musty smell,
I like its flavor none too well,
But Yorick's brain was far from dull,
Though Hamlet pah! 'd, and dropped his skull.

Why, here comes rain! The sky grows dark, —
Was that the roll of thunder? Hark!
The shop affords a safe retreat,
A chair extends its welcome seat,

The tradesman has a civil look
(I've paid, impromptu, for my book),
The clouds portend a sudden shower, —
I'll read my purchase for an hour.

. . . .

What have I rescued from the shelf?
A Boswell, writing out himself!
For though he changes dress and name,
The man beneath is still the same,
Laughing or sad, by fits and starts,
One actor in a dozen parts,
And whatsoe'er the mask may be,
The voice assures us, *This is he.*

I say not this to cry him down;
I find my Shakespeare in his clown,
His rogues the selfsame parent own;
Nay! Satan talks in Milton's tone!
Where'er the ocean inlet strays,
The salt sea wave its source betrays;
Where'er the queen of summer blows,
She tells the zephyr, "I'm the rose!"

And his is not the playwright's page;
His table does not ape the stage;
What matter if the figures seen
Are only shadows on a screen,
He finds in them his lurking thought,
And on their lips the words he sought,
Like one who sits before the keys
And plays a tune himself to please.

And was he noted in his day?
Read, flattered, honored? Who shall say?

Poor wreck of time the wave has cast
To find a peaceful shore at last,
Once glorying in thy gilded name
And freighted deep with hopes of fame,
Thy leaf is moistened with a tear,
The first for many a long, long year!

For be it more or less of art
That veils the lowliest human heart
Where passion throbs, where friendship
  glows,
Where pity's tender tribute flows,
Where love has lit its fragrant fire,
And sorrow quenched its vain desire,
For me the altar is divine,
Its flame, its ashes, — all are mine!

And thou, my brother, as I look
And see thee pictured in thy book,
Thy years on every page confessed
In shadows lengthening from the west,
Thy glance that wanders, as it sought
Some freshly opening flower of thought,
Thy hopeful nature, light and free,
I start to find myself in thee!

. . . .

Come, vagrant, outcast, wretch forlorn
In leather jerkin stained and torn,
Whose talk has filled my idle hour
And made me half forget the shower,
I'll do at least as much for you,
Your coat I'll patch, your gilt renew,
Read you — perhaps — some other time.
Not bad, my bargain! Price one dime!

SONGS OF MANY SEASONS

1862-1874

OPENING THE WINDOW

Thus I lift the sash, so long
Shut against the flight of song;
All too late for vain excuse, —
Lo, my captive rhymes are loose!

Rhymes that, flitting through my brain,
Beat against my window-pane,
Some with gayly colored wings,
Some, alas! with venomed stings.

Shall they bask in sunny rays?
Shall they feed on sugared praise?
Shall they stick with tangled feet
On the critic's poisoned sheet?

Are the outside winds too rough?
Is the world not wide enough?
Go, my wingèd verse, and try, —
Go, like Uncle Toby's fly!

PROGRAMME

OCTOBER 7, 1874

Reader — gentle — if so be
Such still live, and live for me,
Will it please you to be told
What my tenscore pages hold?

Here are verses that in spite
Of myself I needs must write,
Like the wine that oozes first
When the unsqueezed grapes have burst.

Here are angry lines, "too hard!"
Says the soldier, battle-scarred.
Could I smile his scars away
I would blot the bitter lay,

Written with a knitted brow,
Read with placid wonder now.
Throbbed such passion in my heart?
Did his wounds once really smart?

Here are varied strains that sing
All the changes life can bring,
Songs when joyous friends have met,
Songs the mourner's tears have wet.

See the banquet's dead bouquet,
Fair and fragrant in its day;
Do they read the selfsame lines, —
He that fasts and he that dines?

Year by year, like milestones placed,
Mark the record Friendship traced.
Prisoned in the walls of time
Life has notched itself in rhyme:

As its seasons slid along,
Every year a notch of song,
From the June of long ago,
When the rose was full in blow,

Till the scarlet sage has come
And the cold chrysanthemum.
Read, but not to praise or blame;
Are not all our hearts the same?

For the rest, they take their chance, —
Some may pay a passing glance;
Others, — well, they served a turn, —
Wherefore written, would you learn?

Not for glory, not for pelf,
Not, be sure, to please myself,
Not for any meaner ends, —
Always "by request of friends."

Here's the cousin of a king, —
Would I do the civil thing?
Here's the first-born of a queen:
Here's a slant-eyed Mandarin.

Would I polish off Japan?
Would I greet this famous man,
Prince or Prelate, Sheik or Shah? —
Figaro çi and Figaro là!

Would I just this once comply? —
So they teased and teased till I
(Be the truth at once confessed)
Wavered — yielded — did my best.

Turn my pages, — never mind
If you like not all you find;
Think not all the grains are gold
Sacramento's sand-banks hold.

Every kernel has its shell,
Every chime its harshest bell,
Every face its weariest look,
Every shelf its emptiest book,

Every field its leanest sheaf,
Every book its dullest leaf,
Every leaf its weakest line, —
Shall it not be so with mine?

Best for worst shall make amends,
Find us, keep us, leave us friends
Till, perchance, we meet again.
Benedicite. — Amen!

IN THE QUIET DAYS

AN OLD-YEAR SONG

As through the forest, disarrayed
By chill November, late I strayed,
A lonely minstrel of the wood
Was singing to the solitude;
I loved thy music, thus I said,
When o'er thy perch the leaves were spread;
Sweet was thy song, but sweeter now
Thy carol on the leafless bough.
  Sing, little bird! thy note shall cheer
  The sadness of the dying year.

When violets pranked the turf with blue
And morning filled their cups with dew,
Thy slender voice with rippling trill
The budding April bowers would fill,
Nor passed its joyous tones away
When April rounded into May:
  Thy life shall hail no second dawn, —
  Sing, little bird! the spring is gone.

And I remember — welladay! —
Thy full-blown summer roundelay,
As when behind a broidered screen
Some holy maiden sings unseen;
With answering notes the woodland rung,
And every treetop found a tongue.
  How deep the shade! the groves how fair!
  Sing, little bird! the woods are bare.

The summer's throbbing chant is done
And mute the choral antiphon;
The birds have left the shivering pines
To flit among the trellised vines,
Or fan the air with scented plumes
Amid the love-sick orange-blooms,
  And thou art here alone, — alone, —
  Sing, little bird! the rest have flown.

The snow has capped yon distant hill,
At morn the running brook was still,
From driven herds the clouds that rise
Are like the smoke of sacrifice;
Erelong the frozen sod shall mock
The ploughshare, changed to stubborn rock,
  The brawling streams shall soon be dumb, —
  Sing, little bird! the frosts have come.

Fast, fast the lengthening shadows creep,
The songless fowls are half asleep,
The air grows chill, the setting sun
May leave thee ere thy song is done,
The pulse that warms thy breast grow cold,
Thy secret die with thee, untold:
  The lingering sunset still is bright, —
  Sing, little bird! 't will soon be night.

DOROTHY Q.

A FAMILY PORTRAIT

I cannot tell the story of Dorothy Q. more simply in prose than I have told it in verse, but I can add something to it.
Dorothy was the daughter of Judge Edmund Quincy, and the niece of Josiah Quincy, junior, the young patriot and orator who died just before the American Revolution, of which he

was one of the most eloquent and effective promoters. The son of the latter, Josiah Quincy, the first mayor of Boston bearing that name, lived to a great age, one of the most useful and honored citizens of his time.

The canvas of the painting was so much decayed that it had to be replaced by a new one, in doing which the rapier thrust was of course filled up.

GRANDMOTHER'S mother: her age, I guess,
Thirteen summers, or something less;
Girlish bust, but womanly air;
Smooth, square forehead with uprolled hair;
Lips that lover has never kissed;
Taper fingers and slender wrist;
Hanging sleeves of stiff brocade;
So they painted the little maid.

On her hand a parrot green
Sits unmoving and broods serene.
Hold up the canvas full in view, —
Look! there 's a rent the light shines through,
Dark with a century's fringe of dust, —
That was a Red-Coat's rapier-thrust!
Such is the tale the lady old,
Dorothy's daughter's daughter, told.

Who the painter was none may tell, —
One whose best was not over well;
Hard and dry, it must be confessed,
Flat as a rose that has long been pressed;
Yet in her cheek the hues are bright,
Dainty colors of red and white,
And in her slender shape are seen
Hint and promise of stately mien.

Look not on her with eyes of scorn, —
Dorothy Q. was a lady born!
Ay! since the galloping Normans came,
England's annals have known her name;
And still to the three-hilled rebel town
Dear is that ancient name's renown,
For many a civic wreath they won,
The youthful sire and the gray-haired son.

O Damsel Dorothy! Dorothy Q.!
Strange is the gift that I owe to you;
Such a gift as never a king
Save to daughter or son might bring, —
All my tenure of heart and hand,
All my title to house and land;
Mother and sister and child and wife
And joy and sorrow and death and life!

What if a hundred years ago
Those close-shut lips had answered No,
When forth the tremulous question came
That cost the maiden her Norman name,
And under the folds that look so still
The bodice swelled with the bosom's thrill?
Should I be I, or would it be
One tenth another, to nine tenths me?

Soft is the breath of a maiden's YES:
Not the light gossamer stirs with less;
But never a cable that holds so fast
Through all the battles of wave and blast,
And never an echo of speech or song
That lives in the babbling air so long!
There were tones in the voice that whispered then
You may hear to-day in a hundred men.

O lady and lover, how faint and far
Your images hover, — and here we are,
Solid and stirring in flesh and bone, —
Edward's and Dorothy's — all their own, —
A goodly record for Time to show
Of a syllable spoken so long ago! —
Shall I bless you, Dorothy, or forgive
For the tender whisper that bade me live?

It shall be a blessing, my little maid!
I will heal the stab of the Red-Coat's blade,
And freshen the gold of the tarnished frame,
And gild with a rhyme your household name;
So you shall smile on us brave and bright
As first you greeted the morning's light,
And live untroubled by woes and fears
Through a second youth of a hundred years.

THE ORGAN-BLOWER

DEVOUTEST of my Sunday friends,
The patient Organ-blower bends;
I see his figure sink and rise,
(Forgive me, Heaven, my wandering eyes!)
A moment lost, the next half seen,
His head above the scanty screen,
Still measuring out his deep salaams
Through quavering hymns and panting psalms.

No priest that prays in gilded stole,
To save a rich man's mortgaged soul;
No sister, fresh from holy vows,
So humbly stoops, so meekly bows;
His large obeisance puts to shame
The proudest genuflecting dame,
Whose Easter bonnet low descends
With all the grace devotion lends.

O brother with the supple spine,
How much we owe those bows of thine!
Without thine arm to lend the breeze,
How vain the finger on the keys!
Though all unmatched the player's skill,
Those thousand throats were dumb and
  still:
Another's art may shape the tone,
The breath that fills it is thine own.

Six days the silent Memnon waits
Behind his temple's folded gates;
But when the seventh day's sunshine falls
Through rainbowed windows on the walls,
He breathes, he sings, he shouts, he fills
The quivering air with rapturous thrills;
The roof resounds, the pillars shake,
And all the slumbering echoes wake!

The Preacher from the Bible-text
With weary words my soul has vexed
(Some stranger, fumbling far astray
To find the lesson for the day);
He tells us truths too plainly true,
And reads the service all askew, —
Why, why the — mischief — can't he look
Beforehand in the service-book?

But thou, with decent mien and face,
Art always ready in thy place;
Thy strenuous blast, whate'er the tune,
As steady as the strong monsoon;
Thy only dread a leathery creak,
Or small residual extra squeak,
To send along the shadowy aisles
A sunlit wave of dimpled smiles.

Not all the preaching, O my friend,
Comes from the church's pulpit end!
Not all that bend the knee and bow
Yield service half so true as thou!
One simple task performed aright,
With slender skill, but all thy might,
Where honest labor does its best,
And leaves the player all the rest.

This many-diapasoned maze,
Through which the breath of being strays,
Whose music makes our earth divine,
Has work for mortal hands like mine.
My duty lies before me. Lo,
The lever there! Take hold and blow!
And He whose hand is on the keys
Will play the tune as He shall please.

AFTER THE FIRE

[The great Boston fire occurred November
9–10, 1872.]

WHILE far along the eastern sky
I saw the flags of Havoc fly,
As if his forces would assault
The sovereign of the starry vault
And hurl Him back the burning rain
That seared the cities of the plain,
I read as on a crimson page
The words of Israel's sceptred sage: —

*For riches make them wings, and they
Do as an eagle fly away.*

O vision of that sleepless night,
What hue shall paint the mocking light
That burned and stained the orient skies
Where peaceful morning loves to rise,
As if the sun had lost his way
And dawned to make a second day, —
Above how red with fiery glow,
How dark to those it woke below!

On roof and wall, on dome and spire,
Flashed the false jewels of the fire;
Girt with her belt of glittering panes,
And crowned with starry-gleaming vanes,
Our northern queen in glory shone
With new-born splendors not her own,
And stood, transfigured in our eyes,
A victim decked for sacrifice!

The cloud still hovers overhead,
And still the midnight sky is red;
As the lost wanderer strays alone
To seek the place he called his own,
His devious footprints sadly tell
How changed the pathways known so
  well;
The scene, how new! The tale, how old
Ere yet the ashes have grown cold!

Again I read the words that came
Writ in the rubric of the flame:
Howe'er we trust to mortal things,
Each hath its pair of folded wings;
Though long their terrors rest unspread
Their fatal plumes are never shed;
At last, at last, they stretch in flight,
And blot the day and blast the night!

Hope, only Hope, of all that clings
Around us, never spreads her wings;
Love, though he break his earthly chain,
Still whispers he will come again;
But Faith that soars to seek the sky
Shall teach our half-fledged souls to fly,
And find, beyond the smoke and flame,
The cloudless azure whence they came!

AT THE PANTOMIME

18—: REWRITTEN 1874

THE house was crammed from roof to floor,
Heads piled on heads at every door;
Half dead with August's seething heat
I crowded on and found my seat,
My patience slightly out of joint,
My temper short of boiling-point,
Not quite at *Hate mankind as such*,
Nor yet at *Love them overmuch*.

Amidst the throng the pageant drew
Were gathered Hebrews not a few,
Black-bearded, swarthy, — at their side
Dark, jewelled women, orient-eyed:
If scarce a Christian hopes for grace
Who crowds one in his narrow place,
What will the savage victim do
Whose ribs are kneaded by a Jew?

Next on my left a breathing form
Wedged up against me, close and warm;
The beak that crowned the bistred face
Betrayed the mould of Abraham's race, —
That coal-black hair, that smoke-brown hue, —
Ah, cursèd, unbelieving Jew!
I started, shuddering, to the right,
And squeezed — a second Israelite!

Then woke the evil brood of rage
That slumber, tongueless, in their cage;
I stabbed in turn with silent oaths
The hook-nosed kite of carrion clothes,
The snaky usurer, him that crawls
And cheats beneath the golden balls,
Moses and Levi, all the horde,
Spawn of the race that slew its Lord.

Up came their murderous deeds of old,
The grisly story Chaucer told,
And many an ugly tale beside
Of children caught and crucified;
I heard the ducat-sweating thieves
Beneath the Ghetto's slouching eaves,
And, thrust beyond the tented green,
The lepers cry, "Unclean!   Unclean!"

The show went on, but, ill at ease,
My sullen eye it could not please,
In vain my conscience whispered, "Shame!
Who but their Maker is to blame?"
I thought of Judas and his bribe,
And steeled my soul against their tribe:
My neighbors stirred; I looked again
Full on the younger of the twain.

A fresh young cheek whose olive hue
The mantling blood shows faintly through;
Locks dark as midnight, that divide
And shade the neck on either side;
Soft, gentle, loving eyes that gleam
Clear as a starlit mountain stream; —
So looked that other child of Shem,
The Maiden's Boy of Bethlehem!

And thou couldst scorn the peerless blood
That flows unmingled from the Flood, —
Thy scutcheon spotted with the stains
Of Norman thieves and pirate Danes!
The New World's foundling, in thy pride
Scowl on the Hebrew at thy side,
And lo! the very semblance there
The Lord of Glory deigned to wear!

I see that radiant image rise,
The flowing hair, the pitying eyes,
The faintly crimsoned cheek that shows
The blush of Sharon's opening rose, —
Thy hands would clasp his hallowed feet
Whose brethren soil thy Christian seat,
Thy lips would press his garment's hem
That curl in wrathful scorn for them!

A sudden mist, a watery screen,
Dropped like a veil before the scene;
The shadow floated from my soul,
And to my lips a whisper stole, —
"Thy prophets caught the Spirit's flame,
From thee the Son of Mary came,
With thee the Father deigned to dwell, —
Peace be upon thee, Israel!"

A BALLAD OF THE BOSTON TEA-PARTY

The tax on tea, which was considered so odious and led to the act on which *A Ballad of the Boston Tea Party* is founded, was but a small matter, only twopence in the pound. But it involved a principle of taxation, to which the Colonies would not submit. Their objection was not to the amount, but the claim. The East India Company, however, sent out a number of tea-ships to different American ports, three of them to Boston.

The inhabitants tried to send them back, but in vain. The captains of the ships had consented, if permitted, to return with their cargoes to England, but the consignees refused to discharge them from their obligations, the custom house to give them a clearance for their return, and the governor to grant them a passport for going by the fort. It was easily seen that the tea would be gradually landed from the ships lying so near the town, and that if landed it would be disposed of, and the purpose of establishing the monopoly and raising a revenue effected. To prevent the dreaded consequence, a number of armed men, disguised like Indians, boarded the ships and threw their whole cargoes of tea into the dock. About seventeen persons boarded the ships in Boston harbor, and emptied three hundred and forty-two chests of tea. Among these "Indians" was Major Thomas Melville, the same who suggested to me the poem, *The Last Leaf*.

Read at a meeting of the Massachusetts Historical Society in 1874.

No! never such a draught was poured
  Since Hebe served with nectar
The bright Olympians and their Lord,
  Her over-kind protector, —
Since Father Noah squeezed the grape
  And took to such behaving
As would have shamed our grandsire ape
  Before the days of shaving, —
No! ne'er was mingled such a draught
  In palace, hall, or arbor,
As freemen brewed and tyrants quaffed
  That night in Boston Harbor!
It kept King George so long awake
  His brain at last got addled,
It made the nerves of Britain shake,
  With sevenscore millions saddled;
Before that bitter cup was drained,
  Amid the roar of cannon,
The Western war-cloud's crimson stained
  The Thames, the Clyde, the Shannon;
Full many a six-foot grenadier
  The flattened grass had measured,
And many a mother many a year
  Her tearful memories treasured;
Fast spread the tempest's darkening pall,
  The mighty realms were troubled,
The storm broke loose, but first of all
  The Boston teapot bubbled!

An evening party, — only that,
  No formal invitation,
No gold-laced coat, no stiff cravat,
  No feast in contemplation,
No silk-robed dames, no fiddling band,
  No flowers, no songs, no dancing, —
A tribe of red men, axe in hand, —
  Behold the guests advancing!
How fast the stragglers join the throng,
  From stall and workshop gathered!
The lively barber skips along
  And leaves a chin half-lathered;
The smith has flung his hammer down, —
  The horseshoe still is glowing;
The truant tapster at the Crown
  Has left a beer-cask flowing;
The cooper's boys have dropped the adze,
  And trot behind their master;
Up run the tarry ship-yard lads, —
  The crowd is hurrying faster, —
Out from the Millpond's purlieus gush
  The streams of white-faced millers,
And down their slippery alleys rush
  The lusty young Fort-Hillers;
The ropewalk lends its 'prentice crew, —
  The tories seize the omen:
"Ay, boys, you 'll soon have work to do
  For England's rebel foemen,
'King Hancock,' Adams, and their gang,
  That fire the mob with treason, —
When these we shoot and those we hang
  The town will come to reason."

On — on to where the tea-ships ride!
  And now their ranks are forming, —
A rush, and up the Dartmouth's side
  The Mohawk band is swarming!
See the fierce natives! What a glimpse
  Of paint and fur and feather,
As all at once the full-grown imps
  Light on the deck together!
A scarf the pigtail's secret keeps,
  A blanket hides the breeches, —
And out the cursèd cargo leaps,
  And overboard it pitches!

O woman, at the evening board
  So gracious, sweet, and purring,
So happy while the tea is poured,
  So blest while spoons are stirring,
What martyr can compare with thee,
  The mother, wife, or daughter,
That night, instead of best Bohea,
  Condemned to milk and water!

Ah, little dreams the quiet dame
  Who plies with rock and spindle
The patient flax, how great a flame
  Yon little spark shall kindle!
The lurid morning shall reveal
  A fire no king can smother
Where British flint and Boston steel
  Have clashed against each other!
Old charters shrivel in its track,
  His Worship's bench has crumbled,
It climbs and clasps the union-jack,
  Its blazoned pomp is humbled,
The flags go down on land and sea
  Like corn before the reapers;
So burned the fire that brewed the tea
  That Boston served her keepers!

The waves that wrought a century's wreck
  Have rolled o'er whig and tory;
The Mohawks on the Dartmouth's deck
  Still live in song and story;
The waters in the rebel bay
  Have kept the tea-leaf savor;
Our old North-Enders in their spray
  Still taste a Hyson flavor;

And Freedom's teacup still o'erflows
  With ever fresh libations,
To cheat of slumber all her foes
  And cheer the wakening nations!

NEARING THE SNOW-LINE

1870

SLOW toiling upward from the misty vale,
  I leave the bright enamelled zones below;
No more for me their beauteous bloom shall glow,
  Their lingering sweetness load the morning gale;
Few are the slender flowerets, scentless, pale,
  That on their ice-clad stems all trembling blow
Along the margin of unmelting snow;
  Yet with unsaddened voice thy verge I hail,
White realm of peace above the flowering line;
  Welcome thy frozen domes, thy rocky spires!
O'er thee undimmed the moon-girt planets shine,
On thy majestic altars fade the fires
That filled the air with smoke of vain desires,
  And all the unclouded blue of heaven is thine!

IN WAR TIME

TO CANAAN

A PURITAN WAR-SONG

AUGUST 12, 1862

This poem, published anonymously in the Boston Evening Transcript, was claimed by several persons, three, if I remember correctly, whose names I have or have had, but never thought it worth while to publish.

WHERE are you going, soldiers,
  With banner, gun, and sword?
We 're marching South to Canaan
  To battle for the Lord!
What Captain leads your armies
  Along the rebel coasts?
The Mighty One of Israel,
  His name is Lord of Hosts!
To Canaan, to Canaan
  The Lord has led us forth,
To blow before the heathen walls
  The trumpets of the North!

What flag is this you carry
  Along the sea and shore?
The same our grandsires lifted up, —
  The same our fathers bore!
In many a battle's tempest
  It shed the crimson rain, —

What God has woven in his loom
  Let no man rend in twain!
To Canaan, to Canaan
  The Lord has led us forth,
To plant upon the rebel towers
  The banners of the North!

What troop is this that follows,
  All armed with picks and spades?
These are the swarthy bondsmen, —
  The iron-skin brigades!
They'll pile up Freedom's breastwork,
  They'll scoop out rebels' graves;
Who then will be their owner
  And march them off for slaves?
    To Canaan, to Canaan
    The Lord has led us forth,
    To strike upon the captive's chain
    The hammers of the North!

What song is this you're singing?
  The same that Israel sung
When Moses led the mighty choir,
  And Miriam's timbrel rung!
To Canaan! To Canaan!
  The priests and maidens cried:
To Canaan! To Canaan!
  The people's voice replied.
    To Canaan, to Canaan
    The Lord has led us forth,
    To thunder through its adder dens
    The anthems of the North!

When Canaan's hosts are scattered,
  And all her walls lie flat,
What follows next in order?
  The Lord will see to that!
We'll break the tyrant's sceptre, —
  We'll build the people's throne, —
When half the world is Freedom's,
  Then all the world's our own!
    To Canaan, to Canaan
    The Lord has led us forth,
    To sweep the rebel threshing-floors,
    A whirlwind from the North!

"THUS SAITH THE LORD, I OFFER THEE THREE THINGS"

1862

IN poisonous dens, where traitors hide
  Like bats that fear the day,
While all the land our charters claim
Is sweating blood and breathing flame,
Dead to their country's woe and shame,
  The recreants whisper STAY!

In peaceful homes, where patriot fires
  On Love's own altars glow,
The mother hides her trembling fear,
The wife, the sister, checks a tear,
To breathe the parting word of cheer,
  Soldier of Freedom, GO!

In halls where Luxury lies at ease,
  And Mammon keeps his state,
Where flatterers fawn and menials crouch,
The dreamer, startled from his couch,
Wrings a few counters from his pouch,
  And murmurs faintly WAIT!

In weary camps, on trampled plains
  That ring with fife and drum,
The battling host, whose harness gleams
Along the crimson-flowing streams,
Calls, like a warning voice in dreams,
  We want you, Brother! COME!

Choose ye whose bidding ye will do, —
  To go, to wait, to stay!
Sons of the Freedom-loving town,
Heirs of the Fathers' old renown,
The servile yoke, the civic crown,
  Await your choice TO-DAY!

The stake is laid! O gallant youth
  With yet unsilvered brow,
If Heaven should lose and Hell should win,
On whom shall lie the mortal sin,
That cries aloud, *It might have been?*
  God calls you — answer NOW.

NEVER OR NOW

AN APPEAL

1862

LISTEN, young heroes! your country is calling!
Time strikes the hour for the brave and the true!
Now, while the foremost are fighting and falling,
  Fill up the ranks that have opened for you!

You whom the fathers made free and defended,
  Stain not the scroll that emblazons their fame!
You whose fair heritage spotless descended,
  Leave not your children a birthright of shame!

Stay not for questions while Freedom stands gasping!
  Wait not till Honor lies wrapped in his pall!
Brief the lips' meeting be, swift the hands' clasping, —
  "Off for the wars!" is enough for them all!

Break from the arms that would fondly caress you!
  Hark! 't is the bugle-blast, sabres are drawn!
Mothers shall pray for you, fathers shall bless you,
  Maidens shall weep for you when you are gone!

Never or now! cries the blood of a nation,
  Poured on the turf where the red rose should bloom;
Now is the day and the hour of salvation, —
  Never or now! peals the trumpet of doom!

Never or now! roars the hoarse-throated cannon
  Through the black canopy blotting the skies;
Never or now! flaps the shell-blasted pennon
  O'er the deep ooze where the Cumberland lies!

From the foul dens where our brothers are dying,
  Aliens and foes in the land of their birth, —
From the rank swamps where our martyrs are lying
  Pleading in vain for a handful of earth, —

From the hot plains where they perish outnumbered,
  Furrowed and ridged by the battle-field's plough,
Comes the loud summons; too long you have slumbered,
  Hear the last Angel-trump, — Never or Now!

HYMN

WRITTEN FOR THE GREAT CENTRAL FAIR IN PHILADELPHIA, 1864

[This hymn was to have been sung at the Inaugural Ceremonies June 7, but an accident to the singers' platform prevented its use in that form.]

FATHER, send on Earth again
Peace and good-will to men;
Yet, while the weary track of life
Leads thy people through storm and strife,
Help us to walk therein.

Guide us through the perilous path;
Teach us love that tempers wrath;
Let the fountain of mercy flow
Alike for helpless friend and foe,
Children all of Thine.

God of grace, hear our call;
Bless our gifts, Giver of all;
The wounded heal, the captive restore,
And make us a nation evermore
Faithful to Freedom and Thee.

ONE COUNTRY

1865

ONE country! Treason's writhing asp
Struck madly at her girdle's clasp,
And Hatred wrenched with might and main
To rend its welded links in twain,
While Mammon hugged his golden calf
Content to take one broken half,
While thankless churls stood idly by
And heard unmoved a nation's cry!

One country! "Nay," — the tyrant crew
Shrieked from their dens, — "it shall be two!
Ill bodes to us this monstrous birth,
That scowls on all the thrones of earth,
Too broad yon starry cluster shines,
Too proudly tower the New-World pines,
Tear down the 'banner of the free,'
And cleave their land from sea to sea!"

One country still, though foe and "friend"
Our seamless empire strove to rend;
Safe! safe! though all the fiends of hell
Join the red murderers' battle-yell!
What though the lifted sabres gleam,
The cannons frown by shore and stream, —
The sabres clash, the cannons thrill,
In wild accord, One country still!

One country! in her stress and strain
We heard the breaking of a chain!
Look where the conquering Nation swings
Her iron flail, — its shivered rings!
Forged by the rebels' crimson hand,
That bolt of wrath shall scourge the land
Till Peace proclaims on sea and shore
One Country now and evermore!

GOD SAVE THE FLAG!

1865

WASHED in the blood of the brave and the blooming,
  Snatched from the altars of insolent foes,
Burning with star-fires, but never consuming,
  Flash its broad ribbons of lily and rose.

Vainly the prophets of Baal would rend it,
  Vainly his worshippers pray for its fall;
Thousands have died for it, millions defend it,
  Emblem of justice and mercy to all:

Justice that reddens the sky with her terrors,
  Mercy that comes with her white-handed train,
Soothing all passions, redeeming all errors,
  Sheathing the sabre and breaking the chain.

Borne on the deluge of old usurpations,
  Drifted our Ark o'er the desolate seas,
Bearing the rainbow of hope to the nations,
  Torn from the storm-cloud and flung to the breeze!

God bless the Flag and its loyal defenders,
  While its broad folds o'er the battle-field wave,
Till the dim star-wreath rekindle its splendors,
  Washed from its stains in the blood of the brave!

HYMN

AFTER THE EMANCIPATION PROCLAMATION

1865

GIVER of all that crowns our days,
With grateful hearts we sing thy praise;
Through deep and desert led by Thee,
Our promised land at last we see.

Ruler of Nations, judge our cause!
If we have kept thy holy laws,
The sons of Belial curse in vain
The day that rends the captive's chain.

Thou God of vengeance! Israel's Lord!
Break in their grasp the shield and sword.
And make thy righteous judgments known
Till all thy foes are overthrown!

Then, Father, lay thy healing hand
In mercy on our stricken land;
Lead all its wanderers to the fold,
And be their Shepherd as of old.

So shall one Nation's song ascend
To Thee, our Ruler, Father, Friend,
While Heaven's wide arch resounds again
With Peace on earth, good-will to men!

HYMN

FOR THE FAIR AT CHICAGO

1865

O GOD! in danger's darkest hour,
  In battle's deadliest field,
Thy name has been our Nation's tower,
  Thy truth her help and shield.

Our lips should fill the air with praise,
  Nor pay the debt we owe,
So high above the songs we raise
  The floods of mercy flow.

Yet Thou wilt hear the prayer we speak,
  The song of praise we sing, —
Thy children, who thine altar seek
  Their grateful gifts to bring.

Thine altar is the sufferer's bed,
  The home of woe and pain,
The soldier's turfy pillow, red
  With battle's crimson rain.

No smoke of burning stains the air,
  No incense-clouds arise;
Thy peaceful servants, Lord, prepare
  A bloodless sacrifice.

Lo! for our wounded brothers' need,
  We bear the wine and oil;
For us they faint, for us they bleed,
  For them our gracious toil!

O Father, bless the gifts we bring!
  Cause Thou thy face to shine,
Till every nation owns her King,
  And all the earth is thine.

UNDER THE WASHINGTON ELM, CAMBRIDGE

APRIL 27, 1861

EIGHTY years have passed, and more,
  Since under the brave old tree
Our fathers gathered in arms, and swore
They would follow the sign their banners bore,
  And fight till the land was free.

Half of their work was done,
  Half is left to do,—
Cambridge, and Concord, and Lexington!
When the battle is fought and won,
  What shall be told of you?

Hark! — 't is the south-wind moans,—
  Who are the martyrs down?
Ah, the marrow was true in your children's bones
That sprinkled with blood the cursèd stones
  Of the murder-haunted town!

What if the storm-clouds blow?
  What if the green leaves fall?
Better the crashing tempest's throe
Than the army of worms that gnawed below;
  Trample them one and all!

Then, when the battle is won,
  And the land from traitors free,
Our children shall tell of the strife begun
When Liberty's second April sun
  Was bright on our brave old tree!

FREEDOM, OUR QUEEN

LAND where the banners wave last in the sun,
Blazoned with star-clusters, many in one,
Floating o'er prairie and mountain and sea;
Hark! 't is the voice of thy children to thee!

Here at thine altar our vows we renew
Still in thy cause to be loyal and true,—
True to thy flag on the field and the wave,
Living to honor it, dying to save!

Mother of heroes! if perfidy's blight
Fall on a star in thy garland of light,
Sound but one bugle-blast! Lo! at the sign
Armies all panoplied wheel into line!

Hope of the world! thou hast broken its chains,—
Wear thy bright arms while a tyrant remains,
Stand for the right till the nations shall own
Freedom their sovereign, with Law for her throne!

Freedom! sweet Freedom! our voices resound,
Queen by God's blessing, unsceptred, uncrowned!
Freedom, sweet Freedom, our pulses repeat,
Warm with her life-blood, as long as they beat!

Fold the broad banner-stripes over her breast,—
Crown her with star-jewels Queen of the West!
Earth for her heritage, God for her friend,
She shall reign over us, world without end!

ARMY HYMN

"OLD HUNDRED"

O Lord of Hosts! Almighty King!
Behold the sacrifice we bring!
To every arm thy strength impart,
Thy spirit shed through every heart!

Wake in our breasts the living fires,
The holy faith that warmed our sires;
Thy hand hath made our Nation free;
To die for her is serving Thee.

Be Thou a pillared flame to show
The midnight snare, the silent foe;
And when the battle thunders loud,
Still guide us in its moving cloud.

God of all Nations! Sovereign Lord!
In thy dread name we draw the sword,
We lift the starry flag on high
That fills with light our stormy sky.

From treason's rent, from murder's stain,
Guard Thou its folds till Peace shall
   reign, —
Till fort and field, till shore and sea,
Join our loud anthem, Praise to Thee!

PARTING HYMN

"DUNDEE"

Father of Mercies, Heavenly Friend,
  We seek thy gracious throne;
To Thee our faltering prayers ascend,
  Our fainting hearts are known!

From blasts that chill, from suns that
    smite,
  From every plague that harms;
In camp and march, in siege and fight,
  Protect our men-at-arms!

Though from our darkened lives they take
  What makes our life most dear,
We yield them for their country's sake
  With no relenting tear.

Our blood their flowing veins will shed,
  Their wounds our breasts will share;
Oh, save us from the woes we dread,
  Or grant us strength to bear!

Let each unhallowed cause that brings
  The stern destroyer cease,
Thy flaming angel fold his wings,
  And seraphs whisper Peace!

Thine are the sceptre and the sword,
  Stretch forth thy mighty hand, —
Reign Thou our kingless nation's Lord,
  Rule Thou our throneless land!

THE FLOWER OF LIBERTY

What flower is this that greets the morn,
Its hues from Heaven so freshly born?
With burning star and flaming band
It kindles all the sunset land:
Oh tell us what its name may be, —
Is this the Flower of Liberty?
  It is the banner of the free,
  The starry Flower of Liberty!

In savage Nature's far abode
Its tender seed our fathers sowed;
The storm-winds rocked its swelling bud,
Its opening leaves were streaked with
    blood,
Till lo! earth's tyrants shook to see
The full-blown Flower of Liberty!
  Then hail the banner of the free,
  The starry Flower of Liberty!

Behold its streaming rays unite,
One mingling flood of braided light, —
The red that fires the Southern rose,
With spotless white from Northern snows,
And, spangled o'er its azure, see
The sister Stars of Liberty!
  Then hail the banner of the free,
  The starry Flower of Liberty!

The blades of heroes fence it round,
Where'er it springs is holy ground;
From tower and dome its glories spread;
It waves where lonely sentries tread;
It makes the land as ocean free,
And plants an empire on the sea!
  Then hail the banner of the free,
  The starry Flower of Liberty!

Thy sacred leaves, fair Freedom's flower,
Shall ever float on dome and tower,
To all their heavenly colors true,
In blackening frost or crimson dew, —

And God love us as we love thee,
Thrice holy Flower of Liberty!
Then hail the banner of the free,
The starry FLOWER OF LIBERTY!

THE SWEET LITTLE MAN

DEDICATED TO THE STAY-AT-HOME RANGERS

Now, while our soldiers are fighting our battles,
Each at his post to do all that he can,
Down among rebels and contraband chattels,
What are you doing, my sweet little man?

All the brave boys under canvas are sleeping,
All of them pressing to march with the van,
Far from the home where their sweethearts are weeping;
What are you waiting for, sweet little man?

You with the terrible warlike mustaches,
Fit for a colonel or chief of a clan,
You with the waist made for sword-belts and sashes,
Where are your shoulder-straps, sweet little man?

Bring him the buttonless garment of woman!
Cover his face lest it freckle and tan;
Muster the Apron-String Guards on the Common,
That is the corps for the sweet little man!

Give him for escort a file of young misses,
Each of them armed with a deadly rattan;
They shall defend him from laughter and hisses,
Aimed by low boys at the sweet little man.

All the fair maidens about him shall cluster,
Pluck the white feathers from bonnet and fan,
Make him a plume like a turkey-wing duster, —
That is the crest for the sweet little man!

Oh, but the Apron-String Guards are the fellows!
Drilling each day since our troubles began, —
"Handle your walking-sticks!" "Shoulder umbrellas!"
That is the style for the sweet little man!

Have we a nation to save? In the first place
Saving ourselves is the sensible plan, —
Surely the spot where there's shooting's the worst place
Where I can stand, says the sweet little man.

Catch me confiding my person with strangers!
Think how the cowardly Bull-Runners ran!
In the brigade of the Stay-at-Home Rangers
Marches my corps, says the sweet little man.

Such was the stuff of the Malakoff-takers,
Such were the soldiers that scaled the Redan;
Truculent housemaids and bloodthirsty Quakers,
Brave not the wrath of the sweet little man!

Yield him the sidewalk, ye nursery maidens!
Sauve qui peut! Bridget, and right about! Ann; —
Fierce as a shark in a school of menhadens,
See him advancing, the sweet little man!

When the red flails of the battle-field's threshers
Beat out the continent's wheat from its bran,
While the wind scatters the chaffy secesshers,
What will become of our sweet little man?

When the brown soldiers come back from the borders,
How will he look while his features they scan?
How will he feel when he gets marching orders,
Signed by his lady love? sweet little man!

Fear not for him, though the rebels expect him, —
Life is too precious to shorten its span;
Woman her broomstick shall raise to protect him,
    Will she not fight for the sweet little man?

Now then, nine cheers for the Stay-at-Home Ranger!
Blow the great fish-horn and beat the big pan!
First in the field that is farthest from danger,
    Take your white-feather plume, sweet little man!

UNION AND LIBERTY

FLAG of the heroes who left us their glory,
Borne through their battle-fields' thunder and flame,
Blazoned in song and illumined in story,
    Wave o'er us all who inherit their fame!
    Up with our banner bright,
    Sprinkled with starry light,
    Spread its fair emblems from mountain to shore,
    While through the sounding sky
    Loud rings the Nation's cry, —
    UNION AND LIBERTY! ONE EVERMORE!

Light of our firmament, guide of our Nation,
Pride of her children, and honored afar,
Let the wide beams of thy full constellation
    Scatter each cloud that would darken a star!
    Up with our banner bright, etc.

Empire unsceptred! what foe shall assail thee,
Bearing the standard of Liberty's van?
Think not the God of thy fathers shall fail thee,
    Striving with men for the birthright of man!
    Up with our banner bright, etc.

Yet if, by madness and treachery blighted,
Dawns the dark hour when the sword thou must draw,
Then with the arms of thy millions united,
    Smite the bold traitors to Freedom and Law!
    Up with our banner bright, etc.

Lord of the Universe! shield us and guide us,
Trusting Thee always, through shadow and sun!
Thou hast united us, who shall divide us?
    Keep us, oh keep us the MANY IN ONE!
    Up with our banner bright,
    Sprinkled with starry light,
    Spread its fair emblems from mountain to shore,
    While through the sounding sky
    Loud rings the Nation's cry, —
    UNION AND LIBERTY! ONE EVERMORE!

SONGS OF WELCOME AND FAREWELL

AMERICA TO RUSSIA

AUGUST 5, 1866

Read by Hon. G. V. Fox at a dinner given to the Mission from the United States, St. Petersburg.

THOUGH watery deserts hold apart
The worlds of East and West,
Still beats the selfsame human heart
In each proud Nation's breast.

Our floating turret tempts the main
    And dares the howling blast
To clasp more close the golden chain
    That long has bound them fast.

In vain the gales of ocean sweep,
    In vain the billows roar
That chafe the wild and stormy steep
    Of storied Elsinore.

She comes! She comes! her banners dip
    In Neva's flashing tide,
With greetings on her cannon's lip,
    The storm-god's iron bride!

Peace garlands with the olive-bough
    Her thunder-bearing tower,

And plants before her cleaving prow
  The sea-foam's milk-white flower.

No prairies heaped their garnered store
  To fill her sunless hold,
Not rich Nevada's gleaming ore
  Its hidden caves infold,

But lightly as the sea-bird swings
  She floats the depths above,
A breath of flame to lend her wings,
  Her freight a people's love!

When darkness hid the starry skies
  In war's long winter night,
One ray still cheered our straining eyes,
  The far-off Northern light!

And now the friendly rays return
  From lights that glow afar,
Those clustered lamps of Heaven that burn
  Around the Western Star.

A nation's love in tears and smiles
  We bear across the sea,
O Neva of the banded isles,
  We moor our hearts in thee!

WELCOME TO THE GRAND DUKE ALEXIS

MUSIC HALL, DECEMBER 6, 1871

Sung to the Russian national air by the children of the public schools.

SHADOWED so long by the storm-cloud of danger,
  Thou whom the prayers of an empire defend,
Welcome, thrice welcome! but not as a stranger,
  Come to the nation that calls thee its friend!

Bleak are our shores with the blasts of December,
  Fettered and chill is the rivulet's flow;
Throbbing and warm are the hearts that remember
  Who was our friend when the world was our foe.

Look on the lips that are smiling to greet thee,
  See the fresh flowers that a people has strewn:
Count them thy sisters and brothers that meet thee;
  Guest of the Nation, her heart is thine own!

Fires of the North, in eternal communion,
  Blend your broad flashes with evening's bright star!
God bless the Empire that loves the Great Union;
  Strength to her people! Long life to the Czar!

AT THE BANQUET TO THE GRAND DUKE ALEXIS

DECEMBER 9, 1871

ONE word to the guest we have gathered to greet!
The echoes are longing that word to repeat, —
It springs to the lips that are waiting to part,
For its syllables spell themselves first in the heart.

Its accents may vary, its sound may be strange,
But it bears a kind message that nothing can change;
The dwellers by Neva its meaning can tell,
For the smile, its interpreter, shows it full well.

That word! How it gladdened the Pilgrim of yore
As he stood in the snow on the desolate shore!
When the shout of the sagamore startled his ear
In the phrase of the Saxon, 't was music to hear!

Ah, little could Samoset offer our sire, —
The cabin, the corn-cake, the seat by the fire;
He had nothing to give, — the poor lord of the land, —
But he gave him a WELCOME, — his heart in his hand!

The tribe of the sachem has melted away,
But the word that he spoke is remembered to-day,
And the page that is red with the record of shame
The tear-drops have whitened round Samoset's name.

The word that he spoke to the Pilgrim of old
May sound like a tale that has often been told;
But the welcome we speak is as fresh as the dew, —
As the kiss of a lover, that always is new!

Ay, Guest of the Nation! each roof is thine own
Through all the broad continent's star-bannered zone;
From the shore where the curtain of morn is uprolled,
To the billows that flow through the gateway of gold.

The snow-crested mountains are calling aloud;
Nevada to Ural speaks out of the cloud,
And Shasta shouts forth, from his throne in the sky,
To the storm-splintered summits, the peaks of Altai!

You must leave him, they say, till the summer is green!
Both shores are his home, though the waves roll between;
And then we'll return him, with thanks for the same,
As fresh and as smiling and tall as he came.

But ours is the region of arctic delight;
We can show him auroras and pole-stars by night;
There's a Muscovy sting in the ice-tempered air,
And our firesides are warm and our maidens are fair.

The flowers are full-blown in the garlanded hall, —
They will bloom round his footsteps wherever they fall;
For the splendors of youth and the sunshine they bring
Make the roses believe 't is the summons of Spring.

One word of our language he needs must know well,
But another remains that is harder to spell;
We shall speak it so ill, if he wishes to learn
How we utter *Farewell*, he will have to return!

AT THE BANQUET TO THE CHINESE EMBASSY

AUGUST 21, 1868

BROTHERS, whom we may not reach
Through the veil of alien speech,
Welcome! welcome! eyes can tell
What the lips in vain would spell, —
Words that hearts can understand,
Brothers from the Flowery Land!

We, the evening's latest born,
Hail the children of the morn!
We, the new creation's birth,
Greet the lords of ancient earth,
From their storied walls and towers
Wandering to these tents of ours!

Land of wonders, fair Cathay,
Who long hast shunned the staring day,
Hid in mists of poet's dreams
By thy blue and yellow streams, —
Let us thy shadowed form behold, —
Teach us as thou didst of old.

Knowledge dwells with length of days;
Wisdom walks in ancient ways:
Thine the compass that could guide
A nation o'er the stormy tide,
Scourged by passions, doubts, and fears,
Safe through thrice a thousand years!

Looking from thy turrets gray
Thou hast seen the world's decay, —
Egypt drowning in her sands, —
Athens rent by robbers' hands, —
Rome, the wild barbarian's prey,
Like a storm-cloud swept away:

Looking from thy turrets gray
Still we see thee. Where are they?
And lo! a new-born nation waits,
Sitting at the golden gates
That glitter by the sunset sea, —
Waits with outspread arms for thee!

Open wide, ye gates of gold,
To the Dragon's banner-fold!
Builders of the mighty wall,
Bid your mountain barriers fall!
So may the girdle of the sun
Bind the East and West in one,

Till Mount Shasta's breezes fan
The snowy peaks of Ta Sieue-Shan, —
Till Erie blends its waters blue
With the waves of Tung-Ting-Hu, —
Till deep Missouri lends its flow
To swell the rushing Hoang-Ho!

AT THE BANQUET TO THE JAPANESE EMBASSY

AUGUST 2, 1872

We welcome you, Lords of the Land of the Sun!
The voice of the many sounds feebly through one;
Ah! would 't were a voice of more musical tone,
But the dog-star is here, and the song-birds have flown.

And what shall I sing that can cheat you of smiles,
Ye heralds of peace from the Orient isles?
If only the Jubilee — Why did you wait?
You are welcome, but oh! you 're a little too late!

We have greeted our brothers of Ireland and France,
Round the fiddle of Strauss we have joined in the dance,
We have lagered Herr Saro, that fine-looking man,
And glorified Godfrey, whose name it is Dan.

What a pity! we 've missed it and you 've missed it too,
We had a day ready and waiting for you;
We 'd have shown you — provided, of course, you had come —
You 'd have heard — no, you would n't, because it was dumb.

And then the great organ! The chorus's shout!
Like the mixture teetotalers call "Cold without " —
A mingling of elements, strong, but not sweet;
And the drum, just referred to, that "could n't be beat."

The shrines of our pilgrims are not like your own,
Where white Fusiyama lifts proudly its cone,
(The snow-mantled mountain we see on the fan
That cools our hot cheeks with a breeze from Japan.)

But ours the wide temple where worship is free
As the wind of the prairie, the wave of the sea;
You may build your own altar wherever you will,
For the roof of that temple is over you still.

One dome overarches the star-bannered shore;
You may enter the Pope's or the Puritan's door,
Or pass with the Buddhist his gateway of bronze,
For a priest is but Man, be he bishop or bonze.

And the lesson we teach with the sword and the pen
Is to all of God's children, "We also are men!
If you wrong us we smart, if you prick us we bleed,
If you love us, no quarrel with color or creed!"

You 'll find us a well-meaning, free-spoken crowd,
Good-natured enough, but a little too loud, —
To be sure, there is always a bit of a row
When we choose our Tycoon, and especially now.

You 'll take it all calmly, — we want you
    to see
What a peaceable fight such a contest can
    be,
And of one thing be certain, however it
    ends,
You will find that our voters have chosen
    your friends.

If the horse that stands saddled is first in
    the race,
You will greet your old friend with the
    weed in his face;
And if the white hat and the White House
    agree,
You 'll find H. G. really as loving as he.

But oh, what a pity — once more I must
    say —
That we could not have joined in a "Japan-
    ese day"!
Such greeting we give you to-night as we
    can;
Long life to our brothers and friends of
    Japan!

The Lord of the mountain looks down from
    his crest
As the banner of morning unfurls in the
    West;
The Eagle was always the friend of the
    Sun;
You are welcome! — The song of the cage-
    bird is done.

BRYANT'S SEVENTIETH BIRTH-
DAY

NOVEMBER 3, 1864

O EVEN-HANDED Nature! we confess
This life that men so honor, love, and bless
Has filled thine olden measure. Not the
    less

We count the precious seasons that remain;
Strike not the level of the golden grain,
But heap it high with years, that earth
    may gain

What heaven can lose, — for heaven is rich
    in song:
Do not all poets, dying, still prolong
Their broken chants amid the seraph throng,

Where, blind no more, Ionia's bard is seen,
And England's heavenly minstrel sits be-
    tween
The Mantuan and the wan-cheeked Floren-
    tine?

This was the first sweet singer in the
    cage
Of our close-woven life. A new-born age
Claims in his vesper song its heritage:

Spare us, oh spare us long our heart's de-
    sire!
Moloch, who calls our children through the
    fire,
Leaves us the gentle master of the lyre.

We count not on the dial of the sun
The hours, the minutes, that his sands have
    run;
Rather, as on those flowers that one by
    one

From earliest dawn their ordered bloom
    display
Till evening's planet with her guiding ray
Leads in the blind old mother of the day,

We reckon by his songs, each song a
    flower,
The long, long daylight, numbering hour
    by hour,
Each breathing sweetness like a bridal
    bower.

His morning glory shall we e'er forget?
His noontide's full-blown lily coronet?
His evening primrose has not opened yet;

Nay, even if creeping Time should hide the
    skies
In midnight from his century-laden eyes,
Darkened like his who sang of Paradise,

Would not some hidden song-bud open
    bright
As the resplendent cactus of the night
That floods the gloom with fragrance and
    with light?

How can we praise the verse whose music
    flows
With solemn cadence and majestic close,
Pure as the dew that filters through the
    rose?

How shall we thank him that in evil days
He faltered never, — nor for blame, nor
  praise,
Nor hire, nor party, shamed his earlier
  lays?

But as his boyhood was of manliest hue,
So to his youth his manly years were true,
All dyed in royal purple through and
  through!

He for whose touch the lyre of Heaven is
  strung
Needs not the flattering toil of mortal
  tongue:
Let not the singer grieve to die unsung!

Marbles forget their message to mankind:
In his own verse the poet still we find,
In his own page his memory lives enshrined,

As in their amber sweets the smothered
  bees, —
As the fair cedar, fallen before the breeze,
Lies self-embalmed amidst the mouldering
  trees.

Poets, like youngest children, never grow
Out of their mother's fondness. Nature
  so
Holds their soft hands, and will not let
  them go,

Till at the last they track with even feet
Her rhythmic footsteps, and their pulses
  beat
Twinned with her pulses, and their lips re-
  peat

The secrets she has told them, as their
  own:
Thus is the inmost soul of Nature known,
And the rapt minstrel shares her awful
  throne!

O lover of her mountains and her woods,
Her bridal chamber's leafy solitudes,
Where Love himself with tremulous step
  intrudes,

Her snows fall harmless on thy sacred
  fire:
Far be the day that claims thy sounding
  lyre
To join the music of the angel choir!

Yet, since life's amplest measure must be
  filled,
Since throbbing hearts must be forever
  stilled,
And all must fade that evening sunsets gild,

Grant, Father, ere he close the mortal eyes
That see a Nation's reeking sacrifice,
Its smoke may vanish from these blackened
  skies!

Then, when his summons comes, since come
  it must,
And, looking heavenward with unfaltering
  trust,
He wraps his drapery round him for the
  dust,

His last fond glance will show him o'er his
  head
The Northern fires beyond the zenith
  spread
In lambent glory, blue and white and
  red, —

The Southern cross without its bleeding
  load,
The milky way of peace all freshly strowed,
And every white-throned star fixed in its
  lost abode!

A FAREWELL TO AGASSIZ

[Written on the eve of Agassiz's journey to Brazil in 1865.]

How the mountains talked together,
Looking down upon the weather,
When they heard our friend had planned his
Little trip among the Andes!
How they 'll bare their snowy scalps
To the climber of the Alps
When the cry goes through their passes,
"Here comes the great Agassiz!"
"Yes, I'm tall," says Chimborazo,
"But I wait for him to say so, —
That's the only thing that lacks, — he
Must see me, Cotopaxi!"
"Ay! ay!" the fire-peak thunders,
"And he must view my wonders!
I'm but a lonely crater
Till I have him for spectator!"
The mountain hearts are yearning,
The lava-torches burning,
The rivers bend to meet him,

The forests bow to greet him,
It thrills the spinal column
Of fossil fishes solemn,
And glaciers crawl the faster
To the feet of their old master!
Heaven keep him well and hearty,
Both him and all his party!
From the sun that broils and smites,
From the centipede that bites,
From the hail-storm and the thunder,
From the vampire and the condor,
From the gust upon the river,
From the sudden earthquake shiver,
From the trip of mule or donkey,
From the midnight howling monkey,
From the stroke of knife or dagger,
From the puma and the jaguar,
From the horrid boa-constrictor
That has scared us in the pictur',
From the Indians of the Pampas
Who would dine upon their grampas,
From every beast and vermin
That to think of sets us squirmin',
From every snake that tries on
The traveller his p'ison,
From every pest of Natur',
Likewise the alligator,
And from two things left behind him, —
(Be sure they'll try to find him,)
The tax-bill and assessor, —
Heaven keep the great Professor!
May he find, with his apostles,
That the land is full of fossils,
That the waters swarm with fishes
Shaped according to his wishes,
That every pool is fertile
In fancy kinds of turtle,
New birds around him singing,
New insects, never stinging,
With a million novel data
About the articulata,
And facts that strip off all husks
From the history of mollusks.

And when, with loud Te Deum,
He returns to his Museum,
May he find the monstrous reptile
That so long the land has kept ill
By Grant and Sherman throttled,
And by Father Abraham bottled,
(All specked and streaked and mottled
With the scars of murderous battles,
Where he clashed the iron rattles
That gods and men he shook at,)
For all the world to look at!

God bless the great Professor!
And Madam, too, God bless her!
Bless him and all his band,
On the sea and on the land,
Bless them head and heart and hand,
Till their glorious raid is o'er,
And they touch our ransomed shore!
Then the welcome of a nation,
With its shout of exultation,
Shall awake the dumb creation,
And the shapes of buried æons
Join the living creature's pæans,
Till the fossil echoes roar;
While the mighty megalosaurus
Leads the palæozoic chorus, —
God bless the great Professor,
And the land his proud possessor, —
Bless them now and evermore!

AT A DINNER TO ADMIRAL FARRAGUT

JULY 6, 1865

Now, smiling friends and shipmates all.
  Since half our battle 's won,
A broadside for our Admiral!
  Load every crystal gun!
Stand ready till I give the word, —
  You won't have time to tire, —
And when that glorious name is heard,
  Then hip! hurrah! and fire!

Bow foremost sinks the rebel craft, —
  Our eyes not sadly turn
And see the pirates huddling aft
  To drop their raft astern;
Soon o'er the sea-worm's destined prey
  The lifted wave shall close, —
So perish from the face of day
  All Freedom's banded foes!

But ah! what splendors fire the sky!
  What glories greet the morn!
The storm-tost banner streams on high,
  Its heavenly hues new-born!
Its red fresh dyed in heroes' blood,
  Its peaceful white more pure,
To float unstained o'er field and flood
  While earth and seas endure!

All shapes before the driving blast
  Must glide from mortal view;

Black roll the billows of the past
  Behind the present's blue,
Fast, fast, are lessening in the light
  The names of high renown, —
Van Tromp's proud besom fades from
    sight,
  And Nelson's half hull down!

Scarce one tall frigate walks the sea
  Or skirts the safer shores
Of all that bore to victory
  Our stout old commodores;
Hull, Bainbridge, Porter, — where are
    they?
  The waves their answer roll,
"Still bright in memory's sunset ray, —
  God rest each gallant soul!"

A brighter name must dim their light
  With more than noontide ray,
The Sea-King of the "River Fight,"
  The Conqueror of the Bay, —
Now then the broadside! cheer on cheer
  To greet him safe on shore!
Health, peace, and many a bloodless year
  To fight his battles o'er!

AT A DINNER TO GENERAL GRANT

JULY 31, 1865

WHEN treason first began the strife
  That crimsoned sea and shore,
The Nation poured her hoarded life
  On Freedom's threshing-floor;
From field and prairie, east and west,
  From coast and hill and plain,
The sheaves of ripening manhood pressed
  Thick as the bearded grain.

Rich was the harvest; souls as true
  As ever battle tried;
But fiercer still the conflict grew,
  The floor of death more wide;
Ah, who forgets that dreadful day
  Whose blot of grief and shame
Four bitter years scarce wash away
  In seas of blood and flame?

Vain, vain the Nation's lofty boasts,
  Vain all her sacrifice!
"Give me a man to lead my hosts,
  O God in heaven!" she cries.

While Battle whirls his crushing flail,
  And plies his winnowing fan, —
Thick flies the chaff on every gale, —
  She cannot find her man!

Bravely they fought who failed to win, —
  Our leaders battle-scarred, —
Fighting the hosts of hell and sin,
  But devils die always hard!
Blame not the broken tools of God
  That helped our sorest needs;
Through paths that martyr feet have trod
  The conqueror's steps He leads.

But now the heavens grow black with
    doubt,
  The ravens fill the sky,
"Friends" plot within, foes storm with-
    out,
  Hark, — that despairing cry,
"Where is the heart, the hand, the brain
  To dare, to do, to plan?"
The bleeding Nation shrieks in vain, —
  She has not found her man!

A little echo stirs the air, —
  Some tale, whate'er it be,
Of rebels routed in their lair
  Along the Tennessee.
The little echo spreads and grows,
  And soon the trump of Fame
Has taught the Nation's friends and foes
  The "man on horseback"'s name.

So well his warlike wooing sped,
  No fortress might resist
His billets-doux of lisping lead,
  The bayonets in his fist, —
With kisses from his cannons' mouth
  He made his passion known
Till Vicksburg, vestal of the South,
  Unbound her virgin zone.

And still where'er his banners led
  He conquered as he came,
The trembling hosts of treason fled
  Before his breath of flame,
And Fame's still gathering echoes grew
  Till high o'er Richmond's towers
The starry fold of Freedom flew,
  And all the land was ours.

Welcome from fields where valor fought
  To feasts where pleasure waits;

A Nation gives you smiles unbought
  At all her opening gates!
Forgive us when we press your hand, —
  Your war-worn features scan, —
God sent you to a bleeding land;
  Our Nation found its man!

TO H. W. LONGFELLOW

BEFORE HIS DEPARTURE FOR EUROPE,
MAY 27, 1868

Our Poet, who has taught the Western
    breeze
  To waft his songs before him o' er the
    seas,
Will find them wheresoe'er his wander-
    ings reach
Borne on the spreading tide of English
    speech
Twin with the rhythmic waves that kiss the
    farthest beach.

Where shall the singing bird a stranger
    be
  That finds a nest for him in every
    tree?
How shall he travel who can never go
Where his own voice the echoes do not
    know,
Where his own garden flowers no longer
    learn to grow?

Ah! gentlest soul! how gracious, how
    benign
  Breathes through our troubled life that
    voice of thine,
Filled with a sweetness born of happier
    spheres,
That wins and warms, that kindles, soft-
    ens, cheers,
That calms the wildest woe and stays the
    bitterest tears!

Forgive the simple words that sound
    like praise;
  The mist before me dims my gilded
    phrase;
Our speech at best is half alive and cold,
And save that tenderer moments make
    us bold
Our whitening lips would close, their tru-
    est truth untold.

We who behold our autumn sun be-
    low
  The Scorpion's sign, against the Archer's
    bow,
Know well what parting means of friend
    from friend;
After the snows no freshening dews de-
    scend,
And what the frost has marred, the sun-
    shine will not mend.

So we all count the months, the weeks,
    the days,
  That keep thee from us in unwonted
    ways,
Grudging to alien hearths our widowed
    time;
And one has shaped a breath in artless
    rhyme
That sighs, "We track thee still through
    each remotest clime."

What wishes, longings, blessings, prayers
    shall be
  The more than golden freight that floats
    with thee!
And know, whatever welcome thou shalt
    find, —
Thou who hast won the hearts of half
    mankind, —
The proudest, fondest love thou leaves
    still behind!

TO CHRISTIAN GOTTFRIED EHRENBERG

FOR HIS "JUBILÆUM" AT BERLIN, NO-
VEMBER 5, 1868

This poem was written at the suggestion of
Mr. George Bancroft, the historian.

Thou who hast taught the teachers of man-
    kind
  How from the least of things the might-
    iest grow,
What marvel jealous Nature made thee
    blind,
  Lest man should learn what angels long
    to know?
Thou in the flinty rock, the river's flow,
  In the thick-moted sunbeam's sifted
    light

Hast trained thy downward-pointed tube
    to show
Worlds within worlds unveiled to mortal
    sight,
Even as the patient watchers of the
    night, —
The cyclope gleaners of the fruitful
    skies, —
Show the wide misty way where heaven is
    white
All paved with suns that daze our won-
    dering eyes.

Far o'er the stormy deep an empire lies,
  Beyond the storied islands of the blest,
That waits to see the lingering day-star
    rise;
  The forest-cinctured Eden of the West;
Whose queen, fair Freedom, twines her
    iron crest
  With leaves from every wreath that mor-
    tals wear,
But loves the sober garland ever best
  That science lends the sage's silvered
    hair; —
Science, who makes life's heritage more
    fair,
  Forging for every lock its mastering
    key,
Filling with life and hope the stagnant
    air,
  Pouring the light of Heaven o'er land
    and sea!
From her unsceptred realm we come to
    thee,
  Bearing our slender tribute in our hands;
Deem it not worthless, humble though it
    be,
  Set by the larger gifts of older lands:
The smallest fibres weave the strongest
    bands, —
  In narrowest tubes the sovereign nerves
    are spun, —
A little cord along the deep sea-sands
  Makes the live thought of severed na-
    tions one:
Thy fame has journeyed westering with
    the sun,
  Prairies and lone sierras know thy name

And the long day of service nobly done
  That crowns thy darkened evening with
    its flame!

One with the grateful world, we own thy
    claim, —
  Nay, rather claim our right to join the
    throng
Who come with varied tongues, but hearts
    the same,
  To hail thy festal morn with smiles and
    song;
Ah, happy they to whom the joys belong
  Of peaceful triumphs that can never die
From History's record, — not of gilded
    wrong,
  But golden truths that, while the world
    goes by
With all its empty pageant, blazoned high
  Around the Master's name forever shine!
So shines thy name illumined in the sky, —
  Such joys, such triumphs, such remem-
    brance thine!

A TOAST TO WILKIE COLLINS

FEBRUARY 16, 1874

THE painter's and the poet's fame
Shed their twinned lustre round his name,
To gild our story-teller's art,
Where each in turn must play his part.

What scenes from Wilkie's pencil sprung,
The minstrel saw but left unsung!
What shapes the pen of Collins drew,
No painter clad in living hue!

But on our artist's shadowy screen
A stranger miracle is seen
Than priest unveils or pilgrim seeks, —
The poem breathes, the picture speaks!

And so his double name comes true,
They christened better than they knew,
And Art proclaims him twice her son, —
Painter and poet, both in one!

MEMORIAL VERSES

FOR THE SERVICES IN MEMORY OF ABRAHAM LINCOLN

CITY OF BOSTON, JUNE 1, 1865

CHORAL: "LUTHER'S JUDGMENT HYMN"

O THOU of soul and sense and breath
  The ever-present Giver,
Unto thy mighty Angel, Death,
  All flesh thou dost deliver;
What most we cherish we resign,
For life and death alike are thine,
  Who reignest Lord forever!

Our hearts lie buried in the dust
  With him so true and tender,
The patriot's stay, the people's trust,
  The shield of the offender;
Yet every murmuring voice is still,
As, bowing to thy sovereign will,
  Our best-loved we surrender.

Dear Lord, with pitying eye behold
  This martyr generation,
Which thou, through trials manifold,
  Art showing thy salvation!
Oh let the blood by murder spilt
Wash out thy stricken children's guilt
  And sanctify our nation!

Be thou thy orphaned Israel's friend,
  Forsake thy people never,
In One our broken Many blend,
  That none again may sever!
Hear us, O Father, while we raise
With trembling lips our song of praise,
  And bless thy name forever!

FOR THE COMMEMORATION SERVICES

CAMBRIDGE, JULY 21, 1865

FOUR summers coined their golden light in leaves,
  Four wasteful autumns flung them to the gale,
Four winters wore the shroud the tempest weaves,
  The fourth wan April weeps o'er hill and vale;

And still the war-clouds scowl on sea and land,
  With the red gleams of battle staining through,
When lo! as parted by an angel's hand,
  They open, and the heavens again are blue!

Which is the dream, the present or the past?
  The night of anguish or the joyous morn?
The long, long years with horrors overcast,
  Or the sweet promise of the day new-born?

Tell us, O father, as thine arms infold
  Thy belted first-born in their fast embrace,
Murmuring the prayer the patriarch breathed of old, —
  "Now let me die, for I have seen thy face!"

Tell us, O mother, — nay, thou canst not speak,
  But thy fond eyes shall answer, brimmed with joy, —
Press thy mute lips against the sunbrowned cheek,
  Is this a phantom, — thy returning boy?

Tell us, O maiden, — ah, what canst thou tell
  That Nature's record is not first to teach, —
The open volume all can read so well,
  With its twin rose-hued pages full of speech?

And ye who mourn your dead, — how sternly true
  The crushing hour that wrenched their lives away,
Shadowed with sorrow's midnight veil for you,
  For them the dawning of immortal day!

Dream-like these years of conflict, not a
    dream!
Death, ruin, ashes tell the awful tale,
Read by the flaming war-track's lurid
    gleam:
    No dream, but truth that turns the na-
        tions pale!

For on the pillar raised by martyr hands
    Burns the rekindled beacon of the right,
Sowing its seeds of fire o'er all the lands, —
    Thrones look a century older in its light!

Rome had her triumphs; round the con-
    queror's car
    The ensigns waved, the brazen clarions
        blew,
And o'er the reeking spoils of bandit war
    With outspread wings the cruel eagles
        flew;

Arms, treasures, captives, kings in clanking
    chains
    Urged on by trampling cohorts bronzed
        and scarred,
And wild-eyed wonders snared on Libyan
    plains,
    Lion and ostrich and camelopard.

Vain all that prætors clutched, that consuls
    brought
    When Rome's returning legions crowned
        their lord;
Less than the least brave deed these hands
    have wrought,
    We clasp, unclinching from the bloody
        sword.

Theirs was the mighty work that seers
    foretold;
    They know not half their glorious toil
        has won,
For this is Heaven's same battle, — joined
    of old
    When Athens fought for us at Mara-
        thon!

Behold a vision none hath understood!
    The breaking of the Apocalyptic seal;
Twice rings the summons. — Hail and fire
    and blood!
    Then the third angel blows his trumpet-
        peal.

Loud wail the dwellers on the myrtled
    coasts,
    The green savannas swell the maddened
        cry,
And with a yell from all the demon hosts
    Falls the great star called Wormwood
        from the sky!

Bitter it mingles with the poisoned flow
    Of the warm rivers winding to the shore,
Thousands must drink the waves of death
    and woe,
    But the star Wormwood stains the heav-
        ens no more!

Peace smiles at last; the Nation calls her
    sons
    To sheathe the sword; her battle-flag
        she furls,
Speaks in glad thunders from unshotted
    guns,
    No terror shrouded in the smoke-wreath's
        curls.

O ye that fought for Freedom, living, dead,
    One sacred host of God's anointed Queen,
For every holy drop your veins have shed
    We breathe a welcome to our bowers of
        green!

Welcome, ye living! from the foeman's
    gripe
    Your country's banner it was yours to
        wrest, —
Ah, many a forehead shows the banner-
    stripe,
    And stars, once crimson, hallow many a
        breast.

And ye, pale heroes, who from glory's bed
    Mark when your old battalions form in
        line,
Move in their marching ranks with noise-
    less tread,
    And shape unheard the evening counter-
        sign,

Come with your comrades, the returning
    brave;
    Shoulder to shoulder they await you here;
These lent the life their martyr-brothers
    gave, —
    Living and dead alike forever dear!

EDWARD EVERETT

"OUR FIRST CITIZEN"

Read at the meeting of the Massachusetts Historical Society, January 30, 1865.

WINTER'S cold drift lies glistening o'er his breast;
  For him no spring shall bid the leaf unfold:
What Love could speak, by sudden grief oppressed,
  What swiftly summoned Memory tell, is told.

Even as the bells, in one consenting chime,
  Filled with their sweet vibrations all the air,
So joined all voices, in that mournful time,
  His genius, wisdom, virtues, to declare.

What place is left for words of measured praise,
  Till calm-eyed History, with her iron pen,
Grooves in the unchanging rock the final phrase
  That shapes his image in the souls of men?

Yet while the echoes still repeat his name,
  While countless tongues his full-orbed life rehearse,
Love, by his beating pulses taught, will claim
  The breath of song, the tuneful throb of verse, —

Verse that, in ever-changing ebb and flow,
  Moves, like the laboring heart, with rush and rest,
Or swings in solemn cadence, sad and slow,
  Like the tired heaving of a grief-worn breast.

This was a mind so rounded, so complete,
  No partial gift of Nature in excess,
That, like a single stream where many meet,
  Each separate talent counted something less.

A little hillock, if it lonely stand,
  Holds o'er the fields an undisputed reign;
While the broad summit of the table-land
  Seems with its belt of clouds a level plain.

Servant of all his powers, that faithful slave,
  Unsleeping Memory, strengthening with his toils,
To every ruder task his shoulder gave,
  And loaded every day with golden spoils.

Order, the law of Heaven, was throned supreme
  O'er action, instinct, impulse, feeling, thought;
True as the dial's shadow to the beam,
  Each hour was equal to the charge it brought.

Too large his compass for the nicer skill
  That weighs the world of science grain by grain;
All realms of knowledge owned the mastering will
  That claimed the franchise of its whole domain.

Earth, air, sea, sky, the elemental fire,
  Art, history, song, — what meanings lie in each
Found in his cunning hand a stringless lyre,
  And poured their mingling music through his speech.

Thence flowed those anthems of our festal days,
  Whose ravishing division held apart
The lips of listening throngs in sweet amaze,
  Moved in all breasts the selfsame human heart.

Subdued his accents, as of one who tries
  To press some care, some haunting sadness down;
His smile half shadow; and to stranger eyes
  The kingly forehead wore an iron crown.

He was not armed to wrestle with the storm,

To fight for homely truth with vulgar
    power;
Grace looked from every feature, shaped
    his form, —
The rose of Academe, — the perfect
    flower!

Such was the stately scholar whom we
    knew
In those ill days of soul-enslaving calm,
Before the blast of Northern vengeance
    blew
Her snow-wreathed pine against the
    Southern palm.

Ah, God forgive us! did we hold too cheap
The heart we might have known, but
    would not see,
And look to find the nation's friend asleep
Through the dread hour of her Geth-
    semane?

That wrong is past; we gave him up to
    Death
With all a hero's honors round his name;
As martyrs coin their blood, he coined his
    breath,
And dimmed the scholar's in the pa-
    triot's fame.

So shall we blazon on the shaft we raise, —
Telling our grief, our pride, to unborn
    years, —
"He who had lived the mark of all men's
    praise
Died with the tribute of a Nation's tears."

SHAKESPEARE

TERCENTENNIAL CELEBRATION

APRIL 23, 1864

"WHO claims our Shakespeare from that
    realm unknown,
Beyond the storm-vexed islands of the
    deep,
Where Genoa's roving mariner was blown?
Her twofold Saint's-day let our England
    keep;
Shall warring aliens share her holy task?"
    The Old World echoes ask.

O land of Shakespeare! ours with all thy
    past,
Till these last years that make the sea
    so wide,
Think not the jar of battle's trumpet-blast
Has dulled our aching sense to joyous
    pride
In every noble word thy sons bequeathed
    The air our fathers breathed!

War-wasted, haggard, panting from the
    strife,
We turn to other days and far-off lands,
Live o'er in dreams the Poet's faded life,
Come with fresh lilies in our fevered
    hands
To wreathe his bust, and scatter purple
    flowers, —
    Not his the need, but ours!

We call those poets who are first to mark
Through earth's dull mist the coming of
    the dawn, —
Who see in twilight's gloom the first pale
    spark,
While others only note that day is gone;
For him the Lord of light the curtain rent
    That veils the firmament.

The greatest for its greatness is half known,
Stretching beyond our narrow quadrant-
    lines, —
As in that world of Nature all outgrown
Where Calaveras lifts his awful pines,
And cast from Mariposa's mountain-wall
    Nevada's cataracts fall.

Yet heaven's remotest orb is partly ours,
Throbbing its radiance like a beating
    heart;
In the wide compass of angelic powers
The instinct of the blindworm has its part;
So in God's kingliest creature we behold
    The flower our buds infold.

With no vain praise we mock the stone-
    carved name
Stamped once on dust that moved with
    pulse and breath,
As thinking to enlarge that amplest fame
Whose undimmed glories gild the night
    of death:
We praise not star or sun; in these we see
    Thee, Father, only thee!

Thy gifts are beauty, wisdom, power, and
    love:
  We read, we reverence on this human
    soul, —
Earth's clearest mirror of the light above, —
  Plain as the record on thy prophet's scroll,
When o'er his page the effluent splendors
    poured,
  Thine own "Thus saith the Lord!"

This player was a prophet from on high,
  Thine own elected. Statesman, poet,
    sage,
For him thy sovereign pleasure passed them
    by;
  Sidney's fair youth, and Raleigh's ripened
    age,
Spenser's chaste soul, and his imperial
    mind
  Who taught and shamed mankind.

Therefore we bid our hearts' Te Deum
    rise,
  Nor fear to make thy worship less divine,
And hear the shouted choral shake the
    skies,
  Counting all glory, power, and wisdom
    thine;
For thy great gift thy greater name adore,
  And praise thee evermore!

In this dread hour of Nature's utmost
    need,
  Thanks for these unstained drops of
    freshening dew!
Oh, while our martyrs fall, our heroes bleed,
  Keep us to every sweet remembrance
    true,
Till from this blood-red sunset springs new-
    born
  Our Nation's second morn!

IN MEMORY OF JOHN AND ROBERT WARE

Read at the annual meeting of the Massa-
chusetts Medical Society, May 25, 1864.

No mystic charm, no mortal art,
  Can bid our loved companions stay;
The bands that clasp them to our heart
Snap in death's frost and fall apart;
  Like shadows fading with the day,
    They pass away.

The young are stricken in their pride,
  The old, long tottering, faint and fall;
Master and scholar, side by side,
Through the dark portals silent glide,
  That open in life's mouldering wall
    And close on all.

Our friend's, our teacher's task was done,
  When Mercy called him from on high;
A little cloud had dimmed the sun,
The saddening hours had just begun,
  And darker days were drawing nigh:
    'T was time to die.

A whiter soul, a fairer mind,
  A life with purer course and aim,
A gentler eye, a voice more kind,
We may not look on earth to find.
  The love that lingers o'er his name
    Is more than fame.

These blood-red summers ripen fast;
  The sons are older than the sires;
Ere yet the tree to earth is cast,
The sapling falls before the blast;
  Life's ashes keep their covered fires, —
    Its flame expires.

Struck by the noiseless, viewless foe,
  Whose deadlier breath than shot or shell
Has laid the best and bravest low,
His boy, all bright in morning's glow,
  That high-souled youth he loved so well,
    Untimely fell.

Yet still he wore his placid smile,
  And, trustful in the cheering creed
That strives all sorrow to beguile,
Walked calmly on his way awhile:
  Ah, breast that leans on breaking reed
    Must ever bleed!

So they both left us, sire and son,
  With opening leaf, with laden bough:
The youth whose race was just begun,
The wearied man whose course was run,
  Its record written on his brow,
    Are brothers now.

Brothers! — The music of the sound
  Breathes softly through my closing strain;
The floor we tread is holy ground,
Those gentle spirits hovering round,
  While our fair circle joins again
    Its broken chain.

HUMBOLDT'S BIRTHDAY

CENTENNIAL CELEBRATION, SEPTEMBER 14, 1869

BONAPARTE, AUGUST 15, 1769.— HUMBOLDT, SEPTEMBER 14, 1769

Ere yet the warning chimes of midnight sound,
  Set back the flaming index of the year,
Track the swift-shifting seasons in their round
    Through fivescore circles of the swinging sphere !

Lo, in yon islet of the midland sea
  That cleaves the storm-cloud with its snowy crest,
The embryo-heir of Empires yet to be,
    A month-old babe upon his mother's breast.

Those little hands that soon shall grow so strong
  In their rude grasp great thrones shall rock and fall,
Press her soft bosom, while a nursery song
    Holds the world's master in its slender thrall.

Look ! a new crescent bends its silver bow;
  A new-lit star has fired the eastern sky;
Hark ! by the river where the lindens blow
    A waiting household hears an infant's cry.

This, too, a conqueror ! His the vast domain,
  Wider than widest sceptre-shadowed lands;
Earth and the weltering kingdom of the main
    Laid their broad charters in his royal hands.

His was no taper lit in cloistered cage,
  Its glimmer borrowed from the grove or porch;
He read the record of the planet's page
    By Etna's glare and Cotopaxi's torch.

He heard the voices of the pathless woods;
  On the salt steppes he saw the starlight shine;
He scaled the mountain's windy solitudes,
    And trod the galleries of the breathless mine.

For him no fingering of the love-strung lyre,
  No problem vague, by torturing schoolmen vexed;
He fed no broken altar's dying fire,
    Nor skulked and scowled behind a Rabbi's text.

For God's new truth he claimed the kingly robe
  That priestly shoulders counted all their own,
Unrolled the gospel of the storied globe
    And led young Science to her empty throne.

While the round planet on its axle spins
  One fruitful year shall boast its double birth,
And show the cradles of its mighty twins,
    Master and Servant of the sons of earth.

Which wears the garland that shall never fade,
  Sweet with fair memories that can never die ?
Ask not the marbles where their bones are laid,
    But bow thine ear to hear thy brothers' cry: —

"Tear up the despot's laurels by the root,
  Like mandrakes, shrieking as they quit the soil ?
Feed us no more upon the blood-red fruit
    That sucks its crimson from the heart of Toil !

" We claim the food that fixed our mortal fate, —
  Bend to our reach the long-forbidden tree !
The angel frowned at Eden's eastern gate, —
    Its western portal is forever free !

" Bring the white blossoms of the waning year,
  Heap with full hands the peaceful conqueror's shrine

Whose bloodless triumphs cost no sufferer's tear!
Hero of knowledge, be our tribute thine!"

POEM

AT THE DEDICATION OF THE HALLECK MONUMENT, JULY 8, 1869

Say not the Poet dies!
Though in the dust he lies,
He cannot forfeit his melodious breath,
Unsphered by envious death!
Life drops the voiceless myriads from its roll;
Their fate he cannot share,
Who, in the enchanted air
Sweet with the lingering strains that Echo stole,
Has left his dearer self, the music of his soul!

We o'er his turf may raise
Our notes of feeble praise,
And carve with pious care for after eyes
The stone with "Here he lies;"
He for himself has built a nobler shrine,
Whose walls of stately rhyme
Roll back the tides of time,
While o'er their gates the gleaming tablets shine
That wear his name inwrought with many a golden line!

Call not our Poet dead,
Though on his turf we tread!
Green is the wreath their brows so long have worn, —
The minstrels of the morn,
Who, while the Orient burned with new-born flame,
Caught that celestial fire
And struck a Nation's lyre!
These taught the western winds the poet's name;
Theirs the first opening buds, the maiden flowers of fame!

Count not our Poet dead!
The stars shall watch his bed,
The rose of June its fragrant life renew
His blushing mound to strew,
And all the tuneful throats of summer swell
With trills as crystal-clear
As when he wooed the ear
Of the young muse that haunts each wooded dell,
With songs of that "rough land" he loved so long and well!

He sleeps; he cannot die!
As evening's long-drawn sigh,
Lifting the rose-leaves on his peaceful mound,
Spreads all their sweets around,
So, laden with his song, the breezes blow
From where the rustling sedge
Frets our rude ocean's edge
To the smooth sea beyond the peaks of snow.
His soul the air enshrines and leaves but dust below!

HYMN

FOR THE CELEBRATION AT THE LAYING OF THE CORNER-STONE OF HARVARD MEMORIAL HALL, CAMBRIDGE, OCTOBER 6, 1870

Not with the anguish of hearts that are breaking
Come we as mourners to weep for our dead;
Grief in our breasts has grown weary of aching,
Green is the turf where our tears we have shed.

While o'er their marbles the mosses are creeping,
Stealing each name and its legend away,
Give their proud story to Memory's keeping,
Shrined in the temple we hallow to-day.

Hushed are their battle-fields, ended their marches,
Deaf are their ears to the drum-beat of morn, —
Rise from the sod, ye fair columns and arches!
Tell their bright deeds to the ages unborn!

Emblem and legend may fade from the portal,
Keystone may crumble and pillar may fall;
They were the builders whose work is immortal,
Crowned with the dome that is over us all!

HYMN

FOR THE DEDICATION OF MEMORIAL HALL AT CAMBRIDGE, JUNE 23, 1874

WHERE, girt around by savage foes,
Our nurturing Mother's shelter rose,
Behold, the lofty temple stands,
Reared by her children's grateful hands!

Firm are the pillars that defy
The volleyed thunders of the sky;
Sweet are the summer wreaths that twine
With bud and flower our martyrs' shrine.

The hues their tattered colors bore
Fall mingling on the sunlit floor
Till evening spreads her spangled pall,
And wraps in shade the storied hall.

Firm were their hearts in danger's hour,
Sweet was their manhood's morning flower
Their hopes with rainbow hues were bright, —
How swiftly winged the sudden night!

O Mother! on thy marble page
Thy children read, from age to age,
The mighty word that upward leads
Through noble thought to nobler deeds.

TRUTH, heaven-born TRUTH, their fearless guide,
Thy saints have lived, thy heroes died;
Our love has reared their earthly shrine,
Their glory be forever thine!

HYMN

AT THE FUNERAL SERVICES OF CHARLES SUMNER, APRIL 29, 1874

SUNG BY MALE VOICES TO A NATIONAL AIR OF HOLLAND

ONCE more, ye sacred towers,
Your solemn dirges sound;
Strew, loving hands, the April flowers,
Once more to deck his mound.
A nation mourns its dead,
Its sorrowing voices one,
As Israel's monarch bowed his head
And cried, "My son! My son!"

Why mourn for him? — For him
The welcome angel came
Ere yet his eye with age was dim
Or bent his stately frame;
His weapon still was bright,
His shield was lifted high
To slay the wrong, to save the right, —
What happier hour to die?

Thou orderest all things well;
Thy servant's work was done;
He lived to hear Oppression's knell,
The shouts for Freedom won.
Hark! from the opening skies
The anthem's echoing swell, —
"O mourning Land, lift up thine eyes!
God reigneth. All is well!"

RHYMES OF AN HOUR

AN IMPROMPTU

AT THE WALCKER DINNER UPON THE COMPLETION OF THE GREAT ORGAN FOR BOSTON MUSIC HALL IN 1863

I ASKED three little maidens who heard the organ play,
Where all the music came from that stole our hearts away:

"I know," — said fair-haired Edith, — "it was the autumn breeze
That whistled through the hollows of all those silver trees."

"No, child!" — said keen-eyed Clara, —
"it is a lion's cage, —
They woke him out of slumber, — I heard him roar and rage."

"Nay,"—answered soft-voiced Anna,—
"'t was thunder that you heard,
And after that came sunshine and singing of a bird."

"Hush, hush, you little children, for all of you are wrong,"
I said, "my pretty darlings,—it was no earthly song;
A band of blessed angels has left the heavenly choirs,
And what you heard last evening were seraph lips and lyres!"

ADDRESS

FOR THE OPENING OF THE FIFTH AVENUE THEATRE, NEW YORK, DECEMBER 3, 1873

HANG out our banners on the stately tower!
It dawns at last — the long-expected hour!
The steep is climbed, the star-lit summit won,
The builder's task, the artist's labor done;
Before the finished work the herald stands,
And asks the verdict of your lips and hands!

Shall rosy daybreak make us all forget
The golden sun that yester-evening set?
Fair was the fabric doomed to pass away
Ere the last headaches born of New Year's Day;
With blasting breath the fierce destroyer came
And wrapped the victim in his robes of flame;
The pictured sky with redder morning blushed,
With scorching streams the naiad's fountain gushed,
With kindling mountains glowed the funeral pyre,
Forests ablaze and rivers all on fire, —
The scenes dissolved, the shriveling curtain fell,
Art spread her wings and sighed a long farewell!

Mourn o'er the Player's melancholy plight, —
Falstaff in tears, Othello deadly white, —
Poor Romeo reckoning what his doublet cost,
And Juliet whimpering for her dresses lost, —
Their wardrobes burned, their salaries all undrawn,
Their cues cut short, their occupation gone!

"Lie there in dust," the red-winged demon cried,
"Wreck of the lordly city's hope and pride!"
Silent they stand, and stare with vacant gaze,
While o'er the embers leaps the fitful blaze;
When, lo! a hand, before the startled train,
Writes in the ashes, "It shall rise again, —
Rise and confront its elemental foes!"
The word was spoken, and the walls arose,
And ere the seasons round their brief career
The new-born temple waits the unborn year.

Ours was the toil of many a weary day
Your smiles, your plaudits, only can repay;
We are the monarchs of the painted scenes,
You, you alone the real Kings and Queens!
Lords of the little kingdom where we meet,
We lay our gilded sceptres at your feet,
Place in your grasp our portal's silvered keys
With one brief utterance: *We have tried to please.*
Tell us, ye sovereigns of the new domain,
Are you content — or have we toiled in vain?

With no irreverent glances look around
The realm you rule, for this is haunted ground!
Here stalks the Sorcerer, here the Fairy trips,
Here limps the Witch with malice-working lips,
The Graces here their snowy arms entwine,
Here dwell the fairest sisters of the Nine, —
She who, with jocund voice and twinkling eye,

OPENING OF THE FIFTH AVENUE THEATRE

Laughs at the brood of follies as they fly;
She of the dagger and the deadly bowl,
Whose charming horrors thrill the trembling soul;
She who, a truant from celestial spheres,
In mortal semblance now and then appears,
Stealing the fairest earthly shape she can —
Sontag or Nilsson, Lind or Malibran;
With these the spangled houri of the dance, —
What shaft so dangerous as her melting glance,
As poised in air she spurns the earth below,
And points aloft her heavenly-minded toe!

What were our life, with all its rents and seams,
Stripped of its purple robes, our waking dreams?
The poet's song, the bright romancer's page,
The tinselled shows that cheat us on the stage
Lead all our fancies captive at their will;
Three years or threescore, we are children still.
The little listener on his father's knee,
With wandering Sindbad ploughs the stormy sea,
With Gotham's sages hears the billows roll
(Illustrious trio of the venturous bowl,
Too early shipwrecked, for they died too soon
To see their offspring launch the great balloon);
Tracks the dark brigand to his mountain lair,
Slays the grim giant, saves the lady fair,
Fights all his country's battles o'er again
From Bunker's blazing height to Lundy's Lane;
Floats with the mighty captains as they sailed,
Before whose flag the flaming red-cross paled,
And claims the oft-told story of the scars
Scarce yet grown white, that saved the stripes and stars!

Children of later growth, we love the PLAY,
We love its heroes, be they grave or gay,
From squeaking, peppery, devil-defying Punch
To roaring Richard with his camel-hunch;
Adore its heroines, those immortal dames,
Time's only rivals, whom he never tames,
Whose youth, unchanging, lives while thrones decay
(Age spares the Pyramids — and Dejazet);
The saucy-aproned, razor-tongued soubrette,
The blond-haired beauty with the eyes of jet,
The gorgeous Beings whom the viewless wires
Lift to the skies in strontian-crimsoned fires,
And all the wealth of splendor that awaits
The throng that enters those Elysian gates.

See where the hurrying crowd impatient pours,
With noise of trampling feet and flapping doors,
Streams to the numbered seat each pasteboard fits
And smooths its caudal plumage as it sits;
Waits while the slow musicians saunter in,
Till the bald leader taps his violin;
Till the old overture we know so well,
Zampa or Magic Flute or William Tell,
Has done its worst — then hark! the tinkling bell!
The crash is o'er — the crinkling curtain furled,
And lo! the glories of that brighter world!

Behold the offspring of the Thespian cart,
This full-grown temple of the magic art,
Where all the conjurers of illusion meet,
And please us all the more, the more they cheat.
These are the wizards and the witches too
Who win their honest bread by cheating you
With cheeks that drown in artificial tears
And lying skull-caps white with seventy years,
Sweet-tempered matrons changed to scolding Kates,
Maids mild as moonbeams crazed with murderous hates,
Kind, simple souls that stab and slash and slay
And stick at nothing, if it's in the play!

Would all the world told half as harm-
  less lies!
Would all its real fools were half as wise
As he who blinks through dull Dundreary's
  eyes!
Would all the unhanged bandits of the age
Were like the peaceful ruffians of the
  stage!
Would all the cankers wasting town and
  state,
The mob of rascals, little thieves and
  great,
Dealers in watered milk and watered
  stocks,
Who lead us lambs to pasture on the
  rocks, —
Shepherds — Jack Sheppards — of their
  city flocks, —
The rings of rogues that rob the luckless
  town,
Those evil angels creeping up and down
The Jacob's ladder of the treasury stairs, —
Not stage, but real Turpins and Ma-
  caires, —
Could doff, like us, their knavery with
  their clothes,
And find it easy as forgetting oaths!

  Welcome, thrice welcome to our virgin
    dome,
The Muses' shrine, the Drama's new-found
  home!
Here shall the Statesman rest his weary
  brain,
The worn-out Artist find his wits again;
Here Trade forget his ledger and his cares,
And sweet communion mingle Bulls and
  Bears;
Here shall the youthful Lover, nestling
  near
The shrinking maiden, her he holds most
  dear,
Gaze on the mimic moonlight as it falls
On painted groves, on sliding canvas walls,
And sigh, "My angel! What a life of
  bliss
We two could live in such a world as
  this!"
Here shall the timid pedants of the schools,
The gilded boors, the labor-scorning fools,
The grass-green rustic and the smoke-
  dried cit,
Feel each in turn the stinging lash of wit,
And as it tingles on some tender part
Each find a balsam in his neighbor's smart;

So every folly prove a fresh delight
As in the picture of our play to-night.

Farewell! The Players wait the Prompt-
  er's call;
Friends, lovers, listeners! Welcome one
  and all!

A SEA DIALOGUE

NOVEMBER 10, 1864

Cabin Passenger   *Man at Wheel*

CABIN PASSENGER

FRIEND, you seem thoughtful. I not won-
  der much
That he who sails the ocean should be sad.
I am myself reflective. When I think
Of all this wallowing beast, the Sea, has
  sucked
Between his sharp thin lips, the wedgy
  waves,
What heaps of diamonds, rubies, emeralds,
  pearls;
What piles of shekels, talents, ducats,
  crowns,
What bales of Tyrian mantles, Indian
  shawls,
Of laces that have blanked the weavers'
  eyes,
Of silken tissues, wrought by worm and
  man,
The half-starved workman, and the well-
  fed worm;
What marbles, bronzes, pictures, parch-
  ments, books;
What many-lobuled, thought-engendering
  brains;
Lie with the gaping sea-shells in his
  maw, —
I, too, am silent; for all language seems
A mockery, and the speech of man is vain.
O mariner, we look upon the waves
And they rebuke our babbling. "Peace!"
  they say, —
"Mortal, be still!" My noisy tongue is
  hushed,
And with my trembling finger on my lips
My soul exclaims in ecstasy —

MAN AT WHEEL
                              Belay!

A SEA DIALOGUE

CABIN PASSENGER

Ah yes! "Delay," — it calls, "nor haste to break
The charm of stillness with an idle word!"
O mariner, I love thee, for thy thought
Strides even with my own, nay, flies before.
Thou art a brother to the wind and wave;
Have they not music for thine ear as mine,
When the wild tempest makes thy ship his lyre,
Smiting a cavernous basso from the shrouds
And climbing up his gamut through the stays,
Through buntlines, bowlines, ratlines, till it shrills
An alto keener than the locust sings,
And all the great Æolian orchestra
Storms out its mad sonata in the gale?
Is not the scene a wondrous and —

MAN AT WHEEL

Avast!

CABIN PASSENGER

Ah yes, a vast, a vast and wondrous scene!
I see thy soul is open as the day
That holds the sunshine in its azure bowl
To all the solemn glories of the deep.
Tell me, O mariner, dost thou never feel
The grandeur of thine office, — to control
The keel that cuts the ocean like a knife
And leaves a wake behind it like a seam
In the great shining garment of the world?

MAN AT WHEEL

Belay y'r jaw, y' swab! y' hoss-marine!
(*To the Captain.*)
Ay, ay, Sir! Stiddy, Sir! Sou'wes' b'sou'!

CHANSON WITHOUT MUSIC

BY THE PROFESSOR EMERITUS OF DEAD AND LIVE LANGUAGES

PHI BETA KAPPA. — CAMBRIDGE, 1867

You bid me sing, — can I forget
 The classic ode of days gone by, —
How belle Fifine and jeune Lisette
 Exclaimed, "Anacreōn, gerōn ei"?
"Regardez donc," those ladies said, —
 "You 're getting bald and wrinkled too:
When summer's roses all are shed,
 Love 's nullum ite, voyez-vous!"

In vain ce brave Anacreon's cry,
 "Of Love alone my banjo sings"
(Erōta mounon). "Etiam si, —
 Eh b'en?" replied the saucy things, —
"Go find a maid whose hair is gray,
 And strike your lyre, — we sha'n't complain:
But parce nobis, s'il vous plaît, —
 Voilà Adolphe! Voilà Eugène!"

Ah, jeune Lisette! Ah, belle Fifine!
 Anacreon's lesson all must learn;
O kairos oxūs; Spring is green,
 But Acer Hyems waits his turn!
I hear you whispering from the dust,
 "Tiens, mon cher, c'est toujours so, —
The brightest blade grows dim with rust,
 The fairest meadow white with snow!"

You do not mean it! *Not* encore?
 Another string of playday rhymes?
You 've heard me — nonne est? — before,
 Multoties, — more than twenty times;
Non possum, — vraiment, — pas du tout,
 I cannot! I am loath to shirk;
But who will listen if I do,
 My memory makes such shocking work?

Ginōsko. Scio. Yes, I 'm told
 Some ancients like my rusty lay,
As Grandpa Noah loved the old
 Red-sandstone march of Jubal's day.
I used to carol like the birds,
 But time my wits has quite unfixed,
Et quoad verba, — for my words, —
 Ciel! Eheu! Whe-ew! — how they 're mixed!

Mehercle! Zeu! Diable! how
 My thoughts were dressed when I was young,
But tempus fugit! see them now
 Half clad in rags of every tongue!
O philoi, fratres, chers amis!
 I dare not court the youthful Muse,
For fear her sharp response should be,
 "Papa Anacreon, please excuse!"

Adieu! I've trod my annual track
How long!— let others count the miles,—
And peddled out my rhyming pack
To friends who always paid in smiles.
So, laissez-moi! some youthful wit
No doubt has wares he wants to show;
And I am asking, "Let me sit,"
Dum ille clamat, "Dos pou sto!"

FOR THE CENTENNIAL DINNER

OF THE PROPRIETORS OF BOSTON PIER,
OR THE LONG WHARF, APRIL 16, 1873

DEAR friends, we are strangers; we never before
Have suspected what love to each other we bore;
But each of us all to his neighbor is dear,
Whose heart has a throb for our time-honored pier.

As I look on each brother proprietor's face,
I could open my arms in a loving embrace;
What wonder that feelings, undreamed of so long,
Should burst all at once in a blossom of song!

While I turn my fond glance on the monarch of piers,
Whose throne has stood firm through his eightscore of years,
My thought travels backward and reaches the day
When they drove the first pile on the edge of the bay.

See! The joiner, the shipwright, the smith from his forge,
The redcoat, who shoulders his gun for King George,
The shopman, the 'prentice, the boys from the lane,
The parson, the doctor with gold-headed cane,

Come trooping down King Street, where now may be seen
The pulleys and ropes of a mighty machine;

The weight rises slowly; it drops with a thud;
And, lo! the great timber sinks deep in the mud!

They are gone, the stout craftsmen that hammered the piles,
And the square-toed old boys in the three-cornered tiles;
The breeches, the buckles, have faded from view,
And the parson's white wig and the ribbon-tied queue.

The redcoats have vanished; the last grenadier
Stepped into the boat from the end of our pier;
They found that our hills were not easy to climb,
And the order came, "Countermarch, double-quick time!"

They are gone, friend and foe, — anchored fast at the pier,
Whence no vessel brings back its pale passengers here;
But our wharf, like a lily, still floats on the flood,
Its breast in the sunshine, its roots in the mud.

Who — who that has loved it so long and so well —
The flower of his birthright would barter or sell?
No: pride of the bay, while its ripples shall run,
You shall pass, as an heirloom, from father to son!

Let me part with the acres my grandfather bought,
With the bonds that my uncle's kind legacy brought,
With my bank-shares,— old "Union,"
whose ten per cent stock
Stands stiff through the storms as the Eddystone rock;

With my rights (or my wrongs) in the "Erie,"— alas!
With my claims on the mournful and "Mutual Mass.;"

With my " Phil. Wil. and Balt.," with my
 "C. B. and Q.;"
But I never, no never, will sell out of
 you.

We drink to thy past and thy future to-
 day,
Strong right arm of Boston, stretched out
 o'er the bay.
May the winds waft the wealth of all na-
 tions to thee,
And thy dividends flow like the waves of
 the sea !

A POEM SERVED TO ORDER

PHI BETA KAPPA, JUNE 26, 1873

THE Caliph ordered up his cook,
And, scowling with a fearful look
 That meant, — We stand no gammon, —
" To-morrow, just at two," he said,
" Hassan, our cook, will lose his head,
 Or serve us up a salmon."

"Great sire," the trembling *chef* replied,
" Lord of the Earth and all beside,
 Sun, Moon, and Stars, and so on " —
(Look in Eothen, — there you 'll find
A list of titles. Never mind;
 I have n't time to go on:)

" Great sire," and so forth, thus he spoke,
" Your Highness must intend a joke;
 It does n't stand to reason
For one to order salmon brought,
Unless that fish is sometimes caught,
 And also is in season.

" Our luck of late is shocking bad,
In fact, the latest catch we had
 (We kept the matter shady),
But, hauling in our nets, — alack !
We found no salmon, but a sack
 That held your honored Lady ! "

" Allah is great ! " the Caliph said,
" My poor Zuleika, you are dead,
 I once took interest in you."
" Perhaps, my Lord, you 'd like to know
We cut the lines and let her go."
 " Allah be praised ! Continue."

" It is n't hard one's hook to bait,
And, squatting down, to watch and wait,
 To see the cork go under;
At last suppose you 've got your bite,
You twitch away with all your might, —
 You 've hooked an eel, by thunder ! "

The Caliph patted Hassan's head :
" Slave, thou hast spoken well," he said,
 " And won thy master's favor.
Yes; since what happened t' other morn
The salmon of the Golden Horn
 Might have a doubtful flavor.

" That last remark about the eel
Has also justice that we feel
 Quite to our satisfaction.
To-morrow we dispense with fish,
And, for the present, if you wish,
 You 'll keep your bulbous fraction."

" Thanks ! thanks ! " the grateful *chef* re-
 plied,
His nutrient feature showing wide
 The gleam of arches dental:
" To cut my head off would n't pay,
I find it useful every day,
 As well as ornamental."

Brothers, I hope you will not fail
To see the moral of my tale
 And kindly to receive it.
You know your anniversary pie
Must have its crust, though hard and
 dry,
 And some prefer to leave it.

How oft before these youths were born
I 've fished in Fancy's Golden Horn
 For what the Muse might send me !
How gayly then I cast the line,
When all the morning sky was mine,
 And Hope her flies would lend me !

And now I hear our despot's call,
And come, like Hassan, to the hall, —
 If there 's a slave, I am one, —
My bait no longer flies, but worms !
I 've caught — Lord bless me ! how he
 squirms !
 An eel, and not a salmon !

THE FOUNTAIN OF YOUTH

READ AT THE MEETING OF THE HARVARD ALUMNI ASSOCIATION, JUNE 25, 1873

THE fount the Spaniard sought in vain
  Through all the land of flowers
Leaps glittering from the sandy plain
  Our classic grove embowers;
Here youth, unchanging, blooms and smiles,
  Here dwells eternal spring,
And warm from Hope's elysian isles
  The winds their perfume bring.

Here every leaf is in the bud,
  Each singing throat in tune,
And bright o'er evening's silver flood
  Shines the young crescent moon.
What wonder Age forgets his staff
  And lays his glasses down
And gray-haired grandsires look and laugh
  As when their locks were brown!

With ears grown dull and eyes grown dim
  They greet the joyous day
That calls them to the fountain's brim
  To wash their years away.
What change has clothed the ancient sire
  In sudden youth? For, lo!
The Judge, the Doctor, and the Squire
  Are Jack and Bill and Joe!

And be his titles what they will,
  In spite of manhood's claim
The graybeard is a school-boy still
  And loves his school-boy name;
It calms the ruler's stormy breast
  Whom hurrying care pursues,
And brings a sense of peace and rest,
  Like slippers after shoes.

And what are all the prizes won
  To youth's enchanted view?
And what is all the man has done
  To what the boy may do?
O blessed fount, whose waters flow
  Alike for sire and son,
That melts our winter's frost and snow
  And makes all ages one!

I pledge the sparkling fountain's tide,
  That flings its golden shower
With age to fill and youth to guide,
  Still fresh in morning flower!

Flow on with ever-widening stream,
  In ever-brightening morn, —
Our story's pride, our future's dream,
  The hope of times unborn!

NO TIME LIKE THE OLD TIME

1865

THERE is no time like the old time, when
  you and I were young,
When the buds of April blossomed, and the
  birds of spring-time sung!
The garden's brightest glories by summer
  suns are nursed,
But oh, the sweet, sweet violets, the flowers
  that opened first!

There is no place like the old place, where
  you and I were born,
Where we lifted first our eyelids on the
  splendors of the morn
From the milk-white breast that warmed
  us, from the clinging arms that bore,
Where the dear eyes glistened o'er us that
  will look on us no more!

There is no friend like the old friend, who
  has shared our morning days,
No greeting like his welcome, no homage
  like his praise:
Fame is the scentless sunflower, with gaudy
  crown of gold;
But friendship is the breathing rose, with
  sweets in every fold.

There is no love like the old love, that we
  courted in our pride;
Though our leaves are falling, falling, and
  we're fading side by side,
There are blossoms all around us with the
  colors of our dawn,
And we live in borrowed sunshine when the
  day-star is withdrawn.

There are no times like the old times, —
  they shall never be forgot!
There is no place like the old place, — keep
  green the dear old spot!
There are no friends like our old friends, —
  may Heaven prolong their lives!
There are no loves like our old loves, —
  God bless our loving wives!

A HYMN OF PEACE

SUNG AT THE "JUBILEE," JUNE 15, 1869, TO THE MUSIC OF KELLER'S "AMERICAN HYMN"

Angel of Peace, thou hast wandered too long!
  Spread thy white wings to the sunshine of love!
Come while our voices are blended in song, —
  Fly to our ark like the storm-beaten dove!
Fly to our ark on the wings of the dove, —
  Speed o'er the far-sounding billows of song,
Crowned with thine olive-leaf garland of love, —
  Angel of Peace, thou hast waited too long!

Joyous we meet, on this altar of thine
  Mingling the gifts we have gathered for thee,
Sweet with the odors of myrtle and pine,
  Breeze of the prairie and breath of the sea, —
Meadow and mountain and forest and sea!
  Sweet is the fragrance of myrtle and pine,
Sweeter the incense we offer to thee,
  Brothers, once more round this altar of thine!

Angels of Bethlehem, answer the strain!
  Hark! a new birth-song is filling the sky! —
Loud as the storm-wind that tumbles the main
  Bid the full breath of the organ reply, —
Let the loud tempest of voices reply, —
  Roll its long surge like the earth-shaking main!
Swell the vast song till it mounts to the sky! —
  Angels of Bethlehem, echo the strain!

BUNKER-HILL BATTLE AND OTHER POEMS

1874-1877

GRANDMOTHER'S STORY OF BUNKER-HILL BATTLE

AS SHE SAW IT FROM THE BELFRY

The story of Bunker Hill battle is told as literally in accordance with the best authorities as it would have been if it had been written in prose instead of in verse. I have often been asked what steeple it was from which the little group I speak of looked upon the conflict. To this I answer that I am not prepared to speak authoritatively, but that the reader may take his choice among all the steeples standing at that time in the northern part of the city. Christ Church in Salem Street is the one I always think of, but I do not insist upon its claim. As to the personages who made up the small company that followed the old corporal, it would be hard to identify them, but by ascertaining where the portrait by Copley is now to be found, some light may be thrown on their personality.

Daniel Malcolm's gravestone, splintered by British bullets, may be seen in the Copp's Hill burial-ground.

'T is like stirring living embers when, at eighty, one remembers
All the achings and the quakings of "the times that tried men's souls;"
When I talk of *Whig* and *Tory*, when I tell the *Rebel* story,
To you the words are ashes, but to me they 're burning coals.

I had heard the muskets' rattle of the April running battle;
Lord Percy's hunted soldiers, I can see their red coats still;
But a deadly chill comes o'er me, as the day looms up before me,
When a thousand men lay bleeding on the slopes of Bunker's Hill.

'T was a peaceful summer's morning, when the first thing gave us warning
Was the booming of the cannon from the river and the shore:
"Child," says grandma, "what's the matter, what is all this noise and clatter?
Have those scalping Indian devils come to murder us once more?"

Poor old soul! my sides were shaking in the midst of all my quaking,
To hear her talk of Indians when the guns began to roar:
She had seen the burning village, and the slaughter and the pillage,
When the Mohawks killed her father with their bullets through his door.

Then I said, "Now, dear old granny, don't you fret and worry any,
For I'll soon come back and tell you whether this is work or play;
There can't be mischief in it, so I won't be gone a minute" —
For a minute then I started. I was gone the livelong day.

No time for bodice-lacing or for looking-glass grimacing;
Down my hair went as I hurried, tumbling half-way to my heels;
God forbid your ever knowing, when there's blood around her flowing,
How the lonely, helpless daughter of a quiet household feels!

In the street I heard a thumping; and I knew it was the stumping
Of the Corporal, our old neighbor, on that wooden leg he wore,

With a knot of women round him, — it was
  lucky I had found him,
So I followed with the others, and the Cor-
  poral marched before.

They were making for the steeple, — the
  old soldier and his people;
The pigeons circled round us as we climbed
  the creaking stair.
Just across the narrow river — oh, so close
  it made me shiver! —
Stood a fortress on the hill-top that but
  yesterday was bare.

Not slow our eyes to find it; well we knew
  who stood behind it,
Though the earthwork hid them from us,
  and the stubborn walls were dumb:
Here were sister, wife, and mother, looking
  wild upon each other,
And their lips were white with terror as
  they said, THE HOUR HAS COME!

The morning slowly wasted, not a morsel
  had we tasted,
And our heads were almost splitting with
  the cannons' deafening thrill,
When a figure tall and stately round the
  rampart strode sedately;
It was PRESCOTT, one since told me; he
  commanded on the hill.

Every woman's heart grew bigger when
  we saw his manly figure,
With the banyan buckled round it, stand-
  ing up so straight and tall;
Like a gentleman of leisure who is stroll-
  ing out for pleasure,
Through the storm of shells and cannon-
  shot he walked around the wall.

At eleven the streets were swarming, for
  the redcoats' ranks were forming;
At noon in marching order they were
  moving to the piers;
How the bayonets gleamed and glistened,
  as we looked far down, and listened
To the trampling and the drum-beat of the
  belted grenadiers!

At length the men have started, with a
  cheer (it seemed faint-hearted),
In their scarlet regimentals, with their
  knapsacks on their backs,

And the reddening, rippling water, as after
  a sea-fight's slaughter,
Round the barges gliding onward blushed
  like blood along their tracks.

So they crossed to the other border, and
  again they formed in order;
And the boats came back for soldiers, came
  for soldiers, soldiers still:
The time seemed everlasting to us women
  faint and fasting, —
At last they're moving, marching, marching
  proudly up the hill.

We can see the bright steel glancing all
  along the lines advancing, —
Now the front rank fires a volley, — they
  have thrown away their shot;
For behind their earthwork lying, all the
  balls above them flying,
Our people need not hurry; so they wait
  and answer not.

Then the Corporal, our old cripple (he would
  swear sometimes and tipple), —
He had heard the bullets whistle (in the
  old French war) before, —
Calls out in words of jeering, just as if they
  all were hearing, —
And his wooden leg thumps fiercely on the
  dusty belfry floor: —

"Oh! fire away, ye villains, and earn King
  George's shillin's,
But ye'll waste a ton of powder afore a
  'rebel' falls;
You may bang the dirt and welcome, they're
  as safe as Dan'l Malcolm
Ten foot beneath the gravestone that you've
  splintered with your balls!"

In the hush of expectation, in the awe and
  trepidation
Of the dread approaching moment, we are
  well-nigh breathless all;
Though the rotten bars are failing on the
  rickety belfry railing,
We are crowding up against them like the
  waves against a wall.

Just a glimpse (the air is clearer), they are
  nearer, — nearer, — nearer,
When a flash — a curling smoke-wreath —
  then a crash — the steeple shakes —

The deadly truce is ended; the tempest's
  shroud is rended;
Like a morning mist it gathered, like a
  thundercloud it breaks!

Oh the sight our eyes discover as the blue-
  black smoke blows over!
The red-coats stretched in windrows as a
  mower rakes his hay;
Here a scarlet heap is lying, there a head-
  long crowd is flying
Like a billow that has broken and is shiv-
  ered into spray.

Then we cried, "The troops are routed!
  they are beat — it can't be doubted!
God be thanked, the fight is over!" — Ah!
  the grim old soldier's smile!
"Tell us, tell us why you look so?" (we
  could hardly speak, we shook so), —
"Are they beaten? Are they beaten?
  ARE they beaten?"— "Wait a
  while."

Oh the trembling and the terror! for too
  soon we saw our error:
They are baffled, not defeated; we have
  driven them back in vain;
And the columns that were scattered, round
  the colors that were tattered,
Toward the sullen, silent fortress turn their
  belted breasts again.

All at once, as we are gazing, lo the roofs
  of Charlestown blazing!
They have fired the harmless village; in an
  hour it will be down!
The Lord in heaven confound them, rain
  his fire and brimstone round them, —
The robbing, murdering red-coats, that
  would burn a peaceful town!

They are marching, stern and solemn; we
  can see each massive column
As they near the naked earth-mound with
  the slanting walls so steep.
Have our soldiers got faint-hearted, and in
  noiseless haste departed?
Are they panic-struck and helpless? Are
  they palsied or asleep?

Now! the walls they're almost under!
  scarce a rod the foes asunder!
Not a firelock flashed against them! up
  the earthwork they will swarm!

But the words have scarce been spoken,
  when the ominous calm is broken,
And a bellowing crash has emptied all the
  vengeance of the storm!

So again, with murderous slaughter, pelted
  backwards to the water,
Fly Pigot's running heroes and the
  frightened braves of Howe;
And we shout, "At last they're done for,
  it's their barges they have run for:
They are beaten, beaten, beaten; and the
  battle's over now!"

And we looked, poor timid creatures, on
  the rough old soldier's features,
Our lips afraid to question, but he knew
  what we would ask:
"Not sure," he said; "keep quiet, — once
  more, I guess, they'll try it —
Here's damnation to the cut-throats!" —
  then he handed me his flask,

Saying, "Gal, you're looking shaky; have
  a drop of old Jamaiky;
I'm afeard there'll be more trouble afore
  the job is done;"
So I took one scorching swallow; dreadful
  faint I felt and hollow,
Standing there from early morning when
  the firing was begun.

All through those hours of trial I had
  watched a calm clock dial,
As the hands kept creeping, creeping, —
  they were creeping round to four,
When the old man said, "They're forming
  with their bagonets fixed for storm-
  ing:
It's the death-grip that's a-coming, — they
  will try the works once more."

With brazen trumpets blaring, the flames
  behind them glaring,
The deadly wall before them, in close array
  they come;
Still onward, upward toiling, like a dragon's
  fold uncoiling, —
Like the rattlesnake's shrill warning the
  reverberating drum!

Over heaps all torn and gory — shall I tell
  the fearful story,
How they surged above the breastwork, as
  a sea breaks over a deck;

How, driven, yet scarce defeated, our worn-
out men retreated,
With their powder-horns all emptied, like
the swimmers from a wreck?

It has all been told and painted; as for me,
they say I fainted,
And the wooden-legged old Corporal
stumped with me down the stair:
When I woke from dreams affrighted the
evening lamps were lighted, —
On the floor a youth was lying; his bleeding
breast was bare.

And I heard through all the flurry, "Send
for WARREN! hurry! hurry!
Tell him here 's a soldier bleeding, and
he 'll come and dress his wound!"
Ah, we knew not till the morrow told its
tale of death and sorrow,
How the starlight found him stiffened on
the dark and bloody ground.

Who the youth was, what his name was,
where the place from which he came
was,
Who had brought him from the battle, and
had left him at our door,
He could not speak to tell us; but 't was
one of our brave fellows,
As the homespun plainly showed us which
the dying soldier wore.

For they all thought he was dying, as they
gathered round him crying, —
And they said, "Oh, how they 'll miss him!"
and, "What *will* his mother do?"
Then, his eyelids just unclosing like a child's
that has been dozing,
He faintly murmured, "Mother!" — and
— I saw his eyes were blue.

"Why, grandma, how you 're winking!"
Ah, my child, it sets me thinking
Of a story not like this one. Well, he
somehow lived along;
So we came to know each other, and I
nursed him like a — mother,
Till at last he stood before me, tall, and
rosy-cheeked, and strong.

And we sometimes walked together in the
pleasant summer weather, —
"Please to tell us what his name was?"
Just your own, my little dear, —

There 's his picture Copley painted: we be-
came so well acquainted,
That — in short, that 's why I 'm grandma,
and you children all are here!

AT THE "ATLANTIC" DINNER

DECEMBER 15, 1874

I SUPPOSE it 's myself that you 're making
allusion to
And bringing the sense of dismay and con-
fusion to.
Of course *some* must speak, — they are al-
ways selected to,
But pray what 's the reason that I am ex-
pected to?
I 'm not fond of wasting my breath as those
fellows do
That want to be blowing forever as bellows
do;
Their legs are uneasy, but why will you jog
any
That long to stay quiet beneath the mahog-
any?

Why, why call *me* up with your battery of
flatteries?
You say "He writes poetry," — that 's what
the matter is!
"It costs him no trouble — a pen full of
ink or two
And the poem is done in the time of a
wink or two;
As for thoughts — never mind — take the
ones that lie uppermost,
And the rhymes used by Milton and Byron
and Tupper most;
The lines come so easy! at one end he jin-
gles 'em,
At the other with capital letters he shingles
'em,
Why, the thing writes itself, and before
he 's half done with it
He hates to stop writing, he has such good
fun with it!"

Ah, that is the way in which simple ones
go about
And draw a fine picture of things they
don't know about!
We all know a kitten, but come to a cata-
mount
The beast is a stranger when grown up to
that amount,

(A stranger we rather prefer should n't
 visit us,
A *felis* whose advent is far from felici-
 tous.)
The boy who can boast that his trap has
 just got a mouse
Must n't draw it and write underneath
 "hippopotamus;"
Or say unveraciously, "This is an ele-
 phant,"—
Don't think, let me beg, these examples
 irrelevant,—
What they mean is just this — that a thing
 to be painted well
Should always be something with which
 we 're acquainted well.

You call on your victim for "things he has
 plenty of,—
Those copies of verses no doubt at least
 twenty of;
His desk is crammed full, for he always
 keeps writing 'em
And reading to friends as his way of de-
 lighting 'em!"
I tell you this writing of verses means busi-
 ness,—
It makes the brain whirl in a vortex of
 dizziness:
You think they are scrawled in the languor
 of laziness —
I tell you they 're squeezed by a spasm of
 craziness,
A fit half as bad as the staggering vertigos
That seize a poor fellow and down in the
 dirt he goes!

And therefore it chimes with the word's
 etymology
That the sons of Apollo are great on apol-
 ogy,
For the writing of verse is a struggle mys-
 terious
And the gayest of rhymes is a matter that 's
 serious.
For myself, I 'm relied on by friends in ex-
 tremities,
And I don't mind so much if a comfort to
 them it is;
'T is a pleasure to please, and the straw
 that can tickle us
Is a source of enjoyment though slightly
 ridiculous.

I am up for a — something — and since
 I 've begun with it,
I must give you a toast now before I have
 done with it.
Let me pump at my wits as they pumped
 the Cochituate
That moistened — it may be — the very
 last bit you ate:
Success to our publishers, authors and
 editors,
To our debtors good luck, — pleasant
 dreams to our creditors;
May the monthly grow yearly, till all we
 are groping for
Has reached the fulfilment we 're all of us
 hoping for;
Till the bore through the tunnel — it makes
 me let off a sigh
To think it may possibly ruin my pro-
 phecy —
Has been punned on so often 't will never
 provoke again
One mild adolescent to make the old joke
 again;
Till abstinent, all-go-to-meeting society
Has forgotten the sense of the word ine-
 briety;
Till the work that poor Hannah and Bridget
 and Phillis do
The humanized, civilized female gorillas do;
Till the roughs, as we call them, grown
 loving and dutiful,
Shall worship the true and the pure and
 the beautiful,
And, preying no longer as tiger and vulture
 do,
All read the "Atlantic" as persons of cul-
 ture do!

"LUCY"

FOR HER GOLDEN WEDDING, OCTOBER
18, 1875

[The subject of this poem was a familiar fig-
ure in the household of Dr. Holmes's father, and
was married while living there to a farmer.]

"LUCY."— The old familiar name
 Is now, as always, pleasant,
Its liquid melody the same
 Alike in past or present;
Let others call you what they will,
 I know you 'll let me use it;
To me your name is Lucy still,
 I cannot bear to lose it.

What visions of the past return
 With Lucy's image blended!

What memories from the silent urn
  Of gentle lives long ended!
What dreams of childhood's fleeting morn,
  What starry aspirations,
That filled the misty days unborn
  With fancy's coruscations!

Ah, Lucy, life has swiftly sped
  From April to November;
The summer blossoms all are shed
  That you and I remember;
But while the vanished years we share
  With mingling recollections,
How all their shadowy features wear
  The hue of old affections!

Love called you. He who stole your heart
  Of sunshine half bereft us;
Our household's garland fell apart
  The morning that you left us;
The tears of tender girlhood streamed
  Through sorrow's opening sluices;
Less sweet our garden's roses seemed,
  Less blue its flower-de-luces.

That old regret is turned to smiles,
  That parting sigh to greeting;
I send my heart-throb fifty miles,
  Through every line 't is beating;
God grant you many and happy years,
  Till when the last has crowned you
The dawn of endless day appears,
  And heaven is shining round you!

HYMN

FOR THE INAUGURATION OF THE STATUE OF GOVERNOR ANDREW, HINGHAM, OCTOBER 7, 1875

BEHOLD the shape our eyes have known!
It lives once more in changeless stone;
So looked in mortal face and form
Our guide through peril's deadly storm.

But hushed the beating heart we knew,
That heart so tender, brave, and true,
Firm as the rooted mountain rock,
Pure as the quarry's whitest block!

Not his beneath the blood-red star
To win the soldier's envied scar;
Unarmed he battled for the right,
In Duty's never-ending fight.

Unconquered will, unslumbering eye,
Faith such as bids the martyr die,
The prophet's glance, the master's hand
To mould the work his foresight planned,

These were his gifts; what Heaven had lent
For justice, mercy, truth, he spent,
First to avenge the traitorous blow,
And first to lift the vanquished foe.

Lo, thus he stood; in danger's strait
The pilot of the Pilgrim State!
Too large his fame for her alone, —
A nation claims him as her own!

A MEMORIAL TRIBUTE

READ AT THE MEETING HELD AT MUSIC HALL, FEBRUARY 8, 1876, IN MEMORY OF DR. SAMUEL G. HOWE

I

LEADER of armies, Israel's God,
  Thy soldier's fight is won!
Master, whose lowly path he trod,
  Thy servant's work is done!

No voice is heard from Sinai's steep
  Our wandering feet to guide;
From Horeb's rock no waters leap;
  No Jordan's waves divide;

No prophet cleaves our western sky
  On wheels of whirling fire;
No shepherds hear the song on high
  Of heaven's angelic choir:

Yet here as to the patriarch's tent
  God's angel comes a guest;
He comes on heaven's high errand sent,
  In earth's poor raiment drest.

We see no halo round his brow
  Till love its own recalls,
And, like a leaf that quits the bough,
  The mortal vesture falls.

In autumn's chill declining day,
  Ere winter's killing frost,
The message came; so passed away
  The friend our earth has lost.

Still, Father, in thy love we trust;
  Forgive us if we mourn
The saddening hour that laid in dust
  His robe of flesh outworn.

II

How long the wreck-strewn journey seems
  To reach the far-off past
That woke his youth from peaceful dreams
  With Freedom's trumpet-blast!

Along her classic hillsides rung
  The Paynim's battle-cry,
And like a red-cross knight he sprung
  For her to live or die.

No trustier service claimed the wreath
  For Sparta's bravest son;
No truer soldier sleeps beneath
  The mound of Marathon;

Yet not for him the warrior's grave
  In front of angry foes;
To lift, to shield, to help, to save,
  The holier task he chose.

He touched the eyelids of the blind,
  And lo! the veil withdrawn,
As o'er the midnight of the mind
  He led the light of dawn.

He asked not whence the fountains roll
  No traveller's foot has found,
But mapped the desert of the soul
  Untracked by sight or sound.

What prayers have reached the sapphire
    throne,
  By silent fingers spelt,
For him who first through depths unknown
  His doubtful pathway felt,

Who sought the slumbering sense that lay
  Close shut with bolt and bar,
And showed awakening thought the ray
  Of reason's morning star!

Where'er he moved, his shadowy form
  The sightless orbs would seek,
And smiles of welcome light and warm
  The lips that could not speak.

No labored line, no sculptor's art,
  Such hallowed memory needs;
His tablet is the human heart,
  His record loving deeds.

III

The rest that earth denied is thine, —
  Ah, is it rest? we ask,
Or, traced by knowledge more divine,
  Some larger, nobler task?

Had but those boundless fields of blue
  One darkened sphere like this;
But what has heaven for thee to do
  In realms of perfect bliss?

No cloud to lift, no mind to clear,
  No rugged path to smooth,
No struggling soul to help and cheer,
  No mortal grief to soothe!

Enough; is there a world of love,
  No more we ask to know;
The hand will guide thy ways above
  That shaped thy task below.

JOSEPH WARREN, M.D.

1875

TRAINED in the holy art whose lifted shield
  Wards off the darts a never-slumbering
    foe,
  By hearth and wayside lurking, waits to
    throw,
Oppression taught his helpful arm to wield
The slayer's weapon: on the murderous field
The fiery bolt he challenged laid him low,
Seeking its noblest victim. Even so
The charter of a nation must be sealed!
  The healer's brow the hero's honors
    crowned,
From lowliest duty called to loftiest deed.
  Living, the oak-leaf wreath his temples
    bound;
Dying, the conqueror's laurel was his meed,
Last on the broken ramparts' turf to bleed
  Where Freedom's victory in defeat was
    found.

OLD CAMBRIDGE

JULY 3, 1875

[Upon the occasion of the Centennial celebration of Washington taking command of the American army. It was on this occasion that Lowell read his ode, *Under the Old Elm.*]

AND can it be you 've found a place
Within this consecrated space,
　That makes so fine a show,
For one of Rip Van Winkle's race?
　And is it really so?
Who wants an old receipted bill?
Who fishes in the Frog-pond still?
Who digs last year's potato hill? —
　That 's what he 'd like to know!

And were it any spot on earth
Save this dear home that gave him birth
　Some scores of years ago,
He had not come to spoil your mirth
　And chill your festive glow;
But round his baby-nest he strays,
With tearful eye the scene surveys,
His heart unchanged by changing days, —
　That 's what he 'd have you know.

Can you whose eyes not yet are dim
Live o'er the buried past with him,
　And see the roses blow
When white-haired men were Joe and Jim
　Untouched by winter's snow?
Or roll the years back one by one
As Judah's monarch backed the sun,
And see the century just begun? —
　That 's what he 'd like to know!

I come, but as the swallow dips,
Just touching with her feather-tips
　The shining wave below,
To sit with pleasure-murmuring lips
　And listen to the flow
Of Elmwood's sparkling Hippocrene,
To tread once more my native green,
To sigh unheard, to smile unseen, —
　That 's what I 'd have you know.

But since the common lot I 've shared
(We all are sitting "unprepared,"
　Like culprits in a row,
Whose heads are down, whose necks are bared
　To wait the headsman's blow),
I 'd like to shift my task to you,
By asking just a thing or two
About the good old times I knew, —
　Here 's what I want to know:

The yellow meetin' house — can you tell
Just where it stood before it fell
　Prey of the vandal foe, —
Our dear old temple, loved so well,
　By ruthless hands laid low?
Where, tell me, was the Deacon's pew?
Whose hair was braided in a queue?
(For there were pig-tails not a few,) —
　That 's what I 'd like to know.

The bell — can you recall its clang?
And how the seats would slam and bang?
　The voices high and low?
The basso's trump before he sang?
　The viol and its bow?
Where was it old Judge Winthrop sat?
Who wore the last three-cornered hat?
Was Israel Porter lean or fat? —
　That 's what I 'd like to know.

Tell where the market used to be
That stood beside the murdered tree?
　Whose dog to church would go?
Old Marcus Reemie, who was he?
　Who were the brothers Snow?
Does not your memory slightly fail
About that great September gale? —
Whereof one told a moving tale,
　As Cambridge boys should know.

When Cambridge was a simple town,
Say just when Deacon William Brown
　(Last door in yonder row),
For honest silver counted down,
　His groceries would bestow? —
For those were days when money meant
Something that jingled as you went, —
No hybrid like the nickel cent,
　I 'd have you all to know,

But quarter, ninepence, pistareen,
And fourpence hapennies in between,
　All metal fit to show,
Instead of rags in stagnant green,
　The scum of debts we owe;
How sad to think such stuff should be
Our Wendell's cure-all recipe, —
Not Wendell H., but Wendell P., —
　The one you all must know!

I question — but you answer not —
Dear me! and have I quite forgot
　How fivescore years ago,

Just on this very blessed spot,
  The summer leaves below,
Before his homespun ranks arrayed
In green New England's elm-bough shade
The great Virginian drew the blade
  King George full soon should know!

O George the Third! you found it true
Our George was more than *double you*,
  For nature made him so.
Not much an empire's crown can do
If brains are scant and slow, —
Ah, not like that his laurel crown
Whose presence gilded with renown
Our brave old Academic town,
  As all her children know!

So here we meet with loud acclaim
To tell mankind that here he came,
  With hearts that throb and glow;
Ours is a portion of his fame
  Our trumpets needs must blow!
On yonder hill the Lion fell,
But here was chipped the eagle's shell, —
That little hatchet did it well,
  As all the world shall know!

WELCOME TO THE NATIONS

PHILADELPHIA, JULY 4, 1876

BRIGHT on the banners of lily and rose
Lo! the last sun of our century sets!
Wreathe the black cannon that scowled on
  our foes,
  All but her friendships the nation for-
    gets!
  All but her friends and their welcome
    forgets!
These are around her; but where are her
  foes?
Lo, while the sun of her century sets,
Peace with her garlands of lily and rose!

Welcome! a shout like the war trumpet's
  swell
  Wakes the wild echoes that slumber
    around!
Welcome! it quivers from Liberty's bell;
  Welcome! the walls of her temple re-
    sound!
  Hark! the gray walls of her temple re-
    sound!
Fade the far voices o'er hillside and dell;

Welcome! still whisper the echoes
  around;
Welcome! still trembles on Liberty's bell!

Thrones of the continent! isles of the
  sea!
  Yours are the garlands of peace we en-
    twine;
Welcome, once more, to the land of the
  free,
  Shadowed alike by the palm and the
    pine;
  Softly they murmur, the palm and the
    pine,
  "Hushed is our strife, in the land of the
    free;"
  Over your children their branches en-
    twine,
Thrones of the continents! isles of the sea!

A FAMILIAR LETTER

TO SEVERAL CORRESPONDENTS

YES, write, if you want to, there's nothing
  like trying;
  Who knows what a treasure your casket
    may hold?
I 'll show you that rhyming 's as easy as
  lying,
  If you 'll listen to me while the art I un-
    fold.

Here 's a book full of words; one can
  choose as he fancies,
  As a painter his tint, as a workman his
    tool;
Just think! all the poems and plays and
  romances
  Were drawn out of this, like the fish
    from a pool!

You can wander at will through its sylla-
  bled mazes,
  And take all you want, — not a copper
    they cost, —
What is there to hinder your picking out
  phrases
  For an epic as clever as "Paradise
    Lost"?

Don't mind if the index of sense is at zero,
  Use words that run smoothly, whatever
    they mean;

A FAMILIAR LETTER

Leander and Lilian and Lillibullero
   Are much the same thing in the rhyming
      machine.

There are words so delicious their sweet-
   ness will smother
   That boarding-school flavor of which
      we're afraid, —
There is "lush" is a good one, and "swirl"
   is another, —
   Put both in one stanza, its fortune is
      made.

With musical murmurs and rhythmical
   closes
   You can cheat us of smiles when you've
      nothing to tell;
You hand us a nosegay of milliner's roses,
   And we cry with delight, "Oh, how
      sweet they *do* smell!"

Perhaps you will answer all needful condi-
   tions
   For winning the laurels to which you
      aspire,
By docking the tails of the two preposi-
   tions
   I' the style o' the bards you so greatly
      admire.

As for subjects of verse, they are only too
   plenty
   For ringing the changes on metrical
      chimes;
A maiden, a moonbeam, a lover of twenty
   Have filled that great basket with bush-
      els of rhymes.

Let me show you a picture — 't is far from
   irrelevant —
   By a famous old hand in the arts of de-
      sign;
'T is only a photographed sketch of an
   elephant, —
   The name of the draughtsman was Rem-
      brandt of Rhine.

How easy! no troublesome colors to lay
   on,
   It can't have fatigued him, — no, not in
      the least, —
A dash here and there with a hap-hazard
   crayon,
   And there stands the wrinkled-skinned,
      baggy-limbed beast.

Just so with your verse, — 't is as easy as
   sketching, —
   You can reel off a song without knitting
      your brow,
As lightly as Rembrandt a drawing or
   etching;
   It is nothing at all, if you only know how.

Well; imagine you've printed your volume
   of verses:
   Your forehead is wreathed with the gar-
      land of fame,
Your poems the eloquent school-boy re-
   hearses,
   Her album the school-girl presents for
      your name;

Each morning the post brings you auto-
   graph letters;
   You'll answer them promptly, — an
      hour is n't much
For the honor of sharing a page with your
   betters,
   With magistrates, members of Congress,
      and such.

Of course you're delighted to serve the
   committees
   That come with requests from the coun-
      try all round,
You would grace the occasion with poems
   and ditties
   When they've got a new schoolhouse,
      or poorhouse, or pound.

With a hymn for the saints and a song for
   the sinners,
   You go and are welcome wherever you
      please;
You're a privileged guest at all manner of
   dinners,
   You've a seat on the platform among
      the grandees.

At length your mere presence becomes a
   sensation,
   Your cup of enjoyment is filled to its brim
With the pleasure Horatian of digitmon-
   stration,
   As the whisper runs round of "That's
      he!" or "That's him!"

But remember, O dealer in phrases sono-
   rous,
   So daintily chosen, so tunefully matched,

Though you soar with the wings of the cherubim o'er us,
The *ovum* was human from which you were hatched.

No will of your own with its puny compulsion
Can summon the spirit that quickens the lyre;
It comes, if at all, like the Sibyl's convulsion
And touches the brain with a finger of fire.

So perhaps, after all, it's as well to be quiet
If you've nothing you think is worth saying in prose,
As to furnish a meal of their cannibal diet
To the critics, by publishing, as you propose.

But it's all of no use, and I'm sorry I've written, —
I shall see your thin volume some day on my shelf;
For the rhyming tarantula surely has bitten,
And music must cure you, so pipe it yourself.

UNSATISFIED

"Only a housemaid!" She looked from the kitchen,
Neat was the kitchen and tidy was she;
There at her window a sempstress sat stitching;
"Were I a sempstress, how happy I'd be!"

"Only a Queen!" She looked over the waters, —
Fair was her kingdom and mighty was she;
There sat an Empress, with Queens for her daughters;
"Were I an Empress, how happy I'd be!"

Still the old frailty they all of them trip in!
Eve in her daughters is ever the same;
Give her all Eden, she sighs for a pippin;
Give her an Empire, she pines for a name!

HOW THE OLD HORSE WON THE BET

DEDICATED BY A CONTRIBUTOR TO THE COLLEGIAN, 1830, TO THE EDITORS OF THE HARVARD ADVOCATE, 1876

Unquestionably there is something a little like extravagance in *How the Old Horse won the Bet*, which taxes the credulity of experienced horsemen. Still there have been a good many surprises in the history of the turf and the trotting course.

The Godolphin Arabian was taken from ignoble drudgery to become the patriarch of the English racing stock.

Old Dutchman was transferred from between the shafts of a cart to become a champion of the American trotters in his time.

"Old Blue," a famous Boston horse of the early decades of this century, was said to trot a mile in less than three minutes, but I do not find any exact record of his achievements.

Those who have followed the history of the American trotting horse are aware of the wonderful development of speed attained in these last years. The lowest time as yet recorded is by Maud S., in 2.08¾.

'T was on the famous trotting-ground,
The betting men were gathered round
From far and near; the "cracks" were there
Whose deeds the sporting prints declare:
The swift g. m., Old Hiram's nag,
The fleet s. h., Dan Pfeiffer's brag,
With these a third — and who is he
That stands beside his fast b. g.?
Budd Doble, whose catarrhal name
So fills the nasal trump of fame.
There too stood many a noted steed
Of Messenger and Morgan breed;
Green horses also, not a few;
Unknown as yet what they could do;
And all the hacks that know so well
The scourgings of the Sunday swell.

Blue are the skies of opening day;
The bordering turf is green with May;
The sunshine's golden gleam is thrown
On sorrel, chestnut, bay, and roan;
The horses paw and prance and neigh,
Fillies and colts like kittens play,
And dance and toss their rippled manes
Shining and soft as silken skeins;
Wagons and gigs are ranged about,

And fashion flaunts her gay turn-out;
Here stands — each youthful Jehu's dream —
The jointed tandem, ticklish team!
And there in ampler breadth expand
The splendors of the four-in-hand;
On faultless ties and glossy tiles
The lovely bonnets beam their smiles;
(The style 's the man, so books avow;
The style 's the woman, anyhow);
From flounces frothed with creamy lace
Peeps out the pug-dog's smutty face,
Or spaniel rolls his liquid eye,
Or stares the wiry pet of Skye, —
O woman, in your hours of ease
So shy with us, so free with these!

"Come on! I'll bet you two to one
I'll make him do it!" "Will you? Done!"

What was it who was bound to do?
I did not hear and can't tell you, —
Pray listen till my story 's through.
Scarce noticed, back behind the rest,
By cart and wagon rudely prest,
The parson's lean and bony bay
Stood harnessed in his one-horse shay —
Lent to his sexton for the day;
(A funeral — so the sexton said;
His mother's uncle's wife was dead.)

Like Lazarus bid to Dives' feast,
So looked the poor forlorn old beast;
His coat was rough, his tail was bare,
The gray was sprinkled in his hair;
Sportsmen and jockeys knew him not,
And yet they say he once could trot
Among the fleetest of the town,
Till something cracked and broke him down, —
The steed's, the statesman's, common lot!
"And are we then so soon forgot?"
Ah me! I doubt if one of you
Has ever heard the name "Old Blue,"
Whose fame through all this region rung
In those old days when I was young!

"Bring forth the horse!" Alas! he showed
Not like the one Mazeppa rode;
Scant-maned, sharp-backed, and shaky-kneed,
The wreck of what was once a steed,

Lips thin, eyes hollow, stiff in joints;
Yet not without his knowing points.
The sexton laughing in his sleeve,
As if 't were all a make-believe,
Led forth the horse, and as he laughed
Unhitched the breeching from a shaft,
Unclasped the rusty belt beneath,
Drew forth the snaffle from his teeth,
Slipped off his head-stall, set him free
From strap and rein, — a sight to see!

So worn, so lean in every limb,
It can't be they are saddling him!
It is! his back the pig-skin strides
And flaps his lank, rheumatic sides;
With look of mingled scorn and mirth
They buckle round the saddle-girth;
With horsy wink and saucy toss
A youngster throws his leg across,
And so, his rider on his back,
They lead him, limping, to the track,
Far up behind the starting-point,
To limber out each stiffened joint.

As through the jeering crowd he past,
One pitying look Old Hiram cast;
"Go it, ye cripple, while ye can!"
Cried out unsentimental Dan;
"A Fast-Day dinner for the crows!"
Budd Doble's scoffing shout arose.

Slowly, as when the walking-beam
First feels the gathering head of steam,
With warning cough and threatening wheeze
The stiff old charger crooks his knees;
At first with cautious step sedate,
As if he dragged a coach of state;
He 's not a colt; he knows full well
That time is weight and sure to tell;
No horse so sturdy but he fears
The handicap of twenty years.

As through the throng on either hand
The old horse nears the judges' stand,
Beneath his jockey's feather-weight
He warms a little to his gait,
And now and then a step is tried
That hints of something like a stride.

"Go!" — Through his ear the summons stung
As if a battle-trump had rung;
The slumbering instincts long unstirred

Start at the old familiar word;
It thrills like flame through every limb, —
What mean his twenty years to him?
The savage blow his rider dealt
Fell on his hollow flanks unfelt;
The spur that pricked his staring hide
Unheeded tore his bleeding side;
Alike to him are spur and rein, —
He steps a five-year-old again!

Before the quarter pole was past,
Old Hiram said, "He's going fast."
Long ere the quarter was a half,
The chuckling crowd had ceased to laugh;
Tighter his frightened jockey clung
As in a mighty stride he swung,
The gravel flying in his track,
His neck stretched out, his ears laid back,
His tail extended all the while
Behind him like a rat-tail file!
Off went a shoe, — away it spun,
Shot like a bullet from a gun;
The quaking jockey shapes a prayer
From scraps of oaths he used to swear;
He drops his whip, he drops his rein,
He clutches fiercely for a mane;
He'll lose his hold — he sways and reels —
He'll slide beneath those trampling heels!
The knees of many a horseman quake,
The flowers on many a bonnet shake,
And shouts arise from left and right,
"Stick on! Stick on!" "Hould tight! Hould tight!"
"Cling round his neck and don't let go —
That pace can't hold — there! steady! whoa!"
But like the sable steed that bore
The spectral lover of Lenore,
His nostrils snorting foam and fire,
No stretch his bony limbs can tire;
And now the stand he rushes by,
And "Stop him! — stop him!" is the cry.
Stand back! he's only just begun —
He's having out three heats in one!

"Don't rush in front! he'll smash your brains;
But follow up and grab the reins!"
Old Hiram spoke. Dan Pfeiffer heard,
And sprang impatient at the word;
Budd Doble started on his bay,
Old Hiram followed on his gray,
And off they spring, and round they go,
The fast ones doing "all they know."
Look! twice they follow at his heels,
As round the circling course he wheels,
And whirls with him that clinging boy
Like Hector round the walls of Troy;
Still on, and on, the third time round!
They're tailing off! they're losing ground!
Budd Doble's nag begins to fail!
Dan Pfeiffer's sorrel whisks his tail!
And see! in spite of whip and shout,
Old Hiram's mare is giving out!
Now for the finish! at the turn,
The old horse — all the rest astern —
Comes swinging in, with easy trot;
By Jove! he's distanced all the lot!

That trot no mortal could explain;
Some said, "Old Dutchman come again!"
Some took his time, — at least they tried,
But what it was could none decide;
One said he couldn't understand
What happened to his second hand;
One said 2.10; *that* could n't be —
More like two twenty-two or three;
Old Hiram settled it at last;
"The time was two — too dee-vel-ish fast!"

The parson's horse had won the bet;
It cost him something of a sweat;
Back in the one-horse shay he went;
The parson wondered what it meant,
And murmured, with a mild surprise
And pleasant twinkle of the eyes,
"That funeral must have been a trick,
Or corpses drive at double-quick;
I should n't wonder, I declare,
If brother — Jehu — made the prayer!"

And this is all I have to say
About that tough old trotting bay,
Huddup! Huddup! G'lang! Good day!

Moral for which this tale is told:
A horse *can* trot, for all he's old.

AN APPEAL FOR "THE OLD SOUTH"

"While stands the Coliseum, Rome shall stand;
When falls the Coliseum, Rome shall fall."

[Written in the spirit of *Old Ironsides*. There was danger that the historic church in Boston would be destroyed, since it stood on land very valuable for commercial purposes, and the congregation worshipping in it had built a new meeting-house in the dwelling-house part of the city. The building was saved almost wholly through the intervention of public-spirited women, headed by Mrs. Mary Hemenway, who not only contributed most of the money needed, but afterward made the church the centre of important work in the teaching of history.]

FULL sevenscore years our city's pride —
 The comely Southern spire —
Has cast its shadow, and defied
 The storm, the foe, the fire;
Sad is the sight our eyes behold;
 Woe to the three-hilled town,
When through the land the tale is told —
 "The brave 'Old South' is down!"

Let darkness blot the starless dawn
 That bears our children tell,
"Here rose the walls, now wrecked and gone,
 Our fathers loved so well;
Here, while his brethren stood aloof,
 The herald's blast was blown
That shook St. Stephen's pillared roof
 And rocked King George's throne!

"The home-bound wanderer of the main
 Looked from his deck afar,
To where the gilded, glittering vane
 Shone like the evening star,
And pilgrim feet from every clime
 The floor with reverence trod,
Where holy memories made sublime
 The shrine of Freedom's God!"

The darkened skies, alas! have seen
 Our monarch tree laid low,
And spread in ruins o'er the green,
 But Nature struck the blow;
No scheming thrift its downfall planned,
 It felt no edge of steel,
No soulless hireling raised his hand
 The deadly stroke to deal.

In bridal garlands, pale and mute,
 Still pleads the storied tower;
These are the blossoms, but the fruit
 Awaits the golden shower;
The spire still greets the morning sun, —
 Say, shall it stand or fall?
Help, ere the spoiler has begun!
 Help, each, and God help all!

THE FIRST FAN

READ AT A MEETING OF THE BOSTON BRIC-À-BRAC CLUB, FEBRUARY 21, 1877

WHEN rose the cry "Great Pan is dead!"
 And Jove's high palace closed its portal,
The fallen gods, before they fled,
 Sold out their frippery to a mortal.

"To whom?" you ask. I ask of you.
 The answer hardly needs suggestion;
Of course it was the Wandering Jew, —
 How could you put me such a question?

A purple robe, a little worn,
 The Thunderer deigned himself to offer;
The bearded wanderer laughed in scorn, —
 You know he always was a scoffer.

"Vife shillins! 't is a monstrous price;
 Say two and six and further talk shun."
"Take it," cried Jove; "we can't be nice, —
 'T would fetch twice that at Leonard's auction."

The ice was broken; up they came,
 All sharp for bargains, god and goddess,
Each ready with the price to name
 For robe or head-dress, scarf or bodice.

First Juno, out of temper, too, —
 Her queenly forehead somewhat cloudy;
Then Pallas in her stockings blue,
 Imposing, but a little dowdy.

The scowling queen of heaven unrolled
 Before the Jew a threadbare turban:
"Three shillings." "One. 'T will suit some old
 Terrific feminine suburban."

But as for Pallas, — how to tell
 In seemly phrase a fact so shocking?
She pointed, — pray excuse me, — well,
 She pointed to her azure stocking.

And if the honest truth were told,
 Its heel confessed the need of darning;
"Gods!" low-bred Vulcan cried, "behold!
 There! that's what comes of too much larning!"

Pale Proserpine came groping round,
　Her pupils dreadfully dilated
With too much living underground —
　A residence quite overrated;

"This kerchief's what you want, I know, —
　Don't cheat poor Venus of her cestus, —
You'll find it handy when you go
　To — you know where; it's pure asbestus."

Then Phœbus of the silver bow,
　And Hebe, dimpled as a baby,
And Dian with the breast of snow,
　Chaser and chased — and caught, it may be:

One took the quiver from her back,
　One held the cap he spent the night in,
And one a bit of *bric-à-brac*,
　Such as the gods themselves delight in.

Then Mars, the foe of human kind,
　Strode up and showed his suit of armor;
So none at last was left behind
　Save Venus, the celestial charmer.

Poor Venus! What had she to sell?
　For all she looked so fresh and jaunty,
Her wardrobe, as I blush to tell,
　Already seemed but quite too scanty.

Her gems were sold, her sandals gone, —
　She always would be rash and flighty, —
Her winter garments all in pawn,
　Alas for charming Aphrodite!

The lady of a thousand loves,
　The darling of the old religion,
Had only left of all the doves
　That drew her car one fan-tailed pigeon.

How oft upon her finger-tips
　He perched, afraid of Cupid's arrow,
Or kissed her on the rosebud lips,
　Like Roman Lesbia's loving sparrow!

"My bird, I want your train," she cried;
　"Come, don't let's have a fuss about it;
I'll make it beauty's pet and pride,
　And you'll be better off without it.

"So vulgar! Have you noticed, pray,
　An earthly belle or dashing bride walk,
And how her flounces track her way,
　Like slimy serpents on the sidewalk?

"A lover's heart it quickly cools;
　In mine it kindles up enough rage
To wring their necks. How can such fools
　Ask men to vote for woman suffrage?"

The goddess spoke, and gently stripped
　Her bird of every caudal feather;
A strand of gold-bright hair she clipped,
　And bound the glossy plumes together,

And lo, the Fan! for beauty's hand,
　The lovely queen of beauty made it;
The price she named was hard to stand,
　But Venus smiled: the Hebrew paid it.

Jove, Juno, Venus, where are you?
　Mars, Mercury, Phœbus, Neptune, Saturn?
But o'er the world the Wandering Jew
　Has borne the Fan's celestial pattern.

So everywhere we find the Fan, —
　In lonely isles of the Pacific,
In farthest China and Japan, —
　Wherever suns are sudorific.

Nay, even the oily Esquimaux
　In summer court its cooling breezes, —
In fact, in every clime 't is so,
　No matter if it fries or freezes.

And since from Aphrodite's dove
　The pattern of the fan was given,
No wonder that it breathes of love
　And wafts the perfumed gales of heaven!

Before this new Pandora's gift
　In slavery woman's tyrant kept her,
But now he kneels her glove to lift, —
　The fan is mightier than the sceptre.

The tap it gives how arch and sly!
　The breath it wakes how fresh and grateful!
Behind its shield how soft the sigh!
　The whispered tale of shame how fateful!

Its empire shadows every throne
　And every shore that man is tost on;
It rules the lords of every zone,
　Nay, even the bluest blood of Boston!

But every one that swings to-night,
Of fairest shape, from farthest region,
May trace its pedigree aright
To Aphrodite's fan-tailed pigeon.

TO RUTHERFORD BIRCHARD HAYES

AT THE DINNER TO THE PRESIDENT, BOSTON, JUNE 26, 1877

How to address him? awkward, it is true:
Call him " Great Father," as the Red Men do?
Borrow some title? this is not the place
That christens men Your Highness and Your Grace;
We tried such names as these awhile, you know,
But left them off a century ago.

His Majesty? We 've had enough of that:
Besides, that needs a crown; he wears a hat.
What if, to make the nicer ears content,
We say His Honesty, the President?

Sir, we believed you honest, truthful, brave,
When to your hands their precious trust we gave,
And we have found you better than we knew,
Braver, and not less honest, not less true!
So every heart has opened, every hand
Tingles with welcome, and through all the land
All voices greet you in one broad acclaim,
Healer of strife! Has earth a nobler name?

What phrases mean you do not need to learn;
We must be civil, and they serve our turn:
" Your most obedient humble " means — means what?
Something the well-bred signer just is not.
Yet there are tokens, sir, you must believe;
There is one language never can deceive:
The lover knew it when the maiden smiled;
The mother knows it when she clasps her child;
Voices may falter, trembling lips turn pale,
Words grope and stumble; this will tell their tale
Shorn of all rhetoric, bare of all pretence,

But radiant, warm, with Nature's eloquence.
Look in our eyes! Your welcome waits you there, —
North, South, East, West, from all and everywhere!

THE SHIP OF STATE

A SENTIMENT

This " sentiment " was read on the same occasion as the *Family Record*, which immediately follows it. The latter poem is the dutiful tribute of a son to his father and his father's ancestors, residents of Woodstock [Connecticut] from its first settlement. [The occasion was the celebration of the Fourth of July, 1877, in accordance with a custom established at Woodstock by Mr. H. C. Bowen.]

THE Ship of State! above her skies are blue,
But still she rocks a little, it is true,
And there *are* passengers whose faces white
Show they don't feel as happy as they might;
Yet on the whole her crew are quite content,
Since its wild fury the typhoon has spent,
And willing, if her pilot thinks it best,
To head a little nearer south by west.
And this they feel: the ship came too near wreck,
In the long quarrel for the quarter-deck,
Now when she glides serenely on her way, —
The shallows past where dread explosives lay, —
The stiff obstructive's churlish game to try:
Let sleeping dogs and still torpedoes lie!
And so I give you all the Ship of State;
Freedom's last venture is her priceless freight;
God speed her, keep her, bless her, while she steers
Amid the breakers of unsounded years;
Lead her through danger's paths with even keel,
And guide the honest hand that holds her wheel!

A FAMILY RECORD

NOT to myself this breath of vesper song,
Not to these patient friends, this kindly throng,
Not to this hallowed morning, though it be

Our summer Christmas, Freedom's jubilee,
When every summit, topmast, steeple, tower,
That owns her empire spreads her starry flower,
Its blood-streaked leaves in heaven's benignant dew
Washed clean from every crimson stain they knew, —
No, not to these the passing thrills belong
That steal my breath to hush themselves with song.

These moments all are memory's; I have come
To speak with lips that rather should be dumb;
For what are words? At every step I tread
The dust that wore the footprints of the dead
But for whose life my life had never known
This faded vesture which it calls its own.
Here sleeps my father's sire, and they who gave
That earlier life here found their peaceful grave.
In days gone by I sought the hallowed ground;
Climbed yon long slope; the sacred spot I found
Where all unsullied lies the winter snow,
Where all ungathered spring's pale violets blow,
And tracked from stone to stone the Saxon name
That marks the blood I need not blush to claim,
Blood such as warmed the Pilgrim sons of toil,
Who held from God the charter of the soil.
I come an alien to your hills and plains,
Yet feel your birthright tingling in my veins;
Mine are this changing prospect's sun and shade,
In full-blown summer's bridal pomp arrayed;
Mine these fair hillsides and the vales between;
Mine the sweet streams that lend their brightening green;
I breathed your air — the sunlit landscape smiled;
I touch your soil — it knows its children's child;

Throned in my heart your heritage is mine;
I claim it all by memory's right divine!
Waking, I dream. Before my vacant eyes
In long procession shadowy forms arise;
Far through the vista of the silent years
I see a venturous band; the pioneers,
Who let the sunlight through the forest's gloom,
Who bade the harvest wave, the garden bloom.
Hark! loud resounds the bare-armed settler's axe, —
See where the stealthy panther left his tracks!
As fierce, as stealthy creeps the skulking foe
With stone-tipped shaft and sinew-corded bow;
Soon shall he vanish from his ancient reign,
Leave his last cornfield to the coming train,
Quit the green margin of the wave he drinks,
For haunts that hide the wild-cat and the lynx.

But who the Youth his glistening axe that swings
To smite the pine that shows a hundred rings?
His features? — something in his look I find
That calls the semblance of my race to mind.
His name? — my own; and that which goes before
The same that once the loved disciple bore.
Young, brave, discreet, the father of a line
Whose voiceless lives have found a voice in mine;
Thinned by unnumbered currents though they be,
Thanks for the ruddy drops I claim from thee!

The seasons pass; the roses come and go;
Snows fall and melt; the waters freeze and flow;
The boys are men; the girls, grown tall and fair,
Have found their mates; a gravestone here and there
Tells where the fathers lie; the silvered hair
Of some bent patriarch yet recalls the time

A FAMILY RECORD

That saw his feet the northern hillside climb,
A pilgrim from the pilgrims far away,
The godly men, the dwellers by the bay.
On many a hearthstone burns the cheerful fire;
The schoolhouse porch, the heavenward pointing spire
Proclaim in letters every eye can read,
Knowledge and Faith, the new world's simple creed.
Hush ! 't is the Sabbath's silence-stricken morn:
No feet must wander through the tasselled corn;
No merry children laugh around the door,
No idle playthings strew the sanded floor;
The law of Moses lays its awful ban
On all that stirs; here comes the tithing-man !
    At last the solemn hour of worship calls;
Slowly they gather in the sacred walls;
Man in his strength and age with knotted staff,
And boyhood aching for its week-day laugh,
The toil-worn mother with the child she leads,
The maiden, lovely in her golden beads, —
The popish symbols round her neck she wears,
But on them counts her lovers, not her prayers, —
Those youths in homespun suits and ribboned queues,
Whose hearts are beating in the high-backed pews.
The pastor rises; looks along the seats
With searching eye; each wonted face he meets;
Asks heavenly guidance; finds the chapter's place
That tells some tale of Israel's stubborn race;
Gives out the sacred song; all voices join,
For no *quartette* extorts their scanty coin;
Then while both hands their black-gloved palms display,
Lifts his gray head, and murmurs, " Let us pray ! "
    And pray he does ! as one that never fears
To plead unanswered by the God that hears;
What if he dwells on many a fact as though
Some things Heaven knew not which it ought to know, —
Thanks God for all his favors past, and yet,
Tells Him there 's something He must not forget;
Such are the prayers his people love to hear, —
See how the Deacon slants his listening ear !
    What ! look once more ! Nay, surely there I trace
The hinted outlines of a well-known face !
Not those the lips for laughter to beguile,
Yet round their corners lurks an embryo smile,
The same on other lips my childhood knew
That scarce the Sabbath's mastery could subdue.
Him too my lineage gives me leave to claim, —
The good, grave man that bears the Psalmist's name.

    And still in ceaseless round the seasons passed;
Spring piped her carol; Autumn blew his blast;
Babes waxed to manhood; manhood shrunk to age;
Life's worn-out players tottered off the stage;
The few are many; boys have grown to men
Since Putnam dragged the wolf from Pomfret's den;
Our new-old Woodstock is a thriving town;
Brave are her children; faithful to the crown;
Her soldiers' steel the savage redskin knows;
Their blood has crimsoned his Canadian snows.
And now once more along the quiet vale
Rings the dread call that turns the mothers pale;
Full well they know the valorous heat that runs
In every pulse-beat of their loyal sons;
Who would not bleed in good King George's cause
When England's lion shows his teeth and claws ?
    With glittering firelocks on the village green
In proud array a martial band is seen;
You know what names those ancient rosters hold, —

Whose belts were buckled when the drum-
   beat rolled, —
But mark their Captain! tell us, who is
   he?
On his brown face that same old look I
   see!
Yes! from the homestead's still retreat he
   came,
Whose peaceful owner bore the Psalmist's
   name;
The same his own. Well, Israel's glorious
   king
Who struck the harp could also whirl the
   sling, —
Breathe in his song a penitential sigh
And smite the sons of Amalek hip and
   thigh:
These shared their task; one deaconed out
   the psalm,
One slashed the scalping hell-hounds of
   Montcalm;
The praying father's pious work is done,
Now sword in hand steps forth the fighting
   son.
On many a field he fought in wilds afar;
See on his swarthy cheek the bullet's scar!
There hangs a murderous tomahawk; be-
   neath,
Without its blade, a knife's embroidered
   sheath;
Save for the stroke his trusty weapon dealt
His scalp had dangled at their owner's
   belt;
But not for him such fate; he lived to see
The bloodier strife that made our nation
   free,
To serve with willing toil, with skilful
   hand,
The war-worn saviors of the bleeding land.
His wasting life to others' needs he gave, —
Sought rest in home and found it in the
   grave.
See where the stones life's brief memorials
   keep,
The tablet telling where he "fell on
   sleep,"—
Watched by a winged cherub's rayless
   eye, —
A scroll above that says we all must die, —
Those saddening lines beneath, the "Night-
   Thoughts" lent:
So stands the Soldier's, Surgeon's monu-
   ment.
Ah! at a glance my filial eye divines
The scholar son in those remembered lines.

The Scholar Son. His hand my foot-
   steps led.
No more the dim unreal past I tread.
O thou whose breathing form was once so
   dear,
Whose cheering voice was music to my ear,
Art thou not with me as my feet pursue
The village paths so well thy boyhood
   knew,
Along the tangled margin of the stream
Whose murmurs blended with thine in-
   fant dream,
Or climb the hill, or thread the wooded vale,
Or seek the wave where gleams yon dis-
   tant sail,
Or the old homestead's narrowed bounds
   explore,
Where sloped the roof that sheds the rains
   no more,
Where one last relic still remains to tell
Here stood thy home, — the memory-haunt-
   ed well,
Whose waters quench a deeper thirst than
   thine,
Changed at my lips to sacramental wine, —
Art thou not with me, as I fondly trace
The scanty records of thine honored race,
Call up the forms that earlier years have
   known,
And spell the legend of each slanted stone?
  With thoughts of thee my loving verse
   began,
Not for the critic's curious eye to scan,
Not for the many listeners, but the few
Whose fathers trod the paths my fathers
   knew;
Still in my heart thy loved remembrance
   burns;
Still to my lips thy cherished name returns;
Could I but feel thy gracious presence near
Amid the groves that once to thee were
   dear!
Could but my trembling lips with mortal
   speech
Thy listening ear for one brief moment
   reach!
How vain the dream! The pallid voyager's
   track
No sign betrays; he sends no message back.
No word from thee since evening's shadow
   fell
On thy cold forehead with my long fare-
   well, —
Now from the margin of the silent sea,
Take my last offering ere I cross to thee!

THE IRON GATE AND OTHER POEMS

1877-1881

THE IRON GATE

[Read at the Breakfast given in honor of Dr. Holmes's Seventieth Birthday by the publishers of the *Atlantic Monthly*, Boston, December 3, 1879.]

WHERE is this patriarch you are kindly greeting?
Not unfamiliar to my ear his name,
Nor yet unknown to many a joyous meeting
   In days long vanished, — is he still the same,

Or changed by years, forgotten and forgetting,
   Dull-eared, dim-sighted, slow of speech and thought,
Still o'er the sad, degenerate present fretting,
   Where all goes wrong, and nothing as it ought?

Old age, the graybeard! Well, indeed, I know him, —
   Shrunk, tottering, bent, of aches and ills the prey;
In sermon, story, fable, picture, poem,
   Oft have I met him from my earliest day:

In my old Æsop, toiling with his bundle, —
   His load of sticks, — politely asking Death,
Who comes when called for, — would he lug or trundle
   His fagot for him? — he was scant of breath.

And sad "Ecclesiastes, or the Preacher," —
   Has he not stamped the image on my soul,
In that last chapter, where the worn-out Teacher
   Sighs o'er the loosened cord, the broken bowl?

Yes, long, indeed, I've known him at a distance,
   And now my lifted door-latch shows him here;
I take his shrivelled hand without resistance,
   And find him smiling as his step draws near.

What though of gilded baubles he bereaves us,
   Dear to the heart of youth, to manhood's prime;
Think of the calm he brings, the wealth he leaves us,
   The hoarded spoils, the legacies of time!

Altars once flaming, still with incense fragrant,
   Passion's uneasy nurslings rocked asleep,
Hope's anchor faster, wild desire less vagrant,
   Life's flow less noisy, but the stream how deep!

Still as the silver cord gets worn and slender,
   Its lightened task-work tugs with lessening strain,
Hands get more helpful, voices, grown more tender,
   Soothe with their softened tones the slumberous brain.

Youth longs and manhood strives, but age remembers,
   Sits by the raked-up ashes of the past,

Spreads its thin hands above the whitening embers
 That warm its creeping life-blood till the last.

Dear to its heart is every loving token
 That comes unbidden ere its pulse grows cold,
Ere the last lingering ties of life are broken,
 Its labors ended and its story told.

Ah, while around us rosy youth rejoices,
 For us the sorrow-laden breezes sigh,
And through the chorus of its jocund voices
 Throbs the sharp note of misery's hopeless cry.

As on the gauzy wings of fancy flying
 From some far orb I track our watery sphere,
Home of the struggling, suffering, doubting, dying,
 The silvered globule seems a glistening tear.

But Nature lends her mirror of illusion
 To win from saddening scenes our age-dimmed eyes,
And misty day-dreams blend in sweet confusion
 The wintry landscape and the summer skies.

So when the iron portal shuts behind us,
 And life forgets us in its noise and whirl,
Visions that shunned the glaring noonday find us,
 And glimmering starlight shows the gates of pearl.

I come not here your morning hour to sadden,
 A limping pilgrim, leaning on his staff, —
I, who have never deemed it sin to gladden
 This vale of sorrows with a wholesome laugh.

If word of mine another's gloom has brightened,
 Through my dumb lips the heaven-sent message came;
If hand of mine another's task has lightened,
 It felt the guidance that it dares not claim.

But, O my gentle sisters, O my brothers,
 These thick-sown snow-flakes hint of toil's release;
These feebler pulses bid me leave to others
 The tasks once welcome; evening asks for peace.

Time claims his tribute; silence now is golden;
 Let me not vex the too long suffering lyre;
Though to your love untiring still beholden,
 The curfew tells me — cover up the fire.

And now with grateful smile and accents cheerful,
 And warmer heart than look or word can tell,
In simplest phrase — these traitorous eyes are tearful —
 Thanks, Brothers, Sisters, — Children, — and farewell!

VESTIGIA QUINQUE RETRORSUM

AN ACADEMIC POEM

1829-1879

Read at the Commencement Dinner of the Alumni of Harvard University, June 25, 1879.

While fond, sad memories all around us throng,
Silence were sweeter than the sweetest song;
Yet when the leaves are green and heaven is blue,
The choral tribute of the grove is due,
And when the lengthening nights have chilled the skies,
We fain would hear the song-bird ere he flies,
And greet with kindly welcome, even as now,
The lonely minstrel on his leafless bough.

This is our golden year, — its golden day;
Its bridal memories soon must pass away;
Soon shall its dying music cease to ring,
And every year must loose some silver string,

Till the last trembling chords no longer thrill, —
Hands all at rest and hearts forever still.

A few gray heads have joined the forming line;
We bear our summons, — "Class of 'Twenty-Nine!'"
Close on the foremost, and, alas, how few!
Are these "The Boys" our dear old Mother knew?
Sixty brave swimmers. Twenty — something more —
Have passed the stream and reached this frosty shore!

How near the banks these fifty years divide
When memory crosses with a single stride!
'T is the first year of stern "Old Hickory"'s rule
When our good Mother lets us out of school,
Half glad, half sorrowing, it must be confessed,
To leave her quiet lap, her bounteous breast,
Armed with our dainty, ribbon-tied degrees,
Pleased and yet pensive, exiles and A. B.'s.

Look back, O comrades, with your faded eyes,
And see the phantoms as I bid them rise.
Whose smile is that? Its pattern Nature gave,
A sunbeam dancing in a dimpled wave;
KIRKLAND alone such grace from Heaven could win,
His features radiant as the soul within;
That smile would let him through Saint Peter's gate
While sad-eyed martyrs had to stand and wait.
Here flits mercurial *Farrar;* standing there,
See mild, benignant, cautious, learned *Ware,*
And sturdy, patient, faithful, honest *Hedge,*
Whose grinding logic gave our wits their edge;
Ticknor, with honeyed voice and courtly grace;
And *Willard,* larynxed like a double bass;
And *Channing,* with his bland, superior look,
Cool as a moonbeam on a frozen brook,
While the pale student, shivering in his shoes,

Sees from his theme the turgid rhetoric ooze;
And the born soldier, fate decreed to wreak
His martial manhood on a class in Greek,
Popkin! How that explosive name recalls
The grand old Busby of our ancient halls!
Such faces looked from Skippon's grim platoons,
Such figures rode with Ireton's stout dragoons;
He gave his strength to learning's gentle charms,
But every accent sounded "Shoulder arms!"

Names, — empty names! Save only here and there
Some white-haired listener, dozing in his chair,
Starts at the sound he often used to hear,
And upward slants his Sunday-sermon ear.

And we — our blooming manhood we regain;
Smiling we join the long Commencement train,
One point first battled in discussion hot, —
Shall we wear gowns? and settled: *We will not.*
How strange the scene, — that noisy boy-debate
Where embryo-speakers learn to rule the State!
This broad-browed youth, sedate and sober-eyed,
Shall wear the ermined robe at Taney's side;
And he, the stripling, smooth of face and slight,
Whose slender form scarce intercepts the light,
Shall rule the Bench where Parsons gave the law,
And sphinx-like sat uncouth, majestic Shaw!
Ah, many a star has shed its fatal ray
On names we loved — our brothers — where are they?
Nor these alone; our hearts in silence claim
Names not less dear, unsyllabled by fame.

How brief the space! and yet it sweeps us back
Far, far along our new-born history's track!

Five strides like this; — the sachem rules the land;
The Indian wigwams cluster where we stand.

The second. Lo! a scene of deadly strife —
A nation struggling into infant life;
Not yet the fatal game at Yorktown won
Where failing Empire fired its sunset gun.
LANGDON sits restless in the ancient chair, —
Harvard's grave Head, — these echoes heard his prayer
When from yon mansion, dear to memory still,
The banded yeomen marched for Bunker's Hill.
Count on the grave triennial's thick-starred roll
What names were numbered on the lengthening scroll, —
Not unfamiliar in our ears they ring, —
Winthrop, Hale, Eliot, Everett, Dexter, Tyng.

Another stride. Once more at 'twenty-nine, —
GOD SAVE KING GEORGE, the Second of his line!
And is *Sir Isaac* living? Nay, not so, —
He followed *Flamsteed* two short years ago, —
And what about the little hump-backed man
Who pleased the bygone days of good Queen Anne?
What, *Pope?* another book he's just put out, —
"The Dunciad," — witty, but profane, no doubt.
Where's *Cotton Mather?* he was always here.
And so he would be, but he died last year.
Who is this preacher our Northampton claims,
Whose rhetoric blazes with sulphureous flames
And torches stolen from Tartarean mines?
Edwards, the salamander of divines.
A deep, strong nature, pure and undefiled;
Faith, firm as his who stabbed his sleeping child;
Alas for him who blindly strays apart,
And seeking God has lost his human heart!

Fall where they might, no flying cinders caught
These sober halls where WADSWORTH ruled and taught.

One footstep more; the fourth receding stride
Leaves the round century on the nearer side.
GOD SAVE KING CHARLES! God knows that pleasant knave
His grace will find it hard enough to save.
Ten years and more, and now the Plague, the Fire,
Talk of all tongues, at last begin to tire;
One fear prevails, all other frights forgot, —
White lips are whispering, — hark! *The Popish Plot!*
Happy New England, from such troubles free
In health and peace beyond the stormy sea!
No Romish daggers threat her children's throats,
No gibbering nightmare mutters "*Titus Oates;*"
Philip is slain, the Quaker graves are green,
Not yet the witch has entered on the scene;
Happy our Harvard; pleased her graduates four;
URIAN OAKES the name their parchments bore.

Two centuries past, our hurried feet arrive
At the last footprint of the scanty five;
Take the fifth stride; our wandering eyes explore
A tangled forest on a trackless shore;
Here, where we stand, the savage sorcerer howls,
The wild cat snarls, the stealthy gray wolf prowls,
The slouching bear, perchance the trampling moose
Starts the brown squaw and scares her red pappoose;
At every step the lurking foe is near;
His Demons reign; God has no temple here!

Lift up your eyes! behold these pictured walls;
Look where the flood of western glory falls

Through the great sunflower disk of blaz-
 ing panes
In ruby, saffron, azure, emerald stains;
With reverent step the marble pavement
 tread
Where our proud Mother's martyr-roll is
 read;
See the great halls that cluster, gathering
 round
This lofty shrine with holiest memories
 crowned;
See the fair Matron in her summer bower,
Fresh as a rose in bright perennial flower;
Read on her standard, always in the van,
"TRUTH," — the one word that makes a
 slave a man;
Think whose the hands that fed her altar-
 fires,
Then count the debt we owe our scholar-
 sires!

Brothers, farewell! the fast declining ray
Fades to the twilight of our golden day;
Some lesson yet our wearied brains may
 learn,
Some leaves, perhaps, in life's thin volume
 turn.
How few they seem as in our waning age
We count them backwards to the title-
 page!
Oh let us trust with holy men of old
Not all the story here begun is told;
So the tired spirit, waiting to be freed,
On life's last leaf with tranquil eye shall
 read
By the pale glimmer of the torch reversed,
Not *Finis*, but *The End of Volume First!*

MY AVIARY

THROUGH my north window, in the wintry
 weather, —
My airy oriel on the river shore, —
I watch the sea-fowl as they flock together
Where late the boatman flashed his
 dripping oar.

The gull, high floating, like a sloop un-
 laden,
Lets the loose water waft him as it will;
The duck, round-breasted as a rustic
 maiden,
Paddles and plunges, busy, busy still.

I see the solemn gulls in council sitting
On some broad ice-floe pondering long
 and late,
While overhead the home-bound ducks are
 flitting,
And leave the tardy conclave in debate,

Those weighty questions in their breasts re-
 volving
Whose deeper meaning science never
 learns,
Till at some reverend elder's look dis-
 solving,
The speechless senate silently adjourns.

But when along the waves the shrill north-
 easter
Shrieks through the laboring coaster's
 shrouds "Beware!"
The pale bird, kindling like a Christmas
 feaster
When some wild chorus shakes the vinous
 air,

Flaps from the leaden wave in fierce re-
 joicing,
Feels heaven's dumb lightning thrill his
 torpid nerves,
Now on the blast his whistling plumage
 poising,
Now wheeling, whirling in fantastic
 curves.

Such is our gull; a gentleman of leisure,
Less fleshed than feathered; bagged
 you'll find him such;
His virtue silence; his employment pleas-
 ure;
Not bad to look at, and not good for
 much.

What of our duck? He has some high-
 bred cousins, —
His Grace the Canvas-back, My Lord
 the Brant, —
Anas and *Anser*, — both served up by
 dozens,
At Boston's *Rocher*, half-way to Na-
 hant.

As for himself, he seems alert and thriv-
 ing, —
Grubs up a living somehow — what, who
 knows?

Crabs? mussels? weeds? — Look quick!
　there's one just diving!
Flop! Splash! his white breast glistens
　— down he goes!

And while he's under — just about a min-
　ute —
I take advantage of the fact to say
His fishy carcase has no virtue in it
The gunning idiot's worthless hire to pay.

He knows you! "sportsmen" from subur-
　ban alleys,
Stretched under seaweed in the treacher-
　ous punt;
Knows every lazy, shiftless lout that sallies
　Forth to waste powder — as *he* says, to
　"hunt."

I watch you with a patient satisfaction,
　Well pleased to discount your predes-
　tined luck;
The float that figures in your sly transac-
　tion
　Will carry back a goose, but not a duck.

Shrewd is our bird; not easy to outwit him!
　Sharp is the outlook of those pin-head
　eyes;
Still, he is mortal and a shot may hit him,
　One cannot always miss him if he tries.

Look! there's a young one, dreaming not
　of danger;
　Sees a flat log come floating down the
　stream;
Stares undismayed upon the harmless
　stranger;
　Ah! were all strangers harmless as they
　seem!

Habet! a leaden shower his breast has shat-
　tered;
　Vainly he flutters, not again to rise;
His soft white plumes along the waves are
　scattered;
　Helpless the wing that braved the tem-
　pest lies.

He sees his comrades high above him flying
　To seek their nests among the island
　reeds;
Strong is their flight; all lonely he is lying
　Washed by the crimsoned water as he
　bleeds.

O Thou who carest for the falling spar-
　row,
　Canst Thou the sinless sufferer's pang
　forget?
Or is thy dread account-book's page so
　narrow
　Its one long column scores thy creatures'
　debt?

Poor gentle guest, by nature kindly
　cherished,
　A world grows dark with thee in blinding
　death;
One little gasp — thy universe has per-
　ished,
　Wrecked by the idle thief who stole thy
　breath!

Is this the whole sad story of creation,
　Lived by its breathing myriads o'er and
　o'er, —
One glimpse of day, then black annihila-
　tion, —
　A sunlit passage to a sunless shore?

Give back our faith, ye mystery-solving
　lynxes!
　Robe us once more in heaven-aspiring
　creeds!
Happier was dreaming Egypt with her
　sphinxes,
　The stony convent with its cross and
　beads!

How often gazing where a bird reposes,
　Rocked on the wavelets, drifting with
　the tide,
I lose myself in strange metempsychosis
　And float a sea-fowl at a sea-fowl's side;

From rain, hail, snow in feathery mantle
　muffled,
　Clear-eyed, strong-limbed, with keenest
　sense to hear
My mate soft murmuring, who, with plumes
　unruffled,
　Where'er I wander still is nestling near;

The great blue hollow like a garment o'er
　me;
　Space all unmeasured, unrecorded time;
While seen with inward eye moves on be-
　fore me
　Thought's pictured train in wordless
　pantomime.

A voice recalls me. — From my window turning
I find myself a plumeless biped still;
No beak, no claws, no sign of wings discerning, —
In fact with nothing bird-like but my quill.

ON THE THRESHOLD

INTRODUCTION TO A COLLECTION OF POEMS BY DIFFERENT AUTHORS

An usher standing at the door
I show my white rosette;
A smile of welcome, nothing more,
Will pay my trifling debt;
Why should I bid you idly wait
Like lovers at the swinging gate?

Can I forget the wedding guest?
The veteran of the sea?
In vain the listener smites his breast, —
"There was a ship," cries he!
Poor fasting victim, stunned and pale.
He needs must listen to the tale.

He sees the gilded throng within,
The sparkling goblets gleam,
The music and the merry din
Through every window stream,
But there he shivers in the cold
Till all the crazy dream is told.

Not mine the graybeard's glittering eye
That held his captive still
To hold my silent prisoners by
And let me have my will;
Nay, *I* were like the three-years' child,
To think you could be so beguiled!

My verse is but the curtain's fold
That hides the painted scene,
The mist by morning's ray unrolled
That veils the meadow's green,
The cloud that needs must drift away
To show the rose of opening day.

See, from the tinkling rill you hear
In hollowed palm I bring
These scanty drops, but ah, how near
The founts that heavenward spring!
Thus, open wide the gates are thrown,
And founts and flowers are all your own!

TO GEORGE PEABODY

DANVERS, 1866

BANKRUPT! our pockets inside out!
Empty of words to speak his praises!
Worcester and Webster up the spout!
Dead broke of laudatory phrases!
Yet why with flowery speeches tease,
With vain superlatives distress him?
Has language better words than these?
THE FRIEND OF ALL HIS RACE, GOD BLESS HIM!

A simple prayer — but words more sweet
By human lips were never uttered,
Since Adam left the country seat
Where angel wings around him fluttered.
The old look on with tear-dimmed eyes,
The children cluster to caress him,
And every voice unbidden cries,
THE FRIEND OF ALL HIS RACE, GOD BLESS HIM!

AT THE PAPYRUS CLUB

A LOVELY show for eyes to see
I looked upon this morning, —
A bright-hued, feathered company
Of nature's own adorning;
But ah! those minstrels would not sing
A listening ear while I lent, —
The lark sat still and preened his wing,
The nightingale was silent;
I longed for what they gave me not —
Their warblings sweet and fluty,
But grateful still for all I got
I thanked them for their beauty.

A fairer vision meets my view
Of Claras, Margarets, Marys,
In silken robes of varied hue,
Like bluebirds and canaries;
The roses blush, the jewels gleam,
The silks and satins glisten,
The black eyes flash, the blue eyes beam,
We look — and then we listen:
Behold the flock we cage to-night —
Was ever such a capture?
To see them is a pure delight;
To hear them — ah! what rapture!

Methinks I hear Delilah's laugh
  At Samson bound in fetters;
"*We* captured!" shrieks each lovelier half,
  "Men think themselves *our* betters!
We push the bolt, we turn the key
  On warriors, poets, sages,
Too happy, all of them, to be
  Locked in our golden cages!"

Beware! the boy with bandaged eyes
  Has flung away his blinder;
He 's lost his mother — so he cries —
  And here he knows he 'll find her:
The rogue! 't is but a new device, —
  Look out for flying arrows
Whene'er the birds of Paradise
  Are perched amid the sparrows!

FOR WHITTIER'S SEVENTIETH BIRTHDAY

DECEMBER 17, 1877

I BELIEVE that the copies of verses I 've spun,
Like Scheherezade's tales, are a thousand and one;
You remember the story, — those mornings in bed, —
'T was the turn of a copper, — a tale or a head.

A doom like Scheherezade's falls upon me
In a mandate as stern as the Sultan's decree:
I 'm a florist in verse, and what *would* people say
If I came to a banquet without my bouquet?

It is trying, no doubt, when the company knows
Just the look and the smell of each lily and rose,
The green of each leaf in the sprigs that I bring,
And the shape of the bunch and the knot of the string.

Yes, — "the style is the man," and the nib of one's pen
Makes the same mark at twenty, and threescore and ten;

It is so in all matters, if truth may be told;
Let one look at the cast he can tell you the mould.

How we all know each other! no use in disguise;
Through the holes in the mask comes the flash of the eyes;
We can tell by his — somewhat — each one of our tribe,
As we know the old hat which we cannot describe.

Though in Hebrew, in Sanscrit, in Choctaw you write,
Sweet singer who gave us the Voices of Night,
Though in buskin or slipper your song may be shod,
Or the velvety verse that Evangeline trod,

We shall say, "You can't cheat us, — we know it is you,"
There is one voice like that, but there cannot be two,
Maëstro, whose chant like the dulcimer rings:
And the woods will be hushed while the nightingale sings.

And he, so serene, so majestic, so true,
Whose temple hypæthral the planets shine through,
Let us catch but five words from that mystical pen,
We should know our one sage from all children of men.

And he whose bright image no distance can dim,
Through a hundred disguises we can't mistake him,
Whose play is all earnest, whose wit is the edge
(With a beetle behind) of a sham-splitting wedge.

Do you know whom we send you, Hidalgos of Spain?
Do you know your old friends when you see them again?
Hosea was Sancho! you Dons of Madrid,
But Sancho that wielded the lance of the Cid!

And the wood-thrush of Essex, — you know
   whom I mean,
Whose song echoes round us while he sits
   unseen,
Whose heart-throbs of verse through our
   memories thrill
Like a breath from the wood, like a breeze
   from the hill,

So fervid, so simple, so loving, so pure,
We hear but one strain and our verdict is
   sure, —
Thee cannot elude us, — no further we
   search, —
'T is Holy George Herbert cut loose from
   his church !

We think it the voice of a seraph that
   sings, —
Alas ! we remember that angels have
   wings, —
What story is this of the day of his birth ?
Let him live to a hundred ! we want him
   on earth !

One life has been paid him (in gold) by
   the sun ;
One account has been squared and another
   begun;
But he never will die if he lingers be-
   low
Till we've paid him in love half the bal-
   ance we owe !

TWO SONNETS: HARVARD

At the meeting of the New York Harvard
Club, February 21, 1878.

"CHRISTO ET ECCLESIÆ." 1700

To GOD'S ANOINTED AND HIS CHOSEN
   FLOCK :
So ran the phrase the black-robed con-
   clave chose
To guard the sacred cloisters that arose
Like David's altar on Moriah's rock.
Unshaken still those ancient arches mock
   The ram's-horn summons of the windy
      foes
   Who stand like Joshua's army while it
      blows
   And wait to see them toppling with the
      shock.

Christ and the Church. *Their* church,
   whose narrow door
Shut out the many, who if over bold
Like hunted wolves were driven from
   the fold,
Bruised with the flails these godly zealots
   bore,
Mindful that Israel's altar stood of old
Where echoed once Araunah's threshing-
   floor.

1643 "VERITAS." 1878

TRUTH: So the frontlet's older legend ran,
   On the brief record's opening page dis-
      played;
   Not yet those clear-eyed scholars were
      afraid
Lest the fair fruit that wrought the woe of
   man
By far Euphrates — where our sire began
   His search for truth, and, seeking, was
      betrayed —
   Might work new treason in their forest
      shade,
Doubling the curse that brought life's
   shortened span.

Nurse of the future, daughter of the past,
   That stern phylactery best becomes thee
      now;
   Lift to the morning star thy marble
      brow !
Cast thy brave truth on every warring
   blast !
   Stretch thy white hand to that forbidden
      bough,
And let thine earliest symbol be thy last !

THE COMING ERA

THEY tell us that the Muse is soon to fly
   hence,
   Leaving the bowers of song that once
      were dear,
Her robes bequeathing to her sister, Science,
   The groves of Pindus for the axe to
      clear.

Optics will claim the wandering eye of
   fancy,
Physics will grasp imagination's wings,
Plain fact exorcise fiction's necromancy,
   The workshop hammer where the min-
      strel sings.

No more with laughter at Thalia's frolics
  Our eyes shall twinkle till the tears run down,
But in her place the lecturer on hydraulics
  Spout forth his watery science to the town.

No more our foolish passions and affections
  The tragic Muse with mimic grief shall try,
But, nobler far, a course of vivisections
  Teach what it costs a tortured brute to die.

The unearthed monad, long in buried rocks hid,
  Shall tell the secret whence our being came;
The chemist show us death is life's black oxide,
  Left when the breath no longer fans its flame.

Instead of crack-brained poets in their attics
  Filling thin volumes with their flowery talk,
There shall be books of wholesome mathematics;
  The tutor with his blackboard and his chalk.

No longer bards with madrigal and sonnet
  Shall woo to moonlight walks the ribboned sex,
But side by side the beaver and the bonnet
  Stroll, calmly pondering on some problem's x.

The sober bliss of serious calculation
  Shall mock the trivial joys that fancy drew,
And, oh, the rapture of a solved equation, —
  One selfsame answer on the lips of two !

So speak in solemn tones our youthful sages,
  Patient, severe, laborious, slow, exact,
As o'er creation's protoplasmic pages
  They browse and munch the thistle crops of fact.

And yet we 've sometimes found it rather pleasant
  To dream again the scenes that Shakespeare drew, —

To walk the hill-side with the Scottish peasant
  Among the daisies wet with morning's dew;

To leave awhile the daylight of the real,
  Led by the guidance of the master's hand,
For the strange radiance of the far ideal, —
  "The light that never was on sea or land."

Well, Time alone can lift the future's curtain, —
  Science may teach our children all she knows,
But Love will kindle fresh young hearts, 't is certain,
  And June will not forget her blushing rose.

And so, in spite of all that Time is bringing, —
  Treasures of truth and miracles of art,
Beauty and Love will keep the poet singing,
  And song still live, the science of the heart.

IN RESPONSE

Breakfast at the Century Club, New York, May, 1879.

SUCH kindness ! the scowl of a cynic would soften,
  His pulse beat its way to some eloquent word,
Alas ! my poor accents have echoed too often,
  Like that Pinafore music you 've some of you heard.

Do you know me, dear strangers — the hundredth time comer
  At banquets and feasts since the days of my Spring ?
Ah ! would I could borrow one rose of my Summer,
  But this is a leaf of my Autumn I bring.

I look at your faces, — I 'm sure there are some from
  The three-breasted mother I count as my own;

You think you remember the place you have come from,
But how it has changed in the years that have flown!

Unaltered, 't is true, is the hall we call "Funnel,"
Still fights the "Old South" in the battle for life,
But we 've opened our door to the West through the tunnel,
And we 've cut off Fort Hill with our Amazon knife.

You should see the new Westminster Boston has builded, —
Its mansions, its spires, its museums of arts, —
You should see the great dome we have gorgeously gilded, —
'T is the light of our eyes, 't is the joy of our hearts.

When first in his path a young asteroid found it,
As he sailed through the skies with the stars in his wake,
He thought 't was the sun, and kept circling around it
Till Edison signalled, "You 've made a mistake."

We are proud of our city, — her fast-growing figure,
The warp and the woof of her brain and her hands, —
But we 're proudest of all that her heart has grown bigger,
And warms with fresh blood as her girdle expands.

One lesson the rubric of conflict has taught her:
Though parted awhile by war's earth-rending shock,
The lines that divide us are written in water,
The love that unites us cut deep in the rock.

As well might the Judas of treason endeavor
To write his black name on the disk of the sun
As try the bright star-wreath that binds us to sever

And blot the fair legend of "Many in One."

We love YOU, tall sister, the stately, the splendid, —
The banner of empire floats high on your towers,
Yet ever in welcome your arms are extended, —
We share in your splendors, your glory is ours.

Yes, Queen of the Continent! All of us own thee, —
The gold-freighted argosies flock at thy call,
The naiads, the sea-nymphs have met to enthrone thee,
But the Broadway of one is the Highway of all!

I thank you. Three words that can hardly be mended,
Though phrases on phrases their eloquence pile,
If you hear the heart's throb with their eloquence blended,
And read all they mean in a sunshiny smile.

FOR THE MOORE CENTENNIAL CELEBRATION

MAY 28, 1879

I

ENCHANTER of Erin, whose magic has bound us,
Thy wand for one moment we fondly would claim,
Entranced while it summons the phantoms around us
That blush into life at the sound of thy name.

The tell-tales of memory wake from their slumbers, —
I hear the old song with its tender refrain, —
What passion lies hid in those honey-voiced numbers!
What perfume of youth in each exquisite strain!

The home of my childhood comes back as
    a vision, —
  Hark! Hark! A soft chord from its
    song-haunted room, —
'T is a morning of May, when the air is
    Elysian, —
  The syringa in bud and the lilac in
    bloom, —

We are clustered around the "Clementi"
    piano, —
  There were six of us then, — there are
    two of us now, —
She is singing — the girl with the silver
    soprano —
  How "The Lord of the Valley" was false
    to his vow;

"Let Erin remember" the echoes are
    calling;
  Through "The Vale of Avoca" the
    waters are rolled;
"The Exile" laments while the night-dews
    are falling;
  "The Morning of Life" dawns again as
    of old.

But ah! those warm love-songs of fresh
    adolescence!
  Around us such raptures celestial they
    flung
That it seemed as if Paradise breathed its
    quintessence
  Through the seraph-toned lips of the
    maiden that sung!

Long hushed are the chords that my boy-
    hood enchanted
  As when the smooth wave by the angel
    was stirred,
Yet still with their music is memory
    haunted,
  And oft in my dreams are their melodies
    heard.

I feel like the priest to his altar return-
    ing, —
  The crowd that was kneeling no longer
    is there,
The flame has died down, but the brands
    are still burning,
  And sandal and cinnamon sweeten the
    air.

II

The veil for her bridal young Summer is
    weaving
  In her azure-domed hall with its tapes-
    tried floor,
And Spring the last tear-drop of May-dew
    is leaving
  On the daisy of Burns and the shamrock
    of Moore.

How like, how unlike, as we view them to-
    gether,
  The song of the minstrels whose record
    we scan, —
One fresh as the breeze blowing over the
    heather,
  One sweet as the breath from an oda-
    lisque's fan!

Ah, passion can glow mid a palace's splendor;
  The cage does not alter the song of the
    bird;
And the curtain of silk has known whispers
    as tender
  As ever the blossoming hawthorn has
    heard.

No fear lest the step of the soft-slippered
    Graces
  Should fright the young Loves from their
    warm little nest,
For the heart of a queen, under jewels and
    laces,
  Beats time with the pulse in the peasant
    girl's breast!

Thrice welcome each gift of kind Nature's
    bestowing!
  Her fountain heeds little the goblet we
    hold;
Alike, when its musical waters are flowing,
  The shell from the seaside, the chalice
    of gold.

The twins of the lyre to her voices had
    listened;
  Both laid their best gifts upon Liberty's
    shrine;
For Coila's loved minstrel the holly-wreath
    glistened;
  For Erin's the rose and the myrtle en-
    twine.

And while the fresh blossoms of summer are braided
For the sea-girdled, stream-silvered, lake-jewelled isle,
While her mantle of verdure is woven unfaded,
While Shannon and Liffey shall dimple and smile,

The land where the staff of Saint Patrick was planted,
Where the shamrock grows green from the cliffs to the shore,
The land of fair maidens and heroes undaunted,
Shall wreathe her bright harp with the garlands of Moore!

TO JAMES FREEMAN CLARKE

APRIL 4, 1880

I BRING the simplest pledge of love,
Friend of my earlier days;
Mine is the hand without the glove,
The heart-beat, not the phrase.

How few still breathe this mortal air
We called by school-boy names!
You still, whatever robe you wear,
To me are always James.

That name the kind apostle bore
Who shames the sullen creeds,
Not trusting less, but loving more,
And showing faith by deeds.

What blending thoughts our memories share!
What visions yours and mine
Of May-days in whose morning air
The dews were golden wine,

Of vistas bright with opening day,
Whose all-awakening sun
Showed in life's landscape, far away,
The summits to be won!

The heights are gained. Ah, say not so
For him who smiles at time,
Leaves his tired comrades down below,
And only lives to climb!

His labors, — will they ever cease, —
With hand and tongue and pen?
Shall wearied Nature ask release
At threescore years and ten?

Our strength the clustered seasons tax, —
For him new life they mean;
Like rods around the lictor's axe
They keep him bright and keen.

The wise, the brave, the strong, we know, —
We mark them here or there,
But he, — we roll our eyes, and lo!
We find him everywhere!

With truth's bold cohorts, or alone,
He strides through error's field;
His lance is ever manhood's own,
His breast is woman's shield.

Count not his years while earth has need
Of souls that Heaven inflames
With sacred zeal to save, to lead, —
Long live our dear Saint James!

WELCOME TO THE CHICAGO COMMERCIAL CLUB

JANUARY 14, 1880

CHICAGO sounds rough to the maker of verse;
One comfort we have — Cincinnati sounds worse;
If we only were licensed to say Chicagó!
But Worcester and Webster won't let us, you know.

No matter, we songsters must sing as we can;
We can make some nice couplets with Lake Michigan,
And what more resembles a nightingale's voice,
Than the oily trisyllable, sweet Illinois?

Your waters are fresh, while our harbor is salt,
But we know you can't help it — it is n't your fault;
Our city is old and your city is new,
But the railroad men tell us we're greener than you.

You have seen our gilt dome, and no doubt
 you 've been told
That the orbs of the universe round it are
 rolled;
But I 'll own it to you, and I ought to know
 best,
That this is n't quite true of all stars of
 the West.

You 'll go to Mount Auburn, — we 'll show
 you the track, —
And can stay there, — unless you prefer to
 come back;
And Bunker's tall shaft you can climb if
 you will,
But you 'll puff like a paragraph praising
 a pill.

You must see — but you *have* seen — our
 old Faneuil Hall,
Our churches, our school-rooms, our sam-
 ple-rooms, all;
And, perhaps, though the idiots must have
 their jokes,
You have found our good people much like
 other folks.

There are cities by rivers, by lakes, and by
 seas,
Each as full of itself as a cheese-mite of
 cheese;
And a city will brag as a game-cock will
 crow:
Don't your cockerels at home — just a
 little, you know ?

But we 'll crow for you now — here 's a
 health to the boys,
Men, maidens, and matrons of fair Illi-
 nois,
And the rainbow of friendship that arches
 its span
From the green of the sea to the blue
 Michigan !

AMERICAN ACADEMY CENTEN-
NIAL CELEBRATION

MAY 26, 1880

SIRE, son, and grandson; so the century
 glides;
 Three lives, three strides, three foot-
 prints in the sand;
Silent as midnight's falling meteor slides
 Into the stillness of the far-off land;
 How dim the space its little arc has
 spanned !

See on this opening page the names re-
 nowned
 Tombed in these records on our dusty
 shelves,
Scarce on the scroll of living memory
 found,
 Save where the wan-eyed antiquarian
 delves;
 Shadows they seem; ah, what are we
 ourselves ?

Pale ghosts of Bowdoin, Winthrop, Wil-
 lard, West,
 Sages of busy brain and wrinkled brow,
Searchers of Nature's secrets unconfessed,
 Asking of all things Whence and Why
 and How —
 What problems meet your larger vision
 now ?

Has Gannett tracked the wild Aurora's
 path ?
 Has Bowdoin found his all-surrounding
 sphere ?
What question puzzles ciphering Philo-
 math ?
 Could Williams make the hidden causes
 clear
 Of the Dark Day that filled the land
 with fear ?

Dear ancient school-boys ! Nature taught
 to them
 The simple lessons of the star and
 flower,
Showed them strange sights; how on a
 single stem, —
 Admire the marvels of Creative
 Power ! —
 Twin apples grew, one sweet, the other
 sour;

How from the hill-top where our eyes be-
 hold
 In even ranks the plumed and bannered
 maize
Range its long columns, in the days of old
 The live volcano shot its angry blaze, —
 Dead since the showers of Noah's watery
 days;

How, when the lightning split the mighty
    rock,
  The spreading fury of the shaft was
    spent !
How the young scion joined the alien stock,
  And when and where the homeless swal-
    lows went
To pass the winter of their discontent.

Scant were the gleanings in those years of
    dearth;
  No Cuvier yet had clothed the fossil
    bones
That slumbered, waiting for their second
    birth;
  No Lyell read the legend of the stones;
Science still pointed to her empty
    thrones.

Dreaming of orbs to eyes of earth un-
    known,
  Herschel looked heavenwards in the
    starlight pale;
Lost in those awful depths he trod alone,
  Laplace stood mute before the lifted
    veil;
While home-bred Humboldt trimmed
    his toy ship's sail.

No mortal feet these loftier heights had
    gained
  Whence the wide realms of Nature we
    descry;
In vain their eyes our longing fathers
    strained
  To scan with wondering gaze the sum-
    mits high
That far beneath their children's foot-
    paths lie.

Smile at their first small ventures as we
    may,
  The school-boy's copy shapes the schol-
    ar's hand,
Their grateful memory fills our hearts to-
    day;
  Brave, hopeful, wise, this bower of peace
    they planned,
While war's dread ploughshare scarred
    the suffering land.

Child of our children's children yet un-
    born,
  When on this yellow page you turn your
    eyes,

Where the brief record of this May-day
    morn
  In phrase antique and faded letters lies,
How vague, how pale our flitting ghosts
    will rise !

Yet in our veins the blood ran warm and
    red,
  For us the fields were green, the skies
    were blue,
Though from our dust the spirit long has
    fled,
  We lived, we loved, we toiled, we
    dreamed like you,
Smiled at our sires and thought how
    much we knew.

Oh might our spirits for one hour return,
  When the next century rounds its hun-
    dredth ring,
All the strange secrets it shall teach to
    learn,
  To hear the larger truths its years shall
    bring,
Its wiser sages talk, its sweeter minstrels
    sing !

THE SCHOOL-BOY

Read at the Centennial Celebration of the foundation of Phillips Academy, Andover.

1778-1878

THESE hallowed precincts, long to mem-
    ory dear,
Smile with fresh welcome as our feet draw
    near;
With softer gales the opening leaves are
    fanned,
With fairer hues the kindling flowers ex-
    pand,
The rose-bush reddens with the blush of
    June,
The groves are vocal with their minstrels'
    tune,
The mighty elm, beneath whose arching
    shade
The wandering children of the forest
    strayed,
Greets the bright morning in its bridal
    dress,
And spreads its arms the gladsome dawn
    to bless.

Is it an idle dream that nature shares
Our joys, our griefs, our pastimes, and our
    cares ?
Is there no summons when, at morning's
    call,
The sable vestments of the darkness fall ?
Does not meek evening's low-voiced *Ave*
    blend
With the soft vesper as its notes ascend ?
Is there no whisper in the perfumed air
When the sweet bosom of the rose is bare ?
Does not the sunshine call us to rejoice ?
Is there no meaning in the storm-cloud's
    voice ?
No silent message when from midnight
    skies
Heaven looks upon us with its myriad eyes ?

Or shift the mirror; say our dreams
    diffuse
O'er life's pale landscape their celestial
    hues,
Lend heaven the rainbow it has never
    known,
And robe the earth in glories not its own,
Sing their own music in the summer breeze,
With fresher foliage clothe the stately
    trees,
Stain the June blossoms with a livelier dye
And spread a bluer azure on the sky, —
Blest be the power that works its lawless
    will
And finds the weediest patch an Eden
    still;
No walls so fair as those our fancies build, —
No views so bright as those our visions
    gild !

So ran my lines, as pen and paper met,
The truant goose-quill travelling like Planchette;
Too ready servant, whose deceitful ways
Full many a slipshod line, alas ! betrays;
Hence of the rhyming thousand not a few
Have builded worse — a great deal — than
    they knew.

What need of idle fancy to adorn
Our mother's birthplace on her birthday
    morn ?
Hers are the blossoms of eternal spring,
From these green boughs her new-fledged
    birds take wing,
These echoes hear their earliest carols sung,
In this old nest the brood is ever young.

If some tired wanderer, resting from his
    flight,
Amid the gay young choristers alight,
These gather round him, mark his faded
    plumes
That faintly still the far-off grove perfumes,
And listen, wondering if some feeble note
Yet lingers, quavering in his weary throat:—
I, whose fresh voice yon red-faced temple
    knew,
What tune is left me, fit to sing to you ?
Ask not the grandeurs of a labored song,
But let my easy couplets slide along;
Much could I tell you that you know too
    well;
Much I remember, but I will not tell;
Age brings experience; graybeards oft are
    wise,
But oh ! how sharp a youngster's ears and
    eyes !

My cheek was bare of adolescent down
When first I sought the academic town;
Slow rolls the coach along the dusty road,
Big with its filial and parental load;
The frequent hills, the lonely woods are
    past,
The school-boy's chosen home is reached
    at last.
I see it now, the same unchanging spot,
The swinging gate, the little garden plot,
The narrow yard, the rock that made its
    floor,
The flat, pale house, the knocker-garnished
    door,
The small, trim parlor, neat, decorous, chill,
The strange, new faces, kind, but grave
    and still;
Two, creased with age, — or what I then
    called age, —
Life's volume open at its fiftieth page;
One, a shy maiden's, pallid, placid, sweet
As the first snowdrop, which the sunbeams
    greet;
One, the last nursling's; slight she was,
    and fair,
Her smooth white forehead warmed with
    auburn hair;
Last came the virgin Hymen long had
    spared,
Whose daily cares the grateful household
    shared,
Strong, patient, humble; her substantial
    frame

Stretched the chaste draperies I forbear to name.
Brave, but with effort, had the school-boy come
To the cold comfort of a stranger's home;
How like a dagger to my sinking heart
Came the dry summons, "It is time to part;
Good-by!" "Goo—ood-by!" one fond maternal kiss. . . .
Homesick as death! Was ever pang like this? . . .
Too young as yet with willing feet to stray
From the tame fireside, glad to get away, —
Too old to let my watery grief appear, —
And what so bitter as a swallowed tear!
One figure still my vagrant thoughts pursue;
First boy to greet me, Ariel, where are you?
Imp of all mischief, heaven alone knows how
You learned it all, — are you an angel now,
Or tottering gently down the slope of years,
Your face grown sober in the vale of tears?
Forgive my freedom if you are breathing still;
If in a happier world, I know you will.
You were a school-boy — what beneath the sun
So like a monkey? I was also one.
Strange, sure enough, to see what curious shoots
The nursery raises from the study's roots!
In those old days the very, very good
Took up more room — a little — than they should;
Something too much one's eyes encountered then
Of serious youth and funeral-visaged men;
The solemn elders saw life's mournful half, —
Heaven sent this boy, whose mission was to laugh,
Drollest of buffos, Nature's odd protest,
A catbird squealing in a blackbird's nest.
Kind, faithful Nature! While the sour-eyed Scot —
Her cheerful smiles forbidden or forgot —
Talks only of his preacher and his kirk, —
Hears five-hour sermons for his Sunday work, —
Praying and fasting till his meagre face
Gains its due length, the genuine sign of grace, —
An Ayrshire mother in the land of Knox
Her embryo poet in his cradle rocks; —
Nature, long shivering in her dim eclipse,

Steals in a sunbeam to those baby lips;
So to its home her banished smile returns,
And Scotland sweetens with the song of Burns!

The morning came; I reached the classic hall;
A clock-face eyed me, staring from the wall;
Beneath its hands a printed line I read:
YOUTH IS LIFE'S SEED-TIME: so the clock-face said:
Some took its counsel, as the sequel showed, —
Sowed, — their wild oats, — and reaped as they had sowed.
How all comes back! the upward slant-ing floor, —
The masters' thrones that flank the central door, —
The long, outstretching alleys that divide
The rows of desks that stand on either side, —
The staring boys, a face to every desk,
Bright, dull, pale, blooming, common, pic-turesque.
Grave is the Master's look; his forehead wears
Thick rows of wrinkles, prints of worrying cares;
Uneasy lie the heads of all that rule,
His most of all whose kingdom is a school.
Supreme he sits; before the awful frown
That bends his brows the boldest eye goes down;
Not more submissive Israel heard and saw
At Sinai's foot the Giver of the Law.
Less stern he seems, who sits in equal state
On the twin throne and shares the empire's weight;
Around his lips the subtle life that plays
Steals quaintly forth in many a jesting phrase;
A lightsome nature, not so hard to chafe,
Pleasant when pleased; rough-handled, not so safe;
Some tingling memories vaguely I recall,
But to forgive him. God forgive us all!

One yet remains, whose well-remembered name
Pleads in my grateful heart its tender claim;

His was the charm magnetic, the bright look
That sheds its sunshine on the dreariest book;
A loving soul to every task he brought
That sweetly mingled with the lore he taught;
Sprung from a saintly race that never could
From youth to age be anything but good,
His few brief years in holiest labors spent,
Earth lost too soon the treasure heaven had lent.

Kindest of teachers, studious to divine
Some hint of promise in my earliest line,
These faint and faltering words thou canst not hear
Throb from a heart that holds thy memory dear.

As to the traveller's eye the varied plain
Shows through the window of the flying train,
A mingled landscape, rather felt than seen,
A gravelly bank, a sudden flash of green,
A tangled wood, a glittering stream that flows
Through the cleft summit where the cliff once rose,
All strangely blended in a hurried gleam,
Rock, wood, waste, meadow, village, hillside, stream, —
So, as we look behind us, life appears,
Seen through the vista of our bygone years.

Yet in the dead past's shadow-filled domain,
Some vanished shapes the hues of life retain;
Unbidden, oft, before our dreaming eyes
From the vague mists in memory's path they rise.
So comes his blooming image to my view,
The friend of joyous days when life was new,
Hope yet untamed, the blood of youth unchilled,
No blank arrear of promise unfulfilled,
Life's flower yet hidden in its sheltering fold,
Its pictured canvas yet to be unrolled.
His the frank smile I vainly look to greet,
His the warm grasp my clasping hand should meet;
How would our lips renew their school-boy talk,
Our feet retrace the old familiar walk!

For thee no more earth's cheerful morning shines
Through the green fringes of the tented pines;
Ah me! is heaven so far thou canst not hear,
Or is thy viewless spirit hovering near,
A fair young presence, bright with morning's glow,
The fresh-cheeked boy of fifty years ago?

Yes, fifty years, with all their circling suns,
Behind them all my glance reverted runs;
Where now that time remote, its griefs, its joys,
Where are its gray-haired men, its bright-haired boys?
Where is the patriarch time could hardly tire, —
The good old, wrinkled, immemorial "squire"?
(An honest treasurer, like a black-plumed swan,
Not every day our eyes may look upon.)
Where the tough champion who, with Calvin's sword,
In wordy conflicts battled for the Lord?
Where the grave scholar, lonely, calm, austere,
Whose voice like music charmed the listening ear,
Whose light rekindled, like the morning star
Still shines upon us through the gates ajar?
Where the still, solemn, weary, sad-eyed man,
Whose care-worn face my wandering eyes would scan, —
His features wasted in the lingering strife
With the pale foe that drains the student's life?
Where my old friend, the scholar, teacher, saint,
Whose creed, some hinted, showed a speck of taint;
He broached his own opinion, which is not
Lightly to be forgiven or forgot;
Some riddle's point, — I scarce remember now, —
Homoi-, perhaps, where they said homo-ou.
(If the unlettered greatly wish to know
Where lies the difference betwixt *oi* and *o*,
Those of the curious who have time may search

Among the stale conundrums of their
    church.)
Beneath his roof his peaceful life I shared,
And for his modes of faith I little cared, —
I, taught to judge men's dogmas by their
    deeds,
Long ere the days of india-rubber creeds.

Why should we look one common faith
    to find,
Where one in every score is color-blind?
If here on earth they know not red from
    green,
Will they see better into things unseen!
Once more to time's old graveyard I
    return
And scrape the moss from memory's
    pictured urn.
Who, in these days when all things go by
    steam,
Recalls the stage-coach with its four-horse
    team?
Its sturdy driver, — who remembers him?
Or the old landlord, saturnine and grim,
Who left our hill-top for a new abode
And reared his sign-post farther down the
    road?
Still in the waters of the dark Shawshine
Do the young bathers splash and think
    they're clean?
Do pilgrims find their way to Indian Ridge,
Or journey onward to the far-off bridge,
And bring to younger ears the story back
Of the broad stream, the mighty Merrimac?
Are there still truant feet that stray beyond
These circling bounds to Pomp's or
    Haggett's Pond,
Or where the legendary name recalls
The forest's earlier tenant, — "Deerjump
    Falls"?
Yes, every nook these youthful feet ex-
    plore,
Just as our sires and grandsires did of
    yore;
So all life's opening paths, where nature
    led
Their father's feet, the children's children
    tread.
Roll the round century's fivescore years
    away,
Call from our storied past that earliest day
When great Eliphalet (I can see him
    now, —
Big name, big frame, big voice, and beet-
    ling brow),

Then *young* Eliphalet, — ruled the rows of
    boys
In homespun gray or old-world cordu-
    roys, —
And save for fashion's whims, the benches
    show
The selfsame youths, the very boys we
    know.
Time works strange marvels: since I trod
    the green
And swung the gates, what wonders I have
    seen!
But come what will, — the sky itself may
    fall, —
As things of course the boy accepts them
    all.
The prophet's chariot, drawn by steeds of
    flame,
For daily use our travelling millions claim;
The face we love a sunbeam makes our
    own;
No more the surgeon hears the sufferer's
    groan;
What unwrit histories wrapped in darkness
    lay
Till shovelling Schliemann bared them to
    the day!
Your Richelieu says, and says it well, my
    lord,
The pen is (sometimes) mightier than the
    sword;
Great is the goosequill, say we all; Amen!
Sometimes the spade is mightier than the
    pen;
It shows where Babel's terraced walls were
    raised,
The slabs that cracked when Nimrod's
    palace blazed,
Unearths Mycenæ, rediscovers Troy, —
Calmly he listens, that immortal boy.
A new Prometheus tips our wands with
    fire,
A mightier Orpheus strains the whispering
    wire,
Whose lightning thrills the lazy winds out-
    run
And hold the hours as Joshua stayed the
    sun, —
So swift, in truth, we hardly find a place
For those dim fictions known as time and
    space.
Still a new miracle each year supplies, —
See at his work the chemist of the skies,
Who questions Sirius in his tortured rays
And steals the secret of the solar blaze;

Hush! while the window-rattling bugles play
The nation's airs a hundred miles away!
That wicked phonograph! hark! how it swears!
Turn it again and make it say its prayers!
And was it true, then, what the story said
Of Oxford's friar and his brazen head?
While wondering Science stands, herself perplexed
At each day's miracle, and asks "What next?"
The immortal boy, the coming heir of all,
Springs from his desk to "urge the flying ball,"
Cleaves with his bending oar the glassy waves,
With sinewy arm the dashing current braves,
The same bright creature in these haunts of ours
That Eton shadowed with her "antique towers."

Boy! Where is he? the long-limbed youth inquires,
Whom his rough chin with manly pride inspires;
Ah, when the ruddy cheek no longer glows,
When the bright hair is white as winter snows,
When the dim eye has lost its lambent flame,
Sweet to his ear will be his school-boy name!
Nor think the difference mighty as it seems
Between life's morning and its evening dreams;
Fourscore, like twenty, has its tasks and toys;
In earth's wide school-house all are girls and boys.

Brothers, forgive my wayward fancy. Who
Can guess beforehand what his pen will do?
Too light my strain for listeners such as these,
Whom graver thoughts and soberer speech shall please.
Is he not here whose breath of holy song
Has raised the downcast eyes of Faith so long?
Are they not here, the strangers in your gates,
For whom the wearied ear impatient waits, —
The large-brained scholars whom their toils release, —
The bannered heralds of the Prince of Peace?

Such was the gentle friend whose youth unblamed
In years long past our student-benches claimed;
Whose name, illumined on the sacred page,
Lives in the labors of his riper age;
Such be whose record time's destroying march
Leaves uneffaced on Zion's springing arch:
Not to the scanty phrase of measured song,
Cramped in its fetters, names like these belong;
One ray they lend to gild my slender line, —
Their praise I leave to sweeter lips than mine.

Homes of our sires, where Learning's temple rose,
While yet they struggled with their banded foes,
As in the West thy century's sun descends,
One parting gleam its dying radiance lends.
Darker and deeper though the shadows fall
From the gray towers on Doubting Castle's wall,
Though Pope and Pagan re-array their hosts,
And her new armor youthful Science boasts,
Truth, for whose altar rose this holy shrine,
Shall fly for refuge to these bowers of thine;
No past shall chain her with its rusted vow,
No Jew's phylactery bind her Christian brow,
But Faith shall smile to find her sister free,
And nobler manhood draw its life from thee.

Long as the arching skies above thee spread,
As on thy groves the dews of heaven are shed,
With currents widening still from year to year,

And deepening channels, calm, untroubled,
  clear,
Flow the twin streamlets from thy sacred
  hill —
Pieria's fount and Siloam's shaded rill!

THE SILENT MELODY

"BRING me my broken harp," he said;
  "We both are wrecks, — but as ye
    will, —
Though all its ringing tones have fled,
  Their echoes linger round it still;
It had some golden strings, I know,
But that was long — how long! — ago.

"I cannot see its tarnished gold,
  I cannot hear its vanished tone,
Scarce can my trembling fingers hold
  The pillared frame so long their own;
We both are wrecks, — awhile ago
It had some silver strings, I know,

"But on them Time too long has played
  The solemn strain that knows no change,
And where of old my fingers strayed
  The chords they find are new and
    strange, —
Yes! iron strings, — I know, — I know, —
We both are wrecks of long ago.

"We both are wrecks, — a shattered
    pair, —
  Strange to ourselves in time's dis-
    guise . . .
What say ye to the lovesick air
  That brought the tears from Marian's
    eyes?
Ay! trust me, — under breasts of snow
Hearts could be melted long ago!

"Or will ye hear the storm-song's crash
  That from his dreams the soldier woke,
And bade him face the lightning flash
  When battle's cloud in thunder
    broke? . . .
Wrecks, — nought but wrecks! — the time
    was when
We two were worth a thousand men!"

And so the broken harp they bring
  With pitying smiles that none could
    blame;
Alas! there's not a single string
  Of all that filled the tarnished frame!
But see! like children overjoyed,
His fingers rambling through the void!

"I clasp thee! Ay . . . mine ancient
    lyre . . .
  Nay, guide my wandering fingers. . . .
    There!
They love to dally with the wire
  As Isaac played with Esau's hair. . . .
Hush! ye shall hear the famous tune
That Marian called the Breath of June!"

And so they softly gather round:
  Rapt in his tuneful trance he seems:
His fingers move: but not a sound!
  A silence like the song of dreams. . . .
"There! ye have heard the air," he cries,
"That brought the tears from Marian's
    eyes!"

Ah, smile not at his fond conceit,
  Nor deem his fancy wrought in vain;
To him the unreal sounds are sweet, —
  No discord mars the silent strain
Scored on life's latest, starlit page —
The voiceless melody of age.

Sweet are the lips of all that sing,
  When Nature's music breathes unsought,
But never yet could voice or string
  So truly shape our tenderest thought
As when by life's decaying fire
Our fingers sweep the stringless lyre!

OUR HOME — OUR COUNTRY

FOR THE TWO HUNDRED AND FIFTI-
ETH ANNIVERSARY OF THE SETTLE-
MENT OF CAMBRIDGE, MASS., DE-
CEMBER 28, 1880

YOUR home was mine, — kind Nature's
    gift;
  My love no years can chill;
In vain their flakes the storm-winds sift,
The snowdrop hides beneath the drift,
  A living blossom still.

Mute are a hundred long-famed lyres,
  Hushed all their golden strings;
One lay the coldest bosom fires,
One song, one only, never tires
  While sweet-voiced memory sings.

No spot so lone but echo knows
  That dear familiar strain;
In tropic isles, on arctic snows,
Through burning lips its music flows
  And rings its fond refrain.

From Pisa's tower my straining sight
  Roamed wandering leagues away,
When lo ! a frigate's banner bright,
The starry blue, the red, the white,
  In far Livorno's bay.

Hot leaps the life-blood from my heart,
  Forth springs the sudden tear;
The ship that rocks by yonder mart
Is of my land, my life, a part, —
  Home, home, sweet home, is here !

Fades from my view the sunlit scene, —
  My vision spans the waves;
I see the elm-encircled green,
The tower, — the steeple, — and, between,
  The field of ancient graves.

There runs the path my feet would tread
  When first they learned to stray;
There stands the gambrel roof that spread
Its quaint old angles o'er my head
  When first I saw the day.

The sounds that met my boyish ear
  My inward sense salute, —
The woodnotes wild I loved to hear, —
The robin's challenge, sharp and clear, —
  The breath of evening's flute.

The faces loved from cradle days, —
  Unseen, alas, how long !
As fond remembrance round them plays,
Touched with its softening moonlight rays,
  Through fancy's portal throng.

And see ! as if the opening skies
  Some angel form had spared
Us wingless mortals to surprise,
The little maid with light-blue eyes,
  White necked and golden haired !

So rose the picture full in view
  I paint in feebler song;
Such power the seamless banner knew
Of red and white and starry blue
  For exiles banished long.

Oh, boys, dear boys, who wait as men
  To guard its heaven-bright folds,
Blest are the eyes that see again
That banner, seamless now, as then, —
  The fairest earth beholds !

Sweet was the Tuscan air and soft
  In that unfading hour,
And fancy leads my footsteps oft
Up the round galleries, high aloft
  On Pisa's threatening tower.

And still in Memory's holiest shrine
  I read with pride and joy,
" For me those stars of empire shine;
That empire's dearest home is mine;
  I am a Cambridge boy ! "

POEM

AT THE CENTENNIAL ANNIVERSARY DINNER OF THE MASSACHUSETTS MEDICAL SOCIETY, JUNE 8, 1881

THREE paths there be where Learning's favored sons,
Trained in the schools which hold her favored ones,
Follow their several stars with separate aim;
Each has its honors, each its special claim.
Bred in the fruitful cradle of the East,
First, as of oldest lineage, comes the Priest;
The Lawyer next, in wordy conflict strong,
Full armed to battle for the right, — or wrong;
Last, he whose calling finds its voice in deeds,
Frail Nature's helper in her sharpest needs.
  Each has his gifts, his losses and his gains,
  Each his own share of pleasures and of pains;
No life-long aim with steadfast eye pursued
Finds a smooth pathway all with roses strewed;
Trouble belongs to man of woman born, —
Tread where he may, his foot will find its thorn.

  Of all the guests at life's perennial feast,
Who of her children sits above the Priest ?
For him the broidered robe, the carven seat,

Pride at his beck, and beauty at his feet,
For him the incense fumes, the wine is
  poured,
Himself a God, adoring and adored!
His the first welcome when our hearts
  rejoice,
His in our dying ear the latest voice,
Font, altar, grave, his steps on all attend,
Our staff, our stay, our all but heavenly
  friend!
  Where is the meddling hand that dares
    to probe
The secret grief beneath his sable robe?
How grave his port! how every gesture
  tells
Here truth abides, here peace forever
  dwells;
Vex not his lofty soul with comments vain;
Faith asks no questions; silence, ye pro-
  fane!
Alas! too oft while all is calm without
The stormy spirit wars with endless *doubt;*
This is the mocking sceptre, scarce con-
  cealed
Behind tradition's bruised and battered
  shield.
He sees the sleepless critic, age by age,
Scrawl his new readings on the hallowed
  page,
The wondrous deeds that priests and pro-
  phets saw
Dissolved in legend, crystallized in law,
And on the soil where saints and martyrs
  trod
Altars new builded to the Unknown God;
His shrines imperilled, his evangels torn,—
He dares not limp, but ah! how sharp his
  thorn!
  Yet while God's herald questions as he
    reads
The outworn dogmas of his ancient creeds,
Drops from his ritual the exploded verse,
Blots from its page the Athanasian curse,
Though by the critic's dangerous art per-
  plexed,
His holy life is Heaven's unquestioned text;
That shining guidance doubt can never
  mar,—
The pillar's flame, the light of Bethlehem's
  star!

Strong is the moral blister that will draw
Laid on the conscience of the Man of Law
Whom blindfold Justice lends her eyes to
  see

Truth in the scale that holds his promised
  fee.
What! Has not every lie its truthful
  side,
Its honest fraction, not to be denied?
Per contra,— ask the moralist,— in sooth
Has not a lie its share in every truth?
Then what forbids an honest man to try
To find the truth that lurks in every lie,
And just as fairly call on truth to yield
The lying fraction in its breast concealed?
So the worst rogue shall claim a ready
  friend
His modest virtues boldly to defend,
And he who shows the record of a saint
See himself blacker than the devil could
  paint.
  What struggles to his captive soul be-
    long
Who loves the right, yet combats for the
  wrong,
Who fights the battle he would fain re-
  fuse,
And wins, well knowing that he ought to
  lose,
Who speaks with glowing lips and look
  sincere
In spangled words that make the worse
  appear
The better reason; who, behind his mask,
Hides his true self and blushes at his
  task,—
What quips, what quillets cheat the in-
  ward scorn
That mocks such triumph? Has he not
  his thorn?
  Yet stay thy judgment; were thy life
    the prize,
Thy death the forfeit, would thy cynic
  eyes
See fault in him who bravely dares de-
  fend
The cause forlorn, the wretch without a
  friend?
Nay, though the rightful side is wisdom's
  choice,
Wrong has its rights and claims a cham-
  pion's voice;
Let the strong arm be lifted for the weak,
For the dumb lips the fluent pleader
  speak;—
When with warm "rebel" blood our
  street was dyed
Who took, unawed, the hated hirelings'
  side?

No greener civic wreath can Adams claim,
No brighter page the youthful Quincy's name!

  How blest is he who knows no meaner strife
Than Art's long battle with the foes of life!
No doubt assails him, doing still his best,
And trusting kindly Nature for the rest;
No mocking conscience tears the thin disguise
That wraps his breast, and tells him that he lies.
He comes: the languid sufferer lifts his head
And smiles a welcome from his weary bed;
He speaks: what music like the tones that tell,
"Past is the hour of danger, — all is well!"
How can he feel the petty stings of grief
Whose cheering presence always brings relief?
What ugly dreams can trouble his repose
Who yields himself to soothe another's woes?
  Hour after hour the busy day has found
The good physician on his lonely round;
Mansion and hovel, low and lofty door,
He knows, his journeys every path explore, —
Where the cold blast has struck with deadly chill
The sturdy dweller on the storm-swept hill,
Where by the stagnant marsh the sickening gale
Has blanched the poisoned tenants of the vale,
Where crushed and maimed the bleeding victim lies,
Where madness raves, where melancholy sighs,
And where the solemn whisper tells too plain
That all his science, all his art, were vain.
  How sweet his fireside when the day is done
And cares have vanished with the setting sun!
Evening at last its hour of respite brings
And on his couch his weary length he flings.

Soft be thy pillow, servant of mankind,
Lulled by an opiate Art could never find;
Sweet be thy slumber, — thou hast earned it well, —
Pleasant thy dreams! Clang! goes the midnight bell!
  Darkness and storm! the home is far away
That waits his coming ere the break of day;
The snow-clad pines their wintry plumage toss, —
Doubtful the frozen stream his road must cross;
Deep lie the drifts, the slanted heaps have shut
The hardy woodman in his mountain hut, —
Why should thy softer frame the tempest brave?
Hast thou no life, no health, to lose or save?
Look! read the answer in his patient eyes, —
For him no other voice when suffering cries;
Deaf to the gale that all around him blows,
A feeble whisper calls him, — and he goes.
  Or seek the crowded city, — summer's heat
Glares burning, blinding, in the narrow street,
Still, noisome, deadly, sleeps the envenomed air,
Unstirred the yellow flag that says "Beware!"
Tempt not thy fate, — one little moment's breath
Bears on its viewless wing the seeds of death;
Thou at whose door the gilded chariots stand,
Whose dear-bought skill unclasps the miser's hand,
Turn from thy fatal quest, nor cast away
That life so precious; let a meaner prey
Feed the destroyer's hunger; live to bless
Those happier homes that need thy care no less!
  Smiling he listens; has he then a charm
Whose magic virtues peril can disarm?
No safeguard his; no amulet he wears,
Too well he knows that Nature never spares
Her truest servant, powerless to defend
From her own weapons her unshrinking friend.

He dares the fate the bravest well might shun,
Nor asks reward save only Heaven's "Well done!"
Such are the toils, the perils that he knows,
Days without rest and nights without repose,
Yet all unheeded for the love he bears
His art, his kind, whose every grief he shares.
  Harder than these to know how small the part
Nature's proud empire yields to striving Art;
How, as the tide that rolls around the sphere
Laughs at the mounds that delving arms uprear, —
Spares some few roods of oozy earth, but still
Wastes and rebuilds the planet at its will,
Comes at its ordered season, night or noon,
Led by the silver magnet of the moon, —
So life's vast tide forever comes and goes,
Unchecked, resistless, as it ebbs and flows.
  Hardest of all, when Art has done her best,
To find the cuckoo brooding in her nest;
The shrewd adventurer, fresh from parts unknown,
Kills off the patients Science thought her own;
Towns from a nostrum-vender get their name,
Fences and walls the cure-all drug proclaim,
Plasters and pads the willing world beguile,
Fair Lydia greets us with astringent smile,
Munchausen's fellow-countryman unlocks
His new Pandora's globule-holding box,
And as King George inquired, with puzzled grin,
"How — how the devil get the apple in?"
So we ask how, — with wonder-opening eyes, —
Such pygmy pills can hold such giant lies!
  Yes, sharp the trials, stern the daily tasks
That suffering Nature from her servant asks;
His the kind office dainty menials scorn,
His path how hard, — at every step a thorn!

What does his saddening, restless slavery buy?
What save a right to live, a chance to die, —
To live companion of disease and pain,
To die by poisoned shafts untimely slain?
  Answer from hoary eld, majestic shades,—
From Memphian courts, from Delphic colonnades,
Speak in the tones that Persia's despot heard
When nations treasured every golden word
The wandering echoes wafted o'er the seas,
From the far isle that held Hippocrates;
And thou, best gift that Pergamus could send
Imperial Rome, her noblest Cæsar's friend,
Master of masters, whose unchallenged sway
Not bold Vesalius dared to disobey;
Ye who while prophets dreamed of dawning times
Taught your rude lessons in Salerno's rhymes,
And ye, the nearer sires, to whom we owe
The better share of all the best we know,
In every land an ever-growing train,
Since wakening Science broke her rusted chain, —
Speak from the past, and say what prize was sent
To crown the toiling years so freely spent!
  List while they speak:
                In life's uneven road
Our willing hands have eased our brothers' load;
One forehead smoothed, one pang of torture less,
One peaceful hour a sufferer's couch to bless,
The smile brought back to fever's parching lips,
The light restored to reason in eclipse,
Life's treasure rescued like a burning brand
Snatched from the dread destroyer's wasteful hand;
Such were our simple records day by day,
For gains like these we wore our lives away.
In toilsome paths our daily bread we sought,
But bread from heaven attending angels brought;
Pain was our teacher, speaking to the heart,
Mother of pity, nurse of pitying art;
Our lesson learned, we reached the peaceful shore

Where the pale sufferer asks our aid no
    more, —
These gracious words our welcome, our
    reward:
Ye served your brothers; ye have served
    your Lord!

HARVARD

[Read at Commencement Dinner, July 1,
1880. The author had that day received
from his Alma Mater the degree of Doctor of
Laws.]

CHANGELESS in beauty, rose-hues on her
    cheek,
Old walls, old trees, old memories all
    around
Lend her unfading youth their charm an-
    tique
And fill with mystic light her holy ground.
Here the lost dove her leaf of promise
    found
While the new morning showed its blush-
    ing streak
Far o'er the waters she had crossed to seek
The bleak, wild shore in billowy forests
    drowned.
Mother of scholars! on thy rising throne
Thine elder sisters look benignant down;
England's proud twins, and they whose
    cloisters own
The fame of Abelard, the scarlet gown
That laughing Rabelais wore, not yet out-
    grown —
And on thy forehead place the New World's
    crown.

RHYMES OF A LIFE-TIME

FROM the first gleam of morning to the
    gray
  Of peaceful evening, lo, a life unrolled !
  In woven pictures all its changes told,
Its lights, its shadows, every flitting ray,
Till the long curtain, falling, dims the day,
  Steals from the dial's disk the sunlight's
    gold,
  And all the graven hours grow dark and
    cold
Where late the glowing blaze of noontide
    lay.
Ah! the warm blood runs wild in youthful
    veins, —
  Let me no longer play with painted fire;
  New songs for new-born days! I would
    not tire
The listening ears that wait for fresher
    strains
In phrase new-moulded, new-forged
    rhythmic chains,
  With plaintive measures from a worn-out
    lyre.

BEFORE THE CURFEW

AT MY FIRESIDE

ALONE, beneath the darkened sky,
  With saddened heart and unstrung lyre,
I heap the spoils of years gone by,
And leave them with a long-drawn sigh,
Like drift-wood brands that glimmering lie,
  Before the ashes hide the fire.

Let not these slow declining days
  The rosy light of dawn outlast;
Still round my lonely hearth it plays,
And gilds the east with borrowed rays,
While memory's mirrored sunset blaze
  Flames on the windows of the past.

March 1, 1888.

AT THE SATURDAY CLUB

About the time when these papers [*The Autocrat*] were published, the Saturday Club was founded, or, rather, found itself in existence, without any organization, almost without parentage. It was natural enough that such men as Emerson, Longfellow, Agassiz, Peirce, with Hawthorne, Motley, Sumner, when within reach, and others who would be good company for them, should meet and dine together once in a while, as they did, in point of fact, every month, and as some who are still living, with other and newer members, still meet and dine. If some of them had not admired each other they would have been exceptions in the world of letters and science. The club deserves being remembered for having no constitution or by-laws, for making no speeches, reading no papers, observing no ceremonies, coming and going at will without remark, and acting out, though it did not proclaim the motto, "Shall I not take mine ease in mine inn?" There was and is nothing of the Bohemian element about this club, but it has had many good times and not a little good talking.

THIS is our place of meeting; opposite
That towered and pillared building: look
    at it;
King's Chapel in the Second George's day,
Rebellion stole its regal name away, —
Stone Chapel sounded better; but at last
The poisoned name of our provincial past
Had lost its ancient venom; then once more
Stone Chapel was King's Chapel as before.
(So let rechristened North Street, when it
    can,
Bring back the days of Marlborough and
    Queen Anne!)
  Next the old church your wandering eye
    will meet —
A granite pile that stares upon the street —
Our civic temple; slanderous tongues have
    said
Its shape was modelled from St. Botolph's
    head,
Lofty, but narrow; jealous passers-by
Say Boston always held her head too high.
  Turn half-way round, and let your look
    survey
The white façade that gleams across the
    way, —
The many-windowed building, tall and wide,
The palace-inn that shows its northern side
In grateful shadow when the sunbeams
    beat
The granite wall in summer's scorching
    heat.
This is the place; whether its name you
    spell
Tavern, or caravansera, or hotel.
Would I could steal its echoes! you should
    find
Such store of vanished pleasures brought to
    mind:
Such feasts! the laughs of many a jocund
    hour
That shook the mortar from King George's
    tower;
Such guests! What famous names its record boasts,

Whose owners wander in the mob of ghosts!
Such stories! Every beam and plank is
  filled
With juicy wit the joyous talkers spilled,
Ready to ooze, as once the mountain pine
The floors are laid with oozed its turpen-
  tine!

A month had flitted since The Club had
  met;
The day came round; I found the table set,
The waiters lounging round the marble
  stairs,
Empty as yet the double row of chairs.
I was a full half hour before the rest,
Alone, the banquet-chamber's single guest.
So from the table's side a chair I took,
And having neither company nor book
To keep me waking, by degrees there crept
A torpor over me, — in short, I slept.
Loosed from its chain, along the wreck-
  strown track
Of the dead years my soul goes travelling
  back;
My ghosts take on their robes of flesh; it
  seems
Dreaming is life; nay, life less life than
  dreams,
So real are the shapes that meet my eyes.
They bring no sense of wonder, no surprise,
No hint of other than an earth-born source;
All seems plain daylight, everything of
  course.
How dim the colors are, how poor and
  faint
This palette of weak words with which I
  paint!
Here sit my friends; if I could fix them so
As to my eyes they seem, my page would
  glow
Like a queen's missal, warm as if the brush
Of Titian or Velasquez brought the flush
Of life into their features. *Ay de mi!*
If syllables were pigments, you should see
Such breathing portraitures as never man
Found in the Pitti or the Vatican.

Here sits our POET, Laureate, if you will.
Long has he worn the wreath, and wears it
  still.
Dead? Nay, not so; and yet they say his
  bust
Looks down on marbles covering royal dust,
Kings by the Grace of God, or Nature's
  grace;

Dead! No! Alive! I see him in his
  place,
Full-featured, with the bloom that heaven
  denies
Her children, pinched by cold New Eng-
  land skies,
Too often, while the nursery's happier few
Win from a summer cloud its roseate hue.
Kind, soft-voiced, gentle, in his eye there
  shines
The ray serene that filled Evangeline's.
  Modest he seems, not shy; content to
    wait
Amid the noisy clamor of debate
The looked-for moment when a peaceful
  word
Smooths the rough ripples louder tongues
  have stirred.
In every tone I mark his tender grace
And all his poems hinted in his face;
What tranquil joy his friendly presence
  gives!
How could I think him dead? He lives!
  He lives!

There, at the table's further end I see
In his old place our Poet's *vis-à-vis*,
The great PROFESSOR, strong, broad-shoul-
  dered, square,
In life's rich noontide, joyous, debonair.
His social hour no leaden care alloys,
His laugh rings loud and mirthful as a
  boy's, —
That lusty laugh the Puritan forgot, —
What ear has heard it and remembers not?
How often, halting at some wide crevasse
Amid the windings of his Alpine pass,
High up the cliffs, the climbing moun-
  taineer,
Listening the far-off avalanche to hear,
Silent, and leaning on his steel-shod staff,
Has heard that cheery voice, that ringing
  laugh,
From the rude cabin whose nomadic walls
Creep with the moving glacier as it crawls!
  How does vast Nature lead her living
    train
In ordered sequence through that spacious
  brain,
As in the primal hour when Adam named
The new-born tribes that young creation
  claimed! —
How will her realm be darkened, losing
  thee,
Her darling, whom we call *our* AGASSIZ!

But who is he whose massive frame be-
    lies
The maiden shyness of his downcast eyes?
Who broods in silence till, by questions
    pressed,
Some answer struggles from his laboring
    breast?
An artist Nature meant to dwell apart,
Locked in his studio with a human heart,
Tracking its caverned passions to their lair,
And all its throbbing mysteries laying bare.
Count it no marvel that he broods alone
Over the heart he studies, — 't is his own;
So in his page, whatever shape it wear,
The Essex wizard's shadowed self is there,—
The great ROMANCER, hid beneath his veil
Like the stern preacher of his sombre tale;
Virile in strength, yet bashful as a girl,
Prouder than Hester, sensitive as Pearl.

From his mild throng of worshippers
    released,
Our Concord Delphi sends its chosen priest,
Prophet or poet, mystic, sage, or seer,
By every title always welcome here.
Why that ethereal spirit's frame describe?
You know the race-marks of the Brahmin
    tribe, —
The spare, slight form, the sloping shoul-
    der's droop,
The calm, scholastic mien, the clerkly
    stoop,
The lines of thought the sharpened features
    wear,
Carved by the edge of keen New England
    air.
    List! for he speaks! As when a king
        would choose
The jewels for his bride, he might refuse
This diamond for its flaw, — find that less
    bright
Than those, its fellows, and a pearl less
    white
Than fits her snowy neck, and yet at last,
The fairest gems are chosen, and made
    fast
In golden fetters; so, with light delays
He seeks the fittest word to fill his phrase;
Nor vain nor idle his fastidious quest,
His chosen word is sure to prove the best.
Where in the realm of thought, whose
    air is song,
Does he, the Buddha of the West, belong?
He seems a wingèd Franklin, sweetly wise,
Born to unlock the secrets of the skies;

And which the nobler calling, — if 't is fair
Terrestrial with celestial to compare, —
To guide the storm-cloud's elemental flame,
Or walk the chambers whence the light-
    ning came,
Amidst the sources of its subtile fire,
And steal their effluence for his lips and
    lyre?
If lost at times in vague aerial flights,
None treads with firmer footstep when he
    lights;
A soaring nature, ballasted with sense,
Wisdom without her wrinkles or pretence,
In every Bible he has faith to read,
And every altar helps to shape his creed.
Ask you what name this prisoned spirit
    bears
While with ourselves this fleeting breath it
    shares?
Till angels greet him with a sweeter one
In heaven, on earth we call him EMERSON.

I start; I wake; the vision is withdrawn;
Its figures fading like the stars at dawn;
Crossed from the roll of life their cher-
    ished names,
And memory's pictures fading in their
    frames;
Yet life is lovelier for these transient gleams
Of buried friendships; blest is he who
    dreams!

OUR DEAD SINGER

H. W. L.

PRIDE of the sister realm so long our own,
    We claim with her that spotless fame of
        thine,
    White as her snow and fragrant as her
        pine!
Ours was thy birthplace, but in every zone
Some wreath of song thy liberal hand has
        thrown
    Breathes perfume from its blossoms,
        that entwine
    Where'er the dewdrops fall, the sun-
        beams shine,
On life's long path with tangled cares o'er-
        grown.
Can Art thy truthful counterfeit com-
    mand, —
    The silver-haloed features, tranquil,
        mild, —

Soften the lips of bronze as when they
    smiled,
Give warmth and pressure to the marble
    hand?
Seek the lost rainbow in the sky it spanned!
    Farewell, sweet Singer! Heaven re-
      claims its child.

Carved from the block or cast in clinging
    mould,
    Will grateful Memory fondly try her
      best
The mortal vesture from decay to wrest;
His look shall greet us, calm, but ah, how
    cold!
No breath can stir the brazen drapery's fold,
    No throb can heave the statue's stony
      breast;
"He is not here, but risen," will stand
    confest
In all we miss, in all our eyes behold.
How Nature loved him! On his placid
    brow,
    Thought's ample dome, she set the sacred
      sign
    That marks the priesthood of her holiest
      shrine,
Nor asked a leaflet from the laurel's bough
That envious Time might clutch or disallow,
    To prove her chosen minstrel's song
      divine.

On many a saddened hearth the evening
    fire
    Burns paler as the children's hour draws
      near, —
    That joyous hour his song made doubly
      dear, —
And tender memories touch the faltering
    choir.
He sings no more on earth; our vain desire
    Aches for the voice we loved so long to
      hear
    In Dorian flute-notes breathing soft and
      clear, —
The sweet contralto that could never tire.
Deafened with listening to a harsher strain,
    The Mænad's scream, the stark barba-
      rian's cry,
    Still for those soothing, loving tones we
      sigh;
Oh, for our vanished Orpheus once again!
The shadowy silence hears us call in vain!
    His lips are hushed; his song shall never
      die.

TWO POEMS TO HARRIET BEECHER STOWE

ON HER SEVENTIETH BIRTHDAY,
JUNE 14, 1882

I. AT THE SUMMIT

SISTER, we bid you welcome, — we who
    stand
    On the high table-land;
We who have climbed life's slippery Alpine
    slope,
And rest, still leaning on the staff of hope,
Looking along the silent Mer de Glace,
Leading our footsteps where the dark cre-
    vasse
Yawns in the frozen sea we all must pass, —
    Sister, we clasp your hand!

Rest with us in the hour that Heaven has
    lent
    Before the swift descent.
Look! the warm sunbeams kiss the glitter-
    ing ice;
See! next the snow-drift blooms the edel-
    weiss;
The mated eagles fan the frosty air;
Life, beauty, love, around us everywhere,
And, in their time, the darkening hours
    that bear
    Sweet memories, peace, content.

Thrice welcome! shining names our missals
    show
    Amid their rubrics' glow,
But search the blazoned record's starry line,
What halo's radiance fills the page like
    thine?
Thou who by some celestial clue couldst
    find
The way to all the hearts of all mankind,
On thee, already canonized, enshrined,
    What more can Heaven bestow!

II. THE WORLD'S HOMAGE

IF every tongue that speaks her praise
For whom I shape my tinkling phrase
    Were summoned to the table,
The vocal chorus that would meet
Of mingling accents harsh or sweet,
From every land and tribe, would beat
    The polyglots at Babel.

Briton and Frenchman, Swede and Dane,
Turk, Spaniard, Tartar of Ukraine,
　Hidalgo, Cossack, Cadi,
High Dutchman and Low Dutchman, too,
The Russian serf, the Polish Jew,
Arab, Armenian, and Mantchoo,
　Would shout, "We know the lady!"

Know her! Who knows not Uncle Tom
And her he learned his gospel from
　Has never heard of Moses;
Full well the brave black hand we know
That gave to freedom's grasp the hoe
That killed the weed that used to grow
　Among the Southern roses.

When Archimedes, long ago,
Spoke out so grandly, "*dos pou sto* —
　Give me a place to stand on,
I'll move your planet for you, now," —
He little dreamed or fancied how
The *sto* at last should find its *pou*
　For woman's faith to land on.

Her lever was the wand of art,
Her fulcrum was the human heart,
　Whence all unfailing aid is;
She moved the earth! Its thunders pealed,
Its mountains shook, its temples reeled,
The blood-red fountains were unsealed,
　And Moloch sunk to Hades.

All through the conflict, up and down
Marched Uncle Tom and Old John Brown,
　One ghost, one form ideal;
And which was false and which was true,
And which was mightier of the two,
The wisest sibyl never knew,
　For both alike were real.

Sister, the holy maid does well
Who counts her beads in convent cell,
　Where pale devotion lingers;
But she who serves the sufferer's needs,
Whose prayers are spelt in loving deeds,
May trust the Lord will count her beads
　As well as human fingers.

When Truth herself was Slavery's slave,
Thy hand the prisoned suppliant gave
　The rainbow wings of fiction.
And Truth who soared descends to-day
Bearing an angel's wreath away,
Its lilies at thy feet to lay
　With Heaven's own benediction.

A WELCOME TO DR. BENJAMIN APTHORP GOULD

ON HIS RETURN FROM SOUTH AMERICA

AFTER FIFTEEN YEARS DEVOTED TO CATALOGUING THE STARS OF THE SOUTHERN HEMISPHERE

Read at the Dinner given at the Hotel Vendome, May 6, 1885.

ONCE more Orion and the sister Seven
　Look on thee from the skies that hailed
　　thy birth, —
How shall we welcome thee, whose home
　　was heaven,
　From thy celestial wanderings back to
　　earth?

Science has kept her midnight taper burning
　To greet thy coming with its vestal
　　flame;
Friendship has murmured, "When art thou
　　returning?"
　"Not yet! Not yet!" the answering
　　message came.

Thine was unstinted zeal, unchilled devotion,
　While the blue realm had kingdoms to
　　explore, —
Patience, like his who ploughed the unfurrowed ocean,
　Till o'er its margin loomed San Salvador.

Through the long nights I see thee ever
　　waking,
　Thy footstool earth, thy roof the hemisphere,
While with thy griefs our weaker hearts
　　are aching,
　Firm as thine equatorial's rock-based
　　pier.

The souls that voyaged the azure depths
　　before thee
　Watch with thy tireless vigils, all unseen, —
Tycho and Kepler bend benignant o'er
　　thee,
　And with his toy-like tube the Florentine, —

He at whose word the orb that bore him
  shivered
To find her central sovereignty disowned,
While the wan lips of priest and pontiff
  quivered,
  Their jargon stilled, their Baal disen-
    throned.

Flamsteed and Newton look with brows
  unclouded,
Their strife forgotten with its faded
  scars, —
(Titans, who found the world of space too
  crowded
  To walk in peace among its myriad
    stars).

All cluster round thee, — seers of earliest
  ages,
Persians, Ionians, Mizraim's learned
  kings,
From the dim days of Shinar's hoary sages
  To his who weighed the planet's fluid
    rings.

And we, for whom the northern heavens
  are lighted,
For whom the storm has passed, the sun
  has smiled,
Our clouds all scattered, all our stars
  united,
  We claim thee, clasp thee, like a long-
    lost child.

Fresh from the spangled vault's o'er-arch-
  ing splendor,
Thy lonely pillar, thy revolving dome,
In heartfelt accents, proud, rejoicing, ten-
  der,
  We bid thee welcome to thine earthly
    home!

TO FREDERICK HENRY HEDGE

AT A DINNER GIVEN HIM ON HIS
EIGHTIETH BIRTHDAY, DECEMBER 12,
1885

With a bronze statuette of John of Bologna's
Mercury, presented by a few friends.

Fit emblem for the altar's side,
  And him who serves its daily need,
The stay, the solace, and the guide
  Of mortal men, whate'er his creed!

Flamen or Auspex, Priest or Bonze,
  He feeds the upward-climbing fire,
Still teaching, like the deathless bronze,
  Man's noblest lesson, — to aspire.

Hermes lies prone by fallen Jove,
  Crushed are the wheels of Krishna's car,
And o'er Dodona's silent grove
  Streams the white ray from Bethlehem's
    star.

Yet snatched from Time's relentless clutch,
  A godlike shape, that human hands
Have fired with Art's electric touch,
  The herald of Olympus stands.

Ask not what ore the furnace knew;
  Love mingled with the flowing mass,
And lends its own unchanging hue,
  Like gold in Corinth's molten brass.

Take then our gift; this airy form
  Whose bronze our benedictions gild,
The hearts of all its givers warm
  With love by freezing years unchilled.

With eye undimmed, with strength unworn,
  Still toiling in your Master's field,
Before you wave the growths unshorn,
  Their ripened harvest yet to yield.

True servant of the Heavenly Sire,
  To you our tried affection clings,
Bids you still labor, still aspire,
  But clasps your feet and steals their
    wings.

TO JAMES RUSSELL LOWELL

This is your month, the month of "perfect
  days,"
Birds in full song and blossoms all ablaze.
Nature herself your earliest welcome
  breathes,
Spreads every leaflet, every bower in-
  wreathes;
Carpets her paths for your returning feet,
Puts forth her best your coming steps to
  greet;
And Heaven must surely find the earth in
  tune
When Home, sweet Home, exhales the
  breath of June.

These blessed days are waning all too
　　fast,
And June's bright visions mingling with
　　the past;
Lilacs have bloomed and faded, and the rose
Has dropped its petals, but the clover blows,
And fills its slender tubes with honeyed
　　sweets;
The fields are pearled with milk-white
　　margarites;
The dandelion, which you sang of old,
Has lost its pride of place, its crown of
　　gold,
But still displays its feathery-mantled
　　globe,
Which children's breath or wandering
　　winds unrobe.
These were your humble friends; your
　　opened eyes
Nature had trained her common gifts to
　　prize;
Not Cam nor Isis taught you to despise
Charles, with his muddy margin and the
　　harsh,
Plebeian grasses of the reeking marsh.
New England's home-bred scholar, well
　　you knew
Her soil, her speech, her people, through
　　and through,
And loved them ever with the love that
　　holds
All sweet, fond memories in its fragrant
　　folds.
Though far and wide your wingèd words
　　have flown,
Your daily presence kept you all our own,
Till, with a sorrowing sigh, a thrill of
　　pride,
We heard your summons, and you left our
　　side
For larger duties and for tasks untried.

How pleased the Spaniards for a while to
　　claim
This frank Hidalgo with the liquid name,
Who stored their classics on his crowded
　　shelves
And loved their Calderon as they did
　　themselves!
Before his eyes what changing pageants
　　pass!
The bridal feast how near the funeral
　　mass!
The death-stroke falls, — the Misereres
　　wail;
The joy-bells ring, — the tear-stained
　　cheeks unveil,
While, as the playwright shifts his pictured
　　scene,
The royal mourner crowns his second
　　queen.

From Spain to Britain is a goodly stride, —
Madrid and London long-stretched leagues
　　divide.
What if I send him, "Uncle S., says he,"
To my good cousin whom he calls "J. B." ?
A nation's servants go where they are
　　sent, —
He heard his Uncle's orders, and he went.
　　By what enchantments, what alluring
　　　arts,
Our truthful James led captive British
　　hearts, —
Whether his shrewdness made their states-
　　men halt,
Or if his learning found their Dons at
　　fault,
Or if his virtue was a strange surprise,
Or if his wit flung star-dust in their eyes, —
Like honest Yankees we can simply guess;
But that he did it all must needs confess.
England herself without a blush may claim
Her only conqueror since the Norman came.
　　Eight years an exile! What a weary
　　　while
Since first our herald sought the mother
　　isle!
His snow-white flag no churlish wrong has
　　soiled, —
He left unchallenged, he returns unspoiled.

Here let us keep him, here he saw the
　　light,
His genius, wisdom, wit, are ours by right;
And if we lose him our lament will be
We have "five hundred" — *not* "as good
　　as he."

TO JOHN GREENLEAF WHITTIER

ON HIS EIGHTIETH BIRTHDAY

1887

FRIEND, whom thy fourscore winters leave
　　more dear
Than when life's roseate summer on thy
　　cheek

Burned in the flush of manhood's manliest
    year,
Lonely, how lonely! is the snowy peak
Thy feet have reached, and mine have
    climbed so near!
Close on thy footsteps 'mid the landscape
    drear
I stretch my hand thine answering grasp to
    seek,
Warm with the love no rippling rhymes
    can speak!
Look backward! From thy lofty height
    survey
Thy years of toil, of peaceful victories
    won,
Of dreams made real, largest hopes out-
    run!
Look forward! Brighter than earth's
    morning ray
Streams the pure light of Heaven's unset-
    ting sun,
The unclouded dawn of life's immortal
    day!

PRELUDE TO A VOLUME PRINTED IN RAISED LETTERS FOR THE BLIND

DEAR friends, left darkling in the long
    eclipse
That veils the noonday, — you whose
    finger-tips
A meaning in these ridgy leaves can find
Where ours go stumbling, senseless, help-
    less, blind,
This wreath of verse how dare I offer you
To whom the garden's choicest gifts are
    due?
The hues of all its glowing beds are ours,
Shall you not claim its sweetest-smelling
    flowers?

Nay, those I have I bring you, — at their
    birth
Life's cheerful sunshine warmed the grate-
    ful earth;
If my rash boyhood dropped some idle
    seeds,
And here and there you light on saucy
    weeds
Among the fairer growths, remember still
Song comes of grace, and not of human
    will:

We get a jarring note when most we try,
Then strike the chord we know not how or
    why;
Our stately verse with too aspiring art
Oft overshoots and fails to reach the
    heart,
While the rude rhyme one human throb
    endears
Turns grief to smiles, and softens mirth to
    tears.
Kindest of critics, ye whose fingers read,
From Nature's lesson learn the poet's
    creed;
The queenly tulip flaunts in robes of flame,
The wayside seedling scarce a tint may
    claim,
Yet may the lowliest leaflets that unfold
A dewdrop fresh from heaven's own chalice
    hold.

BOSTON TO FLORENCE

Sent to "The Philological Circle" of Florence for its meeting in commemoration of Dante, January 27, 1881, the anniversary of his first condemnation.

PROUD of her clustering spires, her new-
    built towers,
Our Venice, stolen from the slumbering
    sea,
A sister's kindliest greeting wafts to
    thee,
Rose of Val d' Arno, queen of all its
    flowers!
Thine exile's shrine thy sorrowing love em-
    bowers,
Yet none with truer homage bends the
    knee,
Or stronger pledge of fealty brings, than
    we,
Whose poets make thy dead Immortal
    ours.
Lonely the height, but ah, to heaven how
    near!
Dante, whence flowed that solemn verse
    of thine
Like the stern river from its Apennine
Whose name the far-off Scythian thrilled
    with fear:
Now to all lands thy deep-toned voice is
    dear,
And every language knows the Song
    Divine!

AT THE UNITARIAN FESTIVAL

MARCH 8, 1882

The waves unbuild the wasting shore;
  Where mountains towered the billows sweep,
Yet still their borrowed spoils restore,
  And build new empires from the deep.
So while the floods of thought lay waste
  The proud domain of priestly creeds,
Its heaven-appointed tides will haste
  To plant new homes for human needs.
Be ours to mark with hearts unchilled
  The change an outworn church deplores;
The legend sinks, but Faith shall build
  A fairer throne on new-found shores.

POEM

FOR THE TWO HUNDRED AND FIFTIETH ANNIVERSARY OF THE FOUNDING OF HARVARD COLLEGE

Twice had the mellowing sun of autumn crowned
The hundredth circle of his yearly round,
When, as we meet to-day, our fathers met:
That joyous gathering who can e'er forget,
When Harvard's nurslings, scattered far and wide,
Through mart and village, lake's and ocean's side,
Came, with one impulse, one fraternal throng,
And crowned the hours with banquet, speech, and song?

Once more revived in fancy's magic glass,
I see in state the long procession pass:
Tall, courtly, leader as by right divine,
Winthrop, our Winthrop, rules the marshalled line,
Still seen in front, as on that far-off day
His ribboned baton showed the column's way.
Not all are gone who marched in manly pride
And waved their truncheons at their leader's side;
Gray, Lowell, Dixwell, who his empire shared,
These to be with us envious Time has spared.

Few are the faces, so familiar then,
Our eyes still meet amid the haunts of men;
Scarce one of all the living gathered there,
Whose unthinned locks betrayed a silver hair,
Greets us to-day, and yet we seem the same
As our own sires and grandsires, save in name.
There are the patriarchs, looking vaguely round
For classmates' faces, hardly known if found;
See the cold brow that rules the busy mart;
Close at its side the pallid son of art,
Whose purchased skill with borrowed meaning clothes,
And stolen hues, the smirking face he loathes.
Here is the patient scholar; in his looks
You read the titles of his learned books;
What classic lore those spidery crow's-feet speak !
What problems figure on that wrinkled cheek !
For never thought but left its stiffened trace,
Its fossil footprint, on the plastic face,
As the swift record of a raindrop stands,
Fixed on the tablet of the hardening sands.
On every face as on the written page
Each year renews the autograph of age;
One trait alone may wasting years defy, —
The fire still lingering in the poet's eye,
While Hope, the siren, sings her sweetest strain, —
Non omnis moriar is its proud refrain.

Sadly we gaze upon the vacant chair;
He who should claim its honors is not there, —
Otis, whose lips the listening crowd enthrall
That press and pack the floor of Boston's hall.
But Kirkland smiles, released from toil and care
Since the silk mantle younger shoulders wear, —
Quincy's, whose spirit breathes the selfsame fire
That filled the bosom of his youthful sire,
Who for the altar bore the kindled torch
To freedom's temple, dying in its porch.

Three grave professions in their sons appear,
Whose words well studied all well pleased will hear:
Palfrey, ordained in varied walks to shine,
Statesman, historian, critic, and divine;
Solid and square behold majestic Shaw,
A mass of wisdom and a mine of law;
Warren, whose arm the doughtiest warriors fear,
Asks of the startled crowd to lend its ear, —
Proud of his calling, him the world loves best,
Not as the coming, but the parting guest.

Look on that form, — with eye dilating scan
The stately mould of nature's kingliest man!
Tower-like he stands in life's unfaded prime;
Ask you his name? None asks a second time!
He from the land his outward semblance takes,
Where storm-swept mountains watch o'er slumbering lakes.
See in the impress which the body wears
How its imperial might the soul declares:
The forehead's large expansion, lofty, wide,
That looks unsilvered vainly strive to hide;
The lines of thought that plough the sober cheek;
Lips that betray their wisdom ere they speak
In tones like answers from Dodona's grove;
An eye like Juno's when she frowns on Jove.
I look and wonder; will he be content —
This man, this monarch, for the purple meant —
The meaner duties of his tribe to share,
Clad in the garb that common mortals wear?
Ah, wild Ambition, spread thy restless wings,
Beneath whose plumes the hidden œstrum stings;
Thou whose bold flight would leave earth's vulgar crowds,
And like the eagle soar above the clouds,
Must feel the pang that fallen angels know
When the red lightning strikes thee from below!

Less bronze, more silver, mingles in the mould
Of him whom next my roving eyes behold;
His, more the scholar's than the statesman's face,
Proclaims him born of academic race.

Weary his look, as if an aching brain
Left on his brow the frozen prints of pain;
His voice far-reaching, grave, sonorous, owns
A shade of sadness in its plaintive tones,
Yet when its breath some loftier thought inspires
Glows with a heat that every bosom fires.
Such Everett seems; no chance-sown wild flower knows
The full-blown charms of culture's double rose, —
Alas, how soon, by death's unsparing frost,
Its bloom is faded and its fragrance lost!

Two voices, only two, to earth belong,
Of all whose accents met the listening throng:
Winthrop, alike for speech and guidance framed,
On that proud day a twofold duty claimed;
One other yet, — remembered or forgot, —
Forgive my silence if I name him not.
Can I believe it? I, whose youthful voice
Claimed a brief gamut, — notes not over choice, —
Stood undismayed before the solemn throng,
And *propria voce* sung that saucy song
Which even in memory turns my soul aghast, —
Felix audacia was the verdict cast.

What were the glory of these festal days
Shorn of their grand illumination's blaze?
Night comes at last with all her starry train
To find a light in every glittering pane.
From "Harvard's" windows see the sudden flash, —
Old "Massachusetts" glares through every sash;
From wall to wall the kindling splendors run
Till all is glorious as the noonday sun.

How to the scholar's mind each object brings
What some historian tells, some poet sings!
The good gray teacher whom we all revered —
Loved, honored, laughed at, and by freshmen feared,
As from old "Harvard," where its light began,
From hall to hall the clustering splendors ran —

Took down his well-worn Æschylus and read,
Lit by the rays a thousand tapers shed,
How the swift herald crossed the leagues between
Mycenæ's monarch and his faithless queen;
And thus he read, — my verse but ill displays
The Attic picture, clad in modern phrase:

On Ida's summit flames the kindling pile,
And Lemnos answers from his rocky isle;
From Athos next it climbs the reddening skies,
Thence where the watch-towers of Macistus rise.
The sentries of Mesapius in their turn
Bid the dry heath in high-piled masses burn,
Cithæron's crag the crimson billows stain,
Far Ægiplanctus joins the fiery train.
Thus the swift courier through the pathless night
Has gained at length the Arachnæan height,
Whence the glad tidings, borne on wings of flame,
" Ilium has fallen!" reach the royal dame.

So ends the day; before the midnight stroke
The lights expiring cloud the air with smoke;
While these the toil of younger hands employ,
The slumbering Grecian dreams of smouldering Troy.

As to that hour with backward steps I turn,
Midway I pause; behold a funeral urn!
Ah, sad memorial! known but all too well
The tale which thus its golden letters tell:

This dust, once breathing, changed its joyous life
For toil and hunger, wounds and mortal strife;
Love, friendship, learning's all-prevailing charms,
For the cold bivouac and the clash of arms.
The cause of freedom won, a race enslaved
Called back to manhood, and a nation saved,
These sons of Harvard, falling ere their prime,
Leave their proud memory to the coming time.

While in their still retreats our scholars turn
The mildewed pages of the past, to learn
With endless labor of the sleepless brain
What once has been and ne'er shall be again,
We reap the harvest of their ceaseless toil
And find a fragrance in their midnight oil.
But let a purblind mortal dare the task
The embryo future of itself to ask,
The world reminds him, with a scornful laugh,
That times have changed since Prospero broke his staff.
Could all the wisdom of the schools foretell
The dismal hour when Lisbon shook and fell,
Or name the shuddering night that toppled down
Our sister's pride, beneath whose mural crown
Scarce had the scowl forgot its angry lines,
When earth's blind prisoners fired their fatal mines?
New realms, new worlds, exulting Science claims,
Still the dim future unexplored remains;
Her trembling scales the far-off planet weigh,
Her torturing prisms its elements betray, —
We know what ores the fires of Sirius melt,
What vaporous metals gild Orion's belt;
Angels, archangels, may have yet to learn
Those hidden truths our heaven-taught eyes discern;
Yet vain is Knowledge, with her mystic wand,
To pierce the cloudy screen and read beyond;
Once to the silent stars the fates were known,
To us they tell no secrets but their own.

At Israel's altar still we humbly bow,
But where, oh where, are Israel's prophets now?
Where is the sibyl with her hoarded leaves?
Where is the charm the weird enchantress weaves?
No croaking raven turns the auspex pale,
No reeking altars tell the morrow's tale;
The measured footsteps of the Fates are dumb,
Unseen, unheard, unheralded, they come,
Prophet and priest and all their following fail.
Who then is left to rend the future's veil?

Who but the poet, he whose nicer sense
No film can baffle with its slight defence,
Whose finer vision marks the waves that stray,
Felt, but unseen, beyond the violet ray? —
Who, while the storm-wind waits its darkening shroud,
Foretells the tempest ere he sees the cloud, —
Stays not for time his secrets to reveal,
But reads his message ere he breaks the seal.
So Mantua's bard foretold the coming day
Ere Bethlehem's infant in the manger lay;
The promise trusted to a mortal tongue
Found listening ears before the angels sung.
So while his load the creeping pack-horse galled,
While inch by inch the dull canal-boat crawled,
Darwin beheld a Titan from "afar
Drag the slow barge or drive the rapid car,"
That panting giant fed by air and flame,
The mightiest forges task their strength to tame.

Happy the poet! him no tyrant fact
Holds in its clutches to be chained and racked;
Him shall no mouldy document convict,
No stern statistics gravely contradict;
No rival sceptre threats his airy throne;
He rules o'er shadows, but he reigns alone.
Shall I the poet's broad dominion claim
Because you bid me wear his sacred name
For these few moments? Shall I boldly clash
My flint and steel, and by the sudden flash
Read the fair vision which my soul descries
Through the wide pupils of its wondering eyes?
List then awhile; the fifty years have sped;
The third full century's opened scroll is spread,
Blank to all eyes save his who dimly sees
The shadowy future told in words like these:

How strange the prospect to my sight appears,
Changed by the busy hands of fifty years!
Full well I know our ocean-salted Charles,
Filling and emptying through the sands and marls
That wall his restless stream on either bank,
Not all unlovely when the sedges rank
Lend their coarse veil the sable ooze to hide
That bares its blackness with the ebbing tide.
In other shapes to my illumined eyes
Those ragged margins of our stream arise:
Through walls of stone the sparkling waters flow,
In clearer depths the golden sunsets glow,
On purer waves the lamps of midnight gleam,
That silver o'er the unpolluted stream.
Along his shores what stately temples rise,
What spires, what turrets, print the shadowed skies!
Our smiling Mother sees her broad domain
Spread its tall roofs along the western plain;
Those blazoned windows' blushing glories tell
Of grateful hearts that loved her long and well;
Yon gilded dome that glitters in the sun
Was Dives' gift, — alas, his only one!
These buttressed walls enshrine a banker's name,
That hallowed chapel hides a miser's shame;
Their wealth they left, — their memory cannot fade
Though age shall crumble every stone they laid.
  Great lord of millions, — let me call thee great,
Since countless servants at thy bidding wait, —
Richesse oblige: no mortal must be blind
To all but self, or look at human kind
Laboring and suffering, — all its want and woe, —
Through sheets of crystal, as a pleasing show
That makes life happier for the chosen few
Duty for whom is something not to do.
  When thy last page of life at length is filled,
What shall thine heirs to keep thy memory build?
Will piles of stone in Auburn's mournful shade
Save from neglect the spot where thou art laid?

Nay, deem not thus; the sauntering stranger's eye
Will pass unmoved thy columned tombstone by,
No memory wakened, not a teardrop shed,
Thy name uncared for and thy date unread.
But if thy record thou indeed dost prize,
Bid from the soil some stately temple rise, —
Some hall of learning, some memorial shrine,
With names long honored to associate thine:
So shall thy fame outlive thy shattered bust
When all around thee slumber in the dust.
Thus England's Henry lives in Eton's towers,
Saved from the spoil oblivion's gulf devours;
Our later records with as fair a fame
Have wreathed each uncrowned benefactor's name;
The walls they reared the memories still retain
That churchyard marbles try to keep in vain.
In vain the delving antiquary tries
To find the tomb where generous Harvard lies:
Here, here, his lasting monument is found,
Where every spot is consecrated ground!
O'er Stoughton's dust the crumbling stone decays,
Fast fade its lines of lapidary praise;
There the wild bramble weaves its ragged nets,
There the dry lichen spreads its gray rosettes;
Still in yon walls his memory lives unspent,
Nor asks a braver, nobler monument.
Thus Hollis lives, and Holden, honored, praised,
And good Sir Matthew, in the halls they raised;
Thus live the worthies of these later times,
Who shine in deeds, less brilliant, grouped in rhymes.
Say, shall the Muse with faltering steps retreat,
Or dare these names in rhythmic form repeat?
Why not as boldly as from Homer's lips
The long array of Argive battle-ships?

When o'er our graves a thousand years have past
(If to such date our threatened globe shall last)
These classic precincts, myriad feet have pressed,
Will show on high, in beauteous garlands dressed,
Those honored names that grace our later day, —
Weld, Matthews, Sever, Thayer, Austin, Gray,
Sears, Phillips, Lawrence, Hemenway, — to the list
Add Sanders, Sibley, — all the Muse has missed.

Once more I turn to read the pictured page
Bright with the promise of the coming age.
Ye unborn sons of children yet unborn,
Whose youthful eyes shall greet that far-off morn,
Blest are those eyes that all undimmed behold
The sights so longed for by the wise of old.
From high-arched alcoves, through resounding halls,
Clad in full robes majestic Science calls,
Tireless, unsleeping, still at Nature's feet,
Whate'er she utters fearless to repeat,
Her lips at last from every cramp released
That Israel's prophet caught from Egypt's priest.
I see the statesman, firm, sagacious, bold,
For life's long conflict cast in amplest mould;
Not his to clamor with the senseless throng
That shouts unshamed, "Our party, right or wrong,"
But in the patriot's never-ending fight
To side with Truth, who changes wrong to right.
I see the scholar; in that wondrous time
Men, women, children, all can write in rhyme.
These four brief lines addressed to youth inclined
To idle rhyming in his notes I find:

Who writes in verse that should have writ in prose
Is like a traveller walking on his toes;
Happy the rhymester who in time has found
The heels he lifts were made to touch the ground.

I see gray teachers, — on their work intent,
Their lavished lives, in endless labor spent,
Had closed at last in age and penury
    wrecked,
Martyrs, not burned, but frozen in neglect,
Save for the generous hands that stretched
    in aid
Of worn-out servants left to die half paid.
Ah, many a year will pass, I thought, ere
    we
Such kindly forethought shall rejoice to
    see, —
Monarchs are mindful of the sacred debt
That cold republics hasten to forget.

I see the priest, — if such a name he
    bears
Who without pride his sacred vestment
    wears;
And while the symbols of his tribe I seek
Thus my first impulse bids me think and
    speak:

Let not the mitre England's prelate wears
Next to the crown whose regal pomp it
    shares,
Though low before it courtly Christians
    bow,
Leave its red mark on Younger England's
    brow.
We love, we honor, the maternal dame,
But let her priesthood wear a modest name,
While through the waters of the Pilgrim's
    bay
A new-born Mayflower shows her keels the
    way.
Too old grew Britain for her mother's
    beads, —
Must we be necklaced with her children's
    creeds?
Welcome alike in surplice or in gown
The loyal lieges of the Heavenly Crown!
We greet with cheerful, not submissive,
    mien
A sister church, but not a mitred Queen!

A few brief flutters, and the unwilling
    Muse,
Who feared the flight she hated to refuse,
Shall fold the wings whose gayer plumes
    are shed,
Here where at first her half-fledged pin-
    ions spread.
    Well I remember in the long ago
How in the forest shades of Fontainebleau,

Strained through a fissure in a rocky cell,
One crystal drop with measured cadence
    fell.
Still, as of old, forever bright and clear,
The fissured cavern drops its wonted tear,
And wondrous virtue, simple folk aver,
Lies in that teardrop of *la roche qui pleure.*
    Of old I wandered by the river's side
Between whose banks the mighty waters
    glide,
Where vast Niagara, hurrying to its fall,
Builds and unbuilds its ever-tumbling wall;
Oft in my dreams I hear the rush and roar
Of battling floods, and feel the trembling
    shore,
As the huge torrent, girded for its leap,
With bellowing thunders plunges down the
    steep.
    Not less distinct, from memory's pic-
        tured urn,
The gray old rock, the leafy woods, return;
Robed in their pride the lofty oaks appear,
And once again with quickened sense I
    hear,
Through the low murmur of the leaves
    that stir,
The tinkling teardrop of *la roche qui pleure.*

So when the third ripe century stands com-
    plete,
As once again the sons of Harvard meet,
Rejoicing, numerous as the seashore sands,
Drawn from all quarters, — farthest dis-
    tant lands,
Where through the reeds the scaly saurian
    steals,
Where cold Alaska feeds her floundering
    seals,
Where Plymouth, glorying, wears her iron
    crown,
Where Sacramento sees the suns go down;
Nay, from the cloisters whence the refluent
    tide
Wafts their pale students to our Mother's
    side, —
Mid all the tumult that the day shall
    bring,
While all the echoes shout, and roar, and
    ring,
These tinkling lines, oblivion's easy prey,
Once more emerging to the light of day,
Not all unpleasing to the listening ear
Shall wake the memories of this bygone
    year,

Heard as I hear the measured drops that flow
From the gray rock of wooded Fontainebleau.

Yet, ere I leave, one loving word for all
Those fresh young lives that wait our Mother's call:
One gift is yours, kind Nature's richest dower, —
Youth, the fair bud that holds life's opening flower,
Full of high hopes no coward doubts enchain,
With all the future throbbing in its brain,
And mightiest instincts which the beating heart
Fills with the fire its burning waves impart.
O joyous youth, whose glory is to dare, —
Thy foot firm planted on the lowest stair,
Thine eye uplifted to the loftiest height
Where Fame stands beckoning in the rosy light,
Thanks for thy flattering tales, thy fond deceits,
Thy loving lies, thy cheerful smiling cheats !
Nature's rash promise every day is broke, —
A thousand acorns breed a single oak,
The myriad blooms that make the orchard gay
In barren beauty throw their lives away;
Yet shall we quarrel with the sap that yields
The painted blossoms which adorn the fields,
When the fair orchard wears its May-day suit
Of pink-white petals, for its scanty fruit ?
Thrice happy hours, in hope's illusion dressed,
In fancy's cradle nurtured and caressed,
Though rich the spoils that ripening years may bring,
To thee the dewdrops of the Orient cling, —
Not all the dye-stuffs from the vats of truth
Can match the rainbow on the robes of youth !

Dear unborn children, to our Mother's trust
We leave you, fearless, when we lie in dust:
While o'er these walls the Christian banner waves
From hallowed lips shall flow the truth that saves;
While o'er those portals *Veritas* you read

No church shall bind you with its human creed.
Take from the past the best its toil has won,
But learn betimes its slavish ruts to shun.
Pass the old tree whose withered leaves are shed,
Quit the old paths that error loved to tread,
And a new wreath of living blossoms seek,
A narrower pathway up a loftier peak;
Lose not your reverence, but unmanly fear
Leave far behind you, all who enter here !

As once of old from Ida's lofty height
The flaming signal flashed across the night,
So Harvard's beacon sheds its unspent rays
Till every watch-tower shows its kindling blaze.
Caught from a spark and fanned by every gale,
A brighter radiance gilds the roofs of Yale;
Amherst and Williams bid their flambeaus shine,
And Bowdoin answers through her groves of pine;
O'er Princeton's sands the far reflections steal,
Where mighty Edwards stamped his iron heel;
Nay, on the hill where old beliefs were bound
Fast as if Styx had girt them nine times round,
Bursts such a light that trembling souls inquire
If the whole church of Calvin is on fire !
Well may they ask, for what so brightly burns
As a dry creed that nothing ever learns ?
Thus link by link is knit the flaming chain
Lit by the torch of Harvard's hallowed plain.

Thy son, thy servant, dearest Mother mine,
Lays this poor offering on thy holy shrine,
An autumn leaflet to the wild winds tost,
Touched by the finger of November's frost,
With sweet, sad memories of that earlier day,
And all that listened to my first-born lay,
With grateful heart this glorious morn I see, —
Would that my tribute worthier were of thee !

POST-PRANDIAL

PHI BETA KAPPA

WENDELL PHILLIPS, ORATOR; CHARLES GODFREY LELAND, POET

1881

"THE Dutch have taken Holland," — so
    the school-boys used to say;
The Dutch have taken Harvard, — no doubt
    of that to-day!
For the Wendells were low Dutchmen, and
    all their vrows were Vans;
And the Breitmanns are high Dutchmen,
    and here is honest Hans.

Mynheers, you both are welcome! Fair
    cousin Wendell P.,
Our ancestors were dwellers beside the
    Zuyder Zee;
Both Grotius and Erasmus were countrymen of we,
And Vondel was our namesake, though he
    spelt it with a V.

It is well old Evert Jansen sought a dwelling over sea
On the margin of the Hudson, where he
    sampled you and me
Through our grandsires and great-grandsires, for you would n't quite agree
With the steady-going burghers along the
    Zuyder Zee.

Like our Motley's John of Barnveld, you
    have always been inclined
To speak, — well, — somewhat frankly, —
    to let us know your mind,
And the Mynheers would have told you to
    be cautious what you said,
Or else that silver tongue of yours might
    cost your precious head.

But we 're very glad you've kept it; it was
    always Freedom's own,
And whenever Reason chose it she found
    a royal throne;
You have whacked us with your sceptre;
    our backs were little harmed,
And while we rubbed our bruises we owned
    we had been charmed.

And you, our *quasi* Dutchman, what welcome should be yours
For all the wise prescriptions that work
    your laughter-cures?
"Shake before taking"? — not a bit, —
    the bottle-cure's a sham;
Take before shaking, and you 'll find it
    shakes your diaphragm.

"Hans Breitmann gif a barty, — vhere is
    dot barty now?"
On every shelf where wit is stored to
    smooth the careworn brow!
A health to stout Hans Breitmann! How
    long before we see
Another Hans as handsome, — as bright a
    man as he!

THE FLÂNEUR

BOSTON COMMON, DECEMBER 6, 1882

DURING THE TRANSIT OF VENUS

I LOVE all sights of earth and skies,
From flowers that glow to stars that shine;
The comet and the penny show,
All curious things, above, below,
Hold each in turn my wandering eyes:
I claim the Christian Pagan's line,
Humani nihil, — even so, —
And is not human life divine?

When soft the western breezes blow,
And strolling youths meet sauntering maids,
I love to watch the stirring trades
Beneath the Vallombrosa shades
Our much-enduring elms bestow;
The vender and his rhetoric's flow,
That lambent stream of liquid lies;
The bait he dangles from his line,
The gudgeon and his gold-washed prize.
I halt before the blazoned sign
That bids me linger to admire
The drama time can never tire,
The little hero of the hunch,
With iron arm and soul of fire,
And will that works his fierce desire, —
Untamed, unscared, unconquered Punch!
My ear a pleasing torture finds
In tones the withered sibyl grinds, —
The *dame sans merci*'s broken strain.
Whom I erewhile, perchance, have known,

When Orleans filled the Bourbon throne,
A siren-singing by the Seine.

But most I love the tube that spies
The orbs celestial in their march;
That shows the comet as it whisks
Its tail across the planets' disks,
As if to blind their blood-shot eyes;
Or wheels so close against the sun
We tremble at the thought of risks
Our little spinning ball may run,
To pop like corn that children parch,
From summer something overdone,
And roll, a cinder, through the skies.

Grudge not to-day the scanty fee
To him who farms the firmament,
To whom the Milky Way is free;
Who holds the wondrous crystal key,
The silent Open Sesame
That Science to her sons has lent;
Who takes his toll, and lifts the bar
That shuts the road to sun and star.
If Venus only comes to time,
(And prophets say she must and shall,)
To-day will hear the tinkling chime
Of many a ringing silver dime,
For him whose optic glass supplies
The crowd with astronomic eyes, —
The Galileo of the Mall.

Dimly the transit morning broke;
The sun seemed doubting what to do,
As one who questions how to dress,
And takes his doublets from the press,
And halts between the old and new.
Please Heaven he wear his suit of blue,
Or don, at least, his ragged cloak,
With rents that show the azure through!

I go the patient crowd to join
That round the tube my eyes discern,
The last new-comer of the file,
And wait, and wait, a weary while,
And gape, and stretch, and shrug, and smile,
(For each his place must fairly earn,
Hindmost and foremost, in his turn,)
Till hitching onward, pace by pace,
I gain at last the envied place,
And pay the white exiguous coin:
The sun and I are face to face;
He glares at me, I stare at him;
And lo! my straining eye has found
A little spot that, black and round,
Lies near the crimsoned fire-orb's rim.
O blessed, beauteous evening star,
Well named for her whom earth adores, —
The Lady of the dove-drawn car, —
I know thee in thy white simar;
But veiled in black, a rayless spot,
Blank as a careless scribbler's blot,
Stripped of thy robe of silvery flame, —
The stolen robe that Night restores
When Day has shut his golden doors, —
I see thee, yet I know thee not;
And canst thou call thyself the same?

A black, round spot, — and that is all;
And such a speck our earth would be
If he who looks upon the stars
Through the red atmosphere of Mars
Could see our little creeping ball
Across the disk of crimson crawl
As I our sister planet see.

And art thou, then, a world like ours,
Flung from the orb that whirled our own
A molten pebble from its zone?
How must thy burning sands absorb
The fire-waves of the blazing orb,
Thy chain so short, thy path so near,
Thy flame-defying creatures hear
The maelstroms of the photosphere!
And is thy bosom decked with flowers
That steal their bloom from scalding showers?
And hast thou cities, domes, and towers,
And life, and love that makes it dear,
And death that fills thy tribes with fear?

Lost in my dream, my spirit soars
Through paths the wandering angels know;
My all-pervading thought explores
The azure ocean's lucent shores;
I leave my mortal self below,
As up the star-lit stairs I climb,
And still the widening view reveals
In endless rounds the circling wheels
That build the horologe of time.
New spheres, new suns, new systems gleam;
The voice no earth-born echo hears
Steals softly on my ravished ears:
I hear them "singing as they shine" —
A mortal's voice dissolves my dream:
My patient neighbor, next in line,
Hints gently there are those who wait.
O guardian of the starry gate,
What coin shall pay this debt of mine?
Too slight thy claim, too small the fee

That bids thee turn the potent key
The Tuscan's hand has placed in thine.
Forgive my own the small affront,
The insult of the proffered dime;
Take it, O friend, since this thy wont,
But still shall faithful memory be
A bankrupt debtor unto thee,
And pay thee with a grateful rhyme.

AVE

PRELUDE TO "ILLUSTRATED POEMS"

FULL well I know the frozen hand has come
That smites the songs of grove and garden dumb,
And chills sad autumn's last chrysanthemum;

Yet would I find one blossom, if I might,
Ere the dark loom that weaves the robe of white
Hides all the wrecks of summer out of sight.

Sometimes in dim November's narrowing day,
When all the season's pride has passed away,
As mid the blackened stems and leaves we stray,

We spy in sheltered nook or rocky cleft
A starry disk the hurrying winds have left,
Of all its blooming sisterhood bereft:

Some pansy, with its wondering baby eyes —
Poor wayside nursling ! — fixed in blank surprise
At the rough welcome of unfriendly skies;

Or golden daisy, — will it dare disclaim
The lion's tooth, to wear this gentler name ?
Or blood-red salvia, with its lips aflame:

The storms have stripped the lily and the rose,
Still on its cheek the flush of summer glows,
And all its heart-leaves kindle as it blows.

So had I looked some bud of song to find
The careless winds of autumn left behind,
With these of earlier seasons' growth to bind.

Ah me ! my skies are dark with sudden grief,
A flower lies faded on my garnered sheaf;
Yet let the sunshine gild this virgin leaf, —

The joyous, blessed sunshine of the past,
Still with me, though the heavens are overcast, —
The light that shines while life and memory last.

Go, pictured rhymes, for loving readers meant;
Bring back the smiles your jocund morning lent,
And warm their hearts with sunbeams yet unspent !

KING'S CHAPEL

READ AT THE TWO HUNDREDTH ANNIVERSARY

Is it a weanling's weakness for the past
That in the stormy, rebel-breeding town,
Swept clean of relics by the levelling blast,
Still keeps our gray old chapel's name of "King's,"
Still to its outworn symbols fondly clings, —
Its unchurched mitres and its empty crown ?

Poor harmless emblems ! All has shrunk away
That made them gorgons in the patriot's eyes;
The priestly plaything harms us not to-day;
The gilded crown is but a pleasing show,
An old-world heirloom, left from long ago,
Wreck of the past that memory bids us prize.

Lightly we glance the fresh-cut marbles o'er;
Those two of earlier date our eyes enthrall:
The proud old Briton's by the western door.
And hers, the Lady of Colonial days,
Whose virtues live in long-drawn classic phrase, —
The fair Francesca of the southern wall.

Ay ! those were goodly men that Reynolds drew,
And stately dames our Copley's canvas holds,

To their old Church, their Royal Master, true,
Proud of the claim their valiant sires had earned,
That "gentle blood," not lightly to be spurned,
  Save by the churl ungenerous Nature moulds.

All vanished! It were idle to complain
  That ere the fruits shall come the flowers must fall;
Yet somewhat we have lost amidst our gain,
Some rare ideals time may not restore, —
The charm of courtly breeding, seen no more,
  And reverence, dearest ornament of all.

Thus musing, to the western wall I came,
  Departing: lo! a tablet fresh and fair,
Where glistened many a youth's remembered name
In golden letters on the snow-white stone, —
Young lives these aisles and arches once have known,
  Their country's bleeding altar might not spare.

These died that we might claim a soil unstained,
  Save by the blood of heroes; their bequests
A realm unsevered and a race unchained.
Has purer blood through Norman veins come down
From the rough knights that clutched the Saxon's crown
  Than warmed the pulses in these faithful breasts?

These, too, shall live in history's deathless page,
  High on the slow-wrought pedestals of fame,
Ranged with the heroes of remoter age;
They could not die who left their nation free,
Firm as the rock, unfettered as the sea,
  Its heaven unshadowed by the cloud of shame.

While on the storied past our memory dwells,
  Our grateful tribute shall not be denied, —

The wreath, the cross of rustling immortelles;
And willing hands shall clear each darkening bust,
As year by year sifts down the clinging dust
  On Shirley's beauty and on Vassall's pride.

But for our own, our loved and lost, we bring
  With throbbing hearts and tears that still must flow,
In full-heaped hands, the opening flowers of spring,
Lilies half-blown, and budding roses, red
As their young cheeks, before the blood was shed
  That lent their morning bloom its generous glow.

Ah, who shall count a rescued nation's debt,
  Or sum in words our martyrs' silent claims?
Who shall our heroes' dread exchange forget, —
All life, youth, hope, could promise to allure
For all that soul could brave or flesh endure?
  They shaped our future; we but carve their names.

HYMN

FOR THE SAME OCCASION

SUNG BY THE CONGREGATION TO THE TUNE OF TALLIS'S EVENING HYMN

O'ERSHADOWED by the walls that climb,
  Piled up in air by living hands,
A rock amid the waves of time,
  Our gray old house of worship stands.

High o'er the pillared aisles we love
  The symbols of the past look down;
Unharmed, unharming, throned above,
  Behold the mitre and the crown!

Let not our younger faith forget
  The loyal souls that held them dear;
The prayers we read their tears have wet,
  The hymns we sing they loved to hear.

The memory of their earthly throne
  Still to our holy temple clings,
But here the kneeling suppliants own
  One only Lord, the King of kings.

Hark! while our hymn of grateful praise
  The solemn echoing vaults prolong,
The far-off voice of earlier days
  Blends with our own in hallowed song:

To Him who ever lives and reigns,
  Whom all the hosts of heaven adore,
Who lent the life his breath sustains,
  Be glory now and evermore!

HYMN—THE WORD OF PROMISE

(BY SUPPOSITION)

AN HYMN SET FORTH TO BE SUNG BY THE GREAT ASSEMBLY AT NEWTOWN, [MASS.] MO. 12. 1. 1636

Written by OLIVER WENDELL HOLMES, eldest son of Rev. ABIEL HOLMES, eighth Pastor of the First Church in Cambridge, Massachusetts.

LORD, Thou hast led us as of old
  Thine Arm led forth the chosen Race
Through Foes that raged, through Floods
    that roll'd,
  To Canaan's far-off Dwelling-Place.

Here is Thy bounteous Table spread,
  Thy Manna falls on every Field,
Thy Grace our hungering Souls hath fed,
  Thy Might hath been our Spear and
    Shield.

Lift high Thy Buckler, Lord of Hosts!
  Guard Thou Thy Servants, Sons and
    Sires,
While on the Godless heathen Coasts
  They light Thine Israel's Altar-fires!

The salvage Wilderness remote
  Shall hear Thy Works and Wonders
    sung;
So from the Rock that Moses smote
  The Fountain of the Desart sprung.

Soon shall the slumbering Morn awake,
  From wandering Stars of Errour freed,
When Christ the Bread of Heaven shall
    break
  For Saints that own a common Creed.

The Walls that fence His Flocks apart
  Shall crack and crumble in Decay,
And every Tongue and every Heart
  Shall welcome in the new-born Day.

Then shall His glorious Church rejoice
  His Word of Promise to recall,—
ONE SHELTERING FOLD, ONE SHEPHERD'S
    VOICE,
  ONE GOD AND FATHER OVER ALL!

HYMN

READ AT THE DEDICATION OF THE OLIVER WENDELL HOLMES HOSPITAL AT HUDSON, WISCONSIN

JUNE 7, 1887

ANGEL of love, for every grief
  Its soothing balm thy mercy brings,
For every pang its healing leaf,
  For homeless want, thine outspread wings.

Enough for thee the pleading eye,
  The knitted brow of silent pain;
The portals open to a sigh
  Without the clank of bolt or chain.

Who is our brother? He that lies
  Left at the wayside, bruised and sore:
His need our open hand supplies,
  His welcome waits him at our door.

Not ours to ask in freezing tones
  His race, his calling, or his creed;
Each heart the tie of kinship owns,
  When those are human veins that bleed.

Here stand the champions to defend
  From every wound that flesh can feel;
Here science, patience, skill, shall blend
  To save, to calm, to help, to heal.

Father of Mercies! Weak and frail,
  Thy guiding hand thy children ask;
Let not the Great Physician fail
  To aid us in our holy task.

Source of all truth, and love, and light,
  That warm and cheer our earthly days,
Be ours to serve Thy will aright,
  Be Thine the glory and the praise!

ON THE DEATH OF PRESIDENT GARFIELD

I

FALLEN with autumn's falling leaf
  Ere yet his summer's noon was past,
Our friend, our guide, our trusted chief, —
  What words can match a woe so vast!

And whose the chartered claim to speak
  The sacred grief where all have part,
Where sorrow saddens every cheek
  And broods in every aching heart?

Yet Nature prompts the burning phrase
  That thrills the hushed and shrouded hall,
The loud lament, the sorrowing praise,
  The silent tear that love lets fall.

In loftiest verse, in lowliest rhyme,
  Shall strive unblamed the minstrel choir, —
The singers of the new-born time,
  And trembling age with outworn lyre.

No room for pride, no place for blame, —
  We fling our blossoms on the grave,
Pale, — scentless, — faded, — all we claim,
  This only, — what we had we gave.

Ah, could the grief of all who mourn
  Blend in one voice its bitter cry,
The wail to heaven's high arches borne
  Would echo through the caverned sky.

II

O happiest land, whose peaceful choice
  Fills with a breath its empty throne!
God, speaking through thy people's voice,
  Has made that voice for once his own.

No angry passion shakes the state
  Whose weary servant seeks for rest,
And who could fear that scowling hate
  Would strike at that unguarded breast?

He stands, unconscious of his doom,
  In manly strength, erect, serene;
Around him Summer spreads her bloom;
  He falls, — what horror clothes the scene!

How swift the sudden flash of woe
  Where all was bright as childhood's dream!
As if from heaven's ethereal bow
  Had leaped the lightning's arrowy gleam.

Blot the foul deed from history's page;
  Let not the all-betraying sun
Blush for the day that stains an age
  When murder's blackest wreath was won.

III

Pale on his couch the sufferer lies,
  The weary battle-ground of pain:
Love tends his pillow; Science tries
  Her every art, alas! in vain.

The strife endures how long! how long!
  Life, death, seem balanced in the scale,
While round his bed a viewless throng
  Await each morrow's changing tale.

In realms the desert ocean parts
  What myriads watch with tear-filled eyes,
His pulse-beats echoing in their hearts,
  His breathings counted with their sighs!

Slowly the stores of life are spent,
  Yet hope still battles with despair;
Will Heaven not yield when knees are bent?
  Answer, O thou that hearest prayer!

But silent is the brazen sky;
  On sweeps the meteor's threatening train,
Unswerving Nature's mute reply,
  Bound in her adamantine chain.

Not ours the verdict to decide
  Whom death shall claim or skill shall save;
The hero's life though Heaven denied,
  It gave our land a martyr's grave.

Nor count the teaching vainly sent
  How human hearts their griefs may share, —
The lesson woman's love has lent,
  What hope may do, what faith can bear!

Farewell! the leaf-strown earth enfolds
  Our stay, our pride, our hopes, our fears,
And autumn's golden sun beholds
  A nation bowed, a world in tears.

THE GOLDEN FLOWER

When Advent dawns with lessening days,
  While earth awaits the angels' hymn;
When bare as branching coral sways
  In whistling winds each leafless limb;
When spring is but a spendthrift's dream,
  And summer's wealth a wasted dower,
Nor dews nor sunshine may redeem, —
  Then autumn coins his Golden Flower.

Soft was the violet's vernal hue,
  Fresh was the rose's morning red,
Full-orbed the stately dahlia grew, —
  All gone! their short-lived splendors shed.
The shadows, lengthening, stretch at noon;
  The fields are stripped, the groves are dumb;
The frost-flowers greet the icy moon, —
  Then blooms the bright chrysanthemum.

The stiffening turf is white with snow,
  Yet still its radiant disks are seen
Where soon the hallowed morn will show
  The wreath and cross of Christmas green;
As if in autumn's dying days
  It heard the heavenly song afar,
And opened all its glowing rays,
  The herald lamp of Bethlehem's star.

Orphan of summer, kindly sent
  To cheer the fading year's decline,
In all that pitying Heaven has lent
  No fairer pledge of hope than thine.
Yes! June lies hid beneath the snow,
  And winter's unborn heir shall claim
For every seed that sleeps below
  A spark that kindles into flame.

Thy smile the scowl of winter braves,
  Last of the bright-robed, flowery train,
Soft sighing o'er the garden graves,
  "Farewell! farewell! we meet again!"
So may life's chill November bring
  Hope's golden flower, the last of all,
Before we hear the angels sing
  Where blossoms never fade and fall!

YOUTH

[Read at the celebration of the thirty-first anniversary of the Boston Young Men's Christian Union, May 31, 1882.]

Why linger round the sunken wrecks
  Where old Armadas found their graves?
Why slumber on the sleepy decks
  While foam and clash the angry waves?
Up! when the storm-blast rends the clouds,
  And winged with ruin sweeps the gale,
Young feet must climb the quivering shrouds,
  Young hands must reef the bursting sail!

Leave us to fight the tyrant creeds
  Who felt their shackles, feel their scars;
The cheerful sunlight little heeds
  The brutes that prowled beneath the stars;
The dawn is here, the day star shows
  The spoils of many a battle won,
But sin and sorrow still are foes
  That face us in the morning sun.

Who sleeps beneath yon bannered mound
  The proudly sorrowing mourner seeks,
The garland-bearing crowd surrounds?
  A light-haired boy with beardless cheeks!
'T is time this "fallen world" should rise;
  Let youth the sacred work begin!
What nobler task, what fairer prize
  Than earth to save and Heaven to win?

HAIL, COLUMBIA!

1798

THE FIRST VERSE OF THE SONG

BY JOSEPH HOPKINSON

"Hail, Columbia! Happy land!
Hail, ye heroes, heaven-born band,
  Who fought and bled in Freedom's cause,
  Who fought and bled in Freedom's cause,
And when the storm of war was gone
Enjoy'd the peace your valor won.
  Let independence be our boast,
  Ever mindful what it cost;
  Ever grateful for the prize,
  Let its altar reach the skies.

THE FOUNTAIN AT STRATFORD-ON-AVON

"Firm — united — let us be,
Rallying round our Liberty;
As a band of brothers join'd,
Peace and safety we shall find."

. . . .

ADDITIONAL VERSES

WRITTEN AT THE REQUEST OF THE COMMITTEE FOR THE CONSTITUTIONAL CENTENNIAL CELEBRATION AT PHILADELPHIA, 1887

Look our ransomed shores around,
Peace and safety we have found!
  Welcome, friends who once were foes!
  Welcome, friends who once were foes,
To all the conquering years have gained,—
A nation's rights, a race unchained!
Children of the day new-born,
Mindful of its glorious morn,
Let the pledge our fathers signed
Heart to heart forever bind!

While the stars of heaven shall burn,
While the ocean tides return,
Ever may the circling sun
Find the Many still are One!

Graven deep with edge of steel,
Crowned with Victory's crimson seal,
  All the world their names shall read!
  All the world their names shall read,
Enrolled with his, the Chief that led
The hosts whose blood for us was shed.
Pay our sires their children's debt,
Love and honor, nor forget
Only Union's golden key
Guards the Ark of Liberty!

While the stars of heaven shall burn,
While the ocean tides return,
Ever may the circling sun
Find the Many still are One!

Hail, Columbia! strong and free,
Throned in hearts from sea to sea!
  Thy march triumphant still pursue!
  Thy march triumphant still pursue
With peaceful stride from zone to zone,
Till Freedom finds the world her own!
Blest in Union's holy ties,
Let our grateful song arise,
Every voice its tribute lend,
All in loving chorus blend!

While the stars in heaven shall burn,
While the ocean tides return,
Ever shall the circling sun
Find the Many still are One!

POEM

FOR THE DEDICATION OF THE FOUNTAIN AT STRATFORD-ON-AVON, PRESENTED BY GEORGE W. CHILDS, OF PHILADELPHIA

[Dated August 29, 1887.]

Welcome, thrice welcome is thy silvery
    gleam,
  Thou long-imprisoned stream!
Welcome the tinkle of thy crystal beads
As plashing raindrops to the flowery
    meads,
As summer's breath to Avon's whispering
    reeds!
From rock-walled channels, drowned in
    rayless night,
  Leap forth to life and light;
Wake from the darkness of thy troubled
    dream,
And greet with answering smile the morning's beam!

No purer lymph the white-limbed Naiad
    knows
  Than from thy chalice flows;
Not the bright spring of Afric's sunny
    shores,
Starry with spangles washed from golden
    ores,
Nor glassy stream Bandusia's fountain
    pours,
Nor wave translucent where Sabrina fair
    Braids her loose-flowing hair,
Nor the swift current, stainless as it rose
Where chill Arveiron steals from Alpine
    snows.

Here shall the traveller stay his weary feet
  To seek thy calm retreat;
Here at high noon the brown-armed reaper
    rest;
Here, when the shadows, lengthening from
    the west,
Call the mute song-bird to his leafy nest,
Matron and maid shall chat the cares away
  That brooded o'er the day,

While flocking round them troops of chil-
　　dren meet,
And all the arches ring with laughter
　　sweet.

Here shall the steed, his patient life who
　　spends
　　　In toil that never ends,
Hot from his thirsty tramp o'er hill and
　　plain,
Plunge his red nostrils, while the torturing
　　rein
Drops in loose loops beside his floating
　　mane;
Nor the poor brute that shares his master's
　　lot
　　　Find his small needs forgot, —
Truest of humble, long-enduring friends,
Whose presence cheers, whose guardian
　　care defends!

Here lark and thrush and nightingale shall
　　sip,
　　　And skimming swallows dip,
And strange shy wanderers fold their lus-
　　trous plumes
Fragrant from bowers that lent their sweet
　　perfumes
Where Pæstum's rose or Persia's lilac
　　blooms;
Here from his cloud the eagle stoop to
　　drink
　　　At the full basin's brink,
And whet his beak against its rounded lip,
His glossy feathers glistening as they drip.

Here shall the dreaming poet linger long,
　　Far from his listening throng, —
Nor lute nor lyre his trembling hand shall
　　bring;
Here no frail Muse shall imp her crippled
　　wing,
No faltering minstrel strain his throat to
　　sing!
These hallowed echoes who shall dare to
　　claim
　　　Whose tuneless voice would shame,
Whose jangling chords with jarring notes
　　would wrong
The nymphs that heard the Swan of Avon's
　　song?

What visions greet the pilgrim's raptured
　　eyes!
　　　What ghosts made real rise!

The dead return, — they breathe, — they
　　live again,
Joined by the host of Fancy's airy train,
Fresh from the springs of Shakespeare's
　　quickening brain!
The stream that slakes the soul's diviner
　　thirst
　　　Here found the sunbeams first;
Rich with his fame, not less shall memory
　　prize
The gracious gift that humbler wants sup-
　　plies.

O'er the wide waters reached the hand
　　that gave
　　　To all this bounteous wave,
With health and strength and joyous beauty
　　fraught;
Blest be the generous pledge of friendship,
　　brought
From the far home of brothers' love, un-
　　bought!
Long may fair Avon's fountain flow, en-
　　rolled
　　　With storied shrines of old,
Castalia's spring, Egeria's dewy cave,
And Horeb's rock the God of Israel clave!

Land of our fathers, ocean makes us two,
　　But heart to heart is true!
Proud is your towering daughter in the West,
Yet in her burning life-blood reign confest
Her mother's pulses beating in her breast.
This holy fount, whose rills from heaven
　　descend,
　　　Its gracious drops shall lend, —
Both foreheads bathed in that baptismal
　　dew,
And love make one the old home and the
　　new!

TO THE POETS WHO ONLY READ AND LISTEN

When evening's shadowy fingers fold
　　The flowers of every hue,
Some shy, half-opened bud will hold
　　Its drop of morning's dew.

Sweeter with every sunlit hour
　　The trembling sphere has grown,
Till all the fragrance of the flower
　　Becomes at last its own.

We that have sung perchance may find
  Our little meed of praise,
And round our pallid temples bind
  The wreath of fading bays:

Ah, Poet, who has never spent
  Thy breath in idle strains,
For thee the dewdrop morning lent
  Still in thy heart remains;

Unwasted, in its perfumed cell
  It waits the evening gale;
Then to the azure whence it fell
  Its lingering sweets exhale.

FOR THE DEDICATION OF THE NEW CITY LIBRARY, BOSTON

NOVEMBER 26, 1888

PROUDLY, beneath her glittering dome,
  Our three-hilled city greets the morn;
Here Freedom found her virgin home, —
  The Bethlehem where her babe was born.

The lordly roofs of traffic rise
  Amid the smoke of household fires;
High o'er them in the peaceful skies
  Faith points to heaven her clustering spires.

Can Freedom breathe if ignorance reign?
  Shall Commerce thrive where anarchs rule?
Will Faith her half-fledged brood retain
  If darkening counsels cloud the school?

Let in the light! from every age
  Some gleams of garnered wisdom pour,
And, fixed on thought's electric page,
  Wait all their radiance to restore.

Let in the light! in diamond mines
  Their gems invite the hand that delves;
So learning's treasured jewels shine
  Ranged on the alcove's ordered shelves.

From history's scroll the splendor streams,
  From science leaps the living ray;
Flashed from the poet's glowing dreams
  The opal fires of fancy play.

Let in the light! these windowed walls
  Shall brook no shadowing colonnades,
But day shall flood the silent halls
  Till o'er yon hills the sunset fades.

Behind the ever open gate
  No pikes shall fence a crumbling throne,
No lackeys cringe, no courtiers wait, —
  This palace is the people's own!

Heirs of our narrow-girdled past,
  How fair the prospect we survey,
Where howled unheard the wintry blast
  And rolled unchecked the storm-swept bay!

These chosen precincts, set apart
  For learned toil and holy shrines,
Yield willing homes to every art
  That trains, or strengthens, or refines.

Here shall the sceptred mistress reign
  Who heeds her meanest subject's call,
Sovereign of all their vast domain,
  The queen, the handmaid of them all!

TO JAMES RUSSELL LOWELL

AT THE DINNER GIVEN IN HIS HONOR AT THE TAVERN CLUB, ON HIS SEVENTIETH BIRTHDAY, FEBRUARY 22, 1889

A HEALTH to him whose double wreath displays
The critic's ivy and the poet's bays;
Who stayed not till with undisputed claim
The civic garland filled his meed of fame;
True knight of Freedom, ere her doubtful cause
Rose from the dust to meet the world's applause,
His country's champion on the bloodless field
Where truth and manhood stand for spear and shield!

Who is the critic? He who never skips
The luckless passage where his author slips;
Slides o'er his merits, stumbles at his faults,
Calls him a cripple if he sometimes halts.
Rich in the caustic epithets that sting,
The venom-vitriol malice loves to fling;

His quill a feathered fang at hate's command,
His ink the product of his poison-gland, —
Is this the critic? Call him not a snake, —
This noxious creature, — for the reptile's sake!
He is the critic who is first to mark
The star of genius when its glimmering spark
First pricks the sky, not waiting to proclaim
Its coming glory till it bursts in flame.
He is the critic whose divining rod
Tells where the waters hide beneath the sod;
Whom studious search through varied lore has taught
The streams, the rills, the fountain-heads, of thought;
Who, if some careless phrase, some slipshod clause,
Crack Priscian's skull or break Quintilian's laws,
Points out the blunder in a kindly way,
Nor tries his larger wisdom to display.
Where will you seek him? Wander far and wide,
Then turn and find him seated at your side!

Who is the poet? He who matches rhymes
In the last fashion of the new-born times;
Sweats over sonnets till the toil seems worse
Than Heaven intended in the primal curse;
Work, duties, pleasures, every claim forgets,
To shape his rondeaus and his triolets?
Or is it he whose random venture throws
His lawless whimseys into moonstruck prose,
Where they who worship the barbarian's creed
Will find a rhythmic cadence as they read,
As the pleased rustic hears a tune, or thinks
He hears a tune, in every bell that clinks?
Are these the poets? Though their pens should blot
A thousand volumes, surely such are not.
Who *is* the poet? He whom Nature chose
In that sweet season when she made the rose.

Though with the changes of our colder clime
His birthday will come somewhat out of time,
Through all the shivering winter's frost and chill,
The bloom and fragrance cling around it still.
He is the poet who can stoop to read
The secret hidden in a wayside weed;
Whom June's warm breath with childlike rapture fills,
Whose spirit "dances with the daffodils;"
Whom noble deeds with noble thoughts inspire
And lend his verse the true Promethean fire;
Who drinks the waters of enchanted streams
That wind and wander through the land of dreams;
For whom the unreal is the real world,
Its fairer flowers with brighter dews impearled.
He looks a mortal till he spreads his wings, —
He seems an angel when he soars and sings!
Behold the poet! Heaven his days prolong,
Whom Elmwood's nursery cradled into song!

Who is the patriot? He who deftly bends
To every shift that serves his private ends,
His face all smiling while his conscience squirms,
His back as limber as a canker worm's;
Who sees his country floundering through a drift,
Nor stirs a hand the laboring wheel to lift,
But trusts to Nature's leisure-loving law,
And waits with patience for the snow to thaw?
Or is he one who, called to conflict, draws
His trusty weapon in his country's cause;
Who, born a poet, grasps his trenchant rhymes
And strikes unshrinking at the nation's crimes;
Who in the days of peril learns to teach
The wisest lessons in the homeliest speech;
Whose plain good sense, alive with tingling wit,

Can always find a handle that will fit;
Who touches lightly with Ithuriel spear
The toad close squatting at the people's
  ear,
And bids the laughing, scornful world descry
The masking demon, the incarnate lie?
This, this is he his country well may say
Is fit to share her savior's natal day!
  Think not the date a worn-out king
    assigned
  As Life's full measure holds for all mankind;
  Shall Gladstone, crowned with eighty
    years, withdraw?
See, nearer home, the Lion of the Law —
How Court Street trembles when he leaves
  his den,
Clad in the pomp of *four* score years and
  ten!

Once more the health of Nature's favored
  son,
The poet, critic, patriot, all in one;
Health, honor, friendship, ever round him
  wait
In life's fair field beyond the seven-barred
  gate!

BUT ONE TALENT

Ye who yourselves of larger worth esteem
Than common mortals, listen to my dream,
And learn the lesson of life's cozening
  cheat,
    The coinage of conceit.

— The angel, guardian of my youth and
    age,
Spread out before me an account-book's
    page,
Saying, "This column marks what thou
    dost owe, —
    The gain thou hast to show."

"Spirit," I said, "I know, alas! too well
How poor the tale thy record has to tell.
Much I received, — the little I have
    brought
    Seems by its side as naught.

"Five talents, all of Ophir's purest gold,
These five fair caskets ranged before thee
    hold;
The first can show a few poor shekels' gain,
    The rest unchanged remain.

"Bringing my scanty tribute, overawed,
To Him who reapeth where He hath not
    strawed,
I tremble like a culprit when I count
    My whole vast debt's amount.

"What will He say to one from whom
    were due
Ten talents, when he comes with less than
    two?
What can I do but shudder and await
    The slothful servant's fate?"

— As looks a mother on an erring child,
The angel looked me in the face and
    smiled:
"How couldst thou, reckoning with thyself, contrive
    To count thy talents five?

"These caskets which thy flattering fancies gild
Not all with Ophir's precious ore are
    filled;
Thy debt is slender, for thy gift was small:
    One talent, — that was all.

"This second casket, with its grave pretence,
Is weighty with thine IGNORANCE, dark
    and dense,
Save for a single glowworm's glimmering
    light
    To mock its murky night

"The third conceals the DULNESS that was
    thine.
How could thy mind its lack of wit divine?
Let not what Heaven assigned thee bring
    thee blame;
    Thy want is not thy shame.

"The fourth, so light to lift, so fair to see,
Is filled to bursting with thy VANITY,
The vaporous breath that kept thy hopes
    alive
    By counting one as five.

"These held but little, but the fifth held
    less, —
Only blank vacuum, naked nothingness,

An idiot's portion. He who gave it knows
    Its claimant nothing owes.

"Thrice happy pauper he whose last ac-
    count
Shows on the debtor side the least amount!
The more thy gifts, the more thou needs
    must pay
    On life's dread reckoning day."

— Humbled, not grieving to be undeceived,
I woke, from fears of hopeless debt re-
    lieved:
For sparing gifts but small returns are
    due, —
    Thank Heaven I had so few!

FOR THE WINDOW IN ST. MARGARET'S

IN MEMORY OF A SON OF ARCHDEACON FARRAR

AFAR he sleeps whose name is graven here,
    Where loving hearts his early doom de-
    plore;
Youth, promise, virtue, all that made him
    dear
    Heaven lent, earth borrowed, sorrowing
    to restore.

JAMES RUSSELL LOWELL

1819-1891

THOU shouldst have sung the swan-song
    for the choir
That filled our groves with music till the
    day
Lit the last hilltop with its reddening fire,
    And evening listened for thy lingering
    lay.

But thou hast found thy voice in realms afar
    Where strains celestial blend their notes
    with thine;
Some cloudless sphere beneath a happier
    star
    Welcomes the bright-winged spirit we
    resign.

How Nature mourns thee in the still retreat
    Where passed in peace thy love-enchanted
    hours!

Where shall she find an eye like thine to
    greet
    Spring's earliest footprints on her open-
    ing flowers?

Have the pale wayside weeds no fond re-
    gret
    For him who read the secrets they enfold?
Shall the proud spangles of the field for-
    get
    The verse that lent new glory to their
    gold?

And ye whose carols wooed his infant ear,
    Whose chants with answering woodnotes
    he repaid,
Have ye no song his spirit still may hear
    From Elmwood's vaults of overarching
    shade?

Friends of his studious hours, who thronged
    to teach
    The deep-read scholar all your varied
    lore,
Shall he no longer seek your shelves to
    reach
    The treasure missing from his world-
    wide store?

This singer whom we long have held so
    dear
    Was Nature's darling, shapely, strong,
    and fair;
Of keenest wit, of judgment crystal-clear,
    Easy of converse, courteous, debonair,

Fit for the loftiest or the lowliest lot,
    Self-poised, imperial, yet of simplest
    ways;
At home alike in castle or in cot,
    True to his aim, let others blame or
    praise.

Freedom he found an heirloom from his
    sires;
Song, letters, statecraft, shared his years
    in turn;
All went to feed the nation's altar-fires
    Whose mourning children wreathe his
    funeral urn.

He loved New England, — people, lan-
    guage, soil,
    Unweaned by exile from her arid breast.

Farewell awhile, white-handed son of toil,
  Go with her brown-armed laborers to thy rest.

Peace to thy slumber in the forest shade!
  Poet and patriot, every gift was thine;
Thy name shall live while summers bloom and fade,
  And grateful Memory guard thy leafy shrine!

IN MEMORY OF JOHN GREENLEAF WHITTIER

DECEMBER 17, 1807 — SEPTEMBER 7, 1892

THOU, too, hast left us. While with heads bowed low,
  And sorrowing hearts, we mourned our summer's dead,
The flying season bent its Parthian bow,
  And yet again our mingling tears were shed.

Was Heaven impatient that it could not wait
  The blasts of winter for earth's fruits to fall?
Were angels crowding round the open gate
  To greet the spirits coming at their call?

Nay, let not fancies, born of old beliefs,
  Play with the heart-beats that are throbbing still,
And waste their outworn phrases on the griefs,
  The silent griefs that words can only chill.

For thee, dear friend, there needs no high-wrought lay,
  To shed its aureole round thy cherished name, —
Thou whose plain, home-born speech of *Yea and Nay*
  Thy truthful nature ever best became.

Death reaches not a spirit such as thine, —
  It can but steal the robe that hid thy wings;
Though thy warm breathing presence we resign,
  Still in our hearts its loving semblance clings.

Peaceful thy message, yet for struggling right, —
  When Slavery's gauntlet in our face was flung, —
While timid weaklings watched the dubious fight
  No herald's challenge more defiant rung.

Yet was thy spirit tuned to gentle themes
  Sought in the haunts thy humble youth had known.
Our stern New England's hills and vales and streams, —
  Thy tuneful idyls made them all their own.

The wild flowers springing from thy native sod
  Lent all their charms thy new-world song to fill, —
Gave thee the mayflower and the golden-rod
  To match the daisy and the daffodil.

In the brave records of our earlier time
  A hero's deed thy generous soul inspired,
And many a legend, told in ringing rhyme,
  The youthful soul with high resolve has fired.

Not thine to lean on priesthood's broken reed;
  No barriers caged thee in a bigot's fold;
Did zealots ask to syllable thy creed,
  Thou saidst "Our Father," and thy creed was told.

Best loved and saintliest of our singing train,
  Earth's noblest tributes to thy name belong.
A lifelong record closed without a stain,
  A blameless memory shrined in deathless song.

Lift from its quarried ledge a flawless stone;
  Smooth the green turf and bid the tablet rise,
And on its snow-white surface carve alone
  These words, — he needs no more, —
    HERE WHITTIER LIES.

TO THE TEACHERS OF AMERICA

[During a session in Boston of the National Educational Association, in February, 1893, Mr. Houghton and other publishers gave a reception for the purpose of introducing resident authors to the members of the association. It was on this occasion, February 23, 1893, that Dr. Holmes read the following verses.]

TEACHERS of teachers! Yours the task,
Noblest that noble minds can ask,
High up Aonia's murmurous mount,
To watch, to guard the sacred fount
  That feeds the streams below;
To guide the hurrying flood that fills
A thousand silvery rippling rills
  In ever-widening flow.

Rich is the harvest from the fields
That bounteous Nature kindly yields,
But fairer growths enrich the soil
Ploughed deep by thought's unwearied toil
  In Learning's broad domain.
And where the leaves, the flowers, the fruits,
Without your watering at the roots,
  To fill each branching vein?

Welcome! the Author's firmest friends,
Your voice the surest Godspeed lends,
Of you the growing mind demands
The patient care, the guiding hands,
  Through all the mists of morn.
And knowing well the future's need,
Your prescient wisdom sows the seed
  To flower in years unborn.

HYMN

WRITTEN FOR THE TWENTY-FIFTH ANNIVERSARY OF THE REORGANIZATION OF THE BOSTON YOUNG MEN'S CHRISTIAN UNION, MAY 31, 1893

TUNE, "DUNDEE"

OUR Father! while our hearts unlearn
  The creeds that wrong thy name,
Still let our hallowed altars burn
  With Faith's undying flame!

Not by the lightning-gleams of wrath
  Our souls thy face shall see,
The star of Love must light the path
  That leads to Heaven and Thee.

Help us to read our Master's will
  Through every darkening stain
That clouds his sacred image still,
  And see Him once again,

The brother man, the pitying friend
  Who weeps for human woes,
Whose pleading words of pardon blend
  With cries of raging foes.

If 'mid the gathering storms of doubt,
  Our hearts grow faint and cold,
The strength we cannot live without
  Thy love will not withhold.

Our prayers accept; our sins forgive;
  Our youthful zeal renew;
Shape for us holier lives to live,
  And nobler work to do!

FRANCIS PARKMAN

SEPTEMBER 16, 1823 — NOVEMBER 8, 1893

Read at the memorial meeting of the Massachusetts Historical Society.

HE rests from toil; the portals of the tomb
  Close on the last of those unwearying hands
That wove their pictured webs in History's loom,
  Rich with the memories of three distant lands.

One wrought the record of the Royal Pair
  Who saw the great Discoverer's sail unfurled,
Happy his more than regal prize to share,
  The spoils, the wonders, of the sunset world.

There, too, he found his theme; upreared anew,
  Our eyes beheld the vanished Aztec shrines,
And all the silver splendors of Peru
  That lured the conqueror to her fatal mines.

Nor less remembered he who told the tale
  Of empire wrested from the strangling
    sea;
Of Leyden's woe, that turned his readers
    pale,
  The price of unborn freedom yet to be;

Who taught the New World what the Old
    could teach;
  Whose silent hero, peerless as our
    own,
By deeds that mocked the feeble breath of
    speech
  Called up to life a State without a
    Throne.

As year by year his tapestry unrolled,
  What varied wealth its growing length
    displayed!
What long processions flamed in cloth of
    gold!
  What stately forms their flowing robes
    arrayed!

Not such the scenes our later craftsman
    drew;
  Not such the shapes his darker pattern
    held;
A deeper shadow lent its sober hue,
  A sadder tale his tragic task compelled.

He told the red man's story; far and wide
  He searched the unwritten records of his
    race;
He sat a listener at the Sachem's side,
  He tracked the hunter through his wild-
    wood chase.

High o'er his head the soaring eagle
    screamed;
  The wolf's long howl rang nightly;
    through the vale

Tramped the lone bear; the panther's eye-
    balls gleamed;
  The bison's gallop thundered on the gale.

Soon o'er the horizon rose the cloud of
    strife, —
  Two proud, strong nations battling for
    the prize, —
Which swarming host should mould a na-
    tion's life,
  Which royal banner float the western
    skies.

Long raged the conflict; on the crimson sod
  Native and alien joined their hosts in
    vain;
The lilies withered where the Lion trod,
  Till Peace lay panting on the ravaged
    plain.

A nobler task was theirs who strove to win
  The blood-stained heathen to the Chris-
    tian fold,
To free from Satan's clutch the slaves of
    sin;
  Their labors, too, with loving grace he
    told.

Halting with feeble step, or bending o'er
  The sweet-breathed roses which he loved
    so well,
While through long years his burdening
    cross he bore,
  From those firm lips no coward accents
    fell.

A brave, bright memory! his the stainless
    shield
  No shame defaces and no envy mars!
When our far future's record is unsealed,
  His name will shine among its morning
    stars.

POEMS FROM OVER THE TEACUPS

TO THE ELEVEN LADIES

WHO PRESENTED ME WITH A SILVER LOVING CUP ON THE TWENTY-NINTH OF AUGUST, M DCCC LXXXIX

"Who gave this cup?" The secret thou wouldst steal
Its brimming flood forbids it to reveal:
No mortal's eye shall read it till he first
  Cool the red throat of thirst.

If on the golden floor one draught remain,
Trust me, thy careful search will be in vain;
Not till the bowl is emptied shalt thou know
  The names enrolled below.

Deeper than Truth lies buried in her well
Those modest names the graven letters spell
Hide from the sight; but wait, and thou shalt see
  Who the good angels be

Whose bounty glistens in the beauteous gift
That friendly hands to loving lips shall lift:
Turn the fair goblet when its floor is dry, —
  Their names shall meet thine eye.

Count thou their number on the beads of Heaven:
Alas! the clustered Pleiads are but seven;
Nay, the nine sister Muses are too few, —
  The Graces must add two.

"For whom this gift?" For one who all too long
Clings to his bough among the groves of song;
Autumn's last leaf, that spreads its faded wing
  To greet a second spring.

Dear friends, kind friends, whate'er the cup may hold,
Bathing its burnished depths, will change to gold:
Its last bright drop let thirsty Mænads drain,
  Its fragrance will remain.

Better love's perfume in the empty bowl
Then wine's nepenthe for the aching soul;
Sweeter than song that ever poet sung,
  It makes an old heart young!

THE PEAU DE CHAGRIN OF STATE STREET

How beauteous is the bond
In the manifold array
Of its promises to pay,
While the eight per cent it gives
And the rate at which one lives
  Correspond!

But at last the bough is bare
Where the coupons one by one
Through their ripening days have run,
And the bond, a beggar now,
Seeks investment anyhow,
  Anywhere!

CACOETHES SCRIBENDI

If all the trees in all the woods were men;
And each and every blade of grass a pen;
If every leaf on every shrub and tree
Turned to a sheet of foolscap; every sea
Were changed to ink, and all earth's living tribes
Had nothing else to do but act as scribes,
And for ten thousand ages, day and night,
The human race should write, and write, and write,

Till all the pens and paper were used up,
And the huge inkstand was an empty cup,
Still would the scribblers clustered round its brink
Call for more pens, more paper, and more ink.

THE ROSE AND THE FERN

LADY, life's sweetest lesson wouldst thou learn,
  Come thou with me to Love's enchanted bower:
High overhead the trellised roses burn;
Beneath thy feet behold the feathery fern, —
  A leaf without a flower.

What though the rose leaves fall? They still are sweet,
  And have been lovely in their beauteous prime,
While the bare frond seems ever to repeat,
" For us no bud, no blossom, wakes to greet
  The joyous flowering time!"

Heed thou the lesson. Life has leaves to tread
  And flowers to cherish; summer round thee glows;
Wait not till autumn's fading robes are shed,
But while its petals still are burning red
  Gather life's full-blown rose!

I LIKE YOU AND I LOVE YOU

I LIKE YOU met I LOVE YOU, face to face;
  The path was narrow, and they could not pass.
  I LIKE YOU smiled; I LOVE YOU cried, Alas!
And so they halted for a little space.

"Turn thou and go before," I LOVE YOU said,
  " Down the green pathway, bright with many a flower;
Deep in the valley, lo! my bridal bower
Awaits thee." But I LIKE YOU shook his head.

Then while they lingered on the span-wide shelf
That shaped a pathway round the rocky ledge,
I LIKE YOU bared his icy dagger's edge,
And first he slew I LOVE YOU, — then himself.

LA MAISON D'OR

(BAR HARBOR)

FROM this fair home behold on either side
  The restful mountains or the restless sea:
So the warm sheltering walls of life divide
  Time and its tides from still eternity.

Look on the waves: their stormy voices teach
  That not on earth may toil and struggle cease.
Look on the mountains: better far than speech
  Their silent promise of eternal peace.

TOO YOUNG FOR LOVE

  Too young for love?
  Ah, say not so!
Tell reddening rosebuds not to blow!
Wait not for spring to pass away, —
Love's summer months begin with May!
  Too young for love?
  Ah, say not so!
  Too young? Too young?
  Ah, no! no! no!

  Too young for love?
  Ah, say not so,
While daisies bloom and tulips glow!
June soon will come with lengthened day
To practise all love learned in May.
  Too young for love?
  Ah, say not so!
  Too young? Too young?
  Ah, no! no! no!

THE BROOMSTICK TRAIN; OR, THE RETURN OF THE WITCHES

If there are any anachronisms or other inaccuracies in this story, the reader will please to remember that the narrator's memory is liable to be at fault, and if the event recorded interests him, will not worry over any little slips or stumbles.

The terrible witchcraft drama of 1692 has been seriously treated, as it well deserves to be. The story has been told in two large volumes by the Rev. Charles Wentworth Upham, and in a small and more succinct volume, based upon his work, by his daughter-in-law, Caroline E. Upham.

The delusion, commonly spoken of as if it belonged to Salem, was more widely diffused through the towns of Essex County. Looking upon it as a pitiful and long dead and buried superstition, I trust my poem will no more offend the good people of Essex County than Tam O'Shanter worries the honest folk of Ayrshire.

The localities referred to are those with which I am familiar in my drives about Essex County.

LOOK out! Look out, boys! Clear the track!
The witches are here! They've all come back!
They hanged them high, — No use! No use!
What cares a witch for a hangman's noose?
They buried them deep, but they would n't lie still,
For cats and witches are hard to kill;
They swore they should n't and would n't die, —
Books said they did, but they lie! they lie!

A couple of hundred years, or so,
They had knocked about in the world below,
When an Essex Deacon dropped in to call,
And a homesick feeling seized them all;
For he came from a place they knew full well,
And many a tale he had to tell.
They longed to visit the haunts of men,
To see the old dwellings they knew again,
And ride on their broomsticks all around
Their wide domain of unhallowed ground.

In Essex county there 's many a roof
Well known to him of the cloven hoof;
The small square windows are full in view
Which the midnight hags went sailing through,
On their well-trained broomsticks mounted high,
Seen like shadows against the sky;
Crossing the track of owls and bats,
Hugging before them their coal-black cats.

Well did they know, those gray old wives,
The sights we see in our daily drives:
Shimmer of lake and shine of sea,
Browne's bare hill with its lonely tree,
(It was n't then as we see it now,
With one scant scalp-lock to shade its brow;)
Dusky nooks in the Essex woods,
Dark, dim, Dante-like solitudes,
Where the tree-toad watches the sinuous snake
Glide through his forests of fern and brake;
Ipswich River; its old stone bridge;
Far off Andover's Indian Ridge,
And many a scene where history tells
Some shadow of bygone terror dwells, —
Of "Norman's Woe" with its tale of dread,
Of the Screeching Woman of Marblehead,
(The fearful story that turns men pale:
Don't bid me tell it, — my speech would fail.)

Who would not, will not, if he can,
Bathe in the breezes of fair Cape Ann, —
Rest in the bowers her bays enfold,
Loved by the sachems and squaws of old?
Home where the white magnolias bloom,
Sweet with the bayberry's chaste perfume,
Hugged by the woods and kissed by the sea!
Where is the Eden like to thee?
For that "couple of hundred years, or so,"
There had been no peace in the world below;
The witches still grumbling, "It is n't fair;
Come, give us a taste of the upper air!
We 've had enough of your sulphur springs,
And the evil odor that round them clings;
We long for a drink that is cool and nice, —
Great buckets of water with Wenham ice;
We 've served you well up-stairs, you know;
You 're a good old — fellow — come, let us go!"

I don't feel sure of his being good,
But he happened to be in a pleasant mood, —
As fiends with their skins full sometimes are, —

(He'd been drinking with "roughs" at a Boston bar.)
So what does he do but up and shout
To a graybeard turnkey, "Let 'em out!"

To mind his orders was all he knew;
The gates swung open, and out they flew.
"Where are our broomsticks?" the beldams cried.
"Here are your broomsticks," an imp replied.
"They've been in — the place you know — so long
They smell of brimstone uncommon strong;
But they've gained by being left alone, —
Just look, and you'll see how tall they've grown."
"And where is my cat?" a vixen squalled.
"Yes, where are our cats?" the witches bawled,
And began to call them all by name:
As fast as they called the cats, they came:
There was bob-tailed Tommy and long-tailed Tim,
And wall-eyed Jacky and green-eyed Jim,
And splay-foot Benny and slim-legged Beau,
And Skinny and Squally, and Jerry and Joe,
And many another that came at call, —
It would take too long to count them all.
All black, — one could hardly tell which was which,
But every cat knew his own old witch;
And she knew hers as hers knew her, —
Ah, didn't they curl their tails and purr!

No sooner the withered hags were free
Than out they swarmed for a midnight spree;
I couldn't tell all they did in rhymes,
But the Essex people had dreadful times.
The Swampscott fishermen still relate
How a strange sea-monster stole their bait;
How their nets were tangled in loops and knots,
And they found dead crabs in their lobster-pots.
Poor Danvers grieved for her blasted crops,
And Wilmington mourned over mildewed hops.
A blight played havoc with Beverly beans, —
It was all the work of those hateful queans!
A dreadful panic began at "Pride's,"
Where the witches stopped in their midnight rides,
And there rose strange rumors and vague alarms
'Mid the peaceful dwellers at Beverly Farms.

Now when the Boss of the Beldams found
That without his leave they were ramping round,
He called, — they could hear him twenty miles,
From Chelsea beach to the Misery Isles;
The deafest old granny knew his tone
Without the trick of the telephone.
"Come here, you witches! Come here!" says he, —
"At your games of old, without asking me!
I'll give you a little job to do
That will keep you stirring, you godless crew!"

They came, of course, at their master's call,
The witches, the broomsticks, the cats, and all;
He led the hags to a railway train
The horses were trying to drag in vain.
"Now, then," says he, "you've had your fun,
And here are the cars you've got to run.
The driver may just unhitch his team,
We don't want horses, we don't want steam;
You may keep your old black cats to hug,
But the loaded train you've got to lug."

Since then on many a car you'll see
A broomstick plain as plain can be;
On every stick there's a witch astride, —
The string you see to her leg is tied.
She will do a mischief if she can,
But the string is held by a careful man,
And whenever the evil-minded witch
Would cut some caper, he gives a twitch.
As for the hag, you can't see her,
But hark! you can hear her black cat's purr,
And now and then, as a car goes by,
You may catch a gleam from her wicked eye.
Often you've looked on a rushing train,
But just what moved it was not so plain.
It couldn't be those wires above,
For they could neither pull nor shove;

Where was the motor that made it go
You couldn't guess, *but now you know.*

Remember my rhymes when you ride again
On the rattling rail by the broomstick train!

TARTARUS

While in my simple gospel creed
That "God is Love" so plain I read,
Shall dreams of heathen birth affright
My pathway through the coming night?
Ah, Lord of life, though spectres pale
Fill with their threats the shadowy vale,
With Thee my faltering steps to aid,
How can I dare to be afraid?

Shall mouldering page or fading scroll
Outface the charter of the soul?
Shall priesthood's palsied arm protect
The wrong our human hearts reject,
And smite the lips whose shuddering cry
Proclaims a cruel creed a lie?
The wizard's rope we disallow
Was justice once, — is murder now!

Is there a world of blank despair,
And dwells the Omnipresent there?
Does He behold with smile serene
The shows of that unending scene,
Where sleepless, hopeless anguish lies,
And, ever dying, never dies?
Say, does He hear the sufferer's groan,
And is that child of wrath his own?

O mortal, wavering in thy trust,
Lift thy pale forehead from the dust!
The mists that cloud thy darkened eyes
Fade ere they reach the o'erarching skies!
When the blind heralds of despair
Would bid thee doubt a Father's care,
Look up from earth, and read above
On heaven's blue tablet, God is Love!

AT THE TURN OF THE ROAD

The glory has passed from the goldenrod's plume,
The purple-hued asters still linger in bloom:
The birch is bright yellow, the sumachs are red,
The maples like torches aflame overhead.

But what if the joy of the summer is past,
And winter's wild herald is blowing his blast?
For me dull November is sweeter than May,
For my love is its sunshine, — she meets me to-day!

Will she come? Will the ring-dove return to her nest?
Will the needle swing back from the east or the west?
At the stroke of the hour she will be at her gate;
A friend may prove laggard, — love never comes late.

Do I see her afar in the distance? Not yet.
Too early! Too early! She could not forget!
When I cross the old bridge where the brook overflowed,
She will flash full in sight at the turn of the road.

I pass the low wall where the ivy entwines;
I tread the brown pathway that leads through the pines;
I haste by the boulder that lies in the field,
Where her promise at parting was lovingly sealed.

Will she come by the hillside or round through the wood?
Will she wear her brown dress or her mantle and hood?
The minute draws near, — but her watch may go wrong;
My heart *will* be asking, What keeps her so long?

Why doubt for a moment? More shame if I do!
Why question? Why tremble? Are angels more true?
She would come to the lover who calls her his own
Though she trod in the track of a whirling cyclone!

I crossed the old bridge ere the minute had passed.
I looked: lo! my Love stood before me at last.

Her eyes, how they sparkled, her cheeks,
    how they glowed,
As we met, face to face, at the turn of the
    road!

INVITÂ MINERVÂ

I find the burden and restrictions of rhyme more and more troublesome as I grow older. There are times when it seems natural enough to employ that form of expression, but it is only occasionally; and the use of it as a vehicle of the commonplace is so prevalent that one is not much tempted to select it as the medium for his thoughts and emotions. The art of rhyming has almost become a part of a high-school education, and its practice is far from being an evidence of intellectual distinction. Mediocrity is as much forbidden to the poet in our days as it was in those of Horace, and the immense majority of the verses written are stamped with hopeless mediocrity.

When one of the ancient poets found he was trying to grind out verses which came unwillingly, he said he was writing *Invitâ Minervâ*.

VEX not the Muse with idle prayers,—
    She will not hear thy call;
She steals upon thee unawares,
    Or seeks thee not at all.

Soft as the moonbeams when they sought
    Endymion's fragrant bower,
She parts the whispering leaves of thought
    To show her full-blown flower.

For thee her wooing hour has passed,
    The singing birds have flown,
And winter comes with icy blast
    To chill thy buds unblown.

Yet, though the woods no longer thrill
    As once their arches rung,
Sweet echoes hover round thee still
    Of songs thy summer sung.

Live in thy past; await no more
    The rush of heaven-sent wings;
Earth still has music left in store
    While Memory sighs and sings.

READINGS OVER THE TEACUPS

FIVE STORIES AND A SEQUEL

[In his volume, *Songs in Many Keys*, Dr. Holmes had a division, *Pictures from Occasional Poems*. He discarded his sub-title in the Riverside Edition, but took from the group under that title five stories and reproduced them in a new setting under the above title.]

TO MY OLD READERS

You know "The Teacups," that congenial set
Which round the Teapot you have often met;
The grave DICTATOR, him you knew of old, —
Knew as the shepherd of another fold:
Grayer he looks, less youthful, but the same
As when you called him by a different name.
  Near him the MISTRESS, whose experienced skill
Has taught her duly every cup to fill;
"Weak;" "strong;" "cool;" "lukewarm;" "hot as you can pour;"
"No sweetening;" "sugared;" "two lumps;" "one lump more."
  Next, the PROFESSOR, whose scholastic phrase
At every turn the teacher's tongue betrays,
Trying so hard to make his speech precise
The captious listener finds it overnice.
  Nor be forgotten our ANNEXES twain,
Nor HE, the owner of the squinting brain,
Which, while its curious fancies we pursue,
Oft makes us question, "Are we crack-brained too?"
  Along the board our growing list extends,
As one by one we count our clustering friends, —
The youthful DOCTOR waiting for his share
Of fits and fevers when his crown gets bare;
In strong, dark lines our square-nibbed pen should draw
The lordly presence of the MAN OF LAW;
Our bashful TUTOR claims a humbler place,
A lighter touch, his slender form to trace.
Mark the fair lady he is seated by, —
Some say he is her lover, — some deny, —
Watch them together, — time alone can show
If dead-ripe friendship turns to love or so.
Where in my list of phrases shall I seek
The fitting words of NUMBER FIVE to speak?
Such task demands a readier pen than mine, —
What if I steal the Tutor's Valentine?
  Why should I call her gracious, winning, fair?
Why with the loveliest of her sex compare?
Those varied charms have many a Muse inspired;
At last their worn superlatives have tired;
Wit, beauty, sweetness, each alluring grace,
All these in honeyed verse have found their place;
I need them not, — two little words I find
Which hold them all in happiest form combined;
No more with baffled language will I strive, —
All in one breath I utter: Number Five!
  Now count our teaspoons — if you care to learn
How many tinkling cups were served in turn, —
Add all together, you will find them ten, —
Our young MUSICIAN joined us now and then.

Our bright DELILAH you must needs recall,
The comely handmaid, youngest of us all;
Need I remind you how the little maid
Came at a pinch to our Professor's aid, —
Trimmed his long locks with unrelenting shears
And eased his looks of half a score of years?

Sometimes, at table, as you well must know,
The stream of talk will all at once run low,
The air seems smitten with a sudden chill,
The wit grows silent and the gossip still;
This was our poet's chance, the hour of need,
When rhymes and stories we were used to read.
 One day a whisper round the teacups stole, —
"*No scrap of paper in the silver bowl!*"
(Our "poet's corner" may I not expect
My kindly reader still may recollect?)
 "What! not a line to keep our souls alive?"
Spoke in her silvery accents Number Five.
"No matter, something we must find to read, —
Find it or make it, — yes, we must indeed!
Now I remember I have seen at times
Some curious stories in a book of rhymes, —
How certain secrets, long in silence sealed,
In after days were guessed at or revealed.
Those stories, doubtless, some of you must know, —
They all were written many a year ago;
But an old story, be it false or true,
Twice told, well told, is twice as good as new;
Wait but three sips and I will go myself,
And fetch the book of verses from its shelf."
 No time was lost in finding what she sought, —
Gone but one moment, — lo! the book is brought.
 "Now, then, Professor, fortune has decreed
That you, this evening, shall be first to read, —
Lucky for us that listen, for in fact
Who reads this poem must know how to act."

Right well she knew that in his greener age
He had a mighty hankering for the stage.
The patient audience had not long to wait;
Pleased with his chance, he smiled and took the bait;
Through his wild hair his coaxing fingers ran, —
He spread the page before him and began.

THE BANKER'S SECRET

[When first published this bore the title *The Banker's Dinner.*]

THE Banker's dinner is the stateliest feast
The town has heard of for a year, at least;
The sparry lustres shed their broadest blaze,
Damask and silver catch and spread the rays;
The florist's triumphs crown the daintier spoil
Won from the sea, the forest, or the soil;
The steaming hot-house yields its largest pines,
The sunless vaults unearth their oldest wines;
With one admiring look the scene survey,
And turn a moment from the bright display.

 Of all the joys of earthly pride or power,
What gives most life, worth living, in an hour?
When Victory settles on the doubtful fight
And the last foeman wheels in panting flight,
No thrill like this is felt beneath the sun;
Life's sovereign moment is a battle won.
 But say what next? To shape a Senate's choice,
By the strong magic of the master's voice;
To ride the stormy tempest of debate
That whirls the wavering fortunes of the state.
 Third in the list, the happy lover's prize
Is won by honeyed words from women's eyes.
If some would have it first instead of third,
So let it be, — I answer not a word.

The fourth, — sweet readers, let the thoughtless half
Have its small shrug and inoffensive laugh;
Let the grave quarter wear its virtuous frown,
The stern half-quarter try to scowl us down;
But the last eighth, the choice and sifted few,
Will hear my words, and, pleased, confess them true.

Among the great whom Heaven has made to shine,
How few have learned the art of arts, — to dine!
Nature, indulgent to our daily need,
Kind-hearted mother! taught us all to feed;
But the chief art, — how rarely Nature flings
This choicest gift among her social kings!
Say, man of truth, has life a brighter hour
Than waits the chosen guest who knows his power?
He moves with ease, itself an angel charm, —
Lifts with light touch my lady's jewelled arm,
Slides to his seat, half leading and half led,
Smiling but quiet till the grace is said,
Then gently kindles, while by slow degrees
Creep softly out the little arts that please;
Bright looks, the cheerful language of the eye,
The neat, crisp question and the gay reply, —
Talk light and airy, such as well may pass
Between the rested fork and lifted glass; —
With play like this the earlier evening flies,
Till rustling silks proclaim the ladies rise.
His hour has come, — he looks along the chairs,
As the Great Duke surveyed his iron squares.
That's the young traveller, — is n't much to show, —
Fast on the road, but at the table slow.
Next him, — you see the author in his look, —
His forehead lined with wrinkles like a book, —
Wrote the great history of the ancient Huns, —
Holds back to fire among the heavy guns.
Oh, there's our poet seated at his side,
Beloved of ladies, soft, cerulean-eyed.
Poets are prosy in their common talk,
As the fast trotters, for the most part, walk.
And there's our well-dressed gentleman, who sits,
By right divine, no doubt, among the wits,
Who airs his tailor's patterns when he walks,
The man that often speaks, but never talks.
Why should he talk, whose presence lends a grace
To every table where he shows his face?
He knows the manual of the silver fork,
Can name his claret — if he sees the cork, —
Remark that "White-top" was considered fine,
But swear the "Juno" is the better wine; —
Is not this talking? Ask Quintilian's rules;
If they say No, the town has many fools.
Pause for a moment, — for our eyes behold
The plain unsceptred king, the man of gold,
The thrice illustrious threefold millionnaire;
Mark his slow-creeping, dead, metallic stare;
His eyes, dull glimmering, like the balance-pan
That weighs its guinea as he weighs his man.
Who's next? An artist in a satin tie
Whose ample folds defeat the curious eye.
And there's the cousin, — must be asked, you know, —
Looks like a spinster at a baby-show.
Hope he is cool, — they set him next the door, —
And likes his place, between the gap and bore.
Next comes a Congressman, distinguished guest!
We don't count him, — they asked him with the rest;
And then some white cravats, with well-shaped ties,
And heads above them which their owners prize.

Of all that cluster round the genial board,
Not one so radiant as the banquet's lord.
Some say they fancy, but they know not why,

A shade of trouble brooding in his eye,
Nothing, perhaps, — the rooms are over-
  hot, —
Yet see his cheek, — the dull-red burning
  spot, —
Taste the brown sherry which he does not
  pass, —
Ha! That is brandy; see him fill his glass!
  But not forgetful of his feasting friends,
To each in turn some lively word he sends;
See how he throws his baited lines about,
And plays his men as anglers play their
  trout.

With the dry sticks all bonfires are be-
  gun;
Bring the first fagot, proser number one!
A question drops among the listening crew
And hits the traveller, pat on Timbuctoo.
We're on the Niger, somewhere near its
  source, —
Not the least hurry, take the river's course
Through Kissi, Foota, Kankan, Bammakoo,
Bambarra, Sego, so to Timbuctoo,
Thence down to Youri; — stop him if we
  can,
We can't fare worse, — wake up the Con-
  gressman!
The Congressman, once on his talking legs,
Stirs up his knowledge to its thickest dregs;
Tremendous draught for dining men to
  quaff!
Nothing will choke him but a purpling
  laugh.
A word, — a shout, — a mighty roar, — 't is
  done;
Extinguished; lassoed by a treacherous pun.
  A laugh is priming to the loaded soul;
The scattering shots become a steady roll,
Broke by sharp cracks that run along the
  line,
The light artillery of the talker's wine.
The kindling goblets flame with golden
  dews,
The hoarded flasks their tawny fire diffuse,
And the Rhine's breast-milk gushes cold
  and bright,
Pale as the moon and maddening as her
  light;
With crimson juice the thirsty southern sky
Sucks from the hills where buried armies
  lie,
So that the dreamy passion it imparts
Is drawn from heroes' bones and lovers'
  hearts.

But lulls will come; the flashing soul
  transmits
Its gleams of light in alternating fits.
The shower of talk that rattled down amain
Ends in small patterings like an April's
  rain;
The voices halt; the game is at a stand;
Now for a solo from the master-hand!
  'T is but a story, — quite a simple
  thing, —
An *aria* touched upon a single string,
But every accent comes with such a grace
The stupid servants listen in their place,
Each with his waiter in his lifted hands,
Still as a well-bred pointer when he stands.
A query checks him: "Is he quite exact?"
  (This from a grizzled, square-jawed man
  of fact.)
The sparkling story leaves him to his fate,
Crushed by a witness, smothered with a
  date,
As a swift river, sown with many a star,
Runs brighter, rippling on a shallow bar.
The smooth divine suggests a graver doubt;
A neat quotation bowls the parson out;
Then, sliding gayly from his own display,
He laughs the learned dulness all away.
  So, with the merry tale and jovial song,
The jocund evening whirls itself along,
Till the last chorus shrieks its loud *encore*,
And the white neckcloths vanish through
  the door.

One savage word! — The menials know
  its tone,
And slink away; the master stands alone.
"Well played, by —— ;" breathe not what
  were best unheard;
His goblet shivers while he speaks the
  word, —
"If wine tells truth, — and so have said
  the wise, —
It makes me laugh to think how brandy
  lies!
Bankrupt to-morrow, — millionnaire to-
  day, —
The farce is over, — now begins the play!"
  The spring he touches lets a panel glide;
An iron closet lurks beneath the slide,
Bright with such treasures as a search
  might bring
From the deep pockets of a truant king.
Two diamonds, eyeballs of a god of bronze,
Bought from his faithful priest, a pious
  bonze,

A string of brilliants; rubies, three or four;
Bags of old coin and bars of virgin ore;
A jewelled poniard and a Turkish knife,
Noiseless and useful if we come to strife.
 Gone ! As a pirate flies before the wind,
And not one tear for all he leaves behind !
From all the love his better years have
 known
Fled like a felon, — ah ! but not alone !
The chariot flashes through a lantern's
 glare, —
Oh the wild eyes ! the storm of sable hair !
Still to his side the broken heart will
 cling, —
The bride of shame, the wife without the
 ring:
Hark, the deep oath, — the wail of frenzied woe, —
Lost ! lost to hope of Heaven and peace
 below !

He kept his secret; but the seed of crime
Bursts of itself in God's appointed time.
The lives he wrecked were scattered far
 and wide;
One never blamed nor wept, — she only
 died.
None knew his lot, though idle tongues
 would say
He sought a lonely refuge far away,
And there, with borrowed name and altered mien,
He died unheeded, as he lived unseen.
The moral market had the usual chills
Of Virtue suffering from protested bills;
The White Cravats, to friendship's memory true,
Sighed for the past, surveyed the future
 too;
Their sorrow breathed in one expressive
 line, —
"Gave pleasant dinners; who has got his
 wine ? "

The reader paused, — the Teacups knew
 his ways, —
He, like the rest, was not averse to praise.
Voices and hands united; every one
Joined in approval : " Number Three, well
 done ! "

"Now for the Exile's story; if my wits
Are not at fault, his curious record fits
Neatly as sequel to the tale we 've heard;

Not wholly wild the fancy, nor absurd
That this our island hermit well might be
That story's hero, fled from over sea.
Come, Number Seven, we would not have
 you strain
The fertile powers of that inventive brain.
Read us 'The Exile's Secret;' there's
 enough
Of dream-like fiction and fantastic stuff
In the strange web of mystery that invests
The lonely isle where sea birds build their
 nests."

"Lies ! naught but lies ! " so Number
 Seven began, —
No harm was known of that secluded man.
He lived alone, — who would n't if he
 might,
And leave the rogues and idiots out of
 sight ?
A foolish story, — still, I 'll do my best, —
The house was real, — don't believe the
 rest.
How could a ruined dwelling last so long
Without its legends shaped in tale and
 song ?
Who was this man of whom they tell the
 lies ?
Perhaps — why not ? — NAPOLEON ! in disguise, —
So some said, kidnapped from his ocean
 coop,
Brought to this island in a coasting sloop, —
Meanwhile a sham Napoleon in his place
Played Nap. and saved Sir Hudson from
 disgrace.
Such was one story; others used to say,
"No, — not Napoleon, — it was Marshal
 Ney."
" Shot ? " Yes, no doubt, but not with balls
 of lead,
But balls of pith that never shoot folks
 dead.
He wandered round, lived South for many
 a year,
At last came North and fixed his dwelling
 here.
Choose which you will of all the tales that
 pile
Their mingling fables on the tree-crowned
 isle.
Who wrote this modest version I suppose
That truthful Teacup, our Dictator, knows;
Made up of various legends, it would seem,
The sailor's yarn, the crazy poet's dream.

Such tales as this, by simple souls received,
At first are stared at and at last believed;
From threads like this the grave historians try
To weave their webs, and never know they lie.
Hear, then, the fables that have gathered round
The lonely home an exiled stranger found.

THE EXILE'S SECRET

[Originally entitled *The Island Ruin*.]

YE that have faced the billows and the spray
Of good St. Botolph's island-studded bay,
As from the gliding bark your eye has scanned
The beaconed rocks, the wave-girt hills of sand,
Have ye not marked one elm-o'ershadowed isle,
Round as the dimple chased in beauty's smile, —
A stain of verdure on an azure field,
Set like a jewel in a battered shield?
Fixed in the narrow gorge of Ocean's path,
Peaceful it meets him in his hour of wrath;
When the mailed Titan, scourged by hissing gales,
Writhes in his glistening coat of clashing scales,
The storm-beat island spreads its tranquil green,
Calm as an emerald on an angry queen.
  So fair when distant should be fairer near;
A boat shall waft us from the outstretched pier.
The breeze blows fresh; we reach the island's edge,
Our shallop rustling through the yielding sedge.
  No welcome greets us on the desert isle;
Those elms, far-shadowing, hide no stately pile:
Yet these green ridges mark an ancient road;
And lo! the traces of a fair abode;
The long gray line that marks a garden-wall,
And heaps of fallen beams, — fire-branded all.

Who sees unmoved, a ruin at his feet,
The lowliest home where human hearts have beat?
Its hearthstone, shaded with the bistre stain
A century's showery torrents wash in vain;
Its starving orchard, where the thistle blows
And mossy trunks still mark the broken rows;
Its chimney-loving poplar, oftenest seen
Next an old roof, or where a roof has been;
Its knot-grass, plantain, — all the social weeds,
Man's mute companions, following where he leads;
Its dwarfed, pale flowers, that show their straggling heads,
Sown by the wind from grass-choked garden-beds;
Its woodbine, creeping where it used to climb;
Its roses, breathing of the olden time;
All the poor shows the curious idler sees,
As life's thin shadows waste by slow degrees,
Till naught remains, the saddening tale to tell,
Save home's last wrecks, — the cellar and the well?

  And whose the home that strews in black decay
The one green-glowing island of the bay?
Some dark-browed pirate's, jealous of the fate
That seized the strangled wretch of "Nix's Mate"?
Some forger's, skulking in a borrowed name,
Whom Tyburn's dangling halter yet may claim?
Some wan-eyed exile's, wealth and sorrow's heir,
Who sought a lone retreat for tears and prayer?
Some brooding poet's, sure of deathless fame,
Had not his epic perished in the flame?
Or some gray wooer's, whom a girlish frown
Chased from his solid friends and sober town?
Or some plain tradesman's, fond of shade and ease,
Who sought them both beneath these quiet trees?

Why question mutes no question can unlock,
Dumb as the legend on the Dighton rock?
One thing at least these ruined heaps declare, —
They were a shelter once; a man lived there.

But where the charred and crumbling records fail,
Some breathing lips may piece the half-told tale;
No man may live with neighbors such as these,
Though girt with walls of rock and angry seas,
And shield his home, his children, or his wife,
His ways, his means, his vote, his creed, his life,
From the dread sovereignty of Ears and Eyes
And the small member that beneath them lies.

They told strange things of that mysterious man;
Believe who will, deny them such as can;
Why should we fret if every passing sail
Had its old seaman talking on the rail?
The deep-sunk schooner stuffed with Eastern lime,
Slow wedging on, as if the waves were slime;
The knife-edged clipper with her ruffled spars,
The pawing steamer with her mane of stars,
The bull-browed galliot butting through the stream,
The wide-sailed yacht that slipped along her beam,
The deck-piled sloops, the pinched chebacco-boats,
The frigate, black with thunder-freighted throats,
All had their talk about the lonely man;
And thus, in varying phrase, the story ran.

His name had cost him little care to seek,
Plain, honest, brief, a decent name to speak,
Common, not vulgar, just the kind that slips
With least suggestion from a stranger's lips.

His birthplace England, as his speech might show,
Or his hale cheek, that wore the red-streak's glow;
His mouth sharp-moulded; in its mirth or scorn
There came a flash as from the milky corn,
When from the ear you rip the rustling sheath,
And the white ridges show their even teeth.
His stature moderate, but his strength confessed,
In spite of broadcloth, by his ample breast;
Full-armed, thick-handed; one that had been strong,
And might be dangerous still, if things went wrong.
He lived at ease beneath his elm-trees' shade,
Did naught for gain, yet all his debts were paid;
Rich, so 't was thought, but careful of his store;
Had all he needed, claimed to have no more.

But some that lingered round the isle at night
Spoke of strange stealthy doings in their sight;
Of creeping lonely visits that he made
To nooks and corners, with a torch and spade.
Some said they saw the hollow of a cave;
One, given to fables, swore it was a grave;
Whereat some shuddered, others boldly cried,
Those prowling boatmen lied, and knew they lied.
They said his house was framed with curious cares,
Lest some old friend might enter unawares;
That on the platform at his chamber's door
Hinged a loose square that opened through the floor;
Touch the black silken tassel next the bell,
Down, with a crash, the flapping trap-door fell;
Three stories deep the falling wretch would strike,
To writhe at leisure on a boarder's pike.

By day armed always; double-armed at night,
His tools lay round him; wake him such as might.
A carbine hung beside his India fan,

His hand could reach a Turkish ataghan;
Pistols, with quaint-carved stocks and barrels gilt,
Crossed a long dagger with a jewelled hilt;
A slashing cutlass stretched along the bed; —
All this was what those lying boatmen said.
Then some were full of wondrous stories told
Of great oak chests and cupboards full of gold;
Of the wedged ingots and the silver bars
That cost old pirates ugly sabre-scars;
How his laced wallet often would disgorge
The fresh-faced guinea of an English George,
Or sweated ducat, palmed by Jews of yore,
Or double Joe, or Portuguese moidore;
And how his finger wore a rubied ring
Fit for the white-necked play-girl of a king.
But these fine legends, told with staring eyes,
Met with small credence from the old and wise.

Why tell each idle guess, each whisper vain?
Enough: the scorched and cindered beams remain.
He came, a silent pilgrim to the West,
Some old-world mystery throbbing in his breast;
Close to the thronging mart he dwelt alone;
He lived; he died. The rest is all unknown.

Stranger, whose eyes the shadowy isle survey,
As the black steamer dashes through the bay,
Why ask his buried secret to divine?
He was thy brother; speak, and tell us thine!

Silence at first, a kind of spell-bound pause;
Then all the Teacups tinkled their applause;
When that was hushed no sound the stillness broke
Till once again the soft-voiced lady spoke:

"The Lover's Secret, — surely that must need
The youngest voice our table holds to read.
Which of our two 'Annexes' shall we choose?
Either were charming, neither will refuse;
But choose we must, — what better can we do
Than take the younger of the youthful two?"

True to the primal instinct of her sex,
"Why, that means *me*," half whispered each Annex.
"What if it does?" the voiceless question came,
That set those pale New England cheeks aflame;
"Our old-world scholar may have ways to teach
Of Oxford English, Britain's purest speech, —
She shall be youngest, — youngest *for to-day*, —
Our dates we'll fix hereafter as we may;
All rights reserved, — the words we know so well,
That guard the claims of books which never sell."

The British maiden bowed a pleased assent,
Her two long ringlets swinging as she bent;
The glistening eyes her eager soul looked through
Betrayed her lineage in their Saxon blue.
Backward she flung each too obtrusive curl
And thus began, — the rose-lipped English girl.

THE LOVER'S SECRET

[When first published this poem was entitled *The Mysterious Illness.*]

WHAT ailed young Lucius? Art had vainly tried
To guess his ill, and found herself defied.
The Augur plied his legendary skill;
Useless; the fair young Roman languished still.
His chariot took him every cloudless day
Along the Pincian Hill or Appian Way;
They rubbed his wasted limbs with sulphurous oil,
Oozed from the far-off Orient's heated soil;
They led him tottering down the steamy path
Where bubbling fountains filled the thermal bath;

Borne in his litter to Egeria's cave,
They washed him, shivering, in her icy wave.
They sought all curious herbs and costly stones,
They scraped the moss that grew on dead men's bones,
They tried all cures the votive tablets taught,
Scoured every place whence healing drugs were brought,
O'er Thracian hills his breathless couriers ran,
His slaves waylaid the Syrian caravan.
At last a servant heard a stranger speak
A new chirurgeon's name; a clever Greek,
Skilled in his art; from Pergamus he came
To Rome but lately; GALEN was the name.
The Greek was called: a man with piercing eyes,
Who must be cunning, and who might be wise.
He spoke but little, — if they pleased, he said,
He'd wait awhile beside the sufferer's bed.
So by his side he sat, serene and calm,
His very accents soft as healing balm;
Not curious seemed, but every movement spied,
His sharp eyes searching where they seemed to glide;
Asked a few questions, — what he felt, and where?
"A pain just here," "A constant beating there."
Who ordered bathing for his aches and ails?
"Charmis, the water-doctor from Marseilles."
What was the last prescription in his case?
"A draught of wine with powdered chrysoprase."
Had he no secret grief he nursed alone?
A pause; a little tremor; answer, — "None."
Thoughtful, a moment, sat the cunning leech,
And muttered "Eros!" in his native speech.
In the broad atrium various friends await
The last new utterance from the lips of fate;
Men, matrons, maids, they talk the question o'er,
And, restless, pace the tessellated floor.
Not unobserved the youth so long had pined
By gentle-hearted dames and damsels kind;
One with the rest, a rich Patrician's pride,
The lady Hermia, called "the golden-eyed;"
The same the old Proconsul fain must woo,
Whom, one dark night, a masked sicarius slew;
The same black Crassus over roughly pressed
To hear his suit, — the Tiber knows the rest.
(Crassus was missed next morning by his set;
Next week the fishers found him in their net.)
She with the others paced the ample hall,
Fairest, alas! and saddest of them all.
At length the Greek declared, with puzzled face,
Some strange enchantment mingled in the case,
And naught would serve to act as counter-charm
Save a warm bracelet from a maiden's arm.
Not every maiden's, — many might be tried;
Which not in vain, experience must decide.
Were there no damsels willing to attend
And do such service for a suffering friend?
The message passed among the waiting crowd,
First in a whisper, then proclaimed aloud.
Some wore no jewels; some were disinclined,
For reasons better guessed at than defined;
Though all were saints, — at least professed to be, —
The list all counted, there were named but three.
The leech, still seated by the patient's side,
Held his thin wrist, and watched him, eagle-eyed.
Aurelia first, a fair-haired Tuscan girl,
Slipped off her golden asp, with eyes of pearl.
His solemn head the grave physician shook;
The waxen features thanked her with a look.

Olympia next, a creature half divine,
Sprung from the blood of old Evander's line,
Held her white arm, that wore a twisted chain
Clasped with an opal-sheeny cymophane.
In vain, O daughter! said the baffled Greek.
The patient sighed the thanks he could not speak.
Last, Hermia entered; look, that sudden start!
The pallium heaves above his leaping heart;
The beating pulse, the cheek's rekindled flame,
Those quivering lips, the secret all proclaim.
The deep disease long throbbing in the breast,
The dread enchantment, all at once confessed!
The case was plain; the treatment was begun;
And Love soon cured the mischief he had done.

Young Love, too oft thy treacherous bandage slips
Down from the eyes it blinded to the lips!
Ask not the Gods, O youth, for clearer sight,
But the bold heart to plead thy cause aright.
And thou, fair maiden, when thy lovers sigh,
Suspect thy flattering ear, but trust thine eye;
And learn this secret from the tale of old:
No love so true as love that dies untold.

"Bravo, Annex!" they shouted, every one, —
"Not Mrs. Kemble's self had better done."
"Quite so," she stammered in her awkward way, —
Not just the thing, but something she must say.

The teaspoon chorus tinkled to its close
When from his chair the MAN OF LAW arose,
Called by her voice whose mandate all obeyed,
And took the open volume she displayed.
Tall, stately, strong, his form begins to own
Some slight exuberance in its central zone, —
That comely fulness of the growing girth
Which fifty summers lend the sons of earth.
A smooth, round disk about whose margin stray,
Above the temples, glistening threads of gray;
Strong, deep-cut grooves by toilsome decades wrought
On brow and mouth, the battle-fields of thought;
A voice that lingers in the listener's ear,
Grave, calm, far-reaching, every accent clear, —
(Those tones resistless many a foreman knew
That shaped their verdict ere the twelve withdrew;)
A statesman's forehead, athlete's throat and jaw,
Such the proud semblance of the Man of Law.
His eye just lighted on the printed leaf,
Held as a practised pleader holds his brief.
One whispered softly from behind his cup,
" He does not read, — his book is wrong side up!
He knows the story that it holds by heart, —
So like his own! How well he'll act his part!"
Then all were silent; not a rustling fan
Stirred the deep stillness as the voice began.

THE STATESMAN'S SECRET

[Formerly *The Disappointed Statesman*.]

WHO of all statesmen is his country's pride,
Her councils' prompter and her leaders' guide?
He speaks; the nation holds its breath to hear;
He nods, and shakes the sunset hemisphere.
Born where the primal fount of Nature springs
By the rude cradles of her throneless kings,

In his proud eye her royal signet flames,
By his own lips her Monarch she proclaims.
  Why name his countless triumphs, whom to meet
Is to be famous, envied in defeat?
The keen debaters, trained to brawls and strife,
Who fire one shot, and finish with the knife,
Tried him but once, and, cowering in their shame,
Ground their hacked blades to strike at meaner game.
The lordly chief, his party's central stay,
Whose lightest word a hundred votes obey,
Found a new listener seated at his side,
Looked in his eye, and felt himself defied,
Flung his rash gauntlet on the startled floor,
Met the all-conquering, fought, — and ruled no more.
  See where he moves, what eager crowds attend!
What shouts of thronging multitudes ascend!
If this is life, — to mark with every hour
The purple deepening in his robes of power,
To see the painted fruits of honor fall
Thick at his feet, and choose among them all,
To hear the sounds that shape his spreading name
Peal through the myriad organ-stops of fame,
Stamp the lone isle that spots the seaman's chart,
And crown the pillared glory of the mart,
To count as peers the few supremely wise
Who mark their planet in the angels' eyes, —
If this is life —
  What savage man is he
Who strides alone beside the sounding sea?
Alone he wanders by the murmuring shore,
His thoughts as restless as the waves that roar;
Looks on the sullen sky as stormy-browed
As on the waves yon tempest-brooding cloud,
Heaves from his aching breast a wailing sigh,
Sad as the gust that sweeps the clouded sky.
Ask him his griefs; what midnight demons plough
The lines of torture on his lofty brow;

Unlock those marble lips, and bid them speak
The mystery freezing in his bloodless cheek.
His secret? Hid beneath a flimsy word;
One foolish whisper that ambition heard;
And thus it spake: "Behold yon gilded chair,
The world's one vacant throne, — thy place is there!"
  Ah, fatal dream! What warning spectres meet
In ghastly circle round its shadowy seat!
Yet still the Tempter murmurs in his ear
Thè maddening taunt he cannot choose but hear:
"Meanest of slaves, by gods and men accurst,
He who is second when he might be first!
Climb with bold front the ladder's topmost round,
Or chain thy creeping footsteps to the ground!"
  Illustrious Dupe! Have those majestic eyes
Lost their proud fire for such a vulgar prize?
Art thou the last of all mankind to know
That party-fights are won by aiming low?
Thou, stamped by Nature with her royal sign,
That party-hirelings hate a look like thine?
Shake from thy sense the wild delusive dream!
Without the purple, art thou not supreme?
And soothed by love unbought, thy heart shall own
A nation's homage nobler than its throne!

Loud rang the plaudits; with them rose the thought,
"Would he had learned the lesson he has taught!"
Used to the tributes of the noisy crowd,
The stately speaker calmly smiled and bowed;
The fire within a flushing cheek betrayed,
And eyes that burned beneath their penthouse shade.

"The clock strikes ten, the hours are flying fast, —
Now, Number Five, we've kept you till the last!"

What music charms like those caressing tones
Whose magic influence every listener owns, —
Where all the woman finds herself expressed,
And Heaven's divinest effluence breathes confessed?
Such was the breath that wooed our ravished ears,
Sweet as the voice a dreaming vestal hears;
Soft as the murmur of a brooding dove,
It told the mystery of a mother's love.

THE MOTHER'S SECRET

[Originally *A Mother's Secret*.]

How sweet the sacred legend — if unblamed
In my slight verse such holy things are named —
Of Mary's secret hours of hidden joy,
Silent, but pondering on her wondrous boy!
Ave, Maria! Pardon, if I wrong
Those heavenly words that shame my earthly song!
The choral host had closed the Angel's strain
Sung to the listening watch on Bethlehem's plain,
And now the shepherds, hastening on their way,
Sought the still hamlet where the Infant lay.
They passed the fields that gleaning Ruth toiled o'er, —
They saw afar the ruined threshing-floor
Where Moab's daughter, homeless and forlorn,
Found Boaz slumbering by his heaps of corn;
And some remembered how the holy scribe,
Skilled in the lore of every jealous tribe,
Traced the warm blood of Jesse's royal son
To that fair alien, bravely wooed and won.
So fared they on to seek the promised sign,
That marked the anointed heir of David's line.
At last, by forms of earthly semblance led,
They found the crowded inn, the oxen's shed.
No pomp was there, no glory shone around
On the coarse straw that strewed the reeking ground;
One dim retreat a flickering torch betrayed, —
In that poor cell the Lord of Life was laid!
The wondering shepherds told their breathless tale
Of the bright choir that woke the sleeping vale;
Told how the skies with sudden glory flamed,
Told how the shining multitude proclaimed,
"Joy, joy to earth! Behold the hallowed morn!
In David's city Christ the Lord is born!
'Glory to God!' let angels shout on high,
'Good-will to men!' the listening earth reply!"
They spoke with hurried words and accents wild;
Calm in his cradle slept the heavenly child.
No trembling word the mother's joy revealed, —
One sigh of rapture, and her lips were sealed;
Unmoved she saw the rustic train depart,
But kept their words to ponder in her heart.

Twelve years had passed; the boy was fair and tall,
Growing in wisdom, finding grace with all.
The maids of Nazareth, as they trooped to fill
Their balanced urns beside the mountain rill,
The gathered matrons, as they sat and spun,
Spoke in soft words of Joseph's quiet son.
No voice had reached the Galilean vale
Of star-led kings, or awe-struck shepherd's tale;
In the meek, studious child they only saw
The future Rabbi, learned in Israel's law.
So grew the boy, and now the feast was near
When at the Holy Place the tribes appear.
Scarce had the home-bred child of Nazareth seen
Beyond the hills that girt the village green;
Save when at midnight, o'er the starlit sands,
Snatched from the steel of Herod's murdering bands,

A babe, close folded to his mother's breast,
Through Edom's wilds he sought the sheltering West.
  Then Joseph spake: "Thy boy hath largely grown;
Weave him fine raiment, fitting to be shown;
Fair robes beseem the pilgrim, as the priest;
Goes he not with us to the holy feast?"
  And Mary culled the flaxen fibres white;
Till eve she spun; she spun till morning light.
The thread was twined; its parting meshes through
From hand to hand her restless shuttle flew,
Till the full web was wound upon the beam;
Love's curious toil, — a vest without a seam!
They reach the Holy Place, fulfil the days
To solemn feasting given, and grateful praise.
At last they turn, and far Moriah's height
Melts in the southern sky and fades from sight.
All day the dusky caravan has flowed
In devious trails along the winding road;
(For many a step their homeward path attends,
And all the sons of Abraham are as friends.)
Evening has come, — the hour of rest and joy, —
Hush! Hush! That whisper, — "Where is Mary's boy?"
  Oh, weary hour! Oh, aching days that passed
Filled with strange fears each wilder than the last, —
The soldier's lance, the fierce centurion's sword,
The crushing wheels that whirl some Roman lord,
The midnight crypt that sucks the captive's breath,
The blistering sun on Hinnom's vale of death!
  Thrice on his cheek had rained the morning light;
Thrice on his lips the mildewed kiss of night,
Crouched by a sheltering column's shining plinth,
Or stretched beneath the odorous terebinth.

  At last, in desperate mood, they sought once more
The Temple's porches, searched in vain before;
They found him seated with the ancient men, —
The grim old rufflers of the tongue and pen, —
Their bald heads glistening as they clustered near,
Their gray beards slanting as they turned to hear,
Lost in half-envious wonder and surprise
That lips so fresh should utter words so wise.
  And Mary said, — as one who, tried too long,
Tells all her grief and half her sense of wrong, —
"What is this thoughtless thing which thou hast done?
Lo, we have sought thee sorrowing, O my son!"
  Few words he spake, and scarce of filial tone,
Strange words, their sense a mystery yet unknown;
Then turned with them and left the holy hill,
To all their mild commands obedient still.
  The tale was told to Nazareth's sober men,
And Nazareth's matrons told it oft again;
The maids retold it at the fountain's side,
The youthful shepherds doubted or denied;
It passed around among the listening friends,
With all that fancy adds and fiction lends,
Till newer marvels dimmed the young renown
Of Joseph's son, who talked the Rabbis down.
  But Mary, faithful to its lightest word,
Kept in her heart the sayings she had heard,
Till the dread morning rent the Temple's veil,
And shuddering earth confirmed the wondrous tale.

Youth fades; love droops; the leaves of friendship fall:
A mother's secret hope outlives them all.

Hushed was the voice, but still its accents thrilled
The throbbing hearts its lingering sweetness filled.
The simple story which a tear repays
Asks not to share the noisy breath of praise.
A trance-like stillness, — scarce a whisper heard,
No tinkling teaspoon in its saucer stirred;
A deep-drawn sigh that would not be suppressed,
A sob, a lifted kerchief told the rest.

"Come now, Dictator," so the lady spoke,
"You too must fit your shoulder to the yoke;
You'll find there's something, doubtless, if you look,
To serve your purpose, — so, now take the book."
"Ah, my dear lady, you must know full well,
'Story, God bless you, I have none to tell.'
To those five stories which these pages hold
You all have listened, — every one is told.
There's nothing left to make you smile or weep, —
A few grave thoughts may work you off to sleep."

THE SECRET OF THE STARS

Is man's the only throbbing heart that hides
The silent spring that feeds its whispering tides?
Speak from thy caverns, mystery-breeding Earth,
Tell the half-hinted story of thy birth,
And calm the noisy champions who have thrown
The book of types against the book of stone!

Have ye not secrets, ye refulgent spheres,
No sleepless listener of the starlight hears?
In vain the sweeping equatorial pries
Through every world-sown corner of the skies,
To the far orb that so remotely strays
Our midnight darkness is its noonday blaze;
In vain the climbing soul of creeping man
Metes out the heavenly concave with a span,
Tracks into space the long-lost meteor's trail,
And weighs an unseen planet in the scale;
Still o'er their doubts the wan-eyed watchers sigh,
And Science lifts her still unanswered cry:
"Are all these worlds, that speed their circling flight,
Dumb, vacant, soulless, — baubles of the night?
Warmed with God's smile and wafted by his breath,
To weave in ceaseless round the dance of Death?
Or rolls a sphere in each expanding zone,
Crowned with a life as varied as our own?"

Maker of earth and stars! If thou hast taught
By what thy voice hath spoke, thy hand hath wrought,
By all that Science proves, or guesses true,
More than thy poet dreamed, thy prophet knew, —
The heavens still bow in darkness at thy feet,
And shadows veil thy cloud-pavilioned seat!
Not for ourselves we ask thee to reveal
One awful word beneath the future's seal;
What thou shalt tell us, grant us strength to bear;
What thou withholdest is thy single care.
Not for ourselves; the present clings too fast,
Moored to the mighty anchors of the past;
But when, with angry snap, some cable parts,
The sound re-echoing in our startled hearts, —
When, through the wall that clasps the harbor round,
And shuts the raving ocean from its bound,
Shattered and rent by sacrilegious hands,
The first mad billow leaps upon the sands, —
Then to the Future's awful page we turn,
And what we question hardly dare to learn.
Still let us hope! for while we seem to tread
The time-worn pathway of the nations dead,
Though Sparta laughs at all our warlike deeds,
And buried Athens claims our stolen creeds,

Though Rome, a spectre on her broken throne,
Beholds our eagle and recalls her own,
Though England fling her pennons on the breeze
And reign before us Mistress of the seas, —
While calm-eyed History tracks us circling round
Fate's iron pillar where they all were bound,
Still in our path a larger curve she finds,
The spiral widening as the chain unwinds!
Still sees new beacons crowned with brighter flame
Than the old watch-fires, like, but not the same!
No shameless haste shall spot with bandit-crime
Our destined empire snatched before its time.
Wait, — wait, undoubting, for the winds have caught
From our bold speech the heritage of thought;
No marble form that sculptured truth can wear
Vies with the image shaped in viewless air;
And thought unfettered grows through speech to deeds,
As the broad forest marches in its seeds.
What though we perish ere the day is won?
Enough to see its glorious work begun!
The thistle falls before a trampling clown,
But who can chain the flying thistle-down?
Wait while the fiery seeds of freedom fly,
The prairie blazes when the grass is dry!
 What arms might ravish, leave to peaceful arts,
Wisdom and love shall win the roughest hearts;
So shall the angel who has closed for man
The blissful garden since his woes began
Swing wide the golden portals of the West,
And Eden's secret stand at length confessed!

The reader paused; in truth he thought it time, —
Some threatening signs accused the drowsy rhyme.
The Mistress nodded, the Professor dozed,
The two Annexes sat with eyelids closed, —
Not *sleeping*, — no! But when one shuts one's eyes,
That one hears better no one, sure, denies.
The Doctor whispered in Delilah's ear,
Or seemed to whisper, for their heads drew near.
Not all the owner's efforts could restrain
The wild vagaries of the squinting brain, —
Last of the listeners Number Five alone
The patient reader still could call his own.

"Teacups, arouse!" 'T was thus the spell I broke;
The drowsy started and the slumberers woke.
"The sleep I promised you have now enjoyed,
Due to your hour of labor well employed.
Swiftly the busy moments have been passed;
This, our first 'Teacups,' must not be our last.
Here, on this spot, now consecrated ground,
The Order of 'The Teacups' let us found!
By winter's fireside and in summer's bower
Still shall it claim its ever-welcome hour,
In distant regions where our feet may roam
The magic teapot find or make a home;
Long may its floods their bright infusion pour,
Till time and teacups both shall be no more!"

APPENDIX

I. VERSES FROM THE OLDEST PORTFOLIO

FROM THE "COLLEGIAN," 1830, ILLUSTRATED ANNUALS, ETC.

Nescit vox missa reverti. — HORAT. *Ars Poetica*.
Ab iis quæ non adjuvant quam mollissime oportet pedem referre. — QUINTILIAN, L. VI. C. 4.

THESE verses have always been printed in my collected poems, and as the best of them may bear a single reading, I allow them to appear, but in a less conspicuous position than the other productions. A chick, before his shell is off his back, is hardly a fair subject for severe criticism. If one has written anything worth preserving, his first efforts may be objects of interest and curiosity. Other young authors may take encouragement from seeing how tame, how feeble, how commonplace were the rudimentary attempts of the half-fledged poet. If the boy or youth had anything in him, there will probably be some sign of it in the midst of his imitative mediocrities and ambitious failures.

These "first verses" of mine, written before I was sixteen, have little beyond a common academy boy's ordinary performance. Yet a kindly critic said there was one line which showed a poetical quality:

"The boiling ocean trembled into calm."

One of these poems — the reader may guess which — won fair words from Thackeray. The *Spectre Pig* was a wicked suggestion which came into my head after reading Dana's *Buccaneer*. Nobody seemed to find it out, and I never mentioned it to the venerable poet, who might not have been pleased with the parody.

This is enough to say of these unvalued copies of verses.

FIRST VERSES

PHILLIPS ACADEMY, ANDOVER, MASS., 1824 OR 1825

Translation from The Æneid, Book I.

THE god looked out upon the troubled deep
Waked into tumult from its placid sleep;
The flame of anger kindles in his eye
As the wild waves ascend the lowering sky;
He lifts his head above their awful height
And to the distant fleet directs his sight,
Now borne aloft upon the billow's crest,
Struck by the bolt or by the winds oppressed,
And well he knew that Juno's vengeful ire
Frowned from those clouds and sparkled in that fire.
On rapid pinions as they whistled by
He calls swift Zephyrus and Eurus nigh:
Is this your glory in a noble line
To leave your confines and to ravage mine?
Whom I — but let these troubled waves subside —
Another tempest and I'll quell your pride!
Go — bear our message to your master's ear,
That wide as ocean I am despot here;
Let him sit monarch in his barren caves,
I wield the trident and control the waves!
He said, and as the gathered vapors break
The swelling ocean seemed a peaceful lake;
To lift their ships the graceful nymphs essayed
And the strong trident lent its powerful aid;
The dangerous banks are sunk beneath the main,
And the light chariot skims the unruffled plain.
As when sedition fires the public mind,
And maddening fury leads the rabble blind,
The blazing torch lights up the dread alarm,
Rage points the steel and fury nerves the arm,
Then, if some reverend sage appear in sight,
They stand — they gaze, and check their headlong flight, —
He turns the current of each wandering breast
And hushes every passion into rest, —
Thus by the power of his imperial arm
The boiling ocean trembled into calm;
With flowing reins the father sped his way
And smiled serene upon rekindled day.

THE MEETING OF THE DRYADS

Written after a general pruning of the trees around Harvard College. A little poem, on a similar occasion, may be found in the works of Swift, from which, perhaps, the idea was borrowed; although I was as much surprised as amused to meet with it some time after writing the following lines.

IT was not many centuries since,
When, gathered on the moonlit green,
Beneath the Tree of Liberty,
A ring of weeping sprites was seen.

The freshman's lamp had long been dim,
 The voice of busy day was mute,
And tortured Melody had ceased
 Her sufferings on the evening flute.

They met not as they once had met,
 To laugh o'er many a jocund tale:
But every pulse was beating low,
 And every cheek was cold and pale.

There rose a fair but faded one,
 Who oft had cheered them with her song;
She waved a mutilated arm,
 And silence held the listening throng.

"Sweet friends," the gentle nymph began,
 "From opening bud to withering leaf,
One common lot has bound us all,
 In every change of joy and grief.

"While all around has felt decay,
 We rose in ever-living prime,
With broader shade and fresher green,
 Beneath the crumbling step of Time.

"When often by our feet has past
 Some biped, Nature's walking whim,
Say, have we trimmed one awkward shape,
 Or lopped away one crooked limb?

"Go on, fair Science; soon to thee
 Shall Nature yield her idle boast;
Her vulgar fingers formed a tree,
 But thou hast trained it to a post.

"Go, paint the birch's silver rind,
 And quilt the peach with softer down;
Up with the willow's trailing threads,
 Off with the sunflower's radiant crown!

"Go, plant the lily on the shore,
 And set the rose among the waves,
And bid the tropic bud unbind
 Its silken zone in arctic caves;

"Bring bellows for the panting winds,
 Hang up a lantern by the moon,
And give the nightingale a fife,
 And lend the eagle a balloon!

"I cannot smile, — the tide of scorn,
 That rolled through every bleeding vein,
Comes kindling fiercer as it flows
 Back to its burning source again.

"Again in every quivering leaf
 That moment's agony I feel,
When limbs, that spurned the northern blast,
 Shrunk from the sacrilegious steel.

"A curse upon the wretch who dared
 To crop us with his felon saw!
May every fruit his lip shall taste
 Lie like a bullet in his maw.

"In every julep that he drinks,
 May gout, and bile, and headache be;
And when he strives to calm his pain,
 May colic mingle with his tea.

"May nightshade cluster round his path,
 And thistles shoot, and brambles cling;
May blistering ivy scorch his veins,
 And dogwood burn, and nettles sting.

"On him may never shadow fall,
 When fever racks his throbbing brow,
And his last shilling buy a rope
 To hang him on my highest bough!"

She spoke; — the morning's herald beam
 Sprang from the bosom of the sea,
And every mangled sprite returned
 In sadness to her wounded tree.

THE MYSTERIOUS VISITOR

THERE was a sound of hurrying feet,
 A tramp on echoing stairs,
There was a rush along the aisles, —
 It was the hour of prayers.

And on, like Ocean's midnight wave,
 The current rolled along,
When, suddenly, a stranger form
 Was seen amidst the throng.

He was a dark and swarthy man,
 That uninvited guest;
A faded coat of bottle-green
 Was buttoned round his breast.

There was not one among them all
 Could say from whence he came;
Nor beardless boy, nor ancient man,
 Could tell that stranger's name.

All silent as the sheeted dead,
 In spite of sneer and frown,
Fast by a gray-haired senior's side
 He sat him boldly down.

There was a look of horror flashed
 From out the tutor's eyes;
When all around him rose to pray,
 The stranger did not rise!

A murmur broke along the crowd,
 The prayer was at an end;
With ringing heels and measured tread,
 A hundred forms descend.

Through sounding aisle, o'er grating stair,
 The long procession poured,
Till all were gathered on the seats
 Around the Commons board.

That fearful stranger! down he sat,
 Unasked, yet undismayed;
And on his lip a rising smile
 Of scorn or pleasure played.

He took his hat and hung it up,
 With slow but earnest air;

He stripped his coat from off his back,
  And placed it on a chair.

Then from his nearest neighbor's side
  A knife and plate he drew;
And, reaching out his hand again,
  He took his teacup too.

How fled the sugar from the bowl!
  How sunk the azure cream!
They vanished like the shapes that float
  Upon a summer's dream.

A long, long draught, — an outstretched hand, —
  And crackers, toast, and tea,
They faded from the stranger's touch,
  Like dew upon the sea.

Then clouds were dark on many a brow,
  Fear sat upon their souls,
And, in a bitter agony,
  They clasped their buttered rolls.

A whisper trembled through the crowd, —
  Who could the stranger be?
And some were silent, for they thought
  A cannibal was he.

What if the creature should arise, —
  For he was stout and tall, —
And swallow down a sophomore,
  Coat, crow's-foot, cap, and all!

All sullenly the stranger rose;
  They sat in mute despair;
He took his hat from off the peg,
  His coat from off the chair.

Four freshmen fainted on the seat,
  Six swooned upon the floor;
Yet on the fearful being passed,
  And shut the chapel door.

There is full many a starving man,
  That walks in bottle green,
But never more that hungry one
  In Commons hall was seen.

Yet often at the sunset hour,
  When tolls the evening bell,
The freshman lingers on the steps,
  That frightful tale to tell.

THE TOADSTOOL

There's a thing that grows by the fainting flower,
  And springs in the shade of the lady's bower;
The lily shrinks, and the rose turns pale,
When they feel its breath in the summer gale,
And the tulip curls its leaves in pride,
And the blue-eyed violet starts aside;
But the lily may flaunt, and the tulip stare,
For what does the honest toadstool care?

She does not glow in a painted vest,
And she never blooms on the maiden's breast;
But she comes, as the saintly sisters do,
In a modest suit of a Quaker hue.
And, when the stars in the evening skies
Are weeping dew from their gentle eyes,
The toad comes out from his hermit cell,
The tale of his faithful love to tell.

Oh, there is light in her lover's glance,
That flies to her heart like a silver lance;
His breeches are made of spotted skin,
His jacket is tight, and his pumps are thin;
In a cloudless night you may hear his song,
As its pensive melody floats along,
And, if you will look by the moonlight fair,
The trembling form of the toad is there.

And he twines his arms round her slender stem,
In the shade of her velvet diadem;
But she turns away in her maiden shame,
And will not breathe on the kindling flame;
He sings at her feet through the livelong night,
And creeps to his cave at the break of light;
And whenever he comes to the air above,
His throat is swelling with baffled love.

THE SPECTRE PIG

A BALLAD

It was the stalwart butcher man,
  That knit his swarthy brow,
And said the gentle Pig must die,
  And sealed it with a vow.

And oh! it was the gentle Pig
  Lay stretched upon the ground,
And ah! it was the cruel knife
  His little heart that found.

They took him then, those wicked men,
  They trailed him all along:
They put a stick between his lips,
  And through his heels a thong;

And round and round an oaken beam
  A hempen cord they flung,
And, like a mighty pendulum,
  All solemnly he swung!

Now say thy prayers, thou sinful man,
  And think what thou hast done,
And read thy catechism well,
  Thou bloody-minded one;

For if his sprite should walk by night,
  It better were for thee,
That thou wert mouldering in the ground,
  Or bleaching in the sea.

It was the savage butcher then,
  That made a mock of sin,
And swore a very wicked oath,
  He did not care a pin.

It was the butcher's youngest son, —
His voice was broke with sighs,
And with his pocket-handkerchief
He wiped his little eyes;

All young and ignorant was he,
But innocent and mild,
And, in his soft simplicity,
Out spoke the tender child: —

"Oh, father, father, list to me;
The Pig is deadly sick,
And men have hung him by his heels,
And fed him with a stick."

It was the bloody butcher then,
That laughed as he would die,
Yet did he soothe the sorrowing child,
And bid him not to cry; —

"Oh, Nathan, Nathan, what's a Pig,
That thou shouldst weep and wail?
Come, bear thee like a butcher's child,
And thou shalt have his tail!"

It was the butcher's daughter then,
So slender and so fair,
That sobbed as if her heart would break,
And tore her yellow hair;

And thus she spoke in thrilling tone, —
Fast fell the tear-drops big: —
"Ah! woe is me! Alas! Alas!
The Pig! The Pig! The Pig!"

Then did her wicked father's lips
Make merry with her woe,
And call her many a naughty name,
Because she whimpered so.

Ye need not weep, ye gentle ones,
In vain your tears are shed,
Ye cannot wash his crimson hand,
Ye cannot soothe the dead.

The bright sun folded on his breast
His robes of rosy flame,
And softly over all the west
The shades of evening came.

He slept, and troops of murdered Pigs
Were busy with his dreams;
Loud rang their wild, unearthly shrieks,
Wide yawned their mortal seams.

The clock struck twelve; the Dead hath heard;
He opened both his eyes,
And sullenly he shook his tail
To lash the feeding flies.

One quiver of the hempen cord, —
One struggle and one bound, —
With stiffened limb and leaden eye,
The Pig was on the ground!

And straight towards the sleeper's house
His fearful way he wended;
And hooting owl and hovering bat
On midnight wing attended.

Back flew the bolt, up rose the latch,
And open swung the door,
And little mincing feet were heard
Pat, pat along the floor.

Two hoofs upon the sanded floor,
And two upon the bed;
And they are breathing side by side,
The living and the dead!

"Now wake, now wake, thou butcher man!
What makes thy cheek so pale?
Take hold! take hold! thou dost not fear
To clasp a spectre's tail?"

Untwisted every winding coil;
The shuddering wretch took hold,
All like an icicle it seemed,
So tapering and so cold.

"Thou com'st with me, thou butcher man!" —
He strives to loose his grasp,
But, faster than the clinging vine,
Those twining spirals clasp:

And open, open swung the door,
And, fleeter than the wind,
The shadowy spectre swept before,
The butcher trailed behind.

Fast fled the darkness of the night,
And morn rose faint and dim;
They called full loud, they knocked full long,
They did not waken him.

Straight, straight towards that oaken beam,
A trampled pathway ran;
A ghastly shape was swinging there, —
It was the butcher man.

TO A CAGED LION

Poor conquered monarch! though that haughty glance
Still speaks thy courage unsubdued by time,
And in the grandeur of thy sullen tread
Lives the proud spirit of thy burning clime; —
Fettered by things that shudder at thy roar,
Torn from thy pathless wilds to pace this narrow floor!

Thou wast the victor, and all nature shrunk
Before the thunders of thine awful wrath;
The steel-armed hunter viewed thee from afar,
Fearless and trackless in thy lonely path!
The famished tiger closed his flaming eye,
And crouched and panted as thy step went by!

Thou art the vanquished, and insulting man
  Bars thy broad bosom as a sparrow's wing;
His nerveless arms thine iron sinews bind,
  And lead in chains the desert's fallen king;
Are these the beings that have dared to twine
  Their feeble threads around those limbs of thine?

So must it be; the weaker, wiser race,
  That wields the tempest and that rides the sea,
Even in the stillness of thy solitude.
  Must teach the lesson of its power to thee;
And thou, the terror of the trembling wild,
  Must bow thy savage strength, the mockery of a child!

THE STAR AND THE WATER-LILY

The sun stepped down from his golden throne,
  And lay in the silent sea,
And the Lily had folded her satin leaves,
  For a sleepy thing was she;
What is the Lily dreaming of?
  Why crisp the waters blue?
See, see, she is lifting her varnished lid!
  Her white leaves are glistening through!

The Rose is cooling his burning cheek
  In the lap of the breathless tide;—
The Lily hath sisters fresh and fair,
  That would lie by the Rose's side;
He would love her better than all the rest,
  And he would be fond and true;—
But the Lily unfolded her weary lids,
  And looked at the sky so blue.

Remember, remember, thou silly one,
  How fast will thy summer glide,
And wilt thou wither a virgin pale,
  Or flourish a blooming bride?
"Oh, the Rose is old, and thorny, and cold,
  And he lives on earth," said she;
"But the Star is fair and he lives in the air,
  And he shall my bridegroom be."

But what if the stormy cloud should come,
  And ruffle the silver sea?
Would he turn his eye from the distant sky,
  To smile on a thing like thee?
Oh no, fair Lily, he will not send
  One ray from his far-off throne;
The winds shall blow, and the waves shall flow,
  And thou wilt be left alone.

There is not a leaf on the mountain-top,
  Nor a drop of evening dew,
Nor a golden sand on the sparkling shore,
  Nor a pearl in the waters blue,
That he has not cheered with his fickle smile,
  And warmed with his faithless beam, —
And will he be true to a pallid flower,
  That floats on the quiet stream?

Alas for the Lily! she would not heed,
  But turned to the skies afar,
And bared her breast to the trembling ray
  That shot from the rising star;
The cloud came over the darkened sky,
  And over the waters wide:
She looked in vain through the beating rain,
  And sank in the stormy tide.

ILLUSTRATION OF A PICTURE

"A SPANISH GIRL IN REVERIE"

She twirled the string of golden beads,
  That round her neck was hung, —
My grandsire's gift; the good old man
  Loved girls when he was young;
And, bending lightly o'er the cord,
  And turning half away,
With something like a youthful sigh,
  Thus spoke the maiden gray:—

"Well, one may trail her silken robe,
  And bind her locks with pearls,
And one may wreathe the woodland rose
  Among her floating curls;
And one may tread the dewy grass,
  And one the marble floor,
Nor half-hid bosom heave the less,
  Nor broidered corset more!

"Some years ago, a dark-eyed girl
  Was sitting in the shade, —
There 's something brings her to my mind
  In that young dreaming maid, —
And in her hand she held a flower,
  A flower, whose speaking hue
Said, in the language of the heart,
  'Believe the giver true.'

"And, as she looked upon its leaves,
  The maiden made a vow
To wear it when the bridal wreath
  Was woven for her brow;
She watched the flower, as, day by day,
  The leaflets curled and died;
But he who gave it never came
  To claim her for his bride.

"Oh, many a summer's morning glow
  Has lent the rose its ray,
And many a winter's drifting snow
  Has swept its bloom away;
But she has kept that faithless pledge
  To this, her winter hour,
And keeps it still, herself alone,
  And wasted like the flower."

Her pale lip quivered, and the light
  Gleamed in her moistening eyes;—
I asked her how she liked the tints
  In those Castilian skies?
"She thought them misty,—'t was perhaps
  Because she stood too near;"
She turned away, and as she turned
  I saw her wipe a tear.

A ROMAN AQUEDUCT

The sun-browned girl, whose limbs recline
 When noon her languid hand has laid
Hot on the green flakes of the pine,
 Beneath its narrow disk of shade;

As, through the flickering noontide glare,
 She gazes on the rainbow chain
Of arches, lifting once in air
 The rivers of the Roman's plain; —

Say, does her wandering eye recall
 The mountain-current's icy wave, —
Or for the dead one tear let fall,
 Whose founts are broken by their grave?

From stone to stone the ivy weaves
 Her braided tracery's winding veil,
And lacing stalks and tangled leaves
 Nod heavy in the drowsy gale.

And lightly floats the pendent vine,
 That swings beneath her slender bow,
Arch answering arch, — whose rounded line
 Seems mirrored in the wreath below.

How patient Nature smiles at Fame!
 The weeds, that strewed the victor's way,
Feed on his dust to shroud his name,
 Green where his proudest towers decay.

See, through that channel, empty now,
 The scanty rain its tribute pours, —
Which cooled the lip and laved the brow
 Of conquerors from a hundred shores.

Thus bending o'er the nation's bier,
 Whose wants the captive earth supplied,
The dew of Memory's passing tear
 Falls on the arches of her pride!

FROM A BACHELOR'S PRIVATE JOURNAL

Sweet Mary, I have never breathed
 The love it were in vain to name;
Though round my heart a serpent wreathed,
 I smiled, or strove to smile, the same.

Once more the pulse of Nature glows
 With faster throb and fresher fire,
While music round her pathway flows,
 Like echoes from a hidden lyre.

And is there none with me to share
 The glories of the earth and sky?
The eagle through the pathless air
 Is followed by one burning eye.

Ah no! the cradled flowers may wake,
 Again may flow the frozen sea,
From every cloud a star may break, —
 There comes no second spring to me.

Go, — ere the painted toys of youth
 Are crushed beneath the tread of years;
Ere visions have been chilled to truth,
 And hopes are washed away in tears.

Go, — for I will not bid thee weep, —
 Too soon my sorrows will be thine,
And evening's troubled air shall sweep
 The incense from the broken shrine.

If Heaven can hear the dying tone
 Of chords that soon will cease to thrill,
The prayer that Heaven has heard alone
 May bless thee when those chords are still.

LA GRISETTE

Ah, Clemence! when I saw thee last
 Trip down the Rue de Seine,
And turning, when thy form had past,
 I said, "We meet again," —
I dreamed not in that idle glance
 Thy latest image came,
And only left to memory's trance
 A shadow and a name.

The few strange words my lips had taught
 Thy timid voice to speak,
Their gentler signs, which often brought
 Fresh roses to thy cheek,
The trailing of thy long loose hair
 Bent o'er my couch of pain,
All, all returned, more sweet, more fair:
 Oh, had we met again!

I walked where saint and virgin keep
 The vigil lights of Heaven,
I knew that thou hadst woes to weep,
 And sins to be forgiven;
I watched where Genevieve was laid,
 I knelt by Mary's shrine,
Beside me low, soft voices prayed;
 Alas! but where was thine?

And when the morning sun was bright,
 When wind and wave were calm,
And flamed, in thousand-tinted light,
 The rose of Notre Dame,
I wandered through the haunts of men,
 From Boulevard to Quai,
Till, frowning o'er Saint Etienne,
 The Pantheon's shadow lay.

In vain, in vain; we meet no more,
 Nor dream what fates befall;
And long upon the stranger's shore
 My voice on thee may call,
When years have clothed the line in moss
 That tells thy name and days,
And withered, on thy simple cross,
 The wreaths of Père-la-Chaise!

VERSES FROM THE OLDEST PORTFOLIO

OUR YANKEE GIRLS

Let greener lands and bluer skies,
  If such the wide earth shows,
With fairer cheeks and brighter eyes,
  Match us the star and rose;
The winds that lift the Georgian's veil,
  Or wave Circassia's curls,
Waft to their shores the sultan's sail, —
  Who buys our Yankee girls?

The gay grisette, whose fingers touch
  Love's thousand chords so well;
The dark Italian, loving much,
  But more than *one* can tell;
And England's fair-haired, blue-eyed dame,
  Who binds her brow with pearls; —
Ye who have seen them, can they shame
  Our own sweet Yankee girls?

And what if court or castle vaunt
  Its children loftier born? —
Who heeds the silken tassel's flaunt
  Beside the golden corn?
They ask not for the dainty toil
  Of ribboned knights and earls,
The daughters of the virgin soil,
  Our freeborn Yankee girls!

By every hill whose stately pines
  Wave their dark arms above
The home where some fair being shines,
  To warm the wilds with love,
From barest rock to bleakest shore
  Where farthest sail unfurls,
That stars and stripes are streaming o'er, —
  God bless our Yankee girls!

L'INCONNUE

Is thy name Mary, maiden fair?
  Such should, methinks, its music be;
The sweetest name that mortals bear
  Were best befitting thee;
And she to whom it once was given,
Was half of earth and half of heaven.

I hear thy voice, I see thy smile,
  I look upon thy folded hair;
Ah! while we dream not they beguile,
  Our hearts are in the snare;
And she who chains a wild bird's wing
Must start not if her captive sing.

So, lady, take the leaf that falls,
  To all but thee unseen, unknown:
When evening shades thy silent walls,
  Then read it all alone;
In stillness read, in darkness seal,
Forget, despise, but not reveal!

STANZAS

Strange! that one lightly whispered tone
  Is far, far sweeter unto me,
Than all the sounds that kiss the earth,
  Or breathe along the sea;
But, lady, when thy voice I greet,
Not heavenly music seems so sweet.

I look upon the fair blue skies,
  And naught but empty air I see;
But when I turn me to thine eyes,
  It seemeth unto me
Ten thousand angels spread their wings
Within those little azure rings.

The lily hath the softest leaf
  That ever western breeze hath fanned,
But thou shalt have the tender flower,
  So I may take thy hand;
That little hand to me doth yield
More joy than all the broidered field.

O lady! there be many things
  That seem right fair, below, above;
But sure not one among them all
  Is half so sweet as love; —
Let us not pay our vows alone,
But join two altars both in one.

LINES BY A CLERK

Oh! I did love her dearly,
  And gave her toys and rings,
And I thought she meant sincerely,
  When she took my pretty things.
But her heart has grown as icy
  As a fountain in the fall,
And her love, that was so spicy,
  It did not last at all.

I gave her once a locket,
  It was filled with my own hair,
And she put it in her pocket
  With very special care.
But a jeweller has got it, —
  He offered it to me, —
And another that is not it
  Around her neck I see.

For my cooings and my billings
  I do not now complain,
But my dollars and my shillings
  Will never come again;
They were earned with toil and sorrow,
  But I never told her that,
And now I have to borrow,
  And want another hat.

Think, think, thou cruel Emma,
  When thou shalt hear my woe,
And know my sad dilemma,
  That thou hast made it so.
See, see my beaver rusty,
  Look, look upon this hole,
This coat is dim and dusty;
  Oh let it rend thy soul!

Before the gates of fashion
  I daily bent my knee,
But I sought the shrine of passion,
  And found my idol, — thee.

Though never love intenser
Had bowed a soul before it,
Thine eye was on the censer,
And not the hand that bore it.

THE PHILOSOPHER TO HIS LOVE

Dearest, a look is but a ray
Reflected in a certain way;
A word, whatever tone it wear,
Is but a trembling wave of air;
A touch, obedience to a clause
In nature's pure material laws.

The very flowers that bend and meet,
In sweetening others, grow more sweet;
The clouds by day, the stars by night,
Inweave their floating locks of light;
The rainbow, Heaven's own forehead's braid,
Is but the embrace of sun and shade.

How few that love us have we found!
How wide the world that girds them round!
Like mountain streams we meet and part,
Each living in the other's heart,
Our course unknown, our hope to be
Yet mingled in the distant sea.

But Ocean coils and heaves in vain,
Bound in the subtle moonbeam's chain;
And love and hope do but obey
Some cold, capricious planet's ray,
Which lights and leads the tide it charms
To Death's dark caves and icy arms.

Alas! one narrow line is drawn,
That links our sunset with our dawn;
In mist and shade life's morning rose,
And clouds are round it at its close;
But ah! no twilight beam ascends
To whisper where that evening ends.

Oh! in the hour when I shall feel
Those shadows round my senses steal,
When gentle eyes are weeping o'er
The clay that feels their tears no more,
Then let thy spirit with me be,
Or some sweet angel, likest thee!

THE POET'S LOT

What is a poet's love? —
To write a girl a sonnet,
To get a ring, or some such thing,
And fustianize upon it.

What is a poet's fame? —
Sad hints about his reason,
And sadder praise from garreteers,
To be returned in season.

Where go the poet's lines? —
Answer, ye evening tapers!
Ye auburn locks, ye golden curls,
Speak from your folded papers!

Child of the ploughshare, smile;
Boy of the counter, grieve not,
Though muses round thy trundle-bed
Their broidered tissue weave not.

The poet's future holds
No civic wreath above him;
Nor slated roof, nor varnished chaise,
Nor wife nor child to love him.

Maid of the village inn,
Who workest woe on satin,
(The grass in black, the graves in green,
The epitaph in Latin,)

Trust not to them who say,
In stanzas, they adore thee;
Oh rather sleep in churchyard clay,
With urn and cherub o'er thee!

TO A BLANK SHEET OF PAPER

Wan-visaged thing! thy virgin leaf
To me looks more than deadly pale,
Unknowing what may stain thee yet, —
A poem or a tale.

Who can thy unborn meaning scan?
Can Seer or Sibyl read thee now?
No, — seek to trace the fate of man
Writ on his infant brow.

Love may light on thy snowy cheek,
And shake his Eden-breathing plumes;
Then shalt thou tell how Lelia smiles,
Or Angelina blooms.

Satire may lift his bearded lance,
Forestalling Time's slow-moving scythe,
And, scattered on thy little field,
Disjointed bards may writhe.

Perchance a vision of the night,
Some grizzled spectre, gaunt and thin,
Or sheeted corpse, may stalk along,
Or skeleton may grin!

If it should be in pensive hour
Some sorrow-moving theme I try,
Ah, maiden, how thy tears will fall,
For all I doom to die!

But if in merry mood I touch
Thy leaves, then shall the sight of thee
Sow smiles as thick on rosy lips
As ripples on the sea.

The Weekly press shall gladly stoop
To bind thee up among its sheaves;
The Daily steal thy shining ore,
To gild its leaden leaves.

Thou hast no tongue, yet thou canst speak,
Till distant shores shall hear the sound;

Thou hast no life, yet thou canst breathe
  Fresh life on all around.

Thou art the arena of the wise,
  The noiseless battle-ground of fame;
The sky where halos may be wreathed
  Around the humblest name.

Take, then, this treasure to thy trust,
  To win some idle reader's smile,
Then fade and moulder in the dust,
  Or swell some bonfire's pile.

TO THE PORTRAIT OF "A GENTLEMAN"

IN THE ATHENÆUM GALLERY

[The companion poem, *To the Portrait of "A Lady,"* was retained by Dr. Holmes in his group, *Earlier Poems.*]

It may be so, — perhaps thou hast
  A warm and loving heart;
I will not blame thee for thy face,
  Poor devil as thou art.

That thing thou fondly deem'st a nose,
  Unsightly though it be,
In spite of all the cold world's scorn,
  It may be much to thee.

Those eyes, — among thine elder friends
  Perhaps they pass for blue, —
No matter, — if a man can see,
  What more have eyes to do?

Thy mouth, — that fissure in thy face,
  By something like a chin, —
May be a very useful place
  To put thy victual in.

I know thou hast a wife at home,
  I know thou hast a child,
By that subdued, domestic smile
  Upon thy features mild.

That wife sits fearless by thy side,
  That cherub on thy knee;
They do not shudder at thy looks,
  They do not shrink from thee.

Above thy mantle is a hook, —
  A portrait once was there;
It was thine only ornament, —
  Alas! that hook is bare.

She begged thee not to let it go,
  She begged thee all in vain;
She wept, — and breathed a trembling prayer
  To meet it safe again.

It was a bitter sight to see
  That picture torn away;
It was a solemn thought to think
  What all her friends would say!

And often in her calmer hours,
  And in her happy dreams,
Upon its long-deserted hook
  The absent portrait seems.

Thy wretched infant turns his head
  In melancholy wise,
And looks to meet the placid stare
  Of those unbending eyes.

I never saw thee, lovely one, —
  Perchance I never may;
It is not often that we cross
  Such people in our way;

But if we meet in distant years,
  Or on some foreign shore,
Sure I can take my Bible oath,
  I've seen that face before.

THE BALLAD OF THE OYSTERMAN

It was a tall young oysterman lived by the river-side,
His shop was just upon the bank, his boat was on the tide;
The daughter of a fisherman, that was so straight and slim,
Lived over on the other bank, right opposite to him.

It was the pensive oysterman that saw a lovely maid,
Upon a moonlight evening, a-sitting in the shade;
He saw her wave her handkerchief, as much as if to say,
"I'm wide awake, young oysterman, and all the folks away."

Then up arose the oysterman, and to himself said he,
"I guess I'll leave the skiff at home, for fear that folks should see;
I read it in the story-book, that, for to kiss his dear,
Leander swam the Hellespont, — and I will swim this here."

And he has leaped into the waves, and crossed the shining stream,
And he has clambered up the bank, all in the moonlight gleam;
Oh there were kisses sweet as dew, and words as soft as rain, —
But they have heard her father's step, and in he leaps again!

Out spoke the ancient fisherman, — "Oh, what was that, my daughter?"
"'T was nothing but a pebble, sir, I threw into the water."
"And what is that, pray tell me, love, that paddles off so fast?"
"It's nothing but a porpoise, sir, that's been a-swimming past."

Out spoke the ancient fisherman, — "Now bring
    me my harpoon!
I 'll get into my fishing-boat, and fix the fellow
    soon."
Down fell that pretty innocent, as falls a snow-
    white lamb,
Her hair drooped round her pallid cheeks, like
    seaweed on a clam.

Alas for those two loving ones! she waked not
    from her swound,
And he was taken with the cramp, and in the
    waves was drowned;
But Fate has metamorphosed them, in pity of
    their woe,
And now they keep an oyster-shop for mer-
    maids down below.

A NOONTIDE LYRIC

THE dinner-bell, the dinner-bell
    Is ringing loud and clear;
Through hill and plain, through street and lane,
    It echoes far and near;
From curtained hall and whitewashed stall,
    Wherever men can hide,
Like bursting waves from ocean caves,
    They float upon the tide.

I smell the smell of roasted meat!
    I hear the hissing fry!
The beggars know where they can go,
    But where, oh where shall I?
At twelve o'clock men took my hand,
    At two they only stare,
And eye me with a fearful look,
    As if I were a bear!

The poet lays his laurels down,
    And hastens to his greens;
The happy tailor quits his goose,
    To riot on his beans;
The weary cobbler snaps his thread,
    The printer leaves his pi;
His very devil hath a home,
    But what, oh what have I?

Methinks I hear an angel voice,
    That softly seems to say:
"Pale stranger, all may yet be well,
    Then wipe thy tears away;
Erect thy head, and cock thy hat,
    And follow me afar,
And thou shalt have a jolly meal,
    And charge it at the bar."

I hear the voice! I go! I go!
    Prepare your meat and wine!
They little heed their future need
    Who pay not when they dine.
Give me to-day the rosy bowl,
    Give me one golden dream, —
To-morrow kick away the stool,
    And dangle from the beam!

THE HOT SEASON

THE folks, that on the first of May
    Wore winter coats and hose,
Began to say, the first of June,
    "Good Lord! how hot it grows!"
At last two Fahrenheits blew up,
    And killed two children small,
And one barometer shot dead
    A tutor with its ball!

Now all day long the locusts sang
    Among the leafless trees;
Three new hotels warped inside out,
    The pumps could only wheeze;
And ripe old wine, that twenty years
    Had cobwebbed o'er in vain,
Came spouting through the rotten corks
    Like Joly's best champagne!

The Worcester locomotives did
    Their trip in half an hour;
The Lowell cars ran forty miles
    Before they checked the power;
Roll brimstone soon became a drug,
    And loco-focos fell;
All asked for ice, but everywhere
    Saltpetre was to sell.

Plump men of mornings ordered tights,
    But, ere the scorching noons,
Their candle-moulds had grown as loose
    As Cossack pantaloons!
The dogs ran mad, — men could not try
    If water they would choose;
A horse fell dead, — he only left
    Four red-hot, rusty shoes!

But soon the people could not bear
    The slightest hint of fire;
Allusions to caloric drew
    A flood of savage ire;
The leaves on heat were all torn out
    From every book at school,
And many blackguards kicked and caned,
    Because they said, "Keep cool!"

The gas-light companies were mobbed,
    The bakers all were shot.
The penny press began to talk
    Of lynching Doctor Nott;
And all about the warehouse steps
    Were angry men in droves,
Crashing and splintering through the doors
    To smash the patent stoves!

The abolition men and maids
    Were tanned to such a hue,
You scarce could tell them from their friends,
    Unless their eyes were blue;
And, when I left, society
    Had burst its ancient guards,
And Brattle Street and Temple Place
    Were interchanging cards!

A PORTRAIT

A still, sweet, placid, moonlight face,
  And slightly nonchalant,
Which seems to claim a middle place
  Between one's love and aunt,
Where childhood's star has left a ray
  In woman's sunniest sky,
As morning dew and blushing day
  On fruit and blossom lie.

And yet, — and yet I cannot love
  Those lovely lines on steel ;
They beam too much of heaven above,
  Earth's darker shades to feel ;
Perchance some early weeds of care
  Around my heart have grown,
And brows unfurrowed seem not fair,
  Because they mock my own.

Alas ! when Eden's gates were sealed,
  How oft some sheltered flower
Breathed o'er the wanderers of the field,
  Like their own bridal bower ;
Yet, saddened by its loveliness,
  And humbled by its pride,
Earth's fairest child they could not bless, —
  It mocked them when they sighed.

AN EVENING THOUGHT

WRITTEN AT SEA

If sometimes in the dark blue eye,
  Or in the deep red wine,
Or soothed by gentlest melody,
  Still warms this heart of mine,
Yet something colder in the blood,
  And calmer in the brain,
Have whispered that my youth's bright flood
  Ebbs, not to flow again.

If by Helvetia's azure lake,
  Or Arno's yellow stream,
Each star of memory could awake,
  As in my first young dream,
I know that when mine eye shall greet
  The hillsides bleak and bare,
That gird my home, it will not meet
  My childhood's sunsets there.

Oh, when love's first, sweet, stolen kiss
  Burned on my boyish brow,
Was that young forehead worn as this ?
  Was that flushed cheek as now ?
Were that wild pulse and throbbing heart
  Like these, which vainly strive,
In thankless strains of soulless art,
  To dream themselves alive ?

Alas ! the morning dew is gone,
  Gone ere the full of day ;
Life's iron fetter still is on,
  Its wreaths all torn away ;

Happy if still some casual hour
  Can warm the fading shrine,
Too soon to chill beyond the power
  Of love, or song, or wine !

"THE WASP" AND "THE HORNET"

The two proud sisters of the sea,
  In glory and in doom ! —
Well may the eternal waters be
  Their broad, unsculptured tomb !
The wind that rings along the wave,
  The clear, unshadowed sun,
Are torch and trumpet o'er the brave,
  Whose last green wreath is won !

No stranger-hand their banners furled,
  No victor's shout they heard ;
Unseen, above them ocean curled,
  Safe by his own pale bird ;
The gnashing billows heaved and fell ;
  Wild shrieked the midnight gale ;
Far, far beneath the morning swell
  Were pennon, spar, and sail.

The land of Freedom ! Sea and shore
  Are guarded now, as when
Her ebbing waves to victory bore
  Fair barks and gallant men ;
Oh, many a ship of prouder name
  May wave her starry fold,
Nor trail, with deeper light of fame,
  The paths they swept of old !

"QUI VIVE ?"

" Qui vive ? " The sentry's musket rings,
  The channelled bayonet gleams ;
High o'er him, like a raven's wings
  The broad tricolored banner flings
Its shadow, rustling as it swings
  Pale in the moonlight beams ;
Pass on ! while steel-clad sentries keep
Their vigil o'er the monarch's sleep,
  Thy bare, unguarded breast
Asks not the unbroken, bristling zone
That girds you sceptred trembler's throne ;
  Pass on, and take thy rest !

" Qui vive ? " How oft the midnight air
  That startling cry has borne !
How oft the evening breeze has fanned
The banner of this haughty land,
  O'er mountain snow and desert sand,
  Ere yet its folds were torn !
Through Jena's carnage flying red,
Or tossing o'er Marengo's dead,
  Or curling on the towers
Where Austria's eagle quivers yet,
And suns the ruffled plumage, wet
  With battle's crimson showers !

" Qui vive ? " And is the sentry's cry, —
  The sleepless soldier's hand, —
Are these — the painted folds that fly

And lift their emblems, printed high
On morning mist and sunset sky —
  The guardians of a land?
No! If the patriot's pulses sleep,
How vain the watch that hirelings keep, —
  The idle flag that waves,
When Conquest, with his iron heel,
Treads down the standards and the steel
  That belt the soil of slaves!

A SOUVENIR

YES, lady! I can ne'er forget,
That once in other years we met;
Thy memory may perchance recall
A festal eve, a rose-wreathed hall,
Its tapers' blaze, its mirrors' glance,
Its melting song, its ringing glance; —
Why, in thy dream of virgin joy,
Shouldst thou recall a pallid boy?

Thine eye had other forms to seek,
Why rest upon his bashful cheek?
With other tones thy heart was stirred,
Why waste on him a gentle word?
We parted, lady, — all night long
Thine ear to thrill with dance and song, —
And I — to weep that I was born
A thing thou scarce wouldst deign to scorn.

And, lady! now that years have past,
My bark has reached the shore at last;
The gales that filled her ocean wing,
Have chilled and shrunk thy hasty spring,
And eye to eye, and brow to brow,
I stand before thy presence now ; —
Thy lip is smoothed, thy voice is sweet,
Thy warm hand offered when we meet.

Nay, lady! 't is not now for me
To droop the lid or bend the knee.
I seek thee, — oh thou dost not shun;
I speak, — thou listenest like a nun;
I ask thy smile, — thy lip uncurls,
Too liberal of its flashing pearls ;
Thy tears, — thy lashes sing again, —
My Hebe turns to Magdalen!

O changing youth! that evening hour
Looked down on ours, — the bud — the flower:
Thine faded in its virgin soil,
And mine was nursed in tears and toil;
Thy leaves were withering, one by one,
While mine were opening to the sun.
Which now can meet the cold and storm,
With freshest leaf and hardiest form?

Ay, lady! that once haughty glance
Still wanders through the glittering dance,
She asks in vain from others' pride,
The charity thine own denied ;
And as thy fickle lips could learn
To smile and praise, — that used to spurn,
So the last offering on thy shrine
Shall be this flattering lay of mine!

THE DYING SENECA

HE died not as the martyr dies,
  Wrapped in his living shroud of flame;
He fell not as the warrior falls,
  Gasping upon the field of fame ;
A gentler passage to the grave,
The murderer's softened fury gave.

Rome's slaughtered sons and blazing piles
  Had tracked the purpled demon's path,
And yet another victim lived
  To fill the fiery scroll of wrath ;
Could not imperial vengeance spare
His furrowed brow and silver hair?

The field was sown with noble blood,
  The harvest reaped in burning tears,
When, rolling up its crimson flood,
  Broke the long-gathering tide of years;
His diadem was rent away,
And beggars trampled on his clay.

None wept, — none pitied ; — they who knelt
  At morning by the despot's throne,
At evening dashed the laurelled bust,
  And spurned the wreaths themselves had
    strown;
The shout of triumph echoed wide,
The self-stung reptile writhed and died!

THE LAST PROPHECY OF CASSANDRA

THE sun is fading in the skies,
  And evening shades are gathering fast;
Fair city, ere that sun shall rise,
  Thy night hath come, — thy day is past!

Ye know not, — but the hour is nigh ;
  Ye will not heed the warning breath;
No vision strikes your clouded eye,
  To break the sleep that wakes in death.

Go, age, and let thy withered cheek
  Be wet once more with freezing tears;
And bid thy trembling sorrows speak,
  In accents of departed years.

Go, child, and pour thy sinless prayer
  Before the everlasting throne ;
And He, who sits in glory there,
  May stoop to hear thy silver tone.

Go, warrior, in thy glittering steel,
  And bow thee at the altar's side;
And bid thy frowning gods reveal
  The doom their mystic counsels hide.

Go, maiden, in thy flowing veil,
  And bare thy brow, and bend thy knee;
When the last hopes of mercy fail,
  Thy God may yet remember thee.

Go, as thou didst in happier hours,
  And lay thine incense on the shrine;

And greener leaves, and fairer flowers,
　Around the sacred image twine.

I saw them rise, — the buried dead, —
　From marble tomb and grassy mound;
I heard the spirits' printless tread,
　And voices not of earthly sound.

I looked upon the quivering stream,
　And its cold wave was bright with flame;
And wild, as from a fearful dream,
　The wasted forms of battle came.

Ye will not hear, — ye will not know, —
　Ye scorn the maniac's idle song;
Ye care not! but the voice of woe
　Shall thunder loud, and echo long.

Blood shall be in your marble halls,
　And spears shall glance, and fire shall glow;
Ruin shall sit upon your walls,
　But ye shall lie in death below.

Ay, none shall live, to hear the storm
　Around their blackened pillars sweep;
To shudder at the reptile's form,
　Or scare the wild bird from her sleep.

TO MY COMPANIONS

MINE ancient chair! thy wide-embracing arms
　Have clasped around me even from a boy:
Hadst thou a voice to speak of years gone by,
　Thine were a tale of sorrow and of joy,
Of fevered hopes and ill-foreboding fears,
And smiles unseen, and unrecorded tears.

And thou, my table! though unwearied time
　Hath set his signet on thine altered brow,
Still can I see thee in thy spotless prime,
　And in my memory thou art living now;
Soon must thou slumber with forgotten things,
The peasant's ashes and the dust of kings.

Thou melancholy mug! thy sober brown
　Hath something pensive in its evening hue,
Not like the things that please the tasteless
　　clown,
　With gaudy streaks of orange and of blue;
And I must love thee, for thou art mine own,
Pressed by my lip, and pressed by mine alone.

My broken mirror! faithless, yet beloved,
　Thou who canst smile, and smile alike on all,
Oft do I leave thee, oft again return,
　I scorn the siren, but obey the call;
I hate thy falsehood, while I fear thy truth,
But most I love thee, flattering friend of youth.

Primeval carpet! every well-worn thread
　Has slowly parted with its virgin dye;
I saw thee fade beneath the ceaseless tread,
　Fainter and fainter in mine anxious eye;
So flies the color from the brightest flower,
And heaven's own rainbow lives but for an
　　hour.

I love you all! there radiates from our own,
　A soul that lives in every shape we see;
There is a voice, to other ears unknown,
　Like echoed music answering to its key.
The dungeoned captive hath a tale to tell,
Of every insect in his lonely cell;
And these poor frailties have a simple tone,
That breathes in accents sweet to me alone.

II. ASTRÆA: THE BALANCE OF ILLUSIONS

[THIS poem, first delivered before the ✦ B K society of Yale College, August 14, 1850, was published the same year and only recently disappeared as a separate publication; but upon rearranging his poems for an early collective edition, Dr. Holmes included a group of *Pictures from Occasional Poems*, in which he placed certain excerpts from *Astræa*. These passages were retained without the grouped heading in his final Riverside edition, and are reproduced in this edition. *Astræa*, however, has had an independent life so long that it seems best to reproduce it here, indicating the excerpts in their places.]

WHAT secret charm, long whispering in mine ear,
Allures, attracts, compels, and chains me here,
Where murmuring echoes call me to resign
Their sacred haunts to sweeter lips than mine;
Where silent pathways pierce the solemn shade,
In whose still depths my feet have never
　　strayed;
Here, in the home where grateful children meet
And I, half alien, take the stranger's seat,
Doubting, yet hoping that the gift I bear
May keep its bloom in this unwonted air?
Hush, idle fancy, with thy needless art,
Speak from thy fountains, O my throbbing
　　heart!

Say, shall I trust these trembling lips to tell
The fireside tale that memory knows so well?
How, in the days of Freedom's dread campaign,
A home-bred schoolboy left his village plain,
Slow faring southward, till his wearied feet
Pressed the worn threshold of this fair retreat;
How, with his comely face and gracious mien,
He joined the concourse of the classic green,
Nameless, unfriended, yet by nature blest
With the rich tokens that she loves the best;
The flowing locks, his youth's redundant
　　crown,
Smoothed o'er a brow unfurrowed by a frown;
The untaught smile that speaks so passing
　　plain
A world all hope, a past without a stain;
The clear-hued cheek, whose burning current
　　glows
Crimson in action, carmine in repose;
Gifts such as purchase, with unminted gold,
Smiles from the young and blessings from the
　　old.

Say, shall my hand with pious love restore
The faint, far pictures time beholds no more?
How the grave Senior, he whose later fame
Stamps on our laws his own undying name,
Saw from on high, with half paternal joy,
Some spark of promise in the studious boy,
And bade him enter, with benignant tone,
Those stately precincts which he called his own,
Where the fresh student and the youthful sage
Read by one taper from the common page;
How the true comrade, whose maturer date
Graced the large honors of his ancient State,
Sought his young friendship, which through every change
No time could weaken, no remove estrange;
How the great MASTER, reverend, solemn, wise,
Fixed on his face those calm, majestic eyes,
Full of grave meaning, where a child might read
The Hebraist's patience and the Pilgrim's creed,
But warm with flashes of parental fire
That drew the stripling to his second sire;
How kindness ripened, till the youth might dare
Take the low seat beside his sacred chair,
While the gray scholar, bending o'er the young,
Spelled the square types of Abraham's ancient tongue,
Or with mild rapture stooped devoutly o'er
His small coarse leaf, alive with curious lore:
Tales of grim judges, at whose awful beck
Flashed the broad blade across a royal neck,
Or learned dreams of Israel's long lost child
Found in the wanderer of the western wild.

Dear to his age were memories such as these,
Leaves of his June in life's autumnal breeze;
Such were the tales that won my boyish ear,
Told in low tones that evening loves to hear.

Thus in the scene I pass so lightly o'er,
Trod for a moment, then beheld no more,
Strange shapes and dim, unseen by other eyes,
Through the dark portals of the past arise;
I see no more the fair embracing throng,
I hear no echo to my saddened song,
No more I heed the kind or curious gaze,
The voice of blame, the rustling thrill of praise;
Alone, alone, the awful past I tread
White with the marbles of the slumbering dead;
One shadowy form my dreaming eyes behold
That leads my footsteps as it led of old,
One floating voice, amid the silence heard,
Breathes in my ear love's long unspoken word; —
These are the scenes thy youthful eyes have known;
My heart's warm pulses claim them as its own!
The sapling, compassed in thy fingers' clasp,
My arms scarce circle in their twice-told grasp,
Yet in each leaf of yon o'ershadowing tree
I read a legend that was traced by thee.
Year after year the living wave has beat
These smooth-worn channels with its trampling feet,
Yet in each line that scores the grassy sod
I see the pathway where thy feet have trod.
Though from the scene that hears my faltering lay,
The few that loved thee long have passed away,
Thy sacred presence all the landscape fills,
Its groves and plains and adamantine hills!

Ye who have known the sudden tears that flow, —
Sad tears, yet sweet, the dews of twilight woe, —
When, led by chance, your wandering eye has crossed
Some poor memorial of the loved and lost,
Bear with my weakness as I look around
On the dear relics of this holy ground,
These bowery cloisters, shadowed and serene,
My dreams have pictured ere mine eyes have seen.

And oh, forgive me, if the flower I brought
Droops in my hand beside this burning thought;
The hopes and fears that marked this destined hour,
The chill of doubt, the startled throb of power,
The flush of pride, the trembling glow of shame,
All fade away and leave my FATHER's name!

[Here appears SPRING, ante p. 80.]

What life is this, that spreads in sudden birth
Its plumes of light around a new-born earth?
Is this the sun that brought the unwelcome day,
Pallid and glimmering with his lifeless ray,
Or through the sash that bars you narrow cage
Slanted, intrusive, on the opened page?
Is this soft breath the same complaining gale
That filled my slumbers with its murmuring wail?
Is this green mantle of elastic sod
The same brown desert with its frozen clod,
Where the last ridges of the dingy snow
Lie till the windflower blooms unstained below?

Thus to my heart its wonted tides return
When sullen Winter breaks his crystal urn,
And o'er the turf in wild profusion showers
Its dewy leaflets and ambrosial flowers.
In vacant rapture for a while I range
Through the wide scene of universal change,
Till, as the statue in its nerves of stone
Felt the new senses wakening one by one,
Each long closed inlet finds its destined ray
Through the dark curtain Spring has rent away.
I crush the buds the clustering lilacs bear;
The same sweet fragrance that I loved is there;
The same fresh hues each opening disk reveals;
Soft as of old each silken petal feels;
The birch's rind its flavor still retains,
Its boughs still ringing with the self-same strains;
Above, around, rekindling Nature claims
Her glorious altars wreathed in living flames;
Undimmed, unshadowed, far as morning shines
Feeds with fresh incense her eternal shrines.
Lost in her arms, her burning life I share,
Breathe the wild freedom of her perfumed air,

From Heaven's fair face the long-drawn shadows roll,
And all its sunshine floods my opening soul!
[Here appears THE STUDY, ante p. 82.]
See, while I speak, my fireside joys return,
The lamp rekindles and the ashes burn,
The dream of summer fades before their ray,
As in red firelight sunshine dies away.
A two-fold picture; ere the first was gone,
The deepening outline of the next was drawn,
And wavering fancy hardly dares to choose
The first or last of her dissolving views.

No Delphic sage is wanted to divine
The shape of Truth beneath my gauzy line;
Yet there are truths, — like schoolmates, once well known,
But half remembered, not enough to own, —
That, lost from sight in life's bewildering train,
May be, like strangers, introduced again,
Dressed in new feathers, as from time to time
May please our friends, the milliners of rhyme.

Trust not, it says, the momentary hue
Whose false complexion paints the present view;
Red, yellow, violet stain the rainbow's light,
The prism dissolves, and all again is white.
[Here appears THE BELLS, ante p. 83.]
But how, alas! among our eager race,
Shall smiling candor show her girlish face?
What place is secret to the meddling crew,
Whose trade is settling what we all shall do?
What verdict sacred from the busy fools,
That sell the jargon of their outlaw schools?
What pulpit certain to be never vexed
With libels sanctioned by a holy text?
Where, O my country, is the spot that yields
The freedom fought for on a hundred fields?

Not one strong tyrant holds the servile chain,
Where all may vote and each may hope to reign;
One sturdy cord a single limb may bind,
And leave the captive only half confined,
But the free spirit finds its legs and wings
Tied with unnumbered Lilliputian strings,
Which, like the spider's undiscovered fold,
In countless meshes round the prisoner rolled,
With silken pressure that he scarce can feel,
Clamp every fibre as in bands of steel!

Hard is the task to point in civil phrase
One's own dear people's foolish works or ways;
Woe to the friend that marks a touchy fault,
Himself obnoxious to the world's assault!
Think what an earthquake is a nation's hiss,
That takes its circuit through a land like this;
Count with the census, would you be precise,
From sea to sea, from oranges to ice;
A thousand myriads are its virile lungs,
A thousand myriads its contralto tongues!

And oh, remember the indignant press;
Honey is bitter to its fond caress,
But the black venom that its hate lets fall
Would shame to sweetness the hyena's gall!

Briefly and gently let the task be tried
To touch some frailties on their tender side;
Not to dilate on each imagined wrong,
And spoil at once our temper and our song,
But once or twice a passing gleam to throw
On some rank failings ripe enough to show,
Patterns of others, — made of common stuff, —
The world will furnish parallels enough, —
Such as bewilder their contracted view,
Who make one pupil do the work of two;
Who following nature, where her tracks divide,
Drive all their passions on the narrower side,
And pour the phials of their virtuous wrath
On half mankind that take the wider path.

Nature is liberal to her inmost soul,
She loves alike the tropic and the pole,
The storm's wild anthem, and the sunshine's calm,
The arctic fungus, and the desert palm;
Loves them alike, and wills that each maintain
Its destined share of her divided reign;
No creeping moss refuse her crystal gem,
No soaring pine her cloudy diadem!

Alas! her children, borrowing but in part
The flowing pulses of her generous heart,
Shame their kind mother with eternal strife
At all the crossings of their mingled life;
Each age, each people finds its ready shifts
To quarrel stoutly o'er her choicest gifts.

History can tell of early ages dim,
When man's chief glory was in strength of limb;
Then the best patriot gave the hardest knocks,
The height of virtue was to fell an ox;
Ill fared the babe of questionable mould,
Whom its stern father happened to behold;
In vain the mother with her ample vest
Hid the poor nursling on her throbbing breast;
No tears could save him from the kitten's fate,
To live an insult to the warlike state.

This weakness passed, and nations owned once more,
Man was still human, measuring five feet four,
The anti-cripples ceased to domineer,
And owned Napoleon worth a grenadier.

In these mild times the ancient bully's sport
Would lead its hero to a well known court;
Olympian athletes, though the pride of Greece,
Must face the Justice if they broke the peace,
And valor find some inconvenient checks,
If strolling Theseus met Policeman X.

[Here appears NON-RESISTANCE, ante p. 83.]
Yet when thy champion's stormy task is done,
The frigate silenced and the fortress won,
When toil-worn valor claims his laurel wreath,
His reeking cutlass slumbering in its sheath,
The fierce declaimer shall be heard once more,
Whose twang was smothered by the conflict's roar;

Heroes shall fall that strode unharmed away
Through the red heaps of many a doubtful day,
Hacked in his sermons, riddled in his prayers,
The broadcloth slashing what the broadsword
 spares!

Untaught by trial, ignorance might suppose
That all our fighting must be done with blows;
Alas! not so; between the lips and brain
A dread artillery masks its loaded train;
The smooth portcullis of the smiling face
Veils the grim battery with deceptive grace,
But in the flashes of its opened fire,
Truth, Honor, Justice, Peace and Love expire.

[Here appears THE MORAL BULLY, *ante* p. 84.]

If generous fortune give me leave to choose
My saucy neighbors barefoot or in shoes,
I leave the hero blustering while he dares
On platforms furnished with posterior stairs,
Till prudence drives him to his "earnest" legs
With large bequest of disappointed eggs,
And take the brawler whose unstudied dress
Becomes him better, and protects him less;
Give me the bullying of the scoundrel crew,
If swaggering virtue won't insult me too!

Come, let us breathe; a something not divine
Has mingled, bitter, with the flowing line.
Pause for a moment while our soul forgets
The noisy tribe in panta-loons or -lets;
Nor pass, ungrateful, by the debt we owe
To those who teach us half of all we know,
Not in rude license, or unchristian scorn,
But hoping, loving, pitying, while they warn!

Sweep out the pieces! Round a careless room
The feather-duster follows up the broom;
If the last target took a round of grape
To knock its beauty something out of shape,
The next asks only, if the listener please,
A schoolboy's blowpipe and a gill of peas.

This creeping object, caught upon the brink
Of an old teacup, filled with muddy ink,
Lives on a leaf that buds from time to time
In certain districts of a temperate clime.
O'er this he toils in silent corners snug,
And leaves a track behind him, like a slug;
The leaves he stains a humbler tribe devours,
Thrown off in mouthly or in weekly showers;
Himself kept savage on a starving fare,
Of such exuviæ as his friends can spare.

Let the bug drop, and view him if we can
In his true aspect as a *quasi* man.
The little wretch, whose terebrating powers
Would bore a Paixhan in a dozen hours,
Is called a CRITIC by the heavy friends
That help to pay his minus dividends.

The pseudo-critic-editorial race
Owns no allegiance but the law of place;
Each to his region sticks through thick and
 thin,
Stiff as a beetle spiked upon a pin.

Plant him in Boston, and his sheet he fills
With all the slipslop of his threefold hills,
Talks as if Nature kept her choicest smiles
Within his radius of a dozen miles,
And nations waited till his next Review
Had made it plain what Providence must do.
Would you believe him, water is not damp
Except in buckets with the Hingham stamp,
And Heaven should build the walls of Paradise
Of Quincy granite lined with Wenham ice.

But Hudson's banks, with more congenial
 skies,
Swell the small creature to alarming size:
A gayer pattern wraps his flowery chest,
A sham more brilliant sparkles on his breast,
An eyeglass, hanging from a gilded chain,
Taps the white leg that tips his rakish cane;
Strings of new names, the glories of the age,
Hang up to dry on his exterior page,
Titanic pygmies, shining lights obscure,
His favored sheets have managed to secure,
Whose wide renown beyond their own abode
Extends for miles along the Harlaem road;
New radiance lights his patronizing smile,
New airs distinguish his patrician style,
New sounds are mingled with his fatal hiss,
Oftenest "*provincial*" and "*metropolis.*"

He cry "*provincial*" with imperious brow!
The half-bred rogue, that groomed his mother's
 cow!
Fed on coarse tubers and Æolian beans
Till clownish manhood crept among his teens,
When, after washing and unheard of pains
To lard with phrases his refractory brains,
A third-rate college licked him to the shape,
Not of the scholar, but the scholar's ape!

God bless Manhattan! Let her fairly claim,
With all the honors due her ancient name,
Worth, wisdom, wealth, abounding and to
 spare,
Rags, riots, rogues, at least her honest share;
But not presume, because, by sad mischance,
The mobs of Paris wring the neck of France,
Fortune has ordered she shall turn the poise
Of thirty Empires with her Bowery boys!

The poorest hamlet on the mountain's side
Looks on her glories with a sister's pride;
When the first babes her fruitful ship-yards
 wean
Play round the breasts of Ocean's conquered
 queen,
The shout of millions, borne on every breeze,
Sweeps with EXCELSIOR o'er the enfranchised
 seas!

Yet not too rashly let her think to bind
Beneath her circlet all the nation's mind;
Our star-crowned mother, whose informing
 soul
Clings to no fragment, but pervades the whole,
Views with a smile the clerk of Maiden Lane,
Who takes her ventral ganglion for her brain!
No fables tell us of Minervas born

From bags of cotton or from sacks of corn;
The halls of Leyden Science used to cram,
While dulness snored in purse-proud Amsterdam!

But those old burghers had a foggy clime,
And better luck may come the second time;
What though some churls of doubtful sense declare
That poison lurks in her commercial air,
Her buds of genius dying premature,
From some malaria draining cannot cure;
Nay, that so dangerous is her golden soil,
Whate'er she borrows she contrives to spoil;
That drooping minstrels in a few brief years
Lose their sweet voice, the gift of other spheres;
That wafted singing from their native shore,
They touch the Battery, and are heard no more; —
By those twinned waves that wear the varied gleams
Beryl or sapphire mingles in their streams,
Till the fair sisters o'er her yellow sands,
Clasping their soft and snowy ruffled hands,
Lay on her footstool with their silver keys
Strength from the mountains, freedom from the seas, —
Some future day may see her rise sublime
Above her counters, — only give her time!

When our first Soldiers' swords of honor gild
The stately mansions that her tradesmen build;
When our first Statesmen take the Broadway track,
Our first Historians following at their back;
When our first Painters, dying, leave behind
On her proud walls the shadows of their mind;
When our first Poets flock from farthest scenes
To take in hand her pictured Magazines;
When our first Scholars are content to dwell
Where their own printers teach them how to spell;
When world-known Science crowds toward her gates,
Then shall the children of our hundred States
Hail her a true METROPOLIS of men,
The nation's centre. Then, and not till then!

The song is failing. Yonder clanging tower
Shakes in its cup the more than brimming hour;
The full-length gallery which the fates deny,
A colored Moral briefly must supply.

[Here appears THE MIND'S DIET, *ante* p. 85.]

The song is passing. Let its meaning rise
To loftier notes before its echo dies,
Nor leave, ungracious, in its parting train
A trivial flourish or discordant strain.

These lines may teach, rough-spoken though they be,
Thy gentle creed, divinest Charity!
Truth is at heart not always as she seems,
Judged by our sleeping or our waking dreams.

[Here appears OUR LIMITATIONS, *ante* p. 85.]

The song is hushed. Another moment parts
This breathing zone, this belt of living hearts;
Ah, think not thus the parting moment ends
The soul's embrace of new discovered friends.

Sleep on my heart, thou long expected hour,
Time's new-born daughter, with thine infant dower,
One sad, sweet look from those expiring charms
The clasping centuries strangle in their arms,
Dreams of old halls, and shadowy arches green,
And kindly faces loved as soon as seen!
Sleep, till the fires of manhood fade away,
The sprinkled locks have saddened into gray,
And age, oblivious, blends thy memories old
With hoary legends that his sire has told!

III. NOTES AND ADDENDA

Page 6. *Or gaze upon yon pillared stone.*
The tomb of the Vassall family is marked by a freestone tablet, supported by five pillars, and bearing nothing but the sculptured reliefs of the Goblet and the Sun, — *Vas-Sol* — which designated a powerful family, now almost forgotten.

The exile referred to in the next stanza was a native of Honfleur in Normandy.
Page 15. POETRY.
[On publishing this poem in the edition of 1836, Dr. Holmes wrote as follows in the *Preface:*] The first poem in the collection being somewhat discursive, I will point out, in a few words, its scope and connection. Its object is to express some general truths on the sources and the machinery of poetry; to sketch some changes which may be supposed to have taken place in its history, constituting four grand eras; and to point out some less obvious manifestations of the poetical principle. The stages assigned to the progress of poetry are as follows: —
I. The period of Pastoral and Descriptive Poetry; which allowed a digression upon home, and the introduction of a descriptive lyric.
II. The period of Martial Poetry. At the close of this division are some remarks on our want of a national song, and an attempt is made to enliven the poem by introducing a lyric which deals in martial images and language, although written only for an occasional purpose.
III. The Epic or Historic period of Poetry. Under this division of the subject, the supposed necessity of an American *Iliad* was naturally enough touched upon.
IV. The period of Dramatic Poetry, or that which analyzes, and traces from their origin, the passions excited by certain combinations of circumstances. As this seemed the highest reach of poetical art, so it constitutes the last of my supposed epochs.

The remarks contained in the last division relate to some of the different forms in which poetry has manifested itself, and to a pseudo-poetical race of invalids, whose melancholic notions are due, much oftener than is supposed, to the existence of pulmonary disease, frequently attributed to the morbid state of mind of which it is principally the cause. The allusions introduced at the close will carry their own explanation to all for whom they were intended. I have thus given a general analysis of a poem, which, being written for public delivery, required more variety than is commonly demanded in metrical essays.

Page 15. *Scenes of my youth.*
This poem was commenced a few months subsequently to the author's return to his native village, after an absence of nearly three years.

Page 18. *Gleams like a diamond on a dancing girl.*
A few lines, perhaps deficient in dignity, were introduced at this point, in delivering the poem, and are appended in this clandestine manner for the gratification of some of my audience.

How many a stanza, blushing like the rose,
Would turn to fustian if resolved to prose!
How many an epic, like a gilded crown,
If some bold critic dared to melt it down,
Roll in his crucible a shapeless mass,
A grain of gold-leaf to a pound of brass!
Shorn of their plumes, our moonstruck sonneteers
Would seem but jackdaws croaking to the spheres;
Our gay Lotharios, with their Byron curls,
Would pine like oysters cheated of their pearls!

Woe to the spectres of Parnassus' shade,
If truth should mingle in the masquerade.
Lo, as the songster's pale creations pass,
Off come at once the "Dearest" and "Alas!"
Crack go the lines and levers used to prop
Top-heavy thoughts, and down at once they drop.
Flowers weep for *hours*; Love, shrieking for his *dove*,
Finds not the solace that he seeks — above.
Fast in the mire, through which in happier time
He ambled dryshod on the stilts of rhyme,
The prostrate poet finds at length a tongue
To curse in prose the thankless stars he sung.

And though, perchance, the haughty muse it shames,
How deep the magic of harmonious names!
How sure the story of romance to please,
Whose rounded stanza ends with Heloise!
How rich and full our intonations ride
"On Torno's cliffs, or Pambamarca's side"!
But were her name some vulgar "proper noun,"
And Pambamarca changed to Belchertown,
She might be pilloried for her doubtful fame,
And no enthusiast would arise to blame;
And he who outraged the poetic sense,
Might find a home at Belchertown's expense!

The harmless boys, scarce knowing right from wrong,
Who libel others and themselves in song,
When their first pothooks of poetic rage
Slant down the corners of an album's page,
(Where crippled couplets spread their sprawling charms,
As half-taught swimmers move their legs and arms,)
Will talk of "Hesper on the brow of eve,"
And call their cousins "lovely Genevieve;" —
While thus transformed, each dear deluded maid,
Pleased with herself in novel grace arrayed,
Smiles on the Paris who has come to crown
This newborn Helen in a gingham gown!

Page 19. *The leaflets gathered at your side.*
See THE CAMBRIDGE CHURCHYARD, page 5.
Page 20. *Swept through the world the war-song of Marseilles.*
The music and words of the Marseilles Hymn were composed in one night.
Page 20. *Our nation's anthem pipes a country dance!*
The popular air of "Yankee Doodle," like the dagger of Hudibras, serves a pacific as well as a martial purpose.
Page 21. *Thus mocked the spoilers with his school-boy scorn.*
See OLD IRONSIDES, page 3.
Page 22. *On other shores, above their mouldering towns.*
Daniel Webster quoted several of the verses which follow, in his address at the laying of the corner-stone of the addition to the Capitol at Washington, July 4, 1851.
Page 22. *Bore Ever Ready, faithful to the last.*
"Semper paratus," — a motto of the revolutionary standards.
Page 24. *Thou calm, chaste scholar.*
Charles Chauncy Emerson; died May 9, 1836.
Page 24. *And thou, dear friend.*
James Jackson, Jr., M. D.; died March 29, 1834.
Page 28. THE STEAMBOAT.
Mr. Emerson has quoted some lines from this poem, but somewhat disguised as he recalled them. It is never safe to quote poetry without referring to the original.
Page 44. *As Wesley questioned in his youthful dream.*

Οἵη περ φύλλων γενεή, τοιήδε καὶ ἀνδρῶν.
Iliad, VI. 146.

Wesley quotes this line in his account of his early doubts and perplexities. See Southey's *Life of Wesley*, Vol. II., p. 185.
Page 46. *It tells the turret.*
The churches referred to in the lines which follow are
1. "King's Chapel," the foundation of which was laid by Governor Shirley in 1749.
2. Brattle Street Church, consecrated in 1773. The completion of this edifice, the design of which included a spire, was prevented by the

troubles of the Revolution, and its plain, square tower presented nothing more attractive than a massive simplicity. In the front of this tower, till the church was demolished in 1872, there was to be seen, half embedded in the brick-work, a cannon-ball, which was thrown from the American fortifications at Cambridge, during the bombardment of the city, then occupied by the British troops.

3. The Old South, first occupied for public worship in 1730.

4. Park Street Church, built in 1809, the tall white steeple of which is the most conspicuous of all the Boston spires.

5. Christ Church, opened for public worship in 1723, and containing a set of eight bells, long the only chime in Boston.

Page 54. *The Angel spake: This threefold hill shall be.*

The name first given by the English to Boston was TRI-MOUNTAIN. The three hills upon and around which the city is built are Beacon Hill, Fort Hill, and Copp's Hill.

In the early records of the Colony, it is mentioned, under date of May 6th, 1635, that "A BEACON is to be set on the Sentry hill, at Boston, to give notice to the country of any danger; to be guarded by one man stationed near, and fired as occasion may be." The last beacon was blown down in 1789.

The eastern side of Fort Hill was formerly "a ragged cliff, that seemed placed by nature in front of the entrance to the harbor for the purposes of defence, to which it was very soon applied, and from which it obtained its present name." Its summit is now a beautiful green enclosure.

Copp's Hill was used as a burial-ground from a very early period. The part of it employed for this purpose slopes towards the water upon the northern side. From its many interesting records of the dead I select the following, which may serve to show what kind of dust it holds.

"Here lies buried in a
Stone Grave 10 feet deep
Capt. DANIEL MALCOLM Mercht
who departed this Life
October 23d, 1769,
Aged 44 years,
a true son of Liberty,
a Friend to the Publick,
an Enemy to oppression,
and one of the foremost
in opposing the Revenue Acts
on America."

The gravestone from which I copied this inscription is bruised and splintered by the bullets of the British soldiers.

Page 79. THE PLOUGHMAN.

[The following is the Report referred to in the head-note as furnished by Dr. Holmes, in his capacity as chairman of the committee.]

The committee on the ploughing-match are fully sensible of the dignity and importance of the office entrusted to their judgment. To decide upon the comparative merits of so many excellent specimens of agricultural art is a most delicate, responsible, and honorable duty.

The plough is a very ancient implement. It is written in the English language p-l-o-u-g-h, and, by the association of free and independent spellers, p-l-o-w. It may be remarked that the same gentlemen can, by a similar process, turn their coughs into cows; which would be the cheapest mode of raising live stock, although it is to be feared that they (referring to the cows) would prove but low-bred animals. Some have derived the English word plough from the Greek *ploutos*, the wealth which comes from the former suggesting its resemblance to the latter. But such resemblances between different languages may be carried too far: as for example, if a man should trace the name of the Altamaha to the circumstance that the first settlers were all tomahawked on the margin of that river.

Time and experience have sanctioned the custom of putting only plain, practical men upon this committee. Were it not so, the most awkward blunders would be constantly occurring. The inhabitants of our cities, who visit the country during the fine season, would find themselves quite at a loss if an overstrained politeness should place them in this position. Imagine a trader, or a professional man, from the capital of the State, unexpectedly called upon to act in rural matters. Plough-shares are to him shares that pay no dividends. A coulter, he supposes, has something to do with a horse. His notions of stock were obtained in Faneuil Hall market, where the cattle looked funnily enough, to be sure, compared with the living originals. He knows, it is true, that there is a difference in cattle, and would tell you that he prefers the sirloin breed. His children are equally unenlightened; they know no more of the poultry-yard than what they have learned by having the chicken-pox, and playing on a Turkey carpet. Their small knowledge of wool-growing is lam(b)entable.

The history of one of these summer-visitors shows how imperfect is his rural education. He no sooner establishes himself in the country than he begins a series of experiments. He tries to drain a marsh, but only succeeds in draining his own pockets. He offers to pay for carting off a compost heap; but is informed that it consists of corn and potatoes in an unfinished state. He sows abundantly, but reaps little or nothing, except with the implement which he uses in shaving; a process which is frequently performed for him by other people, though he pays no barber's bill. He builds a wire-fence and paints it green, so that nobody can see it. But he forgets to order a pair of spectacles apiece for his cows, who, taking offence at something else, take his fence in addition, and make an invisible one of it sure enough. And, finally, having bought a machine to chop fodder, which chops off a good slice of his dividends, and two or three children's fingers, he concludes that, instead of cutting feed, he will cut farming; and so sells out to one of those plain, practical farmers, such as you have honored by placing them on your committee: whose pockets are not so full when he starts, but have fewer holes and not so many fingers in them.

It must have been one of these practical men whose love of his pursuits led him to send in to the committee the following lines, which it is hoped will be accepted as a grateful tribute to the noble art whose successful champions are now to be named and rewarded.

Page 99. THE TWO STREAMS.

When a little poem called *The Two Streams* was first printed, a writer in the *New York Evening Post* virtually accused the author of it of borrowing the thought from a baccalaureate sermon of President Hopkins of Williamstown, and printed a quotation from that discourse, which, as I thought, a thief or catchpoll might well consider as establishing a fair presumption that it was so borrowed. I was at the same time wholly unconscious of having met with the discourse or the sentence which the verses were most like, nor do I believe I ever had seen or heard either. Some time after this, happening to meet my eloquent cousin, Wendell Phillips, I mentioned the fact to him, and he told me that *he* had once used the special image said to be borrowed, in a discourse delivered at Williamstown. On relating this to my friend Mr. Buchanan Read, he informed me that *he* too had used the image, — perhaps referring to his poem called *The Twins*. He thought Tennyson had used it also. The parting of the streams on the Alps is poetically elaborated in a passage attributed to "M. Loisne," printed in the *Boston Evening Transcript* for Oct. 23, 1859. Captain, afterwards Sir Francis Head, speaks of the showers parting on the Cordilleras, one portion going to the Atlantic, one to the Pacific. I found the image running loose in my mind, without a halter. It suggested itself as an illustration of the will, and I worked the poem out by the aid of Mitchell's School Atlas. The spores of a great many ideas are floating about in the atmosphere. We no more know where the lichens which eat the names off from the gravestones borrowed the germs that gave them birth. The two match-boxes were just alike; but neither was a plagiarism. — *My Hunt after "the Captain,"* pp. 45, 46.

Page 110. INTERNATIONAL ODE.

This ode was sung in unison by twelve hundred children of the public schools, to the air of "God save the Queen," at the visit of the Prince of Wales to Boston, October 18, 1860.

Page 113. POEMS OF THE CLASS OF '29.

[The following is a roll-call of this celebrated class in Harvard College.]

Joseph Angier
Elbridge Gerry Austin
Reuben Bates
George Tyler Bigelow
William Brigham
John Parker Bullard
William Henry Channing
James Freeman Clarke
Edwin Conant
Frederick William Crocker
Francis Boardman Crowninshield
Edward Linzee Cunningham
Benjamin Robbins Curtis
Curtis Cutler
George Thomas Davis
Jonathan Thomas Davis
Nathaniel Foster Derby
Samuel Adams Devens
George Humphrey Devereux
Nicholas Devereux
Charles Fay
William Emerson Foster
Francis Augustus Foxcroft
Joel Giles
William Gray
Charles Lowell Hancock
Oliver Wendell Holmes
John Hubbard
Solomon Martin Jenkins
Albert Locke
Josiah Quincy Loring
Samuel May
Henry Blake McLellan
Horatio Cook Meriam
Edward Patrick Milliken
William Mixter
Isaac Edward Morse
Benjamin Peirce
George William Phillips
George Washington Richardson
Andrew Ritchie
Chandler Robbins
James Dutton Russell
Howard Sargent
Samuel Francis Smith
Edward Dexter Sohier
Charles Storer Storrow
George Augustus Taylor
John James Taylor
Francis Thomas
James Thurston
John Rogers Thurston
Samuel Ripley Townsend
Josiah Kendall Waite
Joshua Holyoke Ward
Ezra Weston
James Humphrey Wilder
Benjamin Pollard Winslow
William Young

Page 118. THE BOYS.

The members of the Harvard College class of 1829 referred to in this poem are: "Doctor," Francis Thomas; "Judge," G. T. Bigelow, Chief Justice of the Supreme Court of Massachusetts; "Speaker," Hon. Francis B. Crowninshield, Speaker of the Massachusetts House of Representatives; "Mr. Mayor," G. W. Richardson, of Worcester, Mass; "Member of Congress," Hon. George T. Davis; "Reverend," James Freeman Clarke; "boy with the grave mathematical look," Benjamin Peirce; "boy with a three-decker brain," Judge Benjamin R. Curtis, of the Supreme Court of the United States; "nice youngster of excellent pith," S. F. Smith, author of "My Country, 't is of Thee."

A CHRONOLOGICAL LIST OF DR. HOLMES'S POEMS

Page 141. *That lovely, bright-eyed boy.*
William Watson Sturgis.
Who faced the storm so long.
Francis B. Crowninshield.
Our many-featured friend.
George T. Davis.
Page 149. THE CHAMBERED NAUTILUS.
I have now and then found a naturalist who still worried over the distinction between the Pearly Nautilus and the Paper Nautilus, or Argonauta. As the stories about both are mere fables, attaching to the Physalia, or Portuguese man-of-war, as well as to these two molluscs, it seems over-nice to quarrel with the poetical handling of a fiction sufficiently justified by the name commonly applied to the ship of pearl as well as the ship of paper.
Page 151. *The close-clinging dulcamara.*
The "bitter-sweet" of New England is the *Celastrus scandens*, "bourreau des arbres" of the Canadian French.
Page 162. ODE FOR A SOCIAL MEETING.
I recollect a British criticism of the poem "with the slight alterations," in which the writer was quite indignant at the treatment my convivial song had received. No committee, he thought, would dare treat a Scotch author in that way. I could not help being reminded of Sydney Smith, and the surgical operation he proposed, in order to get a pleasantry into the head of a North Briton.
Page 192. *All armed with picks and spades.*
The captured slaves were at this time organized as pioneers.
Page 193. *Father, send on Earth again.*
[This hymn was sung to the tune of " Silent Night "]
Page 245. *This broad-browed youth.*
Benjamin Robbins Curtis.
The stripling smooth of face and slight.
George Tyler Bigelow.
Page 276. PRELUDE TO A VOLUME PRINTED IN RAISED LETTERS FOR THE BLIND.
[This volume was published in 1885 from the Howe Memorial Press in Boston, the *Prelude* there called *Dedication* being dated June 15, of that year. There are ninety-one poems in the collection, and of these the following were designated by Dr. Holmes, who so far aided in the selection: —
The Dorchester Giant.
The September Gale.
The Height of the Ridiculous.
The Living Temple.
The Voiceless.
Martha.
The Flower of Liberty.
Union and Liberty.
The Chambered Nautilus.
Sun and Shadow.
The Deacon's Masterpiece.
Contentment.
Under the Violets.
The Opening of the Piano.
Bill and Joe.
The Old Man Dreams.
The Boys.

Dorothy Q.
The Organ-Blower.
Brother Jonathan's Lament for Sister Caroline.
Poem at the Dedication of the Halleck Monument.
A Farewell to Agassiz.
For the Moore Centennial Celebration.
A Familiar Letter.
The Iron Gate.
My Aviary.
The Silent Melody.]

IV. A CHRONOLOGICAL LIST OF DR. HOLMES'S POEMS

IN this list the attempt has been made to date the poems either by the occasion or by the first printing in periodical form. Whenever the first appearance of a poem has been not precisely determined, the title is printed in italic under the year when the volume first including it was published.

1824, 25. Translation from the Æneid.
1830. The Toadstool.
The Last Prophecy of Cassandra.
To a Caged Lion.
To My Companions.
The Dorchester Giant.
The Spectre Pig.
Reflections of a Proud Pedestrian.
The Mysterious Visitor.
The Meeting of the Dryads.
Evening, by a Tailor.
Stanzas: "Strange! that one lightly whispered tone."
The Height of the Ridiculous.
Old Ironsides.
The Ballad of the Oysterman.
From a Bachelor's Private Journal.
Daily Trials: by a Sensitive Man.
The Treadmill Song.
The Star and the Water-Lily.
To a Blank Sheet of Paper.
A Noontide Lyric.
The Hot Season.
1831. To an Insect.
L'Inconnue.
My Aunt.
The Last Leaf.
1832. The Dilemma.
The Philosopher to his Love.
The Comet.
A Portrait.
"The Wasp" and "The Hornet."
1833. The Dying Seneca.
1836. Poetry: A Metrical Essay.
A Song for the Centennial Celebration of Harvard College.
The Cambridge Churchyard.
To the Portrait of a Lady.
To the Portrait of a Gentleman.
The Music Grinders.

The September Gale.
The Last Reader.
Illustrations of a Picture.
A Roman Aqueduct.
La Grisette.
Lines by a Clerk.
The Poet's Lot.
An Evening Thought.
"Qui Vive?"
A Souvenir.
The Last Prophecy of Cassandra.
1838. The Only Daughter.
1840. The Steamboat.
Departed Days.
The Morning Visit.
1842. Song, written for the Dinner given to Charles Dickens.
Song for a Temperance Dinner.
1843. Terpsichore; an After-Dinner Poem.
1844. Lines, recited at the Berkshire Jubilee.
Verses for After-Dinner.
1845. A Modest Request.
1846. Urania: A Rhymed Lesson.
1848. The Pilgrim's Vision.
Lexington.
On Lending a Punch-Bowl.
The Island Hunting-Song.
Nux Postcœnatica.
The Parting Word.
A Song of Other Days.
A Sentiment.
The Stethoscope Song.
Extracts from a Medical Poem.
1849. The Ploughman.
1850. Dedication of the Pittsfield Cemetery.
Spring.
The Study.
The Bells.
Non-Resistance.
The Moral Bully.
The Mind's Diet.
Our Limitations.
1850-1856. The Banker's Secret.
The Exile's Secret.
The Lover's Secret.
The Statesman's Secret.
The Secret of the Stars.
1851. To Governor Swain.
A Song of "Twenty-Nine."
1852. Questions and Answers.
To an English Friend.
1853. A Poem for the Meeting of the American Medical Association.
After a Lecture on Wordsworth.
After a Lecture on Moore.
After a Lecture on Keats.
After a Lecture on Shelley.
At the Close of a Course of Lectures.
An Impromptu.
1854. The New Eden.
The Hudson.
The Old Man Dreams.
Semi-Centennial Celebration of the New England Society.
1855. A Sentiment.
Farewell: to J. R. Lowell.
Remember — Forget.

1856. For the Meeting of the Burns Club.
Birthday of Daniel Webster.
Ode for Washington's Birthday.
Our Indian Summer.
1857. Album Verses.
Latter-Day Warnings.
A Parting Health: to J. L. Motley.
Sun and Shadow.
Prologue.
Ode for a Social Meeting.
Meeting of the Alumni of Harvard College.
The Parting Song.
1858. Mare Rubrum.
The Chambered Nautilus.
What We all think.
The Last Blossom.
The Living Temple.
Spring has come.
A Good Time Going.
The Two Armies.
Musa.
The Deacon's Masterpiece.
Æstivation.
Contentment.
Prelude.
Parson Turell's Legacy.
The Voiceless.
The Old Man of the Sea.
The Last Look.
Avis.
1859. De Sauty.
For the Burns' Centennial Celebration.
The Boys.
The Opening of the Piano.
The Promise.
At a Birthday Festival.
The Crooked Footpath.
The Mother's Secret.
The Two Streams.
Robinson of Leyden.
St. Anthony the Reformer.
At a Meeting of Friends.
Midsummer.
Iris, Her Book.
Under the Violets.
Hymn of Trust.
Boston Common: Three Pictures.
A Sun-Day Hymn.
The Gray Chief.
1860. In Memory of Charles Wentworth Upham, Jr.
For the Meeting of the National Sanitary Association.
International Ode.
Lines.
1861. A Voice of the Loyal North.
Brother Jonathan's Lament for Sister Caroline.
Prologue to Songs in Many Keys.
Agnes.
Martha.
Vive La France.
Army Hymn.
Parting Hymn.
The Flower of Liberty.
Union and Liberty.

A CHRONOLOGICAL LIST OF DR. HOLMES'S POEMS

Under the Washington Elm, Cambridge.
The Sweet Little Man.
The Old Player.
The Old Man of the Sea.
1862. To My Readers.
J. D. R.
Voyage of the Good Ship Union.
To Canaan: a Puritan War-Song.
" Thus saith the Lord, I offer thee three things."
Never or Now.
1863. "Choose you this day whom ye will serve."
An Impromptu at the Walcker Dinner.
1864. F. W. C.
The Last Charge.
Shakespeare.
In Memory of John and Robert Ware.
Hymn written for the Great Central Fair.
Bryant's Seventieth Birthday.
A Sea Dialogue.
1865. Hymn after the Emancipation Proclamation.
Edward Everett.
Our Oldest Friend.
Sherman's in Savannah.
One Country.
God save the Flag.
Hymn for the Fair at Chicago.
A Farewell to Agassiz.
For the Services in Memory of Abraham Lincoln.
At a Dinner to Admiral Farragut.
At a Dinner to General Grant.
For the Commemoration Services, Cambridge.
No Time Like the Old Time.
1866. My Annual.
America to Russia.
To George Peabody.
1867. All Here.
Chanson Without Music.
1868. Bill and Joe.
Once More.
At the Banquet to the Chinese Embass
To H. W. Longfellow.
To Christian Gottfried Ehrenberg.
1869. The Old Cruiser.
Hymn for the Class Meeting.
Humboldt's Birthday.
Poem at the Dedication of the Halleck Monument.
A Hymn of Peace.
1870. Rip Van Winkle.
Even-Song.
Nearing the Snow-Line.
Hymn for the Celebration at the Laying of the Corner-Stone of Harvard Memorial Hall.
1871. The Smiling Listener.
Dorothy Q.
Welcome to the Grand Duke Alexis.
At the Banquet to the Grand Duke Alexis.
1872. Homesick in Heaven.
Fantasia.

Aunt Tabitha.
Our Sweet Singer.
Wind-Clouds and Star-Drifts.
At the Banquet to the Japanese Embassy.
Epilogue to the Breakfast-Table Series.
The Organ-Blower.
After the Fire.
1873. H. C. M., H. S., J. K. W.
What I have come for.
Address for the Opening of the Fifth Avenue Theatre.
For the Centennial Dinner of the Proprietors of Boston Pier.
A Poem served to Order.
The Fountain of Youth.
1874. Our Banker.
Opening the Window.
Programme.
An Old-Year Song.
At the Pantomime.
A Ballad of the Boston Tea-Party.
A Toast to Wilkie Collins.
Hymn for the Dedication of Memorial Hall at Cambridge.
Hymn at the Funeral Services of Charles Sumner.
At the "Atlantic" Dinner.
1875. For Class Meeting.
Grandmother's Story of Bunker-Hill Battle.
Lucy.
Hymn for the Inauguration of the Statue of Governor Andrew.
Joseph Warren, M. D.
Old Cambridge.
1876. A Familiar Letter.
Ad Amicos.
A Memorial Tribute: S. G. Howe.
Welcome to the Nations.
Unsatisfied.
How the Old Horse won the Bet.
1877. How not to settle it.
The First Fan.
To Rutherford Birchard Hayes.
The Ship of State.
A Family Record.
For Whittier's Seventieth Birthday.
An Appeal for "The Old South."
1878. My Aviary.
Two Sonnets: Harvard.
The Last Survivor.
The School-Boy.
The Silent Melody.
1879. The Archbishop and Gil Blas.
Vestigia Quinque Retrorsum.
The Iron Gate.
In Response.
For the Moore Centennial Celebration.
1880. The Shadows.
The Coming Era.
To James Freeman Clarke.
Welcome to the Chicago Commercial Club.
American Academy Centennial Celebration.
Our Home — Our Country.
1881. Benjamin Peirce.

Poem at the Centennial Anniversary Dinner of the Massachusetts Medical Society.
Post-Prandial, ♦ B K.
Rhymes of a Life-Time.
Boston to Florence.
On the Death of President Garfield.
On the Threshold.
At the Papyrus Club.
1882. In the Twilight.
Our Dead Singer.
Two Poems to Harriet Beecher Stowe.
At the Unitarian Festival.
The Flâneur.
1883. Poem read at the Dinner given to the Author by the Medical Profession of the City of New York.
A Loving-Cup Song.
King's Chapel.
Hymn for the Two Hundredth Anniversary of King's Chapel.
1884. The Girdle of Friendship.
At the Saturday Club.
Ave.
1885. The Lyre of Anacreon.
A Welcome to Dr. Benjamin Apthorp Gould.
To Frederick Henry Hedge.
To James Russell Lowell.
To the Poets who only read and listen.
Prelude to a Volume printed in Raised Letters for the Blind.
1886. The Old Tune.
Poem for the Two Hundred and Fiftieth Anniversary of the Founding of Harvard College.
Hymn — The Word of Promise.

1887. The Broken Circle.
To John Greenleaf Whittier.
Hymn read at the Dedication of the Oliver Wendell Holmes Hospital.
Additional Verses to Hail Columbia.
Poem for the Dedication of the Fountain at Stratford-on-Avon.
1888. The Angel-Thief.
At My Fireside.
For the Dedication of the New City Library, Boston.
The Golden Flower.
1889. After the Curfew.
To James Russell Lowell.
To the Eleven Ladies.
1890. But One Talent.
The Peau de Chagrin of State Street.
Cacoethes Scribendi.
The Rose and the Fern.
I like you and I love you.
La Maison D'Or.
Too Young for Love.
The Broomstick Train.
Tartarus.
At the Turn of the Road.
Invitâ Minervâ.
1891. For the Window in St. Margaret's.
James Russell Lowell.
To My Old Readers.
Readings Over the Teacups, Connecting Passages.
1892. In Memory of John Greenleaf Whittier.
1893. To the Teachers of America.
Hymn for the Twenty-fifth Anniversary of the Boston Young Men's Christian Union.
Francis Parkman.

INDEX OF FIRST LINES

A crazy bookcase, placed before, 183.
A health to dear woman! She bids us untwine, 42.
A health to him whose double wreath displays, 293.
A lovely show for eyes to see, 249.
A prologue? Well, of course the ladies know, 153.
A sick man's chamber, though it often boast, 58.
A still, sweet, placid, moonlight face, 331.
A triple health to Friendship, Science, Art, 63.
Afar he sleeps whose name is graven here, 296.
Ah Clemence! when I saw thee last, 326.
Ah, here it is! the sliding rail, 164.
All overgrown with bush and fern, 109.
Alone, beneath the darkened sky, 269.
Alone! no climber of an Alpine cliff, 175.
An usher standing at the door, 249.
And can it be you 've found a place, 231.
And what shall be the song to-night, 116.
Angel of Death! extend thy silent reign! 87.
Angel of love, for every grief, 288.
Angel of Peace, thou hast wandered too long! 223.
Another clouded night; the stars are hid, 171.
As I look from the isle, o'er its billows of green, 150.
As Life's unending column pours, 59.
As o'er the glacier's frozen sheet, 41.
As the voice of the watch to the mariner's dream, 93.
As through the forest, disarrayed, 186.
Ay, tear her tattered ensign down! 4.

Bankrupt! our pockets inside out! 249.
Behold — not him we knew! 103.
Behold the rocky wall, 100.
Behold the shape our eyes have known! 229.
Brave singer of the coming time, 155.
Brief glimpses of the bright celestial spheres, 172.
Bright on the banners of lily and rose, 232.
"Bring me my broken harp," he said, 263.
Brothers, whom we may not reach, 200.
But what is this? 181.

Changeless in beauty, rose-hues on her cheek, 268.
Chicago sounds rough to the maker of verse, 255.
Clear the brown path, to meet his coulter's gleam! 79.
Come back to your mother, ye children, for shame, 34.

Come, dear old comrade, you and I, 113.
Come! fill a fresh bumper, for why should we go, 162.
Come, heap the fagots! Ere we go, 145.
Come, spread your wings, as I spread mine, 90.

Day hath put on his jacket, and around, 9.
Dear friends, left darkling in the long eclipse, 276.
Dear friends, we are strangers; we never before, 220.
Dear Governor, if my skiff might brave, 89.
Dearest, a look is but a ray, 328.
Devoutest of my Sunday friends, 187.
Do you know the Old Man of the Sea, of the Sea? 109.

Eighty years have passed, and more, 105.
Enchanter of Erin, whose magic has bound us, 253.
Ere yet the warning chimes of midnight sound, 213.

Facts respecting an old arm-chair, 160.
Fallen with autumn's falling leaf, 289.
Farewell, for the bark has her breast to the tide, 97.
Fast as the rolling seasons bring, 122.
Father of Mercies, Heavenly Friend, 196.
Father, send on Earth again, 193.
Fit emblem for the altar's side, 274.
Flag of the heroes who left us their glory, 198.
Flash out a stream of blood-red wine, 117.
For him the Architect of all, 143.
Four summers coined their golden light in leaves, 208.
Friend, whom thy fourscore winters leave more dear, 275.
Friend, you seem thoughtful. I not wonder much, 218.
From my lone turret as I look around, 176.
From the first gleam of morning to the gray, 268.
From this fair home behold on either side, 301.
Full sevenscore years our city's pride, 237.
Full well I know the frozen hand has come, 286.

Giver of all that crowns our days, 194.
Go seek thine earth-born sisters, — thus the Voice, 169.
God bless our Fathers' Land! 110.
Grandmother's mother; her age, I guess, 187.

INDEX OF FIRST LINES

Hang out our banners on the stately tower! 216.
Has there any old fellow got mixed with the boys? 118.
Have I deserved your kindness? Nay, my friends, 68.
Have you heard of the wonderful one-hoss shay, 158.
He died not as the martyr dies, 332.
He rests from toil; the portals of the tomb, 298.
He sleeps not here; in hope and prayer, 165.
He was all sunshine; in his face, 103.
Her hands are cold; her face is white, 163.
Here I sweep these foolish leaves away, 167.
Here's the old cruiser, 'Twenty-nine, 128.
His birthday. — Nay, we need not speak, 107.
How beauteous is the bond, 300.
How long will this harp which you once loved to hear, 125.
"How many have gone?" was the question of old, 142.
How sweet the sacred legend — if unblamed, 317.
How the mountains talked together, 203.
How to address him? awkward, it is true, 239.

I am not humble; I was shown my place, 176.
I asked three little maidens who heard the organ play, 215.
I believe that the copies of verses I've spun, 250.
I bring the simplest pledge of love, 255.
I claim the right of knowing whom I serve, 177.
I don't think I feel much older; I'm aware I'm rather gray, 141.
I give you the health of the oldest friend, 124.
I have come with my verses — I think I may claim, 134.
I hold a letter in my hand, 62.
I like, at times, to hear the steeples' chimes, 138.
I Like you met I Love you, face to face, 301.
I love all sights of earth and skies, 284.
I love to hear thine earnest voice, 7.
I may not rightly call thy name, 100.
I must leave thee, lady sweet! 40.
I pray thee by the soul of her that bore thee, 164.
I remember — why, yes! God bless me! and was it so long ago? 108.
I saw him once before, 5.
I saw the curl of his waving lash, 8.
I sometimes sit beneath a tree, 14.
I stood on Sarum's treeless plain, 147.
I suppose it's myself that you're making allusion to, 227.
I thank you, MR. PRESIDENT, you've kindly broke the ice, 104.
I was sitting with my microscope, upon my parlor rug, 34.
I was thinking last night, as I sat in the cars, 36.
I wrote some lines once on a time, 14.
If all the trees in all the woods were men, 300.
If every tongue that speaks her praise, 272.
If sometimes in the dark blue eye, 331.
I'm ashamed, — that's the fact, — it's a pitiful case, 119.

I'm not a chicken; I have seen, 13.
I'm the fellah that tole one day, 160.
In candent ire the solar splendor flames, 158.
In narrowest girdle, O reluctant Muse, 54.
In poisonous dens, where traitors hide, 192.
In the hour of twilight shadows, 26.
In the little southern parlor of the house you may have seen, 166.
Is it a weanling's weakness for the past, 286.
Is man's the only throbbing heart that hides, 319.
Is thy name Mary, maiden fair? 327.
It is a pity and a shame — alas! alas! I know it is, 136.
It is not what we say or sing, 126.
It may be so, — perhaps thou hast, 329.
It may be, yes, it must be, Time that brings, 130.
It was a tall young oysterman lived by the river-side, 329.
It was not many centuries since, 321.
It was the stalwart butcher man, 323.

Kiss mine eyelids, beauteous Morn, 170.

Lady, life's sweetest lesson wouldst thou learn, 301.
Land where the banners wave last in the sun, 195.
Leader of armies, Israel's God, 229.
Let greener lands and bluer skies, 326.
Let me retrace the record of the years, 174.
Like the tribes of Israel, 124.
Listen, young heroes! your country is calling! 192.
Little I ask; my wants are few, 157.
Look our ransomed shores around, 291.
Look out! Look out, boys! Clear the track! 302.
Lord of all being! throned afar, 163.
Lord, Thou hast led us as of old, 288.
"Lucy." — The old familiar name, 228.

Mine ancient chair! thy wide embracing arms, 333.
My aunt! my dear unmarried aunt! 8.

Nay, blame me not; I might have spared, 1.
New England, we love thee; no time can erase, 96.
No fear lest praise should make us proud! 166.
No life worth naming ever comes to good, 85.
No more the summer floweret charms, 31.
No mystic charm, no mortal art, 212.
No! never such a draught was poured, 190.
Not bed-time yet! The night-winds blow, 144.
Not charity we ask, 100.
Not in the world of light alone, 101.
Not to myself this breath of vesper song, 239.
Not with the anguish of hearts that are breaking, 214.
Now, by the blessed Paphian queen, 7.
Now, men of the North! will you join in the strife, 123.
Now, smiling friends and shipmates all, 204.
Now, while our soldiers are fighting our battles, 197.

INDEX OF FIRST LINES 347

O even-handed Nature! we confess, 202.
O God! in danger's darkest hour, 194.
O Lord of Hosts! Almighty King! 196.
O Love Divine, that stooped to share, 163.
O my lost beauty! — hast thou folded quite, 150.
O Thou of soul and sense and breath, 208.
O'ershadowed by the walls that climb, 287.
Oh for one hour of youthful joy! 115.
Oh! I did love her dearly, 327.
Oh, there are times, 9.
Old Rip Van Winkle had a grandson, Rip, 63.
Old Time, in whose bank we deposit our notes, 135.
Once more Orion and the sister Seven, 273.
Once more, ye sacred towers, 215.
One broad, white sail in Spezzia's treacherous bay, 92.
One country! Treason's writhing asp, 193.
One memory trembles on our lips, 133.
One word to the guest we have gathered to greet! 199.
"Only a housemaid!" She looked from the kitchen, 234.
Our ancient church! its lowly tower, 5.
Our Father! while our hearts unlearn, 298.
Our poet, who has taught the Western breeze, 206.

Perhaps too far in these considerate days, 83.
Poor conquered monarch! though that haughty glance, 324.
Precisely. I see it. You all want to say, 131.
Pride of the sister realm so long our own, 271.
Proud of her clustering spires, her new-built towers, 276.
Proudly, beneath her glittering dome, 293.

"Qui vive?" The sentry's musket rings, 331.

Reader — gentle — if so be, 185.

Say not the Poet dies! 214.
Scarce could the parting ocean close, 94.
Scene, — a back parlor in a certain square, 37.
Scenes of my youth! awake its slumbering fire! 15.
See how yon flaming herald treads, 28.
Sexton! Martha's dead and gone, 104.
Shadowed so long by the storm-cloud of danger, 199.
She came beneath the forest dome, 39.
She gathered at her slender waist, 145.
She has gone, — she has left us in passion and pride, 111.
She twirled the string of golden beads, 325.
Shine soft, ye trembling tears of light, 91.
Sire, son, and grandson; so the century glides, 256.
Sister, we bid you welcome, — we who stand, 272.
Slow toiling upward from the misty vale, 191.
Slowly the mist o'er the meadow was creeping, 28.
Strange! that one lightly whispered tone, 327.
Such kindness! the scowl of a cynic would soften, 252.
Sweet Mary, I have never breathed, 326.

Teachers of teachers! Yours the task, 298.
Tell me, O Provincial! speak, Ceruleo-Nasal! 167.
That age was older once than now, 152.
The Banker's dinner is the stateliest feast, 307.
The Caliph ordered up his cook, 221.
The clock has struck noon; are it thrice tell the hours, 115.
The Comet! He is on his way, 11.
The curtain rose; in thunders long and loud, 85.
The dinner-bell, the dinner-bell, 330.
The dirge is played, the throbbing death-peal rung, 133.
"The Dutch have taken Holland," — so the schoolboys used to say, 284.
The feeble sea-birds, blinded in the storms, 61.
The folks, that on the first of May, 330.
The fount the Spaniard sought in vain, 222.
The friends that are, and friends that were, 120.
The glory has passed from the goldenrod's plume, 304.
The god looked out upon the troubled deep, 321.
The house was crammed from roof to floor, 189.
The land of sunshine and of song! 110.
The minstrel of the classic lay, 146.
The mountains glitter in the snow, 97.
The muse of boyhood's fervid hour, 137.
The noon of summer sheds its ray, 106.
The painter's and the poet's fame, 207
The piping of our slender, peaceful reeds, 72.
The Play is over. While the light, 148.
The pledge of Friendship! it is still divine, 42.
The seed that wasteful autumn cast, 90.
The Ship of State! above her skies are blue, 239.
The snows that glittered on the disk of Mars, 174.
The stars are rolling in the sky, 13.
The stars their early vigils keep, 33.
The summer dawn is breaking, 114.
The sunbeams, lost for half a year, 152.
The sun-browned girl, whose limbs recline, 326.
The sun is fading in the skies, 332.
The sun stepped down from his golden throne, 325.
The tale I tell is gospel true, 73.
The time is racked with birth-pangs; every hour, 180.
The two proud sisters of the sea, 331.
The waves unbuild the wasting shore, 277.
The wreath that star-crowned Shelley gave, 92.
There are three ways in which men take, 12.
There is no time like the old time, when you and I were young, 222.
There was a giant in time of old, 10.
There was a sound of hurrying feet, 322.
There was a young man in Boston town, 60.
There's a thing that grows by the fainting flower, 323.
These hallowed precincts, long to memory dear, 257.
They bid me strike the idle strings, 32.
They tell us that the Muse is soon to fly hence, 251.
This ancient silver bowl of mine, it tells of good old times, 29.
This is our place of meeting; opposite, 269.

INDEX OF FIRST LINES

This is the ship of pearl, which poets feign, 149.
This is your month, the month of "perfect days," 274.
This shred of song you bid me bring, 146.
Thou Gracious Power, whose mercy lends, 129.
Thou shouldst have sung the swan-song for the choir, 296.
Thou, too, hast left us. While with heads bowed low, 297.
Thou who hast taught the teachers of mankind, 206.
Though watery deserts hold apart, 198.
Though young no more, we still would dream, 156.
Three paths there be where Learning's favored sons, 264.
Through my north window, in the wintry weather, 247.
Thus I lift the sash, so long, 185.
Time is a thief who leaves his tools behind him, 147.
'T is like stirring living embers when, at eighty, one remembers, 224.
'T is midnight: through my troubled dream, 120.
'T is sweet to fight our battles o'er, 102.
To God's anointed and his chosen flock, 251.
Too young for love? 301.
Trained in the holy art whose lifted shield, 220.
Truth: So the frontlet's older legend ran, 231.
'T was a vision of childhood that came with its dawn, 94.
'T was on the famous trotting ground, 234.
Twice had the mellowing sun of autumn crowned, 277.

Vex not the Muse with idle prayers, 305.

Wan-visaged thing! thy virgin leaf, 328.
Washed in the blood of the brave and the blooming, 194.
We count the broken lyres that rest, 99.
We sing "Our Country's" song to-night, 120.
We trust and fear, we question and believe, 85.
We welcome you, Lords of the Land of the Sun! 201.
We will not speak of years to-night, 102.
Welcome to the day returning, 98.
Welcome, thrice welcome is thy silvery gleam, 291.
Well, Miss, I wonder where you live, 11.
What ailed young Lucius? Art had vainly tried, 313.
What am I but the creature Thou hast made, 178.
What flower is this that greets the morn, 196.
What if a soul redeemed, a spirit that loved, 182.
What is a poet's love? 328.
What makes the Healing Art divine? 106.

What secret charm, long whispering in mine ear, 333.
Whatever I do, and whatever I say, 171.
When Advent dawns with lessening days, 290.
When Eve had led her lord away, 155.
When evening's shadowy fingers fold, 292.
When legislators keep the law, 155.
When life hath run its largest round, 98.
When o'er the street the morning peal is flung, 83.
When rose the cry "Great Pan is dead!" 237.
When the Puritans came over, 30.
When treason first began the strife, 205.
Where are you going, soldiers, 191.
Where, girt around by savage foes, 215.
Where is this patriarch you are kindly greeting? 243.
Where, oh where, are the visions of morning, 115.
While far along the eastern sky, 188.
While fond, sad memories all around us throng, 244.
While in my simple gospel creed, 304.
Who claims our Shakespeare from that realm unknown, 211.
"Who gave this cup?" The secret thou wouldst steal, 300.
Who is the shepherd sent to lead, 102.
Who of all statesmen is his country's pride, 315.
Why linger round the sunken wrecks, 290.
"*Will I come?*" That *is* pleasant! I beg to inquire, 127.
Winter is past; the heart of Nature warms, 80.
Winter's cold drift lies glistening o'er his breast, 210.

Ye that have faced the billows and the spray, 311.
Ye who yourselves of larger worth esteem, 295.
Yes, dear departed, cherished days, 32.
Yes, dear Enchantress, — wandering far and long, 43.
Yes, lady! I can ne'er forget, 332.
Yes! the vacant chairs tell sadly we are going, going fast, 140.
Yes, tyrants, you hate us, and fear while you hate, 121.
Yes, we knew we must lose him, — though friendship may claim, 151.
Yes, write, if you want to, there's nothing like trying, 232.
Yet in the darksome crypt I left so late, 82.
Yon whey-faced brother, who delights to wear, 84.
You bid me sing, — can I forget, 219.
You know "The Teacups," that congenial set, 306.
You'll believe me, dear boys, 't is a pleasure to rise, 117.
Your home was mine, — kind Nature's gift, 263.

INDEX OF TITLES

[*The titles of the main divisions of this book are set in* SMALL CAPITALS.]

"Ad Amicos," 137.
Address for the Opening of the Fifth Avenue Theatre, 216.
Æstivation, 158.
After a Lecture on Keats, 92.
After a Lecture on Moore, 91.
After a Lecture on Shelley, 92.
After a Lecture on Wordsworth, 90.
After-Dinner Poem, 54.
After the Curfew, 148.
After the Fire, 188.
Agnes, 72.
Album Verses, 155.
All here, 126.
America to Russia, 198.
American Academy Centennial Celebration, 256.
Angel-Thief, The, 147.
Appeal for "The Old South," An, 236.
Archbishop, The, and Gil Blas, 141.
Army Hymn, 196.
Astræa, 333.
At a Meeting of Friends, 108.
At My Fireside, 269.
At the Papyrus Club, 249.
At the Saturday Club, 269.
At the Turn of the Road, 304.
At the Unitarian Festival, 277.
Atlantic Dinner, At the, 227.
Aunt, My, 8.
Aunt Tabitha, 171.
Ave, 286.
Aviary, My, 247.
Avis, 100.

Bachelor's Private Journal, From a, 326.
Ballad of the Boston Tea-Party, A, 190.
Ballad of the Oysterman, The, 329.
Banker's Secret, The, 307.
Banquet to the Chinese Embassy, At the, 200.
Banquet to the Grand Duke Alexis, At the, 199.
Banquet to the Japanese Embassy, At the, 201.
BEFORE THE CURFEW, 209.
Bells, The, 83.
Bill and Joe, 113.
Birthday Festival, At a, 102.
Birthday of Daniel Webster, 98.
Birthday Tribute to J. F. Clarke, A, 102.
Blank Sheet of Paper, To a, 328.
Boston Common, 109.
Boston to Florence, 276.
Boys, The, 118.
Broken Circle, The, 147.
Broomstick Train, The, 301.
Brother Jonathan's Lament, 111.
Bryant's Seventieth Birthday, 202.

BUNKER-HILL BATTLE AND OTHER POEMS (1874-1877), 224.
Burns Centennial Celebration, For the, 107.
But One Talent, 295.

Cacoethes Scribendi, 300.
Caged Lion, To a, 324.
Cambridge Churchyard, The, 5.
Canaan, To, 191.
Centennial Dinner of the Massachusetts Medical Society, 264.
Chambered Nautilus, The, 149.
Chanson without Music, 219.
"Choose You this Day," 121.
Clarke, James Freeman, To, 255.
Close of a Course of Lectures, At the, 93.
Comet, The, 11.
Coming Era, The, 251.
Contentment, 157.
Crooked Footpath, The, 164.

Daily Trials, 9.
De Sauty, 167.
Deacon's Masterpiece, The, 158.
Death of President Garfield, On the, 289.
Dedication of the Fountain at Stratford-on-Avon, 291.
Dedication of the Halleck Monument, Poem at the, 214.
Dedication of the New City Library, Boston, For the, 293.
Dedication of the Pittsfield Cemetery, 87.
Departed Days, 32.
Dilemma, The, 7.
Dinner to Admiral Farragut, At a, 204.
Dinner to General Grant, At a, 205.
Dorchester Giant, The, 10.
Dorothy Q., 186.
Dying Seneca, The, 332.

EARLIER POEMS, 3.
Edward Everett, 210.
Ehrenberg, Christian Gottfried, To, 206.
English Friend, To an, 90.
Epilogue to the Breakfast-Table Series, 183.
Even-Song, 130.
Evening, by a Tailor, 9.
Evening Thought, An, 331.
Exile's Secret, The, 311.
Extracts from a Medical Poem, 61.

Familiar Letter, A, 232.
Family Record, A, 239.
Fantasia, 170.
Farewell to Agassiz, A, 203.

INDEX OF TITLES

Farewell to J. R. Lowell, 97.
First Fan, The, 237.
First Verses, 321.
Flâneur, The, 284.
Flower of Liberty, The, 196.
For Class Meeting, 136.
For the Burns Centennial Celebration, 107.
For the Centennial Dinner of the Proprietors of Boston Pier, 220.
For the Commemoration Services, 208.
For the Dedication of the New City Library, Boston, 293.
For the Meeting of the Burns Club, 97.
For the Meeting of the National-Sanitary Association, 106.
For the Moore Centennial Celebration, 253.
For the Services in Memory of Abraham Lincoln, 208.
For the Window in St. Margaret's, 296.
For Whittier's Seventieth Birthday, 250.
Fountain of Youth, The, 222.
Freedom, Our Queen, 195.
F. W. C., 122.

Garfield, President, On the Death of, 289.
Girdle of Friendship, The, 145.
God save the Flag, 194.
Golden Flower, The, 290.
Good Time Going, A, 155.
Gould, Dr. Benjamin Apthorp, A Welcome to, 273.
Governor Swain, To, 89.
Grandmother's Story of Bunker-Hill Battle, 224.
Gray Chief, The, 102.

H. C. M., H. S., J. K. W., 133.
Hail Columbia! 290.
Harvard, 268.
Harvard College, Poem for the Two Hundred and Fiftieth Anniversary of the Founding of, 277.
Hayes, Rutherford Birchard, To, 239.
Hedge, Frederick Henry, To, 274.
Height of the Ridiculous, The, 14.
Homesick in Heaven, 169.
Hot Season, The, 330.
How not to settle it, 138.
How the Old Horse won the Bet, 234.
Hudson, The, 94.
Humboldt's Birthday, 213.
Hymn after the Emancipation Proclamation, 194.
Hymn at the Funeral Services of Charles Sumner, 215.
Hymn for the Class-Meeting, 129.
Hymn for the Dedication of Memorial Hall at Cambridge, 215.
Hymn for the Fair at Chicago, 194.
Hymn for the Inauguration of the Statue of Governor Andrew, 229.
Hymn for the Laying of the Corner-Stone of Harvard Memorial Hall, 214.
Hymn for the Two Hundredth Anniversary of King's Chapel, 287.
Hymn of Peace, A, 223.
Hymn of Trust, 163.

Hymn read at the Dedication of the Oliver Wendell Holmes Hospital at Hudson, Wisconsin, 288.
Hymn written for the Great Central Fair in Philadelphia, 193.
Hymn written for the Twenty-fifth Anniversary of the Reorganization of the Boston Young Men's Christian Union, 298.
Hymn, The Word of Promise, 288.

I Like you and I Love you, 301.
Illustration of a Picture, 325.
Impromptu, An, 115.
Impromptu at the Walcker Dinner upon the Completion of the Great Organ for Boston Music Hall, An, 215.
In Memory of Charles Wentworth Upham, Jr., 103.
In Memory of John and Robert Ware, 212.
In Memory of John Greenleaf Whittier, 297.
In Response, 252.
IN THE QUIET DAYS, 186.
In the Twilight, 144.
IN WAR TIME, 191.
Indian Summer, Our, 117.
Insect, To an, 7.
International Ode, 110.
Iris, Her Book, 164.
IRON GATE, THE, 243.
Island Hunting-Song, The, 31.
Invitâ Minervâ, 305.

J. D. R., 120.
Joseph Warren, M. D., 230.

King's Chapel. Read at the Two Hundredth Anniversary, 286.

La Grisette, 326.
La Maison d'Or, 301.
Last Blossom, The, 156.
Last Charge, The, 123.
Last Leaf, The, 4.
Last Look, The, 103.
Last Prophecy of Cassandra, 332.
Last Reader, The, 14.
Last Survivor, The, 140.
Latter-Day Warnings, 154.
Lexington, 28.
L'Inconnue, 327.
Lines, 119.
Lines by a Clerk, 327.
Lines recited at the Berkshire Jubilee, 33.
Living Temple, The, 101.
Longfellow, H. W., To, 206.
Lover's Secret, The, 313.
Loving-Cup Song, A, 145.
Lowell, James Russell, To, 274, 293.
Lowell, James Russell, 296.
"Lucy," 228.
Lyre of Anacreon, The, 146.

Mare Rubrum, 117.
Martha, 104.
MEDICAL POEMS, 58.
Meeting of Friends, At a, 108.
Meeting of the Alumni of Harvard College, 104.

INDEX OF TITLES

Meeting of the American Medical Association, 62.
Meeting of the Burns Club, For the, 97.
Meeting of the Dryads, The, 321.
Meeting of the National Sanitary Association, 106.
Memorial Tribute to Dr. Samuel G. Howe, A, 229.
MEMORIAL VERSES, 208.
Midsummer, 167.
Mind's Diet, The, 85.
Modest Request, A, 37.
Moral Bully, The, 84.
Morning Visit, The, 58.
Mother's Secret, The, 317.
Musa, 150.
Music Grinders, The, 12.
My Annual, 125.
My Aunt, 8.
My Aviary, 247.
Mysterious Visitor, The, 322.

Nearing the Snow Line, 191.
Never or Now, 192.
New Eden, The, 94.
Non-Resistance, 83.
Noontide Lyric, A, 330.
No Time like the Old Time, 222.
Nux Postcœnatica, 35.

Ode for a Social Meeting (with alterations), 162.
Ode for Washington's Birthday, 98.
Old Cambridge, 230.
Old Cruiser, The, 128.
Old Ironsides, 3.
Old Man Dreams, The, 115.
Old Man of the Sea, The, 109.
Old Player, The, 85.
Old Tune, The, 146.
Old-Year Song, An, 186.
On Lending a Punch-Bowl, 29.
On the Threshold, 249.
Once More, 127.
One Country, 193.
Only Daughter, The, 32.
Opening of the Piano, The, 166.
Opening the Window, 185.
Organ-Blower, The, 187.
Our Banker, 135.
Our Dead Singer. H. W. L., 271.
Our Home — Our Country, 263.
Our Indian Summer, 117.
Our Limitations, 85.
Our Oldest Friend, 124.
Our Sweet Singer, 133.
Our Yankee Girls, 326.

Pantomime, At the, 189.
Parkman, Francis, 208.
Parson Turell's Legacy, 160.
Parting Health, A, 151.
Parting Hymn, 196.
Parting Song, The, 106.
Parting Word, The, 40.
Peabody, George, To, 249.
Peau de Chagrin of State Street, The, 300.
Peirce, Benjamin, 143.

Philosopher to his Love, The, 328.
Pilgrim's Vision, The, 26.
Ploughman, The, 79.
Poem at the Centennial Dinner of the Massachusetts Medical Society, 264.
Poem for the Dedication of the Fountain at Stratford-on-Avon, 291.
Poem for the Dedication of the Pittsfield Cemetery, 87.
Poem for the Meeting of the American Medical Association, 62.
Poem read at the Dinner given to the Author by the Medical Profession of the City of New York, 68.
Poem served to Order, A, 221.
POEMS FROM THE AUTOCRAT, 149.
POEMS FROM THE PROFESSOR, 163.
POEMS FROM THE POET, 169.
POEMS FROM OVER THE TEACUPS, 300.
POEMS OF THE CLASS OF '29, 113.
POEMS PUBLISHED BETWEEN 1837 AND 1848, 26.
Poet's Lot, The, 328.
Poetry: a Metrical Essay, 15.
Portrait, A, 331.
Portrait of "A Gentleman," To the, 329.
Portrait of a Lady, To the, 11.
Post-Prandial, 284.
Prelude (to Parson Turell's Legacy), 160.
Prelude to a Volume printed in Raised Letters for the Blind, 276.
Programme, 185.
Prologue, 153.
Prologue to Songs in Many Keys, 72.
Promise, The, 100.

Questions and Answers, 115.
"Qui Vive?" 331.

READINGS OVER THE TEACUPS, 306.
Reflections of a Proud Pedestrian, 8.
Remember — Forget, 116.
Rhymed Lesson, A, 43.
Rhymes of a Life-Time, 268.
RHYMES OF AN HOUR, 216.
Rip Van Winkle, M. D., 63.
Robinson of Leyden, 165.
Roman Aqueduct, A, 326.
Rose and the Fern, The, 301.

School-Boy, The, 257.
Sea Dialogue, A, 218.
Secret of the Stars, The, 319.
Semi-Centennial Celebration of the New England Society, 96.
Sentiment, A, 42, 63.
September Gale, The, 13.
Services in Memory of Abraham Lincoln, For the, 208.
Shadows, The, 142.
Shakespeare Tercentennial Celebration, 211.
Sherman's in Savannah, 124.
Ship of State, The, 239.
Silent Melody, The, 263.
Smiling Listener, The, 131.
Song for a Temperance Dinner, 42.
Song for the Centennial Celebration of Harvard College, 30.

INDEX OF TITLES

Song for the Dinner to Charles Dickens, 33.
Song of Other Days, A, 41.
Song of "Twenty-Nine," A, 114.
SONGS IN MANY KEYS, 72.
SONGS OF MANY SEASONS, 185.
SONGS OF WELCOME AND FAREWELL, 198.
Souvenir, A, 332.
Spectre Pig, The, 323.
Spring, 80.
Spring has come, 152.
St. Anthony the Reformer, 166.
St. Margaret's, For the Window in, 296.
Stanzas, 327.
Star and the Water-Lily, The, 325.
Statesman's Secret, The, 315.
Steamboat, The, 28.
Stethoscope Song, The, 60.
Stowe, Harriet Beecher, Two Poems to, 272.
Study, The, 82.
Sun and Shadow, 150.
Sun-Day Hymn, A, 163.
Sweet Little Man, The, 197.

Tartarus, 304.
Teachers of America, To the, 298.
"Thus saith the Lord," 192.
To a Blank Sheet of Paper, 328.
To a Caged Lion, 324.
To an English Friend, 90.
To an Insect, 7.
To Canaan, 191.
To Christian Gottfried Ehrenberg, 206.
To Frederick Henry Hedge, 274.
To George Peabody, 249.
To Governor Swain, 89.
To H. W. Longfellow, 206.
To James Freeman Clarke, 255.
To James Russell Lowell, 274.
To John Greenleaf Whittier, 275.
To My Companions, 333.
To My Old Readers, 306.
To My Readers, 1.
To Rutherford Birchard Hayes, 239.

To the Eleven Ladies, 300.
To the Poets who only read and listen, 292.
To the Portrait of "A Gentleman," 329.
To the Portrait of a Lady, 11.
To the Teachers of America, 298.
Toadstool, The, 323.
Toast to Wilkie Collins, A, 207.
Too Young for Love, 301.
Treadmill Song, The, 13.
Two Armies, The, 59.
Two Poems to Harriet Beecher Stowe, 272.
Two Sonnets: Harvard, 251.
Two Streams, The, 99.

Under the Violets, 163.
Under the Washington Elm, 195.
Union and Liberty, 198.
Unsatisfied, 234.
Upham, Charles Wentworth, Jr., In Memory of, 103.

Verses for After-Dinner, 36.
VERSES FROM THE OLDEST PORTFOLIO, 321.
Vestigia Quinque Retrorsum, 244.
Vive la France, 110.
Voice of the Loyal North, A, 120.
Voiceless, The, 99.
Voyage of the Good Ship Union, 120.

Ware, John and Robert, In Memory of, 212.
Wasp and the Hornet, The, 331.
Welcome to Dr. Benjamin Apthorp Gould. A, 273.
Welcome to the Chicago Commercial Club, 255.
Welcome to the Grand Duke Alexis, 199.
Welcome to the Nations, 232.
What I have come for, 134.
What We all think, 152.
Whittier, John Greenleaf, In Memory of, 297.
Whittier, John Greenleaf, To, 275.
Wind-Clouds and Star-Drifts, 171.

Youth, 290.

BIBLIOLIFE

Old Books Deserve a New Life
www.bibliolife.com

Did you know that you can get most of our titles in our trademark **EasyScript**™ print format? **EasyScript**™ provides readers with a larger than average typeface, for a reading experience that's easier on the eyes.

Did you know that we have an ever-growing collection of books in many languages?

Order online:
www.bibliolife.com/store

Or to exclusively browse our **EasyScript**™ collection:
www.bibliogrande.com

At BiblioLife, we aim to make knowledge more accessible by making thousands of titles available to you – quickly and affordably.

Contact us:
BiblioLife
PO Box 21206
Charleston, SC 29413